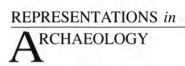

REPRESENTATIONS *in*
ARCHAEOLOGY

EDITED BY *Jean-Claude Gardin and Christopher S. Peebles*

REPRESENTATIONS *in*

ARCHAEOLOGY

INDIANA UNIVERSITY PRESS • *Bloomington and Indianapolis*

The paper used in this publication meets the minimum requirements of American
National Standard for Information Sciences—Permanence of Paper for Printed
Library Materials, ANSI Z39.48-1984.

∞™

Manufactured in the United States of America

Library of Congress Cataloging-in-Publication Data

Representations in archaeology / edited by Jean-Claude Gardin and
    Christopher S. Peebles.
        p.   cm.
    Includes bibliographical references.
    ISBN 0–253–32546–3. — ISBN 0–253–20709–6 (paper)
    1. Archaeology—Philosophy–Congresses. I. Gardin, Jean-Claude.
II. Peebles, Christopher S.
CC72.R47   1992
930.1—dc20   91–24995
1 2 3 4 5   96 95 94 93 92

in memory of
André Leroi-Gourhan

Contents

Acknowledgments

As editors, we offer thanks to all of the authors for the time and effort they took in writing and then revising their contributions. The papers sent by each participant in advance of the seminar were revised and expanded as a result of our week-long discussions. Subsequently, some papers were revised further at our request; some were revised at the request of the reader for Indiana University Press, Professor Don Rice of the University of Virginia, who proved an excellent critic and a sympathetic colleague; some were revised twice, at the request of the reader and then of the editors. We thank the authors for their patience during this three-year process. We also thank Rachel Fryman for drafting many of the illustrations in their final form.

As organizers and participants in the seminar, we thank our co-organizer, Professor Michael Herzfeld, for his skill and labor in our collective behalf. We also thank the staff and Fellows of the Glenn A. Black Laboratory for their hospitality; the Catering Service of the Indiana Memorial Union and the Fireside Inn of Bloomington for fine food and lodging; and Chateau Thomas Winery for demonstrating that the best of California grapes and Hoosier skill can produce the finest of wines. We thank Angus Paul of the *Chronicle of Higher Education* for listening and then reporting on our work with grace and intelligence. Finally, we thank the Centre National de la Recherche Scientifique, France, the National Science Foundation, USA, and the Glenn A. and Ida F. Black Endowment, Indiana University Foundation, for support of this seminar.

REPRESENTATIONS *in*
ARCHAEOLOGY

Jean-Claude Gardin and Christopher S. Peebles

Introduction

Should the proceedings of every colloquium or round table that deals with an interesting subject in the social sciences be published? Their number increases constantly, and it is certainly true that their systematic publication is one of the reasons for the overabundance of edited volumes that disturbs an ever growing number of scholars and the budgets of librarians, particularly those in the social sciences. Archaeology, although among the more restrained disciplines in this regard, nonetheless faces the same problems. There are countless meetings of archaeologists throughout the world every year, gatherings where different views are expressed under a variety of headings: observation techniques, archaeometry, regional or thematic surveys, new schools and concepts, methodology, and so on. One is entitled to wonder about the usefulness of publishing these views, since they often prove local, transient, repetitive, and contingent—in short, limited from almost any perspective, and thus doomed to be ignored or forgotten.

What, then, of the present collection? One major justification for its existence is that it deals with the phenomenon of topical inflation through one of its particular manifestations: the proliferation of "approaches" to the interpretation of archaeological remains that spans more than a decade. We hope that by confronting these new approaches, we will prepare the way for a slight change in course, not so much as a solution to "the explosion of scientific information," with which we both have been concerned over the years, but rather as an incentive to explore more deeply "first principles" that touch upon the foundations of our discipline. Another justification is our ambition to encompass all the trends and "schools" that nowadays compete for a dubious primacy in archaeology. We hope thereby to discover a few good reasons to unburden a discipline that today is more encumbered than it is enriched by the accumulation of so many divergent manifestations.

What was the genesis of this twofold hope? And why did we think it would be better achieved by means of a round table restricted to twenty participants—anglophone and francophone—rather than an international conference open to more participants, all languages, and many nations? It is a tale that can be briefly told. In 1983, the 5th International Institute for Semiotic and Structural Studies was held in Bloomington, Indiana, under the direction of Michael Herzfeld. One course of lectures on the program of this Institute, given by Jean-Claude Gardin, was entitled "Semiotics and Archaeology." The subject covered by this enigmatic title came in the form of two intertwined intellectual strands: (1) the natural or artificial languages used in the representation of archaeological materials

in databases and (2) the operations carried out on the symbols that make up these
languages in order to create or support the interpretative hypotheses relevant to these
archaeological materials. The reference to semiotics, or semiology, if one accepts the
Saussurian term, pointed to the value of systems of representation in approaching or
reconstructing archaeological reasoning. Thomas A. Sebeok, who listens very carefully
each time a semiotic process is evoked, was kind enough to regard this as a fruitful
approach within the wider perspective of general cultural anthropology. It was at this
point that several of the participants conceived of a conference on the potential contributions of semiotics to archaeology and related disciplines. Gardin and Herzfeld took on
the task of organizing it.

It is not surprising that the chosen location was the Bloomington campus of Indiana
University, where, over the past thirty years, Sebeok had built one of the most prestigious
centers for semiotic research and teaching. As for the date, it was postponed for a long
time because the two designated organizers had obligations which, if not more urgent,
were more difficult to put off. Things got a fresh start when a third individual, Christopher
Peebles, a visiting professor who had briefly eluded the weight of accumulated obligations,
was appointed to the faculty of Indiana University. He was added to the project and
began the task of constructing an administrative structure for it. Through telephone calls,
letters, and occasional meetings, Gardin, Herzfeld, and Peebles decided that the most
appropriate formula was a Franco-American round table, organized within the program
of scientific cooperation between the Centre National de la Recherche Scientifique
(CNRS) and the National Science Foundation (NSF). By choosing this path, we were
accepting the restrictions imposed by the two foundations regarding the number and
nationality of the participants: a maximum of twenty, in principle only from France and
the United States, with no visiting auditors. In brief, it could only be a "closed" round
table, in the most restrictive sense of the term. We immediately found many reasons to
be satisfied with these restrictions.

Principal among these reasons was our shared faith in workshops, during which a
small number of researchers discuss working materials distributed in advance rather than
passively listening to papers being read to them by their authors. The other side of the
organizational coin was that our choice of participants was bound to cause criticism: it
was clear from the outset that there were far more than twenty scholars as well informed
and well qualified as we were to make useful contributions to the discussions. Yet we
were limited by the rules of the game to only twenty. As to nationalities, the NSF and
the CNRS agreed to be flexible on one aspect that really mattered to us: the "American"
participation was extended to include English-speaking countries so that we were able
to invite a limited number of colleagues from Great Britain (Christopher Chippindale and
James Doran were invited and were able to participate; Ian Hodder and Colin Renfrew
were invited and initially agreed to attend but were prevented from participating by
unanticipated changes in their schedules); similarly, the "French" participation became
French-speaking, thanks to the presence of Alain Gallay, a distinguished scholar from
Switzerland.

Two detailed project proposals were produced by the organizers: one by Peebles (then
a visiting professor at The Pennsylvania State University) and Herzfeld for the NSF, the
other by Gardin for the CNRS. This first step was very instructive: the two texts,

developed independently on opposite sides of the Atlantic, with little consultation among their authors (except for a short exchange of letters and a few conversations on the subject), showed encouraging convergences. Yet there were also divergences, which confirmed the value we placed on the meeting in the first place and on its organization as an intense, closed seminar that would consume an entire week of 12-hour days.

First, the convergence: both sides stressed the main problem raised by the proliferation of so-called "new" approaches in archaeology. Indeed, how could we accept the great variety of theoretical perspectives relevant to our primary mission—interpretation—without at the same time questioning the very status of a discipline that could so easily embrace such a wide variety of ideas, schools, and paradigms? Conversely, if tolerance of variety does not hamper the attempt to clarify the respective merits of these different approaches, then on which criteria should we base even a relative evaluation?

Then, the differences: they were to be found primarily in the way we viewed the answers to such questions. (1) The American proposal looked the most ambitious at first glance; one could read in it:

> over the last decade, several French, British and North American archaeologists have taken an informed and highly optimistic view of the ability of the archaeological record to produce information that speaks directly and *unambiguously* (emphasis added here) to some aspects of the development of society and culture. Examples that illustrate this methodological optimism are symptomatic of an even broader philosophical convergence among social scientists from the Anglo-Saxon and Continental traditions . . . [namely] the philosophical rapprochement between logical empiricism on the one hand and dialectical and hermeneutic approaches on the other. (following Radnitzky 1973)

Grounds for either a synthesis or a symbiosis were thus outlined, and the objective was to go beyond these two main approaches, which many had seen as incompatible, and find within the human sciences "an outline of a truly cognitive archaeology, rooted [in part] in semiotics." (2) The French proposal was more moderate in tone: in the face of such a "jungle of new approaches . . . —structural, analytical, systemic, social, experimental, symbolic, cognitive, and theoretical archaeologies— . . . is it not time to give this luxuriance a bit of order . . . by clarifying the proper contribution of each to the progress of archaeology, be it 'new' or not?" Then, to "give the discussions a more concrete foundation . . . , three of these 'new' approaches—new in comparison to those belonging to the 'new archaeology' of ten or twenty years ago—would have to be considered, specifically those entitled: symbolic, structural and semiotic." Such was also the desire of the American organizers, who had included these three terms in the title of the planned conference. Yet the French proposal added something that would lead to a much broader and deeper inquiry: "the study of both the merits and the limits of each of these three approaches, supported by concrete case studies, should clarify the utility of considering all known modes of archaeological constructs from the same epistemological perspective."

This final theme gave unity to both proposals—French and American—and provided an intellectual anchor for the discussions that were to follow.

The route from intentions to results, however, is never very certain. As the discussions began, we knew, without any doubt, that a small group of twenty persons over the span of a single week could not expect to outline the unitary epistemological perspective contained in the proposals and in the invitation to the seminar. Moreover, even if we had succeeded, we would have been highly unlikely to convince our colleagues in the archaeological community to accept such sweeping conclusions. Our real objective was, in fact, more modest: we wanted to draw attention to certain epistemological questions that we thought had not been sufficiently debated in archaeology; we thought to fuel the debate by publishing a book made up of the revised versions of the papers prepared in advance of the meeting. The revisions, which were made over the course of the last thirty months, and were subject to the tempo of the authors's fieldwork and the reliability of the post, took into account both the general themes developed during the conference and the specific points that were made about the structure and content of each paper. This book is the result.

The reader will certainly be struck—as we first were—at the apparent heterogeneity of the papers gathered together in this volume. (1) Some raise general *philosophical* questions (Bell, Sperber), about which few of the others seem to be worried. (2) The three types of approaches in the title of the seminar occupy only a part of the book, *semiotics* itself being given little attention (Gardin, Herzfeld, Molino), although it played a major role in the conception of the project. (3) Though the *symbolic* approaches are readily recognizable (Galloway, Kus, Leone and Kryder-Reid), this is not the case for the so-called *structural* approaches: the contributions we have put under this heading are those in which the authors try to make explicit the mental operations that allow us to "make sense" of categories of particular archaeological materials (Aurenche, Perlès, Stordeur). It is clear that constructs of this nature could be easily formulated in the language of structuralism; it is equally clear, to the authors and to ourselves, that such a translation would neither enhance nor diminish the qualities or the defects of these constructs. (4) Our attempt to distribute the papers among the three families of approaches outlined above in fact brings out the uncertainties of their boundaries. Our doubt is all the more relevant because other authors show comparable energy in the elucidation of the inferences that underlie the formation of *concepts*, although making it impossible and even unnecessary to attach any of the three labels—symbolic, structural, or semiotic—to their respective constructions (Davis, Fotiadis, Gallay). (5) Thus, banal as it may seem, the idea gradually dawns that the truly interesting questions, raised by any interpretative approach, are about the mechanisms and the foundations of the arguments linking the empirical base to the speculative superstructure of each hypothesis, conclusion, theory, model, etc. Then we can easily look for possible *formalizations* of these lines of reasoning: sometimes the focus is in the early stages of our apprehension of archaeological materials (Chippindale), sometimes it comprises the actual and conclusive interpretation of them (Roux). Carried far enough, such formalization leads to *computer applications,* whose primary interest is still of an epistemological nature, at least for those who have chosen them as the subject of their reflections (Doran, Francfort, Lagrange).

The variety of these themes is undeniable; far from masking it, we have deliberately emphasized it by the use of italics above: philosophy of interpretation, contribution of semiotic, symbolic, structural, and other approaches in the transition from materials to concepts (or vice versa), the formalization of this process, computer applications—those were the subjects that concerned us in Bloomington from 6 through 10 October 1987. Were they so disparate that communication among the participants would be difficult if not impossible? These fears did in fact strike the organizers at a point just before the seminar actually began. Fortunately they turned out to be unfounded. The nature of the discussions on the themes presented in each of the papers showed the opposite. Indeed, the same questions were raised time and again, despite the diversity of the themes that were tackled; this unity of intellectual purpose will appear once again in the conclusion of the present work. In the Epilogue, we have tried to summarize these recurring questions and the substance of the discussions that took place during the seminar.

Let us now turn to the participants and their papers.[1] As indicated above, we have organized their contributions into four sections, but we have done so in a somewhat different order from that sketched thus far.

(I) We have grouped together works pertaining to the philosophical and semiotic aspects of the new interpretative approaches. The juxtaposition of these two terms may prove surprising. In part, it reflects our desire to pay due tribute to semiotics, since this gathering was organized under its banner. Yet there is more to it than simple filial piety: indeed, one can note that all three specifically semiotic texts (Molino, Herzfeld, Gardin) actually address the same epistemological and methodological questions as the other two texts in this section, which leave out semiotics (Bell and Sperber). We have intermingled them deliberately.

In the first chapter, Jean Molino offers the opinions of a "sheer amateur"—so he writes, being neither an archaeologist nor a prehistorian—on the recent development of *modes* (or fashions) of archaeological interpretation. His "hypothetical competence" as a semiotician—his own words—provides us with a general overview of the subject that evoked envy from the other participants. Moreover, his title, "Archaeology and Symbol Systems," immediately emphasizes the main theme of this book: namely, an attempt to understand the role of the symbolic in archaeology, both as archaeologists attribute it to the "Other," the humans in the past, and as they embody it in archaeological practice in the present, in the here and now.

James Bell (chapter 2) gets to the heart of one major current confrontation between holistic and individualist approaches to explanation. Using this terminology, the author traces recent shifts away from interpretations in terms of structures or processes transcending our free will (holistic approaches), toward those that restore importance to the individual (methodological individualism), making that person's mental processes—even emotional states (empathic approaches)—decisive factors in human history.

Dan Sperber (chapter 3) deals with a related duality by opposing materialist trends in anthropology and history, where mental images are considered only as the products of a higher order of material determinism, to the modern cognitivist trends, which establish more subtle dialectical relationships between cultural representations and the material substratum. He opts for a non-monist materialism: one in which both public and individual (mental) representations are the important objects of study. "Thus to treat representations, whether mental or public, as material causes among other material causes implies rooting the study of thought and of communication in cognitive psychology."

He suggests that analysis of the evolution and diffusion of representations would require interpretive models similar to those used by epidemiology and pathology to chart the clinical course and spread of infectious diseases.

In chapter 4 Michael Herzfeld takes us back to semiotic concerns via archaeological space imagined as a field of decipherable signs (both present and absent) and to the important function of iconicity in this process. His is a semiotic stance informed by symbolic anthropology—a direction that Herzfeld considers most relevant. He sees archaeological interpretation occurring in the context of specific symbolic universes, similar to those whose importance semiotics tries to demonstrate in all communication. Thus the vision of "self-reflection" (reflexivity), cultivated by semiotics in its search for the ideological foundations of all discourse, has a preeminent role to play in the epistemological progress of our discipline as well.

A similar point of view is developed in different terms by Jean-Claude Gardin (chapter 5). He proposes shifting the discussion toward a metatheoretical level where there is less debate about the merits of a particular philosophical approach and more concern for the "manner in which our stock of knowledge about the people and societies of the past is enriched *in practice* [our italics] through the study of material remains." To this end, he suggests the application of logicist analysis to interpretative constructions observed in the archaeological literature, irrespective of the "school" to which the work might express adherence. Gardin, in turn, includes the logicist enterprise within semiotics; that is, within the science of symbolic constructions in general, in the sense given it by Jean Molino (chapter 1). There is, however, an obvious difference between this use of the term and the looser use of "sémiologie" which emerged a few decades ago in the humanities and then in archaeology itself, encompassing structuralist and hermeneutic approaches as well.

(II) The second part brings together studies no less speculative than those in the preceding section, yet the chapters in this section are based on more specific and more concrete archaeological examples. Thus, starting from the logicist analysis of an article by L. R. Binford, Alain Gallay poses a number of epistemological and philosophical questions that are related directly to those raised in Part I, yet he does so as an "artisan" rather than as a philosopher (chapter 6). In so doing, he establishes a list of incisive propositions that are relative to not only the assumptions but also the limits—to him inevitable—of explanation in archaeology. From his perspective, the concepts that are regarded as original in certain approaches—system, structure, symbol—suddenly become trite, and he says so directly in his conclusions.

The study by Whitney Davis (chapter 7) also deals with the foundations and the limits of interpretation in archaeology from the perspective of Paleolithic iconography. He asks: Under what conditions is it possible to attribute meaning to these representations in terms and in ways that are convincing? He suggests a "paleosemiotics" whose function would be to determine the "local knowledge" we need to share about such images in order to establish such conviction. It is, on the one hand, empirical knowledge; on the other, it is theoretical, linked to an anthropology of symbolism in the sense given it by Michael Herzfeld (chapter 4), without which the archaeologist would always be condemned to silence.

The final chapter in this section deals with the problems of inference in the other direction (from the top down), examining particular concepts used in archaeology in order to determine which signs are taken to represent such ideas in concrete form "in the ground," and what are the presuppositions about the relations of signifier and signified thus established. Michael Fotiadis studies the idea of "site" (chapter 8), showing that some theoretical basis is necessary to legitimate a reasoned use of even so common a term. This theory belongs to what the author calls the "ideology of the discipline." It is not a variety of the "social, cultural, or political ideology of the modern West," but rather of knowledge shared by the members of the scientific community; it is expressed through "codes" underlying specialized discourse, in his terms, an "idiom close to natural language."

(III) The six studies in the third part continue these reflections on interpretation, but each originates in a specific archaeological or anthropological research project. Thus the presentation of projects and their results occupies as much space as do general methodological considerations. Consequently the title given to this third part of the volume might come as a surprise. One might legitimately ask: Are these studies really characteristic of either symbolic or structural approaches? The anglophone authors (Mark Leone and Elizabeth Kryder-Reid, Susan Kus, Patricia Galloway) certainly pursue different objectives, yet these objectives all deal with the restoration of appropriate mental representations to particular sociocultural groups. We considered this common trait sufficient to link these six studies to the trends that characterize symbolic archaeology, but it must be understood that our choice of a label does not commit these authors to any position whatsoever. Similarly, the francophone authors (Olivier Aurenche, Danielle Stordeur, Catherine Perlès) are not responsible for our decision to classify their contributions among approaches we consider to be generally structural in character. Certainly, they would reject this and any other label, because the tone of their several papers attempts to place their discourse firmly below (or above) that of any particular "school." The characteristic which they do share is a certain spirit of system, in the best sense of the term, through which they clearly define variables within an observational field and then establish significant correlations—that is to say, correlations constitutive of structures or configurations or structures amenable to interpretation. To restate a point Alain Gallay makes in the conclusion to his paper, and with which we are in agreement: "Any analysis of reality, whatever the domain, implies analysis of the correlations between variables as a first step toward understanding the world around us. In calling itself structural, archaeology has not invented anything new."

The contrast between the "anglophone" and the "francophone" approaches is striking. It certainly reflects a more general division that developed during the seminar and emerged as one of the main themes of the final discussions (see Epilogue). Moiety membership, however, was not generated exclusively on the basis of mother tongue. It would also be wrong to overemphasize the opposition, since it largely results from the difference between the subjects treated by each group: ethnosociological and temporally close in the first case, archaeological and temporally remote in the second.

The study by Mark Leone and Elizabeth Kryder-Reid, for example (chapter 9), is a sociological analysis—from the standpoint of the producers (the archaeologists and historians) and the consumers (local residents and tourists)—of representations of the past presented to the public in the historic towns of Saint Mary's City and Annapolis, Maryland, through various "media" (walking tours, excavations in progress, museums, theater, etc.). The perspective is that of "critical archaeology," a stance developed by Leone and his colleagues over the last decade. This position, with its Marxist reference via Jürgen Habermas, is neither symbolic nor cognitive archaeology, despite certain past connections or sympathies with that school. The goal of Leone and Kryder-Reid is to answer the question: "Does archaeology explore and discover and reexplore and rediscover relationships that occurred in the past? That is, is archaeology about the past? Or does archaeology deal with relationships between the present and the past? That is, is it principally about the present?"

Susan Kus, for her part (chapter 10), doubts the ability of this "we" to erect a framework which can support a double reflection of the world, particularly one that embraces the "Other," even if that framework is founded on a symbolic approach that is pushed to its elusive limits. The example which she presents charts a course that leads to a certain reciprocal intelligibility between two cultures, but it comes from a living society in Madagascar. The emphatic approach to death she depicts would not have been feasible through mere contact with mortuary remains, even if they had been ennobled by the presence of the Egyptian god-king Ramses II speaking with the voice of Charlton Heston, as she so elegantly suggests in her anecdote.

The work of Patricia Galloway (chapter 11) is also founded on ethnological observations, or, to be more precise, on early ethnohistorical accounts of Native Americans in the southern states. Her goal is to establish the limits of what we can learn from the chronicles of sixteenth-century Spaniards about the Native Peoples of the Southeastern United States by comparing these documents with archaeological remains from the same region. She summarizes her discussion, as well as her reasoning, in resolutely modern terms: what matters is the reconstruction of the two bases of knowledge underlying the observed interpretations—in the first case the texts, and in the second the archaeological remains. As in the two preceding studies, the confrontation of these "two sets of world knowledge" is a way of clarifying the conditions under which representations are produced, and also a means of stressing the limits of symbolic analyses for any comprehensive study of past societies.

Let us now turn to the "francophone" studies mentioned above. Here the subject matter and consequently the methods of analysis are quite different from the "anglophone" papers. Nonetheless, these studies also have a certain higher-level unity. They all focus on the eastern Mediterranean and the Neolithic: in consequence, there are neither texts nor informants to support and enrich *our* representation of *their* representations. However, the interpretative processes used are no less interesting than those of earlier papers and are amenable to the same depth and breadth of investigation.

Olivier Aurenche, for example (chapter 12), examines temporal and spatial variation among settlements in the Near East over a period of some 10,000 years. His conclusions, which include significant sociocultural dimensions, may seem impoverished when compared to those of the earlier chapters of this section, but one should not disparage them without indicating at the same time just how and with what data it would have been possible to take them further.

Similarly, some of us might be uneasy at the imbalance between Danielle Stordeur's splendidly documented study of the bone industries in the Levant between the tenth and the sixth millennia (chapter 13) and the nature of the interpretations she draws from their distribution in space and time; it is up to those dissatisfied minds to provide better interpretations of their own based on the same facts, while keeping in mind that such alternative interpretations should be capable of empirical verification or falsification, which, in this case, constitutes the rule of the game.

Catherine Perlès (chapter 14) strives to anticipate such reservations with an attempt to restore the "intentions" of the artisans as they are expressed in the patterned variability of lithic industries; her reasoning, she writes, does not belong to any of the particular approaches with which the seminar, as originally constituted, was concerned—symbolic, structural, semiotic—yet her "cognitive" approach does allow one to "question the matter in these terms." She deals with stone tool assemblages recovered throughout Europe, from the Magdalenian through the Neolithic—a span of more than 20,000 years. In her analysis she constructs a systematic inventory of options open to stone tool makers throughout that temporal span and at various conceptual levels: economic, social, and even symbolic. She characterizes the development of the sequent tool assemblages in terms of a series of "strategies" that are the consequences of intentional acts on the part of the artisans who made and maintained these implements.

(IV) The feature common to the studies in the fourth part is their use of "formal" methods in their analysis of archaeological materials. Christopher Chippindale (chapter 15), examines the modes of production of archaeological materials, yet he does so in ways that refer neither to objective "conditions" nor to subjective "strategies." Instead, his intentions are to construct formal systems—akin to generative grammars—that not only describe one or another category of object or monument but also indicate the specificity of each such construction in terms that will support "social inferences."

Valentine Roux approaches the formalization of archaeological inferences by another route (chapter 16). Her principal point is that the legitimacy of our rewriting operations $p \rightarrow q$ comes essentially from a "knowledge of reference" that we constitute analogically from ethnological observations, indicating that *IF p* is present, *THEN* the presence of *q* can be taken for granted. The example she chooses (the relation between wheel-thrown ceramic production and craft specialization) shows that it takes time and money to give our inferences the empirical foundations necessary to meet the logicist requirements through such ethnological studies.

At first glance, the next paper, by Henri-Paul Francfort (chapter 17), takes the same line, asking: What knowledge bases do archaeologists or anthropologists rely on to characterize a given society as proto-state or proto-urban? Here, the expression "knowledge base" is more than a metaphor: the author, with the collaboration of computer scientists, has endeavored to construct an expert system that reproduces the process of reasoning that leads to such diagnoses. His objective, which goes well beyond that of simple computer simulation, was demonstrated for the seminar participants. The richest part of the presentation illustrated the application of a general theory of measurement in archaeology, an event through which one was able to recognize numerous epistemological and methodological positions debated on other days.

James Doran's contribution (chapter 18) is very close to that offered by Henri-Paul Francfort: to paraphrase Francfort, the central question is just how and to what extent social, economic, and political "key concepts and processes" can be convincingly expressed in computational terms. To this end Doran gives more space and thought to aspects of computers and artificial intelligence than do the other contributors; yet, his ultimate objective goes beyond computer experiments. It remains the elaboration of a "better and more rigorous sociocultural theory," tested in ways that would be congenial to Francfort and the others.

Marie-Salomé Lagrange, who is no less interested in computers than Doran and Francfort (and the editors, for that matter), nonetheless expresses reservations about their uncritical application in archaeology (chapter 19). She writes that "experiment shows that computation does not really take over from thought." The latter requires operations which, even for relatively simple tasks, such as the allocation of monuments to pre-established classes, are beyond the competence of expert systems, including those which are regarded as "classics" of their genre. One of the faculties computers lack is the ability to "learn"; that is, they cannot elaborate upon classifications based on pre-established groups through modification of their own rules of computation. The experiment in automatic learning reported by Lagrange illustrates this gap between artificial and natural intelligence. Nevertheless, she urges us to use the first (artificial intelligence) to deepen our knowledge of the second (natural intelligence). It seems that archaeology, as broadly conceived, currently is the beneficiary of a certain lead in these matters, and it would be a great pity if we lost it.

The paper that ends this series, by Christopher Peebles (chapter 20), could lead to misapprehensions: indeed, it begins on a resolutely negative note, attacking trends that could be most conveniently labeled as "scientism"—logical positivism, operationalism, instrumentalism, and, above all, behaviorism. He does so even though several contributions to this volume, especially those in this very section, might be considered a part of the "schools" that he derides. Thoughts of such invidious comparisons should disappear once he makes clear that he believes archaeology should adopt a form of basic realism once it frees itself from the fetters of unnecessarily reductionistic, mechanistic, self-limiting, ahistorical approaches. Indeed, the main theme of the program he sketches is the study of the mental *representations*, a representational materialism, constituting archaeological matter itself, in the manifold subjective and objective senses of this term. Thus his plea for the inclusion of a "cognitive level of analysis" in prehistoric research fits comfortably with the ideas of most participants. It comprises a search for the inter-subjective representations through which we try to penetrate the symbolic worlds of people of the past, yet it also includes objective representations inasmuch as we strive in their application to invest them with criteria of "reality," in the study of culture as well as nature.

(V) Most of the general philosophical positions that were present at the beginning of the seminar were in evidence as it ended, yet in the interval they had been reworked and reinforced through the examination and discussion of a variety of empirical works. After five days and evenings filled with discussions, the participants met on Saturday morning and brought the proceedings full circle. This short final session allowed them an opportunity to sum up the results of the seminar, each from his or her own perspective. Moreover, it was agreed that if necessary the authors would revise their contributions in light of these discussions. We will not encumber this thick volume with a summary of these "debates." It is, however, the function of our Epilogue, the fifth and final part of the volume, to summarize the main themes around which these final discussions were organized. As prologue both to the papers that follow and to the Epilogue that comes after, we can suggest that the substance of these discussions comprised broadly shared intellectual commitments to the "rationality" of those "others" from the past as well as those with us in the present.

NOTE

1. One participant, Carole Crumley, had committed her paper for publication elsewhere: "A Dialectical Critique of Hierarchy," in *Power Relations and State Formation,* Thomas C. Patterson and Christine Galley, eds., pp. 155–169, American Anthropological Association, Washington, D.C., 1987.

REFERENCE

Radnitzky, G. 1973. *Contemporary Schools of Metascience.* Henry Regnery Company, Chicago.

PART I

Philosophical and Semiotic Points of View

Archaeology and Symbol Systems

The most distinctive aspect of the social sciences and humanities *(des "sciences humaines")* is without doubt their recurrent tendency to revert to models of true sciences—those pure and hard disciplines—based on the models of the natural sciences. It is an old tendency, sometimes as old as the disciplines themselves, and it would be difficult to list all the pseudosciences which have successively obstructed research, from Gall's phrenology to Hennequin's "scientific criticism" (1888). The reason for this is that at any given time, a scientific model is considered to represent the ideal method. Consequently, disciplines that are uncertain about their status and their methods try to imitate this model. For the past fifty years, the most striking example has been linguistics, a discipline which thought it had become a formal science capable of reaching the rigor and productivity found in logic or mathematics; it is obvious, however, that its results—although significant—did not meet expectations.

The "New Archaeology,"[1] whose date of birth can be symbolically fixed in 1968, the year when books by the Binfords and Clarke were published (Binford and Binford 1968; Clarke 1968), is to archaeology what generative grammar has been to linguistics: it marks the moment when, under the influence of works by specialists in epistemology and the history of sciences (e.g., Nagel 1961 and Kuhn 1962), archaeology started pondering explicit problems in method. This is one of the basic points on which L. R. Binford again insists in 1977: "The most commonly cited and debated point I have tried to emphasize is that to be productive, a scientist must operate with a self-conscious awareness of the ideas and assumptions by which he proceeds" (Binford 1977:1). It is precisely because of the importance given to methodological considerations that a volume like the present one can find a place; it is for the same reason that a sheer amateur was invited to contribute a paper; that is, because it was believed that his hypothetical competence in semiotics would entitle him to participate in an undertaking whose purpose was to create an outline of a truly cognitive archaeology rooted in semiotics. All I have to do now is to play my part, that of a semiotician, to whom by definition nothing that belongs to the sign is unknown, and to submit a few tentative reflections on the relationships between archaeology and semiotics.

First, I will clarify my conception of semiotics. This changing and varied field, with its uncertain disciplinary status, lacks unity; without doubt, there are as many semiologies or forms of semiotics (the name itself is not fully established) as there are semioticians, and thus it is wiser to say where I stand so as to avoid confusions and ambiguities (see Molino, 1973, 1975, 1978, 1985a, 1985b). I will summarize this conception, which I call the semiology of symbolic forms, under three headings: (1) the definition and (2) the functions of the sign and (3) the existential mode of symbols.

1. *Definition of the sign*. The most accurate definition of the sign in general—this term henceforth will refer to different species of a same kind—is without doubt that of the Scholastics, *stat aliquid pro aliquo*: something stands for something else, takes the place of something else, plays the part of something else, refers to something else other than itself. The starting point of an authentic semiotics can only be found in a conception of the sign inspired by Peirce: a sign is something that means something to somebody, in any respect or in any way. It is intended for somebody, that is, it creates in this person's mind an equivalent or perhaps a more developed sign. The specific sign it has created is what Peirce calls the "interpretant" of the first sign. Any object, any reality can only be described through other signs which are the "interpretants" of the original sign. From this conception the following points ensue: (i) We should remember that the sign represents its object, refers to its object, yet only through other signs, which are the "interpretants"; (ii) this cross-reference from one sign to other signs is infinite.

2. *Functions of the sign*. First, two general views of the sign must be distinguished. These two views bring about two types of semiologies, which will be called the semiology of communication and the semiology of representation. As will be seen, we are not exactly dealing with the distinction between semiology of communication and semiology of signification already suggested by Prieto (1966) and Mounin (1970). In the first case, the sign is defined as the instrument of human communication; this has been the most common definition since linguistics and various human sciences first used the model suggested by theories of information and communication. This notion of sign is the basis for semiologies as different as those of Prieto and Eco. In the second case, the sign is considered as a substitute whose function is primarily cognitive. Let us consider language as an example: Should it really be accepted, as linguists often state, that the primary function of language is communication? As a matter of fact, language is an instrument far too complicated, perhaps unnecessarily complicated, to provide for simple communication needs, which, as is shown by the evolution of communication systems among animals, are well provided for by structurally different organizations. In this case the anthropologists' point of view is much more enlightening; with Leroi-Gourhan (1964, 1965), we would be more correct in thinking that language and instrument progress in a parallel and related way: "In other words, based on a formula identical to that of Primates, man builds concrete tools and symbols, all of them representing a product of the same process or, rather, relying on the same fundamental equipment of the mind. This leads us to consider not only that language is as characteristic of humankind as the tool, but also that they are both an expression of the same property of humankind . . . " (Leroi-Gourhan 1964:162–163).

3. *Existential mode of symbols*. All species of signs are characterized by a specific existential mode: signs appear as material existence, as production, and as reception.

First, the sign is production, not emission as is usually said when using the misleading communication model. Language does not encode a preexisting meaning, because, as pointed out by R. Ruyer (1954), where would this meaning first be and how could there be new meanings if all we did was to convey a meaning already present? The existence of the sign is *poïetic*, if by *poïetic* we understand the conditions and operations that lead to the creation of something that would not have existed unless someone had brought into being something irreducibly new. In a way, it can be said that work is of and exists through the sign, as much as work is of and exists through the tool. This is why, having been produced, the sign exists materially as an object of the world among the other objects of the world: image, word, rite, work of art, or scientific theory. It is because it is endowed with a material existence that the sign offers access to knowledge and also can be analyzed as an object. It offers access to knowledge inasmuch as thought objectivizes itself in the sign, permitting the constant dialectic of the sign and the operation that alone ensures progress of knowledge; the number objectivizes the operations carried out on collections of objects, thus allowing the objectivized operations to become in turn objects of more complex operations. Once objectivized, the sign can be studied like any other object of the world: its different components can be analyzed and dissected, as can be the various configurations of which the sign is a part.

Meanwhile, however, one should not forget that this object is only one aspect of the sign, something that gives some control over it but which is not sufficient to constitute it: we are facing a mere trace of the results of past operations and of the possibilities of new operations to come. In addition, the sign has an "aesthetic" existence; this means that it is received, or, more precisely, reproduced, by someone. Any symbolic object presupposes an exchange in which production and consumption, transmitter and receiver are neither interchangeable nor share the same view of the object that they thus constitute differently. As Valéry observed, there is no guarantee of an exact and direct correspondence between the effect produced by a work of art and its creator's intentions. Although existing as production, as an object in the world, and as reproduction, the sign is also reference: reference to the world and to the infinity of its interpretants.

Is this fundamental structure of the sign purely formal? Without doubt it is not so, since it appears as the consequence of a common origin, which will be called the symbolic function. Specialists in aphasia were the first to assume the existence of this function. To Hughlings Jackson (1932), not only language but also writing and pantomime are representative behaviors; they belong to the same function, which allows representation through signs or images. For Head (1926), a particular type of behavior exists, which he calls an activity of formulation and symbolic expression and in which a symbol, either linguistic or not, plays a role between the initiation and the execution of an act; within this category of activity we find behaviors as diverse as language and writing, as well as calculation, music, plans and itineraries, designs, dates, and so on.

Although specialists in psychopathology are led to assume the existence of this symbolic function to account for the phenomena they encounter, developmental, child psychologists point to that manifestation of the different aspects of this same capacity, which consists in being able to represent something signified—object, event, conceptual scheme, etc.—by means of a differentiated "signifiant" whose sole purpose is to provide this representation: language, mental image, symbolic gesture, etc. (Piaget and Inhelder 1968). The emergence and development of this symbolic function in the child can be followed precisely; at the end of the sensorimotor period, at around eighteen months of age, it shows itself in the approximately simultaneous apparition of five types of representative behaviors: delayed imitation, symbolic game or fiction game, design, mental image, and language. Since these various behaviors imply, at the same moment, the same strategy of representation by means of signs and symbols, it is legitimate to assume the existence of a symbolic function, as real as are the nutritive or reproductive functions to the living being. Thus, the hypothesis of a symbolic function allows us to escape the dilemma in which the humanities are caught much too often nowadays: either the symbolic constitutes another irreducible and mysteriously creative world, the beyond (of the world) that Nietzsche thought he had overcome, or the symbolic is but a ghostly world, a pale reflection of the world here below and its interests. The symbolic function is the enabling condition for a positive science of culture and can be regarded, in turn, as an anthropological property; man—according to the anthropologist Leslie A. White (1949)—is not so much a rationalizing animal, but a "symboling animal" who creates symbols at the same time as he creates tools.

Just as one can follow the ontogenesis of the symbolic function, one may, with more or less verisimilitude, reconstruct its phylogenesis. We may hypothesize that along with more and more sophisticated tools—the only vestiges of the different stages of evolution—more and more complicated and efficient systems of symbols should appear (see Leroi-Gourhan 1964; Lieberman 1975). The process of hominization should not be regarded as a sudden transition, from nothingness to the whole, which would have entailed successively a technical and then a cultural evolution, both of which came only after a purely physical evolution: tools, language, social organization, art, and religion were factors in the hominization process rather than merely consequences of it; thus, they are not superstructures of an evolution that would have happened independently, but an integral part of the evolution and transformation process (see Geertz 1973:55–83). This interpretation seems to be confirmed by recent discoveries in paleontology, since some anthropologists do not hesitate to attribute technique, but also reflection and language, to *Homo habilis* (from 4 million to 1.6 million years ago): "Schematically, it could be said that the first man appears as a superior Primate of dry savannas, a biped, opportunistic omnivore, social artisan, cunning and cautious, lucid and talkative. Man is present, in all his functional and behavioral characteristics" (Coppens 1983:120). The symbolic function, thus, is anything but mysterious, even if we are far from understanding its organization. J. P. Changeux's "mental objects" (Changeux 1983) provide us with a sketch and a model of what could be a neurology of the symbolic function. The symbolic is therefore an autonomous field of the "existent" to which it would be absurd to deny the independence usually granted to technique or social and economic organization. For both technique and society exist only through the presence of the symbolic.

The symbol is as autonomous, as productive, as the tool. Such are the facts on which a semiology must necessarily be built, and they constitute a general theory of symbolic processes. Symbol and tool share numerous properties, first in the sense that they both constitute victory of "mediation" over reality, as mentioned by P. Janet (1935, 1936). Instead of directly facing reality, humankind turns away so as to achieve a better triumph over it. What is the tool if not a mediator of behavior? The same configuration can be found in the symbol. Instead of being lost in the present, instead of immediately living in the here and now of a world that has no temporal horizon, humankind organizes experience by distancing the self from the world in and through the symbol: as the tool represents distance from the object, the symbol represents distance from reality. There is mediation and distance, hence the possibility of a projection toward the past (memory) and toward the future (daydreaming, imagination, technical, artistic, and scientific creation). Animals challenge reality with their claws; humankind takes a detour by making cudgels so as to better act on reality. It is the same for the symbol: humans neither represent nor reflect the world, they build it through symbols. This conception and Marx's formula in the *German Ideology*—"Wherever a relationship can be found, this relationship exists for me"—are poles apart. In fact, Marx denies mediation: not only mediation of the symbol inserted between humans and the world, but also any social mediation. His denial of symbolic mediation lies in the fact that his thought is still part of the old myth of social transparency in a free society, where generic humankind will be self-sufficient and will enjoy the pure reflection that the world and others provide. The essential question remains: If a hammer does not reflect the world, yet acts upon it, why should this be different for the symbol?

Let us now try to see, at some personal risk and peril, what the situation of archaeology looks like in terms of this semiology of symbolic forms. I will first consider the evolution of the discipline. Here we encounter one of the characteristics which, from the very beginning, distinguishes the social from the natural sciences: specialists in natural sciences do not wonder about the underlying logic of their discipline, nor do they need to—unless they personally feel like knowing it. The same is not true for social sciences: nothing is more serious than forgetting, for censored tradition very often tends to reappear where it is least expected. Nothing is more dangerous than the theme, now commonplace, of a scientific revolution that would allow a discipline to start anew and reconstruct everything on absolute and completely new foundations. Indeed, previous stages in archaeology progressively elaborated questions, methods, and different types of answers that are still broadly valid. Therefore, it is essential to consider once again, even in schematic form, moments in the evolution of the discipline in order to separate what is living from what is dead, what may be kept from what has to be abandoned.

Archaeology progressively modified its ontology. A preliminary remark should be made about this issue: as Vico pointed out in his *Scienza nuova* (1953 [original 1744]), human works are realities whose existence cannot be questioned; they may be the only ones to have this particular status, which, in this case, forces us to adopt a realistic metaphysics. In accordance with a Cartesian approach, we could either question the existence of the external world or wonder about the existential status of the phenomenon or the thing in itself. We cannot doubt the existence of human works any more than we can doubt "I think, therefore I am."

Archaeology started out by considering monuments. This last word is to be taken in the particular meaning of remarkable works showing an artistic or symbolic value, whatever their nature—architecture, sculpture, mosaic. This stand follows the tradition established in Europe by the archaeology of Classical Greece and Rome. We will later emphasize the specific nature of the different archaeologies, or more specifically of the different divisions of archaeology, according to the type of civilization that each considers. Clearly, classical archaeology can be defined by its origin in a particular relationship to values. We may repeat Max Weber's formula: vestiges of classical civilizations are the origin of our culture, therefore they are not like any other reality. They carry a meaning and a value as models; they are works whose apprehension must be, in the last resort, aesthetic. Let it be mentioned here that, despite its striking inadequacies, this perspective should not be irrevocably rejected: monuments are also "things of beauty" and their aesthetic dimension is part of their symbolic reality.

Archaeology then switched from the monument to the object: tools and manufactured objects—dishes, pieces of pottery, implements, etc. Here, functional dimensions take over: What are tools and manufactured objects used for? Humankind appears through the differential preservation of traces as a maker, as *Homo faber*, whose archaeology tries to restore the productive activity of the species. A third and last stage is characterized by a maximal generalization: archaeology finally considers everything that humans have left as vestiges of their existence; it considers all traces, whatever their nature. Food remnants, pollen, bone splinters, flint fragments, use-wear on teeth and on flint blades, coprolites, footprints, marks left by any activity or gesture. Anything is of value to an archaeology that more appropriately may be called *ichnology*, the "study of traces," the name given to the discipline that studies the fossilized traces left by living organisms. Incidentally, it should be noted that in order to interpret these traces, ichnology has gotten into the habit of resorting to aktuopaleontology, a discipline that analyzes modifications to the seashore caused by the action of living beings, just as archaeology today resorts to ethnology to interpret traces left by human cultures. This is one example from the many instances of partial similarity between the natural and the human sciences. Of course, it should be added that this transformation of ontology cannot be separated from the reformulation of excavation techniques.

As its ontology changed, archaeology changed the questions it asked of its material. One could thus witness the process that P. Veyne (1971; 1984: chapter 10) called, for history in general, a "lengthening of the questionnaire." Traditional archaeology developed around three essential problems: the identification, classification, and chronology of monuments and objects. Identification answers the following question: What is this? What is this monument, this vase, this tool? Identification consists either of placing the object in a known category or of defining a new category on the basis of the object's hypothetical function. However, we must stress the fact that the problems posed by identification can be extremely different, depending on the cultures under study and the object under analysis. Identification is made easier if the archaeologist has written or printed texts at hand. It becomes a matter of connecting two types of reality. If the analyst does not have any such supplementary source of information, the only possible procedure is by *analogy*, and we see here the fundamental role played by deductive reasoning in the archaeologist's approach, a reasoning which also can take the form of abductive reasoning as defined by Peirce. In addition, a distinction must be made between a monument or an object with figures—in the sense of figurative art—and nonfigurative objects. In the first case the problem is one of representation, which involves the symbolic dimension right at the start. In the general case, identification is closely linked to classification, since *ipso facto* it places the object in a category of objects which are intuitively regarded as analogous.

At this point, it is useful to introduce the notion of *series*, which comes first from epigraphy and then from economic history, since it undoubtedly provides one of the fundamental concepts of all historic disciplines and the human sciences in general. In these domains, the basic datum cannot be an isolated object, for an isolated object is nothing and does not have any meaning: as Eduard Gehrard used to say, whoever has seen one monument has not seen any, whoever has seen thousands of them has seen only one of them. The difference from natural sciences is as follows: there exist, and even more clearly at the first stages of science, some natural kinds which allow us to take an entity of the natural world—stone, vegetable, or animal—as the neutral and ordinary representative of its kind. On the other hand, *there are no natural species of human artifacts*; hence the importance of notions like that of "style," which, in the humanities, is the equivalent of the natural species. It is thus possible to understand the determining importance of classification, which not only means placing a specific object in a well-defined group, but also has a constitutive function. In this way classifications and series make up the object and the elementary fact. They are neither the object nor the trace, but the series in which they are integrated and constituted as fact.

The third fundamental question posed by traditional archaeology was chronology, whose status appeared as paradoxical and, in certain respects, was linked to the previous questions by a vicious circle. Since without texts archaeology had no way of fulfilling the first duty of the historian, that of establishing chronology, the identification and constitution of series were almost exclusively aimed at dating the object or the series by integrating them in a higher-order series of primarily chronological value. At this point in its development, archaeology corresponded fairly well to the goals history had set itself in its classical age: historical facts should be established, which is to say that they should be dated. We will see how various factors led beyond these goals of traditional archaeology; it should be stressed, however, that these questions still have a meaning that cannot be ignored. Identification, classification, and dating are still the basis of archaeological inquiry.

The questionnaire has indeed been lengthened, and the positions of old questions have been changed. With the discovery of new dating techniques, archaeology has been able—at least in the case of archaeology without texts—to develop chronology independently of the constitution of the object; the most fortunate consequence has been to liberate the mind of the archaeologist. Once relieved of the obsessive duty of dating, he or she could turn to new questions. Thus the evolution of archaeological ontology and the lengthening of the questionnaire develop in parallel; the interest given to traces in all their various forms is but one aspect of the slow mutation that transformed the discipline of history into a social science. It is not only ethnology—as is often said when speaking about ethnoarchaeology—but also sociology and all the social sciences which now suggest or dictate their questions to the archaeologist. Thus, a crucial change has taken place in the very orientation of archaeological work, and this new archaeology—in a broad sense, not in that of a restricted adherence to a particular school—falls within the general framework of the social sciences. Its main problem becomes this: From traces left by human groups, how can their social existence be reconstructed? Two difficulties arise.

First, can we be sure that traces answer questions posed by the present study of societies? Certainly, a dialectical relationship between social sciences and archaeological traces may be considered; if questions are reformulated by the social sciences, they also have to be adapted to the limitations of reconstruction actually permitted by the traces. Furthermore, taking traces into account imposes new questions on present societies, particularly about the kind of traces left by a living society and their relationships with the activity of that society. Too often, a certain anthropological triumphalism imposed questions the archaeologist could not answer in an interesting way, thus ignoring the infrangible principle of historical method according to which there are no good questions in history other than those which can be answered in a plausible and legitimate way.

The second difficulty is concerned with the symbolic as we previously defined it (and is not to be confused with the orientations of Hodder's [1982, 1987] symbolic archaeology). The traditional study of monuments called upon a very elaborate symbolism rooted in religious references; the dominant tendency in the contemporary analysis of traces is materialistic functionalism according to which no system of symbols of any sort plays a part in the interpretation. In this way, one directly switches from traces to ecological and economic factors that are supposed to determine the forms and processes of social organization. If there is a lesson to be learned from the evolution of history, it is the need to switch from economic and social history to the history of mentalities—as linguistics was forced, by an inevitable drift, to switch from syntax to semantics in order to account for these selfsame syntactical facts that face it. For traces never directly express an external constraint: they are the product of a culture, of a mediation through signs and symbols. Then, if man is a "symboling animal"—according to Leslie White's formula (1949)—the mediation through the symbol is an obligation for the specialist in archaeology.

One must avoid establishing *a priori* a unique and immediate type of explanation for social activities as they are crystallized in traces; one must also beware of ambiguities in terminology, for example that of the term "meaning" as applied to ecological or economic function. The meanings of human activity are numerous and complex: explicit or implicit, conscious or unconscious, ritual or innovative, public or private. They cannot be reduced to any external foundation, be it idealistic or materialistic, structural or practical. Any social practice is symbolic through and through, and there is no tool, no activity, no product that is truly empty of meaning. Whatever may be the limits of the evidence provided by traces, it is essential to consider this symbolic dimension as the most important one and to construct hypotheses that allow one to restore its meaning, at least in part. Traces have been produced by members of a given culture and this production indissociably combines actions and meanings, deeds and thoughts.

The present condition of archaeology is explained not only by its evolution, but also—as I mentioned at the beginning of this chapter—by the extent of its theoretical concerns and by the determination displayed by new archaeologists to achieve a more scientific status. In this broad movement, which covers all historical and social disciplines, it is of primary importance to keep one's head and to distinguish elements and problems that have too often been confused in the past. Reflections on the new archaeology are at the confluence of very diverse methods and achievements. First, there is the introduction of specific scientific techniques, such as carbon-14 and palynology. Their development has sometimes led to the belief that "auxiliary sciences" ensure the validity of the global interpretative process, which, however, went beyond them on all sides and cannot be based on them. Then, the quantitative revolution occurred, an event more important than the progress just mentioned, and gave birth to what is here and there referred to as archaeometry. This development constituted a natural and predictable step in the evolution of the discipline. Moreover, it probably was stimulated by the influence of geography, for the points of contact and the parallels between the progress of the two disciplines are striking and should be analyzed in detail. Let us just indicate a few points of convergence: concern about the quantitative study of space and its organization, the use of notions borrowed from systems theory, the elaboration of models, and an emphasis on explanation (see, for example, Harvey 1969; Chorley and Haggett 1967; Haggett 1965). We will return to some of these themes in a moment; meanwhile, let us recall the problems posed by the quantitative approach in archaeology. The main difficulty here lies in the sampling issue: the representativity of quantified elements (see Gardin 1979; Gallay 1986). It is therefore important to be cautious about acceptance of quantitative treatments whose archaeological foundations are quite uncertain.

A third element is the fascination exerted by the hypothetico-deductive model of scientific method in its classical neo-positivist version (see, for example, Hempel and Oppenheim 1948; Nagel 1961). It is interesting to note that this hypothetico-deductive model triumphed in the "soft" disciplines—linguistics and the new archaeology—while it was subjected to more and more serious criticism in natural sciences, criticism that eventually led to its renunciation (see, for example works by Goodman, Hanson, Feyerabend, Kuhn, and Popper, and the references in Brown 1977). It is not surprising, then, that Binford, in one of his latest books (1983), distanced himself from this aspect of new archaeology. Two additional remarks will suffice: in the first place, the physical sciences do not show as much concern for the purity of their methods, whereas nothing is more worrying than a desire for purity and scientific "standing" in a domain where results are so often doubtful; second, the most fruitful direction of research does not consist in competing with a method whose purity is inaccessible and misleading, but in elaborating a specific method which respects the complexity of archaeological facts.

The last factor to have influenced the orientation taken by theories of archaeology is the model of social sciences, and of quantitative sociology in particular (see, for example, Lazarsfeld, in Lazarsfeld and Rosenberg 1955). The goals of the New Archaeology could be summarized—in a new formula—by saying that it tries to answer sociological questions while using its own forms of conceptualization and quantitative treatment of data (see, for example, the general introduction in Binford 1977:1–10).

It seems to us that these various influences, although exerting a positive effect and provoking a profound renewal in the goals and methods of archaeology, also have had harmful consequences. Put bluntly, the discipline tried to put on clothes not intended for it to wear. Maybe, in the near future, it will be able to devise a method more adapted to its goals and means. Let us state tentatively what we think constitutes the different levels of analysis of archaeological data. The identification of traces is often neglected by the most extreme supporters of new archaeology; we previously encountered this level and saw that it was tightly linked to problems of definition and classification. Yet two types of problems must be distinguished, depending on whether we are dealing with isolated, elementary objects or with configurations. Although the first problem, that of elementary objects, was passed on from old to new archaeology without much change, it can be said that the major contribution of the new archaeology is in the realm of the second, that of the configuration of objects. We believe that under the influence of geography, archaeology gave primary importance to phenomena concerning the human appropriation of space. Indeed, regardless of which perspective was adopted—in this respect, one could oppose Hodder's symbolic archaeology (Hodder 1978, 1982, 1987) to Flannery's or Binford's anthropological and materialistic archaeology—the main feature has been the decisive role attributed to space: settlements, households, hunting itineraries, exchange routes all become major concerns in textless archaeology.

It is at this moment that actualism comes into play; this injunction points to the fact that we should observe present cultures in order to establish links between social activities and traces of spatial occupation. The totally original aspect of the questions raised is then clear: the correlations we have to elicit cannot be compared with the correlations established in sociology, for we have no means to know these activities except through the traces they have left behind. The most fruitful lesson of actualist comparison seems to have been the recognition of the ambiguity of traces: traces can mean something completely different than what we naïvely wanted them to mean; in some sense, we are more and more aware of the fact that we do not know what specific activities the traces we uncover correspond to. Actualist comparisons mainly contributed to a broadening of the range of possible answers and plausible hypotheses.

Up to this point, we have only considered synchronic analyses. However, from its very beginning, archaeology aimed at historical goals. Beyond chronology, traditional archaeology tried to account for transformations. Most of the time its model of interpretation was based on two principles which were more or less explicit: (1) that there is an almost direct correspondence between cultures and certain specific aspects of artifacts left by each of them; and (2) that evolution happens through diffusion and borrowing. Once again, the contribution of New Archaeologies in this domain seems to be negative (which does not in anyway detract from its interest) and has led to two opposite principles: (1) cultures leave heterogeneous traces and there is no direct correspondence between styles and cultures; (2) diffusion and borrowing are not enough to explain transformations and cannot be relied on to reconstruct evolutionary sequences. The new archaeology substituted a new problem for these principles that bore a relationship to the neo-evolutionism of American cultural anthropology. What mattered now was to account for processes which lead from one stage to another within social evolution (see, for example, Forrester 1969; Chorley and Kennedy 1971) and which were based on systematic models of materialist inspiration—that is to say, models where ecological and demographic constraints played a determining role. These problems are undoubtedly interesting and reflect preoccupations that the archaeologist should always have in mind; yet difficulties arise from the fact that the data are too underdetermined and uncertain for these complex models to be validated.

We thus are led to discuss the notion of model as it is commonly used in archaeology. A preliminary observation is necessary: the books with the term "model" in their titles (Clarke 1972 and Renfrew 1973) do not give a precise idea of what a model represents in archaeology. This lack of specificity comes about because archaeology is a complex and heterogeneous discipline which can only artificially be assigned a unique and coherent method. Indeed, it is important to react against the misleading ideal, too long supported by neo-positivism and embodied in the *International Encyclopedia of Unified Science*, about the so-called unity of science. This position is a myth, and its rejection holds true not only for the various sciences but also for each one of them individually. An Aristotelian perspective, according to which knowledge has an indefinitely branched structure, would be more appropriate (see Fodor 1975). On the one hand, archaeology does not have to fall within the compass of a hypothetical unified scientific method; on the other, it must resort to diverse operations, hypotheses, models, and theories, depending on the questions and domains addressed. The identification of traces calls for models other than those of classification, the interpretation of spatial configurations, or the evolution of cultures; similarly, models must change from classical to protohistoric and prehistoric archaeology. Archaeological data appear as a set of objects and traces that the archaeologist tries to identify, classify, organize, interpret, and explain. This is what we call the neutral or material level of existence of symbolic realities. Analytical operations, too, are symbolic constructions, yet these constructions cannot be reduced to a single model, no matter how sophisticated it might be.

Up to this point, we have proceeded as if the facts available to the archaeologist were immediate and indisputable. This conception was the basis for positivism and neo-positivism: there were some empirical objective and independent data as well as a formal discourse which constituted the absolute foundation of a scientific approach. This conception is inaccurate. There is no such thing as a pure empirical basis, and any datum is inextricably linked to theoretical hypotheses which can be more or less explicit. Data are partly observed and partly constructed, a point made by historians of science about the period when even physicists (see Duhem 1914) were beginning to question the naïvely objectivist models of scientific method. There is, in all domains of knowledge, a role played by the cultural subject, and this intervention can be observed not only in the natural sciences but also in the historical and social disciplines. We shall limit ourselves, however, to the problems posed by the presence of the observer-analyst in the constitution of human data. From this perspective, the situation is considerably different. All the human sciences work on traces, and to date it seems impossible to accomplish the epistemological break which, in the seventeenth century, gave birth to the natural sciences by separating object and subject, primary "objective" qualities (extent and movement) and secondary qualities linked to the subject perception. When analyzing human evidence, the scientist faces data that are homogeneous to his own perception: he is in an *"esthésique,"* sensuous position; that is, he perceives and reproduces data which he modifies according to his knowledge, and no principle of separation enables him to distinguish between objective properties and subjective properties in the phenomenon perceived. One then can understand the recurrent nature of interpretative theories of human facts. By interpretative theories we mean the conceptions based on Marxism and the sociology of knowledge as well as the diverse forms of hermeneutics. Indeed, in all cases, knowledge of the object is fundamentally and implacably linked to the situation of the knowing subject. One of the latest versions of this orientation can be found, for example, in the philosophical synthesis implemented by Rorty (1979), in which pragmatism, hermeneutics, existentialism, and deconstruction meet to dissolve epistemology and replace it with the dialogical interpretation of cultures.

The cultural subject certainly intervenes in the construction of evidence, the selection of facts, and the subject's own relationship, at the other extremity of archaeological work, to values such as the accumulation and exhibition of the remains (collections, museum displays, etc.). Yet, the whole point is to know what kind of impact this intervention has on archaeology as well as on the different senses of man. I shall make a distinction between two problems, one ontological, the other methodological. Regarding the first problem, we must find out whether there *exists* an archaeological object, independent of the cultural subject studying it. The latest fashion in this domain seems to be the antirealism supported by thinkers as different as Goodman (1978), Putman in his second version (the "internal realism," 1981), and van Fraassen (1980).

Bearing this ontological problem in mind, we previously recalled that, according to Vico, the most certain existence is the existence of traces and human works: the analysis and interpretation of traces might be ambiguous and uncertain, but not so their existence. More generally, it is necessary to return to a realistic ontology (see Hacking 1983) that has nothing to do with an objectivist epistemology. Within the humanities, the question becomes clearer if placed in the perspective of a semiology of symbolic forms: traces and works exist, and this "entitivity" is what ensures the objective reality of a material or neutral level of these traces. This material level makes an analysis possible without determining it in a univocal way. This underdetermination of analysis comes from factors linked to the multiple and laminated existence of traces: at a material level, the trace is—as is any ontic presence—the medium and starting point of an infinite analysis, which can be taken into account by distinct models. The trace, however, is also the result of an activity as perceived and reproduced by a subject. To each of these perspectives corresponds a new dimension of analysis which is irreducible to the others. The consequences of such a situation seem to be important for archaeology and are closely akin to the recent warnings stated by Gallay (1986). The configurations brought out at the material level of the existence of traces do not necessarily correspond to the *poïetic* configurations of the social activities that produced these traces.

The situation is thus similar to the relationships between material level and *"esthésique"* strategy or, to reformulate the problem as a simple question: Is what we set as a pertinent configuration of traces only an artifact of our reconstruction? We are not dealing here with the somewhat secondary problem that hermeneutics and critical theories address and that can often only lead to whirlings of signification without any increase in knowledge. What matters now is to know whether and how one can be assured of the relevance of a configuration. Finally, we would like to insist on one fundamental aspect of this work whose signification is underestimated most of the time: we will call it the criticism of traces. If a criticism of texts has existed for a long time, and has been progressively elaborated by philological tradition (see Molino 1985a), it is not certain that the much more recent criticism of traces has reached the same degree of development.

Criticism proceeds negatively: its aim is to rid the text of its additions and its errors, and to find its original form. Recently, archaeology seems to have made an important move toward the settling of a criticism of traces by considering the various mechanisms through which the traces left by a culture have been transmitted and modified: What processes transformed the deposits into the shape in which we find them today? (see Binford 1981; Binford and Bertram 1977; Brain 1981). Thus, a criticism of traces which appears to be the equivalent of the *Ars critica* of the Renaissance is developing in archaeology; it is the only way of founding archaeology on a methodology comparable to the one philology and history have used to acquire a scientific status.

The symbolic appears in archaeological practice according to the three complementary modalities which define the triple existential mode of human facts. First, the archaeologist faces data in an *"esthésique"* capacity, perceiving and reconstructing phenomena. Only a specific criticism—as in the case of history—makes it possible to go beyond the contradiction of hermeneutics and guarantees, at least negatively, the relevance of data. From these data, the archaeologist identifies, classifies, and extracts configurations, and presents more or less explicit, more or less formal symbolic models of these data and their organization: this is the analysis of the material or neutral level of traces. However, at one time or the other, the third dimension of the symbolic, the *poïetic* dimension, must come into play: traces acquire meaning only if related to the human activities that produced them. It is this triple anchorage that links archaeology to the semiology of symbolic forms.

NOTE

1. Hereafter rendered in lower case and without quotation marks (ed.).

REFERENCES

Binford, L. R. (ed.) 1977. *For Theory Building in Archaeology*. Academic Press, New York.
——1981. *Bones: Ancient Men and Modern Myths*. Academic Press, New York.
——1983. *In Pursuit of the Past*. Thames and Hudson, London.
Binford, L. R., and J. B. Bertram 1977. "Bone frequencies and attritional processes," in L. R. Binford (ed.), *For Theory Building in Archaeology*, pp. 77–156. Academic Press, New York.
Binford, S. R., and L. R. Binford (eds.) 1968. *New Perspectives in Archaeology*. Aldine, Chicago.
Brain, C. K. 1981. *The Hunters or the Hunted? An Introduction to African Cave Taphonomy*. University of Chicago Press, Chicago.
Brown, H. I. 1977. *Perception, Theory and Commitment: The New Philosophy of Science*. Precedent Publishing, Chicago
Changeux, J.-P. 1983. *L'homme neuronal*. Librairie Arthème Fayard, Paris.
——1985. *Neuronal Man*. Pantheon, New York.
Chaunu, P. 1974. *Histoire, science sociale*. S.E.D.E.S., Paris

Chorley, R. J., and P. Haggett (eds.) 1967. *Models in Geography*. Methuen, London.
Chorley, R. J., and B. A. Kennedy 1971. *Physical Geography: A System Approach*. Prentice Hall, Englewood Cliffs, NJ.
Clarke, D. L. 1968. *Analytical Archaeology*. Methuen, London.
———(ed.) 1972. *Models in Archaeology*. Methuen, London.
Coppens, Y. 1983. *Le sinqe, l'Afrique et l'homme*. Librairie Arthème Fayard, Paris.
Duhem, P. 1914. *La théorie physique*, 2nd ed. Marcel Riviére, Paris.
Fodor, J. A. 1975. *The Language of Thought*. Thomas Y. Crowell, New York.
Forrester, J. W. 1969. *Urban Dynamics*. MIT Press, Cambridge, MA.
Gallay, A. 1986. *L'archéologie demain*. Belfont, Paris.
Gardin, J.-C. 1979. *Une archéologie théorique*. Hachette, Paris.
———1980. *Archaeological Constructs*. Cambridge University Press, Cambridge.
Geertz, C. 1973. *The Interpretation of Cultures*. Basic Books, New York.
Goodman, N. 1978. *Ways of Worldmaking*. Hackett Publishing Co., Indianapolis, IN.
Hacking, I. 1983. *Representing and Intervening*. Cambridge University Press, Cambridge.
Haggett, P. 1965. *Locational Analysis in Human Geography*. Edward Arnold, London.
Harvey, D. 1969. *Explanation in Geography*. Edward Arnold, London.
Head, H. 1926. *Aphasia and Kindred Disorders of Speech*. Cambridge University Press, Cambridge.
Hempel, C. G., and P. Oppenheim 1948. "Studies in the logic of explanation," *Philosophy of Science* **15**, 135–175.
Hennequin, E. 1888. *La critique scientifique: analyse sociologique*. Perrin, Paris.
Hodder, I. (ed.) 1978. *The Spatial Organisation of Culture*. Duckworth, London.
———1982. *Symbols in Action*. Cambridge University Press, Cambridge.
———1987. *Reading the Past*. Cambridge University Press, Cambridge.
Jackson, J. H. 1932. *Selected Writings*. Hodder-Stoughton, London.
Janet, P. 1935. *Les débuts de l'intelligence*. Flammarion, Paris.
———1936. *L'intelligence avant le langage*. Flammarion, Paris.
Kuhn, T. S. 1962. *The Structure of Scientific Revolutions*. The University of Chicago Press, Chicago.
Lazarsfeld, P. F., and M. Rosenberg (eds.) 1955. *The Language of Social Research*. The Free Press, Glencoe, IL.
Leroi-Gourhan, A. 1964. *Le geste et la parole. Vol. 1, Technique et langage*. Albin Michel, Paris.
———1965. *Le geste et la parole. Vol. 2, La mémoirie et les rythmes*. Albin Michel, Paris.
Lieberman, P. 1975. *On the Origins of Language: An Introduction to the Evolution of Human Speech*. Macmillan, New York.
Molino, J. 1973. "Critique sémiologique de l'idéologie," *Sociologie et Sociétés*, Montréal **2/5**, 17–44.
———1975. "Fait musical et sémiologie de la musique," *Musique en Jeu* **17**, 37–62.
———1978. "Note sur la situation du symbolique," *L'Arc* **72**, 20–25.
———1985a. "Pour une histoire de l'interprétation: les étapes de l'herméneutique," *Philosophiques* **XII 1 and 2**, 73–103 and 281–314.
———1985b. "Per una semiologia come teoria delle forme simboliche," *Materiali filosofici* **15**, 9–26.
Mounin, G. 1970. *Introduction à la sémiologie*. Les Editions de Minuit, Paris.
Nagel, E. 1961. *The Structure of Science*. Harcourt, Brace & World, New York.
Piaget, J., and B. Inhelder 1968. *La psychologie de l'enfant*. Presses Universitaires de France, Paris.
Prieto, L. J. 1966. *Messages et signaux*. Presses Universitaires de France, Paris.
Putnam, H. 1981. *Reason, Truth and History*. Cambridge University Press, Cambridge.
Renfrew, C. (ed.) 1973. *The Explanation of Cultural Change: Models in Prehistory*. Duckworth, London.
Robert, L. 1961. "Epigraphie," in *L'histoire et ses méthodes*, pp. 453–497. Gallimard, Paris.
Rorty, R. 1979. *Philosophy and the Mirror of Nature*. Princeton University Press, Princeton, NJ.
Ruyer, R. 1954. *La cybernétique et l'origine de l'information*. Flammarion, Paris.

van Fraassen, B. C. 1980. *The Scientific Image*. Oxford University Press, Oxford.
Veyne, P. 1971. *Comment on écrit l'histoire*. Éditions du Seuil, Paris.
————1984. *Writing History*. Wesleyan University Press, Middletown, CT.
Vico, G. 1953 [orig. 1744]. *(Scienza nuova) Principes d'une science nouvelle*. Nagel, Paris.
White, L. A. 1949. *The Science of Culture*. Grove Press, New York.

On Capturing Agency in Theories
About Prehistory

Incorporating human agency into theories about prehistory has moved high on the list of priorities amongst theoretical archaeologists, prompting reference to a cognitive revolution in studies of prehistory. This paper explores the methods of incorporating agency in theories about prehistory. It intends to leave archaeologists with methodological criteria helpful for including agency in their theory building.

Different types of explanation either constrain or encourage inclusion of the ideas, decisions, and actions of humans. At one extreme are methodological approaches which exclude agency entirely, and at the other extreme are approaches which embrace agency uncritically. The extremes form the ends of a continuum, however. It will be convenient to chop the explanatory continuum into three parts, each with a quite distinct role for human agency.

The first type of explanation—*holistic* explanation—invokes only forces transcendent to human agency. Holistic approaches assume that what humans think, wish, desire, believe, or will is not a factor, or at least not a significant factor, in the development or structure of human organization. The second—*individualistic* explanation—invokes human agency: the thoughts, decisions, and other willful elements of humans. Individualistic approaches assume that thoughts and decisions have had a major impact on the structure and change of human organizations. The third—*empathetic* explanation—reconstructs not only thoughts and decisions, but also elements like affective states, spiritual orientations, and experiential meanings. Empathetic approaches assume the inner experience of humans is worthy of study for its own sake, and also provides a handle for interpreting human culture. The methodological assumptions underlying each of the three types of explanation are, in order, holistic method, individualistic method, and empathetic method.

Much can be gained by understanding the divergent rationales and contrasting guidelines of the three approaches. The strengths and limitations of each are clarified by thorough comprehension of the alternatives. Knowledge of each is also indispensable for shifting approaches, and for amalgamating elements from amongst them. For the most part, however, methodological debate in archaeology has centered on the holistic and empathetic approaches, between which there is a vast gulf. Use of individualistic method as an alternative for building archaeological theory is in its infancy.

It has long been recognized that individualistic elements should not be ignored in archaeological theory (Collingwood 1946; Leone 1982). More recently the importance of individualistic elements has been recognized not just by those critical of holistic approaches (Deetz 1977; Hodder 1985, 1986), but even some closely identified with holistic approaches (Flannery 1968, 1973; Renfrew 1982, 1987). There also have been probing discussions of ways to identify individuality, such as in prehistoric technology (Hill and Gunn 1977). Despite recognition of the importance of agency, and calls to incorporate individualistic elements in archaeological theory, there has yet been no comprehensive discussion of the potential and limitations of methodological individualism for archaeological theory. This lacuna has persisted even though individualistic method has an established tradition in anthropology, and especially in economic anthropology (Halperin 1984, 1985).

1. Holistic, Individualistic, and Empathetic Approaches

Below are sketches of each of the three approaches. They will provide the background to launch a more detailed review.

Prehistory commonly means history without the benefit of written records. That fact has encouraged students of prehistory—particularly archaeologists—to sidestep, or at least deemphasize, speculation about the thoughts and decisions of prehistoric peoples. Avoiding such human elements in theories about the past has dovetailed with the holistic approaches to explanation that dominate the social sciences; i.e., with the assumptions that superhuman forces underlie social structure and that humans have no agency over them. In short, to understand either static structure or dynamic change with holistic method is to search for forces transcending humans. Crude Marxist interpretations and processual explanations are holistic.

Incidentally, the meaning of holism as it is used here is different from that used in anthropology. The anthropological meaning of holism is that particular aspects of a culture, such as rituals or eating, can be understood only within the context of the culture as a whole.

Another goal in archaeological theory is to incorporate elements like thoughts and decisions into theories about prehistoric peoples. Incorporating such human elements rests on a number of assumptions. It assumes that thoughts and decisions do have agency— they are not just reflections of, or "superstructure" upon, underlying forces. It also assumes that collective actions and shared institutions are best interpreted as the products of the decisions and actions of individuals. These assumptions and related ideas constitute individualistic method, or *methodological individualism*. Cognitive archaeology, for example, the goal of which is to understand the thoughts, decisions, and similar ideational facets of prehistoric people, breaks sharply with holistic method by employing individualistic method. That schism is dramatic, and its ramifications are likely to shake the foundations of theory building in archaeology.

Attempts to reconstruct the feelings, hopes, experiential meanings, and other affective and spiritual elements of prehistoric peoples often utilize empathetic method: use of personal intuition to understand the inner lives of other people. Empathetic method assumes there is common structure to human experience. The common structure is the "bridge" that justifies an investigator's claims about the experiences of other people. Since there is a shared structure to experience, the feelings, hopes, and experiential meanings of an investigator are assumed to be similar to those of a target group. Emic approaches to theory building normally employ elements of empathetic method.

2. Holistic Method vs. Individualistic Method

Religious inclinations, or disinclinations, can be set aside when reading the following exchange between an atheist and a believer:

Atheist: "Can you not see that the church is designed to control your life? Its theological doctrine mandates that you accept it as the broadcaster of wisdom, telling you what you can and cannot do. You also are expected to serve it, both in time and with money, in order to gain 'salvation,' whatever that is. You are expected to participate in its rituals, and submit to the proclamations of its prelate—that person who is supposedly in closer contact with its deity, if there is one. In other words, you are but a pawn of institutionalized religion, and if you wish to understand it you must see through your delusion of belief to realize how it represses and exploits you."

Believer: "That's not at all how I conceive of my commitment. God has given me many blessings, and my church is an incarnate messenger of His word. I feel neither repressed nor exploited. As a matter of fact, I have willingly given my life to God and his agent, the Church, and am thankful to have made the decision to do so."

Which of the above positions is correct? Overlooking one's own predispositions, the answer is rather trivial: they both are correct. Each offers insight and understanding, although from quite disparate perspectives. What would clearly be a mistake, in my view, is uncritical adoption of one to the exclusion of the other.

The position of the atheist is purely holistic. It is also considered "scientific" by many. Its scientific status can seem especially assured to those strongly influenced by methodological visions that emphasize the function of institutions in repressing people. Marxist interpretations are an example.

To a holist, the expostulations of the believer are subjective, emotional, and impressionistic to the point of being irrational. The convictions of the believer, however, should not be simply dismissed because they do not fit a precast view of science. The thoughts and commitments of the believer can be interpreted as his choices, and those choices can be interpreted to be the reason for the existence of churches and other religious institutions.

To give serious attention to the believer's view, one must break from holistic method. The grip of holism is not easily severed, however. Its heritage is powerful in our intellectual tradition, especially since it is so often identified with the "scientific" study of mankind. The reasons will emerge in the upcoming section.

3. Holism

The principal tenets of holism can be summarized quite briefly. Holism is the belief that forces transcending humans explain the thoughts, decisions, and actions of men, and that social structure and change are explained by those transcendent forces. Human agency has no significant influence on the holistic forces. Although this characterization of holism is extreme, holistic tendencies can dominate theory building to the point where individualistic and empathetic alternatives are excluded. The reasons are historical as well as intellectual.

Holistic Roots in the Bronze Age

The view that man is not in control of his own destiny, either individually or collectively, extends far back into the religious and cultural heritage of civilization. It has been argued that such religious or quasi-religious beliefs were prominent in the Bronze Age, in Mycenaen Greece (1400–1100 B.C.). At that time there may have been no concept of a free will, much less a workable theory of rationality. Man's affairs were deemed to be in the hands of the gods, and even the latter seemed to have little if any control over their own lives. In other words, fatalism prevailed, even before the notion itself was formulated (Snell 1982; also see Herzfeld 1982, for an ethnographic interpretation of fatalism in contemporary Greek culture).

Fatalistic views are by no means limited to the past, as almost any observer of contemporary culture can attest. Consider apocalyptic religions, which assume the future is determined, usually featuring a catastrophic event, and that we can only submit to that future. Another fatalistic view is the crude Communist doctrine that inexorable economic "laws" dictate that collective socialism will replace capitalism. In short, the assumption that superhuman forces underlie human affairs is as old as mankind and yet as contemporary as the present.

Hegel, Marx, Comte

While the roots of holism can be traced into the misty past of mankind, especially in religious and social outlooks, in the nineteenth century it came to be identified with attempts to uncover "scientific" explanations of human institutions (Hayek 1972). In technical idiom, this new version of holism assumes sociological determinism, the view that humans are passive pawns shaped by social forces.

That forces transcending humans are the "real" levers controlling our lives, and which dominate us whether we like it or not, much less choose them or not, is a concept that can be traced to a number of thinkers of the last century. Hegel, Marx, and Comte figure prominently amongst them. Below are comments on each.

Hegel (1770–1831) maintained that the world is a product of what he called the *Weltgeist* (world spirit), or *Geist* for short. The manifestation of the *Geist* in space is "nature" and its manifestation in time is "history." In short, all structure and change are the product of the *Geist*. The *Geist* transcends human control. In Hegel's view, it controls us. We may deceive ourselves into thinking that we are agents of our own intentional action, and that those actions make a difference in the course of events. The *Geist* is the real causal agent, however. In other words, humans are puppets and their strings are pulled by the *Geist* (Hegel 1977).

Marx (1818–1883), who frequently acknowledged his intellectual debt to Hegel, adopted the latter's view that transcendent forces control both the structure and the dynamics of society. In Marx's view the force is not an idea, like the *Geist* (Hegel was an *idealist)*, but is matter, especially economic structure (Marx was a *materialist.*) The economic structure of a society is the primary determinant of human phenomena—social, religious, cultural—and economic systems develop and disappear without regard to the plans, hopes, and control of humans. A "scientific" study of mankind, according to the Marxist view, must be focused upon the material forces (Marx and Engels 1961). The spread of holism in the contemporary world has perhaps been due more to Marx than to anyone else. Along for the ride was, and still is, the belief that "scientific" explanations must be holistic.

Incidentally, the expressions materialism, cultural materialism, and Marxist are no small cause of confusion in the archaeological literature. *Materialism* is simply the view that humans, prehistoric or otherwise, are predominately occupied with activities to provide for subsistence. In other words, human activity is mainly economic activity, a corollary of which is that the economic dimension of all institutions is crucially significant. Another entirely different meaning of materialism is that archaeological theory should always be answerable to the material record. It is the view that theories in archaeology should have an empirical foundation. *Cultural materialism* is the view that all cultural phenomena are the epiphenomena of the economic orientation of man. Marx and many Marxists embrace cultural materialism. In the archaeological literature the meaning is similar, with the caveat that it does not carry with it some other Marxist historical and social doctrines, such as the inevitability of changes in economic systems. Marvin Harris is the pivotal articulator of cultural materialism in archaeological theory (Harris 1979). The label *Marxist* in theoretical archaeology is normally reserved for theories which place ideational elements in dialectical relationship with economic factors. Marxist theory in archaeology is also sometimes—but not always—associated with Marxist historical and social doctrines, such as the belief that a class with advantages in a given economic system will exploit classes less privileged in the system.

The Marxist heritage has left the impression that holistic forces are always materialistic. It is important to realize, however, that holistic forces can also be idealistic. Hegel's *Weltgeist* is an example. "High structuralism" in contemporary anthropology also gives holism an idealistic slant. High structuralism assumes that universal patterns in human mentality are the primary levers in the formation of human social organization (Lévi-Strauss 1966). Humans have no more control over those patterns than they do over economic forces, according to structuralist interpretations. Typical of holistic approaches, uncovering universals—in this case, patterns of the mind—is a primary goal. Another goal of high structuralism, however, is to uncover meaning in the lives of people. That is why structuralist approaches also have empathetic elements.

Auguste Comte (1798–1857) is another Continental thinker whose intellectual influence on contemporary social science cannot be overestimated. He also left a heritage of holism, and identified science with holism. A number of elements constitute Comte's holistic view. Comte coined the expression "positivism" from the French verb *positer*—to posit. Specifically, he maintained that all scientific knowledge must be derivable strictly from what is posited to the senses; speculation about causes or other metaphysical entities beyond what is posited to the senses should be excluded from science. The anti-metaphysical face of Comte's view of knowledge contrasts strongly with the economic metaphysics in the Marxist view, but the similarities in the two traditions are even more striking. Comte, like Marx, believed there were universal laws of social organization that transcend human agency and hence are not malleable. Just as for the Marxists, a science of man requires uncovering those universal laws (Comte 1968; Martineau 1855).

In short, Comte as well as Marx endorsed holistic approaches to the study of man, and each identified science with his particular approach. Since the Marxist and Comtean traditions have been immensely influential in the development of the social sciences, it is hardly surprising that holistic approaches tend to dominate, and that holistic approaches are commonly identified as "scientific."

Marxist Theories, Processual Theories

Some meat can be added to the skeleton of holism with a few examples. These will also provide substance for a discussion of the advantages and disadvantages of holistic approaches.

Marxist theories place ideational elements—thought, ideas, religious belief, and other cognitive factors—in dialectical relation with material elements—economic structure and the roles into which it forces people. The underlying assumption is that the material elements dictate and constrain the formation and change of the ideational elements. At the extreme—in "vulgar" Marxism—the material elements determine the ideational elements, the latter being only a "superstructure" upon the former. In a modified form, the material and ideational components interact, although material factors dominate.

Of particular importance to the present discussion is that Marxist theories deemphasize the role of human agency, and discount it completely at the extreme. Explanations of social structure and change are not found in the agency of humans, but rather in economic institutions. Thoughts, decisions, and other ideational elements—"consciousness," to use Marxist terminology—are interpreted to be the product of a person's role in the economic structure of society rather than as pivotal in the formation of that structure. That is why Marxist explanations remain largely holistic despite the interest of some Marxists in the cognitive side of humans (Leone 1982; Tilley 1981).

Processual theories are another well-known example of holistic explanation. Processual theories—theories which explain change from one state of affairs to another state of affairs—normally assume that the causes of change transcend human agency. Systemic approaches, which explain change in terms of endogenous dynamics (the "system") rather than exogenous factors, have been particularly favored amongst processual archaeologists.

In Marxist approaches the crucial dynamics are taken away from the will of humans and are attributed to institutions, whereas in processual theories humans are removed even further because institutions themselves are interpreted to be products of entities like systems (Flannery 1968). As a result, processual approaches have provided even less room for the agency of humans than Marxist approaches (Hodder 1986).

Another reason for the exclusion of human agency is that processual explanations have been identified with positivistic method, the anti-metaphysical slant of which excludes from scientific scrutiny speculative elements such as "minds." The belief that positivism underlies processual approaches, and the attempt by some (Binford 1972) to employ positivism rigorously, have put a further methodological constraint on the inclusion of human agency in processual explanations.

Incidentally, processual archaeology should be identified with refutationist rather than positivistic method (Bell 1987). Some processual problems can also be approached with individualistic method, as will be argued later in this paper. Individualistic method also has refutationist roots.

Some Benefits and Limits of Holistic Explanation

An advantage of holistic approaches is that the normal source for interpreting the thoughts, feelings, and decisions of humans—the written record—can be sidestepped. Since archaeological study focuses on prehistory, or history before written records, this advantage can hardly be overemphasized.

Another advantage is that a sizable portion of the artifactual record is appropriate for building and assessing holistic explanations. Marxist approaches, for example, rely heavily upon utensils, tools, and anything else which might have been instrumental in the productive life of prehistoric peoples. Such artifacts often dominate the record. For the same reason, many processual theories address economic organization and change, or at least incorporate economic factors if the goal is to explain other types of social change.

The above advantages might tempt the conclusion that only holistic approaches are appropriate if theories are to be assessed against the artifactual record. But there are two serious drawbacks to accepting that conclusion. Holistic approaches cannot account for the agency of humans, and cannot adequately explain social change unpredictable by holistic means. The example below will bring out strengths of holistic approaches. Those strengths will also reveal the two pitfalls.

The long-term cycles of economic expansion and contraction associated with Nicolai Kondratieff—called Kondratieff cycles—are played out over fifty- to sixty-year periods regardless of catastrophic events or disruptive humans (Schumpeter 1964). Even the Second World War, one of the greatest manmade catastrophes in history, and Adolf Hitler, one of the most disruptive humans of all time, did not substantially alter the advent of economic expansion predicted by Kondratieff theory. World War II was emphatically not the cause of the expansion, as is popularly believed, because the upswing in capitalization and economic activity during and after the war was already in place before the war commenced. The drastic upheaval of the war was only a ripple that might have accelerated the economic expansion in North America by a few years and delayed it in Europe by a few years. In short, the Second World War in general and Hitler in particular could just as well have been nonexistent, neither having more than a transitory effect on the Kondratieff wave of expansion.

If events like the Second World War and someone like Hitler had little or no effect on the march of economic expansion, then no unique events ever alter economic forces and no humans have agency. The conclusion is that only holistic approaches should be used when developing theories about human social organization and change.

But wait. Humans are agents, and not all events can be predicted. The first lacuna of holism—inability to account for human agency—would require ignoring the fact that Hitler's impact was startling, and that the Second World War did have important consequences. There has been a near-universal disgust with fascism, at least in one of its more virulent forms. There has been a partial but significant unification of most of Western Europe. Unification of Europe was one of Hitler's dreams, although its present structure is not what he had envisioned. The point is that human thoughts, decisions, and actions—and the events flowing from them—do "make a difference."

It is reasonable to overlook the difficulties in holism when one's theoretical goals can be pursued in spite of them. Hitler's agency and the war were insignificant for Kondratieff economic cycles. On the other hand, the Second World War drastically affected the lives of hundreds of millions of people and many political, social, and economic events. If one's theoretical goals require incorporating such effects, then holistic approaches may not be adequate. Those wed to holistic approaches can be blind to that fact. Instead of employing a non-holistic approach, they are likely to consider the agency of humans and the unpredictability of certain events to be unfit for "scientific" investigation, and hence they ignore them.

The second lacuna—that holistic method cannot adequately account for unpredictable change—is related to the first. Ideas and decisions, and the actions following from them, can bring about change. But ideas are sometimes new, and not always predictable. Nor are the changes resulting from new ideas always predictable. These points have been made by Karl Popper in *The Poverty of Historicism* (1957). Popper argues that new scientific ideas grow from the weaknesses of received ones. Since it is not often possible to predict where crucial weaknesses will be found in received ideas, he reasons that the shape of new ideas is likewise unpredictable. Since ideas in science lead to new technology, and technology has an enormous impact on events, future events are likewise unpredictable (Popper 1957).

The unpredictability of change is magnified by the fact that actions have unintended consequences which sometimes prevail over the intended consequences. In human affairs, events are usually the product of unintended consequences as well as intended ones. That many phenomena are unintended will be discussed further when reviewing methodological individualism.

There is yet another reason why the unpredictability of human events is overlooked. When restructuring the past, in which events have already transpired, it can seem as if there were no room for alternative occurrences. As a result, what has occurred can appear to have been "determined." That is why theories built upon historical investigation are prejudiced toward the predictability of events. Historical disciplines like archaeology are slanted toward holistic approaches for this reason alone.

By the way, historians not shackled by a deterministic prejudice often produce the most interesting accounts of events. A notable example are the war histories of A. J. P. Taylor (1965, 1966). Taylor reconstructs wartime situations as perceived by the pivotal humans, tracing the rationale for their decisions and pointing out the consequences— often unintended—that followed. There is always the suggestion that alternate decisions might have yielded drastically different turns in the course of the war. Taylor's approach to historical reconstruction suggests that archaeologists and others intimately involved with making interpretations of the past need not be shackled by a deterministic prejudice.

In sum, holistic approaches do not adequately account for the role of human agency, nor can they incorporate the unpredictability that characterizes so many human events. Are there other approaches which might overcome these lacunae, at least partially? There are. A promising one is the individualistic approach, the subject of the next section.

4. Methodological Individualism

Individualistic method does provide room for human agency and a framework within which unpredictable change can be explored. Another strength is its refutationist guidelines, which encourage the formulation of testable theories, in this case testable theories about thoughts and decisions. The principal drawback is that individualistic method can be applied only to a limited—albeit important—range of theories.

Tenets of Methodological Individualism

Methodological individualism is a set of related ideas. It can be understood from a number of perspectives, depending upon which thesis or theses are chosen as a focus. For the purposes of this paper two theses will be emphasized: (1) that thoughts do have agency: that ideas and decisions, implicit and explicit, are crucial in the development of human societies; (2) that collective actions and entities, such as institutional structure and change, are the product of the decisions and actions of individuals.

That ideas make a difference in human affairs seems *prima facie* valid; it cannot be effectively denied. More important than arguing for the agency of humans is to ask what misconceptions lead to the conclusion that agency is insignificant. Two are reviewed below.

The first is the scientistic tendency to identify science exclusively with one type of method, in this case to identify science with holistic method. Even if human agency is not denied, it is not regarded as legitimate in scientific theories. As already pointed out, some explanations of social organization and change require no reference to human agency. It does not follow, however, that no explanations require reference to human agency.

The second misconception is to interpret methodological assumptions as empirical statements rather than as heuristic tools. If method is interpreted empirically, attention turns immediately to whether methodological components are "true" or "false," such as whether humans really do have minds (individualism) or not (holism). Arguing whether methodological views are true or false, though, is about as sensible as debating whether hammers or saws are true or false. Method is a tool, and thus debate should focus on delineating those situations in which a methodological approach could be productive, and those in which it might not be productive. Individualistic method can be fruitfully employed to build and assess theories when the theoretical problem-situation suggests that the thoughts and decisions of humans have been important. Holistic approaches can be productive when human agency need not be incorporated into theories.

The second thesis of individualistic method is that collective actions and entities are the product of the decisions and actions of individuals. For example, instead of citing a collective "spirit" as the cause of well-known events in late eighteenth-century France, individualistic method implies that the actions of many individuals, regardless of motives and ideas, dovetailed into a partially collective movement referred to as the "French Revolution." Individualists avoid reifying collective notions such as the "spirit" of the revolution, or a "collective" movement, into causal entities. Instead, collectives are interpreted as derivative, the result of the decisions and actions of individual human beings. Even if some individuals do act because of dedication to a hypostatized entity, such as the "spirit" of a revolution, they do so out of their own choice.

A corollary is that the collective actions of individuals can be interpreted as the product of different and incompatible motives. More mileage can be squeezed from the example of the French Revolution. Some people may have joined the events because of commitment to revolutionary ideals, others because they feared the consequences of not doing so, yet others because they hoped for pecuniary gain, others because of the excitement, others because those close to them were involved, and others for a myriad of further reasons and motives, including spontaneous involvement with no motive whatsoever.

That a variety of motives underlie collective action provides a framework for explaining change, and particularly unpredictable change. Under given conditions collective actions can be dominated and directed by the ideas and motives of some individuals. As conditions fluctuate, however, others with alternative ideas and motives can rise to dominate. The result can be change, and even drastic change, in the collective actions of a group. That is why a revolution can turn into a monster quite discordant with the ideas which might initially have made it appealing.

It can now be seen that the two themes underlying individualistic method are closely related. The ideas and decisions of individuals explain change, but there are normally a wide variety of ideas and motives amongst individuals. Changing conditions encourage dominant motives and ideas to fade while facilitating others to emerge. The result, not surprisingly, is unpredictable change.

Unintended Consequences

Unpredictable changes are also unintended. That is intuitively obvious, but individualistic method can be better understood through an explicit discussion of three reasons why unintended consequences often arise in human affairs.

The first reason was discussed above: collective actions are the product of numerous and inconsistent motives and ideas. As conditions change, dominant ideas and motives tend to recede, while others ascend to dominate. The second reason was also outlined above: new and unpredictable ideas can and do arise. They can lead to decisions unforeseen prior to the advent of the new ideas. The results are consequences unintended from the perspective of prior conditions.

Projecting the future without accounting for how altered conditions might impinge upon decision making is called *static analysis*. To project future revenue from new tax laws without accounting for how the new tax laws will affect consumer and investment decisions is an example. Individualists consider static analysis a grave mistake.

A third reason for unintended consequences is that knowledge of the motives and ideas of individuals is scanty. One must be particularly careful when analyzing collective action, the common behavioral features of which seldom if ever imply that the motives and goals of the participants are the same.

In brief, then, there are numerous reasons for the prevalence of unintended consequences, even in a world where individual humans act intentionally. Of particular note is what is not an explanation of unintended consequences: there is no resort to transcendent forces beyond the realm of human agency. Individualists part company with holists at this point.

Even though holists and individualists both recognize that much of what occurs lies beyond the intentions of humans, the reasons are markedly different. Holists persist in believing that the future would be predictable if only the right universal "laws" were found. Individualists, on the other hand, contend that predicting the future is tenuous at best and is intrinsically impossible in most cases. For individualists the future is open, to use philosophical terminology (Popper 1945). No appeal to holistic forces will ever enable all social structure and transformation to be predicted.

That the future is open provides another criticism of the search for universals such as "covering laws" in historical fields like archaeology. If the future is open, such "laws" are always suspect.

Knowledge of Individuals

Knowledge of the ideas and motives of particular individuals is scanty. This point is extremely important in the individualist framework: it implies that assumptions about people's goals and decisions should be made only with considerable caution if at all. The corollary is that policies based upon such assumptions—collectivist policies, for example—should be avoided. The case against assuming knowledge of individuals, and its constraints on the use of individualistic method, will be discussed in more detail below. An explanation of how individualistic method can be and is effectively employed within those constraints will follow.

It certainly is possible to catch glimpses of the ideas and motives of some people, especially of those with whom one is personally close. For a more distant set of people, however, and especially a larger set—even when there is collective action—individualistic method cautions against assuming such knowledge. Furthermore, if one must be careful about presupposing knowledge of the ideas and motives of living people, one must be all the more so for those no longer on this earth and especially for those for whom there is little or no written record.

If the agency of humans is significant in the structure and transformations of human institutions, and yet knowledge of their ideas and motives can only be fragmentary, then individualistic tools for investigating human institutions would seem poor at best. In light of this argument, it would not be surprising if individualistic approaches were ignored or abandoned in favor of holistic ones.

Indeed, individualistic method is constrained by the opaqueness and variability of individual ideas and motives. It can be effectively used, however, in those realms of human activity where the ideas and/or motives are shared. That is why it can be fruitfully employed to analyze the rudimentary economic behavior of individuals: all individuals need to make decisions about obtaining food and shelter and, in more developed economies, about other material goods and services such as medicine, transportation, education. That individualistic method has an established tradition in economic anthropology is not surprising, then. Nor is it surprising in archaeology that it has been effectively employed to analyze the decisions of individuals in the pursuit of game and other foodstuffs in hunter-gatherer societies (Mithen 1987), or in the making and management of tools for such pursuits (papers by Francfort, Perlès, and Roux in this volume). Individualistic method would be less useful for analyzing the choices made by individuals for certain colors of clothing, however, or for their tastes in music. In such realms necessity does not constrain the variety of choice. Decision making can thus be more capricious, and, as a result, far more variegated. Besides the economic realm, individualistic approaches can be employed to investigate other types of ideas shared by groups of people, such as ideas in mathematics and/or science. It comes as no surprise, then, that cognitive archaeology is focused on ideas shared by a group rather than on ideas which are less public and agreed upon (Renfrew 1987).

Ideas, decisions, and actions can and often do become constituents in the lives of people to the point where they seem to function in many people's lives like rocks, weather, and other such naturalistic entities. In philosophical terminology, that is a reason why cognitive elements are amenable to a realist interpretation: the view that ideas are attempts to describe the actual world. A corollary is that ideas become actual elements in the sphere of human decision and action, just like rocks or other naturalistic entities (Popper 1972, 1983). "Traditions," for example, can and do become factors which both guide and constrain the lives of individuals. Traditions turn into "ideologies" when they are accepted and acted upon to the point where counterevidence is ignored or dismissed without critical reflection. Indeed, the reality of cognitive elements is demonstrated by the prevalence of ideological thinking, in which ideas are more "real" than any evidence that can be marshaled against them.

Despite being real elements in our world, cognitive elements are amenable to change, even drastic change. Even ideologies come and go, sometimes with rather surprising speed. In other words, ideas shared by individuals, or decisions and actions common to different individuals, are not the same as holistic forces impinging upon individuals. Holistic forces are always beyond the control of humans and in principle never change. That is why holistic approaches assume a future trajectory predictable from a model of an antecedent past, necessitating the belief that there is a model to make the predictions. Vulgar Marxist approaches assume that the future of human institutions is predictable from economic laws, for example. The ideas of humans cannot interfere because they are themselves a product of economic factors. Approaches which assume there are laws binding at all times for all societies ("covering laws") are another example of the same belief.

The difference between the malleable status of shared ideas, decisions, and actions of individualistic approaches and the nonmalleable status of forces impinging on humans in holistic approaches cannot be overemphasized. Carole Crumley, for example, uses an individualistic approach in her study of regional development of the Burgundy region of France (Crumley and Marquardt 1987). The interplay between ideational elements and material conditions is appropriately called a "dialectical" approach, rather than a Marxist approach, thus avoiding the political and holistic overtones of the latter. On the other hand, the methodological recommendations in the recent book by Shanks and Tilley on approaches to understanding the prehistoric past are more individualistic than holistic. For that reason labeling them "Marxist" might be misleading (Shanks and Tilley 1987).

It should be clear by now that the "individual" in individualistic method is a *generic* individual: some individual or other rather than a particular individual. For example, it is assumed that a decision to hunt fauna rather than gather flora under specified conditions by the hunter-gatherers in the studies of Steven Mithen would be a decision made by most hunter-gatherers of the Périgord rather than just the decision of some particular individual (Mithen 1987).

Applications of individualistic method in studies of the prehistoric past are limited to the generic individual. When a particular individual becomes a study of prehistorians, however, the goal is usually to identify particular individuals with their products (Hill and Gunn 1977). The goal is similar to that of an art historian attempting to identify the painter responsible for a landscape scene. This is different from the goal of using individualistic method, which is to explain social structure and change as the product of human agency. Both focus on individuals, but the particular individual should not be confused with the generic individual assumed in methodological individualism.

It is obvious by this point that the term "individualism" can be confusing. The choice of the word is plausible: to emphasize that human agency is what really counts in human institutions, and to contrast that with the pawnlike conception of humans in holistic views. Understandably, individualism has become identified with the dignity of the individual and respect for individuality, and is associated with the social, economic, and political institutions that encourage those qualities. In America that meaning is conveyed by the expression "rugged individualism." Otherwise, however, "individualism" may be an unfortunate choice. It does not connote that we know much about individual ideas or motives; quite the contrary, it cautions us against assuming such knowledge. It does not connote that individuals must act on ideas and motives different from those of others; we can and do act on shared values. It does not even connote that people must act on ideas, or values, or any such things. They might simply react or act spontaneously in some other irrational way. The historical comments below will shed more light on the confusing word "individualism."

5. Historical Roots of Methodological Individualism

Understanding the background to individualistic method will help unravel the confusions surrounding the meaning of "individualism." It will also shed light on why the individualistic outlook can fan such strong emotions.

The roots of methodological individualism are frequently traced to the "Austrian" school of economics. The Austrian school was founded in the late nineteenth century by Carl Menger. Menger argued against the labor theory of value espoused by such diverse thinkers as Karl Marx and Adam Smith. The labor theory of value assumes that the value of a product is, or at least should be, equal to the human effort expended in its production. Menger contended that the value of a product is "subjective"—due to demand for it; the labor invested in a product is only tangentially related to its value and sometimes is irrelevant.

After the First World War a number of members of the Austrian school dedicated themselves to exposing the faults of collectivist economic organization. Eugen von Böhm-Bawerk was one. Even better known was Ludwig von Mises. Not surprisingly, Mises argued for the advantages of free-market economic structure (Mises 1949, 1962). Friedrich von Hayek, Mises's protégé, has become the foremost spokesman of the Austrian school. Hayek clearly recognized the significance of the individualistic assumptions which underlie free-market theory. He has made those assumptions explicit, argued for them, and traced the ramifications of the assumptions on economic theory and social policy. More will be said about Hayek shortly.

Methodological individualism is also associated with Karl Popper. Popper recognized the kinship of the individualistic outlook and his refutationist view of science. He used both in his criticisms of holistic interpretations of history, such as vulgar Marxism. Popper also employed methodological individualism in the development of his social philosophy.

The similarity between the individualistic views of Hayek and Popper is more than coincidental. They have known each other and have shared ideas for decades. Popper even dedicated *The Open Society and its Enemies* (1945) to Hayek.

In *The Road to Serfdom* (1944) and more explicitly in the *Counter-Revolution of Science* (1972), Hayek attacks holistic approaches in the social sciences and social policies based on holistic assumptions. In place of holistic approaches he advocates individualistic method. He offers a number of arguments for individualistic method. For example, he argues that the prerequisites for happiness vary greatly amongst individuals. One person may need wealth, whereas an ascetic lifestyle is crucial for another. Furthermore, humans have only limited knowledge of what is significant in the lives of different people, at least beyond the obvious need for food and a modicum of shelter. He concluded that humans should be constrained as little as possible in working out their own destinies.

Hayek also developed a set of arguments that are specifically economic. For example, the complexity and constant flux of an economy make it impossible to implement efficient and effective collective plans. The more complex an economy becomes, the less feasible becomes planning. Instead of collectivization, Hayek argues for a free market: a market determined by the ensemble of decisions of individuals and freely associating groups of individuals. In short, Hayek's social and economic arguments for free markets presuppose an individualistic outlook on people and institutions. He concluded that the best social structure within which individuals can maximize choices in pursuing their own goals is a liberal democratic society, the center of which is a free-market economy.

Popper's arguments for methodological individualism are also interwoven with his criticisms of holistic method. In *The Open Society and Its Enemies* (1945) and in *The Poverty of Historicism* (1957) Popper warns of the dangers of social and political theories based upon holistic assumptions. Such theories can become self-fulfilling prophecies, but only by intervening in the flow of human events; that is, by using dictatorial means. Popper argues for individualistic method in the social sciences, and the benefits of social and political policies framed within an individualistic outlook.

Individualistic Method and Refutationist Method

Popper has been prominent in the development of methodological individualism for another reason: individualistic method is closely associated with refutationist method. Some important similarities between individualistic method in the social sciences and refutationist method in the physical sciences are outlined below.

Implicit in the refutationist view is that much about theories remains opaque to us. The parts of theories we know best are those which potentially clash with reality; that is, where theories are refutable and thus can be tested. Individualistic method provides the warning that we know little about the variegated motives and ideas upon which individuals make their choices. What an individual can know, however, is when his or her ideas clash with reality. Scientific knowledge advances by developing theories which supersede errors in mistaken theories. Individuals learn by developing better ideas when others fail. The unpredictability of the future of knowledge from the refutationist perspective is similar to the unpredictability of the future of human events implied by individualistic method. The interpretation of scientific knowledge as a human creation and changeable by human agency is similar to the individualistic view of social institutions as human creations and as changeable by humans. Finally, the importance of a social framework in which ideas can be asserted boldly, but also criticized severely, is best guarded by attitudes implied by individualistic method, in which the value of a variety of ideas and goals is paramount. In short, individualistic method for the social sciences is the close relative of refutationist method in the physical sciences.

Individualistic Method and Social Policy

As a formula for social policy, individualistic method can be summarized as follows: leave individuals as free from constraint as possible in all realms of their lives. Individualistic method thus buttresses liberal democracy and free-market economic organization. Not surprisingly, then, individualistic method is also a formula with which to fight against collectivization, whether it be the collectivization of ideas or of production. Holism, on the other hand, tends to buttress collectivization in a number of ways: by the assumptions that humans are pawns of forces transcendent to them and that differences amongst individuals are minimal relative to those leveling forces. Furthermore, since holists often believe that those forces can be understood, they also believe that the future is predictable and hence can be controlled by humans.

In brief, then, individualistic assumptions legitimate free-market economies and holistic assumptions justify socialized economies. That is why commitment to individualism or holism can take on the drumbeat of conviction. The danger is all the greater, however, that conviction can also be drummed into ideology. Ideological attachment to either individualistic or holistic approaches will surely stifle the flexibility necessary for judicious use of either, in archaeology or in any other realm. Fortunately there is medicine. It is prescribed below.

If an archaeologist is uncomfortable with either holistic or individualistic method, and the reason is not based upon an assessment of its advantages and/or disadvantages for his or her theoretical interests in archaeology, then it would be helpful to make an honest appraisal of the influence of one's own political-social orientation. Political and social commitment can be beneficial intellectually by providing the impetus to pursue certain types of theories. Someone particularly interested in the feminist movement, for example, might investigate the role of women in prehistoric societies, or someone intrigued with socialist policies might attempt to understand welfare structure in prehistoric societies. If political and social commitment excludes consideration of an approach which seems contrary to that commitment, however, theory development can be constrained. Commitment can blind one to the disadvantages of the approach wed to one's own political and social convictions, as well as mask the advantages of the alternative approach. Awareness of that danger, and the courage to counter it, will facilitate theory development.

Two alternative reconstructions of the historical background of individualistic method should be mentioned here. The first focuses on unintended consequences, the second on the individuality and agency of humans.

That human institutions and events are a mixed product of purposeful human actions with unintended consequences is attributable to Max Weber (1864–1920). Methodological individualism can thus be interpreted as an outgrowth of the Weberian tradition (Weber 1962). Karl Marx preceded Weber and can also be given a historical note because of his focus on the unintended consequences of economic activity. As pointed out earlier, Marx's philosophy is largely holistic: the unintended consequences of economic activity were explained by economic laws not controlled by individuals. Furthermore, regimes which have identified with Marxism are not noted for embracing the dignity of the individual or other values and institutions normally associated with an individualistic outlook. Despite the irony, it is no historical mirage to trace a crucial element of methodological individualism to Karl Marx because of his emphasis on the role of the unintended consequences of human actions.

A focus on the individuality of humans and on individual responsibility is the hallmark of existentialism, and especially that of Jean-Paul Sartre (Sartre 1957, 1964). It is also illuminating, then, to link the emergence of individualistic method with the existentialist movement that grew before World War II and exploded onto the scene in its wake. That interpretation of the historical roots of individualism has been given by Mark Patton (1986).

6. Holistic Method and Individualistic Method as Tools

The decision to employ either holistic or individualistic method should depend upon its promise for generating and improving explanations in a given problem-situation. A problem-situation is the context which makes an explation interesting. Normally an explanation arouses interest when it illuminates or contradicts the empirical record, ramifies or conflicts with another explanation, or bears upon a broad metaphysical outlook (Popper 1983). It is not uncommon for an explanation to be interesting for two or more of the reasons above. For example, the evolutionary theories of Darwin provided a shock to archaeologists for all three reasons. It conflicted with accepted chronology for the pre-history of man, it was inconsistent with the accepted theory of Archbishop Ussher (1581–1656) that the origin of man dated from 4004 B.C., and it challenged the standard biblical account of the origins of life and mankind.

Some problems addressed by archaeology posit that institutions, social structure, and social dynamics are best interpreted as transcendent to human agency, with little if any dependence upon the thoughts, will, or acts of individuals. For investigation in those realms holistic methods are appropriate. In other problem-situations such institutions, structure, and dynamics are more fruitfully interpreted as the intended and unintended products of human agency. For archaeologists plagued with deciding how to spend one's time and energy, is there a more specific guideline to help one decide which broad approach to follow?

It is clear there is no algorithm or effective procedure which will guarantee a proper decision. One can clarify theoretical goals, however, and then make a decision on method relative to the goals. For example, if there is to be an interpretation of the longer-range trading patterns within a region of prehistoric settlements, relationships amongst popu-lations, tools, agricultural productivity, and other such parameters without concern for other particularities in the settlement cultures would suggest holistic approaches. In such cases holistic assumptions might deliver comprehensive and testable explanations. It must be remembered that goals can change, however, and often in unforeseen ways. Suppose that in the course of investigating field data to test a holistic explanation for the problem-situation above, one discovers a rather startling rise in the trade of a certain type of figurine. It seems to function as an icon, and may thus indicate a significant alteration in thought patterns. The discovery could provide the impetus to use individualistic method. One might search for theories, and evidence that could bear upon them, about a cognitive change.

In short, there are investigative situations in which holistic approaches are promising and others in which individualistic method are promising. It cannot be decided *a priori* which is preferable, but a particular context can indicate which might be best pursued, at least initially. Furthermore, approaches can be switched when necessary. Although holistic and individualistic method are inconsistent, they can be used as complements, as in the example above. Switching is no more surprising than a carpenter using a saw for cutting wood, and then resorting to a hammer to nail it to a sideboard. Uncritical attachment to one approach or the other can prevent a switch to a more productive alternative.

As discussed in §5 above, social and political viewpoints are one reason for uncritical attachment to either holistic or individualistic approaches. There is also an intellectual reason for embracing one approach and avoiding the other: method that is fruitful in one area is assumed, ofttimes mistakenly, to be fruitful in all areas. Another reason is profes-sional: adherence to a particular method can identify a subspecialty. While there is need for professional niches, defining them by method carries the danger of excluding con-sideration of alternative methods which might prove useful. Yet another reason is that methodological commitment can provide the trigger for obtaining grant money, which at times is more dependent upon the proposed method than upon the theoretical goals to be pursued.

Despite the multiple pressures, there is no need to be caught in an ideological trap over method. Simply remember that method is a tool, chosen in light of one's research goals, and that method can and should change. That orientation, along with keeping one's professional, political, and social proclivities in abeyance, should help one assess and use both holistic and individualistic approaches. Nimble use of multiple approaches is more difficult to practice than to preach, of course, but it certainly is possible.

7. Methodological Individualism and Theoretical Archaeology

Some implications of individualistic assumptions for theoretical archaeology will be explored in this and the following sections. First will be a review of ways that understanding the individualistic outlook can be helpful for those who use only holistic approaches. Second will be an outline of the potential for applying individualistic method when building theories about prehistoric social organization and change. Explaining social structure via individual decision making is one area of use. Another is the use of individualistic method in reconstructing ideas in prehistory.

Improving Holistic Approaches by Understanding Individualistic Method

Holistic approaches are unlikely to have borne their last fruit. Despite the obituary notice implied by the expression "postprocessual" archaeology, processual approaches and Marxist ones as well may only be yielding initial harvests. The qualities of holistic theories which make them amenable to the study of prehistoric peoples—such as not requiring written records and a potentially abundant material record for theory assessment—are not always characteristic of individualistic approaches. The material remains which bear witness to the ideas and decisions of prehistoric peoples are not generally obvious or even accessible. For those who wish for these or other reasons to continue pursuing holistic approaches, however, much can still be gained by understanding individualistic method. There are a number of reasons.

First, familiarity with individualistic approaches can serve as a reminder that holistic approaches, which do not deal with personal experience, cannot yield a "complete" understanding of human culture. Realizing that should help prevent ideological attachment to holism.

Second, holistic method will be inadequate for explaining some significant phenomena—such as a remarkable change anomalous within holistic frameworks. Awareness of the potential for individualistic approaches makes it less tempting to treat such anomalies in an *ad hoc* fashion, such as blindly assuming that more holistic research will inevitably account for the anomaly, downplaying the significance of the anomaly, or ignoring it all together. One might not personally choose to attack the anomaly with individualistic tools, but could at least recognize that an individualistic alternative might be fruitful.

Incidentally, there is no reason not to attempt to resolve an anomaly through holistic means. A resolution might be found, after all. That is far different than explaining it away by *ad hoc* strategems, however, which would likely be more tempting if one were ideologically wed to holistic approaches.

Decisions at the Level of the Individual

Explanations of prehistoric data which incorporate decisions of individuals are one fruitful use of individualistic method. The ongoing studies of Steven Mithen on the decision making of hunter-gatherers in pursuit of food is an example already mentioned. Instead of building theories on a database referring only to cumulative group behavior, Mithen uses theories about the choices of individuals to explain the cumulative behavior. It is analogous to explaining gas pressure and volume at the macro-level by the action of molecules at the micro-level. Mithen has used the artifactual record to test his theories. This is important because individualistic theories, like holistic theories, must be assessed against the material record, and be improvable in light of it. As mentioned previously, that is one reason why use of individualist method to explore individual choice will often focus on economic activity, for which there is a reasonable chance to find material remains.

It is also worth stating again that individualistic theories generally must focus upon a prehistoric activity which is largely the same for most individuals under given conditions. A particular hunter-gatherer in the Périgord region of Southwest France in Mithen's studies, for example, is likely to have the same nutritional needs as other hunter-gatherers and also know the same traditional hunting techniques as other hunter-gatherers. Whether one had brown hair and liked shorter women, for example, would not likely have any effect on the hunting activities of either one.

In sum, exploring individual decisions amongst prehistoric peoples requires a focus on activities which leave a substantial material record and activities common to people rather than particularities that leave no material record and differentiate people from each other. For both reasons economic activity will often provide the field of study, and the decisions of a generic individual, rather than particular individuals, will be investigated.

Using individualistic method to explore decision making does require that the choices of individuals be stipulated, but it does not require speculation about the ideas behind those choices. A hunter-gatherer, for example may choose to pursue game instead of gather root plants, but one need not know whether he "thought" abstractly about the consequences of his choices, or made them spontaneously without thought, or anything in between. Individualistic method also can be used to speculate about the thoughts of prehistoric peoples, however. That is one aim of cognitive archaeology.

8. Methodological Individualism in Cognitive Archaeology

The broad goal of cognitive archaeology is to incorporate mental, ideational, symbolic, and other such elements into theories about prehistoric peoples. Within that broad framework, however, is a panorama of specific goals. At one extreme are attempts to capture such abstruse elements as the feelings of prehistoric peoples, their experiential lives, and the range of meanings which engulfed their existence (see paper by Susan Kus in this volume). At the other extreme are guarded attempts to gain at least small glimpses into some of the ideas held by prehistoric peoples (Renfrew 1982). In between are attempts to capture at least some of the symbolic elements in the lives of prehistoric peoples.

All types of cognitive theories include individualistic components. That is why they are not amenable to holistic approaches, which by definition exclude human agency as significant in human institutions. The broad goals of capturing feelings and experiential meanings can hardly avoid empathetic method, at least to some extent. The more confined goal of building theories about the ideas of prehistoric peoples is more amenable to the refutationist constraints of individualistic method. Use of individualistic method in cognitive archaeology will be explored in this section. Empathetic method and the broader goals for which it is employed will be discussed later.

Calls to understand the thoughts of prehistoric peoples, and attempts to do so, have a long history in archaeology (Collingwood 1946; Leone 1982; Hodder 1986). Exploring thoughts within the confines of individualistic method, however, is quite recent. The most explicit example is the methodological proposals for cognitive archaeology offered by Colin Renfrew. Renfrew's attention to methodological constraints, and his careful use of an individualistic approach—even though he does not call it that—make his work particularly exemplary for discussion.

Renfrew's brand of cognitive archaeology was formulated in the early 1980's, first in *Towards an Archaeology of the Mind* (1982) and then in a more recent paper (1987). Both papers are replete with methodological comment as well as illustrative examples of cognitive insights. This section will discuss and simplify the methodological guidelines in Renfrew's work. For the examples themselves the reader is referred directly to his papers. In addition, a number of methodological papers at a session of the 1986 Theoretical Archaeology Group Conference were addressed to Renfrew's approach, including an early draft of this paper, an early draft of the paper by Christopher Peebles in this volume, and another paper by Renfrew himself.

Immediately below are comments on reasons for exploring prehistoric ideas. It is crucial to be familiar with those goals to understand why Renfrew, a devoted processual archaeologist, would turn to an individualistic approach. The discussion will then turn to the individualistic method within Renfrew's approach to cognitive archaeology.

Goals of Cognitive Archaeology

A primary reason for turning to cognitive archaeology is interest in how people may have thought. That in itself would justify pursuing theories about the cognition of prehistoric peoples. There are other reasons, however. One is the belief that ideas have been crucial in human affairs, at least some of the time. It follows that to gain a more complete picture of prehistoric peoples, we must take into account the ideas that animated their lives. A further reason for exploring the cognition of prehistoric peoples is to search for adequate explanations of change in prehistoric societies. This reason is not as obvious as the others.

Explaining change in human societies has been a dominant goal of theoretical archaeologists during the past few decades. The goal of processual archaeology is to explain change, after all, and that is a goal of Marxist approaches as well. As has been seen, however, both processual and Marxist explanations are holistic: they assume that the significant dynamics of change transcend human thought and decision. That is a strength of holism, but its Achilles' heel as well. Holistic approaches assume the future is predictable from the past and also assume there must be a holistic resolution to any anomalous event.

As already argued, the future is not always predictable. The refutationist view that the future is "open" has already been presented. There is additional evidence for this view, however, from sources as diverse as new ideas in systems theory and mathematics, and as old as the intuitive notion that the ideas and decisions of humans do play a role in creating change. More is said below.

Some systems are complex systems, systems which change in ways not explicable from past structure or dynamics. Parameters of the past and present in these systems are not adequate to explain how they change, which is why they tend toward "chaos." Interestingly enough, many complex systems do reorder themselves, but in unpredictable forms.

A primary source of insights and ideas on complex systems has been the work of Ilya Prigogine. Following his work in thermodynamics, Prigogine and his protégés have been employing complex systems to understand social organization and change (Prigogine 1980). Some are already exploring the potential for interpreting prehistoric social organization and change as complex systems (van der Leeuw 1981). Another source of conceptual and even practical breakthroughs is the mathematical fractal theory of Benoit Mandelbrot (1982) and others (Peitgen and Richter 1986). It has been possible to delineate form in the path of a lightning bolt, for example, which had been thought to be totally chaotic.

Yet another way to explain unpredictable change in prehistoric societies is to view change as the result of human agency. The focus on prehistoric cognition, then, can serve processual goals. It is another way of searching for new explanations of change in prehistoric societies. This is a less obvious but significant reason for interest in cognitive archaeology. It will, I predict, lead more and more processual archaeologists to individualistic method.

Employing Refutationist Method

Another reason that processual archaeologists can find individualistic approaches attractive is that the latter share the refutationist method employed in effective processual archaeology. Three related characteristics of refutationism are crucial for employment of methodological individualism: recognition that only glimpses into the ideas of other people are possible, that theories about ideas must be testable, and that the theories are about ideas and not empathetic projections. Renfrew gives careful attention to all three. Each is discussed below.

It has been pointed out that formulating and assessing theories about the ideas of prehistoric peoples is frustrated by the lack of a written record. Quite surprisingly, the sparse material record does hide an advantage. Individualistic method assumes that only glimpses of the many thoughts of people are available even in a contemporary setting, much less a prehistoric one. The upshot of having only a sprinkling of material remains for theory building and testing, and a methodological prescription which warns against presumptuous claims about people's ideas and motives, is that attempts to "restructure" anything approaching a "world view" or "totality of thought" would be highly suspect.

Renfrew is quite insistent that cognitive archaeologists recognize that statements about the ideas of prehistoric people can give only partial insights (Renfrew 1982, 1987).

Building theories about the thoughts of prehistoric peoples must be done in such a way that they can be tested against the material record—that is, the theories need to be refutable. In order that the theories be testable, it is important to separate more speculative elements of theories about ideas from those which are more refutable. The best way is to make a logicist analysis of the ideas, to use the terminology of Jean-Claude Gardin (see paper by Gardin in this volume). A logicist analysis separates the components of the ideas and the inferential steps connecting them. Renfrew does such an analysis in his theorizing about cognition, thus enabling distinctions to be made between what can be known with reasonable confidence and what is more speculative. The logicist analysis leaves a "cognitive map" or *mappa* (Renfrew's terminology), at least part of which can be tested against the material record and the components of which can be assessed for consistency. Through testing and assessment the cognitive map can be improved.

When employing individualistic method in cognitive archaeology one is confined to making statements *about* ideas. This contrasts sharply with empathetic approaches in which one projects into the experience of others. More is said below.

Statements open to empirical assessment can be *distanced* (author's terminology) from the investigator; that is, they can become objects for theoretical exploration regardless of the cultural and other presuppositions of the investigator. When the presuppositions of the investigator do become parts of a cognitive map, they can at least be made explicit and opened to assessment by logistic analysis. This is markedly different from projecting one's own ideas into the minds of others. Projected ideas become *self-referential*—that is, the "truth" of the idea is the product of the person making the claim. The danger is amplified in archaeological contexts precisely because there is usually no written record against which to check a self-referential claim.

In short, while the refutationist guidelines of individualistic method limit the range of statements that can be made about the ideas of people, that limitation enables the statements to be testable. The self-reference inherent in the much more sweeping claims made with empathetic approaches can lessen or even eliminate the possibility of testing.

In practice, distinguishing between testable statements about ideas and nontestable self-referential claims is not always easy. When using individualistic method one should try to form statements that can be tested against the record, assessed for consistency with other statements about ideas, and evaluated in further ways as well, such as by comparing them with other available cultural information. There will always be a "subjective" side to the statements. An example is the impetus provided by an investigator's interests— such as in science, religion, or economics—to explore certain cognitive elements as opposed to others. Regardless, distancing ones own proclivities by logicist analysis, and testing theories against the available record, both help minimize the subjective input of an investigator.

Careful methodological use of individualism is also exemplified in the work of Henri-Paul Francfort and his group at the Centre National de la Recherche Scientifique in Paris. They are exploring, at the level of the generic individual, the manufacture, maintenance, and management of tools in prehistory (see papers by Francfort, Perlès, and Roux in this volume). Their models even enable one to recognize symbolic use of tools: disruption of the normal patterns for choice of materials and style can indicate a symbolic role that overrides the usual utilitarian function of tools (see paper by Perlès in this volume). The work of this group demonstrates the methodological care of individualism: the recognition that only partial insights into the ideas of the generic individuals are possible, the use of logicist analysis to distinguish those ideas more firmly corroborated by the artifactual record from those which are not, and the careful separation of statements about the ideas from self-referential projections.

9. Empathetic Method and Individualistic Method

The goal of reconstructing the feelings, hopes, and other affective and spiritual elements in the experiential lives of prehistoric peoples is much broader than that of gaining insight into some of their ideas. Typically one turns to empathetic method: use of personal intuition to understand the inner lives of other people. Empathetic method assumes there is a common structure to human experience. That common structure is the "bridge" that justifies claims about the experiences of other people: the structure of an investigator's experience is assumed to be similar to that of others, including prehistoric peoples. The trouble is that empathetic reconstructions are far too broad to be made within the refutationist constraints of individualistic method and hence cannot be coaxed from the artifactual record with confidence. Empathetic method is like individualistic method that has lost its refutationist rudder; that is, individualistic method that has transcended the bounds within which statements can be effectively tested.

It is important to bear in mind that empathetic method is seldom encountered in pure form. It is instead a generic expression used to cover quite a range of approaches. At one extreme it merges with individualistic method, adopting the goals and constraints of the latter. It is in that sense that Melas, for example, understands "empathetic" method (Melas n.d.). Likewise, the method recommended by Mark Patton (1986) is based upon individualistic assumptions. At the other extreme empathic method incorporates the broad goals and intuitive approach that characterize pure empathy. At this extreme it is assumed one can "know" how others think and feel via intuitions that are self-referential. The structuralism of Lévi-Strauss tips in this direction (Lévi-Strauss 1966). More often than not there will be an amalgamation of individualistic and empathetic elements, as is the case with Hodder's "contextual structuralism" for uncovering the experience of prehistoric peoples (Hodder 1986; Bell 1987).

In this section the pure form of empathetic method will be briefly discussed. The reason is not because it is commonly employed, but because understanding it can help one recognize and avoid empathetic tendencies when using individualistic method.

To begin, empathetic method does have a number of similarities with individualistic method. Both are contraries to the holistic focus on transhuman forces and dynamics. Advocates of empathetic and individualistic method both recognize that holistic approaches cannot possibly capture the full richness of human life and activity, and particularly not the experiential side. They would likely find, for example, more telling insight in the testimony of the Believer than in that the Atheist earlier in this paper.

Human agency is important to each. The ideas, decisions, and other human elements are not considered insignificant in the organization of human institutions.

Beyond the similarities between individualistic and empathetic method, however, lie differences in goals, and approaches to the goals. First, empathetic method is aimed at painting a comprehensive portrait of the affective, spiritual, cognitive, and other elements in human experience. Individualistic method is restricted to building theories about those elements for which the material record can provide some evidence, such as decision making, cognition, and the rudiments of symbolic meaning. Second, empathetic approaches are not used for the processual goal of explaining change. The empathetic assumption that there are unchanging universal structures of the human mind draws out elements that are static rather than dynamic, and hence are not fruitful for explaining change. Methodological individualism, on the other hand, implies that the thoughts, decisions, and actions of people are in flux, and can be used to explain change. Third and finally, empathetic method does not provide feasible ways of refuting claims, whereas individualistic method does. That is why empathetic approaches do not easily yield conjectures upon which assessments can be made and exploited for improvement. Empathetic portraits are more like a final product rather than a sketch that can be tested, altered, and hence used to gain further understanding and insight.

Incidentally, pure empathetic approaches are sometimes called *high structuralism*, the type of structuralism in which underlying universals in human experience are not only assumed but are stipulated explicitly and are claimed to dominate the generation of cultural forms and human institutions. Lévi-Strauss's high structuralism is the best-known example. High structuralist approaches are like holistic approaches: humans are viewed as pawns of forces which transcend their control. The difference is that internal structural categories of the mind impinge upon humans rather than external forces.

Conclusion

Methodological individualism has been the focus of this paper. Understanding its potential and limitations required discussion of holistic and empathetic approaches as well. As usual when studying a methodological approach, comparison with the alternatives increases understanding of its benefits and weaknesses, helping one make more judicious methodological choices.

Empathetic approaches have commonly been assumed to be the only alternative to holistic approaches. Individualistic method as an alternative is making its way onto the theoretical scene in archaeology, however. It sometimes shares common ground with holism, such as the processual goal of explaining social structure and change. It also shares with empathetic method the focus on human agency as a crucial component in explaining human life and institutions. Individualistic method is refutationist. For that reason it is designed to produce explanations that are testable against the data, and hence revisable in light of the data, qualities which it shares with some processual approaches but which are largely lost in empathetic approaches.

In the eyes of many only holistic approaches merit the label "scientific." That view is not implausible: processual theories are ones in which error can be found and exploited to gain further understanding and new insight. The training that numerous archaeologists receive within the context of the social sciences can reinforce the belief that holistic assumptions are the only route to a "scientific" study of man. Individualistic method, which is also rooted in the refutationist view of science, can be used to formulate, test, and improve at least some theories which incorporate ideas and decision making. It also has the potential to explain major transformations in human societies not explicable by holistic means. For these reasons methodological individualism should take its place among the theory-building tools of archaeologists.

REFERENCES

Bell, J. A. 1987. "Reason vs. relativism: Review of Ian Hodder's *Reading the Past*," *Archaeological Review of Cambridge* **6**, 75–86.
Binford, L. R. 1972. *An Archaeological Perspective*. Academic Press, New York.
Collingwood, R. G. 1946. *The Idea of History*. Clarendon Press, Oxford.
Comte, A. 1968. *System of Positive Polity*. B. Franklin, New York.
Crumley, C. L., and W. H. Marquardt (eds.) 1987. *Regional Dynamics: Burgundy as Polity and Province*. Academic Press, Orlando, FL.
Deetz, J. 1977. *In Small Things Forgotten*. Anchor Books, New York.
Flannery, K. V. 1968. "Culture history vs. cultural process: A debate in American archaeology," *Scientific American* **217**, 119–122.
———1973. "Archaeology with a capital S," in C. L. Redman (ed.), *Research and Theory in Current Archaeology*, pp. 47–53. Willey Intersciences, New York.
Halperin, R. H. 1984. "Polanyi, Marx, and the institutional paradigm in economic anthropology," *Research in Economic Anthropology* **6**, 245–272.
———1985. "The concept of the formal in economic anthropology," *Research in Economic Anthropology* **7**, 339–368.
Harris, M. 1979. *Cultural Materialism: The Struggle for a Science of Culture*. Random House, New York.
Hayek, F. A. von 1944. *The Road to Serfdom*. University of Chicago Press, Chicago.
———1972. *The Counter-Revolution of Science: Studies of the Abuse of Reason*. Liberty Press, Indianapolis, IN.
Hegel, G. W. F. 1977. *Phenomenology of Spirit*. A. U. Miller (tr.). Clarendon House, New York.
Herzfeld, M. 1982. "The etymology of excuses: Aspects of rhetorical performance in Greece," *American Ethnologist* **9**, 644–663.
Hill, J. N., and J. Gunn (eds.) 1977. *The Individual in Prehistory: Studies of Variability in Style in Prehistoric Technologies*. Academic Press, New York.
Hodder, I. 1985. "Post-processual archaeology," *Advances in Archaeological Method and Theory* **8**, 1–26.
———1986. *Reading the Past: Current Approaches to Interpretation in Archaeology*. Cambridge University Press, Cambridge.
Honigman, J. J. 1977. *Understanding Culture*. Greenwood Press, Westport, CT.
van der Leeuw, S. E. (ed.) 1981. *Archaeological Approaches to the Study of Complexity*. **CINGVLA VI**. Albert Egges Van Giffen Instituut voor Prae-en Protohistorie, Universiteit van Amsterdam.
Leone, M. P. 1982. "Some opinions about recovering mind," *American Antiquity* **47**, 742–760.
Lévi-Strauss, C. 1966. *The Savage Mind*. University of Chicago Press, Chicago.
Mandelbrot, B. B. 1982. *The Fractal Geometry of Nature*. Freeman, San Francisco.
Martineau, H. 1855. *The Positive Philosophy of Auguste Comte*. Blanchard, New York.

Marx, K., and F. Engels 1961. *The Communist Manifesto*. New York Labor News, New York.

Melas, E. M. n.d. *Post-Positivist Archaeology*. Manuscript in possession of author.

Mises, L. von 1949. *Human Actions: A Treatise on Economics*. Yale University Press, New Haven, CT.

———1962. *The Free and Prosperous Commonwealth; an Exposition of the Ideas of Classical Liberalism*. Van Norstrand, Princeton, NJ.

Mithen, S. J. 1987. "Modelling decision making and learning by low latitude hunter gatherers," *European Journal of Operational Research* **30**, 240–242.

Patton, M. 1986. "Questioning the fundamentals; the epistemological basis of a social arcaheology," paper delivered at the World Congress of Archaeology, Southampton.

Peitgen, H. O., and P. H. Richter 1986. *The Beauty of Fractals: Images of Complex Dynamical Systems*. Springer-Verlag, Berlin.

Popper, K. R. 1945. *The Open Society and Its Enemies*. Routledge, London.

———1957. *The Poverty of Historicism*. Routledge and Kegan Paul, London.

———1972. *Objective Knowledge: An Evolutionary Approach*. Clarendon Press, Oxford.

———1983. *Realism and the Aim of Science*. Hutchinson, London.

Prigogine, I. 1980. *From Being to Becoming: Time and Complexity in the Physical Sciences*. W. H. Freeman, San Francisco.

Renfrew, C. 1982. *Towards an Archaeology of Mind*. Cambridge University Press, Cambridge.

———1987. "Problems in the modelling and socio-cultural systems," *European Journal of Operational Research* **30**, 179–192.

Sartre, J.-P. 1957. *Existentialism and Human Emotions*. Philosophical Library, New York.

———1964. *Being and Nothingness*. Citadel Press, New York.

Schumpeter, J. A. 1964. *Business Cycles: A Theoretical, Historical, and Statistical Analysis of the Capitalist Process*. McGraw-Hill, New York.

Shand, A. H. 1984. *The Capitalist Alternative: An Introduction to Neo-Austrian Economics*. New York University Press, New York.

Shanks, M., and C. Tilley 1987. *Reconstructing Archaeology: Theory and Practice*. Cambridge University Press, Cambridge.

Snell, B. 1982. *The Discovery of the Mind in Greek Philosophy and Literature*. Dover Publications, New York.

Taylor, A. J. P. 1965. *English History, 1914–1945*. Oxford University Press, Oxford.

———1966. *From Sarajevo to Potsdam*. Thames and Hudson, London.

Tilley, C. 1981. "Conceptual frameworks for the explanation of sociocultural change," in I. Hodder, G. Isaac, and N. Hammond (eds.), *Pattern of the Past: Studies in Honor of David Clarke*, pp. 363–386. Cambridge University Press, Cambridge.

Weber, M. 1962. *Basic Concepts in Sociology*. Citadel Press, New York.

Culture and Matter

The Ontological Issue

When analyzing a particular science, a crucial distinction must be made between the kind of data it collects and uses as evidence, and what it is about. Physics is not about meter readings, psychology is not about experimental results, anthropology is not about field observations, and archaeology is not about vestiges. In a naïve rational reconstruction, one might assume that what a science is about is given first, and relevant data is sought out, but, in practice, things are more muddled. In anthropology and archaeology in particular, it is easier to characterize the kinds of data we collect than the kind of things or properties our sciences are about. We have lots of evidence, but to a large extent, we don't know what it is evidence for.

Because they collect different kinds of data, anthropologists and archaeologists tend to study different societies, or the same societies at different periods of their history. But at a more abstract level, anthropology and archaeology are both, not exclusively but to a large extent, about sociocultural things. What kind of things are sociocultural things? How do they fit in the world and how do they relate to things other sciences are about? These are ontological, hence philosophical questions, but, because they have practical implications for our work, we shouldn't ignore them. What is at stake is the way we may, or must, collaborate with other disciplines, and the extent to which what we have to say may fit in a general and consistent (though, of course, fragmentary) picture of the world.

The natural sciences achieve a high level of mutual consistency and interaction in part because they are all grounded in the same materialist ontology (a technically more appropriate term would be "physicalist," but "materialist" is more familiar to social scientists, and nothing in this discussion hinges on such technicalities). Materialism is a monism, a view according to which everything that exists is of one and the same substance, in the most general sense of the term. Materialism assumes that that substance is one studied by physicists, that everything that exists obeys the laws of physics. Materialism contrasts with idealism, which is another kind of monism, and with various forms of ontological pluralism (Cartesian dualism, vitalism, emergentism, etc.) according to which there are several kinds of substances obeying different causal laws. Now that advances in biology have rendered vitalism obsolete, supporters of ontological pluralism are found only in philosophy and in the social sciences.

In the social sciences, both ontological ideas and ontological practice are, to put it mildly, unsatisfactory. In practice, anything goes: the world of the social sciences is crowded with entities the ontological status of which is left undefined. Power, the state, ideology, religion, magic, sacrifice, myth, social classes, casts, nations, kinship, marriage, norms, values, social cohesion, cultural integration, anomy: to what substance do all these objects or properties pertain? How do they fit in the world? Ontological views encountered in the social sciences do not even come near answering such questions. These views are of three types: two types of materialism, one empty, the other self-contradictory, and ontological pluralism, according to which the social domain is ontologically autonomous.[1]

The thesis of the ontological autonomy of the social domain is generally expressed as a series of denials: social facts are not biological facts, they are not psychological facts, they are not a sum of individual facts. But what, then, are they? How are they located in space and time? What causal laws do they obey? How do they interact with other kinds of facts? There are no well-argued answers to these questions. The obvious effect of assuming that there are ontological thresholds between the mental and the biological and between the social and the mental is to insulate biology, psychology, and the social sciences from one another, and to reject as *a priori* mistaken any contribution and, even more, any criticism coming from without. To achieve this dubious result one need not develop in any detail the idea of ontological pluralism; postulating it is enough.

Empty materialism consists in stating that everything is material, including sociocultural phenomena, and in leaving it at that. Well and fine, but as long as you do not begin to reflect about the material existence of sociocultural phenomena, as long as you keep invoking cause-effect relationships among them without even trying to imagine what material processes might bring about these relationships, you are merely paying lip service to materialism. You may use for that a number of standard metaphors which evoke the material character of sociocultural phenomena: the mechanical metaphors of social "forces," the astronomical metaphor of "revolution," the geological metaphor of "stratification," and the many biological metaphors of cultural "life," "reproduction," etc. None of these metaphors, however, has ever been developed into a materialistically plausible model. Such empty materialism helps one evade accusations of idealism or of ontological pluralism. It remains otherwise without effect on one's research practice.

Self-contradictory materialism generally issues from ill-digested Marxism. This kind of materialism is made up of two claims. The first claim is the same as that of empty materialism: everything that is, including social and cultural phenomena, is material. The second claim is that the material side of the social domain, roughly ecology and economy, determine its nonmaterial side, roughly politics and culture. The contradiction is blatant: the first claim is monistic; the second, which contrasts a material and a nonmaterial or less material or ideal side of the social domain, is dualistic. If materialist monism is right, then everything is material: law and religion and art, no less than forces or relationships of production. From a truly materialist point of view, effects cannot be less material than their causes.

There are two ways to eschew the contradiction in this kind of materialism. The first consists in giving up monism (and therefore materialism in the usual sense) and in adopting ontological dualism. At this price—but what a price!—it might be conceivable (I am not sure how) that material things determine nonmaterial ones. The second way out of the contradiction is truer to Marxism (Engels's version at least). It consists in robbing the second claim, that of economic determinism, of any ontological import: one aspect of the material world determines another aspect of the material world; maybe so, but ontology, and in particular the kind of materialism on which the natural sciences are founded, has nothing to do with it. What remains then, on the ontological side, is the first claim: everything that is is material; but this is just standard empty materialism.

Is there an alternative? Can we go beyond lazy dualism and empty or self-contradictory materialism? Part of the answer is suggested by recent developments is psychology.

The Ontology of Cognition

In psychology too, the choice had long seemed to be between dualism—mental facts and neurological facts are of two radically different natures—and empty materialism. There were materialist metaphors—the biological metaphors of Freud, the mechanical metaphor of Piagetian "equilibration," for instance—but no materialist model. Only the behaviorists drew practical conclusions from their materialism; but what conclusions: unable to give a materialist account of mental phenomena, they tried to banish them from the psychological domain!

In the mid-thirties, the mathematician Alan Turing conceived of a materially implementable device that could process information. Even more important, a Turing machine, as the device came to be known, can, demonstrably, perform any operation on encoded information that any other finite physical device, whatever its organization, and whatever the way it encodes information, may perform. To put it bluntly, Turing's discovery provided a way of understanding how matter can think. It took another twenty years, the development of computers, and important advances in neurology, for the impact of Turing's discovery on psychology to be felt and for the "cognitive revolution" to start.[2]

Even then, the cognitive revolution meant different things to different people. For some, it merely meant that mental processes could legitimately be studied again, after decades of behaviorist stricture. Hardly a revolution, that. For more innovative participants in the movement, it meant something else: mental processes could be studied, yes, but studying them now implied showing how they could be material processes. This in turn implied decomposing them in elementary subprocesses, the material implementation of which, for instance on a computer, had become unproblematic.

The same mental process, say the performance of a syllogism, can be programmed in different ways, and differently compiled on different computers; or it can take place in a human brain, and, there too, possibly in different ways. A material model of a mental process may be materially very different from the underlying brain process. Still, the very possibility of providing material models of mental processes changes the field: the question is not anymore whether mental processes are material; it is what material processes they are. The models cognitive psychologists try to develop, besides establishing the material possibility of the mental processes they represent, can also be seen as more or less fine-grained hypotheses about their actual material form (with testable implications for reaction times, breakdown patterns, etc.).

What is involved in cognitive psychology so understood is a minimal form of materialism; the underlying ontological claim is merely that every token mental process is a token material process: for instance, every case of a syllogistic reasoning by a human is a case of a brain process. This minimal materialism (known as "token-physicalism") contrasts with a stronger form ("type-physicalism") according to which every type of mental process is a type of physical process: for instance, the class of mental processes which can be described as human syllogistic reasoning (if there is such a class) is at the same time a definite class (rather than an indefinite set) of brain processes. Whereas strong versions of materialism imply that psychological categories can be either reduced to, or eliminated in favor of, neurological categories, minimal materialism does not imply reductionism.[3]

The minimal materialism involved in current cognitive research is nevertheless true materialism. It is a materialism with practical consequences: it imposes strong constraints on acceptable psychological models. It is a materialism with theoretical implications: mental processes are attributed causal powers in virtue of their material properties. Identifying these properties, however difficult, becomes an intelligible task.

The Ontology of Culture

Now, I don't believe that the solution cognitive psychologists have found to their ontological problem can be simply copied to solve the ontological problem of the social sciences. The material locus of psychological processes is obvious enough, and it is homogeneous: token psychological processes are token neurological processes. By contrast, if sociocultural processes have a material form, then it is a heterogeneous one: it involves neurological processes too, but also other biological processes and environmental processes. Nevertheless, the psychological case suggests an alternative to the maximalist materialism without practical consequences, the Judgment Day reductionism allowing till then ontological havoc, currently found in the social sciences. Let us emulate the minimal materialism of cognitive psychology and try to describe sociocultural phenomena so as to render manifest, not their actual material character, but merely the possibility of their material instantiation. This should be enough of a challenge for a time.

Sociocultural phenomena are, in part, made of bodily movements of individuals and of environmental changes resulting from these movements. For instance, people are beating drums, or erecting a building, or slaughtering an animal. The material character of these phenomena is, so far, unproblematic. But we must go further. Is it a musical exercise, a drummed message, or a ritual? Is it a public, a religious, or a private building? Is it an act of butchery or a sacrifice? In order to answer, one must, one way or another, take into account the representations involved in these behaviors. Whatever one's theoretical or methodological framework, representations play an essential role in defining sociocultural phenomena. But what kind of material objects are representations?

Let us note, to begin with, that two types of representations are involved: mental representations and public representations. Beliefs, intentions, preferences are mental representations. Until the cognitive revolution, the ontological status of mental representations was obscure. Signals, utterances, texts, pictures are public representations. Public representations have an obviously material aspect. However, describing this aspect—the sounds of speech, the shapes and colors of a picture—leaves out the most important, the fact that these material traces can be interpreted: they represent something for someone.

To account for the fact that public representations are interpretable, one must assume the existence of an underlying system, e.g., a language, a code, an ideology. In the semiotic and semiological traditions, these underlying interpretation systems have been described in abstract rather than in psychological terms, and indeed their existence has often been considered extrapsychological. With such an approach, the material existence of these systems remains obscure. As a result, the material properties which make public representations interpretable, and the material existence of sociocultural phenomena described with reference to public representations, remain obscure too. One may also view underlying interpretation systems as complex mental representations; this is, for instance, what Noam Chomsky does when he describes a grammar as a mental device. This second approach brings us back to the psychology of mental representations, and therefore to the new perspectives opened by the development of the cognitive sciences.

The true difficulty in developing even a minimal materialism in the social sciences came from the role representations unavoidably play in them. However, in psychology, the material character of mental representations has changed from the status of a total mystery to that of an intelligible problem. The question is whether the social sciences can redefine their notion of a representation on the basis of the cognitive notion of a representation. What I would like to do now is suggest how this can be done, and how, as a result, the whole ontology of the social sciences can be purified, how truly materialist social sciences become conceivable.

An Epidemiology of Representation

Just as one can say that a human population is inhabited by a much larger population of viruses, one can say that it is inhabited by a much larger population of mental representations. Most of these representations are found in only one individual. Some, however, get communicated, i.e., first transformed by the communicator into public representations, and then retransformed by the audience into mental representations. A very small proportion of these communicated representations get communicated repeatedly. Through communication (or, in other cases, through imitation), some representations spread out in a human population and may end up being instantiated in every member of the population for several generations. Such widespread and enduring representations are paradigmatic cases of cultural representations.

The question becomes now why are some representations, so to speak, contagious, either generally, or in specific contexts. To answer such a question is to develop a kind of "epidemiology of representations" (see Sperber 1985a, 1985b). The epidemiological metaphor can help us, provided we see its limits. One limit is self-evident: we certainly do not want to imply that cultural representations are in any sense pathological. Another limit, though less obvious, is much more important: while pathogenic agents such as viruses and bacteria reproduce in the process of transmission and only occasionally undergo a mutation, representations are transformed almost every time they are transmitted and remain stable only in certain limiting cases. A cultural representation in particular is made of many versions, mental and public ones. Each mental version results from the interpretation of a public representation which itself is an expression of a mental representation.

One might choose as a topic of study these causal consecutions made of mental and public representations, and try to explain how the mental states of human organisms may cause them to modify their environment, in particular by producing signs, and how such modifications of their environment may cause a modification of the mental states of other human organisms. The ontology of such an undertaking resembles that of epidemiology. It is a rather heterogeneous ontology, since psychological and ecological phenomena are mixed together, just as in epidemiology pathological and ecological phenomena are mixed. In both cases, what is to be explained is the distribution of individual conditions, pathological or psychological. In both cases the explanation takes into account both the state of the individuals and that of their common environment, which is itself largely modified by the behavior of the individuals.

In spite of its heterogeneity, the ontology of an epidemiology of representations is strictly materialist: mental representations are brain states described in functional terms, and it is the interaction between brains, organisms, and environment which explains the distribution of these representations.

Another way in which the epidemiological metaphor may be helpful is in suggesting the kind of theoretical objectives we may reasonable aim at. Because of the ontological heterogeneity of epidemiological phenomena, there is no such thing as a general epidemiological theory. The distributions of different pathological conditions, say malaria, thalassemia, and influenza, may have quite different explanations. As a result, what we find in epidemiology is a variety of different models with greater or lesser generality, and a common methodology. Similarly, I doubt very much that we should, in the study of sociocultural phenomena, aim at a grand general theory.

Different types of representations may have their distribution explained in quite different ways. For the time being at least, a realistic and ambitious enough aim would be to develop materialistically plausible explanatory models of the distribution of, for instance, various folk-classifications, myths, techniques, art forms, rituals, legal rules, etc. Models with the greatest possible generality, provided they are truly explanatory, are of course to be preferred. However, aiming from the start at a holistic theory, as many social scientists are prone to do, results, for practical, and possibly also for substantive, reasons in no theory at all.

Let me very briefly illustrate the epidemiological approach with a couple of examples.

Myth

Take a myth, say the Bororo myth of the bird-nester which Lévi-Strauss uses as the starting point of his Mythologiques. In a traditional approach, this myth is a canonical version arrived at by selectively synthesizing the various collected versions. Such a canonical version is an abstract object, without existence in the society studied. It may serve an expository purpose, but, as it stands, it neither calls for, nor provides an explanation. Lévi-Strauss himself departs from this traditional approach: for him, to study a myth is to study the relationships of "transformation" (i.e., the way in which resemblances and differences are patterned) between the different versions of the myth and between the myth and other myths. With this approach, neither a single version nor a synthesis of several versions is an appropriate object of study. A myth should be considered, rather, as the set of all its versions.

The ontological status of a myth as a set of versions, and the explanatory value of analysing the relationships of transformations between these versions are unclear, but they can be clarified in an epidemiological perspective. What I suggest, in a nutshell, is to try to model not the set, but the consecution linking the different versions of the myth, and for this, to consider not just the public versions but also the mental ones (without which there would be no causal consecution). Of course, we have records of only a few of the public versions and none of the mental ones, but complementing observations with hypotheses about unobserved, and even unobservable entities is plain normal science.

Studying a myth in this perspective, we have three types of objects:

1) Narratives, i.e., public representations which can be observed and recorded, but which can only be interpreted by taking into account:

2) Stories, i.e., mental representations of events, which can be expressed as, or constructed from narratives.

3) Causal consecutions: . . . -narrative-story-narrative- . . .

Every token of one of these three types is a material object. Every token of a narrative is a specific acoustic event. Every token of a story is a specific brain state. A consecution causally linking such specific material things is, of course, itself a material thing.

The causal explanation of the existence of these public narratives and these mental stories is provided by the description of their consecution. The explanation of the consecution calls for a model where both psychological and ecological factors will come into play. For instance, a crucial ecological factor would be the absence in the society considered of the kind of external memory stores writing provides: oral representations, unlike written ones, are environmental events rather than environmental states. A crucial psychological factor would be the organization of spontaneous human memory. The interaction of these two factors would help explain why a given narrative with an easily memorized structure is transmitted with little variation in an oral tradition.

What about the concept of a myth in all this? A consecution of versions is of course no more a myth than an epidemic of influenza is a case of influenza. Unlike a case of influenza, which is influenza even without an epidemic, each mental story, or each public narrative, is itself cultural, and hence mythical, only to the extent that it belongs to such a consecution. No material object, therefore, is intrinsically a myth. At best, talking of "myth" may serve to draw attention to a body of related data. But the basic concept needed in studying these data is that of a causal consecution of narratives and stories. A truly materialist ontology leads to a reconceptualization of the domain.

The fact that, in a nonliterate population, we find narratives that can be considered versions of one another (and are so considered by the natives) is what leads us to identify a "myth." Other cultural forms, "beliefs," "folk-classifications," "traditional techniques," are also characterized by a wide distribution of very similar representations. The ontological purification of the concepts involved in the study of such phenomena is simple enough. It consists in ridding ontology of the abstract synthetic version of these representations and of keeping only the many public and mental versions, and their consecution.

Marriage

The ontology of social institutions, which are the subject matter par excellence of the social sciences, raises further problems. For there to be a state, a market, a church, a ritual, it is not necessary that every individual who participates in the institution should have a mental version of it; indeed, in most cases the very idea is meaningless. Institutions are neither public nor mental representations. How, then, could an epidemiology of representations help provide a materialist account of institutions?

Well, an epidemiology of representations is not about representations but about the process of their distribution. In some cases, similar representations, for example, versions of the same myth, are distributed by a repetitive consecution of public and mental representations; in other cases many different representations are involved in the same distribution process, the distribution of some representations playing a causal role in the distribution of others. The communication of given representations in given parts of the social network makes possible the communication of other representations in other parts of the network. Institutional phenomena, I maintain, are characterized by such complex consecutions.

Take a simple example, which I simplify even further: civil marriage in France today. The classical approach would consist of defining it as a ceremony establishing a jural link of a certain type between a woman and a man. If, as natives of today's France we have no problem using these notions, as scientists we should be puzzled by the ontological status of a ceremony, of a jural link, and therefore of marriage itself. The epidemiological approach provides a solution to the puzzle.

The material process which the natives describe by saying that, say, Pierre and Marie got married involves two levels or representations. At the higher level, there is a representation of a course of action: a certain number of preconditions being fulfilled, a civil officer "pronounces a man and a woman united by marriage." The basic public version of this representation is a chapter of the *Code Civil*, the origin and distribution of which is, to a large extent a matter of public record. Note that what this higher-level representation describes is a type of lower-level representation and the conditions under which it can be produced and distributed. The civil officer who pronounces Pierre and Marie husband and wife produces such a lower-level representation in accordance with the higher-level one. This lower-level representation can then be reproduced, paraphrased, elaborated, etc. Anyone who now says that Pierre and Marie are married is not describing an actual material fact, but restating the civil officer's original representation. Anyone who states the rights and duties of Pierre and Marie as married people is producing a more or less faithful and specific version of a higher-level, general representation, the original version of which is again in the *Code Civil*.

"Marriage," "rights," "duties," are immaterial entities existing in the ontology of the natives, hence in our everyday ontology. In our materialist ontology for scientific use, on the other hand, there exist only mental or public representations of marriage in general, of particular marriages, and of rights and duties, and the consecution of these representations. The representations natives have of immaterial entities are themselves quite material. The distribution of these representations can have effects on the behavior of the natives which are very similar to the effects they themselves attribute—wrongly— to the immaterial state of affairs represented. The difference of ontologies is not incompatible, therefore, with a certain degree of correspondence between the two descriptions, that of the native and that of the scientist.

Concluding Remarks

I have deliberately chosen, as illustrations of the epidemiological approach, two types of cultural phenomena which leave few or no vestiges for archaeologists to study. What I have argued is that they are no less material than other cultural phenomena such as toolmaking or cave painting, vestiges of which outlive the individuals and even the societies which produce them. Whether our evidence is made of archaeological vestiges or of anthropological observations, our data are fragmentary; they are just more or less so. In both cases, our task is to develop hypotheses about those elements which we were unable to observe (either because we were not at the right time at the right place, or because, being mental, they are unobservable) so as to situate our data in the causal consecution which alone explains them.

The program I am suggesting is not without precursors. The diffusionist approach in anthropology and archaeology was concerned with a causal explanation of the distribution in space and time of cultural items. One of its weaknesses was the poverty of its psychological assumptions. A comparable weakness is found in several recent biologically inspired approaches to culture, where the mind/brain is seen essentially as a reproduction device.[4] The most obvious lesson of recent cognitive work is that recall is not storage in reverse, and comprehension is not expression in reverse. Memory and communication transform information. Thus, to treat representations, whether mental or public, as material causes among other material causes implies rooting the study of thought and of communication in cognitive psychology.[5]

An epidemiology of representations would establish a relationship of mutual relevance between the cognitive and the social sciences, similar to that between pathology and epidemiology. This relationship would in no way be one of reduction of the social to the psychological. Sociocultural facts, on this approach, are ecological patterns of psychological facts: they do not reduce to psychological facts but cannot either be defined independently of them. It should be clear that such an epidemiological approach to culture has practical implications for anthropology and archaeology. Determining what these implications are will require, for each type of sociocultural phenomena, some creative work. This, I know, will deter some, and, I hope, will attract others.

NOTES

An earlier, somewhat different, French version of this paper was published as Sperber 1987.

1. Methodological individualism, represented in this volume by James Bell's contribution, is a way to exert some ontological restraint. However the "individual" methodological individualists seem to have in mind is a Cartesian subject who believes, decides, and acts, rather than a cognitively endowed organism that processes information and controls its own movements. This view of the individual raises ontological problems of its own.

2. Gardner 1985 is the first history of the cognitive revolution, and one particularly useful to social scientists because of the author's interest in the relationship between cognition and culture.

3. For a discussion of these ontological issues see in particular Fodor 1981, Cummins 1983, Churchland 1984.

4. See Cavalli-Sforza and Feldman 1981, Dawkins 1976, Lumsden and Wilson 1981, Boyd and Richerson 1985.

5. For a cognitively grounded approach to human communication, see Sperber and Wilson 1986.

REFERENCES

Boyd, R., and P. J. Richerson 1985. *Culture and the Evolutionary Process*. University of Chicago Press, Chicago.
Cavalli-Sforza, L. L., and M. W. Feldman 1981. *Cultural Transmission and Evolution: A Quantitative Approach*. Princeton University Press, Princeton, NJ.
Churchland, P. M. 1984. *Mind and Consciousness*. MIT Press, Cambridge, MA.
Cummins, R. 1983. *The Nature of Psychological Explanation*. MIT Press, Cambridge, MA.
Dawkins, R. 1976. *The Selfish Gene*. Oxford University Press, Oxford.
Fodor, J. 1981. *Representations: Philosophical Essays on the Foundations of Cognitive Science*. MIT Press, Cambridge, MA.
Gardner, H. 1985. *The Mind's New Science: A History of the Cognitive Revolution*. Basic Books, New York.
Lumsden, C. J., and E. O. Wilson 1981. *Genes, Mind and Culture*. Harvard University Press, Cambridge, MA.
Sperber, D. 1985a. *On Anthropological Knowledge*. Cambridge University Press, Cambridge.
———1985b. "Anthropology and psychology: Towards an epidemiology of representations," *Man* (n.s.) **20,** 73–89.
———1987. "Les sciences cognitives, les sciences sociales et le matérialisme," *Le Débat* **47,** 103–115.
Sperber, D., and D. Wilson 1986. *Relevance: Communication and Cognition*. Harvard University Press, Cambridge, MA.

Metapatterns

ARCHAEOLOGY AND THE USES OF EVIDENTIAL SCARCITY

Of Others Past and Present

Archaeology is one of the scholarly zones in which identity—human, cultural, local—is the motivating issue. While this means that the discipline carries a heavy and potentially unstable ideological load, it also offers great opportunities for critical reflection both within archaeology and in relation to the social sciences with which it has the most symbiotic ties. Archaeology has conventionally looked to social and cultural anthropology as a source of ideas and insight to a much greater extent than that discipline has sought inspiration in archaeology. Whether we take the Kroeberian component in Clarke's (1968:113, 278–279) critique of archaeological taxonomy, the ethnoarchaeological reconstructions of experimental archaeologists (Coles 1979), or the inclusion of social anthropologists as critical members of survey research teams (see Jacobsen 1985), we encounter a consistent pattern. Because anthropologists who deal with contemporaneous populations have the advantage of being able to interrogate "informants," most archaeologists today assume that, at the very least, their sociocultural colleagues can help them establish the limits of plausibility in reconstructing the past. And that, truth to tell, is no small gift.

But the characteristic archaeological encounter with absence also has a great deal to teach social anthropologists. Such evidential scarcity both imposes analytical caution and presses the search for possible modes of interpretation. Imagine an ethnographer denied access to the very possibility of linguistic interaction and you have an accurate picture of the worst constraint on the archaeological recovery of culture. The comparative ease of access that even an imperfect or excessively formal knowledge of the field language seems to grant led many prestructuralist ethnographers to treat all meaning in terms of a linguistic and implicitly referential model ("this object device is [always] a symbol; the symbol means X"). Yet, sensitive analyses of the relationship between material objects, their meaning, and their reproduction in the play of language (e.g., Parmentier 1987) shows that the premise of pure referentiality is no more apposite for nonlinguistic symbols than it is for language. Systematicity is strategic; an ordered past represents a game successfully played—irritating instabilities. Any notion of meaning not embedded in political process and agency claims not merely synchronic status (which is an acceptable analytical device), but freedom from history itself. As such, it is unlikely to serve either archaeology or ethnography well. What is more, the search for language-like meaning in the archaeological record can hardly be other than quixotic. Semantic (or, in Peircean terms, "symbolic"[1]) meaning, which plays so large a part in the more interpretation-oriented varieties of social and cultural anthropology, is easily the least accessible; it can only be deciphered—and then partially—when written records provide the necessary commentary.

Archaeology has had to confront the inadequacies of its evidential base much more seriously than has any other field of cultural study. Its lack of some kinds of evidence places it more obviously, and therefore more accessibly, at the disposal of ideologies that can exploit both its incapacities and its symbolic association with an unusually strong intimation of scholarly disinterestedness and removal from current political concerns. Once perceived, however, that potential liability can function in a very productive way, because it permits a clearer vision of the ways in which ideology permeates description. In a dialectical relationship between ethnography and excavation (to focus on the specifically empirical aspects of the relevant disciplines), the archaeologist's hermeneutic dilemmas provide a limiting case for those of the social scientist.

Crucial to this reflexive, interdisciplinary comparison is the archaeologist's very reliance on observation itself—a probably inevitable "visualism," to use Fabian's (1983) critical term, that too easily equates an unproblematized resemblance between objects with "relations" between hypostatized "cultures." Clarke's (1968:230–286) early critique of this use of "culture" in archaeology anticipated the problem, but treated it as a failure of precision rather than as an instructive pointer to the entailment of the archaeological investigator in the delineation of the object of study. Yet it is clear, as J. G. D. Clark's exposé of the "invasion hypothesis" in British prehistory shows (see below), that archaeological concepts of social and cultural boundedness may have a great deal to do with the global political models through which the scholar deals with contemporary experience.

Resemblances and Absences

Archaeology predicates typological relationships primarily upon selective resemblance (iconicity). Such criteria as stratigraphy and surface surveying also require that these be enmeshed in relations of contiguity and distance—spatial forms of indexicality that may then be translated into temporal sequences. Archaeological activity is truly interpretational—a limiting case of ethnographic descriptions as Sperber (1985:22; cf. also 1975:141) has described the latter: as "[conceptual] representations of conceptual representations." Not only are archaeologists often confronted by absences, but these absences may themselves have been significant as parts of a larger pattern of presence-within-absence, as in the spaces to which a building is oriented: what may strike the cultural outsider as random and natural features "may acquire architectonic significance by virtue of their space-shaping and space-defining properties, as these are differentially appropriated by different cultures" (Preziosi 1979:5).[2] We cannot easily interpret such absences even when we know that they are, so to speak, present. Yet the ability to spot the conversion of the natural into the cultural, which is perhaps the most radical and universal mode of boundary creation, is crucial to the whole business of doing archaeology (see also the discussion by Kus [1982:52–53]). It is what unites the practice of archaeology to the praxis that the archaeologist indirectly confronts, and makes nonsense of any Cartesian separation of the cognizing investigator from the "objects" of scientific discourse. An instructive historical curiosity is the "eolith" controversy.

The eolith controversy has left an indelible—if often unacknowledged mark—in the form of a cautious distrust of overinterpretation. Archaeology foregrounds the limits of interpretation precisely because its absences are better defined and harder to ignore than those of contemporaneous ethnography. Archaeology may thus be expected to provide some insight into those aspects of ethnographic practice that reduce nonverbal observations to verbal explanations or even, less dramatically, to the merest descriptions. Let us begin, then, with the extreme case of the eolith controversy. Here, Eco's (1976:22–26) frankly speculative and generic discussion of prehistoric stone tools is entirely germane. Eco addresses what we might call the problem of *"arti-factuality."* His interest is indivisibly in both material culture and economics. His discussion therefore provides a useful starting point for any attempt to bring the accessibly material and the imponderables of symbolic production into a common framework.

Social Facts and Arti-Facts

Eco's argument runs, in summary, as follows. Our hominid antecedents may have used natural objects as tools, but can only be said to have possessed culture when two coincident conditions were satisfied: when Australopithecine hominids came to recognize (or, better, to "re-cognize") objects subsequently encountered as tokens of a common type; and when at the same time they also acquired the capacity to name them in the light of this recognized interconnection in such a manner that the *connotation* of the name became the function of the tool. (One can see immediately how important this is for the argument about human identity: it addresses the question of reflexive thinking, taken by some authorities to be the benchmark of human emergence and instantiated in tool-production [Kitahara-Frisch 1980:220].) In order to demonstrate the encompassing capacity of his framework, Eco then applies it to the Marxist analysis of economic exchanges: for "stone," read "commodity"; for the equivalence relationship between stones, read "exchange value"; and let the "name" of that value be "money." He thus shows that the process of economic exchange rests on the same relationship between tokens standing for a signified, abstract—and therefore "ideological"—type as does the patterning of material artifacts. As he subsequently points out (1976:221), there are cases in which "the 'recognized' object expresses a content although the referent does not exist"—in short, the human trait of cognizing absence.

Although symbolism is usually represented as the most arbitrary form of semiotic relationship, it is in fact only the most *obviously* arbitrary; iconic relations, by contrast, because they either "look natural" or can be "naturalized," are, ironically, a good deal *more* labile, and lend themselves with particular ease to totalizing cultural ideologies

(Herzfeld 1986b). It is not that iconic relationships are actually less arbitrary than, say, symbolic ones; they are, however, iconic in virtue of their *appearing* to be so. Thus, as Eco observes (1976:190), iconicity is a cultural relationship. It is not a naturally given property of relations between objects, because, as a signifying relationship, it requires a social context. Archaeologists should recognize the force of this argument, for it is precisely the point of the controversy about eoliths: were they cultural or natural objects? The decision, as Eco would presumably agree, depended on a recognition of pattern, and that required the identification of more than a single specimen—not just by their putative manufacturers, but, more to the point, by present-day archaeologists, who therefore had to presuppose an ability to recognize the original manufacturers' own patterns of significance. Even assuming a sufficiency of material support, however, and leaving aside the question of how that statistical measure is to be determined or confirmed, we do not escape the ideological issue. Distinguishing human from natural activity is an act of self-determination.

Iconic relationships work well in nationalistic ideologies because they provide the means of collapsing diachronic *continuity* (a relationship of cultural form through time) into *identity* (a relationship of cultural form *outside* time)—the reverse of the normative process in analytical archaeology, which seeks to extrapolate temporal from iconic and spatial relationships. In an adapted version of Bourdieu's (1977) terms, they bring about a reduction of social strategies to cultural rules; and rules, again, are what Eco wants us to look for—relations between relations, or what we might call *metapatterns*. These are what, for example, Fernandez (1977:11), in writing of the mutual reproduction of social structure and architectonic form among the Fang of Gabon, calls "structural replications at various levels and various arenas in Fang life." Such patterns allow individual agents to organize the otherwise chaotic indeterminacies of social existence. The recognition of a recurrent design is thus not simply an understanding of what is out there; it is a reading of a reading.

One of the most ambitious attempts to "read" early stone tools illustrates precisely how the search for pattern becomes a search for identity—not necessarily a wrongheaded enterprise, indeed probably an inevitable one, but one of whose conceptual motivation we should be as aware as we can. Wynn (1979) has attempted to argue, on the basis of a Piagetian model, that the makers of early Acheulean handaxes were as intelligent and as capable of logical inference as modern humans. He reaches this conclusion on the basis of an examination of the artifacts' geometric properties: "whole-part relations, qualitative displacement, spatio-temporal substitution and symmetry" (1979:383). Wynn's argument, typical in this regard of the archaeological predicament, has to operate in the absence of a known social context. Its appeal to universals by an ontogenetic derivation of phylogeny bypasses referential semantics, but recovers a complex of indexical and iconic relations. The semantics are probably irrecoverable (it is not clear what Kitahara-Frisch [1980] means by calling the handaxes "symbolic"); if they were "good to think," we no longer know how. Tools, like social facts, are constructed not only by those who are "in" them, but also by those whose discourse is "about" them. The eoliths provide a limiting case, an ultimately unsuccessful one, of archaeology as a construction of human identity. The best defense against this ideological quicksand is the search for metapatterns and the principled abandonment of a search for pure reference.

Although the eolith controversy is by now past history, and usually serves few present-day purposes other than amusement, the language in which it was conducted speaks to extremely current preoccupations with otherness and time, and the nature of the debate also serves as a salutary reminder that the underlying preoccupation—the association of recognizable form with cultural identity—has not substantially changed. As with both Eco's and Wynn's arguments, the emergence of human intelligence is tied to the predictability of form. The problem of the eoliths was most aptly phrased by the (now nameless) French scholar who remarked, "Man made one, God made ten thousand— God help the man who tries to see the one in the ten thousand" (quoted by Oakley 1957:201).

In fact, scholars who believed in the human origin of the eoliths preferred to see the ten thousand as one—as a single category, that is, in which typological unity could only be achieved by assuming a "primitive" lack of technological differentiation: an early version of the cognitivist argument of Wynn, but also a striking illustration of one of the key facets of the ideology of European identity. In that identity, the non-European Other was typified by formless undifferentiatedness, while the European's versatility was *recognizable* (form-full?[3]) everywhere (see Herzfeld 1987:77–78, 81). Thus, the importance of the eoliths lay in the "evidence" they supplied, not merely to speculations about the intrinsically interesting question of when humanity emerged, but also to the argument that primitives of any era either could produce nothing recognizable at all or could only produce a single form that was (a) close to nature and (b) lacking to an extreme degree the variability of disciplined form that marks the *Kultur* of civilized (i.e., European) humanity.

Miles Burkitt (1933:103), a true believer, insisted that the term *eolith* was wrongly and maliciously used of natural objects that merely bore "a certain *resemblance* to humanly worked tools" (my emphasis); but, though he prematurely crowed that the eolithic "discoveries" at Foxhall had at last added even the skeptical Abbé Breuil to "the growing company of those prehistorians who believed in *the existence of man* as early as late tertiary times" (1933:103; my emphasis), the latter dismissed the entire phenomenon in summary fashion: "All that remains of the many attempts to find traces of an Eolithic stage . . . of human identity is a 'posthumous' list" (Breuil and Lantier 1965:55). Breuil, perhaps unwittingly, put his finger on the problem: *all* archaeological taxonomy is made up of such "posthumous lists," but the disagreement always centers on just where *we* are able to cognize a sufficient degree of iconicity to justify the creation of a taxon. This is the most all-embracing version of the tendentious tactic that we can see most fully in the various nineteenth-century attempts, from Greece to Finland, to legislate continuity with an ancient past as the basis for the creation and maintenance of the nation-state.

The debate was protracted and acrimonious. The protagonists were not simply arguing about whether these or other objects were humanly produced, but were concerned to document the origins of humankind—a concept that depended on circular definitions such as Oakley's preemptive "man the toolmaker." What one found depended on what one believed. MacCurdy, an early eolith enthusiast, reported of a visit to a site near Harmignies (1905: 460; my emphasis):

After being told where to look, my search was rewarded. The first find was a typical Reutelian hammerstone . . . characteristic also of that particular locality, *since* it bore marks of having been much used. It is a flint nodule that had been but slightly altered by chance flaking before being utilized. Only one of the old surfaces of fracture has been preserved. The rest of the exterior either retains the original modular crust or has been modified by artificial chipping. One end and one margin are thoroughly battered by use.

Methods have changed vastly since the heyday of the eolith craze, but the essential dilemma remains. If we are able to identify artifactuality only through the recognition of repetitive patterns of structure and use (though the latter can now be determined by extraordinarily sophisticated techniques), and if the identification of truly semiotic relations depends upon our own ability to recognize these patterns, then the assumption that only human beings can make tools is nominalistic and circular. It also conflicts with ethological evidence. This order of pattern recognition, however, is an essential part of the popularly received definition of what a human being is, since it is also inextricably entailed in the notion of intellectual activity itself. At the same time, in order not to step over the brink of infinite self-castigation, we should remember that it was scholars who have also challenged and undermined this definition.

Eco's comparison of handaxe form with economic relations is far from frivolous. If the essence of archaeological recognition is a "blind" (i.e., noninterpretable) type-token relationship, then we should be searching in the archaeological record not for symbolic meanings, but for ordered sets of relationships (see also Hodder 1982:7). In that regard, the material evidence of an economic relationship should be as "real" as a handaxe. But we usually—though not necessarily with complete justification—treat the significance of handaxes as primarily practical and accessible; the very name that we give them indicates our predilection for function over meaning (but cf. Conkey 1980:231–232). This is not true of economic or other forms of social relationship. Especially in the quest for evidence of social organization, our chances of locating a patrilineal descent system or a marriage rule in prehistoric remains are minimal; but underlying such relations are what Ardener (1971) called "paradigmatic structures," which organize more general principles.

Because these structures are liable to appear in more than one domain of cultural expression, they are also more likely to prove accessible. This is an old idea; we meet it, for example, in Durkheim and Mauss's work on primitive classification, although Needham (1963) rightly adjures us to reject those authors' sociocentrism and to avoid privileging one domain of conceptual organization over the others. In the case of Acheulean handaxes, we do not possess enough other "pieces" of symbolic expression to make that sort of comparative judgment. What we are perhaps able to do is note the recurrence of *combinations* of patterns. The contemporaneous ethnographer can again do this more easily, through the medium of language. Many ethnographic analyses of space would indeed have been impossible without linguistic clues to both the internal indexical relations between the parts of the space concerned and the external parallels—clues that tell us what to compare with what (see, for example, Bourdieu 1973, 1977:89; Herzfeld 1985:149–156; Joseph and Joseph 1987:58–85; Needham 1962:87–96). But this makes a multiplicity of *levels of contrast* all the more requisite when the relative transparency of linguistic representation is lacking.

The tendency to fall into the trap that Needham identified is rife in anthropological writing; archaeology is an exemplary antidote because the archaeologist has no direct access to the level of social specificity. Social anthropologists, by contrast, too easily make the mistake of characterizing whole societies by the dominant mode of social organization (e.g., "a patrilineal society") and assume that all else follows. In Ardener's terms, they mistake syntagmatic instantiation for the encompassing, paradigmatic structure; thus, for example, many writers have assumed that conflict (a syntagmatic relation) was the primary form of opposition (a paradigmatic principle) (Ardener 1971). As Fernandez (1977:9–11) has shown, principles of opposition, which in political life can take the form of conflict but may also be expressed through less violent means, appear characteristically in architectonic forms, from buildings to dance arrangements. In a closely related development, the followers of Evans-Pritchard reduced his understanding of *segmentation*—the relativistic and hierarchical ordering of levels of social knowledge and inclusiveness—to a typological commonplace, and constricted its use to the analysis of so-called acephalous, unilineal societies. Yet this eminently "paradigmatic" concept can lead us to understand the relativity of social relations through *cultural form*—an argument that treats social and artifactual production within a common framework.[4]

Reflexive Boundaries and Visual Penetrations

Only a very old-fashioned form of relativism would insist that the construal of iconicity as culturally patterned must preclude a general human ability to recognize certain types of similarity.[5] Social anthropologists have long recognized that people can *learn* to perceive iconic relations that relate to culturally specific practices (e.g., the "translation" needed to relate a photograph to a known face; see Forge 1968). But they do not need anthropologists to teach them; if they did, ethnography itself would be impossible.

Here again, archaeology sets an instructive example. To take one example of a theme that archaeology did much to popularize, and which has fed some anthropological fantasies about pan-Mediterranean horn symbolism, it appears that the much vaunted Minoan "horns of consecration" may have started life as a stylized cooking-pot support (Diamant and Rutter 1969)! In practice, it is by recognizing similarity/difference that—whether as ethnographers, as archaeologists, or simply as members of a culture concerned with who "we" are—we turn singular connections (indexical contingency) into perceptible patterns (iconicity). Perhaps the most extreme example of this process is the discovery/ invention of *national* culture as something having a *natural* language, a *birthright*, and bureaucratic processes of *naturalization*. In classifying artifacts, we are engaged in conceptual activity similar to that of their manufacturers. In classifying the evidence for different kinds of social structure in the archaeological record, then, we must acknowledge that we are engaged in an ideologically motivated reading of ideological motivations— a more pointed version, this, of Sperber's "[conceptual] representations of conceptual representations."

Eco suggests that the animal/human discrimination represents a kind of "lower limit of semiotics" (1976:9), and so recognizes its value in exploring the boundaries of human identity. Much the same can be said, at the level of ethnic or geopolitical distinction, about all the academic disciplines that deal with culture and society. Discrimination between cultures is but a subset of distinguishing between humanity and its several categorical opposites; and it is always based upon a diagnostic use of iconic relationships (like us/not like us). What seems arbitrary and unique to specific cultures, then, is not the capacity for using iconicity as such, but the selection of diagnostic iconicities as invested with symbolic meaning for the purposes of intercultural differentiation. Cultures become identifiable to us through the construction of boundaries (see also Clarke 1968:242); but the apparent fixity of those boundaries is the rhetorical byproduct of a continuing process (Drummond 1980). This fixity is often represented as an abolition of temporal process through the reification of time. Nationalistic ideologies, for example, construct connections between past and present in the form of a hypostatized "cultural continuity," the effect of which is to create a hermetically circular argument: a past created in the image of the present justifies the present. To such manipulations of temporal process, iconicity is a considerable boon. Backgrounding its culturally contingent aspects, it serves the process of naturalization/nationalization that, in the social sciences, takes the form of the reification of "cultures." That process is enabled by the capacity for self-naturalizing that characterizes iconicity—the feature, that is, which explains why it is so hard to see iconicity as a signifying practice rather than as a presupposable condition.

While iconicity is not necessarily a visual relation, it is characteristically and necessarily the visual forms of iconicity that most concern archaeologists. Archaeologists proceed from visual similarities to hypotheses about social homogeneity and differentiation. If, as Fabian (1983) has argued, the visualist tradition of representation has generated some of the more repressive aspects of cultural relativism, this must constitute a further problem for archaeological interpretation, which in the nature of things relies very heavily on visual properties. It is probably no coincidence that archaeological treatment of social organization, for example, often presupposes a rigidly evolutionist typology of socio-political organization and change (e.g., Milisauskas 1978:30–31, 118–121, etc.). Thus, the absences that archaeology seeks to recover must be filtered through a visualist bias which, virtually inevitable even in contemporaneous ethnographic analysis, is absolutely central to the very existence of archaeology. Structuralist approaches to archaeology will not escape that dilemma; the very essence of the structuralist concern with transformational series of binary oppositions is a visualist metaphor.

Influences and Invasions

Archaeologists have long recognized, in a nontechnical sense, both the risks that this state of affairs entails and its potential value as a check against excessive confidence in the generalizing of ethnographic judgment into larger principles of social-structural change. Well before the current concern with reflexivity got under way in social and cultural anthropology, J. G. D. Clark raised the issue both in his illuminating discussion of the ways in which archaeological museums could be used to serve the propaganda ends of totalitarian régimes (1939:189–212), and in his more specific critique of the "invasion hypothesis" in post–World War II British archaeology (1966).

The latter is an especially revealing piece of work. Here, Clark argues that a kind of national sense of modesty had led the British to resist acknowledging any degree of cultural innovation in (especially) successive phases of the British Iron Age. It should be noted that archaeologists are extremely nervous of independent invention as an explanation; it violates the taxonomic need for continuity. Read, for example the caution in these lines from a Mediterraneanist source (Trump 1980:72; my emphases):

> Crete, though *certainly not backward* at this period, seems also to have *followed an independent line*. Its medium-to-dark, fine burnished pottery, with some incised and dotted decoration, continued at a high technical level, with *extraordinarily little trace of overseas contact of any kind*.

As Vitelli (1984:125) has emphasized, an experimental approach to archaeology can make one productively suspicious of such monolithic senses of "influence."

Clark, however, while appearing to anticipate this proper suspicion, still saw influence as an either/or proposition. He argued that the British "invasion hypothesis" expressed a collective national modesty about cultural achievement in a land where no one wants to be thought "clever." The very antithesis of a claim to cultural originality, the "invasion hypothesis" is, to invoke a literary point of comparison, an "anxiety of influence" (Bloom 1973) in reverse.

One could argue, however, that the stance of modesty is actually something quite different from what it appears to be; that it is, in fact, a characteristic instance of the rhetoric of disinterestedness, in which Clark's criticism of the British national self-image ironically instantiates the very complaint of false modesty that he addresses to it (cf. the instructive parallel in the rhetoric of Evans-Pritchard [Rosaldo 1986]). Raising the possibility of artistic sensibilities among the British, Clark—himself a considerable connoisseur of modern art—asks "why 'waves of imported coinages' . . . should of themselves be taken to reflect the pattern of Belgic migrations to Britain" (1966:187). Clark noted that to see British precursors as concerned with the less practical, more artistic side of social life conflicted with the prevailing cultural ethos. In the process, although he does not highlight the fact, Clark evidently recognized the tendency to arrogate precursors to a possessive genealogy: by forcing the Iron Age to conform to the etiquette of modesty, archaeologists had effectively expropriated a totally unresisting discourse to their own ironies of identity. But Clark's comment amounts to a strikingly similar tactic in its own right. The "obsession" (as he called it) with proving invasions at every turn leads to forgetting "the lives of the people who . . . *in unbroken succession* occupied and shaped the culture of the British Isles" (1966:173; my emphasis)—a claim that ironically echoes some irredentist folklores of Balkan and other nations bent on proving their irreducibly autochthonous antiquity. By restoring a claim to cultural originality, Clark proposes an alternative tactic, more in keeping with his own interests and epoch, for maintaining the distinctiveness of British culture. This is distinctiveness by invention rather than by a bluff "national character" that conflates the Roman and Anglo-Saxon; but it is a claim to continuity nonetheless.

It is worth pointing out that Clark's fulminations, more particularly those that he unleashed against the "veritable chauvinism of prehistory" in Nazi Germany (1966:172; cf. 1939:201–206), remain apposite to this day. But no discourse (including this one) can be ideologically neutral, and Clark's view that in imperial Britain only a sort of benign absentmindedness held sway demonstrates quite clearly the unself-conscious entailment of the privileged, powerful observer in the competitive process of boundary construction. The irony emerges with most force at the point where Clark is speaking of ways in which his critique of the "invasion hypothesis" might be misconstrued (1966:173):

> It is not suggested . . . that British archaeologists should relapse into the stale nostalgia of a Celtic fringe. The imperial past made us citizens of the world and as such we have gained a sense of proportion that one trusts will always be retained.

Celtic fringes, citizens of the world: we find here, as so often, the confluence of local hauteur and international scientism that marks the twin emergence of folklore and social anthropology as disciplines about, respectively, indigenous and exotic "others." The model is apparently, as so often, the Roman imperium.

There is a further irony in Clark's discussion that merits comment here, and also anticipates an analytical issue to be addressed more fully later in this paper. British awareness of a dual cultural heritage—essentially Germanic ("Anglo-Saxon") and Latin—has provided two historical models, the first of which expresses the introspective pride of a people in its rude, untutored ways: "basic Anglo-Saxon" is, for example, a common euphemism for obscene language. The Latinate dimension is the aspect of self-display: formal culture, expressing a perfection of language and thought. Such dualities exist in many cultures. They essentially place in complementary opposition two histories as emblematic of familiar and formal culture, respectively.

In earlier explorations of this phenomenon of "disemia" (Herzfeld 1982, 1987:95–151), I discussed the tensions between "Byzantine/Turkish" and "Classical/Hellenic" elements in modern Greek culture. There, the "orientalizing" elements are clearly associated with the intimate dimension, "European" neoclassicism with national self-exhibition in response to the demanding protectorate of European Great Powers. Greece, however, is a country without pretensions to colonial power; its people passed from Turkish rule to *de facto* Western economic and political suzerainty. In Britain, however, still (at the time of Evans-Pritchard's and Clark's early careers) the paramount global colonial presence, we might expect a reversal, whereby the image of the bluff (and unassuming) Anglo-Saxon would be adumbrated to the equally bluff Latin soldier-architect—a Roman rather than a French image, however. This is the disemia of the powerful, rather than of the powerless: a rhetoric, in fact, of cultural modesty rather than the aggressive nationalism of a small and highly dependent Balkan country. But Clark, in challenging it, seems to express the British cultural revival that surged into life on the ruins of empire. Ultimately, his position is just as fully embedded—whose, indeed, is not?—in the dialectic of cultural identity.

Ideology and the Uses of the Past

Clark's insights, despite (and to some extent because of) their own entailment in a particular vision, remain valuable as a cautionary illustration. Ideology indubitably plays a powerful role in the practice and reuse of archaeology. Reuse is perhaps the more accessible case (see Herzfeld 1986a; Lowenthal 1986); and wherever archaeology has intervened in people's lives for the purposes of reconstructing a "heritage" that they do not entirely share, the discipline itself becomes conceptually reconstructed. I should like to address a case in point from my own ethnographic research.

In Rethemnos (Rethemno[6]), on the island of Crete, the demands of the national Archaeological Service that all Venetian- and Turkish-period houses be conserved in the most literal, austere manner have provoked a reorganization of the (archaeologically constructed) facts of periodicity as symbols of acceptance and rejection. Houses of either period are called "Venetian" (and therefore "European," and so ideologically positive) by those who have scented useful profits in the tourist trade and do not have to live in them themselves any more, but "Turkish" by those condemned by poverty, inertia, or lack of opportunity to staying in them and to fighting for every minor structural or ornamental alteration (Herzfeld 1991). The latter also speak of "archaeology" as a "cancer" and as a "gangrene" and use the name "archaeology" itself—semantically conflated with the bureaucratic service that bears it—as a derogatory term. One might argue—and both the bureaucrats of the Archaeological Service and many of their detractors do so argue—that this is a comment not on the discipline as such, but on its expropriation by a government agency. But to accept this perspective as definitive misses an important point: that archaeology *as a social practice* is today, perhaps more than ever, entailed in the daily lives of those over whose heads—and protests—it has long been carried out, whether as a justification for irredentism or as a consolidation of existing territorial claims.

Some interesting differences of opinion between bureaucrats and citizens affect the flow of events. The inhabitants of the Old Town did not, for the most part, show any appreciation of the antiquity of their houses. They felt bound to these dwellings by considerations of family pride—considerations, what is more, that were often only one or two generations deep. "My father's house" is an affective term in a community many of whose newer immigrants hail from villages with strongly agnatic and patri- and/or virilocal values. In many parts of the Greek-speaking world (see, e.g., Loizos 1975), demographic pressures have brought a shift from virilocal residence to uxorilocality; this may be the reflection less of economic manipulation alone than of the entire array of power considerations that identify good grooms or brides with promising alliances (see Sant Cassia 1982). In Rethemnos the shift has been unequivocally to uxorilocal residence; but this accompanies, if anything, an intensification of androcentrism at the ideological level.

In that ideology, "tradition" means a set of values and ideas handed down through generations of men. No matter that the actual agents of transmission may have been women, or that the women's dowries may be the source of what their sons then describe as the "paternal home." Townspeople profess themselves acutely conscious of the stereotypical Cretan "character," whose predominant features include an uncompromising androcentrism, as well as a resistance to the bureaucratically imposed values and practices of the state. Many inhabitants of the Old Town of Rethemnos are thus hostile toward the regulation of their collective scheduled monument, the more so in that the Archaeological Service imposes—they maintain—a conformity of design that fits ill with their aesthetic of individualistic expression and pride in atomized ownership as well as with their dislike of scholastic precision. In short, they reject the mass production of iconicity, and with it a great deal of ideological baggage that does not belong, they suspect, in the principled nonconformism of their own social milieu.

The wealth that tourism has brought the town is scant consolation for those who, unable to take direct advantage of it, have also been unable to move into more comfortable and less heavily regulated homes. They have become hostages to the economic success of already wealthier fellow-citizens, and their resentment is logically expressed as *difference*—the fracturing of bureaucratic unity and iconicity, and the stylistic reproduction of household autonomy. A bureaucratic *cultural* definition of tradition, which the relatively well-to-do now find it opportune to "buy into," confronts the local *social* understanding of tradition head on.

Thus, we find successful entrepreneurs out-neoclassicizing the establishment (by gluing fake-Classical pilasters on the outside of a dress shop, for example), while the relatively unsuccessful only appeal to the official ideology in that their attacks on "Turkish houses" fit the nationalist terminology of earlier governments. But now, to their chagrin, they find that the government insists on preserving even the traces of the hated Turkish past, so even this discursive stratagem will no longer serve. The preservation of the "enemy's" monuments, an invasion of the national home,[7] mirrors the official callousness to the social ideology of ownership—an ideology on which, for the reasons sketched above, the male pride of the houseowner depends.

This example of the ideological use of archaeology is not, of course, only a scholarly one. Indeed, in the ample evidence that archaeology serves political ends, it may not often be scholars who play the most obvious role (for a historical example, see Silberman 1982). But the Rethemnos case illustrates an important point: the tendency, especially (but not exclusively) under bureaucratic conditions, for a preemptive definition of culture to yield standardization that in turn expresses the power (as well as cultural-ideological rationale) of those who are able to enforce it. The Rethemniotes' personal distaste for conformity is the introverted face of their own particular disemia. It may be fractious and atomistic; but it is familiar—indeed, the emphasis on family and self is the source of its attractiveness in real social life. The other face of that disemia is acceptance of the officially promoted cultural and social unity. The more a resident is practically able to identify with the bearers of official and economic power, the more that individual will adopt the official standardization of what Venetian houses looked like and, with it, the official line that under both Venetian and Turkish rule the masons were mostly Greek anyway (for which there is indeed some evidence).

We shall return below to the subject of disemia. I would like to note here, however, that a hypothetical archaeologist excavating the Old Town a few centuries from now would probably find evidence of this standardization, and would note that its failure is in direct relation to two factors: the poverty of the dwellings, and the interiority of the

space. Each building's physical interior both symbolizes and actualizes cultural familiarity. Ideology leaves its traces.

Recovering Structures

It is never clear how much we can rely on the seeming evidence for rules of social
organization in a record where verbal exegesis is beyond recall. Worse, "[i]deals of
personal conduct are just as impermanent as ideals of social organization" (Collingwood
1939:65). But individualistic concepts of personal conduct are a crucial element in the
European ideology—the social equivalent to the cultural versatility I mentioned earlier.

As a result, an even vestigially survivalist perspective will have us looking for "social
organization" in more "tribal" (i.e., not verbally accessible) forms of culture, in part
because we presuppose (a) that anthropological models of "tribal" organization are
appropriate for prehistory (a denial of coevalness operating in reverse: distance in time
is converted into distance in moral space); (b) that these models are social rather than
cultural; and (c) that individual action (or the role of agency) is archaeologically irrecoverable. This misuse of ethnographically derived models springs in part from a weakness in the models themselves, already briefly mentioned above: the reification of
particular sets of social "rules" (e.g., patriliny or other forms of kinship) and their
consequent entailment in the *form* of social *and cultural* relationships (for example,
segmentation, in the classic sense developed by Evans-Pritchard [1940] and others). This
situation has produced a focus that is quite inappropriate for archaeologists' purposes.

Cultural discriminations that reproduce themselves in a variety of levels and contexts,
by producing mutually iconic marks on the material record, may index a social relationship
(see also Winter 1977:383). Nonrelative social structures, on the other hand, leave no
identifiable mark because they furnish no internal comparison from which to extrapolate,
and are therefore unlikely to lead us to such insights. Cultural traits signify social in-
clusion/exclusion in a hierarchy of social possibilities. It was probably in reaction to the
sociocentric emphasis of much British anthropology that some British archaeologists—
notably Clarke (1968)—sought their inspiration in American cultural anthropology rather
than in the British social variety. Yet in contemporaneous ethnography it would be safe
to say that cultural variety indexes social distance and vice versa; it is only when the
exegetical possibilities of language are removed that this mutuality is disturbed. For those
who deal with the archaeological record, the cultural must always take primacy; and
only those aspects of social organization that do not require linguistic explanation—in
other words, those aspects which exhibit a sufficiently regular iconicity—that may legitimately be identified.

An archaeologically identifiable social relationship must always exist at more than
one level of inclusiveness; otherwise, it will not be clearly identifiable. The most obvious
model in this mode is what Evans-Pritchard (1940) termed the principle of *segmentation*.
A relativity of inclusiveness might show up on the village ground-plan; but we would
not know what the exact form of the kinship mode was. This is because we would lack
a temporal sequence to give the dimension of action (or agency) to the synchronic and
therefore impenetrable pattern that lies, quite literally in this case, "on the ground" (cf.
also Dresch 1986). Action is inscribed in time; only form is represented, rule-like, as

"timeless" (see Bourdieu 1977:6–15). It is an irony of the archaeological condition that, while the discipline has been brilliantly successful at recovering *longues durées*, its capacity for recovering the syntagms of daily interaction—essential, as Vitelli (1984:125–126) points out, for understanding artifactual variation—has been minimal.

Segmentation is (a) a conceptual *idiom* that organizes kinship but also many other aspects of social and cultural distance, rather than the definiens of a certain type of kinship, and (b) a replication of the tension between collective self-recognition and externally directed display at every level of social inclusion and exclusion. As such, it is of far more general significance than any single pattern of social relationship, whether kinship-based or constituted in some other idiom. I would go further, and argue that segmentation is the uniquely primary basis of *all* social relationships, since its relativistic organization of insider-outsider differentiations is the basis of anything we could conceivably recognize as a structured—that is, patterned and repetitive—social system. Because it is primarily conceptual rather than political in the crudely material sense, moreover, it organizes aesthetic relations as well as the formal social order. For this reason, it may be a great deal more accessible to archaeological analysis than some of the more exclusively social idioms that have been looked for in the past. One would not expect to find patriliny simply from a settlement pattern; one might, however, find *analogies* between patterns of cultural similitude and differentiation at different levels of topographical distance, and this would give a set of binary oppositions clustered around the physical boundaries of inside and outside. Segmentation and disemia are mutually entailed (Herzfeld 1987:153–157), although segmentation is more *apparent* in acephalous political systems (because it does not run counter to the dominant ideology of power) whereas disemia is more likely to take tangible form under conditions of military or economic dominance where cultural forms become invested with positive and negative values that express the mutual antagonism of dominant and subordinate groups.

Disemia: Contrastive Patterns

At each level of social organization, the relations between insiders and outsiders are ordered according to topically distinctive principles, but they always remain predicated on the distinction between the inside and the outside of whatever social group is in question. This is disemia, a mode of organizing social knowledge *through cultural form*. Segmentation and disemia only make sense in terms of each other, as the intersecting axes of cultural hierarchy and contrast, respectively. Together, they give us an aesthetic, ethical, and social economy. The combination should be of special interest to archaeology, since, as a metapattern, it might serve to *identify* the ideologically interior and exterior spaces of what otherwise seems an undecipherable morass.

Obviously, the disemia model cannot say anything about the ideological *modes* (kinship type, rules of association, etc.) of discrimination—that much we have already seen. If, however, we can compare cultural patterns that exist on a strictly local scale with further flung patterns of essentially the same type, we may discover some correlations that would, after all, permit a degree of interpretation that does not depend upon verbal exegesis. If, for example, we find that architectonic exteriors (not always easy to identify as such) are associated with design features thought to have originated in a distant but related culture, in contrast to a more narrowly local interior style, it would be fair to infer some degree of asymmetry in the cultural and political relations between the two societies thus emblematically represented.

In order to illustrate the point, let me now describe some of the ways in which disemia operates in the spatial patterns of a culture already mentioned in this context, modern Greece. There, the tension between interior and exterior design mirrors *uses* of history that in turn express important differentials of power. Larger relations of power are expressed by smaller ones, and vice versa: power differences appear as relations between relations, in short. And these relations—as Dresch's (1986) observations should make us realize—can only be disinterred through a comparison *across time*: segmentation is a matter of relative strategies, and the essence of strategies is that one claims one's own position as eternal. Thus, synchronic structures will be meaningless in the absence of verbal exegesis; they entail an interest in suppressing their own historicity.

Greece as a nation-state came into being under a foreign (Bavarian) monarchy installed by the Great Powers as the main price of the country's nominal independence. Foreign advisers and overseas-trained Greeks introduced neoclassical models in art and architecture, following a model that had already been developed by Greek linguistic philosophers in language (the use of the neoclassical *katharevousa* as an evaluatively "high" register of diglossia). I mention the connection with language for two reasons: first, because the phenomenon was first recognized in that arena (see Ferguson 1959); and second, because it shows rather clearly where the task of the archaeologist investigating this culture would differ from that of the contemporaneous ethnographer. On the latter point, we can say that the highly verbocentric character of discourse about cultural domination protected the false primacy of language in most general discussions of neoclassical "formalism" (Mouzelis 1978) in Greece. But language is not often accessible to the archaeologist; even in a literate and historical culture, the demotic forms are often excluded from written language in the early stages of any diglossic situation.

Architecture, by contrast, would show clear divergences between exterior façades displaying a strongly neoclassical style (or, nowadays, "modern American," or "Swiss chalet style") and interior, domestic rooms organized according to the principles of "traditional" village architecture. Thus, what the hypothetical archaeologist of some future century would attempt to establish is the likely meaning of the relationship between the imported, official culture of neoclassicism on the one hand, and the interior and exterior styles of architecture, artifact design, and space use on the other. Given a diachronic sequence of buildings in, let us say, twentieth-century Athens, our hypothetical archaeologist would then be able to establish a sequence of relationships between style contrasts that connected outside/inside with the larger widespread/local pair. This is a great improvement on traditional archaeological appeals to "influence." It would help to explain why imitation happens at all. For as Bourdieu (1984) has elaborately reminded us, the economy of taste is a matter of power differentials above all else.

It may be argued that the case of Greece is an unusual one; the fact that Greece is also the imputed "source" of the neoclassical mode, even though the latter was virtually invented in Western Europe, certainly makes it so. But functionally similar expressions of the formula—

"dominant : subordinate :: exterior : interior"—

have been identified in Nigeria (Yoruba culture: Vlach 1984), Kenya (Swahili culture: Donley 1982), in Haiti (the "high" model being metropolitan French), the American South (where neoclassical motifs held sway for a long time), Newfoundland (Pocius 1979), and throughout the imperial possessions of pre–World War II Italy. In many of these instances, notably the Greek (Herzfeld 1986a) and Swahili, gender relations reproduce—and are reproduced by—this symbolism of cultural asymmetry. The richness of Greek disemia—and especially the wealth of verbal exegesis—makes it an especially useful example for thinking about the ideological patterning of space in cases where such exegetical advantages are not available. For it is not simply architecture that exhibits strongly disemic characteristics; we find analogous patterns in the spatial distribution of associated artifacts and domestic practices (see especially Iakovidis 1982:31–32 on the use of "low" or "Turkish" terms for humble domestic accessories; Martinidis 1974:145–146 on the fear of consuming food in exterior space—possibly another archaeologically recoverable feature).

Consider again the case of Rethemnos. Townspeople there are quite willing to maintain doorways of obviously Venetian design, and express impatience only with the bureaucrats' unwillingness to permit *interior* renovation and remodeling. But conflict arises even over exterior design. Because the neoclassical "rule" permits anything "European," the addition of plate-glass windows or pseudo-Classical stucco ornaments seems to the townspeople to fall within the same rubric as the preservation of the Renaissance façades. Within the houses, there is a striking contrast between two modes. On the one hand, in the rooms reserved for the formal reception of guests there are pastel reproductions of European and North American landscapes and stylized stitchwork samplers of gentlefolk in eighteenth-century garb, pseudo-Meissen china ornaments and coffee services, and framed photographs of various dignitaries and uniformed or formally clad family members; on the other, in the private rooms the ornaments may be more functional (e.g., kitchen utensils, plastic containers of various kinds), more reminiscent of village life (e.g., tools), or intimately bound up with the spiritual life of the household (especially icons in the Byzantine style,[8] placed in strategic corners of the kitchen and/or bedroom). Interestingly, the old Turkish name for the reception area (*oda*, Greek form *o(n)das*) has now been relegated to the private upstairs rooms, while the main reception room rejoices in the Romance-derived name of *saloni*. Power feeds on display.

This last linguistic point may seem to have little relevance for archaeologists. I mention it here, however, as an important piece of evidence in support of the hypothesis that the physical characteristics of interior/exterior discriminations do reproduce ideological boundaries. The reversal in the fortunes of the name *ondas* reproduces the shift from Ottoman imperial rule to Western economic and political control; it is the linguistic epiphenomenon of an ideological and political shift that has also been inscribed upon the hypothetical type of which each house is a physical token, and that is therefore iconically reproduced in most such houses. Disemia, as the paradigmatic model for the syntagmatic concept of diglossia, is more accessible than the latter in the absence of linguistic access.

I have remarked above on the mutual entailment of disemia and segmentation. It is now necessary to return to an analytical perspective on segmentation, in order to suggest how this model might help archaeologists identify evidence of disemia in the material record. Segmentation, we have seen, is a hierarchical entelechy. This means in practice that the dominant member of each hypotactic pair of terms or groups takes on the emblematic characteristics of the encompassing entity that includes them both. Thus, for example, Scots and English are distinguished from each other in contrast to the Welsh, but may agree to sink their differences in a common "Englishness" when confronting non-British opponents. Many Scots object to this, as do Canadians to the reverse use of the term "American" for collective self-designation by U.S. citizens. Something very similar happens in semantic taxonomies of other kinds—as, for example, in the sexist, because asymmetrical, gloss of "man" for "human."

The point at issue here is that segmentation represents the social embodiment of the principles of semantic taxonomy. I have elsewhere discussed the significance of this convergence of social and semantic classification modes as evidence for the persistence of segmentary tendencies in daily social experience among those who live within even the most formally "pyramidal" political structures. In each case, the reappearance of the one common term at each taxonomic level of inclusion indexes the range of semantic markedness. But there is no reason to confine this observation to exclusively linguistic examples. We may instead, following the pattern already adopted in moving from diglossia to disemia, observe that nonlinguistic signs can also stand for various degrees of social and cultural inclusion/exclusion. Thus, a neoclassical façade indexes a more inclusive—and therefore less marked—concept of Greekness than does the domestic clutter of the interior; but it does so in relation to a cultural norm that is derived from a still more broadly inclusive category ("Europeans") balanced, again, against one of equal inclusiveness ("Orientals," i.e., those of Turkish culture)—where "Turkish" is a derogatory term in the externally derived, official value system of the (heavily dependent) Greek state.

This suggests a much more subtle interpretative device than is furnished by simplistic imputations of cultural "influence." It also allows us to seek evidence of social relations that undergird the more or less irrecoverable specificities of kinship and political order. It may also be that this modern use—ironically, in Greece itself—of "Hellenic" themes might generate a comparative approach to such themes in ancient times—in Sicily, in Punic Carthage, in the Iron Age Hallstatt cultures, in Gandhara; the list is endless. What needs to be examined carefully is the *mode of combination* into which such extraneous elements of Greek culture are inserted. From there it should be instructive to proceed to other examples of cultural "influence," viewed in terms of an unequal access to the available means of disseminating cultural (re)sources.

Questions for the Archaeologist: Metapatterns and Ethnology

My intention in this paper has been to ask some questions that would illuminate problems in social anthropology. Some of these are obvious: What would we do with our interpretative schemata if our verbal capacities were suddenly to disappear? What are the absences in discourse that the humbling example of archaeology brings to our attention?

But there are corresponding questions for the archaeologist too. First and foremost: If disemia is the "horizontal" relation between the relations already implied in the diachronic segmentation model (a model that could otherwise appear in the archaeological record only as an undecipherable synchrony), can it help the archaeologist who wishes to infer something about social groups? Dabrowski (1980:120), for example, takes stylistic variety as evidence of the formation of a self-conscious "we-group." But it could be taken as the opposite, as evidence for a lack of cultural cohesion (one recalls the ingenious arguments of European nationalists whereby potentially divisive regional culture was taken as evidence of a transcendant national versatility or genius). The converse, in situations of stylistic homogeneity, is also a matter of great ambiguity. Only through the identification of metapatterns can we expect to make such statements with increasing confidence. The next move must be toward models that are neither exclusively cultural nor exclusively social, but that, because they organize the *realia* of a now irrecoverable social life, allow the archaeologist to approach social form as a cultural artifact that can be "read" through plausible indexical and iconic relations long after the symbolic/semantic meanings have—alas, but what can we do?—evaporated beyond recall.

While such models are only falsifiable in a negative sense (and this is something they share with experimental archaeology), they have the further value that they pose experiential checks to the overliteralization, through language, that often takes place in contemporaneous ethnography. As an anthropologist, I am concerned with all cultural production. If the bias lies in our own cultural values or ideological predilections, it would be scarcely scientific or empirical—as Eco (1976:29) has pointed out—to ignore that constraint on interpretation, or to reject the possibility that its effects are far greater than we at first conceive. The segmentary model, which played an exoticizing role in structural-functionalism, appears to be quite applicable to all societies including our own (Herzfeld 1987:158). Disemia, while in its most dramatic guise the product of late capitalist economies and bourgeois nationalism, represents the tension between collective self-display and collective self-knowledge that must subsist in any situation where human groups divide themselves into an inferior "them" and a superior "us." Where are there any human groupings in which this does not occur?

Acknowledgments: I would like to record my deep gratitude to the National Endowment for the Humanities, whose award to me of a Fellowship for Independent Study and Research in 1986–87 allowed me to conduct the research in Rethemnos (Rethimno, Rethymnon) on which the discussion of these materials is based. The Endowment is not responsible for any of the opinions or materials presented here. I would also like to thank Claudia Chang for some very pertinent comments on an earlier draft.

NOTES

1. In the Peircean system, the "symbolic" sign function (to use Eco's [1976] gloss on the terminology) is the most arbitrary. Together with indexicality and iconicity, it constitutes a triad that has been of considerable value in ethnographic analysis (e.g., Parmentier 1987).

The terminology is extremely useful in that it allows us to distinguish, as here, between the kinds of symbolic decipherment that proceed on the basis of a formal linguistic analogy and those that seem instead to depend more on context or perceptual analogy. Thus, for example, Knapp (1988:151), whose analysis of Bronze Age Cypriot ideology and power employs a strategy that formally seems close to the metarelational mode advocated here, might have clarified his intentions by avoiding the usual anthropological conflation of these concepts in his comment on the various depictions of an ingot-bearer before a tree:

> Whether the tree represents a religious deity, a secular administration, or, perhaps most likely, the 'fuel' used to produce metallic copper, is not the major issue; it *symbolizes* the societal power that made production socially feasible and economically viable.

This statement does not work well if we accept that a symbolic relationship is primarily an arbitrary one. It is precisely because symbolism in this sense *is* arbitrary that it defies analysis without explicit exegesis; it is one of a kind, at least at some level. The indexical relations between (a) ingot-bearer and tree and (b) ingots and other finds, in combination with the iconic relations between the various finds, are what permits us to speculate on their possible symbolic import. Knapp's argument is important, especially in its justifiable criticism of excessively philological (and hence literalistic) readings of artifacts; but the difficulties arise from the lack of an explicit theory of representation, essential to any discussion of power and ideology.

2. It is not necessary to accept the implicit reification of either space or culture in order to appreciate the force of this remark.

3. The Greek *askhimos*, "ugly," is derived from *a-*, the privative, and *skhima*, "form." Lack of form was clearly a trait of exotic otherness in the European ideology described here; it fits well with Douglas's (1966) discussion of category violation and pollution.

4. See now: Dresch 1986, 1988; Herzfeld 1987:152–185; Karp and Maynard 1983; Maynard 1988. We shall return to this central point of the argument below.

5. For three very different arguments tending in the same direction, see Fabian 1983; Sebeok 1979; Sperber 1985.

6. I use the weak form, although the official *Rethimno* and *Rethymnon* may be more familiar to English-speaking readers.

7. The "house" or "home" is a common metaphor for the national territory, with implications of androcentric ideology regarding contests over rival arenas of domestic possession. See also Herzfeld 1986a.

8. Byzantine art comes under the rubric of "intimate" culture for many Greeks, who see it in opposition to the neoclassical models that have been foisted upon them. On the other hand, given the prestige of the Orthodox Church in Greece, the issue is not a simple one.

REFERENCES

Ardener, E. 1971. "The new anthropology and its critics," *Man* (n.s.) **6**, 201–219.
Bloom, H. 1973. *The Anxiety of Influence: A Theory of Poetry*. Oxford University Press, New York.
Bourdieu, P. 1973 [1971]. "The Berber house," in M. Douglas (ed.), *Rules and Meanings*, pp. 98–110. Penguin, Harmondsworth.
———1977. *Outline of a Theory of Practice*. R. Nice (tr.). Cambridge University Press, Cambridge.
———1984. *Distinction: A Social Critique of the Judgement of Taste*. R. Nice (tr.). Harvard University Press, Cambridge, MA.
Breuil, H., and R. Lantier 1965. *The Men of the Old Stone Age (Palaeolithic and Mesolithic)*. St. Martin's, New York.
Burkitt, M. C. 1933. *The Old Stone Age: A Study of Palaeolithic Times*. Cambridge University Press, Cambridge.
Clark, J. G. D. 1939. *Archaeology and Society*. Methuen, London.

————1966. "The invasion hypothesis in British archaeology," *Antiquity* **40,** 172–189.

Clarke, D. L. 1968. *Analytical Archaeology*. Methuen, London.

Coles, J. M. 1979. *Experimental Archaeology*. Academic Press, New York.

Collingwood, R. G. 1939. *An Autobiography*. Oxford University Press, Oxford.

Conkey, M. W. 1980. "Context, structure, and efficacy in Paleolithic art and design," in M. LeCron Foster and S. H. Brandes (eds.), *Symbol as Sense: New Approaches to the Analysis of Meaning*, pp. 225–248. Academic Press, New York.

Dabrowski, J. 1980. "An attempt at the reconstruction of certain social structures in the population of Lusation culture," in R. Schild (ed.), *Unconventional Archaeology: New Approaches and Goals in Polish Archaeology*, pp. 117–139. Akademii Nauk, Wroclaw.

Diamant, S., and J. Rutter 1969. "Horned objects in Anatolia and the Near East and possible connections with the Minoan 'horns of consecration,' " *Anatolian Studies* **19,** 147–177.

Donley, L. W. 1982. "House power: Swahili space and symbolic markers," in I. Hodder (ed.), *Symbolic and Structural Archaeology*, pp. 63–73. Cambridge University Press, Cambridge.

Douglas, M. 1966. *Purity and Danger: An Analysis of Concepts of Pollution and Taboo*. Routledge & Kegan Paul, London.

Dresch, P. 1986. "The significance of the course events take in segmentary systems," *American Ethnologist* **13,** 309–324.

————1988. "Segmentation: Its roots in Arabia and its flowering elsewhere," *Cultural Anthropology* **3,** 50–67.

Drummond, L. 1980. "The cultural continuum: A theory of intersystems," *Man* (n.s.) **15,** 352–374.

Eco, U. 1976. *A Theory of Semiotics*. Indiana University Press, Bloomington.

Evans-Pritchard, E. E. 1940. *The Nuer: A Description of the Modes of Livelihood and Political Institutions of a Nilotic People*. Clarendon Press, Oxford.

Fabian, J. 1983. *Time and the Other: How Anthropology Constructs Its Object*. Columbia University Press, New York.

Ferguson, C. A. 1959. "Diglossia," *Word* **15,** 325–340.

Fernandez, J. W. 1977. *Fang Architectonics*. ISHI, Philadelphia.

Forge, A. 1968. "Learning to see in New Guinea," in P. Mayer (ed.), *Socialization: The Approach from Social Anthropology* (A. S. A. Monograph **8**), pp. 269–291. Tavistock, London.

Herzfeld, M. 1982. "Disemia," in M. Herzfeld and M. D. Lenhart (comps.), *Semiotics 1980*, pp. 205–215. Plenum, New York.

————1985. *The Poetics of Manhood: Contest and Identity in a Cretan Mountain Village*. Princeton University Press, Princeton, NJ.

————1986a. "On some rhetorical uses of iconicity in cultural ideologies," in P. Bouissac, M. Herzfeld, and R. Posner (eds.), *Iconicity: Essays on the Nature of Culture*, pp. 401–419. Stauffenburg, Tübingen.

————1986b. "Within and without: The category of 'female' in the ethnography of modern Greece," in J. Dubisch (ed.), *Gender and Power in Rural Greece*, pp. 215–233. Princeton University Press, Princeton, NJ.

————1987. *Anthropology through the Looking-Glass: Critical Ethnography in the Margins of Europe*. Cambridge University Press, Cambridge.

————1991. *A Place in History: Social and Monumental Time in a Cretan Village*. Princeton University Press, Princeton

Hodder, I. 1982. "Theoretical archaeology: A reactionary view," in I. Hodder (ed.), *Symbolic and Structural Archaeology*, pp. 1–16. Cambridge University Press, Cambridge.

Iakovidis, K. 1982. *Neoelliniki arkhitektoniki ke astiki idheoloyia*. Dhodhoni, Athens.

Jacobsen, T. W. 1985. "Another modest proposal: Ethnoarchaeology in Greece," in N. C. Wilkie and W. D. E. Coulson (eds.), *Contributions to Aegean Archaeology: Studies in Honor of William A. MacDonald*, pp. 91–107. Center for Ancient Studies, University of Minnesota, Minneapolis.

Joseph, R., and T.B Joseph 1987. *The Rose and the Thorn: Semiotic Structures in Morocco*. University of Arizona Press, Tucson.

Karp, I., and K. Maynard 1983. "Reading *The Nuer*," *Current Anthropology* **24**, 481–503.

Kitahara-Frisch, J. 1980. "Symbolizing technology as a key to human evolution," in M. LeCron Foster and S. H. Brandes (eds.), *Symbol as Sense: New Approaches to the Analysis of Meaning*, pp. 211–223. Academic Press, New York.

Knapp, A. B. 1988. "Ideology, archaeology and polity," *Man* (n.s.) **23**, 133–163.

Kus, S. 1982. "Matters material and ideal," in I. Hodder (ed.), *Symbolic and Structural Archaeology*, pp. 47–62. Cambridge University Press, Cambridge.

Loizos, P. 1975. "Changes in property transfer among Greek Cypriot villagers," *Man* (n.s.) **10**, 503–523.

Lowenthal, D. 1986. "Bias: Making the most of an incurable malady," in A. Carruthers (ed.), *Bias in Museums*, pp. 32–35. Museum Professionals Group, Transactions No. 22, Exeter.

MacCurdy, G. G. 1905. "The Eolithic problem: Rude industries ante-dating the Paleolithic," *American Anthropologist* **7**, 425–479.

Martinidis, P. 1974. *Simioloyia tis Arkhitektytonikis*. University of Thessaloniki, Chair of Building Architecture (no. 39).

Maynard, K. 1988. "On Protestants and pastoralists: The segmentary nature of socio-cultural organization," *Man* (n.s.) **23**, 101–117.

Milisauskas, S. 1978. *European Prehistory*. Academic Press, New York.

Mouzelis, N. P. 1978. *Modern Greece: Facets of Underdevelopment*. Macmillan, London.

Needham, R. 1962. *Structure and Sentiment: A Test Case in Social Anthropology*. University of Chicago Press, Chicago.

———1963. "Introduction," in R. Needham (ed. and tr.), *Emile Durkheim and Marcel Mauss, Primitive Classification*, pp. vii–xlviii. Cohen and West, London.

Oakley, K. P. 1957. "Tools makyth man," *Antiquity* **31**, 99–209.

Parmentier, R. J. 1987. *The Sacred Remains: Myth, History, and Polity in Belau*. University of Chicago Press, Chicago.

Pocius, G. L. 1979. "Hooked rugs in Newfoundland," *Journal of American Folklore* **92**, 273–284.

Preziosi, D. 1979. *The Semiotics of the Built Environment: An Introduction to Architectonic Analysis*. Indiana University Press, Bloomington.

Rosaldo, R. 1986. "From the door of his tent: The fieldworker and the inquisitor," in J. Clifford and G. E. Marcus (eds.), *Writing Culture: The Poetics and Politics of Ethnography*, pp. 77–97. University of California Press, Berkeley.

Sant Cassia, P. 1982. "Property in Greek Cypriot marriage strategies, 1920–1980," *Man* (n.s.) **17**, 643–663.

Sebeok, T. A. 1979. *The Sign and Its Masters*. University of Texas Press, Austin.

Silberman, N. A. 1982. *Digging for God and Country: Exploration, Archeology, and the Secret Struggle for the Holy Land, 1799–1917*. Alfred A. Knopf, New York.

Sperber, D. 1975. *Rethinking Symbolism*. A. L. Morton (tr.). Cambridge University Press, Cambridge.

———1985. *On Anthropological Knowledge*. Cambridge University Press, Cambridge.

Trump, D. H. 1980. *Prehistory of the Mediterranean*. Yale University Press, New Haven, CT.

Vitelli, K. D. 1984. "Greek Neolithic pottery by experiment," in P. M. Rice (ed.), *Pots and Potters: Current Approaches in Ceramic Archaeology*, pp. 113–131. Institute of Archaeology, University of California, Los Angeles, Los Angeles.

Vlach, J. M. 1984. "The Brazilian house in Nigeria: The emergence of a twentieth-century house type," *Journal of American Folklore* **97**, 3–23.

Winter, I. 1977. "Perspective on the 'local style' of Hasuna IVB: A study in reciprocity," *Bibliotheca Mesopotamica* **7**, 371–386.

Wynn, T. 1979. "The intelligence of later Acheulean hominids," *Man* (n.s.) **14**, 371–391.

Semiotic Trends in Archaeology

I propose to examine a number of new or not so new approaches in archaeology, which have in common some relation with semiotics, or semiology. My goal is neither to present a survey nor to reveal differences between the various semiotic trends discussed: these differences are merely a reflection of the diversity of research areas and methods that are today encompassed by semiotics. My real purpose is to show that the analysis of these differences raises interesting questions about "new approaches" in general, whatever they may be. The argument runs as follows. A common feature in most of the works considered under the banner of semiotics is a concern for problems of interpretation in archaeology: What are the reasoning processes followed in the reconstitution of past societies on the basis of material remains? Further, assuming that we "believe" in those reconstitutions, as the Greeks believed in their myths (Veyne 1983), what are the foundations of our beliefs? Questions of that sort are obviously relevant beyond reconstructions of the past based on semiotics: they apply to all kinds of interpretative constructs in archaeology, irrespective of the label which we or the author may choose to designate the approach (or method, school, paradigm, etc.). My purpose is thus to take advantage of semiotic issues as a source of wider debate, on a metatheoretical level, which concerns all the "new approaches" in archaeology. Of interest here are their amazing number, which exist under a variety of names (processual, systemic, structural, contextual, symbolic, cognitive, social, analytical, experimental, dialectical, among others), and the rapidity of their succession over the last twenty years, which cannot but raise some fundamental questions.

1. The Approaches Considered

Having no pretense to present an exhaustive survey, I have chosen to restrict myself to three broad classes of archaeological works related to various currents in semiotics: (a) works inspired by structural linguistics, itself related to the name of Ferdinand de Saussure, and through him to semiology as that scholar conceived it; (b) works more closely connected with logic, and more particularly with the logicist current that once crossed American semiotics in the person of Charles Morris; (c) works characterized by positions similar to those of hermeneutics, even when that name is not used, and which are thus related to one of the most prolific branches of contemporary semiotics or semiology on both sides of the Atlantic.

1.1 Structuralist Currents

I shall not undertake to review all the archaeological works inspired by structuralism. For some, a reference to mental "structures" seems to be enough to relate an interpretative construct to structuralism: thus Hodder (1986: 34ff) mixes Piaget and Chomsky with Leach and Lévi-Strauss in his vision of the sources of structuralist archaeology. I shall take a more restrictive view, by requiring that the process of interpretation be related in some way to the methods of structural linguistics or anthropology: we shall thus remain closer to the methodological perspective offered by Ferdinand de Saussure and Claude Lévi-Strauss, to name but the more illustrious fathers of this essentially francophone semiology, as opposed to the dominantly anglophone semiotics considered below (§1.2).

Even restricted in that way, the semiostructural current carries heterogeneous projects along its course. In a number of them, the reference to semiology rests on the fact that the analysis of archaeological remains calls on *ad hoc* systems of signs, under various name (codes, information languages, attributes lists, etc.). In others, a reference to structuralism is substituted for, or added to, that semiological component, the major concern being with certain kinds of operations carried out on the signs of the descriptive language, artificial or natural, rather than with that language itself considered as an autonomous system of signs.

(A) Projects of the first group can be envisaged from a practical or from a theoretical angle. Practically speaking, their interest lies essentially in documentation: the proposed descriptive systems multiply the number of access points to archaeological information, while bypassing certain deficiencies of natural language (Gardin 1979:82–102). From a theoretical viewpoint, we may regard those systems as a tool for the generation of various taxonomic orders, some of which will perhaps suggest productive interpretations, on a cognitive level (Gardin 1967; this vision of things bears some relation with the way in which Jean Molino introduces his "neutral level" of semiological analysis, applied to all kinds of objects: see his contribution in this volume). In both cases, the reference to structuralism is hardly necessary: its only justification lies in our habit of considering any sort of formal or quasi-formal analysis of human product or behavior as one of the distinctive marks of a structural approach (see for example Hodder 1986:36ff, where "Formal analysis" is the title of a section in the chapter devoted to structuralist archaeology).

(B) Projects of the second group, however, do make use of the expected methodology: the semiological system is in this case the ground for a series of operations of the kind used in structural analysis—e.g., grouping signs in distinctive units of a higher order, establishing relations between those units (such as binary oppositions, or more complex arrangements of the kind "x : y :: p : q" etc.), proposing transformation formulas from one area of observation to another, etc. My purpose is not to review exercises of that sort in archaeology (see Hodder 1986:34–54); I shall only raise one or two questions about them that will recur more than once in the present paper. One of them is this: Have we reached a point where we can measure the contribution of structuralist projects in that twofold sense (categories A and B) to the progress of archaeological knowledge? This question hides another one: In which way can we evaluate this contribution, without any personal prejudice or bias? I shall not be bold enough to answer the first question, which I would rather reserve for our discussions. As for the second question, however, we do have means at our disposal to measure the value of the kind of constructs concerned, provided that we agree on their ultimate goals. Let us begin with the formal analyses in class A, for example: some of them have no other function than to improve the efficiency of information retrieval in given sectors of archaeology; tests are available in this case as devised by information scientists in the last decades, and it is only up to us, archaeologists, to use them in our own field. As a way to stimulate a discussion on this point, I am ready to confess that the application of such tests to my own information projects, many years ago, would tend to show that they were not terribly useful.

We can examine in the same spirit the taxonomic constructs that constitute the other group in class A. If their function is heuristic, as is usually argued, the evaluation process consists in verifying that the semiological systems used have indeed been instrumental in the discovery of one or more meaningful orders in the archaeological domains concerned that might not have been discovered otherwise.

But how shall we decide that a given order is meaningful? This is the problem raised in the works of Class B: structural models are indeed hypotheses which we form on the meaning of formal configurations observed in a given field of archaeological investigation. If the exercise is not to be totally arbitrary, in this case as in those which we shall discuss below, it has to be amenable to some kind of judgments on the relative strength or weaknesses of interpretations. Beyond so-called formal criteria (coherence, convergence, etc.), which are in fact formally ill-defined, we shall have to aim sooner or later at empirical tests, in one or other of the following senses: either the traditional confrontation with new data, or, for those who resent this old-fashioned brand of positivism, some form of social consensus, as a substitute for that of the unavailable "Indian." In both cases, the evaluation can be regarded as "objective," insofar as we are expected to agree on the "success" of a given interpretation, in a given slice of time and space, according to the first or to the second criterion. To be sure, we should expect that a certain lapse of time would be needed to reach unanimity; the surprising fact is on the contrary that we can agree so quickly on a prior empirical observation, namely that our structural exercises tend to be ignored by the larger part of the profession, and that they seldom leave any trace in the advance of established knowledge in archaeology. This view may have to be qualified in the light of possible counterevidence. I doubt, however, that we can evade the issue, even if it is stated in milder terms.

1.2 Logicist Trends

The difference between semiology and semiotics is sometimes explained by ethnocultural features: semiology would be the name given to the generalization of linguistic analysis in the Saussurian perspective, encompassing all kinds of communication systems or behavior; semiotics would rather convey the Peircean vision of a science of interpretation, one more or less logically oriented. The former would be dominantly European and francophone, the latter American and anglophone. This dichotomy, already hinted at, is not, to me, very convincing: counterexamples abound, on both sides of the Atlantic, as well as cases of hybridization in which the two trends are inextricably mixed (for example, Meyer 1983; Betti 1984). The distinction, besides, is not essential for my purpose: I shall only consider the impact of those logical or logicist approaches in the archaeological literature, as I did in the case of structuralist interpretations, without concern for finer distinctions in terms of schools of semiotics.

The first observation is that traces of the impact are rather scarce. The impressive work of C. S. Peirce, for instance, led a historian to write interesting pages on what a "logic of historical thought" might look like (Fischer 1971); but the matter has been left there, and there seems to be no comparable book in archaeology. In the same way, some anthropologists are now tempted by the Peircean approach to interpretation, to the point of presenting it as the basis of a new "semiotic anthropology" (Singer 1984); but again, no similar project seems to exist in archaeology, except those which I shall discuss below in connection with hermeneutics, without much relation to the philosophy of C. S. Peirce (§1.3).

My exploration would therefore have stopped short, had I not chosen some twenty-five years ago to place under the banner of semiology the seminar which I had been invited to give at the Ecole des Hautes Etudes en Sciences Sociales on the analysis of interpretation processes in the humanities. "Semiology and Computers," such was the title which I gave then to this program; it has not changed to this day. Its origin can be described in a few words: I had been interested, in the 1950s, in the use of information processing techniques, as they were called then, first in archaeology, then in the broader field of the human sciences. At that time, two major categories of problems had emerged: (a) semiological issues, inevitably present in the constitution or consultation of databases; (b) computing issues, in a formal rather than in a mechanical sense, that became apparent as we tried to produce or reproduce on computers a wide range of constructs derived from such bases (scholarly catalogues, typologies, classifications of objects in space and time, functional interpretations, etc.). Those two components were a prefiguration of the dual expression now common in artificial intelligence, viz., representation and processing of knowledge. It is easy to fuse the two designations into one, "semiological representation and computer processing," thereby confirming, if need be, the close relationship between the two projects.

I shall not recount the history of our work along this twofold path (Gardin 1985a): the only point of concern here is the place of semiotics in the picture. To be quite honest, it is more of an honorific position, devoid of technical import; the basis for it is a rather simple argument, which I shall summarize under four points. (1) Archaeology, like any science, is dependent on the use of *ad hoc* languages or semiological systems for the "formulation" of its objects of study and their interpretation. (2) These systems are first identical with or closely related to natural language, but they tend gradually to evolve into autonomous systems, as the descriptive and interpretative tools of discipline become more complex. (3) To any archaeological commentary we can thus associate a system of knowledge representation (descriptive data and interpretative concepts), more or less widely shared, which belongs in essence to the set of "systems of signs" encompassed in semiology. (4) More specifically, the idea of studying such systems is reminiscent of a project which took shape some fifty years ago in the head of a few logicians, one of whom can be counted among the best-known semioticians: I have in mind the International

Encyclopedia of Unified Science, originally inspired by the work of R. Carnap on the logical analysis of the language of science, as a way to reach a better understanding of its mechanisms and foundations. One of the coauthors of the program was Charles Morris; his place among the founders of semiotics is well known. His famous *Theory of Signs* was one of the rare volumes published as part of the International Encyclopedia of Unified Science (1938).

The disproportion between this ambitious project and our narrow program is self-evident: the most I have ever suggested is a family resemblance, which is sufficient to relate our work to this logical or logicist current, but which does not take us any further. The reason is that we do not find in semiotics as developed by Charles Morris, any more than in the semiotics of C. S. Peirce, even the sketch of a procedure that we might use for our purpose, limited though it may be. Thus the study of the mechanisms and foundations of interpretation in archaeology remains in the last analysis an archaeological matter; semiology is only present, as is the reference to computers, to indicate a perspective, a point of view, rather than the main field of interest.

We now have to raise the same question posed above with respect to structuralist trends: Are we in a position to evaluate the contribution of logicism to the progress of archaeological knowledge? I see no other way to measure the relative merits of any "new approach" than by considering the traces which it has left in the accumulation of more or less established facts and theories about ancient societies. In the case of logicism, this requirement may seem premature: most of our essays have been focused on archaeological work already published, less to question them than to gain some expertise in displaying their semiological structure, in the sense indicated above. The gain in substantial knowledge is then clearly meager; but we may wish to take into account the secondary effects of such endeavors. To give but one example, I would take the case of my work in progress on the archaeology of Central Asia: it tends to take up a new shape, both in substance and form, as I try to elicit the "semio-" systems and the "-logical" operations which underlie my own reasoning processes in that particular context (example in Gardin et al. 1987:59–91).

But what is the worth of the end product? Will our constrained unimaginative reconstitutions, our dreary schematizations still arouse any interest? Can we safely assume that the best minds will want to indulge in such exercises when expert systems will make them accessible to all? Alain Gallay writes, to the point: "we suspect that the reduction of our cognitive ambitions would be so sizable and their questioning so fundamental that very few scholars (including myself) would dare to accept them, in the present cultural context." But then, to put it in Shakespearean terms: "or else, what follows?" For the status quo seems to be just as unacceptable once its weaknesses have been acknowledged.

This is the kind of questions which I should like to see discussed in archaeology, with or without reference to semiotics, yet grateful to semiotics for having led us to them. I shall propose further on a number of possible answers, for my own part, in order to foster this debate.

1.3 Hermeneutic Trends

In the course of these discussions, we should certainly expect that a stand will be taken against "science and technology" (the latter being indeed present in the foregoing perspective by way of expert systems), based on the usual arguments, e.g.: (1) the limits of logical positivism, especially for the understanding of human affairs; (2) the anachronistic nature of such a trust in science, at a time when eminent scholars keep unveiling its indeterminacies, its errors (with inevitable references to Popper, Kuhn, Feyerabend, Holton, and others); (3) the neglect of the inner factors of human behavior, either conscious (intentions, beliefs, values) or not (desires, phantasms, pulsions); (4) our inability, therefore, to apprehend the singularity of historical phenomena, the ontological dimension of knowledge, etc. (I have published elsewhere a more detailed exercise *in anticipatio*, to use a scholastic term, which presents both the current objections to logicism and my answers to them: Gardin 1981:307–331).

The enduring vigor of those criticisms in the last decades, as well as the fact that they are held, rightly or wrongly, to be widely shared, gives all its weight to the third semiotic current in my list, one strongly opposed to the logicist perspective: namely, the hermeneutic approach, illustrated in particular by the more recent books by Ian Hodder and others, and situated both in Britain and in the USA. Let me first justify my labels: there is hardly any reference to semiotics in those books, except through ritual allusions to Ferdinand de Saussure or Charles Peirce, a ritual in which we all engage in similar contexts. In fact, the word "semiotics" is absent in the index of Hodder's last book on "Current approaches to interpretation in archaeology" (1986); and I have not found it either anywhere in the text. It may therefore seem strange to mention the man, the school, or the book in a survey of semiotic trends in archaeology (see, however, Gardin 1983 for a somewhat different picture in Hodder's earlier publications). The same argument holds for the hermeneutic label itself, as used in the title of this paragraph; my only excuse for using it so confidently is the amazing convergence between the positions defended with talent by C. Renfrew, I. Hodder, and others, under various names (cognitive archaeology, symbolic archaeology, contextual archaeology), and the major theses which characterize the hermeneutic current in contemporary semiotics. The following pages will be devoted to a demonstration of this convergence.

I shall not bore the reader with a reminder of these positions on the archaeological side: many of our colleagues know them, some from the "inside," from having contributed to their formulation. Let us begin instead with the theses of hermeneutics, as presented with more and more consistency in some circles of semiotics, and show in passing their reflection in symbolic, cognitive, or contextual archaeology (abridged hereafter SCC). The major stands seems to be the following (for a more detailed presentation, containing also the references to the works on hermeneutics upon which this account is based, see Gardin 1985b:12–17).

(I) The Nature/Culture duality, under different formulations.   —The guiding principle is that human behavior and its products are of another essence than the phenomena studied in the natural sciences and are therefore not amenable to the same interpretative approach. We are thus invited to admit that our reasoning in sciences should follow different forms when dealing with one order or the other; this dichotomy is expressed through the well-known oppositions between Understanding vs. Explanation, or in other languages *Verständnis* vs. *Aufklärung*, Comprehension vs. Explication, etc. The basis for this first point is usually an indictment of the totalitarian aspects of "Science and Technology," using some or all of the arguments which I recalled earlier under that title.

I do not think that I need bother the reader with references showing that a similar stand is taken in SCC archaeology against the "positivist ideology," whether under that name or others.

(II) The place of the subject, both as an actor and as an observer in the human field. —The specificity of the sciences of culture which has just been examined acquires here more substance. First, we should pay due respect to the role that distinct persons or groups play in history, with their respective conscience, representations, beliefs, systems of value—individual or collective—in brief, all the elements of the "inner world" associated with each, that it is precisely the function of the human sciences to disclose in their own ways. What distinguishes those sciences then—and this is the second point— is that they accept, or sometimes prescribe, that the observer should form part of the phenomena under study. This view is expressed in different fashions, such as the unavoidable bias of our categories in interpretation, the necessary part of empathy in the process, the difficulty of disassociating the scientist from its object, and so on.

It is easy to recognize in this twofold argument one of the most common claims of SCC archaeology, similarly concerned with "the inside of things," in accord with Collingwood's often quoted expression: i.e., the need to reach the subjective elements that play their part in the genesis and development of human actions. Such is the objective of "the archaeology of mind" recommended by Renfrew (1982), as well as by Hodder in his quest of the "meaning content" buried in the material remains of societies, present or past (1986:118–146).

(III) Validation, revised. —A necessary correlate of those positions is a questioning of the methods used for the validation of theories in natural sciences. Whole books have been written on this subject in the literature of hermeneutics: quite logically, new validation criteria are proposed, which we may call, undisparagingly, subjective, in keeping with the interpretations which they are intended to confirm. For instance, we shall declare that the explanation of a poem by a given scholar is "good" if the scholar feels some kind of satisfaction or plenitude, as he unravels it, which is in its own way an indisputable sign of its "value" (Howard 1982:161). Alternatively, if we regard this procedure as a little loose, we shall replace this individual measure of value by a collective one, by calling on the arbitration of a group, differently named: "interpretive community" (Schauber and Spolsky 1986:29), "discursive society" (Foucault 1971: 42–43), "textual community" (Stock 1983: chap. 2), etc.; or again the arbitration of a fictitious individual, regarded as the representative of a larger group: "informed reader," "super-reader," "implied reader" etc. (Gardin 1982:13 note 2).

This original conception of validation is by no means presented as applicable only to the sciences of literature or art: the hermeneutic process of interpretation extends to all kinds of human phenomena (Ricoeur 1981), and validation criteria associated with it are therefore to be used also in historical or anthropological explanation. The SCC archaeology again seems to share the same views: one of its most distinguished representatives, having first stressed the centrality of the validation issue in symbolic archaeology (Hodder 1982:viii), soon found a solution of the hermeneutical sort by calling on social consensus, the adhesion of believers (Hodder 1984); his later position on the subject is still more liberal, to the point of proposing to forget it altogether ("how do we then proceed to validate? Well, one answer is to say that we don't": Hodder 1986:93).

(IV) Multi-interpretation, inevitable.   —Hermeneuticians have not been slow to acknowledge the logical consequence of this liberalism: namely, that the same objects, the
same phenomena can give rise to varying interpretations in any number, and that there
is no real way to choose among them. Each one of them is indeed "validated" to the
extent that it satisfies its author or some of its readers. It is therefore wise to admit that
in such conditions "the conflict of interpretations is inevitable and insurmountable," as
claimed recently by one of the leading authorities in hermeneutics (Valdes 1984). We
can moreover verify it at any time by observing the quasi-exponential growth of interpretations currently produced about the same objects of study in the sciences of man,
from Baudelaire's poem "Les Chats" (Plottel 1983) to the origins at the First World
War (Joll 1984). We would be hard-pressed if we were under an obligation to disprove
all previous interpretations of any given object before adding our own.

It stands to reason that SCC archaeology is bound to follow the same logic and admit
in the same way that between its own interpretations, conflict is inevitable and insurmountable. I shall again quote Hodder, always lucid: "varied alternative pasts exist and
involve many individuals and groups, in relation to the changing interpretations of establishment archaeologists" (1986:163).

2. Relations among the Trends Mentioned Thus Far

Placing the three approaches which I have discussed in the same class, under a common
semiotic label, may legitimately be regarded as somewhat artificial. Yet, the three of
them have a common denominator which justifies in a sense this label: they all tend to
cast some light, in one way or other, on "mentalities," differently conceived. The
structures discussed in the first case (§1.1) are mental organizations that are supposed
to determine the behaviors of certain groups or the products of such behaviors; in the
same way, the symbolic systems considered in the third case (§1.3) are constituents of
mentalities, even if of a looser kind than required in structuralist methodology. As for
our logicist schematizations (§1.2), their goal is to elicit the worldviews upon which our
interpretations are founded in archaeology, which is again one way to contribute to the
knowledge of mentalities, but on the observer's side this time, rather than that of the
observed.

This unifying viewpoint has its virtues. One of them is that it strengthens the case
for grouping the three approaches under a common title: the study of "mentalities" or
"worldviews," which is indeed one of the ways in which semiotics is trying to regain
some unity. A more substantial virtue is that we should now see more clearly the part
which these approaches may play in the progress of archaeology; this is what I want to
show in the remaining pages of this paper.

Let me begin with a trivial observation: there is a risk, when discussing new approaches in archaeology, that "trees will hide the forest." The vast majority of archaeologists throughout the world have never heard and will probably never hear of semiotic
trends in our discipline; and the interpretations which this majority produces in the field
owe precious little to these trends, even though they constitute the larger and more solid

part of our knowledge about past societies. Other participants in this conference have made the same observation (see for instance Alain Gallay, this volume). Its meaning, to me, is not that our "innovations" are vain, but rather that they should be reset in a different perspective, which incidentally may help to reduce the fuss made about some of them. For instance, it is clear that the structural and the hermeneutic approaches, each announced in turn as a "revolution," in fact only concern the higher part of the pyramid of knowledge in archaeology: hypotheses are formulated at levels of inference that are seldom reached in "traditional archaeology," but that are also more difficult to control. Moreover, these high-flown interpretations are still largely dependent on the lower parts of the evidentiary pyramid; and their life expectancy seems to be considerable shorter, judging from the fact that so many of them are ignored or forgotten outside the narrow limits of time and space within which they have enjoyed for a while some luster.

As for the logicist approach, it is anything but a revolution; on the contrary, from the outset it was heralded as an aspect of the standard ways of science, in which we strive to come to a better understanding of mechanisms and foundations of interpretation, in a metatheoretical perspective. This last clause explains why it would make little sense to draw comparisons between the logicist approach, applicable to theoretical constructs of any sort, on the one hand, and the structuralist or hermeneutic program on the other, which specializes in particular families of interpretation. Strangely enough, this elementary difference of "type," in the Russellian sense, was first ill-understood: the first reviewers of the logicist program insisted that it could only be sterile, since it declared itself "neutral" with respect to the different schools that were then competing on the archaeological scene as others do today. The use of expert systems has changed all this. Schematizations of reasoning processes once translated into the forms of an expert system, as knowledge bases, become all of a sudden praiseworthy, on the sole basis of "having been implemented on computers" (Gardin et al. 1987:234–236). Paradoxically, this turn of the tide occurs at a moment when the logicist program is losing the "neutrality" which had first harmed it. The following section deals with this twofold evolution.

3. Back to the Foundations of Interpretation in Archaeology

The value of computer applications in this area is that they compel us to study the mechanisms of our reasoning processes so that we can express them in the language of expert systems. We are thus led to elicit, on the one hand, the systems of representation which underlie the formulation of the data in the "fact" base; on the other hand, we must explicitly specify the rewrite operations that are used to link the facts to the hypotheses, or conversely, the "rule" base to the facts. The logicist program pursues no other goals; by extending it into the realm of artificial intelligence, we gain a means to test the value of the reasoning processes that have been observed in the literature, in the following way. The idea is to produce computer-based interpretations of new data, in a given universe of discourse, using a knowledge base that embodies the same process, expressed as inference rules. By assessing the plausibility of "artificial" theories in that sense, *according to any criteria*, we can measure the relative value of the "natural" interpretation processes that have been used to build up the knowledge base.

Let us leave aside the possible validation criteria and examine what happens when the test is negative—i.e., when the artificial interpretation is rejected, either because it is disproved or weakened by empirical counterexamples, or more simply because we find it improper, unpleasing, insufficient, or any qualification of that sort, in the spirit of validation in hermeneutics. The new factor is that we are now better equipped than before to explore the possible sources of rejection. For one thing, we are pressed to go beyond the mere fact of rejection and undertake such explorations, as part of the game of science, instead of merely contemplating it as the inevitable and insurmountable consequence of the conflict of interpretations. Then, we are directed to a number of specific elements as possible causes of the rejection, e.g.: (1) the distinctive features used in the representation system are inadequate, in one way or another (degree of generality, definition, etc.); (2) the system itself is incomplete, relevant features have been omitted that would have barred the unwanted interpretation or opened the way to a more satisfactory one; (3) some of the rules of inference are improper, because they authorize or prescribe undesirable derivations; (4) the knowledge base is incomplete, a number of rewrite rules are missing that would have led to more fruitful interpretations, and so on.

Whatever the case may be, the analysis of the "deficiencies" of expert systems, in the above sense, necessarily leads to a progress in our knowledge, even if only by disclosing its limitations. An effective way to show it is to consider the case of multiple interpretations in concrete situations: given a set of premises **p,** different derivations have been recorded, **q1, q2. . . . qn,** in the same knowledge base. In other words, different authors (experts)—or the same author in different circumstances—draw different consequents **q** from the same antecedent **p.** Let us stress that the phenomenon should not be understood as affecting the relation between the initial propositions (**P0**) and the terminal propositions (**Pn**) in the schematization of a global construct, considered on a macroscopic scale; it concerns the relation between two groups of *consecutive* propositions, (**Pi**) → (**Pi**) + **1,** on the minimal scale of reduction. Multiple interpretation in this second sense is not the one which usually comes to mind in the human sciences; it refers to the more interesting case of atomic or primitive operations that make up the architecture of scholarly constructs, including univocal ones in the first sense. For ambiguous or multivocal inferences at this elementary level, **p** → **q1 . . . qn,** can very well occur through the cumulation of global constructs of any sort, including some that link different sets of (**P0**) and (**Pn**) and do not therefore conflict with one another (on this cumulation process, see Lagrange and Renaud 1987). The problem of multiple interpretation then takes on a totally different dimension; and the major question becomes this one: What do we do when we observe that our interpretations, considered globally (i.e., from (**P0**) to (**Pn**)), rest on operations that are ambiguous, at the elementary level of rewrite or derivation rules **p** → **q**? There are two possible answers: one is that we do nothing—following from this, Hodder's suggestion regarding the related problem of validation (see above). The other is that we try to reduce such ambiguities, either as a matter of scientific deontology or as a source of intellectual pleasure, according to our temperament. The reduction mechanism is straightforward: when confronted with a situation such as

$$p \rightarrow q1 \ OR \ q2 \ OR \ q3. \ldots \ OR \ qn,$$

we should look for additional conditions which, combined with the left part of the rule, will eliminate the disjunctions of the right part. We then obtain a set of rules such as:

p in context C1 $\rightarrow$ **q1**
p in context C2 $\rightarrow$ **q2**
.
.
.
.
p in context Cn $\rightarrow$ **qn**.

Conditions, contexts, these terms are interchangeable, as are others which also happen to begin with a C, complements, criteria, supplementary clauses, etc. They all denote the same function of C, which is to indicate the data that have to be added to the premises of a multivocal rule in order to replace it by a set of univocal rules of the type **p Ci** $\rightarrow$ **qi**. The progress of knowledge to which I was referring above lies in this movement toward "local" rules that are not in conflict with one another, *hic et nunc*, and away from rules that are too general to meet that condition. I have shown elsewhere (Gardin 1989) that this way of contextualizing our inferences was by no means in contradiction with the quest for "universal" rules of reasoning in science; we only have to state more clearly what we mean by the "universal." It is a standard requirement in logic that the formulation of a rule should be accompanied by a delineation of its "domain," i.e., the universe of discourse in which the rule is applicable. Consequently, all well-formed rules are universal, within the limits of their domain. The difficulty lies in defining those domains or at least in circumscribing them in the empirical world.

This is precisely what the very logic of schematizations and experts systems impels us to do, at least in my understanding of their proper use in scientific research. The logicist approach then looks like a return to foundational issues; we raise them apropos of all kinds of interpretive constructs without any preference or prejudice for or against particular classes of them, SCC or other's. Essentially, the major question is this: On what bases do we rest our belief that after having observed or established **p,** we should be authorized to rewrite **q**? No deep reflection is needed to perceive that our "bases" are in fact of different sorts, e.g.: (1) the explicit mention of analogies, or precedents, found in history or ethnology; (2) an implicit call on the part of "natural logic" in argumentation, or again "common sense," even though we are left in the dark as to the content of each term and the real extension of "natural" or "naïve" inferences; (3) ideological or cultural presuppositions of the interpretant, conscious or not, and so on. We should finally recall that our languages or systems of representation themselves play an essential part in the reasoning processes, as we use them in a more or less self-critical fashion to formulate empirical or theoretical propositions in the course of interpretation. It is not surprising that the study of foundations to that depth may seem tedious, arid, difficult; does it follow that it is sterile?

4. Prospective Views

Although the logicist approach consists in studying the foundations of interpretive constructs "without any preference or prejudice for or against particular classes of them," in my own words, the exercise is neither a contemplative nor a speculative one. The kind of epistemology to which we refer is a "practical epistemology" (Gardin 1981), of an applied sort, which has not much to do with the epistemology of philosophers. It is bound eventually to acquire a normative aspect as it makes us more aware of the empirical or social limits of our interpretations. Some scholars consider this kind of exploration— "establishing boundary conditions"—as the major task of the human sciences in the next decades (Fiske and Shweder 1986:11, 19, etc.). I would not go as far in the case of archaeology: the urgency of salvage programs creates more pressing obligations; yet, I am prone to think that among archaeologists who devote some of their time and abilities to the new approaches, a current will develop in favor of those which contribute most actively to this growing awareness of the foundations and limitations of archaeological theories of all kinds, without much concern for the successive schools and "revolutions" to which they are related. In fact, this evolution is already visible, I believe, through a number of signs which we may choose to interpret in that sense, as I shall now propose.

4.1 Cognitive Science

One of the most conspicuous indicators of impending change is the expansion of the cognitive sciences, of which artificial intelligence is a part. I have no doubt that expert systems will soon be fashionable in archaeology, if such is not already the case; we shall therefore have to bear with all kinds of "applications" of such systems, for good or evil, just as we had to live in the 1960s and the 1970s with all kinds of computer applications of mathematical methods, themselves producing returns unequal to the effort invested in them. However, those exercises have at least one virtue: they increase our expertise in the analysis of reasoning processes, even if they yield few other practical consequences. Archaeology would thus seem to take part in the introspective movement of the cognitive sciences, with its insistent questioning of the mechanisms and foundations of our symbolic activity across all its possible manifestations. Among these we find—according to the broader scholars—not only the theoretical constructs of the natural sciences but also artistic or literary constructs from the universe of culture. Both groups may be said to illustrate the wide range of possible words, to use this popular expression, even though they respectively call on modes of thought that are radically different, to the point of constituting two distinct genres, "two natural kinds," in Bruner's words (1986:3–54). I shall examine in a moment the case of the third genre which SCC archaeology claims to be, at least in Hodder's definition, "neither science nor art" (1986:x), on a par with hermeneutics; for the moment, however, let us concentrate on this convergence between the epistemological questions raised by logicist analyses in archaeology and the more general questions studied by cognitivists in a broader perspective.

Other scholars have noted this potential relation between cognitive sciences and archaeology, e.g., C. S. Peebles, in this volume, and the difference in our respective viewpoints is again a Russellian difference of "type." My understanding of his paper is that Peebles finds in the cognitive sciences a number of positions which can serve the purpose of an "archaeology of mind," in Renfrew's sense: the symbolic constructs and modes of thought that are of concern to Peebles are those of peoples of the past. As for me, I draw from the cognitive sciences an incitation to study the symbolic constructs and modes of thought of scholars such as ourselves, when we talk about those peoples in scientific discourse—a possible object of discourse being then the reconstitution of symbolic constructs and modes of thought of peoples of the past. The two programs are by no means mutually exclusive, as shown by this very last sentence; but obviously, the fact that they both make a reference to the cognitive world is not a reason to confound them.

Do we have to stress that in this crossing of archaeology with the cognitive sciences, in the logicist perspective, the interesting element is not the use of computers, but the logicist analysis itself, whether or not instantiated in the design of a knowledge-based system? Eminent cognitivists express the same view, in their own way, even when they are totally dedicated to computers (Pylyshyn 1984:260). Is it also necessary to say once more that logicist schematizations make no pretence of being THE proper representation of organized knowledge, nor of its genesis in an archaeologist's mind? On this point too, some parallels would have to be drawn with cognitivist positions, in which an emphasis is laid on the fact that the functional architectures developed in artificial intelligence have no clear relation, to say the least, with "natural" structures of knowledge in the human mind, however we see them (Pylyshyn 1984:268–269).

4.2 Practical Epistemology

A second significant feature in support of my views on the prospects of practical epistemology is the fact that a number of its positions, which were first regarded as unacceptable, now tend to be commonplace or at least tolerated, according to the case, in archaeology. The major source of earlier criticism, as I mentioned above, was our neutrality with respect to the substance of theories or to the philosophy of the various schools in contemporary archaeology. This position was a correlate of our will to reach first a better understanding of "what they are" and "what they do," in practical terms (Gardin 1981:3–15), without *a priori* bias for or against any one of them in particular. This higher perspective first irritated many scholars: it doomed our undertaking—"very French," according to one reviewer—to the status of a shallow, trivial, verbose exercise. Opinions seem different today, as illustrated by this very conference and the substance of its working papers. Many of them seem to share a concern for "measure," in the polysemous sense of the word advocated, for instance, by H.-P. Francfort, even if the ways proposed to reach that goal do not all follow, God forbid, the philosophy of logicism and expert systems.

Other positions, which were regarded as retrograde ten or fifteen years ago, also tend to be accepted today, in ways that nullify many of the objections raised then against logicism. These positions were and still are essentially positions of dissent with respect to most of the theses then considered as distinctive of the more advanced archaeology. Let me mention for instance, in random order: (1) the idea that the search for "general laws'' is the ultimate goal of science; (2) the primacy of various ''systems'' in the explanation of human behavior; (3) a certain distrust directed toward the so-called traditional methods of historical inquiry, considered as unable to apprehend the laws and systems in question; (4) conversely, a blind trust in the virtues of methods regarded as ''scientific,'' either in the form of overall modes of reasoning (such as the hypothetico-deductive method), or with reference to specific tools, essentially related to mathematics and computers, etc. There is not much left today of these articles of the neo-archaeological faith; any contrary position therefore tends to be regarded as ''post-processual,'' ''post-modern,'' ''post-positivist'' (for example see Hodder 1986:147ff), even if it happens to have been expressed in any number of texts prior to those local ''revolutions.'' Never mind, however, the ambiguity of our reconciliations: the good thing is that the road has been opened, or reopened, to a more eclectic approach of the foundations of interpretation in archaeology, of the kind recommended by Alain Gallay in his excellent defense and illustration of ''Archaeology tomorrow'' (1986).

4.3 Changes in Publication Practices

Finally, I wish to mention a third fact in support of my own projections, which is the growing attention paid to a problem apparently more down-to-earth than the former ones, but in my view directly related to them, namely, the form of our publications. Many years ago I made a plea for the development of what I called pompously ''a new rhetoric'' better suited to the presentation of our materials and ideas than our traditional forms of writing (Gardin and Lagrange 1975). I later undertook to formulate in more detail some of its principles (Gardin 1979:244–273). My present position on the subject would be more radical: I envisage a time, not too far ahead—say, a few decades—when we may be led to use modes of communication other than our traditional publications, at least for some categories of archaeological facts or ideas. Logicist schematizations and expert systems, in our primitive use of them, already prompt us to raise the question (Gardin 1986), even through no clear-cut answers are yet in view. The interesting thing is that the same question is now being raised in a much broader context. Archaeology may be an extreme case, because of the high costs of its publications when compared to the relatively small number of readers; but all scientific and technical disciplines are in fact confronted with the same probable evolution of our habits in that area, under the joint pressure of two kinds of innovations. The more visible ones are technological innovations: we are all aware of the current projections of information scientists, who predict the end of printed documents and libraries, regarded as anachronistic ways of communication, to the benefit of knowledge information processing systems (KIPS), under this designation or another, providing more efficient and less costly forms of access to specialized knowledge (see, for example, Kilgour 1984). The other kind of innovations, less spectacular but much more radical, has to do with our linguistic habits. We can already observe, in restricted universes of discourse, the emergence of ''artificial'' forms of symbolic expression as substitutes for expressions which we regarded as ''natural,'' only by virtue of the fact that they were closely related to a natural language or another. As the phenomenon spreads—and we have little reason to doubt that it will—we may be led to revise the very content of the opposition ''natural/artificial'' in general, whether applied to language, as in our present discussion, or elsewhere to intelligence, to logic (Gardin 1987b), or to computation itself—see for example the original ideas developed by Pylyshyn on "natural computation" in machines (1984:269).

Many may feel doubts as to the realism of such anticipations, or an urge to oppose them in the name of humanism; let me only recall that the same long-term views have first been formulated with as much vigor and sympathy by an anthropologist whom we can hardly regard as a barbarian, André Leroi-Gourhan (1964–5: vol. 2, p. 259). It may also be of interest to observe that as respectable and established an institution as the British Library has recently chosen the relation between "Expert systems and scholarly publications" as one of the research topics which now deserve to receive its attention (Gardin 1987a).

5. Conclusion

The preceding prospects are my personal conclusion with respect to the contribution of semiotic trends to the progress of archaeology; but it may be wise to add a few words to dispel one or two possible misunderstandings.

The trilogy from which I started—structuralism, logicism, hermeneutics—has gradually been replaced by a dichotomy: on one side, structuralist and hermeneutic currents, abundant, generous, and rich in interpretations of the most subtle, imaginative, but also mostly undecidable sort; on the other, the logicist current, parsimonious, meager, poor in words and in ideas within the narrow limits allowed by the game of symbolic manipulations under empirical control. From this dichotomy, I then went on to draw a more general contrast between this latter kind of construction, where empirical validation is more important than the approach followed—to the point where the interest of the latter is a function of the former—with all kinds of interpretative comments characterized by a premium on innovations of perspective, with little or no concern for their possible (or impossible) refutations.

The first source of misunderstanding I fear lies in the temptation one might have to introduce judgments of value into this picture. I do not wish to weaken my presentation of the dichotomy, which I regard as fundamental: we are effectively dealing with two distinct genres, "two natural kinds," to again quote a distinction made by J. Bruner. However, like Bruner, I shun away from establishing any hierarchy of worthiness between the genres, both of which contribute to the enrichment of knowledge; I would only add a reservation which Bruner, more liberal, might not endorse. The rules of the first genre are well known: they are those of the "logico-scientific paradigm," as he calls it; as for the rules of the second genre, which he labels as "narrative," he says, " . . . we know precious little." This is also my view; but it does not follow that when we present our views of the second kind on the meaning of archaeological remains, they can be more or less anything we wish them to be. We also know precious little about the rules which enable us to distinguish a good novel from a bad one, here and now; this does not prevent us from having our views on the matter, personal or collective. I draw this analogy purposely; for in the last analysis I see no other possible affiliation, for the second genre, than to Literature with a capital **L**. In other words, if it is today more or less admitted that the writings of the second genre must essentially please us, here and now (see §1.3, III), we hardly have any other choice than to assimilate them to literary works, in the best hypothesis. The qualities expected in both cases are indeed comparable in two respects: (1) we can infer their existence from the success of certain works and the lack of success of others here and now, (2) but we do not know how to define them other than retrospectively, or, as far as the present is concerned, through comments that can easily be shown to be tautological and without any generative value.

This point of view assigns to the interpretations of SCC archaeology a place of distinction: they must carry our conviction through means that we cannot regard anymore as accessible to everyone; nor do we require anymore that they should be amenable to rationalizations in terms of rules of inference or rules of production. We are back to the situation which I described on the first page, following Paul Veyne, and the analogy which he suggests between the tales of historians and the myths of storytellers: according to him, we should today adhere to the former as others formerly believed in the latter, for reasons which are not related to the "logico-scientific paradigm" but which do not exclude them. Failing which, we would have to define the rules of a third genre freed from the constraints of that paradigm as well as from the demands of literature, in brief, a genre which would be, in Hodder's own terms, "neither science nor art," but which would have to clarify which aspects of its own symbolic manipulations distinguish it from both. A difficult task if there ever was one, as we have seen; all the more difficult if we bear in mind that this obligation extends to another distinction, namely between those scholarly interpretations of the third genre, neither scientific nor literary, and the laymen's interpretations produced by the thousand in nonspecialized journals and books by all kinds of enlightened observers of human behavior. We would thus have to define *four* genres, instead of three. The more traditional reduction to two saves us from this predicament. Its shortcoming, if it is one, is that it reestablishes "Literature" as an honorable way of conveying knowledge about the past. I would rather regard this as an advantage, since such a restoration carries with it an obligation that the works of the alternative genre should display additional qualities, which can only reinforce it.

Another source of misunderstanding disappears in the same process; it concerns the passion which the logicist approach and its followers are supposed to display for "Science and Technology" despite the associated ills—positivism, reductionism, mechanicism, etc., to which should be added their alleged inability to grasp the historical, social, ideological dimensions of the phenomena studied in archaeology (supra, §1.3). Admittedly, in the dual picture which I have just proposed, the "logico-scientific paradigm" seems to be the marked pole of the opposition. This is true, but for a contingent reason, namely, that I do not happen to have myself, to my regret, the qualities required to contribute to the success of the other genre, given the high standards which I personally associate with the label "literary." Had it been otherwise, I should have presented a defense and illustration of the literary approach, as the marked pole, but with a twofold difference with respect to the positions of advocates of the third genre. First, I would have stressed the stronger requirements which interpretations or more generally commentaries of this nature have to meet in order to avoid the risk of drifting toward the fourth genre, as hinted above. Then, I would have included in my argumentation a no less vigorous defence of the other pole, "logico-scientific," under its most severe forms—

logicism, for instance—while confessing my inability to illustrate it myself, for lack of the proper talent.

This difference of perspective is perhaps my only quarrel with SCC archaeology; or more generally with any "new approach" presented in a monolithic, exclusive fashion, without regard for the major duality discussed above. Yet I am quite ready to come to any other understanding of our differences that might emerge from further discussions.

REFERENCES

Betti, E. 1984. "The epistemological problem of understanding as an aspect of the general problem of knowledge," in G. Shapiro and A. Sica (eds.), *Hermeneutics*, pp. 25–53. University of Massachusetts Press, Amherst.

Bruner, J. 1986. *Actual Minds, Possible Worlds*. Harvard University Press, Cambridge, MA.

Fischer, D. H. 1971. *Historians' Fallacies: Toward a Logic of Historical Thought*. Routledge & Kegan Paul, London.

Fiske, D. W., and R. A. Shweder (eds.) 1986. *Metatheory in Social Science: Pluralism and Subjectivities*. University of Chicago Press, Chicago.

Foucault, M. 1971. *L'ordre du discours*. Gallimard, Paris.

Gallay, A. 1986. *L'archéologie demain*. Belfond, Paris.

Gardin, J.-C. 1967. "Methods for the descriptive analysis of archaeological materials," *American Antiquity* **32,** 13–30.

———1979. *Une archéologie théoreque*. Hachette, Paris

———1980. *Archaeological Constructs: An Aspect of Archaeological Theory*. Cambridge University Press, Cambridge.

———1981. "Vers une épistémologie pratique," in J.-C. Gardin et al., *La logique du plausible*, pp. 3–91. Editions de la Maison des Sciences de l'Homme, Paris. (2nd ed. 1987.)

———1982. "Lectures plurielles et sciences singuliéres de la littérature," *Diogène* **111,** 3–14.

———1983. "L'archéologie entre en sémiotique" [a review of I Hodder (ed.), *Symbolic and Structural Archaeology*], *Semiotica* **45–3/4,** 339–344.

———1985a. "Sémiologie et informatique," *Degrés*, 13e année, no. 42–43, pp. b1–b23.

———1985b. "Fondements possibles de la sémologie," *Recherches sémiotiques/Semiotic Inquiry (RSSI)* **5,** 1–31.

———1986. [La publication en archéologie], *Mélanges de l'Ecole Française de Rome*, tome 98–1, pp. 265–372.

———1987a. *Expert Systems and Scholarly Publications*. The British Library, London.

———1987b. "La logique, naturelle ou autre, dans les constructions de sciences humaines," *Revue européenne de sciences sociales* [a special number in honor of J.-B. Grize, M. J. Borel (ed.)], pp. 179–195.

———1989. "The role of local knowledge in archaeological interpretation," in S. J. Shennan (ed.), *Archaeological Approaches to Cultural Identity*, pp. 110–122. Unwin Hyman, London.

Gardin, J.-C. and M.-S. Lagrange 1975. *Essais d'analyse du discours archéologique*. Editions du C.N.R.S. (Centre de Recherches Archéologiques), Paris.

Gardin, J.-C. et al. 1981. *La logique du plausible*. Edition de la Maison des Sciences de l'Homme, Paris. (2nd ed. 1987.)

———1987. *Systèmes experts et sciences humaines: le cas de l'archéologie*. Eyrolles, Paris. English translation: *Artificial Intelligence and Expert Systems: Case Studies in the Knowledge Domain of Archaeology*. Ellis Horwood, Ltd., Chichester, UK.

Hodder, I. (ed.) 1982. *Symbolic and Structural Archaeology*. Cambridge University Press, Cambridge.

Hodder, I. 1984. "Archaeology in 1984," *Antiquity* **58,** 25–32.

————1986. *Reading the Past: Current Approaches to Interpretation in Archaeology*. Cambridge University Press, Cambridge.

Howard, R. 1982. *Three Faces of Hermeneutics: An Introduction to Current Theories of Understanding*. University of California Press, Berkeley.

Joll, J. 1984. *The Origins of the First World War*. Longmans, London.

Kilgour, F. 1984. *Beyond Bibliography*. The British Library, London.

Lagrange, M.-S., and M. Renaud 1987. "Superikon, essai de cumul de six expertises en iconographie," in J.-C. Gardin et al., *Systèmes experts et sciences humaines: le cas de l'archéologie*, pp. 191–229. Eyrolles, Paris.

Leroi-Gourhan, A. 1964–65. *Le geste et la parole*, 2 vol. Albin Michel, Paris.

Meyer, M. 1983. *Meaning and Reading: A Philosophical Essay on Language and Literature*. John Benjamins, Amsterdam.

Morris, C. 1938. *Foundations of a Theory of Signs*. University of Chicago Press, Chicago.

Plottel, J.-P. 1983. "The battle of Baudelaire's 'Les Chats,'" *Romantic Review* **74,** 91–103.

Pylyshyn, Z. W. 1984. *Computation and Cognition: Toward a Foundation for Cognitive Science*. MIT Press, Cambridge, MA.

Renfrew, C. 1982. *Toward an Archaeology of Mind*. Cambridge University Press, Cambridge.

Ricoeur, P. 1981. *Hermeneutics and the Human Sciences*. J. Thompson (ed.). Cambridge University Press, Cambridge.

Schauber, E., and E. Spolsky, 1986. *The Bounds of Interpretation: Linguistic Theory and Literary Text*. Stanford University Press, Palo Alto, CA.

Singer, M. 1984. *Man's Glassy Essence: Explorations in Semiotic Anthropology*. Indiana University Press, Bloomington.

Stock, B. 1983. *The Implications of Literacy: Written Language and Modes of Interpretation in the 11th and 12th Centuries*. Princeton University Press, Princeton, NJ.

Valdes, B. 1984. "Semiotic analysis as a basis for hermeneutic interpretation," A course presented at the 5th International Institute of Semiotic and Structrual Studies, Toronto.

Veyne, P. 1983. *Le Grecs croyaient-ils à leurs mythes?* Seuil, Paris.

PART II

The Foundations and Limits of Interpretation

On the Study of Habitat Structures

REFLECTIONS CONCERNING THE
ARCHAEOLOGY-ANTHROPOLOGY-SCIENCE TRANSITION

The profusion of the so-called "new archaeologies" is a sign of the present confusion concerning the epistemological status of the discipline. One cannot help being struck by the distance separating the constantly renewed theoretical considerations of certain archaeologists from the concrete practice of research, which never seems to borrow anything from the grand theoretical syntheses but nevertheless progresses empirically on the path of knowledge. Confronted with this situation we asked ourselves in our book *L'archéologie demain* (Gallay, 1986) whether the examination would not enable us to understand the empirical basis of archaeology better and thereby bring a greater coherence, a new-found lucidity, and consequently a greater efficiency to research.

In our view the understanding of reality, whatever its nature, must take into account certain constraints which are the same in all disciplines. It is worthwhile now and again to reflect on what makes the unity of what we call science, particularly in cases where the object of the research concerns phenomena developing through time and which are therefore subjected, like archaeology, to history. In this perspective we cannot fail to be struck by the common epistemological problems raised by disciplines such as cosmogony in astrophysics, plate tectonics in geology, or evolutionary biology in the life sciences.

The objectives of these disciplines are to be located at the junction of three specific bodies of knowledge, and it is essential that the articulation among the three be fully understood (fig. 1):

1. history, which is the reconstitution of scenarios of diachronic evolution, and which is founded on the basis of information that must remain forever incomplete;

2. the regularities that one can induce empirically by examining the scenarios of history based on one's overall intuition that our own world possesses a measure of coherence;

3. and the laws that to some extent permit us to understand a number of aspects of reality and to explain the presence of certain regularities even though these do not give us a grasp of specific historical developments as such.

Without going into all the problems raised by the integration within archaeology of historical (scenarios), anthropological (regularities), and scientific approaches, we would

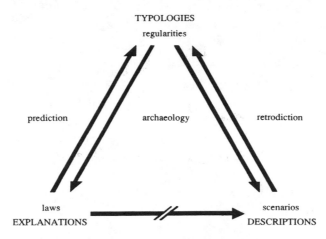

Figure 1. Central position of archaeology in relation to the three possible approaches to complex phenomena which present a temporal dimension. The understanding of particular mechanisms (laws) permits prediction of empirical regularities which, in turn, are used to complete our knowledge of historical scenarios according to the principle of retrodiction. However, direct "explanation" of historical phenomena remains unattainable.

like to insist above all on the third aspect of the question that we only touched on in our book and which raises the problem of the *status of explanation in archaeology*.

L'archéologie demain is situated almost entirely on the axis linking scenarios and regularities, which appeared to us at the time to totally exhaust the field covered by the practice of archaeology. It now seems possible to present more clearly, if not to resolve, the question of the presence and articulation of the third pole in the understanding of reality, that of the definition of laws.

The basis of our reflection stems from an article that L. R. Binford (1978) devotes to the ethnoarchaeological study of an Eskimo camp, and where this author very clearly presents, in a criticism of Yellen's (1977) study of !Kung campsites, the question of explanation in archaeology. In this context we too have had the opportunity to take up this same question during a recent study of the Tuareg campsites of the Hoggar (Gallay, in press). These three studies constitute the concrete material with which we illustrate our view.

1. The Theses Contained in *L'archéologie demain*

To begin with, I will sketch, without additional comment, the main theses developed in my book.

1. Human facts are not more complex than the facts of nature and in particular not more complex than the facts of life. There is no reason to place them in opposition one

to the other. It is therefore possible, at least at a certain level, to try to identify an epistemology common to all three.

2. Archaeological remains constitute just a small fraction of human reality. Even if we can grant them a certain representativeness it is nonetheless totally utopian to believe that the latter will enable the reconstitution of all the aspects of past realities. It is probable that the new archaeologies put forward these last years are animated by an unbounded ambition disproportionate to the documentation actually available.

3. It is not possible to develop a theory of archaeology that does not take into account living reality. Just as the study of pollen is based on the knowledge acquired in botany and cannot be conceived of as developing in isolation, so archaeology cannot be considered apart from ethnoarchaeology, the only discipline (along with experimental archaeology) able to ensure its own legitimacy and efficiency in its approach to the past. The present reflection therefore will be entirely situated in this actualist perspective.

4. A certain amount of overlap exists between the triple opposition scenarios/regularities/laws and the stages of archaeological research as distinguished by J.-C. Gardin (1979): description, typology, explanation. The presentation of the scenarios of history shows an eminently descriptive character. The perception of regularities is always the result of a typological approach. Finally, higher-order explanations often call on mechanisms whose importance will be recognized when we attempt to clarify the notion of law.

5. Scenarios of history must be considered as undetermined, a characteristic of any open system evolving through time. In this perspective the laws likely to be brought to light apply only to the regularities observed, and have the power of predicting only the latter. The laws discovered will therefore have an extremely limited application in the global understanding of history.

6. We posit a contrast between the power of laws to predict regularities and the power of regularities to "retrodict" scenarios. This last term, borrowed from Paul Veyne (1984), adequately denotes the procedure of the historian in reconstituting or restoring the past.

In a general way the position taken in *L'archéologie demain* was limited to the possible command of an empirical knowledge that described scenarios and brought to light regularities permitting a certain hold on reality. This "artisanal" knowledge, however, left wide open the question of explanation. This problem, which must now be dealt with, is the object of the present reflection.

2. Processing of Data. Investigating the Notion of Dependence

A few preliminary remarks should be sufficient to show that the identification of regularities is an everyday exercise in many disciplines. The empirical regularities described by archaeologists fit with the typologies defined by J.-C. Gardin (1979). They refer to the correspondences established between intrinsic characteristics (physical, geometrical, semeiological) and extrinsic characteristics (place, time, function) or the correspondences within these two big classes of phenomena. All the cases presented are in fact correlation phenomena, about which we should like to emphasize three facts:

1. These correlations can appear in three forms, and in the following order of descending accuracy:

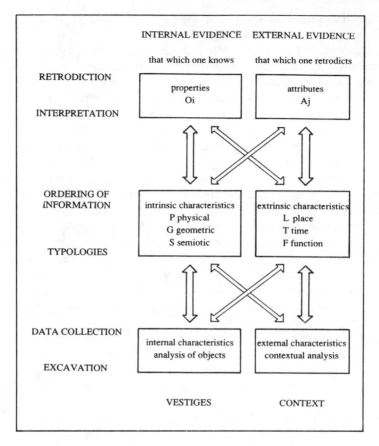

Figure 2. Summary diagram of the usual method of analysis which permits interpretation in archaeology. These interpretations are founded most often on principles of regularity and in no way constitute explanations in the scientific sense.

— Calculated correlations can be proposed for two types of continuous or discontinuous phenomena. We then try to specify the function y = f(x) linking two domains of reality.

— At the intermediate level of accuracy is a simple typology integrating two or several domains of reality, each one being the object of a partition. There is then correlation between classes belonging to distinct phenomena, for example between an x form of ceramic (intrinsic characteristic of a geometrical type), and a manufacturing shop situated in time and in space (extrinsic characteristic of time and place).

— Confronted with more discursive reasoning, we can finally try to specify the implicitly retained relationships by transcribing them in the following form: "if . . . then, or if **Pi** then **Pi + 1**."

These three forms are in fact the diversified expressions of the same empirical approach to the notion of regularities.

2. It is essential to remember that bringing to light a correlation between two phenomena does not necessarily provide the explanation of the phenomenon: "y function of x" does not imply that x is the cause of y. It is necessary therefore to make a fundamental distinction between "explanation" as presented in our book (see especially Gallay 1986 fig. 42, and fig. 2 of this article), which results from the exercise of "retrodiction," and explanation in the scientific sense, a notion to which we shall return later in this paper.

3. All types of correlations deserve to be drawn with care and precision.

It is advisable, therefore, especially in the field of ethnoarchaeology, to elevate, by all possible means, the methods used to form correlations. The principal steps toward this end should be:

3.1. the explanation of the modes of discursive reasoning, with the help of propositional networks of the types "If **Pi** then **Pi + 1**" (essentially a logicist analysis of the archaeological record as it applies to expert systems);

3.2. the setting up of a typological reference framework (establishing the concordance between logical classes); and

3.3. the establishment of calculated correlations, correlations that cannot be confused with the "*coefficients de vraisemblance*" used in certain expert systems (we shall return to these later in the paper).

This approach can be considered as a structural analysis because it tries to clarify the relationships linking the various components of a systemic reality.

To illustrate these points, a logicist analysis of an article by Lewis Binford (1978) gives us a good idea of what a structural analysis of a system, in this case a hunting stand, can be. The analysis of the article (where the distinctions made by the author are not always clear) permits us to distinguish three levels (fig. 3).

1. The camp can be considered as an open system where the following components interact:

— the activities present in the entire camp (B)
— the duration of occupancy of the camp (C)
— the number of camp occupants (D)
— the artifacts present (E)
— the various zones (surfaces) where the observed activities are carried out (F).

All these components are correlated to all of the others by links that we shall now explain.

2. The strategies of discard or deposition modes (G) which generate the observed spatial dispositions.

3. The spatial structure after abandonment, a simplified system, suspended in time and composed of only two components: the artifacts (H, remains) and the surfaces occupied by them (I).

One of Binford's first tasks was therefore to try to specify the relationships linking the various aspects of the reality in order to elucidate the systemic reality. He undertook as a first stage in the analysis a simple processing of data. It would seem, however, that the analysis should have gone beyond the simple bivariate correlations of the remains of a single camp. These data deserve a more extensive analysis, and the observations should

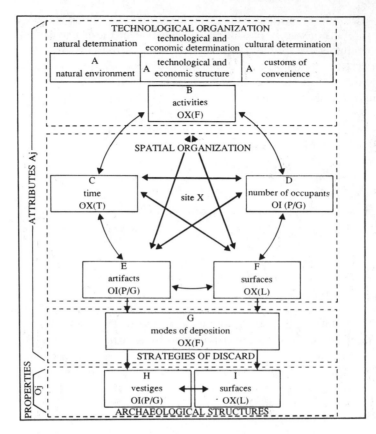

Figure 3. Reconstruction of the descriptive parameters used by Binford in his work with an Eskimo camp, the Mask site (1978). The ordering of the data is founded on the opposition between internal characteristics (OI) and external characteristics (OX). See Figure 2 for a complete list of the symbols employed.

have been extended to other camps. It is not apparent how science can progress through the study of a single case.

3. Explanation: Criticism of the Notion of Regularity

In the history of science it is commonplace to stress how one should be suspicious of perceived regularities and to point out the pitfalls of common sense. Uncritical acceptance and commonsense accounts of various regularities abound in archaeology, even when the facts are supported by knowledge acquired in the fields of ethnoarchaeology or experimental archaeology. The examination of the development of scientific knowledge shows on the other hand that the most profound theories are often counterintuitive. To go beyond the phenomenological approach to reality constitutes a requirement that should not be avoided by any scientific discipline, including archaeology.

To explain in science means to search for the mechanisms responsible for the observed phenomena, which amounts to asking how something works. Everyone knows how knowledge has progressed concerning the structure and functioning of the solar system:

1. Ptolemy's geocentric model reporting on empirical regularities (sunrise and sunset).

2. Copernicus's heliocentric model remaining at the descriptive stage.

3. Attempt at the introduction of descriptive laws, with Kepler.

4. First explanation of the phenomenon by Newton through the laws of gravitation and inertia.

5. Riemann explains gravitation by the gravitational fields.

6. Einstein integrates the preceding developments into the theory of relativity.

In our opinion this example provides a good illustration of how empirically perceived regularities can at first be based on a poor knowledge of reality (geocentric system), even when they have a power to predict reality (rising and setting of the sun), and justifies in our eyes the necessity to go beyond this empirical framework through a sound comprehension of the underlying mechanisms. In our opinion the passage from ordering the data to explanation implies a search for the mechanisms responsible for the observed regularities.

We believe the two ethnoarchaeological studies on the subject of hunting stands mentioned earlier will put our case in the proper perspective. Yellen (1977), in his work on sixteen Bushman camps, demonstrates that it is possible to establish the number of occupants and the duration of their occupancy through the analysis of the remains left on the ground. The integration of discrete variables—remains, surfaces occupied by the remains, duration of occupancy, number of occupants, etc.—provides predictive equations which permit, through analysis of the remains, a way of establishing the duration of occupancy and the number of occupants.

Binford (1978) attempts to apply these formulas to the Mask site, an Eskimo hunting stand, and demonstrates the inadequacy of Yellen's formulas in the case of the Eskimo. For Binford this situation is easily explained when one takes into account the mechanisms behind the introduction of artifacts to the sites; the economic systems of the two populations are totally different. The error therefore comes from the fact that Yellen seemed content to present unexplained correlations, and as a result has overestimated the general scope of his model. Unfortunately, Binford remains quite evasive as to the exact nature of the mechanisms he considers important for the creation of the structure of archaeological remains at the Mask site. Among those to which he seems to grant causal efficacy, we may mention the influence of the natural environment, the nature of the economic system, and, by reading between the lines, the comfort habits of the group (variables labeled "A" in the diagram, fig. 3).

Further thoughts on this question come from our study of the Tuareg campsites of the Hoggar (fig. 4.; see Gallay, in press). In this case we can in fact bring to bear on the observed spatial dispositions two important notions, that of an operational chain (fig 5) and that of body technics (fig. 6). These concepts permit us to specify the origin of behaviors and, what is more, to explain the spatial structures encountered.

The notion of operational chain was proposed by Leroi-Gourhan in his book *Le geste*

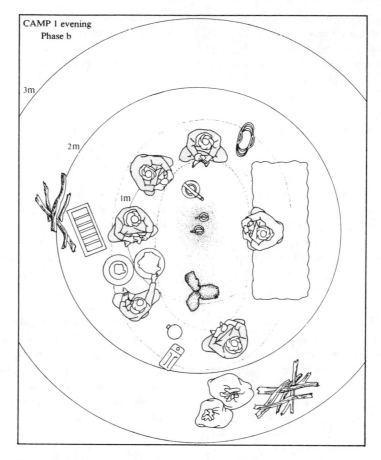

Figure 4. A Tuareg camp in the Hoggar (seating plan around the fire).
Several descriptive reconstructions of this type allow clarification of
spatial regularities present in the spatial distribution of artifacts.

et la parole (1964) and includes both the *motivations* that lie behind the development of
any kind of activity and the operations themselves (which can be compared to *automatic
programs* acquired through experience and education).

In the case at hand, these operational chains are placed solely within the framework
of consumption techniques (alimentation). To these mechanisms are added a certain
number of constraints linked to M. Mauss's notion of body technics (1936, taken up
again in 1960), and to comfort habits, which we shall not address here.

Without providing a final, all-encompassing explanation, this approach nevertheless
enables us to progress somewhat toward an understanding of the phenomena in question.
At the very least, it opens a path in that direction. Equally it offers the advantage of
disclosing certain links that might be established with neighboring disciplines, especially
comparative technology and human ethology.

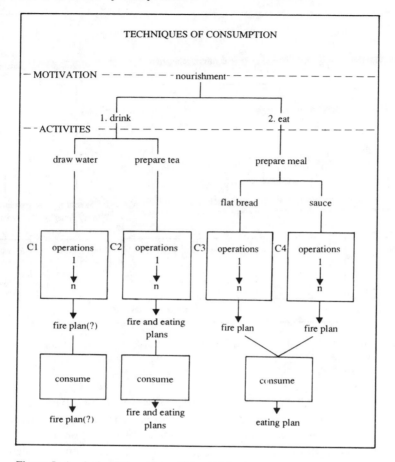

Figure 5. Analysis of the steps which explain the spatial distribution of artifacts in the Tuareg camps studied. The men seat themselves either in a circle around the fire (fire plan) or regroup a bit to the side to eat (eating plan).

4. Explanation: Notion of Plausibility

We know that the explanations provided by archaeologists are for the most part only plausible and not genuine (Gardin et al. 1981), and more often than not it is impossible to choose between several interpretations of the same phenomenon. We know that this situation is due to the limited nature of archaeological remains, a fact often emphasized in archaeological discourse. It is also due to a much more general epistemological situation which is encountered in many other disciplines. The interpretative problems that archaeologists try to resolve are in fact *inverse problems* of the type "What are the phenomena responsible for the observed situation?" and not of the type "What are the consequences and effects of such phenomena?"

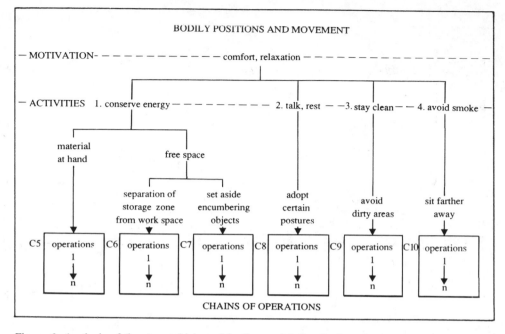

Figure 6. Analysis of the steps which explain the spatial distribution of artifacts in the Tuareg camps studied. The knowledge of bodily positions and movement allows a fuller understanding of the mechanisms in question.

We know that this kind of problem is particularly difficult to solve because it admits of several possible and sometimes conflicting solutions. One of the great deficiencies in contemporary archaeology is the failure to recognize this situation and the belief that one is only faced with direct problems implying univocal solutions. We can illustrate these difficulties by again referring to Binford's article. His analysis suggests that from the observation of remains (relationships between variables H and I) one can go back to the activities responsible for the observed structure (B variables), then further back to the underlying mechanisms (A variables); more precisely:

$$
\begin{array}{rl}
\text{from P0:} & \text{archaeological facts (remains and spaces)} \\
\text{through P1:} & \text{modes of disposal (strategies of abandonment)} \\
\text{P2:} & \text{relational structure OI (P/G)} - \text{OX (L/T)} \\
\text{and P3:} & \text{activities (A variables)} \\
\text{up to P4:} & \text{deterministic, functioning, mechanisms.}
\end{array}
$$

As one progresses from P0 through P4 the range of possibilities obviously increases at each stage until one reaches the point of provoking a totally inextricable situation. Researchers who work on explanations of discursive reasoning in archaeology, and who try to reformulate this reasoning in the form of expert systems, understand the situation all too well.

Anxious to take the particular circumstances of archaeological discourse into account, they attempted to introduce a *"coefficient de vraisemblance"* (CV) to show the degree of feasibility of "**Pi → Pi + 1**" type transitions identified in the studies they analyzed (Lagrange and Renaud 1983, 1984, 1987).

This coefficient, which varies from 0 to 1, can correspond to the following values:

CV = 1.0: rules of formal logic or semantic rules always true.
CV = 0.9: rules unanimously accepted by the experts.
CV = 0.7: the most credible rules.
CV = 0.5: acceptable rules.

These coefficients give rise to calculations which evaluate the credibility of the end product of the estimation. With each transition these coefficients can in fact be modified by weakening when one rises in the hierarchy of transitions toward high-level interpretations according to the formula: CV of the fact created by a rule (CV_{Pi+1}) = minimum of the CV of facts satisfying the conditions of rule (CV1) multiplied by the CV of the action which created the fact (CV2); that is to say:

$$CV_{Pi+1} = CV1 \times CV2.$$

We can also raise the value of a particular CV when one ends up with the same fact through different means. In this case CV1 is the CV of the fact already established, and CV2 is the CV of the new fact produced. The formula becomes:

$$CV_{Pi+1} = CV1 + CV2 - CV1 \times CV2.$$

Lagrange and Renaud rightly insist on the highly subjective nature of such notations, but they nevertheless recognize their practical use when wanting to "confirm" an interpretation (quotation marks are the authors'):

> Although the CVs only constitute, in our opinion, a "warning"—they particularly stress the weak points of an interpretative construction—, note that their efficient use in a process of cumulative estimation is a problem not to be ignored. (Lagrange and Renaud, 1987:217)

This approach deserves consideration because it goes beyond the simple problem of method and raises the whole question of the relevance of explanations.

The proposed procedure and precise calculations carried out on the coefficients give the impression, in fact, that one can measure the degree of probability of hypothesis, that is to say, one can measure the probability of truth.

Before the discussion proceeds much further, it is advisable to sum up the various interpretations that have been given of the concept of probability, regrouped here into five classes, based on notes in the author's possession, from a course given at the University of Geneva in 1986–1987 by Mario Bunge from the McGill University in Montreal:

Formal interpretation: the concept of probability is defined axiomatically.

Scientific interpretation: in the case of a phenomenon governed by random laws, probability measures the possibility for **x** to happen. The scientific interpretation of probability therefore implies that chance is an integral part of reality, which is more and more frequently accepted.

Therefore, the probability theories only apply to cases where the nature of the phenomena is sufficiently well known to enable us to establish the existence of chance.

Logical interpretation: probability measures the likelihood of a relationship existing between a hypothesis and an empirical datum. This conception, retained by Carnap in his theory of confirmation, is not justified, because there is no objective way to attribute probabilities to propositions; it has nevertheless given rise to a wealth of literature.

Subjectivistic interpretation: probability measures the extent of our knowledge. This interpretation is acceptable only if one is a supporter of an absolutely classical determinism. One then admits that chance does not exist and that it is only a product of our ignorance. Everything is determined. Imprecise observations can only come from the observer. This position must be rejected, however, if one admits that chance is a part of reality.

Frequentist interpretation: probability corresponds to the limit reached by relative frequencies when N tends toward infinity. Yet, one should note that the concept of frequency is distinct from the concept of probability. A frequency is defined from a finite number of measures within the framework of a well-determined sampling procedure. Frequency is therefore only an estimator (there are others) of the probability to which it is linked by the law of numbers: the deviation between relative frequency and corresponding probability tends toward zero when N tends toward infinity.

In our opinion, the *"coefficient of vraisemblance"* of Lagrange and Renaud is most closely related to the logical interpretation of the concept of probability. It is therefore not a concept open to a scientific approach, a point we think would be willingly recognized by the authors.

This evaluation, if correct, has an important consequence at the epistemological level. It shows that there is in fact no way to estimate the degree of truth of an interpretation objectively, outside of the possibilities of a direct confrontation with reality. This situation implies that the proposed interpretation is reflected univocally in the material facts, which is, as we have seen, far from being the case.

We come therefore to a fundamental question:

Where should we stop in the processes of successive inferences? Is it useful for knowledge to attain those interpretative levels where it is impossible to test the degree of truth in an objective manner?

We think that it seems more reasonable:

— to stop the inferential processes as soon as the number of alternatives present become too considerable. Consequently, only thoroughly mastered local problems should be tackled; and
— to limit oneself to those inferences which can be validated through the evidence of material facts.

It is difficult today to evaluate what the consequences would be if these attitudes were adopted as a part of the daily practice of archaeology, but we suspect that the reduction of our cognitive ambitions would be so great and the question about the foundations of the discipline so fundamental that very few scientists (including ourselves) would even dare, in the present cultural context, to continue working.

5. Arbitrary Cultural Choices

When one examines higher-level explanations that are capable of accounting for the mechanisms responsible for the observed regularities in the archaeological record, one most frequently finds that the phenomena to be explained have been linked to the context of their natural environment, to technoeconomics, or to human ethology. All are functionalist explanations, capable only of broad application. It is obvious that the cultural behaviors in question are equally determined by other factors, particularly ideological factors linked to the "conceptions of the world" of the societies that are the subject of study. Hodder (1982) advocates the primordial role of these factors in the construction of the cultural characteristics studied by the archaeologist at the same time that he wages intellectual warfare upon functional interpretations.

We can complete what has already been said on the question of explanations in archaeology by the following two remarks:

1. Obviously there is no question of ignoring the presence of "arbitrary" cultural choices linked to ideological factors and impregnating the totality of the various spheres of culture. On the other hand, we think that the "arbitrary" character (cf. the conception of the symbol with Lévi-Strauss) of these manifestations rules out any possibility of a scientific approach. This domain is not accessible to archaeological research. It lies in the sublunary realm in the sense given to this term by Veyne (1984).

2. Nevertheless, one can question whether certain ideological features do present certain functional components susceptible to being understood. Testart's work (1986) on the role of the ideology of blood in the sexual division of labor among the "hunter-gatherers" opens up horizons in this perspective which are worth exploring.

When we try to interpret the spatial dispositions observed in the Tuareg camps through certain technological chains and comfort habits of the group, we do not deny the presence of ideological factors. We are simply compelled to consider them as "noise" of unknown intensity distorting the phenomena that we wish to bring to light.

6. Conclusions

In concentrating on the problem of explanation in archaeology, we have attempted to demonstrate the following:

1. that the analysis of regularities implies a structural approach where all relationships between variables must be precisely specified;

2. that there is no way of testing the degree of truth of an explanation beyond searching for an univocal relationship between the proposed hypothesis and a material fact susceptible of being brought to light by archaeology;

3. that, given this situation, it is advisable to limit our ambitions drastically, to only those hypotheses capable of supporting a validation of this nature;

4. that it is necessary, through ethnoarchaeology and experimental archaeology, to try to discover the mechanisms that lie at the origin of observed regularities; and

5. that, consequently, the only realistic high-level interpretations are those of a functionalist type, and that it is out of the question to set up a so-called symbolic archaeology if one admits the arbitrary nature of the "signifying-signified" relationship.

Consequently, structural and symbolic approaches in archaeology entail the following concerns.

The Notion of Structure

The notion of structure pertains to the notion of system. In our world, as it happens, most phenomena are systemic. We are dealing therefore with banalities. Any analysis of reality, whatever the domain, implies analysis of the correlations between variables as a first step toward understanding the world around us. In calling itself structural, archaeology has not invented anything new. We like to think that it is only placing itself within an analytical framework whose efficiency has been tested for a long time in other fields of science.

The Notion of Symbol

If by symbols we mean the ideological bases governing certain aspects of the cultures studied, and if these symbols are considered to be arbitrary, then we are getting away from the only domain susceptible of being reasonably mastered by archaeologists. If, on the contrary, symbols are the languages elaborated by the observers to understand and master reality, then we find ourselves up against a banality as we did with the notion of structure, since any comprehension of a phenomenon implies the elaboration of a language which is capable of mastering it.

In conclusion, we do not see what the novelty and specificity of a so-called structural and symbolic archaeology could possibly be. These terms, and what they imply, seem useless as soon as one endeavors to place archaeology in the context of other scientific disciplines centered on the study of phenomena developing through time.

REFERENCES

Binford, L. R. 1978. "Dimensional analysis of behavior and site structure: Learning from an Eskimo hunting stand," *American Antiquity* **43,** 330–361.

Gallay, A. 1986. *L'archéologie demain*. Belfond, Paris.

———in press. "Vivre autour du feu," *Recherches d'une problématique d'analyse archéologique*. Bulletin du Centre Genevois d'Anthropologie, 1.

Gardin, J.-C. 1979. *Une archéologie théorique*. Hachette, Paris.

Gardin, J.-C., M.-S. Lagrange, J.-M. Martin, J. Molino, and J. Natali 1981. *La logique du plausible. Essais d'épistémologie pratique*. Maison des Sciences de l'Homme, Paris.

Gardin, J.-C., O. Guillaume, P. Q. Herman, A. Hesnard, M.-S. Lagrange, M. Renaud, E. Zadora-Rio 1987. *Systèmes experts et sciences humaines; le cas de l'archéologie*. Eyrolles, Paris.

Hodder, I. 1982. "Theoretical archaeology: A reactionary view," in I. Hodder (ed.), *Symbolic and Structural Archaeology*, pp. 1–16. Cambridge University Press, Cambridge.

Lagrange, M.-S., and M. Renaud 1983. *Simulation du raisonnement archéologique au moyen d'un système expert: le système Snark*. Ecole européenne "Informatique et mathématiques appliquées en archéologie" (Montpellier, July 1983). Document dactylographié.

———1984. *Superikon. Un essai de cumul de six expertises en icongraphie: érudition ou trivialité?* C.N.R.S. (document de travail No 6), Paris.

———1987. "Cas No 6: Superikon, essai de cumul de six expertises en iconographie," in J.-C. Gardin, et al., *Systèmes experts et sciences humaines*, pp. 191–229. Eyrolles, Paris.

Leroi-Gourhan, A. 1964–1965. *Le geste et la parole*. Albin Michel, Paris.

Mauss, M. 1936. "Les techniques du corps," in M. Mauss 1960, *Sociologie et anthropologie*, pp. 363–386. Presses Universitaires du France, Paris.

Testart, A. 1986. *Essai sur les fondements de la division sexuelle du travail chez les chasseurs-cueilleurs*. Ecole des Hautes Etudes en sciences sociales (Cahiers de l'Homme, NS 25), Paris.

Veyne, P. 1977. *Comment on écrit l'histoire*. Seuil, Paris.

———1984. *Writing History*. M. Moore-Rinvolucri (tr.). Wesleyan University Press, Middletown, CT.

Yellen, J. E. 1977. *Archaeological Approaches to the Present; Models for Reconstructing the Past*. Academic Press, New York.

Finding Symbols in History

Some notoriously demanding passages of Wittgenstein's *Philosophical Investigations* (1968) raise a skeptical puzzle any theories or histories of human symbol-making will ignore at their peril. Stated in one of its strongest forms (and not worrying about Wittgenstein's own exact sense), it is this: although some overt behavior may represent (e.g., denote or depict) something to you and me, having a conventional 'meaning' for us in a 'language' we share, there is no guarantee that, and no final test to determine whether, that same overt behavior—as we could ever perceive and study it—'means' the same thing, or anything at all, to someone else. For example, you and I might represent something by the way in which we blink our eyes and grunt; however, someone else is just blinking and grunting. Or, to take Kripke's example (1982:8–9), by writing the mark/sign ' + ' you and I 'mean' the addition function or 'plus,' but someone else by the same sign ' + ' actually means something else, say, 'quus,' a function in which x quus y = x plus y, if x, y are less than 57, but otherwise (always) = 5. Obviously you and I could not even tell that our 'rule' for using ' + ' diverges from his in any (qu)adding of integers less than 57; we do not detect that his (or our?) rule is 'bent' (Blackburn 1984). We can imagine other, perhaps even more extreme, examples in which no possible test we could ever make would ever settle the possibility that our practices diverge or, more profoundly, that one of us actually lacks 'practice' altogether (see further Davis n.d.).

In this short chapter I cannot explore all the implications of the skeptical puzzle (see Kripke 1982) for art history and the anthropology or archaeology of symbols. For my purposes, I will use it to assert that no empirical or experimental scrutiny of a behavior (like grunting) or a morphology (like a mark) as it were 'on the ground' or 'in front of our noses' can definitively establish that it is a sign (symbol, representation) and/or what its referent might be for its producer. Because it looks like a picture does not mean it is; because it seems to depict my dog does not mean it does. We need to know something further about it. I will interweave a specific form of the skeptical puzzle with a specific kind of answer or avoidance maneuver. However, I hope it will be obvious that my strategy, suitably rewritten, could be made fully general; it can be phrased for any symbols.

Twenty-five thousand or more years ago, for the first time someone entered the cave of Gargas, a small self-contained cavern close to the 700m elevation near the present-day village of Aventignan in the French Pyrenees. Within 50m of the entrance, the cave became fairly dark, and at 100m, making a turn to the left, completely so; our visitor lighted his way with oil or fat burning in a stone lamp. Fortunately the cave was smooth and dry, though from time to time animals had inhabited it. The sharp-clawed cave bear had even scratched on its walls. Although our visitor may have known other caves in the region, we do not know what purposes animated his first visit to Gargas. But one of his actions—and, of course, perhaps one of his purposes—was to draw, or, more precisely, to make marks (Leroi-Gourhan 1967:307–308, Barrière 1976, 1984).

Oozing from hidden fissures, water carrying fine silts of calcium carbonate had deposited panels of moist *Montmilch* on many surfaces of the cave. With his fingers together, our visitor gouged straight and curving traces, or with one finger only traced somewhat more complicated zigzags and swirls (Barrière 1976). We cannot say exactly how long this activity was kept up—perhaps for generations (the fundamental general study is Bednarik 1986). Finally someone traced a simple line in the minimal form of a bison's forequarters—its horns, head, and muzzle (e.g., Barrière 1976:I, 151, for such images). Later the whole outline was drawn, including details of eyes, fetlocks, hooves, and incised with a sharp stone on the harder surfaces of the cave walls. Horses, reindeer, various species of antelope, and other animals were depicted with increasing differentiation, detail, and modulation, and in individually recognizable styles. At least for this people in this part of the world, about 20,000 B.C., image making had been born.

It is the ring of inevitability in this narrative I wish to subvert—or, more exactly, its sufficiency in helping us to understand what it could be for image making to be born. For although I accept that some narrative of the crystallization of symbolic technologies and conventions underwrites the history of all arts, and by some is regarded as the history of art, the status of these 'first' images in traditions is puzzling.

I must make the obvious reminder that the cave of Gargas is not the origin of image making. It is being used here as one example of how image making originates. Images were certainly made elsewhere and perhaps earlier, like the simple but seemingly unmistakable depictions of animals on portable limestone blocks from rock shelters in the Périgord, the earliest dated to about 30,000 B.C. (Delluc and Delluc 1978), or other animal figures painted on stone from the Apollo XI Cave in Namibia, dated at the earliest to about 24,000 B.C. (Lewis-Williams 1983: figs. 42–43; Willcox 1984:231–237). We cannot know whether images were made by earlier hominids in a perishable medium, like bark painting or sand drawing. In the preserved media, *Homo sapiens neanderthalensis* produced nonfigurative graphics (e.g., Marshack 1976), and on the present view, image making is associated with the technologically 'modern' Upper Paleolithic culture of *H. sapiens sapiens*. In fact, *sapiens sapiens* has often been defined as just that creature which makes images and uses other complex symbol systems (Preziosi 1982, Davis 1986). But for our purposes, the whole question of the absolutely 'first' image in chronological terms is a red herring.

Although they were broadly related to and descended from earlier Upper Paleolithic people, there is no direct evidence that the people of Gargas had learned about earlier images. (However, they did make other kinds of images; the wall engravings are in part 'dated' by a tendentious association with one figure on incised plaquettes found in the cave.) Theoretically, a feral child or a Robinson Crusoe, completely cut off from society or tradition, or both, could make images (Davis n.d.); theoretically, image making in-augurates time and time again in history. Though Gargas is a useful example, the same general puzzles arise for any real inaugural image making, whenever and wherever we find it archaeologically.

For an inaugural image, our problem is not external—the problem of identifying its stylistic affiliations or formal sources—but rather internal. Since he had never seen one before, how did the first image maker know how to make an image? By hypothesis, no one had told him what they are or how they can be used.

Now in our initial narrative, the visitor to the cave simply began tracing lines re-sembling the silhouettes of bison, horses, and other creatures. But this description fails to come to grips with two issues. First, as a projection of a three-dimensional object, a two-dimensional visual display is ambiguous. According to any standard of projective fidelity, it can correctly represent any number of different real objects (Hagen 1986). What, then, accounts for the particular judgment that, for example, a square depicts a cube and not some other kind of six-sided object? (This is the kind of question the skeptical puzzle would dramatize.) Second, that a visual display happens to resemble some real object does not guarantee it depicts that object. (The skeptical puzzle also worries this point.) Shadows and mirror 'images' resemble the objects which produce them, but are not necessarily representations of those objects. All kinds of patterns, like Leonardo's mottled wall, resemble various objects fortuitously. (On the vexed question of resemblance-in-representation, see variously Goodman 1976, ch. 1; Manns 1971; Tversky and Gati 1978.) How is it, then, that the simple curves in the cave of Gargas, resembling animal profiles (as well as resembling many other things), were also apparently taken to stand for just those aspects of animals? How is it, in other words, that we could recognize them as images?

The obvious answer to both questions is that the marks in Gargas, whatever they may look like to us, were (or were not) produced as depictions of particular objects. However, this answer provokes a vicious regress. It seems to imply that the image maker already knows what an image is and how to produce it. Where was this knowledge acquired? Unqualified, this 'conventionalist' answer cannot apply to the first image maker (see further Davis 1987, and for a potential solution to the paradoxes and regresses of conventionalism, Lewis 1967).

Let us look more carefully at what was happening in Gargas. Nondepictional tracing—the 'digital flutings' and scribbles made with one or more fingers in the soft *Montmilch*—accumulated on the walls, covering long panels. The tracing has internal rhythms of its own. Although a good deal more should be said about it, for our purposes some fraction of it results in marks which can be seen as certain objects—like panels of digital tracing thought by some observers to contain animal forms (e.g., Barrière 1976: I, 136, pls. 23, 35, 39). Similar complex and suggestive marking can be found in other archaeological contexts, for instance, among the incised blocks of the Périgord (Delluc and Delluc 1978, 1985), and, of course, in the scribbling of simians (e.g., Schiller 1951; Morris 1961; Smith 1973; see generally Davis 1986, 1987). That such marks in some contexts can be mistaken for real things derives directly from the fact that the perceptual system sometimes arrives at mistaken interpretations of the information it picks up in reflected light (Gibson

1979; Marr 1982); although it is in itself a complex phenomenon, for our purposes we can take 'seeing-as' to be an 'automatic' (autonomous) operation of the visual system responding to perceptual ambiguity (Wilkerson 1973a, 1973b; Wollheim 1980: 205–226; Budd 1986).

Like any psychological event, if it has no overt manifestations seeing-as is inaccessible to direct observation. Whether it occurred ten seconds or ten thousand years ago, it is, as it were, 'outside' history—that is, the material evidence of overt human behavior as it is preserved in a fragmentary way in the archaeological record of actions performed and things made. Although it took place in history, seeing-as often has no history.

Recall now that just because someone momentarily sees a mark as an object is not enough for it to depict that object. In the flickering semidarkness, our visitor to the cave may have momentarily mistaken some of the marks—whether made by him or anyone else—as animal forms, but they were not necessarily thereby representations of animals.

Still, if he looked again our visitor could at least learn that what he took to be something else is just and only a mark, morphologically indiscernible as it might be from any of the marks he (or anyone else) had been making all along, for whatever purpose or lack of purpose. In this, he would already learn that he can make the mark not just and only as a mark but also as a mark which can be seen as an object. If and when he remakes that or that kind of mark for seeing-as—knowing it is just a mark but interested in its object-resembling properties—then he is making an image (see in detail Davis n.d.). Mark becomes remark. And insofar as this marking and remarking is a kind of making and remaking, it has a history: we can find it archaeologically.

We will never know, then, whether many of the tracings in Gargas were ever seen as objects. Their recognizability to us as images (or not) is—as the skeptical puzzle reminds us—no evidence one way or another; our seeing-as may have nothing to do with someone else's. Furthermore, we do not even know why the marks, seen-as or not, were being made in the first place—perhaps, as Barrière (1976) and many others have supposed, merely as 'spontaneous graffitomania' (see Bednarik 1986).

But for some tracings, we can observe the continual replication of an object-resembling mark. At Gargas, drawn vertically, a double S-curve can be seen as the curving horns, forehead and muzzle, and neck of a bison. Drawn horizontally, the same curve can be seen as the horns, humped back, and rising tail or descending hindquarters (e.g., Barrière 1976: I, fig. 43, nos. 10, 11). Gargas exhibits a good deal of replication and variation of this particular form. The curves are repeated in the whole or in part of their length to give two horns; two curves are placed at angles to each other to produce a half- or two-thirds-complete outline; the final flips of each curve can be neatly fitted or superimposed; fingerholes establish an eye; a few strokes create legs or tail; the whole contour may be finished off by a second horizontal (ventral) curve below the first (dorsal) one (Davis 1987: fig. 10). As marks, these elaborations are indiscernible from what had already appeared in (hypothetically) nondepictional or even nonsemantic tracing. We can infer that they were in fact being made for seeing-as—i.e., as images—because in replication the object-resembling properties were preserved in the transition from surface to surface or the translation from one tool and medium to another. (Similarly, we could infer they were being made as 'notations' if other kinds of properties, like the discreteness and disjunction of 'characters,' were held constant in use and reuse, in replications; see Marshack 1977, 1984.) But, to reiterate, the very first mark in this and the other replicatory sequences was not made as an image but only as a mark.

Although this analysis solves the logical paradox of regress, it has potentially troublesome implications. Because of the possibility of ambiguity, fortuitous resemblance, and the variability of seeing-as, no amount of study of the visual properties of a mark can definitively tell us whether it is an image and precisely what it is an image of. Despite the apparently bizarre consequences of this result (surely we just know that the Sistine Chapel paintings are images—otherwise what in the world could they be doing up there?), an interpreter must know the whole chain of replication and variation of all the properties of the mark right back to the initial moment of seeing-as in his or in someone else's 'psychological' experience. For depiction, this claim is a close (but not exact) parallel for so-called 'causal' or 'historical' theories of the reference of proper names and natural kind terms (Putnam 1975; Schwartz 1977; Evans 1979; Kripke 1980; Devitt 1982); in the successful production and perception of symbolic reference, an interpreter does not so much have a correct and complete 'description for' or 'belief about' a sign (Russell 1956 is the *locus classicus*) as a more or less hazy understanding of its history of first application ('baptism'), transmission, and change. If I may hideously oversimplify (see Davis n.d.), he does not so much decipher as excavate a language. The point, of course, applies to someone within or outside a particular community of language users or sign makers.

Now sometimes we can study this whole closed cycle of production, from 'baptism' on, in an experimental setting—with simians in a laboratory, infants in a playpen, or draftsmen in a workshop. Most important, we can observe ourselves at work: we can see our own images (notations, etc.) for what they are images (notations) of, irrespective of someone else's ability to pick this up. Otherwise, however, it will be difficult to identify the sequence and structure of the relevant chains of replication.

For one thing, each variant in a chain is necessarily separated from preceding and following variants by some span of space or lag of time. An interpreter's archaeological survey of sign production has to be extremely comprehensive to pick them all up. For another, some properties of the morphology are reproduced in succeeding variants, often becoming inextricably incorporated (drawn over or built into the latest variant), while others, not reproduced, are abandoned or destroyed. We are left archaeologically with a complex morphology, presenting itself as a single unitary 'artifact,' which is simultaneously a selection and palimpsest of many variations—and the garbage of the studio contains a good deal of what we would like to know.

It is the task of so-called 'archaeopsychology' or 'paleosemiotics' to sort out these relations: archaeopsychology becomes the interpretations of both dimensions of the Artifact-Sign, and especially of the interrelation or identity of artifactuality and representationality, on the basis of formal theories about this interrelation and pursuing direct or indirect evidence for it in well-defined cultural and historical contexts. Although it is obvious that this task requires rigorously formulated and in some manner or other empirically or theoretically defensible theories about both representation (e.g., semiosis; interpretation; reference) and artifactuality (e.g., morphology; style; sequence and distribution), it will be enormously complex; admitting both evolutionary and cultural-relativistic premises, perhaps no fully general assertions will be possible.

At any rate, at Gargas and in other unusual art historical or archaeological cases, we can sometimes circumvent the immediate difficulties. Because the paleolithic engraver was removing matter from a surface rather than adding to it, he could not easily change or erase his work; it tends to accumulate in one place. We can therefore watch a chain of replications forming as a palimpsest with an internal 'stratigraphy' all the way back to the initial variation of a nondepictional trace. For instance, in the deepest chamber of Gargas, the Panel of the Great Bull (Barrière 1976: II, pl. 56 etc.) exhibits many complete and incomplete animal forms superimposed on one another. Individual lines are reused to establish new images. Several images can share a single line. (We would not predict such morphologies if superimposition were 'random,' i.e., with the later engraver taking no account of the work of the earlier.) A number of more complete forms can be resolved, but some seem to be arrested in replicatory development—an elk with a subtly modulated contour; horses with forehead or muzzle apparently attempted twice, or redrawn by a later artist; two bison; a heavily worked ibex with outline deeply scraped and interior filled in, with three 'versions' of its head; and the Great Bull himself, created partly by a carved line and partly by a much finer incised line, perhaps preliminary to heavier cutting (see in detail Davis n.d.:ch. 1, sect. 8, for 'chains of replication' in Aurignacian and pre-Magdalenian portable and parietal graphics).

Replication is simply the sequential production of similar artifacts substitutable for one another in some specific context of use (Davis n.d.). The general notion of a chain of replications, somewhat parallel to linguistic philosophers' concept of a 'history of reference' (Kripke 1980:95) or 'designation chain' (Devitt 1982), goes by various names already in art history and archaeology. For example, Kubler (1962) called it a 'form class,' descending from a 'prime object,' an artifact with no formal antecedents. It is perhaps equivalent to what some art historians mean by style, a set of similarities among artifacts explained by their common historical descent (Davis 1990), although style encompasses artifacts which do not represent (reference necessarily has a style, but not vice versa) (Davis n.d.:ch. 2). A variety of sophisticated formal, comparative, and statistical methods are required to understand these chains, classes, or sets (e.g., Sneath and Sokal 1973; Clarke 1978; Hennig 1979).

Often we assume, circularly, that some property of a visual display does or should signify something, perhaps because similar-looking properties in other displays do. We make up a psychological event—a perceptual episode, a belief or intention or rule—to account for it. But as the possibility of ambiguity and of fortuitous resemblance entails, we cannot know in advance which property of the display was seen as something else and what this something exactly was. On my analysis, depiction occurs within a chain of replications. Therefore the interpretation of any image is necessarily historical: it requires that the interpreter know how the mark/sign was produced and its various properties seen/interpreted. Surely in a sense this is good news for art history: it provides us with a strictly logical justification for the very existence of art history itself.

However, there is bad news built in here. the epistemic conditions for interpretability are extremely strict, and the evidence generally poor. Without full archaeological knowledge of its history, the interpreter cannot be certain what a mark signifies. More worrying still, the initial moment of seeing-as itself, investing the whole chain with that particular significance, as a psychological event is actually inaccessible to direct archaeological investigation. It can only be reconstructed inferentially as that perceptual episode (whether or not it is our episode or recognizable to us) which would best explain the whole package of formal and contextual properties of the chain.

Emile Durkheim complained that we are in trouble whenever we have to offer a psychological explanation of anything—and indeed there has been a tendency in modern anthropology to see 'rules' or 'codes' of interpretation as somehow suprapsychological, in 'the culture' or some other reified supraindividual entity. Without worrying the metapsychological questions, in ordinary social situations people do readily infer or learn the relevant archaeological knowledge about making marks—just as they learn how the words of a language have been and are to be used. Images are labeled; their properties are pointed out; particular denotations and connotations are socially discussed. Supposedly this knowledge becomes conventional or institutional. The social group takes it for granted that certain properties of a visual display are to be interpreted in a certain way; 'rules' and 'codes' as it were come to replace actual historical understanding and investigation. As art historians, our task is simply to reconstruct that local common knowledge about images. One strand in the so-called social history of art—although not explicitly Durkheimian—has set out to do just that (although with literally hundreds of versions, the *locus classicus* is still Baxandall 1972).

I have been using the example of a paleolithic cave in part to suggest that if conventional knowledge about images and the archaeology of their production is vastly removed from us, then our interpretative task is just that much harder and the results that much less complete. Despite intriguing speculation (e.g., Leroi-Gourhan 1967, Conkey 1983), we really have no idea exactly in what sense the cave drawings and paintings represented aspects of their makers' world. The images of folk, 'outsider,' or 'eccentric' artists, of other cultural marginals, or of the mad are similarly detached, in varying degrees, from conventional routines of interpretation; their significance is equally hard to reconstruct (I do not claim, of course, that their significance is like that of prehistoric art). But these are platitudes, pointing only to the practical limitations of art historical or other 'archaeological' evidence. Insofar as such images are images at all, they are part of a chain of replications; in theory, they have some history establishing some signification. But I have been making a stronger claim. With a first image, wherever and whenever we find it, there is no preexisting history of replication to anchor it, no history of interpretation in which it is deciphered. It is as it were a novel remark in an unknown language. (Although I will not develop the point, it seems to me that all accounts of images in a 'tradition,' which in a way postpone the 'diachronic' problem of origins for a 'synchronic' or 'structural' analysis, are exposed to the skeptical puzzle and concomitant difficulties of conventionalism; recent art historical writing—e.g., Sauerländer 1983, Clark 1985—problematizes the notion of 'tradition' or 'art history.')

Paleolithic images on portable blocks or cave walls may be the first images in some absolute chronological sense, but this is inessential to the argument. Throughout history, chains of replication are continuously inaugurated in novel episodes of seeing-as. Many of these chains are firmly embedded in existing practices, guided by rules like those in the modern West for perspective projection. These are undoubted realities of social life—about the power of institutions—to be explained in a variety of ways. But there is no logical restriction on when and where seeing-as will take place—no restrictions on the mark or which object-resembling properties can be replicated, or even, of course, on how resemblance itself is judged. Wherever and whenever people make marks, or work matter in any way, a visual form may inaugurally take on semantic significance of any kind.

Let us put together our results. Art historians often assume that images are readily recognizable as such, somehow in advance of art historical research on and interpretation of them. However, it is a kind of art history—the archaeology of replication—which establishes them as images in the first place. To understand what an image signifies, an interpreter must know exactly in what way the properties of a visual display were produced for seeing-as. Because of the possibility of ambiguity and of fortuitous resemblance, no amount of inspecting the display itself, 'empirically' recording its 'attributes,' can possibly provide this information. The interpreter must have what I called 'archaeological' knowledge about the replication of seeing-as. Such knowledge is often coordinated conventionally and passed on institutionally, although this is hardly even a reliable generality and there are no promises about how easy it will be to reconstruct any part of the history. It might be enough to determine that the physical properties and context of the artifact (its apparent morphology, distribution, mode of manufacture, deposition, or preservation, etc.) are most compellingly and comprehensively explained by supposing that it is a sign and/or a sign with such-and-such a representational value. Of course, without even knowing the precise meaning of the sign, we can still make useful, pointed statements, or collect information, about the 'archaeological' place of apparently representational activity in a society—e.g., about its chronology, frequency, distribution, socioeconomic or other behavioral correlates, and so forth. But however it is codified by its users or reconstructed by us, knowledge about images is inaugurally anchored in a psychological event 'outside,' the moment of taking a mark for something in the world, forever inaccessible to us archaeologically.

I do not feel threatened by this result and hope for an archaeology vigorously embracing rather than avoiding it. By phrasing the problems of art history or an anthropology of symbols as I have done here, I am merely questioning a conception of art history as a fully empirical enterprise—the usual positivism awkwardly accompanying a final mysticism. We can certainly gather the facts about the making of marks, and image making is something people do with the marks they have made; the more empirical precision about both, the better. But when mark first becomes image, when a mark remarks, there is no fact of the matter to be located archaeologically.

What kind of history or archaeology is it that could never dig up and display its central event? It is, I think, a history which necessarily offers not only the facts about its objects but also a theory about itself—a systematic organizing hypothesis, like those of Darwin or Freud, about how the present inherits its form from the past and why the past is—or is not—coherent. On my account, symbolic meaning is a particular function of how the present inherits its forms—it is a form of the archaeological coherence of making. 'Seeing as' and 'replication' might remind us in various ways of mutation and selection or trauma and repetition. My own hunch is that this hypothesis, whatever its final form, will arise for art history from the study of perception and visual cognition, and for other sign systems from the study of other cognitive domains. Be that as it may, symbols without history are a puzzle only when history is without theory.

Acknowledgments: The ideas presented here have undergone several formulations. Two were presented at the World Archaeological Congress, Southampton, 1986, and the Annual Meeting of the College Art Association, Boston, 1987; Peter Ucko was a particularly helpful critic of that material, and I thank Unwin Hyman for permission to use material from the Southampton paper. At the NSF/CNRS symposium, comments by Mark Leone, Dan Sperber, and others were crucial in helping me modify some of my earlier phrasings.

REFERENCES

Barrière, C. 1976. *L'art pariétal paléolithique de la grotte de Gargas*. British Archaeological Reports, BAR Supplementary Volume 14 (2 vols.), Oxford.
———1984. "Gargas," in A. Leroi-Gourhan (ed.), *L'art des cavernes: Atlas des grottes ornées paléolithiques françaises*, pp. 514–522. Imprimerie Nationale, Paris.
Baxandall, M. 1972. *Painting and Experience in Fifteenth Century Italy: A Primer in the Social History of Pictorial Style*. Clarendon Press, Oxford.
Bednarik, R. J. 1986. "Parietal finger markings in Europe and Australia," *Rock Art Research* **3**, 30–61.
Blackburn, S. 1984. *Spreading the Word: Groundings in the Philosophy of Language*. Clarendon Press, Oxford.
Budd, M. 1986. "Wittgenstein on seeing aspects," *Mind* **96**, 1–17.
Clark, T. J. 1985. *The Painting of Modern Life: Paris in the Art of Manet and His Followers*. Knopf, New York.
Clarke, D. 1978. *Analytical Archaeology*, 2nd ed. Columbia University Press, New York.
Conkey, M. W. 1983. "On the origins of Paleolithic art: A review and some critical thoughts," in E. Trinkaus (ed.), *The Mousterian Legacy: Human Biocultural Change in the Upper Pleistocene*, pp. 201–227. British Archaeological Reports, BAR International Series 164, Oxford.
Davis, W. 1986. "The origins of image making," *Current Anthropology* **27**, 193–215.
———1987. "Replication and depiction in Paleolithic art," *Representations* **19**, 109–44.
———1990. "Style and history in art history," in M. W. Conkey and C. Hastorf (eds.), *The Uses of Style in Archaeology*. Cambridge University Press, Cambridge.
———n.d. *Seeing Through the Culture: The Possibility of the History of Art*. In preparation.
Delluc, B., and G. Delluc 1978. "Les manifestations graphiques Aurignaciennes sur support rocheux des environs des Eyzies (Dordogne)," *Gallia Préhistoire* **21**, 213–438.
———1985. "De l'empreinte au signe," *Dossiers de l'archéologie* **90**, 56–62.
Devitt, M. 1982. *Designation*. Columbia University Press, New York.
Evans, G. 1979. *Varieties of Reference*. Clarendon, Oxford.
Gibson, J. J. 1979. *The Ecological Theory of Perception*. Houghton Mifflin, Boston.
Goodman, N. 1976. *Languages of Art: An Approach to the Theory of Symbols*, 2nd ed. Hackett, Indianapolis, IN.
Hagen, M. 1986. *Varieties of Realism*. Cambridge University Press, Cambridge.
Hennig, W. 1979. *Phylogenetic Systematics*. D. D. Davis and R. Zangerl (tr.). University of Illinois Press, Urbana.
Kripke, S. 1980. *Naming and Necessity*, 2nd ed. Harvard University Press, Cambridge, MA.

———1982. *Wittgenstein on Rules and Private Language*. Harvard University Press, Cambridge, MA.

Kubler, G. 1962. *The Shape of Time: Remarks on the History of Things*. Yale University Press, New Haven, CT.

Leroi-Gourhan, A. 1967. *Treasures of Prehistoric Art*. N. Guterman (tr.). Abrams, New York.

Lewis, D. 1967. *Convention: A Philosophic Study*. Harvard University Press, Cambridge, MA.

Lewis-Williams, J. D. 1983. *The Rock Art of Southern Africa*. Cambridge University Press, Cambridge.

Manns, J. W. 1971. "Representation, relativism, and resemblance," *Journal of Aesthetics and Art Criticism* **11,** 281–287.

Marr, D. 1982. *Vision: A Computational Investigation into the Human Representation and Processing of Visual Information*. Freeman, San Francisco.

Marshack, A. 1976. "Some implications of the Paleolithic symbolic evidence for the origin of language," *Current Anthropology* **17,** 274–82.

———1977. "The meander as a system: The analysis and recognition of iconographic units in Upper Paleolithic compositions," in P. J. Ucko (ed.), *Form in Indigenous Art*, pp. 286–317. Australian Institute of Aboriginal Studies, Canberra.

———1984. "Concepts théoriques conduisant à de nouvelles méthodes analytiques, de nouveaux procédés de recherche et catégories de données," *L'Anthropologie* **88,** 85–100.

Morris, D. 1961. *The Biology of Art: A Study of the Picture-Making Behaviour of the Great Apes and Its Relationship to Human Art*. Knopf, New York.

Preziosi, D. 1982. "Constru(ct)ing the origins of art," *Art Journal* **42,** 320–325.

Putnam, H. 1975. "The meaning of 'meaning,' " in *Mind, Language, and Reality: Philosophical Papers II*. Cambridge University Press, Cambridge.

Russell, B. 1956. *Logic and Knowledge*, R. C. Marsh (ed.). Allen & Unwin, London.

Sauerländer, W. 1983. "From stilus to style: Reflections on the fate of a notion," *Art History* **6,** 253–270.

Schiller, P. 1951. "Figural preferences in the drawings of a chimpanzee," *Journal of Comparative and Physiological Psychology* **44,** 101–111.

Schwartz, S. (ed.) 1977. *Naming, Necessity, and Natural Kinds*. Cornell University Press, Ithaca, NY.

Smith, D. A. 1973. "Systematic study of chimpanzee drawing," *Journal of Comparative and Physiological Psychology* **82,** 406–414.

Sneath, P. H. A., and R. R. Sokal 1973. *Principles of Numerical Taxonomy*, 2nd ed. Freeman, San Francisco.

Tversky, A., and I. Gati. 1978. "Studies of similarity," in E. Rosch and B. Lloyd (eds.), *Cognition and Categorization*, pp. 79–98. Erlbaum, Hillsdale, NJ.

Wilkerson, T. E. 1973a. "Representation, illusion and aspects," *British Journal of Aesthetics* **18,** 45–58.

———1973b. "Seeing-as," *Mind* **82,** 481–496.

Willcox, A. 1984. *The Rock Art of Africa*. Holmes & Meier, New York.

Wittgenstein, L. 1968. *Philosophical Investigations*. G. E. M. Anscombe (tr.), 3rd ed. Basil Blackwell, Oxford.

Wollheim, R. 1980. *Art and Its Objects*, 2nd ed. Cambridge University Press, Cambridge.

Units of Data as Deployment of Disciplinary Codes

1. The Scope of the Paper

The title above conveys the viewpoint adopted in this paper rather than its scope. The latter is quite limited: I focus, in the first place, on a fundamental empirico-analytical unit of today's archaeology, the concept of site, and undertake to identify its semantic dimensions (meaning, or content) and specify its ontological status. Matters of meaning and ontology are likely to be regarded as meta-archaeological, belonging perhaps to the jurisdiction of the philosopher, but only marginally relevant to the work of the practicing archaeologist. Since, then, this exercise unfolds along a disciplinary boundary, I am also forced to consider that boundary and trace the presuppositions upon which it is founded.

My data are samples of the archaeological literature. The language in which we present to each other our research is my empirical universe. It is from that language that I try to retrieve the meaning and ontological status of the site concept and the makings of the disciplinary boundary.

I have chosen to concentrate on the concept of site for convenience. Thanks to the emphasis on regional research in recent decades, and to the highly significant discourse on method of surface survey generated in the context of such research, it is easy to find in the literature opinions about the meaning and status of the concept.[1] Most of what follows, however, could also be said with regard to any other of our fundamental empirico-analytical units (e.g., activity area, stratigraphic unit, component).

2. Sites as Instrumental Measurements

It is an irony that a purely theoretical exercise should have at its focus a concept so often treated as self-evident: in the first instance, "site" is for archaeology a primitive, defined *by ostension*. Early in our training, that is, we are taken to the field and *shown* by a seasoned archaeologist what a site looks like. We soon become experts in recognizing sites, although such expertise, if gained, for example, in the American Southwest, can prove embarrassing when we switch our fieldwork to, for example, temperate Europe. The fact that sites in different parts of the world display different observable features may be disconcerting in interregional comparisons and in global perspectives. It cannot, however, pose serious problems about the meaning of "site" or the ontological status of the things given that name. As long as it is defined by ostension, whether in the Southwest, in Europe, or elsewhere, "site" remains one of the discipline's primitive terms: its meaning is identical with the ostensible referent, and the latter is nothing short of a real entity and, above all, directly accessible through the senses. Note that if such an attitude is adopted in the context of field research, (a) any definition of the site other than by ostension is superfluous; (b) any description of the procedures whereby sites are identified in the field (i.e., distinguished from one another and from non-sites) also is superfluous; and (c) the entities named sites can in fact be given any other name, including neologisms, since the meaning of the name chosen depends on the referent alone.

Many reports of regional surfaces surveys—a context in which questions about the site concept are appropriate—are consistent with the viewpoint I just outlined. Such reports are reticent with regard to site definition and to procedures of site identification, although they may be quite explicit about other aspects of survey method, such as sampling rationale and design (e.g., Dickson 1979; Cherry 1982). In those cases, I construe the surveyors' attitude to be that sites are self-evident and readily identifiable on the basis of a mental (visual) template which the researchers have acquired through training and field experience.

In most cases today, however, the surveyors take care to devise an operational definition of the site (e.f., Doelle 1977:202). They may also discuss the relationship of that definition to a more abstract concept (a "theoretical" definition of the site), itself relevant to the questions the project sets out to investigate. The operational definitions entail essentially sets of procedures and empirical criteria that will ensure unambiguous identification of sites in the field, control over biases, and intersubjective evaluation of the results. Those are, of course, the guarantees that the "mental template approach" to site identification cannot provide. Above all, the adoption of operational definitions is in keeping with the realization that sites do not normally occur as conspicuous and clearly bounded entities in space; rather, cultural residue is continuously, though not evenly, distributed over the landscape (e.g., Dunnell and Dancey 1983:272; Cherry et al. 1988:159). The radical solution to this situation is to describe one's survey universe in terms of changing frequency of cultural residue through space rather than in terms of sites and empty spaces between them (e.g., Davis et al. 1984). The record so produced is a three-dimensional graph or contour map, showing "peaks" and "troughs," and it need contain no mention whatsoever of sites. Such a record awaits further interpretation, however, and decisions must eventually be made about which "peaks" represent sites and where their boundaries are to be drawn. The important point is that site identification here proceeds on the basis of explicit operational criteria (or so is the claim: see Fotiadis n.d.), with considerable emphasis being placed on quantifiable aspects of the research universe (e.g., Binford 1972; Gallant 1986).

A yet more critical point emerges, howeveer, from this relatively recent adoption of operationalist rigor by the discipline: "site" can no longer be a primitive defined by mere ostension. It has become, instead, a problematical term, to be clarified only through a long sequence of operations. The ontological status of the concept is thereby implicitly challenged. An important conceptual change has been taking place (compare, e.g., the discussions of the site in Hole and Heizer 1969:77–81 and 130–133, and in Keller and Rupp 1983:26–30), with consequences for the discipline that have yet to be appreciated. Let us give consideration to this issue.

Do operational definitions make claims about the ontological status of sites? A definition such as "a site is . . . any locus of cultural material, artifacts or facilities" (Plog and Hill 1971) is somewhat different from the familiar "length is something we can measure with a yardstick" (a typical example of operational definition; cf. Gorsky 1981:151–160). In one sense, a site here is merely the product of the procedures entailed by the particular definition, "synonymous with the corresponding set of operations" (see Joergensen 1951:56). Yet, in archaeological discourse, that and similar definitions are commonly associated with a realist ontological position. Sites defined with operationalist rigor, that is, are thought of as "hard facts," perhaps because the definitions refer to material artifacts. Such realist thinking is iterated in the language of the archaeological text (e.g., one *discovers, finds or locates* sites; for explicit references to the site as "objective reality" see, e.g., Gibbon 1984:47 and 57; Dean 1978:104). I imagine one might object that those are merely metaphors, convenient figures of speech, which I (mis)interpret literally. Metaphors they are, but "merely" they are not. I am of the persuasion that metaphor is the principal means by which we render our concepts meaningful (Lakoff and Johnson 1980). Conversely, then, we are in a position to explore the meaning of our concepts by attending to the metaphors in which those concepts participate.

The insistence on the objective status of sites requires further comment. Let us consider again the operational definition of the site quoted above. It appears at first that this definition entails no operations, making instead some kind of ontological claim. While, however, no operations for identifying sites are explicitly mentioned, such operations can easily be conceived, given one interpretation or another of "cultural material, artifacts, or facilities." If, for example, those terms are interpreted as "visually and tactually identifiable objects, having certain shapes, colors, textures, etc.," the procedure entailed by the definition is to go and look for and handle such objects. If "cultural material" is extended to "human-generated anomalies of soil chemistry" (McManamon 1984:227), the set of procedures would also include coring and obtaining soil samples, conducting laboratory tests, and comparing the results by means of tables or graphs in order to identify anomalies. In the latter example a coherent research design would be employed, involving mechanical tools, chemical reactions, graphic devices, and, possibly, digitizing equipment. Although this design is endowed with immense authority in our society (authority derived from its status as science), one or another application of it may yield ambiguous results. Doubts may arise, that is, as to the nature of the outcome of the procedure—is it a site, some other kind of anomaly, or, even, an anomaly at all? Specifically, the ambiguity amounts to this: Is a site-as-anomaly identified through this procedure a site in the sense we understand the concept through alternative procedures, e.g., excavation or surface reconnaissance?

Ambiguities of this kind can, of course, be easily resolved (one can, after all, resort to the alternative procedures), and the possibility of a plurality of concepts of the site, each concept being unique to a particular procedure, does not arise in contemporary archaeology. Moreover, it does not follow from the above example that a site identified on the basis of an operational definition is merely "synonymous with the corresponding set of operations" (cf. above); the operations entailed might still provide clues as to what a site is, or, most certainly, we will assign to the site, by analogy and by metaphor, one or another ontological status for heuristic and other purposes. What does follow is that our concept of the site is structured to a great extent by the procedure we employ to identify sites and by whatever analogy or metaphor we adopt in our effort to understand what a site is. Any objectivity or "hard facts" left to the concept are, therefore, rather transient, contingent upon a distinctive disciplinary apparatus that encompasses metaphors, analogies, and instrumental operations.

The role of language aside, this view has strong affinities with the empiricist philosophy of science. Now, archaeology has been predominantly empiricist and behaviorist for nearly two decades, yet, with a few exceptions (see below), the discipline has resisted the idea that sites are not objective, "hard" data. Such resistance calls for an explanation, which, however, is too complex a task to be accomplished in a few paragraphs. I will only venture here a suggestion, identifying a relevant, if peripherally, condition. Unlike several fields (e.g., astronomy, biology, chemistry) where an elaborate apparatus has traditionally intervened between the investigator and the investigated, in archaeology we have for generations approached our empirical universe primarily, and most of the time exclusively, with the senses—vision and touch. Our colleagues in the sciences had from time to time to wonder about the sorts of reality registered by their instruments, a kind of concern which more recently became the paramount subject of philosophy of science; we, on the other hand, have had the privilege of seeing our sites and touching (kicking, crushing, etc.) the artifacts constituting them. Our empirical universe has been this "common sense reality." Hence, to raise doubts about the reality of sites would amount to nothing less than disputing the immense authority of common sense reality. Instruments traditionally employed in archaeology, such as the photographic camera or the measuring tape, could by no means engender doubts of the ontological sort, since those were precisely the instruments that had come to lend authority to the common sense reality. (Consider, for example, the role of photographs in everyday life as proofs of existence.) It would also be naïve at this point to expect that the increasing use of remote sensing tools in archaeology will render the site ontologically more problematic.

This argument, however, emphasizes the role of the instruments of fieldwork—whether sensory organs or scientific devices—as if those instruments were objects independent of the less tangible dimensions of cognitive processing, e.g., theory, intellectual tradition, ideology, culture. Any adequate explanation of the discipline's resistance to reconsider the ontology of its units of observation and analysis should address the systematic relationships among all those dimensions and the historical contexts that authorized them. Phrased another way, such an explanation should highlight the history of those dimensions, which would also be its own history. I will return to this issue below (§4), but it should already be clear why such a task cannot be accomplished in a few paragraphs.

3. Sites as Instruments

I have argued above that a realist ontological position with regard to sites, while perfectly compatible with the "mental template approach," is rather problematical in the context of research informed by operationalist principles. Nevertheless, those who have adopted the latter principles in our field have in general overlooked the problem and remained faithful in their writings to the same realist metaphors. Today one might be left with the impression that there is no philosophical gulf of any magnitude between a camp that advocates operationalist rigor and another that opposes it in the name of expedient templates, and that the differences are strictly methodological. If there is any tension of philosophical import, that surfaces in the most self-reflective texts produced in the name of operationalist rigor:

> . . . Like a pair of worn suspenders, the site concept can be stretched so far that it fails to carry any weight at all. In the fieldwork at Reese River, a site (in the traditional sense) might consist of merely an isolated flake on a hillside or a scatter of hundreds of artifacts and features. Perhaps we could even define the *entire valley* as a single site, in which case we are really concerned with "within-site" sampling. But these positions seem to me strained and constricting. Our concepts must be helpful rather than restrictive, so I have scrapped the site concept altogether in this context. The decision is, of course, dictated by the immediate objectives of the survey, and also by the nature of the archaeological remains. (Thomas 1975:63; emphasis in the original)

This often-cited passage expresses most concisely the tension (although other examples could be cited: Cherry 1983:395 and 1984:120; Dunnell and Dancey 1983; Wandsnider and Ebert 1984:10–11; Fotiadis 1985:174–176 and 182–183). We are told, first, that the site concept has a flexible scope, then, that it must be so formulated as to be helpful (in investigating problems), and, finally, that it need not be used where other concepts will or may be more helpful. It begins to look as if the site is a conceptual instrument of research, a disciplinary unit to reckon the past—nothing less and, according to this interpretation of the passage, nothing more. But Thomas is somewhat uneasy about the bottom line of his argument (cf. his comment "But these positions seem to me strained and constricting") and he terminates it abruptly. He never denies that sites also are or may be real entities.

If the tension is resolved in the manner my interpretation of the passage suggests, the geography of concepts unfolding before us is the following:

DATA	SITE	QUERY
(raw material)	(tool)	(finished product)
(sense)	(language)	(meaning)

In general, however, in archaeological discourse site and data are superimposed, "site" at once designating a disciplinary unit of reckoning and a category of empirical object-referents. I may add that site-as-empirical-category can be thought of as formed inductively, while site-as-disciplinary-unit is a theoretical concept, having nothing to do with induction. (I do not mean that "site" has two—much less, opposed—meanings: every time we use the term to refer, we render the referent relevant to a disciplinary query.) That superimposition is not without advantages, but it is also the source of the formidable difficulties we encounter whenever we attempt to define the concept to our colleagues' satisfaction (see, e.g., the round-table discussion in Keller and Rupp 1983:26–

30). If, on the other hand, a distinction is maintained between site and data, those difficulties are eased, but new methodological and philosophical problems arise. The second and third lines of the diagram above, suggesting two possible analogies to the data/site/query geography, provide a glimpse of the philosophical complexities. Few concepts in the Western philosophical tradition are indeed entangled in more problematical relationships than those making up the third line. As for the methodological difficulties, their magnitude can best be appreciated from the following:

> A *site* is a discrete and potentially interpretable locus of cultural materials. . . . By in-
> terpretable we mean that materials of sufficiently great quality and quantity are present for
> at least attempting and usually sustaining inferences about the behavior occurring at the locus.
> (Plog et al. 1978:389; emphasis in the original)

Room is made here for principles of interpretation and for criteria that will ensure uniform application of those principles. Such criteria and principles are still needed when one distinguishes between sites and scatters (or non-sites), since the latter must also be considered as potentially interpretable. The discussion by Plog et al. makes this point explicit.

As I will argue later, the definition of the site by Plog et al. (see also Lightfoot 1986:485–486) comes very close to my view of the site as model of archaeological practice. But it can already be seen in that definition that the concept has empirical referents (here described at a high level of generality as discrete loci of cultural materials) and a dimension that corresponds to the discipline's conceptual apparatus for making sense out of that referent (a potential for interpreting). I am deliberately ''subverting'' here the statement of Plog et al.: they speak of a site as an empirical entity, as an object with properties, including the property of being interpretable. Theirs is a manner of speaking still informed by a commitment to a realist ontology. It is clear, however, that being interpretable is hardly an inherent, empirical property of a discrete locus of cultural materials; it cannot be established as a datum with the aid of a simple operational test universally applicable. The only test imaginable is the archaeologist's attempt at inter-pretation. Moreover, with that attempt, a disciplinary code is brought into play: rather than improvising, the archaeologist deploys a complex apparatus of rules that has been developed through archaeological practice. *A site is constructed by the deployment of the discipline's conceptual apparatus.*

To claim, then, that the site is a disciplinary construct is not a novelty. Nor does it presuppose a distinct philosophical viewpoint, for reified constructs (''analytical tools,'' ''heuristic devices,'' etc.) are perfectly at home in positivist social science. The claim does, however, challenge us to a new question, which can take several forms: What is the construct made of, and how? If the site concept is not as unassailable as are empirical categories, how solid is it, and where does it derive its coherence from? What is the complex apparatus of rules, by the deployment of which sites are constructed? Or, still, if the site as disciplinary unit is, as I claimed above, a theoretical concept, what theory does it belong to? The following is an attempt to give approximate answers to these questions. Quite obviously, if I left the analysis at this point, I would have done nothing more than provide an instantiation of the old empiricist dictum that all observation is theory-laden (e.g., Salmon 1976:376). It is this theory now that comes to be of interest.

4. Archaeology as Social Practice

Not all the things we identify today as sites would have been identified as such a hundred or less years ago. The sites of classical archaeology, for example, for a long time were those places glorified in the process of interpretation of the classical texts. Moreover, one cannot seriously maintain that classical archaeology represented its sites "just as they were." Nor, on the other hand, can it be said that classical archaeology's selective vision and discriminatory practice was arbitrary and unjustifiable. It rather harmonized itself meticulously with aspirations and premises that have yet to be fully illuminated but invariably involved issues of difference—cultural, national, racial, or other (cf. Jenkyns 1980; Herzfeld 1982:10–11 and 1986). It is easy to see today that the sites of classical archaeology were constructed with the aid of a vast ideological apparatus. We might call that ideological apparatus a "theory," if only we remember that such a theory remained transparent in the very focus of the discipline, encoded in the fundamental disciplinary terms.

The question that we expect to hear more and more often in the near future is this: What are the ideologies germane to the construction of sites and similar data-concepts in modern archaeology? (The question has, in fact, already been raised and investigated in the context of American preservation archaeology: Tainter and Lucas 1983.) "Site" no longer evokes—not even among most classical archaeologists—a sanctuary or civic center. As the two definitions quoted earlier make clear, the concept has been rendered in the trails of disciplinary discourse far more comprehensive and abstract. And those definitions appear indeed to be innocent of unspoken ideologies.

Why do, however, those definitions—in fact, all definitions of site in the current archaeological literature—identify so persistently the concept's empirical referent yet contain so few hints that the site also is a disciplinary unit? Could that choice be ideologically informed? Or is it simply a wise choice, since a consideration of the site-as-disciplinary-unit is an "armchair" pursuit, belonging at best in meta-archaeological contexts (e.g., when writing a history of the discipline) but irrelevant to problems of field research (in the context of which almost all definitions of the site have been developed)? I will argue for the inevitable third alternative, namely that the choice is ideology-wise, that if an analysis of the site-as-disciplinary-unit is a meta-archaeological task, it is so only because the theory that lends coherence to that unit also gives rise to a disciplinary boundary and retreats behind it. The site becomes an effective cognitive device for archaeology the moment that the theory upon which that device depends for effectiveness escapes the focus of the discipline. Let us call, then, that theory a disciplinary ideology, and acknowledge the consequences: when the contradictions of that ideology are identified, not only the coherence of our cognitive device will have been eroded but, also, the boundary between archaeology and meta-archaeology will have shifted. Tasks such as the present one may then no longer need be consigned to meta-archaeology but become of central relevance to field research. Today's "meta-archaeology," tomorrow's archaeology—the discontinuity is predicated upon an ephemeral disciplinary ideology.

But the above is too labyrinthine to be of relevance to anything, so I will turn to an example. I found that all extant definitions of the site fail to emphasize essential semantic dimensions of the concept, dimensions that become manifest when we turn our attention from definitions to the usage of "site" in archaeological texts. Specifically, in the definiens of "site" one finds mentions of *locus, spatial cluster of cultural materials and human activity/behavior*. By "site" we routinely mean a special kind of place in the landscape, a place where humans did something, and where their activity left empirically recognizable traces—or such is by definition the convention among colleagues (see references to definitions in McManamon 1984:226–227; Gallant 1986:408). Now let us turn to an excerpt from archaeological text:

> While most sites apparently were relatively small, however, at least some were demonstrably quite large—more than 10 hectares—and were characterized by clear indications of social differentiation and complexity. (Adams 1981:59)

From this sentence one learns, among many other things, that sites have size and, also, a social dimension, a particular state or value of which is "differentiation and complexity." Now, that sites have size is predicated upon (follows logically from) the existing definitions, which stress the spatial referent of the term (see above). In other words, to say "sites have size" expresses an analytic judgment within archaeology. What about social differentiation and complexity? It is difficult to see how they could follow logically from the existing definitions. One would have to perform a long, acrobatic syllogism to show that the social dimension might ultimately be predicated upon such concepts as "cultural materials" or "human activity." Failing this, one must suppose that in "sites have a social dimension" the predicate is not, according to existing definitions, implied in the concept of the subject but is attributed to it on the bases of field observations. In view of that dilemma, let us refrain from classifying "sites have a social dimension" as analytical or synthetic, and search instead for a more revealing classification. Several points of interest emerge here.

(1) That the social dimension of the site concept is not analytically acknowledged and justified by no means automatically indicates poor scientific practice or failure to observe the logical requirements of science. Archaeology is not Euclidean geometry or any other kind of closed deductive theory. In fields with significant experimental components (fields to which archaeology often looks up; see, e.g., Binford 1983:21–22; Gould and Watson 1982:371), conclusions reached experimentally are not always anticipated in the definitions/axioms of the theory. When this happens, the definitions may or may not need revision, but some rethinking clearly has to be done, stimulating further experimentation and further theorizing. (We are thus rapidly led back to the notion that the definition of the site is a heuristic construct.) What could, however, expose us to allegations of poor practice is our *continuing* resistance to speak of the site as a construct with a social dimension.

(2) After all, the social dimension was not discovered by Adams in the floodplain of

the Euphrates and first (in passing) reported by him in 1981. An analogy between site and social concepts appears indeed to be common, long established, disciplinary ground (e.g, Fagan 1988), so that statements such as Adams's cause no bewilderment. In view of this, I will disregard altogether the question whether "sites have a social dimension" is analytic or synthetic. I will instead adopt Eco's term (1976:158–160), and regard "sites have a social dimension" as a *semiotic* judgment. By changing terminologies I am essentially reiterating that "site" denotes above all a disciplinary unit (just as Eco's sign-vehicles of natural language denote cultural units), and I posit that a *code* exists in the disciplinary memory that associates "site" with the semantic field of "society." Any attempt to clarify the concept of site as a disciplinary unit must concern itself with the identification of that code.

(3) To posit the existence of that code is to include in the semantic field of "site" an abstract dimension such as "social unit or system, e.g., a community." Now, one might insist that these are connotations of "site," while the proper denotation of the term is the empirical referent identified in the archaeological definitions (a view completely incongruous with Eco's [1976:55] on denotation and connotation). One might also insist that, even though "site" can be used in certain contexts in lieu (and in the sense) of "social unit," the two are nevertheless completely distinct concepts. Or, finally, one might expect a dictionary of archaeological terms to distinguish between "site$_1$" and "site$_2$," giving under "$_1$" a description of the empirical referent, while under "$_2$" stressing the social dimension. What all these formulations do not reveal, however, is that our concept of site is structured with the help of the much more abstract concept of social unit. Using "site" in a context where "social unit" or "community" would be the proper terms can be regarded as a metaphor. That metaphor, however, is not a mere wordplay, a conventional interchange of signifiers without consequences for the meaning of the terms interchanged. Rather, the metaphor assumes the role of an interpreting device: it permits us to partly understand "site" with the help of (by reference to) "social unit," thereby reinforcing a structural isomorphism between the two concepts.

(4) If the auxiliary concept of social unit is abstract, one expects that it will be understood in turn with the help of other, and probably less abstract, concepts (Lakoff and Johnson 1980, e.g. 61). Being abstract, furthermore, it lends itself to selective interpretation: it can be understood via many alternative concepts. Dominant among such alternatives in contemporary archaeology appears to be the concept of biological organism. Now, the structural isomorphism between the concepts of social unit and organism is so familiar in social science (where it has been, since the 1950s, theoretically amplified as systems theory) and has been so extensively discussed in archaeology that it hardly needs further elaboration. What I wish to stress instead is that the chain "site-social unit-biological organism" can be regarded as a shorthand description and partial identification of the disciplinary code I posited above in (2).

(5) The principle of interpretability so keenly isolated by Plog et al. (see above) can find in this code a more concrete expression. Interpretation consists in the deployment of the code. A discrete locus of cultural materials is interpretable, hence a site, if its constituent empirical elements can be conceptually related to one another in the way the parts of a social unit, and ultimately, of an organism are related. The concepts of social unit and biological organism, that is, provide the archaeologist with a model with which

to structure his/her empirical data. We can think of that process as cognition, and not without justification: it is along that process that the disciplinary query interfaces with the empirical world—whether presented as measurements, patterns registered by remote sensing instruments, or direct sense data—and that world is sorted and transformed to obtain relevance for and become amenable to the query. As cognition, that process remains poorly understood. The critical point for our discussion is that the code functions as a cognitive device; hence, cognition involves not only sense data and instrumental measurements but the disciplinary language as well.

(6) Yet more critical is that the auxiliary concepts of social unit and organism are system-theoretical concepts, constituted not of parts but of parts-in-relationship. That is to say, the parts are fully defined (conceptually constituted) only insofar as they are related to one another—or, at least, it would be arbitrary to exclude those relationships from any consideration of the parts. The implication of this principle is unmistakable: the relationships posited among the physical elements of a locus of cultural materials— the inferences, as Plog et al. call those posited relationships (1978:389)—have no fixed point of origin in the physical elements of the locus. Rather, that point of origin is fixed as the relationships become established. In short, the relationships posited serve *to constitute* the data upon which they are eventually grounded.

The claim, then, that a given discrete locus of cultural materials is a site is founded only when a lattice of relationships among the empirical elements of that locus is established—therefore, in retrospect from the end of the project. The locus is made a site by everything predicated of it. Elaborated in the trails of disciplinary discourse and thus permeated with structure, however, that site is no longer a physical entity, an object-referent, but a semantic unit, a structured semantic field—our disciplinary construct with all its theoretical weight: in the process of interpretation, from a physical object the site is transformed into a concept in the image of the social universe, already interpreted via the biological model. A physicalist conception of matter and space thereby gives way to one that obtains its coherence within a discursive context of social purport.

The passage from Adams quoted earlier may serve to partly illustrate this point. Social differentiation and complexity neither are expected as predicates of a site according to existing definitions of the concept nor are they simple, intuitively clear terms (primitives). They are instead given meaning within a particular discursive/theoretical context, a kind of social evolutionary theory associated with the works of Elman Service, Kent Flannery, and Adams himself (among others). When social differentiation and complexity are predicated of a site, therefore, that site is defined by recourse to that discursive/ theoretical context; it is structured as a semantic field with the aid not of two, independently defined, concepts but with the aid of the entire theory upon which those concepts depend for meaning. For archaeologists unfamiliar with that particular discursive/theoretical context, that predication is likely to be puzzling.

In view of the above, it is difficult to maintain that Adams's sites—in fact, all sites— are objects capable of manifesting themselves in the absence of the disciplinary code. Sites as facts relevant to the archaeological project are reified semantic units. The coherence of those facts does not originate in the object-referent, no matter how sharply that referent may be differentiated from "noise" on the screen of our data processor. Rather, coherence arises in the deployment of the code, the intellectual operations in the course of which the object-referent is invested with structure. It is upon that deployment that archaeology as social science acquires its object.

Does this conclusion imply that our empirical object is constituted "axiomatically," and archaeology is, therefore, unwittingly a "formal" science? Such notions are the toolkit of the empiricist philosopher of science; to adopt them would mean once more switching viewpoints. Instead, a different issue emerges. I argued here that the operations by which archaeology confronts, indeed appropriates, its empirical universe are, in the first place, intellectual. Now, to conclude that the archaeologists' tools are concepts rather than trowels and calipers is, no doubt, news for the public although not for the profession. The critical point consists rather in regarding the disciplinary code as a cognitive device. For to emphasize that codes, in addition to instrumental measurements and sense data, aid us in ordering our empirical universe forces upon us the issue of ideology. Let us, then, return to the code, and highlight its ideological function.

The role of the code in implicating the site concept in ideology may indeed by now be obvious. In the first place, the site is through the code semantically affiliated with the social universe—the universe of ideological tensions par excellence. It is then not surprising at all to find that the code reproduces within itself an aspect of those tensions: its third member ("biological organism") occupies a contradictory position, serving at once to affirm that the site is entangled in ideology, and to deny it. It highlights the particular, and ideologically controversial, standpoint of social evolutionary theory vis-à-vis human societies, namely, that a society is structurally isomorphic with a biological system. At the same time, it removes the site from the ideology-ridden universe of social theory to recast it in the considerably more settled universe of biology.

It follows that the code performs an ideological function: it gives a privileged ontological status to an aspect of the world, thereby denying that privilege to alternative aspects. Specifically, the code guarantees that the social dimension of the site will be understood in terms of a biological model rather than, for instance, a linguistic one. It ensures that notions such as social differentiation and complexity will be analytically defined and operationalized in terms of energy flow networks rather than, for example, in terms of symbolic lattices for marking, classifying, asserting, and denying.

I suspect, however, that the code performs a second, and more crucial, ideological function, namely, to deny its own materiality and render itself transparent to the discipline. Before attempting to demonstrate the validity of this claim, let me place it in the context of my earlier remarks with regard to the rise of the disciplinary boundary between archaeology and meta-archaeology:

(1) The site-as-disciplinary-unit is reified. What is reified, however, is not a sharply demarcated, independent concept but, rather, a structured semantic field, the site as social unit as biological organism—that is, the code;

(2) The reification of the code amounts to an identification of a cognitive device with an empirically accessible object-referent: a potential for interpreting becomes an interpretable entity (see above). That is not a reiteration of the "mental template" approach, for the simple reason that the code is not an inductively formed category, derived from fieldwork, much less a visual image;

(3) But a code identified with an object is no longer a code. It is eliminated and cannot anymore serve as a focus of investigation for the discipline. The only focus of

investigation that remains is the object, now vested with the authority of the code. Archaeology thereby becomes "extroverted," and capable of defining itself by reference to that external object. With its focus pointed away from itself, its goal becomes to test posited relationships among coded empirical facts, rather than to agonize over the constitution of its own codes;

(4) This last disjunction marks the disciplinary boundary: within the boundary (left side of the disjunction) is archaeology, beyond it lies not-archaeology—or, at best, meta-archaeology; and

(5) The reification of the site-as-disciplinary-unit, hence of the code, and of the boundary that separates archaeology from meta-archaeology is predicated upon the semantics of the code. The code, as it were, contains instructions for its self-elimination.

The last item summarizes the second ideological function of the code. To demonstrate that function, then, it is sufficient to demonstrate that the reification of the site is a logical consequence of the semantic dimensions of the code.

In the first place, by emphasizing an affinity between the site and biological systems, the third member of the code places the object of archaeology among the objects of the sciences. The object of archaeology thus acquires something of the materiality of the scientific objects, a materiality that is independent of language, semantics, codes, or intellectual operations. The code, then, could not be constitutive of such an object, for physical matter remains what it is no matter what name we may give it. At best, in that case, the code would be a preliminary formulation, a heuristic device, to be discarded and forgotten after aiding us in discovering the true material properties of our object. It could not, under any circumstances, serve as a focus for the discipline. Any discussion of the code would be strictly meta-archeological, having no bearing on the practice of archaeology.

Thus the code could signal its own demise. For all its parsimony, however, the argument I just presented leaves much to be desired: it only superficially explores the semantic dimensions of the code, and thus fails to identify a salient contradiction among those dimensions. Let us, then, turn again to the code, and posit the presence of yet another link:

$$\text{site} \begin{array}{l} \nearrow \text{social unit–biological organism} \\ \searrow \text{conceptual tool} \end{array}$$

With this addition we have obviously switched semantic systems, from that of disciplinary objects (societies, organisms) to that of disciplinary methods (instruments of research). Nevertheless, the addition is fully justified: the semantic association of "site" with "conceptual tool" is evident from archaeological discourse (see, e.g., the quotation from Thomas 1975, and the references to other authors in §3 above), even though it remains under-coded. We do not, that is, but exceptionally think of our sites as conceptual tools.

It could be argued once more at this point that the code consists throughout of pure methodological devices, constructs of the discipline. As I indicated, however, the code juxtaposes names from two disparate, mutually opposed semantic systems—a contradiction, no doubt symptomatic of the code's ideological function. That contradiction can now be seen to arise from the very names by which the discipline calls its conceptual tools. As soon as those names—"heuristic" or "analytical" devices, "inference," "interpretation," etc.—are added to the code next to "conceptual tool," the contradiction is indeed easily explained: all those names tacitly assert the existence of something *other than* and *prior to* the discipline, something to infer from, to analyze, to interpret or simply to find. Can we still resist the conclusion that the reification of the site *and* the formation of the disciplinary boundary are predicated upon the semantics of the code?

The code, then, escapes the focus of the discipline by stealth, disguised as the object that it, in the first place, helped to carve ("being interpretable"). The skeptic might at this point raise the ultimate objection: Isn't all this just a metaphor? Aren't sites really the products of past societies rather than of the archaeologists' minds? Yes, but what is "society"?—not to ask what is a past society. If the sentence "sites are the products of past societies" has any meaning, that meaning is provided by the disciplinary code. The code alone renders "society" isomorphic with "organism," so that disciplines can conceive of societies as having a life, and therefore a death, and thus becoming extinct and past.

To say that archaeology (mis)takes its model for its data makes the issue appear as an innocent epistemological error, however serious may that error be for scientific practice. From the perspective I have adopted in this paper, that "error" is an essential presupposition of *social* practice.

5. Summary and Comments (The archeologist as bricoleur)

My focus in the previous section has been the operation of a disciplinary ideology, not the broad social, cultural, or political ideology of the modern West. I have not been concerned with the material-political consequences of interpreting the social universe as an ecological system, or of bringing our explanations of past social practices to rest on principles of mechanics and thermodynamics. I have been concerned with the issues that (a) the site concept is constructed in disciplinary discourse with the aid of a code that is ideologically informed; (b) we employ the site concept as a cognitive device to order our empirical universe; hence (c) we order our empirical universe with the aid of a cognitive device that is held together by ideology, yet (d) silently deny the ideological core of our practice; (e) that denial is grounded in the logic of our code, and is, therefore, consistent with our ideology.

Perhaps the most important function of an ideological apparatus is to direct attention away from its own operation, and thus confer its authority to the matter that is operated upon. The apparatus of a social science consists, by necessity, of conceptions of the fabric and workings of human societies. Now, matters social are matter ideological, and matters ideological matter. If our definitions and discussions of the site usually leave unmarked the social content of the concept, the habit is ideologically informed, for that social content is itself ideology. It serves to remove the conceptual apparatus of the discipline from the field of vision of the investigator. The authority of the apparatus is thus transferred to the data, which now assert themselves: the sites become entities, empirical objects external to the disciplinary apparatus. The result is not only an inverted image of the archaeological project, with sites taking the place of facts upon which all theory is to be tested. More critically, a disciplinary boundary is thereby created, that between archaeology and meta-archaeology, between questions of legitimate interest for archaeology and others, such as the sources of coherence of the discipline's concepts, relegated to the margins of the project.

I take the transformation of the site from a physical object to a semantic unit molded on conceptions of the social universe (see above) to be a model of modern archaeological practice, a metaphor for the archaeologist's work. The algorithm for this transformation, whereby a physicalist conception of matter is supplanted by one framed by its social relevance, is wrought in the tropes of disciplinary discourse. That discourse is an idiom contiguous with natural language and permeable by the discourse of other disciplines. The algorithm, then, could be seen as *bricolage*: its constituent concepts have diverse origins and mythical histories—they are rearrangements of concepts already elaborated beyond archaeology, tools adapted but never originally designed for the archaeologist's work.

If I draw this comparison with Lévi-Strauss's *bricoleur*, I do not wish to suggest that archaeology is a science in a primitive stage. Rather I wish to stress that the archaeologist's toolkit is derived from the common materials of language. The operations in which we engage, when we transform the Cartesian space of our field grid to social space, are not instrumental but conceptual; they are not simply *expressed* in a language, they *are* language, subject to the same rules as language and capable of the same functions, including the ideological.

It is out of this conviction that I borrowed from semiotics the notion of code in order to speak about the apparatus of our social science. I also called that apparatus "cognitive," and the deployment of the code "cognition," admitting at once that this is a notion no less mysterious semantically than it is biologically. "Algorithm" was another name I gave to the code, no doubt an ambitious one, for algorithms are thought of as formally logical and semantically empty, in stark contrast with the code. But "algorithm" is also obscure semantically for archaeology, and, in connoting "obscurity," seemed entirely appropriate in the context I placed it. With my choice of such names for the disciplinary apparatus, I have attempted to underline the reflexive, problematical character of that apparatus and of the operations we more often call "analysis," "inference," or simply "archaeological practice." It would be quite naïve at this point to claim that my choices of names, indeed my entire argument, are innocent of ideology. I shall briefly illuminate this last point with reference to two critical concepts, "code" and "discipline."

Does the code exist? The answer is clear: the code exists no more than does the dictionary—that is, the view that language consists of words, building blocks each with specific, sharply demarcated meaning (semantic content). Both the dictionary and the code are constructs, methodological tools, each with concrete utilities, and both are circular: the dictionary defines itself in the entry "dictionary," and the code contains among its links the sign "code." (That is, if the code contains "tool," and the tool is nothing else but the chain of concepts I called "code," then the code also contains its own name.) As I noted, that circularity is an essential presupposition of social practice. If I have made the code the ontological foundation of this exercise, I have also used it as a methodological device. By no means, then, does my view of our units of data as deployment of disciplinary codes stand apart idcologically. In social science, indeed, the opposite of ideology is not absence of ideology, only another ideology. The investment in this exercise, then, has not been the hope that we will strip the site from some metaphysical overburden and reach an undisturbed stratum of data. Rather, the objective has been "the relentless unveiling of the postulates and presuppositions that accompany each construction" (Gardin 1980:125).

Let me turn to "discipline." Quite obviously, I took this as another ontological foundation, as an unproblematic concept/unit, and treated it as if it were a unified mind. My argument would have been impossible without recourse to such a tacit premise. Yet the premise is exceedingly difficult to justify, especially in a decade when dissidence to empiricist practice is mounting on both sides of the North Atlantic, not to mention the archaeologies of the rest of the world. But, after all, archaeology lost its innocence some fifteen years ago (Clarke 1973). Why, then, couldn't it also lose a part of its consciousness?

Acknowledgments: I am very thankful to Jean-Claude Gardin, Michael Herzfeld, and Christopher Peebles, and not only for inviting me to the C.N.R.S.–N.S.F. Conference. All three offered in many occasions encouragement and challenges, without which this paper would have been considerable more muddled.

NOTES

1. The issues raised in that discourse have yet to be settled. As this manuscript is being submitted to the editor, the Society for American Archeology has announced in the program of its 53rd Annual Meeting (1988) two sessions dedicated to the concept of site.

REFERENCES

Adams, R. M. 1981. *Heartland of Cities: Surveys of Ancient Settlement and Land Use on the Central Flood Plain of the Euphrates*. The University of Chicago Press, Chicago.
Binford, L. R. 1972. "Hatchery West: Site definition—surface distribution of cultural items," in L. R. Binford, *An Archaeological Perspective*, pp. 163–181. Seminar Press, New York.
————1983. *In Pursuit of the Past: Decoding the Archaeological Record*. Thames and Hudson, London.
Cherry, J. F. 1982. "A preliminary definition of site distribution on Melos," in C. Renfrew and M. Wagstaff (eds.), *An Island Polity: The Archaeology of Exploitation in Melos*, pp. 10–23. Cambridge University Press, Cambridge.
————1983. "Frogs around the pond: Perspectives on current archaeological survey projects in the Mediterranean region," in D. R. Keller and D. W. Rupp (eds.), *Archaeological Survey in the Mediterranean Area*, pp. 375–416. British Archaeological Reports International Series 155, Oxford.
————1984. "Common sense in Mediterranean survey?" *Journal of Field Archaeology* **11,** 117–120.
Cherry, J. F., J. L. Davis, A. Demitrack, E. Mantzourani, T. F. Strasser, and L. Talalay 1988. "Archaeological survey in an artifact-rich landscape: A Middle Neolithic example from Nemea, Greece," *American Journal of Archaeology* **92,** 159–176.

Clarke, D. 1973. "Archaeology: The loss of innocence," *Antiquity* **47**, 6–18.

Davis, J. L., J. F. Cherry, and E. Mantzourani 1984. "An archaeological survey of northwestern Keos." Paper read at the 86th Meeting of the Archaeological Institute of America, Toronto.

Dean. J. S. 1978. "An evaluation of the initial SARG research design," in R. C. Euler and G. J. Gumerman (eds.), *Investigations of the Southwestern Anthropological Research Group: The Proceedings of the 1976 Conference*, pp. 103–117. Museum of Northern Arizona, Flagstaff.

Dickson, J. S. 1979. *Prehistoric Pueblo Settlement Patterns: The Arroyo Hondo, New Mexico Site Survey*. (Arroyo Hondo Archaeological Series, 2) School of American Research Press, Santa Fe, NM.

Doelle, D. H. 1977. "A multiple survey strategy for cultural resource management studies," in M. B. Schiffer and G. J. Gumerman (eds.), *Conservation Archaeology. A Guide for Cultural Resource Management Studies*, pp. 201–209. Academic Press, New York.

Dunnell, R. C., and W. S. Dancey 1983. "The siteless survey: A regional scale data collection strategy," in M. B. Schiffer (ed.), *Advances in Archaeological Method and Theory* **6**, 267–287. Academic Press, Orlando.

Eco, U. 1976. *A Theory of Semiotics*. Indiana University Press, Bloomington.

Fagan, B. M. 1988. *Archaeology, a Brief Introduction*, 3rd ed. Scott, Foresman and Company, Glennview.

Fotiadis, M. 1985. *Ecology, Economy, and Settlement among Subsistence Farmers in the Serres Basin, Northeastern Greece, 5000–1000 B.C.* Ph.D. Dissertation, Indiana University, Bloomington.

————n.d. "Sites in non-Cartesian coordinates."

Gallant, T. W. 1986. "Background noise' and site definition: A contribution to survey methodology," *Journal of Field Archaeology* **13**, 403–418.

Gardin, J.-C. 1980. *Archaeological Constructs: An Aspect of Theoretical Archaeology*. Cambridge University Press, Cambridge.

Gibbon, G. 1984. *Anthropological Archaeology*. Columbia University Press, New York.

Gorsky, D. P. 1981. *Definition (Logico-Methodological Problems)*. Progress, Moscow.

Gould, R. A., and P. J. Watson 1982. "A dialogue on the meaning and use of analogy in ethnoarchaeological reasoning," *Journal of Anthropological Archaeology* **1**, 355–381.

Herzfeld, M. 1982. *Ours Once More. Folklore, Ideology, and the Making of Modern Greece*. University of Texas Press, Austin.

————1986. "On some rhetorical uses of iconicity in cultural ideologies," in P. Buissac, M. Herzfeld, and R. Posner (eds.), *Iconicity: Essays on the Nature of Culture. Festschrift for Thomas A. Sebeok on His 65th Birthday*, pp. 401–419. Stauffenburg Verlag, Tübingen.

Hole F., and R. F. Heizer 1969. *An Introduction to Prehistoric Archaeology*. Holt, Rinehart, and Winston, New York.

Jenkyns R. 1980. *The Victorians and Ancient Greece*. Harvard University Press, Cambridge, MA.

Joergensen, J. 1951. *The Development of Logical Empiricism*. University of Chicago Press, Chicago.

Keller, D. R., and D. W. Rupp (eds.) 1983. *Archaeological Survey in the Mediterranean Area*. British Archaeological Reports International Series 155, Oxford.

Lakoff, G., and M. Johnson 1980. *Metaphors We Live By*. University of Chicago Press, Chicago.

Lightfoot, K. G. 1986. "Regional surveys in the eastern United States: The strengths and weaknesses of implementing subsurface testing programs," *American Antiquity* **51**, 484–504.

McManamon, F. P. 1984. "Discovering sites unseen," in M. B. Schiffer (ed.), *Advances in Archaeological Method and Theory* **7**, 223–292. Academic Press, Orlando, FL.

Plog, F., and J. Hill 1971. "Explaining variability in the distribution of sites," in G. J. Gumerman (ed.), *The Distribution of Prehistoric Population Aggregates*, pp. 7–36. Prescott College Press, Prescott, AZ.

Plog, S., F. Plog, and W. Wait 1978. "Decision making in modern surveys," in M. B. Schiffer (ed.), *Advances in Archaeological Method and Theory* **1**, 383–421. Academic Press, New York.

Salmon, M. H. 1976. " 'Deductive' versus 'inductive' archaeology," *American Antiquity* **41,** 376–380.

Schiffer, M. B., and G. J. Gumerman 1977. *Conservation Archaeology: A Guide for Cultural Resource Studies*. Academic Press, New York.

Tainter, J. A., and G. J. Lucas 1983. "Epistemology of the significance concept," *American Antiquity* **48,** 707–719.

Thomas, D. H. 1975. "Nonsite sampling in archaeology: Up the creek without a site?" in J. W. Mueler (ed.), *Sampling in Archaeology*, pp. 61–81. University of Arizona Press, Tucson.

Wandsnider, L., and J. I. Ebert 1984. "Accuracy in archaeological surface survey in the Seedskadee project area, southwestern Wyoming," *Haliksa'i: University of New Mexico Contributions to Anthropology* **3,** 9–20.

PART III

Symbolic and Structural Approaches

Mark P. Leone and Elizabeth Kryder-Reid

Critical Perspectives on Work Concerning Charles Carroll of Carrollton

Does archaeology explore and discover and reexplore and rediscover relationships that occurred in the past? That is, is archaeology about the past? Or does archaeology deal with relationships between the present and the past? That is, is it principally about the present? In this essay we work toward an answer to these questions using the assumptions within a critical perspective, principally from Jürgen Habermas, in order to focus on weaknesses in the perspective itself.

Our first obligation is to flesh out our questions so they appear less cryptic and more useful to archaeologists. Is the task of a critical perspective to revise our understanding of the past by introducing political and economic considerations current at the time the data and interpretations were established? Is it our task to deconstruct earlier interpretations, showing them to be functions of political and economic considerations present not in the archaeological past, but current when the earlier interpretation itself was enunciated?

This set of questions includes the problem that every archaeological interpretation is likely to be embedded in or influenced by political considerations. Since that could be so, what is to be done? There are two possibilities. One is to acknowledge the inevitable operation of living factors, look for them, know them, and, having raised them to consciousness, go on about the business of archaeology actively aware of the biases one lives with. This means that one, at the very least, does not lay claim to truer findings as a result of the use of rigorous methods. One lays claim to different findings.

If one chooses this path, then at its end may be the possibility of relativism, the fear that since every discovery is a product of its time and circumstances, knowledge neither progresses nor becomes more firm. It merely changes. Few people accept this as either a necessary or a desirable position. Many argue that in the interplay of data, and of the fit between ideas and what we call facts, and in the recognition of the power of economics and politics, some approximation of reliability is possible. Reliability is used here in the general sense that it stands in opposition to statements that cannot be verified, like fantasies or revelation.

Therefore, the first issue in critical analysis is the possibility of the revision of interpretations of the past to include or expose factors previously excluded for political reasons. We can call this deconstruction.

The second issue is related but seems very different on the surface. Since research is always done in some present and since a present is always going to be projected back onto another time and cultural setting through interpretation, then a critical perspective is to raise to awareness a history of those present influences under which the research is being guided. Thus, from a critical perspective, we do the history or archaeology of the taken-for-granted assumptions that motivate our own research in the first place. The premise of this approach is that if key assumptions are given a history and context, their claims to universal validity can be challenged and other points of view enfranchised.

There is in this second issue the latent matter of a totalitarian attitude that springs from the assumption that one can read the present accurately or neutrally and decide what part of it needs a history, and that any other ongoing research which does not do this is less self-enlightened or illuminated. The claim is that this fear can be relieved by subjecting such a critical approach to public dialogue. But there are two problems with this approach. There is no systematic way we know of to explore the present and then to decide what part of the past would best illuminate it. Ultimately, all hypotheses or hunches come from the present, and to suppose that a better history will be produced by such acknowledgment is yet to be proven, in our opinion. Second, and even more troubling, is that even after a history of controlling biases or ideology is done, how do we know we have produced a more aware, empowering, or democratic society? We have no way to tell.

Our aim in this essay is simple, at least on the surface. It is to frame our work on one archaeological site in such a way that the relationships among three elements are clear. And furthermore, we wish to say that our understanding of the three elements changed as we dug. They are (1) Catholicism in Maryland, (2) the archaeology of the Annapolis property of one of Maryland's leading Catholics, Charles Carroll of Carrollton, a signer of the Declaration of Independence, and (3) an effort to situate the research and the assumptions behind it in public consciousness. Not only did we seek relationships among these three elements but we also acknowledge that the juxtaposition is our choice. We did not have to include Catholicism, patriotism, or the public. But our aim became to see whether we could write archaeology in such a way that we saw material factors in other interpretations more clearly than before, or write archaeology in such a way that the present was more clearly understood. If we succeeded at the first, we would be one more layer of interpretation in the successive scholarship of Annapolis's past. If we succeeded at the second, we might be embroiled in political controversy or might be merely excessively self-referential.

While we say our aim in this essay is simple, the conclusions are not so simple. We know a great deal about the three-way relationship and its elements, particularly the elements. But we feel simultaneously that, on the one hand, we know more than was known before we began and that our contributions provide information of a political kind that has staying power and is not merely relative, and, on the other hand, that we have not contributed much knowledge to the second critical concern. The second should be the past of some unseen assumption that we communicated to the public effectively. Having worked on the three relationships for the four years between 1987 and 1990, our hope is that clearly reporting on them may comprise some guideposts to others concerned with issues of politics in archaeology. We are going to depend on Ray Kemp's appraisal and use of Habermas as a guide from time to time in reporting (1988).

The following description of our decisions begins with some ethnographic work which explicitly formed part of the background for the project we report. We then trace our archaeological interpretation of Charles Carroll of Carrollton, and conclude with reflections on the implications and applications of a critical archaeology.

The ethnographic considerations begin in southern Maryland where the colony was founded in 1634 at Saint Mary's City in what is now the state of Maryland. Saint Mary's City was located on the western shore of Chesapeake Bay, and lasted as the seat of government until the late seventeenth century, when Annapolis became the capital of the colony. The town never had even a thousand people living in it, but was the first in a chain of tobacco port towns along the Chesapeake Bay planned by the government resident in Britain. It represents the beginning of the trading process that linked economic with political power to push population from Saint Mary's to Annapolis and then further north to Baltimore. All this was to colonize the Bay and its vast lands. By the late 1600s Saint Mary's was largely abandoned, and, not long after, the entire town was a ruin with nothing visible above the fields.

Since 1966, Saint Mary's City has been an outdoor history museum. The Saint Mary's City Commission, a state agency, explores the archaeology and history of the seventeenth-century settlement with professional scholars and interprets the information to the public. Some of the interpretation is done through outdoor drama, a form of living history popular in outdoor museums. At Saint Mary's City, outdoor history dramas have been performed during the peak of the summer tourist season, late June, July, and early August. A drama from 1980 serves as a prelude to exploring the link between seventeenth-century Saint Mary's City and current Catholic relations in Maryland, and the implications of political contexts for archaeological work.

The Saint Mary's drama, which took two hours to perform, had about eighteen actors in it. It took place outdoors, in an area where the original Saint Mary's City stood (Miller 1988). The drama attempted to re-create daily life in the colony in the 1660s. Six adjacent locales in the outdoor museum saw action going on simultaneously for about an hour and a quarter, within period settings. These were a printing shop, a tavern, a homestead with attached barnyard, the house of the governor, and a block used to auction newly arrived indentured servants. The focus of action shifted from locale to locale, although there was almost always some activity at every locale. Tourists wandered through all locales and went from one to another depending on what intrigued them. A leitmotif which eventually came to unify all the action was a byplay between a self-identified Protestant who baited Catholic authority and the representatives of the Catholic Lord Baltimore. Beginning as discrete actions centered on genre settings, i.e., conversations about printing techniques and London fashions, husband-wife squabbles, and an auction of a newly arrived indentured woman, the action developed and reached a peak in the central green between all the sets. The climax was the arrest of the Protestant. He had been arguing that because local Indians were threatening, arms should be taken out of locked, Catholic keeping and given out to each able-bodied man, which is to say the Protestant majority. The man was arrested for threatening the base of government. The

Protestant, it became evident as the drama proceeded, played on two points. Protestants, the numerical majority, could not defend themselves and did not trust Catholic officials to keep their word to do so. And Catholics did not allow Protestants full access to their religious practice because there was no Anglican minister for them. Once these twin themes were stated publicly and fully developed by all the actors, Catholic authority hustled the Protestant off for trial on charges of sedition. The trial composed the last part of the drama and lasted between thirty and forty-five minutes.

The trial took place on the ground floor of the principal standing building associated with Saint Mary's City, the late seventeenth-century statehouse, which was reconstructed in 1934 as a memorial to Maryland's tercentenary. While the outdoor drama reached its climax, and before the trial scene began, a costumed sheriff asked a dozen tourists if they would be jury members in the upcoming trial and took the names of those agreeing. Upon the arrest of the Protestant, all the actors and most visitors went the couple hundred yards to the statehouse. The tourists sat in raised theatre-like seats in one part of the chamber while the governor and other actors sat before them as the court. The jury of visitors was called, sworn in, and seated to one side. The trial proceeded with actors as witnesses and then the jury was charged, sent outside alone without any actor participating in its deliberations, made a decision, came in, announced a verdict, and the drama finished regardless of the verdict.

The drama was created from the transcript of a seventeenth-century trial, one of a number of such documents surviving. The whole drama was created by members of the Commission using the most accurate and thoroughly researched documentary and archaeological evidence available. The actors were trained by the staff using word sheets, issue papers, and background papers containing material on the colony, the seventeenth century, and the particular events they were to enact. The degree of authenticity is testified to in numerous ways: the period costumes, actual peoples' and places' names, original events, issues, and language, and, to some extent, original opinions. All these were used as they had been handed down via the written record or corroborated by archaeology.

Once one understands that the past has been as accurately interpreted as is likely possible, then what has the tourist seen beyond accuracy? We offer the following critical deconstruction. Saint Mary's City exists now within St. Mary's County, Maryland. The county is populated by Protestants, who are Episcopalians identified with Old Trinity parish, whose very bricks come from the dismantled seventeenth-century statehouse, in whose place the current church stands. It is also populated by Catholics, who see Saint Mary's City as the original seat of Catholicism in (British) America. Broadly put, the Protestants have more power and control than the Catholics, but the balance is shifting. In colonial times and today, "Protestant" in Maryland meant principally Anglican, now Episcopalian. Catholics were never a majority and also did not control Maryland beyond the first generation; they were disfranchised by the 1680s and never retrieved power. So, Maryland is Catholic in legend more than in fact, and Maryland is religiously more like the rest of the southern colonies.

Southern Maryland is gradually being absorbed by Washington, D.C., an hour and a half away. The symbolic battleground in the struggle for power over land, prices, farming, factories, strangers, and "old wealth" in St. Mary's County is expressed through who shall own, dig, and reconstruct the site of the Jesuit chapel and its cemetery at Saint

Mary's City. The chapel and cemetery were felt by all concerned in the 1980s to be a very important locale. In 1980, the land on which the ruin stood was owned by a Protestant. There were negotiations to excavate the chapel and cemetery by the St. Mary's City Commission. These negotiations helped crystallize the political issue: Protestants felt themselves in control for a long time; historically they have been more or less dominant since the later 1600s. They have had no foil to be dominant against since the Jesuits, major landowners in southern Maryland since the seventeenth century, left a few decades ago. The local population felt that there was continuity between the seventeenth century and the present in their area, with the struggle between Protestants and Catholics a part of that continuity. For a Jesuit chapel to be the focus of public historical activity, then, meant an opportunity for Catholics to make their presence known in what both groups saw as the source of Roman Catholicism in the United States. An original struggle, which had become a metaphor for other issues, was revived by way of discussion and dramatization and now served a new and current issue, which looked like a traditional issue.

The drama in Saint Mary's is, in a sense, a mythical origin story, one that contains the elements of modern conditions in the drama's structure. Within the living environment there is a struggle for sustained political control over the local area, a struggle enunciated as one between Catholics and Protestants and expressed, among other ways, as what shall be done with the archaeological remains of Catholic origins in the vicinity. This struggle, unresolved, was lived out in the trial. The clue to this, including the lack of resolution, can be seen in the decisions of the jury. The verdict on whether the Protestant was or was not guilty of undermining Catholic government was decided by twelve visitors who were sent out unsupervised and uninstructed on what to decide. In the three times Leone saw the drama there were three different verdicts: guilty, not guilty, and undecided. The actors then concluded the drama three different ways. Since this did not occur historically, the drama is a vehicle for seeing the modern community struggle back and forth over the conflict within it.

Another key to the social meaning of the drama consists of some known historical facts. The chapel was a Jesuit establishment, unsupported by the colony's government. Lord Baltimore not only allowed any Christian group to settle and worship in Maryland, but refused public funds for the support of any religion. Thus the chapel was not a state institution and was used by Protestants as well as Catholics. Protestants held services within it, although without a clergyman early on because they could not afford one. The cemetery associated with the chapel contains the indentured servants, who were largely Protestant and who outnumbered the Catholics, and so the site has more Protestants in it than Catholics. Thus, it is quite likely that the Saint Mary's drama is part of the modern struggle for political control. The drama uses the past, not for what the past contained, but for what the past can be made to allow the present to claim.

We do not feel it is crucial here to propose in detail an alternate view of the past of seventeenth-century Saint Mary's City, because our initial effort is an ethnographic deconstruction of the use of the past. T. H. Breen (1980), however, constructs a useful idea which shows just how far modern Maryland may be from seventeenth-century Maryland. In an argument easily applied to Maryland, Breen says colonial Virginians were ahistorical: the past did not influence their thinking; the future could be begun and rebegun endlessly; and the present could untie itself from the past by an act of will. There was no responsibility to the future; neither was there guilt for a poorly used past. The past was not essential for establishing identity in either historical or fictional terms. Change was nothing one worried about or measured, it was not even a category. From this, Breen finds the Chesapeake and other southern colonies populated by "adventurers," self-named in fact and footloose in time.

Breen argues, as other scholars have, that America decided it could learn from the past rather recently, probably in the later nineteenth century, and attributed the lesson to the Puritans of New England, who, with their biblical excursions, self-referential involvement in their own early experiences as precedents, and in their many efforts at chronological record-keeping, are given credit for a modern historical attitude. And we, as visitors to the many places like Saint Mary's all over the country, inherit the assumption: we are what we were. But we do not inherit a true Saint Mary's City. We inherit a recent activity of thinking through organized precedent, and we now use a supposedly old relationship as the content for the precedent. This is the deconstruction.

The ethnography in Saint Mary's City was done before Archaeology in Annapolis, now the focus of this paper, was started, but it raised two issues we believed were important for archaeology in the context of a critical perspective. At Saint Mary's City we were able to situate a current interpretation, including some ambiguities about it, in a context of modern politics and to show that history and archaeology were specifically embedded in the present. Now that we ourselves had a turn at situating our own work on a major Catholic figure and his property, was it our task to understand the politics of our own work or to explore the politics of past work and understanding of the man and land we were considering? Was there something we could say from archaeology that would give some liberating depth to the assumptions governing current research? And second, could we situate older interpretations in their contexts and make the interpretation of the past more comprehensible as a result of introducing political considerations into standing considerations?

In founding Archaeology in Annapolis we made a commitment to a public interpretive program which used archaeology as its substance in order to try to deal with these questions from critical theory. The archaeological project was a joint program between the University of Maryland, College Park, and Annapolis's chief private preservation organization, Historic Annapolis Foundation. Historic Annapolis has an educational component and readily agreed to an interpretive program based on archaeology. The interpretive aspect of the program has been funded since 1982 by the Maryland Humanities Council, a state outlet for federal funds from the National Endowment for the Humanities. Funding for the project and public interpretation comes from the federal government; the state of Maryland, especially through the University of Maryland; the City of Annapolis; Historic Annapolis Foundation; and other sources.

In order to create a technically successful public program, a theater producer, Philip Arnault, was hired. He designed a two-hour guided experience around archaeology. It was to begin with a twenty-minute, twelve-projector-slide program introducing visitors to questions which can be asked of material culture. Then people were to visit a working archaeological site and hear an explanation by an archaeologist who has been trained to talk coherently about archaeological interpretation to the public. Third, a guide book (Leone and Potter 1984) for a self-guided walking tour of a portion of the city concluded the experience. All three components have been completed, and since 1982, archaeologists have given tours to over fifty thousand visitors at seven or more sites open to the public in the center of Annapolis. The first printing of the guidebook sold out quickly and was followed by a second printing, and the slide show (Leone 1986) is finished, but not mounted. It will be shown throughout the state as a videotape transfer available through Maryland's Department of Tourism Development. These combined media compose the means for an interpretation.

The use of critical theory in any field does not necessitate the kind of public museum program we have created in Annapolis. Critical theory is based, however, on a dialogue among equals over the political situation involved (Leone, Potter and Shackel 1987). The dialogue can occur anywhere, but to create and enhance it within a tourist setting such as downtown Annapolis where we were always digging, a public program seemed an ideal adjunct to the museum setting that already existed.

We turn now to an assessment of our own applications of a critical perspective to archaeology, specifically the research surrounding Charles Carroll of Carrollton. In 1987, as part of the 250th anniversary of his birth, Charles Carroll of Carrollton's large city property in Annapolis was made available for excavation and eventually was the site of four seasons of excavations of one of the largest open, intact eighteenth-century landscapes in the city.

Seventeen acres in the heart of the Historic District of Annapolis today belong to the Redemptorist community and house St. Mary's Roman Catholic parish, which was founded in 1825 and has been run by the Redemptorists since 1853. This same land was bought in 1701 by Charles Carroll the Settler, the first of four generations of Charles Carrolls. By 1720 two houses were built there by the Carrolls; by 1770 Charles Carroll of Carrollton had joined both houses and erected one very large typical Anglo-American Palladian house, most of which still stands. Charles Carroll of Carrollton also built an adjoining two-acre landscaped descent or falling garden. It is bordered by a brick wall on the street side and by a broad creek at its base. Much of this waterfront garden remains. Seven thousand pages of Carroll letters and other correspondence survive in Baltimore, making this an unusually rich record for Maryland in the eighteenth century.

In 1987 the first goal of our research design was to use archaeological information to comment on the modern political use of space in the city of Annapolis and to communicate that interpretation to the public. This research was designed to provide a missing political context for Charles Carroll of Carrollton's 250th anniversary as well as an explanation of how large formal garden spaces were used in eighteenth-century Annapolis. Leone and his colleagues (Leone, Ernstein, Kryder-Reid and Shackel 1989; Leone and Shackel 1990) had done several analyses of the 1695 plan for the city of Annapolis and its dozen great late eighteenth-century gardens which attempted to show that the city and later its gardens were three-dimensional "volumes" designed to manage perspective views. These views were of sources of power, i.e., the statehouse and Anglican Church, which were to be enhanced by making them appear to be more central, larger, higher, and grander than they actually were up close. At this point, the planned interpretation had nothing to do with an understanding of either the modern owner of the Carroll property, the Redemptorists, or of older interpretations of Charles Carroll. We did not know that material at the time.

Instead of exploring the ethnography of local Catholicism, which for example runs a large upper-class educational complex, or of older, accepted interpretations of the importance of Charles Carroll of Carrollton, Leone opposed his interpretation to one created for the William Paca Garden. The Wright and Paca analysis (Paca-Steel and Wright 1986) argued that the garden under Historic Annapolis Foundation's care was planned paying attention to two dimensions, more or less as though it were a product of Paca's taste, education, and refinement. That is, they said the garden was unique. In contrast, Leone and Shackel (1990) argued that the Carroll garden was composed by using a set of conventional formulas prevalent at the time and, while Paca was not to be underestimated, his effort was to be seen as standardized, as Georgian houses were. This was a reasonable foil, given critical theory, since Potter (1989; Leone, Potter, and Shackel 1987) had done considerable research to show that space in the city today is used to segregate power centers and ethnic groups but is always handled now by planners and politicians in two dimensions. In fact, each current center of power continues to manage important vistas despite the fact that such impact-manipulation is either ignored or denied. No authority today sees space as having depth or as being an active player in social control.

Most of these points were placed together in a public tour in Charles Carroll's garden through the Maryland Humanities Council. The tour was introduced by an archaeologist and was self-guided after a ten-minute spoken opening. The tour, which could take fifteen to thirty minutes, included a map, a brochure, and six placards and ended with a chance to speak to an archaeologist at a site in the garden. The tour used Carroll's large landscaped formal garden built in the 1770s to illustrate Carroll's understanding and use of principles of natural law, as shown in plane and solid geometry, and in horticulture. The two-acre garden created a number of optical illusions which enhanced the views of his house and served in turn to demonstrate that he could indeed command and control natural law in several ways. The argument concluded that since we were seeing the remains of the work of a man of the Enlightenment, and since society and the state were regarded as natural, law-governed phenomena in the eighteenth century, we were looking at the remains of explicit claims in the garden which would have been understood by many of his contemporaries. They were being made by a man proclaiming his ability to govern at a time when, as a Catholic, he was legally denied that opportunity. Catholics had been disfranchised in Maryland since the late seventeenth century.

We were aware that walking through the garden was the key to experiencing its illusions and impact. Slides, photographs, and maps could not duplicate the visual effect of the managed landscape, where the experience was immediate and convincing. The first point made in the tour of the garden was from the water's edge at the base of the garden.

> The Carroll House, which appears to an observer up close to be a mix of periods with varying qualities of workmanship, appears from here to be a unified block with imposing height. It

begins to look impressive, an impression which grows and intensifies as you walk through the garden. (Kryder-Reid et al. 1987: Placard 1)

The next point is that

> Charles Carroll planned this garden in two ways. On a map, from a bird's-eye view, it is a large triangle. You are standing near the shortest side, which goes through the basement door of the house. The tip of the triangle is to your right 300 feet, at the base of the Eastport bridge. Further, each of the ramps acts as the shortest side of one of a series of similar, smaller triangles formed from the large triangle. Carroll knew surveying and probably also studied enough plane geometry to lay out his garden with these shapes in mind.
>
> The garden is also a volume. Carroll spent at least four years turning the natural slope into a series of descents alternating with flat terraces of varying widths, with his house as seen from the water's edge as the focal point. He understood that human vision could be managed so as to enhance the appearance of the house. He made it appear higher, more distant, and therefore more distinguished, by building a landscape around it that included certain optical illusions. (Kryder-Reid et al. 1987: Placard 1)

This point is continued at the base of the garden's main walkway, the center of the huge waterfront of the property.

> The house appears to be more distant than it actually is, an illusion of depth created by the placement of terraces and falls. The house also appears to have an imposing height, an impression enhanced by the placement of the terraces. To those of Carroll's visitors who recognized the garden as an artificial landscape, it demonstrated its maker's mastery of the principles of geometry, taken to have the status of laws of nature in the 18th century. To any visitor the house would have seemed elevated, distant, and situated in a position of power, testifying to the power of its builder. In these ways Carroll's use of solid geometry to design the garden made his house a powerful social and political statement.
>
> Carroll used plane geometry, horticulture, and landscaping principles to demonstrate his understanding of the laws of nature at the same time he doubled the size of his house, adding the third story, high pitched roof, and tall chimneys, based on his understanding of architectural principles. Simultaneously Carroll reorganized his garden's focal point and the whole visual environment between his house and the water's edge in order to create an image of grandeur. (Kryder-Reid et al. 1987: Placard 2)

The third point we made in the tour through the garden was that people were looking at a space whose meanings had changed through time, and thus Charles Carroll of Carrollton was not the only significant occupant.

> As your mind's eye attempts to picture the Carroll Garden as Carroll built it, you must do a certain amount of mental erasing, since the garden has not been frozen in time. The garden that greeted Carroll's visitors is here, but two feet below the surface. So too is the garden that was a Redemptorist farm 100 years later with cows, fields, and a large grape arbor. Finally, since virtually all the trees and other plantings are relatively new, there is a 20th-century garden here too.
>
> The view you see before you and around you is the sum of the alterations that have created

it. And since one of the strengths of archaeology is its sensitivity to changes through time, an archaeological perspective is an ideal way to think about and understand the different gardens that have occupied this one space. (Kryder-Reid et al. 1987: Placard 4)

This was the way we tried to introduce the idea of continually changing interpretations. We did not introduce political considerations into this picture, partly because we did not know them in 1987 or 1988, and partly because we were not sure of what to say. Then, the tour had two endings. One was the following hypothesis and the second was an invitation to discuss matters with an archaeologist, an invitation frequently taken.

This is the top of the Carroll Garden. Take a look out over the boxwood and toward the water. We think that from this perspective there is a second illusion of depth. We think that the water and the boats appear closer than they actually are. That is, of course, exactly the opposite of the illusion at the bottom of the garden, from which the house appears to be more distant than it actually is. Our hypothesis to explain why these visual effects are here is that while other garden builders in Annapolis used optical illusions to enhance the appearance of their power by making their piece of the world seem bigger, Carroll used the same illusions, in different parts of his garden, to make the rest of the world appear closer.

Why did Carroll build his garden this way and enlarge his house at the same time, both in the 1770s? Consider four things: 1) The dig will show you the remains of an ordinary two-story frame house. There was once another two-story brick house next to it, which was the house Carroll enlarged into the house we see today. 2) Carroll was a Roman Catholic and thus forbidden by Maryland law to hold public office. 3) In the 1770s Carroll's family was one of the richest in the colonies. 4) Carroll signed the Declaration of Independence, treason from the British point of view. Were these four events connected?

Our hypothesis is that by demonstrating his knowledge of and control over the laws of nature in his garden, Carroll was attempting to demonstrate his rights to a powerful place in society, since society was also regarded as having natural order. His garden may have been a demonstration that he should be seen as having or deserving a great deal of say in political affairs, since government, too, was based on natural law. Thus, the order he succeeded in achieving here with optics and horticulture, he was prepared to bring to public affairs. (Kryder-Reid et al. 1987: Placard 5)

This tour was given in the summers of 1987, 1988, and 1989, and it was given as an official part of the Carroll anniversary celebrations in the fall of 1987. About five thousand people, including hundreds of school children, have taken the tour, and it has been well-received. We mention this as an accomplishment because museum educators frequently feel visitors want explanations to be quick, simple, and entertaining. No one complained that the tour was unpatriotic or unflattering to Charles Carroll and few questioned any of our assumptions. There was some debate over the argument about geometry and that was expressed in disagreements in the written evaluations which we were required to request by the Maryland Humanities Council.

The lack of dissension, particularly as we were questioning the simplicity of the analogy between political and natural laws as communicated in a landscape garden, was surprising and alarming. We had attempted to provide all the ingredients of our argument so that they would be more transparent to visitors who might disagree or question them, but the argument appeared to be readily accepted, perhaps because of the seemingly weighty authority of the public program format: the identified archaeologist/expert, the large placards with their brightly colored flags, and the free and readily available brochure to guide the way. We also acknowledge that we provided no foil either in the form of other interpretations of gardens or in the form of our own analysis of the ideology of space in the city.

In response to the absence of discussion or dialogue, the school tours for the 1988 season tried to draw out critical responses by raising explicitly the potential flaws of our argument. The school groups were a particularly appropriate arena for a tour which highlighted opposition, because the captive audience of St. Mary's School children (grades 1–12) had been through a version of the tour presented above the year before. The tour began with questions reviewing the 1987 tour, with a gratifying number of students able to recall the tour's argument. We then solicited ideas about "what history is," and Kryder-Reid and other archaeologists expanded on answers which brought out the interpretive nature of history. In short, the point made was that the way you tell the story affects the story you tell. We then noted what we thought we failed to address the previous year (the Carroll women, Carroll's slaves, etc.) and asked the students why they thought some things are left out of histories and some things are kept in. The answers were generally astounding, especially from the elementary school children: "We leave out things that make us feel bad; we want to make ourselves look good; we can't know everything; we do the stuff that is interesting."

At this point in the tour, we showed them an underground nineteenth-century wine vault and demonstrated how different kinds of evidence (architectural, photographic, artifact) answered different questions. The point, however, was rarely taken in the face of the distractions of being twenty feet underground in a damp, musty vault. The conclusion of the tour was a review and an invitation for the students to question interpretations, whether in tours, exhibits, or books, by considering what is highlighted in a story, what is left out, and why. This tour still had no explicit illustration either of our project's politics or of the biases of earlier interpretations of Carroll and his property.

In terms of the issues of concern to a critical perspective, our public program goals were still clear, and we were able to communicate those goals to a school-age audience, but we were still having trouble placing our own work in an explicit context that would make it a more straightforward subject of debate or dialogue. In terms of a critical perspective, we did not provide a political commentary on earlier interpretations and did not make a clear connection to modern biases within our own context that could have illuminated the ideology of space, or any other ideology. In an attempt to understand the limitations of our own biases and to provide an opposition to our work, we compared the 1987 anniversary celebration of which we were a part to the similar commemoration fifty years earlier. This work has just been finished and has never been put on public display.

In 1937 the 200th anniversary of the birth of Charles Carroll of Carrollton was celebrated, and a volume describing that celebration was published. The 1937 anniversary observance consisted of seven "events" on or around the Signer's birthday. It was funded by a joint resolution of the United States House of Representatives and the Senate as well as the city of Baltimore, the Maryland legislature, and the Catholic Archdiocese of Maryland. The events included a commemoration at the Carroll site in Annapolis, an exhibition of family portraits and heirlooms, a Pontifical Military Field Mass at Doughoregan Manor (another Carroll family estate), ceremonies at the College of West Baden in Indiana, tea at the Lombard Street Carroll House in Baltimore, a grand pageant at Homewood (Carroll's son's house) on the Johns Hopkins campus, and finally, a tablet dedication at the Doughoregan Chapel.

The entire celebration was under the direction of a commission, which gave it some cohesion. The grand scheme presented Carroll the statesman at Annapolis, the family man at the Baltimore Museum of Art, and the religious man at Doughoregan and West Baden, with the Baltimore pageant left as a summary of his entire life (Scharff 1937:v).

In Annapolis, according to the commemorative volume, Carroll's "two principal acts in his political life" were depicted in skits—his First Citizen letters in answer to Daniel Dulany, and the burning of the ship *Peggy Stewart*. But the main part of the event was the speeches by two politicians, whose introductions are the keys to understanding their descriptions of Carroll. The men were introduced as "two outstanding Marylanders, one a statesman and the other a jurist, who represent today, just as Charles Carroll of Carrollton represented in his day and generation, the very highest and best type of Maryland citizenship" (Scharff 1937:5).

The first speaker was the Hon. George L. Radcliffe, U.S. senator and aspiring politician who was to run unsuccessfully for governor eight years later. The senator presented a picture of Carroll as the consummate politician for 1930s Maryland: conservative, yet open to economic and technological innovation. Radcliffe portrayed Carroll as a man who "believed that to be practical a man must have an open mind in regard to suggested changes, but that he needed also a deliberative spirit and a well-balanced mind in weighing new ideas, lest he might lightly discard the wisdom of the ancients" (Scharff 1937:6).

And as if Carroll alone weren't enough of an example, Radcliffe also drew parallels to Washington with his similar "instinctive sense of caution" and "careful and methodical" nature. Yet, Radcliffe maintained, "both were open-minded enough to see the necessity at times for new policies, political and economic" (Scharff 1937:7).

Radcliffe's speech is particularly revealing in light of the circumstances of the late thirties in Maryland. The heavily Democratic state was straining to get out of the Depression, gambling was outlawed, and tax hikes were repeatedly voted down. The Democratic legislature stifled most initiatives of the Republican governor (Quinn 1971:435–436). It is not hard to imagine the point of Radcliffe's persuasion to be, like Carroll, "ever alert to consider new economic and financial ideas but cautious in adopting them" (Scharff 1937:6).

The second address in Annapolis was by the Hon. T. Scott Offutt, lawyer and jurist at the Maryland Court of Appeals. In Offutt's construction, Carroll is first represented as the personification of the American spirit and is then identified with Maryland. Offutt proclaimed that Carroll

> truly represented the spirit of rugged individualism and personal and political independence. . . . Maryland is an old State, its traditions die slowly, and while elsewhere that spirit

has yielded to the advancing collectivism of an industrial age, here it still persists in much of its original strength. Charles Carroll incarnated that spirit. (Scharff 1937:9)

> . . . his memory lives so vividly and so brilliantly with us . . . because his whole life was so interwoven with the struggle of this Nation for independence, and with the history of its first and formative years, that they may not be separated. (Scharff 1937:14)

Offutt continued, explaining that Carroll was still such a prominent figure in Maryland because "he so perfectly exhibited in his life those qualities of heart and mind which the people of this State admire most and love to believe characterize in some degree at least their own lives" (Scharff 1937:9).

For Offutt, Carroll personified revolutionary America. He was not just a patriot, he is patriotism; and he was not just a Marylander, he is Maryland. In the speakers' rhetoric, the past and present are linked and fused. Marylanders are joined with their past and, through it, to the ideals of the present. Maryland's part in the nation is affirmed, and the politicians who can create or at least explicate that link are legitimized.

Of particular interest is the place of the physical landscape—currently our archaeological site—in all this use of the past. While the Carroll grounds did not figure prominently in the celebration, they were recognized as extensions of the Signer's personified patriotism. If Carroll was revered, his house and grounds were relics. The state senator, Ridgely P. Melvin, proclaimed in his welcoming remarks that the celebration was fortunate "in having a setting and an atmosphere that furnish real inspiration for the occasion. . . . we are permitted to assemble here in these beautiful and hallowed grounds, which, appurtenant to the original Carroll mansion, form a shrine of patriotism" (Scharff 1937:5). Furthermore, in the organization of the program, the politicians were presented as the keepers of that shrine.

In 1987 the 250th anniversary of the birth of Charles Carroll of Carrollton was celebrated in sharp relief to the events fifty years earlier. The 1937 anniversary was in large part federally funded; the 1987 event was paid for with state and local funds (Worden 1987). The 1937 celebration was statewide with an additional event in Indiana; the 1987 program was in Annapolis only. The most significant difference is in their designs. The 1937 joint resolution cited Carroll's contributions to the country:

> Charles Carroll of Carrollton pledged his life, his sacred honor, and the largest fortune in America to the success of the Revolution. . . . it is eminently proper and desirable that the United States should officially commemorate this event. (Scharff 1937:1–2)

The commemorative volume justifies itself as

> an attempt to put in appropriate and permanent form a complete record of the entire celebration, so that posterity may know that this generation was not unmindful of the Nation's debt to Charles Carroll of Carrollton. . . . (Scharff 1937:iv)

In contrast to the 1937 paying up of the people's debt to Carroll, the 1987 anniversary was, in many ways, trying to justify Carroll's debt to the people in the form of fund raising for the restoration of the Carroll house and garden. The anniversary coincided with the end of ten years of restoration of the exterior of his house, with efforts underway to raise money for the rest of the restoration plan. Fund-raising efforts were strengthened by demonstrations of both historical significance and a broad-based constituency, both of which were felt to be difficult to come by. In 1937, Carroll's identification as a prominent patriot and founding father was linked to contemporary aspirations of political careers or legislative initiatives. In 1987, the anniversary was a chance to publicize and legitimize the man himself, and in so doing, to justify the expense and effort of the house and garden restoration project.

When Kryder-Reid examined the 1937 anniversary, she found data which showed that interpretations of Carroll had changed, and that both then and now there were separate political factors behind the change. Although the factors in 1937 are not well drawn out yet, they are clearer than those shading today's interpretation. While today we have done relatively little research about the politics of the parish, the priests, or local or regional Catholicism, we do know a great deal about local control of historic preservation and can easily see a shift within the city beginning in the 1960s that emphasizes William Paca, also a signer of the Declaration of Independence. His house and fame became a locally ascendent symbol of upper-class preservationists as they fought to preserve his house. His reputation is now far more important than Carroll's. The rise of historic preservationists who owned Paca's house may be a small part of the story of the flux seen in Carroll's reputation.

We now want to move our discussion to a more general level as well as to summarize our points. We are concerned with the conditions for discourse among equals in a structure free from both internal and external constraints. We aim for a general symmetry among participants in discussion where there is equal opportunity to select and employ argument and response (Kemp 1988:186). This is a paraphrase of Habermas, but reflects the project's commitment to critical theory since 1981. The idea in the paraphrase is an ideal against which to measure our work at Charles Carroll's house and garden.

We have a technique, in using Habermas's categories for describing the conditions for symmetrical discourse, to describe our work. First, did all participants to our program have the same chance to initiate and perpetuate discourse? This question means not so much access to discussion as it does mutual intelligibility. Could we understand each other on equal terms? Since, from the project's beginning we hired a theater producer familiar with neighborhood history projects and made every effort to use ordinary speech, as opposed to jargon, this condition was normally met. Second, is the discourse sincere in the sense of truthful? Were we consistent in what we said, and was the responding public? We believe that this condition was met, since disagreements were always regarded as useful and, indeed, as proof that our aim of fostering discourse was being realized.

Third, could anyone "command and oppose, permit and forbid arguments" (Kemp 1988:186)? Were there one-sided norms; could one side be forbidden to call for justification? Here we begin to realize that while our tour and discussion provided definitions of archaeological procedure and a considerable amount of background on ourselves and Charles Carroll, there was no way a visitor, even a dedicated one, could know enough to challenge effectively what we were doing. The condition of being able to command and oppose, particularly to disagree effectively, was realized occasionally. It required far more detailed knowledge to do this than was readily available. But it is with the fourth condition that we discover our problem. That is, can either side, including a visitor, have the opportunity to provide an alternative explanation or to challenge a given point of the argument? Ideally yes. And we valued it when it happened. But it happened only occasionally.

These four conditions exist in order for a "rationally grounded consensus [to] emerge from . . . discourse" (Kemp 1988:188). It is assumed that this is a ground for democratic action, including democratic access to undertaking politically powerful interpretations of the past in a city where access to interpretations of the past is closely controlled by dominant institutions like the apparatus of state government, the United States Naval Academy, and Historic Annapolis Foundation.

We conclude that in the constraints on give and take and on the inability of visitors and, in part, of ourselves to provide alternative interpretations or to be able to challenge standing validity claims, we did not create the ideal conditions for dialogue. This leads to two considerations: the external constraints on us, and the constraints we imposed on ourselves.

In juxtaposition to the 1937 anniversary celebration and to the St. Mary's City drama, our role in the construction of the history of Charles Carroll is made more transparent. We began to see that an anniversary of the 250th birthday of the Signer was accompanied by secular archaeology, disinterest in Charles Carroll on the part of the clergy who own his property, and no reference to Carroll's religiosity. But we did not give ourselves time to discover why, in terms that would have allowed us to use the material in the public program to question our own or the Carroll Anniversary Committee's claims through archaeology for the validity of restoration. We also failed to explore the immediate ethnographic uses of the past in the Catholic establishment, including its long-standing struggle with Historic Annapolis Foundation over control of the restoration of the Carroll House. This means we did not know the local ideology. We now note the following contrasts which center on the Charles Carroll/St. Mary's parish property, out of which we might have built an ethnography of givens which could have served to provide alternative interpretations. Through the early nineteenth century the property housed the Jesuits, including John Carroll, first American Catholic bishop and founder of Georgetown University. After 1852 it housed the Redemptorists, by the wish of the Carroll family. The Jesuits were regarded as political and intellectual, Redemptorists say they are concerned with spiritual matters. The eighteenth-century connections with the house are with famous men who were foreign-educated, pugnacious, intellectual, overtly political Catholics, and very, very rich. Our tour reinforced this opposition but failed to explain it.

On the other hand, the dig was part of the decade-long archaeological investigation of the city's landscape, both its town plan and its private gardens, and of the archaeological manifestations of emerging capitalism in eighteenth-century Annapolis. Excavating the house and formal garden of the wealthiest resident of Annapolis was an obvious extension of this design. It is tied to an exploration of local ideology and is on continual public display. The interpretive primacy given to the eighteenth-century occupation of the site almost to the exclusion of the nineteenth- and twentieth-century Redemptorist tenure is also compliant with Historic Annapolis Foundation's interest in Annapolis's "golden age,'' but is never discussed. Another factor invisible to the public is the organizational structure of the project. While Leone's interpretations contributed to materialist considerations of Carroll's landscaping efforts, they explicitly avoided a controversy with the Wright/Paca interpretation of the William Paca Garden of Historic Annapolis, cosponsor and a principal source of funding for his own archaeological project.

Perhaps the most compelling reason for our inability to explore ideology and thus either to say or to listen to other validity claims is the low profile in Annapolis today of the Carroll property, the Redemptorists, Charles Carroll of Carrollton's achievements, and local Catholicism. Annapolis is a largely Protestant city, centered geographically on the Episcopal church, on a peninsula settled by Puritans in the 1650s, and made the capital of Maryland explicitly because it was Protestant. The construction of Annapolis's present identity is dependent upon precedent, and that precedent is based in large part upon its eighteenth-century past. The quiet removal of minorities, whether racial or religious, from the history of the town is one of the ways in which the town's preeminent identity as an intact eighteenth-century gem is perpetuated. Parker Potter (1989), coordinator of the project's public program from 1983 to 1988, analyzed the construction of Annapolis histories, yet our own interpretations continue to be products of the same received biases because in the case of the Carroll property we could not and would not engage in acts challenging underlying claims to truth. We did not problematize some givens and we could not aid others in doing so.

Our effort in this essay has been to employ a critical perspective. The core of such a perspective is an exploration of the impact of political factors in the present, and, particularly for archaeologists, in the interpretation of the past. There are, of course, two pasts we have concerned ourselves with. One is previous interpretations, such as the 1937 view of Charles Carroll of Carrollton and the Wright/Paca view of landscape architecture in the Paca garden. Another past is the one we automatically construct as we work in archaeology. Consciousness of the construction process is the end, with communication of it to the public an important concern. From our work over several years we have attempted to (1) situate the political use of Catholicism's history in Maryland, (2) situate and expose to dialogue our own archaeological work on a Catholic property, and (3) describe modern ideology in Annapolis.

We conclude that it is relatively easy to develop hunches about the political aspects of past work, through deconstruction, as was the case with Saint Mary's City, and with the bicentenary of the birth of Charles Carroll of Carrollton. This method guides us very directly to being aware of the influence of political considerations but does not, however, guide us in how to formulate our own research. We also sense the need to communicate these considerations to the public, not only to scholars.

Neither deconstruction nor developing an awareness of political factors in others' and our work was difficult to achieve. The difficulty comes in two areas. One is in a dialogue about political factors, and another is in tracing the effect of such awareness on the results of our research. Such a dialogue is difficult to carry on effectively without creating controversy. The inevitable need for a foil between former work and current work can give rise to comparisons which can be unflattering. Leone avoided such controversy at the Carroll property. Thus, while dialogue did occur, there was often only a pallid foil available to encourage it. Second, it is difficult to describe how awareness of political considerations affects our own work. We know such considerations do, but the paths taken over a multiyear project are hard to follow and then describe. Thus, it is hard to know how political considerations affect archaeology and society precisely, but not hard to know that they do.

Acknowledgments: The data on Saint Mary's City was collected with the help of members of the Saint Mary's City Commission. The Charles Carroll 250th Anniversary Committee was headed by Dr. Robert Worden. The Redemptorist Congregation has aided the archaeological project. The project was supported by the Maryland Humanities Council and sponsored by Historic Annapolis Foundation and the University of Maryland, College Park. Parker Potter helped confirm the structuralist analysis of Charles Carroll's identity in Annapolis, and Robert Preucel brought Ray Kemp's work to our attention.

REFERENCES

Breen, T. H. 1980. *Puritans and Adventurers, Change and Persistance in Early America*. Oxford University Press, New York.

Kemp, R. 1988. "Planning, public hearings, and the politics of discourse," in J. Forester (ed.), *Critical Theory and Public Life*, pp. 177–201. MIT Press, Cambridge, MA.

Kryder-Reid, E., M. P. Leone, B. J. Little, and P. B. Potter, Jr. 1987. *Carroll Garden Placards 1–6*. Annapolis, MD.

Leone, M. P. 1986. *Annapolis: Reflections of the Age of Reason*. Audio-visual program produced by Telesis, Inc. Baltimore, MD.

Leone, M. P., J. H. Ernstein, E. Kryder-Reid, and P. A. Shackel 1989. "Power gardens of Annapolis," *Archaeology* **42**, 35–39, 74–75.

Leone, M. P., and P. B. Potter, Jr. 1984. *Archaeological Annapolis: A Guide to Seeing and Understanding Three Centuries of Change*. Historic Annapolis Inc. and University of Maryland at College Park.

Leone, M. P., P. B. Potter, Jr., and P. A. Shackel 1987. "Toward a critical archaeology," *Current Anthropology* **28**, 283–302.

Leone, M. P., and P. A. Shackel 1990. "Plane and solid geometry in colonial gardens in Annapolis, Maryland," in W. M. Kelso and R. Most (eds.), *Earth Patterns, Essays in Landscape Archaeology*, pp. 153–167. University of Virginia Press, Charlottesville.

Miller, H. M. 1988. "Baroque cities in the wilderness: Archaeology and urban development in the colonial Chesapeake," *Historical Archaeology* **22(2)**, 57–73.

Paca-Steele, B., and St. Clair Wright 1986. "The mathematics of an eighteenth-century wilderness garden," *Journal of Garden History* **6(4)**, 299–320.

Potter, P. B., Jr. 1989. *Archaeology in Public in Annapolis: An Experiment in the Application of Critical Theory to Historical Archaeology*. Ph.D. dissertation, Department of Anthropology, Brown University, Providence, RI.

Quinn, A. W. 1971. "Contemporary Maryland," in M. L. Radoff (ed.), *The Old Line State: A History of Maryland*, pp. 433–462. Maryland Hall of Records, Publication 16, Annapolis, MD.

Scharff, J. H. (ed.) 1937. *The Bicentenary Celebration of the Birth of Charles Carroll of Carrollton*. Lord Baltimore Press, Baltimore, MD.

Worden, R. L. 1987. Application to the Maryland Humanities Council for "Archaeology and the Political Meaning of Charles Carroll of Carrollton." Manuscript on file, Historic Annapolis Foundation, Annapolis, Maryland.

Toward an Archaeology of Body and Soul

> Nothing in man—not even his body—is suffi-
> ciently stable to serve as the basis for self-
> recognition or for understanding other men.
>
> (Michel Foucault 1971: 153)

> On a deeper level, anthropology's concern is nei-
> ther to prove that the primitive is wrong nor to
> side with him against us, but to set itself up on a
> ground where we shall both be intelligible without
> any reduction or rash transposition.
>
> (Maurice Merleau-Ponty 1974: 119)

The original paper for the conference was conceived and partially written in a field situation. Thus it is not surprising that it began with several tales from the field. Anecdotes have frequently served as repositories of anthropological insights. Upon reflection and revision, once again taking place in the field, I have chosen to maintain the original style of exposition. I came to the "problem" that serves as the focus of this paper, not by meticulously tracking it across intellectual traditions, but by it "happening" to me, and I hesitate to let go of its experiential quality. In one sense the "problem's" exposition in this paper maintains a bit of its original flavor, but the style of its exposition is also intended as a meta-commentary on a resonant theme. This is the theme of the credibility of sensuous experience versus the credentialing of logical abstraction.[1] But more of this later as there are two tales to be told now.

One tale is that of an archaeologist venturing into ethnographic fieldwork and the other is the tale of an archaeologist assisting at a public presentation of archaeology. Both of these tales involve "death," the experiencing and the understanding of "death." It is not without interest and irony for this paper, originally presented as part of a conference on semiotics and structuralism in archaeology, that Foucault is said to have argued that "madness, death and sex underlie discourse and resist linguistic appropria-tion" (Dreyfus and Rabinow 1982:vii).[2]

Tale number 1   The week of February 8, 1987
                Andrainjato, Madagascar

The younger sister of Rafotsibe died Sunday. The deceased had expressed the wish that when she died she would like to lie one night in the village where she had passed her married life and one night in the village of her mother, where she had spent her youth. (These villages are within easy walking distance of each other.) The funeral did not take place until Wednesday. February in Madagascar is a hot month in the austral summer of the island. Formaldehyde was not available to inject into the body, and indigenous alternatives involving mixtures of pineapple juice were not used for some reason or another.

Ramatoakely had gone on Tuesday to visit the body in state. She admitted to having drunk a substantial amount of *toaka* (the local home-brewed rum) in order to be able to enter the room since the body was in an advanced state of decomposition. This state had also been a topic of local conversation, especially among the younger women as they went back and forth from the pump to bring the water to be used in the cleansing of the body. (Luckily my control of the local language did not allow me to appreciate the finer details of the description of this phase of the funeral activities.)

Normally burials take place in the afternoon, as there is a symbolic link between the declining sun and the end of life. But given the state of the decomposing body, the burial actually took place in the morning. Appropriate excuses were made by the responsible elders for this breach of tradition. Interestingly enough, one justification given was an appeal to common knowledge about hygiene and health. It was while standing around the collective tomb that I first experienced the smell of a decomposing human body. It is a smell that is overpowering. My research colleague, after inquiring into the etiquette of cigarette smoking during funeral services, returned to our quarters to bring back a pack of cigarettes and matches. I and several local friends stood close to this nonsmoker who had suddenly been transformed into a chain smoker, in order to breathe in the cigarette smoke. The sight of Rafotsibe carrying a handful of "organic matter," scraped from the mats that had held the body, into the tomb certainly contributed to an image of death that I had never experienced previously. All that day I was convinced that this experience had so marked me that I imagined this smell of death following me everywhere. The next day when I remarked on this smell and its lingering presence to one of our informants, he said that this smell does in fact stick to one's clothes and it was not simply a case of an overactive imagination.

My field notes on this incident carry a large question mark as to how far this "smell of death" is critical to the experiencing and the imaging of death in Betsileo society.[3]

Later that week Rafotsibe called me to her side as I was passing by her house, the house where her sister had lain in state on Tuesday and Wednesday. She asked me for some *ranomanitra* (perfume), since the smell of death continued to envelop her as well. To plead her case she invited me to enter the downstairs room which had held her sister's body. I quickly declined, saying that I understood, without the need of demonstration, what she was saying.

It was a later discussion with another anthropologist[4] working on the island that brought a nuance to my attempts to understand the relation of physical experience and emotion to cultural acts and symbolic representations.

A senior member of a family originally from the central highlands of the island now living on the coast in the area where the anthropologist was working had, several years ago, begun construction of a new communal family tomb. Such tombs play critical roles among highland populations in asserting and maintaining both extended family relations and group identity. This individual died before completing the tomb and it was left unfinished for a period of time. At one point another member of this family had a dream in which he was urged to see that this family tomb be completed. Consequently arrangements were made to finish the tomb, and its completion was to be marked by the celebration of a *famadihana*. (This is a festivity where old bodies are rewrapped in new shrouds and, in some cases, as in the one being discussed, are transferred from older family tombs to a newly constructed one. *Famadihana* are considered joyous occasions.)[5] To attend this activity various family members were undertaking travel from the center of the island to the coast, and even from France to Madagascar.

Unfortunately, just before the *famadihana* was to take place, an "aunt" died and had to be placed in the new tomb. The immediate family members were anxious and fearful for the upcoming event because, with the reopening of the tomb with the newly deceased individual in it, the smell of death would still be present. What was at issue here, however, was not so much that the "smell of death" was offensive, it was rather that the smell was a reminder of individual deaths. This situation echoed the words of Rafotsibe when she put off mourning for her sister: one must eventually put aside mourning, not simply to allow the living to go on with their lives, but to allow the dead to be effectively integrated into the community of ancestors on the other side of the grave.[6]

Tale number 2   Friday August 28, 1987
                Memphis, Tennessee

After several years of negotiation, the city of Memphis, Tennessee, was able to host the traveling exhibit of the Egyptian pharaoh Ramses II. Having just arrived back in town less than a week before the closing of the exhibit in Memphis, I did not want to scandalize my students and the members of MSAPA (Mid-South Association of Professional Anthropologists) by being the only resident archaeologist not to have seen the exhibit. Unfortunately, at this late date exhibit catalogues were sold out and the information given on panels over the display cases of the exhibit consisted of several very short and not terribly informative sentences. So, I paid my $2.70 for the pleasure of the recorded company of Charlton Heston as I wondered/wandered through the exhibit hall. (When you come to think of it, who better to "bring to life" the world of the pharaohs than one who has walked and talked with gods and kings.) Any good exhibit of Pharaonic Egypt has its fair share of mummies. Imagine, then, Charlton Heston's biblical voice describing the cult of the dead characteristic of Ramses' time. There were vivid descriptions of the physical preparation of the dead for the afterlife, preparations that included the removal of internal organs through a slit in the left side of the body, stages of fifteen days drying, fifteen days wrapping, and the packaging of various internal organs in separate containers. There were also references to the religious and obsessional need on the part of Egyptians of the period to conquer death in the afterlife through arresting the decomposition of their bodies. The voice of Charlton Heston and the artifactual accoutrements were in place to re-create a historical drama but the sensual and the emotion were not—there was no "smell of death" and for me Ramses is neither god, hero, nor father.

Reflections

Certainly such experiences give us pause to reflect on the grand essentialist question: What do we understand of Death? But there are also questions that can be posed about "local" knowledge and understanding of death, questions that concern us as social scientists. What are the cultural bounds and dimensions of our understanding and experience of death? What possibility is there for us to know "the other's" conceptualization and experience of death? The preceeding two tales, in fact, put a spin on these questions. My experience in Madagascar, easily yet dramatically, undercuts any self-assured belief in a panhuman experience of death's drama. Consequently, the Memphis exhibit's description of the life and death of the Great Ramses, a description that makes explicit appeals to "basic human" hopes and fears, rings false.

Death is a personal drama. It is also a panhuman dilemma subject to alternative cultural explorations. But the intent of this paper is to suggest that a further point for reflection might be drawn from the two tales concerning death. We need to recognize that indigenous symbolic representations and experiences of death play a role in the continuing re-creation of social and cultural orders on the one hand, and that Western conceptualizations of death play a role in professional anthropological attempts to understand the operations of such social and cultural orders.

A review of British social anthropological works on sub-Saharan Africa would more than adequately illustrate the argument that the death of "kings" was troublesome for certain African societies, both at the practical political level of the transfer of power, and at the level of a cultural representation of an indigenous theory of power. The example of the incredible percentage of the gross national product of the New Kingdom under Ramses the Great that was directed toward his funerary rites also helps make the point that death as a concept and as an experience is not without a role in the operations and logics of indigenous social and cultural systems. The indigenous American cultural system is no exception. In a court of law hearsay evidence, that is, testimony of an individual who has not actually witnessed an event but has only "heard tell" of the event by an actual witness to the event, is generally inadmissible. An exception is made for "death-bed" speeches, that is, utterances made by an individual while expiring her/his last breath.[7]

It is also the case that an understanding of "death" slips into our theoretical explanations of the workings of sociocultural systems. For example, the evidence that Neanderthals carefully buried their dead, perhaps with flowers, has been interpreted in terms of the creation of social solidarity under stressful situations. Weber understood that the logic of the legitimacy of charismatic leadership is undermined by the physical decline and eventual death of such leaders. There are numerous other examples where individual deaths, the fear of death, the disregard for personal safety, etc., have entered into our explanations of both historical events and sociocultural processes.

"Death" is not so much the issue here as it is a metonym for a more encompassing argument. It seems to me that we invoke quite often "sensuality," "emotion," "conviction," and the like in social theoretical explanations. We talk about desire for power, about awe before the gods and before kings, about magic as the audacious confrontation of human and natural forces, and about ideological notions of purity and danger being tied to physiological processes. The physical and the emotional are part of our social theoretical discussions just as much as are cold, calculated motives and logics. I do not see how it can be otherwise without reducing humans to automatons or to cerebral essences. (Though various forms of structuralism have been accused of just such reduction and do not seem to mind.) Even if one refuses the need for an appeal to "sensuousness" in "high theory," it is still a professional problem as it does enter into the public presentation of our discipline. We make use of blood, guts, and dirt as well as human dignity to present an image to the public of contemporary and prehistoric "others." We often feel professionally as well as personally compelled to understand why people do such "irrational" things as sacrifice themselves to the lions, betray their allies, or commit infanticide.

Recent trends in archaeology that involve semiotic, structuralist, and symbolic perspectives recognize that "consciousness" has often been left underspecified in the social theory employed by archaeologists. The above discussion is intended to suggest a further point, that an appeal to "sensuousness" (or some combination of the physical and emotional as well as the mental character of human existence), while present in our explanations of social phenomena, has also been left underspecified in our social theory. I would argue that the words of Merleau-Ponty and Foucault that lead off this article announce an important theoretical question for us as well as trace its bounds, if we choose to begin to recognize "sensuality" as an element of our theoretical frameworks. On one side Merleau-Ponty expresses the desire and the possibility of "knowing" the other and oneself without betraying the integrity of the other's experience by encompassing it in too local a frame of understanding. On the other side Foucault challenges the romantic will to understand the other by arguing for the impossibility of transgressing the bounds of our local experience.

Let me be clear about the direction and focus of the argument at this point. "Sensuality" might not be directly recoverable in the archaeological record. This does not then imply that we are free to ignore its place in our theoretical formulations. What do we do with it, though?

Loathing—Logic—Lust

Certainly we archaeologists are intelligent beings attempting to understand ourselves through the material and intellectual products of other intelligent beings. Yet, we are also sensuous beings, and if this point needs stressing we have only to recall that the exercise of our profession calls upon our visual and tactile senses as much as upon our ability to reason symbolically.

The concept of the symbol and of symbolic activity has give form and focus to the school of American anthropology. Perhaps one can partially explain American archaeological interest in structuralism and semiotics in light of this tradition, given American archaeology's close association with cultural anthropology. In a sense, an interest in the "archaeology of the mind" reasserts a heritage of symbolism in face of the ever popular ecological and evolutionary approaches.[8] Yet a theoretical focus placed on the accepting, reflecting, and/or skeptical mind courts an essentialist position of mind and culture, as various critics have pointed out. It also courts a form of intellectual hubris wherein the mind of the modern archaeologist is seen as capable of encompassing the mind of the prehistoric nonarchaeologist. In such a theoretical approach to the individual and to culture, there is neither much room for nor great interest in the enjoying, suffering, and resisting body. The sensuousness of body and soul demands an existential context wherein symbols and symbolic activity find their context and content, not simply their manipulation. It is not just that "the symbolic" must be granted ontological status in our theories, but "sensuous human activity" as well.

So there we have it: Marx has come in through a theoretical back door, for the concept of "praxis" has been defined in terms of sensuous human activity. The term "Marxism" has a way of making people feel uncomfortable, myself included, because it has so often been ensconced in intellectual game playing and power plays. Meriting the title of "Marxist" is not my concern, nor is my concern to explain each and every relevant and irrelevant use of Marx's writings. I am more interested in appreciating some aspects of Marx's thought that might be useful for laying out some basic theoretical field markers so as not to reinvent the theoretical wheel. Marx's insistence on an existential and historical context for social formulations is a first point of appreciation. What seems even more useful conceptually for our purposes is the premise that "social being determines consciousness," with the understanding that social being is constituted through praxis, through sensuous human activity.[9]

If we then take the position that the constitution of body and soul takes place in and is conditioned by a social and historical situation or context, then the skeptical position of Foucault announced on the first page of this article must be dealt with in some fashion. This is the position that we never overlap sufficiently with the context of the "other" to enable understanding across contexts. As anthropologists, historians, and/or social scientists we naïvely deal with this issue by a professional leap of faith in taking the position that

> no society, however foreign it might seem to the observer, can be considered without meaning. (Augé 1979:79)

We should not leap too far and thus jump back into the essentialist camp, however. Merleau-Ponty's position is a first approximation of a position which allows us to reject the skepticism of Foucault as well as the hubris of the essentialist embrace of "the other." We can thus direct our attention to the context of human experience and begin to specify the critical elements of social and historical contexts that influence the creation and manipulation of the symbols and symbolic systems that we use to understand and act upon the world.

Taking Symbols Seriously (though a bit naïvely)[10]

Turner has made an interesting distinction between two "clusters" of cultural symbols (1978:574–575), and I find it suggestive to follow his reasoning for a moment in tracking the question of the content and context of symbols. According to Turner one can place cultural symbols on a continuum, the two poles of which he labels "physiological" and "ideological" or "normative." One critical contrast between the two poles is that of intense and immediate affect on one end and abstract social values and norms on the others. Turner has offered examples of symbols that cluster around these two poles drawn from his work among the Ndembu of Zambia. Symbols that fit more readily into the "physiological" cluster include such things as mother's milk, menstrual blood, and the blood of circumcision. Symbols that fit more readily into the "ideological" or "normative" cluster are such issues as group solidarity and the reciprocity expected among kin. Turner has argued that participation in various rituals effects the transfer of affect from the first cluster of symbols to the second cluster of symbols. This transfer is important for it sustains the social order by "inducing the individual to feel the awesome power of his social obligations instead of regarding them as either remote or a nuisance" (1978:575–576). Taking a hint from Turner's remarks on symbols and the role of ritual activity in creating symbolic systems, I would suggest that our questions on the context and content of sensuous human activity be formulated as questions about the differing contents of these two symbolic clusters and the manner in which the two clusters are linked in cultural practice.

For the sake of initiating discussion I will conceptualize the issue of "context and content" in terms of an opposition, all the while recognizing that lived experience is not encompassed by the logic of exclusive categories. Let me propose the following two poles of socioeconomic context. At one pole we have the cluster of "the state," literacy, class organization, elaborate division of labor, carpentered space, bureaucratic time, and the like. At the other pole we have the logic of gift-giving, emphasis on the ethics of kinship organization, social time and space that overlap with seasons and local ecology, and the like. What follows are a few points to consider if we use this contrast in tracking our problem of the context and content of sensuous human activity.

Within the context of the state, sociopolitical apparatuses, such as bureaucratic structures and permanent offices, become increasingly institutionalized, objectified, and materially manifest. Bourdieu has remarked:

> . . . objectification guarantees the permanence and cumulativity of material and symbolic acquisitions which can then subsist without the agents having to recreate them continuously and in their entirety by deliberate action. (1977:184)

It is less ritual than it is routine that is the form of sensuous human activity that maintains the sociopolitical order in state societies.

It is also worth considering that the "embodiment" that might be said to characterize ritual social activity finds a contrast in the reification and thus externalization of the "state" as blueprint for the social order. Foucault has argued that the "body has become an essential component for the operation of power relations in modern society" (Dreyfus and Rabinow 1982:112) in that such societies take apart and reconstitute the body so as to allow its more effective manipulation and control. Part of the "reconstituting" of the body is its constitution in opposition to mind. This reconstitution is complemented by a differential valuing of various bodies and minds, that is complemented by issues of class, race, literacy, and intellectual labor.

States are societies that permit and encourage full-time specialization, and more specifically and critically, as Marx has remarked, such a division of labor is based on a division of intellectual from manual labor (1977:167–168). Such a "state of affairs" allows for the production, accumulation, and monopolization of increasingly extensive and complex systems of knowledge. Such systems of knowledge are used in the service of state operations, in particular, in the construction of the form and content of the society's "normative" or "ideological" symbols. Such symbolic form and content must be ideologically appropriated to some degree and in some fashion by other participants in the state. With the division of labor, class organization, etc. that are characteristic of state organization, the commonality of immediate sensuous human activity is more severely limited than in nonstate societies. Thus one might begin to understand how, on the one hand, issues of clarity, simplicity, and abstraction and, on the other hand, issues of material and behavioral mapping onto the structures and routines of the state become valued in the production of the symbols and logics that are consciously produced by the "experts" of the states and instructed to the "masses."

Preliminary Conclusions

> Cultures vary greatly in their exploitation of the
> various senses and in the way in which they relate
> their conceptual apparatus to the various senses.
> (Ong 1977: 3)

The task of understanding symbolic and sensuous human activity is formidable. We cannot assume that the contents of the physical-emotional realm of experience are either panhuman or empathically knowable across sociohistorical contexts. Much less can we assume that the abstract normative pole of indigenous social concepts is stable across sociohistorical contexts. Further, the mechanisms that allow the linkage or cross-mapping of these two symbolic clusters is not identical across sociohistorical contexts.

These considerations would seem to argue that the closer we are in features to the sociopolitical context of "the other" the more legible symbols and symbolic systems might be. This is not only because of our proximity in social space and time but also because of the nature of the state. This is to say, there will be a certain array of symbols of the "normative" or "ideological" cluster whose conscious creation and manipulation on the part of indigenous "intellectual specialists" and whose deliberate mapping onto the concrete material products and routines of the state might make them more easily accessible to us. We might use this advantage of symbolic legibility to begin working our way through the constitution and control of sensuous human activity in different sociohistorical contexts rather than mistaking this legibility for a privileged perspective.

This discussion should be viewed as an attempt to formulate a problem focus—the understanding of sensuous human activity. It is also an attempt to offer a few borrowed concepts to chart a bit of the theoretical terrain. While I would defend the importance of this problem concern, I am not ready to defend the specific formulation as it stands in this article. Let the subsequent discussion and critique begin.

NOTES

1. To put this theme another way is to draw attention to the contrast between the "authority" that backs the phrase "I feel it to be so," and the "power" that backs the phrase "I know it to be so."

2. It should be duly noted that I have made a most conservative choice among the three potential categories.

3. The Betsileo are one of eighteen "ethnic" groups that inhabit Madagascar. They are peasant agriculturalists whose primary subsistence activities are the cultivation of wet rice and the raising of cattle. They live in the south-central highlands of the island.

4. Personal communication, Leslie Sharp.

5. Certainly the joy is nuanced by melancholy, but the emotional emphasis of the occasion, nevertheless, is on rejoicing.

6. This research was carried out under the Fulbright Program during the 1986–1987 academic year. I would like to thank my colleague, Victor Raharijaona, Assistant Director of the Musée d'Art et d'Archéologie of Madagascar, for his research collaboration, the people of the Mitongoa/Andrainjato area for their patience and generosity, and the Musée d'Art et d'Archéologie for the loan of field equipment.

7. My thanks to Thomas Kus for drawing my attention to this aspect of the U.S. legal system.

8. I do not intend this remark to denigrate the contributions that ecological and evolutionary theory have made to American archaeology.

9. Raymond Williams (1977) has suggested that we take Marx's premise that "social being determines consciousness" as the central and beginning point of our social theory, rather than the "base-superstructure" model that figures as the central focus of much Marxist-inspired social analysis.

10. Sperber has remarked: "I suggest . . . that the notion of the symbol, at least provisionally, be removed from the vocabulary of the theory of symbolism, and be described only as a native notion" (1975:50).

REFERENCES

Augé, M. 1979. *Symbole, fonction, histoire: les interrogations*. Hachette, Paris.
Bourdieu, P. 1977. *Outline of a Theory of Practice*. Cambridge University Press, Cambridge, MA.

Dreyfus, H., and P. Rabinow 1982. *Michel Foucault: Beyond Structuralism and Hermeneutics*. University of Chicago Press, Chicago.

Foucault, M. 1971. "Nietzsche, genealogy, history," in D. F. Bouchard (ed.), *Michel Foucault: Language, Counter-Memory, Practice: Selected Essays and Interviews*. Cornell University Press, Ithaca, New York

Marx, K. 1977. *Karl Marx: Selected Writings*. D. McLellan (ed.). Oxford University Press, Oxford.

Merleau-Ponty, M. 1974. *Phenomenology, Language and Sociology: Selected Essays of Maurice Merleau-Ponty*. J. O'Neill (ed). Heineman, London.

Ong, W. 1967. *The Presence of the Word: Some Prolegomena for Cultural and Religious History*. Yale University Press, New Haven, CT.

———1977. *Interfaces of the Word: Studies in the Evolution of Consciousness and Culture*. Cornell University Press, Ithaca, NY.

Sperber, D. 1975. *Rethinking Symbolism*. A. L. Morton (tr.). Cambridge University Press, Cambridge.

Turner, V. 1978. "Encounter with Freud: The making of a comparative symbologist," in G. D. Spindler (ed.), *The Making of Psychological Anthropology*, pp. 558–583. University of California Press, Berkeley.

Williams, R. 1977. *Marxism and Literature*. Oxford University Press, Oxford.

The Unexamined Habitus

DIRECT HISTORIC ANALOGY
AND THE ARCHAEOLOGY OF THE TEXT

Ethnographic analogy has long been the archaeologist's mainstay for the interpretation of patterns emerging in material remains. Although great care has not always been shown in its use, many archaeologists, by virtue of their training as social scientists, assume that they know how to accord proper evaluation to ethnographic evidence gathered in the modern period. Where difficulty arises and is seen to arise, as it must in the case of peoples now extinct or heavily acculturated, is in the case of "ethnographic" evidence taken from historical sources rather than living peoples. In spite of the fact that this is recognized as a special case with special problems, archaeologists often abandon the evaluation of such sources to historians, accepting their judgments at face value even in the absence of critical historical work in the relevant field. But although it is part of the historian's task to have a broad knowledge of the cultural and social contexts of his subjects, historians who are competent to handle both sides of a culture-contact situation that occurred in the past are few and far between: most frequently they only interpret the European view of events, while the "natives" remain "people without history" (Wolf 1982). Nor in this context is the problem of narrative history—either that written by modern historians or the narrative sources on which they depend—addressed, though among historiographers it is as hotly debated a problem as are Western interpretative frames in anthropology. Because the issues involved in the use of historical ethnographic analogy have been so little discussed from a theoretical standpoint, I have chosen to examine the documents portraying early contact between European and native in the Southeastern United States as an example of the problem, with a view toward the suggestion of at least a partial solution.

The Southeastern Problem

The meeting of European and Indian in the Southeastern United States in the fifteenth and sixteenth centuries occurred so relatively recently that the outcome of this meeting in the shape of European accounts has exercised an irresistible fascination for students of the prehistory of the region ever since. However embarrassed we may be by the fact that we have met the enemy and he is us, Western anthropologists dealing with the testimony of sixteenth-century Spaniards have presumably felt that their guilty kinship of westernness and conquest made the narratives of the early explorers transparent and therefore usable without question. If Soto and his men were our cultural brothers, their hypocrisy in relating what they saw would be the same as our own, and we could make up for it. This is a fairly commonplace problem in the social sciences. What is not commonplace is the apparently willed blindness with which Southeastern archaeologists have ignored it. Here I will set aside the really serious purely archaeological questions that remain unanswered in the region to focus on just this problem.

Fifty years' archaeological research suggests that the social geography of the Southeastern region in the sixteenth century, when it was first penetrated by European explorers, was a patchwork of varied social organization: agricultural chiefdoms where floodplain widths and richness permitted the so-called Mississippian adaptation that depended upon maize, beans, and squash supplemented by hunting/fishing; possible chiefdoms where gathered resources were rich enough to support elites and minor horticulture was sufficient to make up the difference; and segmented tribal organization where the land did not favor full sedentarism and at least seasonal displacement was necessary to subsistence on hunted and gathered materials. The correlation between organizational complexity and horticultural or agricultural subsistence base is a real one, based upon settlement pattern studies at macro and micro levels (B. Smith 1978).

By the fourteenth century there were several sites assumed to represent multilevel Mississippian chiefdoms situated at strategic points across the Southeast. They were characterized by major centers surrounded by minor centers and small settlements, both thought to be in some sense dependent upon the major centers. These centers all showed evidence of social ranking in the population they served, residence by the society's elite, and craft specialization of some degree.

It is clear that these chiefdoms did not exist in a vacuum and that they communicated with one another. The keystone of this observation is the appearance across the region of a set of artifacts and motifs so mysterious in connotative content that they have been grouped under the rubric of "Southern Cult" or (more "objectively") "Southeastern Ceremonial Complex." Soberer researchers have suggested that these materials represent not a belief system but prestige goods trade, but all agree that they indicate that contact between chiefdoms in the Southeast, by whatever mechanism it was achieved, was widespread and sustained (Galloway 1989).

Yet these chiefdoms were not all contemporary; they could reach the end of a "natural" life span without the help of Europeans, and many of them had done so by the time of contact. All over the Southeast their populations were dispersed and their "ceremonial" centers abandoned at a dateline that is too ill-defined to permit the assignment of a unitary cause but that lies in the near temporal vicinity of the first period of European contact. It is tempting to wish for a unitary cause, and there are those who think they have found it in the diseases brought to the New World by Europeans.

Clearly European disease attacking the vulnerable populations of the New World was a major factor in the reduction of aboriginal populations in morale as well as in numbers. The reduction in numbers is now seen to have been dramatic, as the work of historical demographers shows that a large aboriginal population for the Americas was likely (cf. Dobyns 1983). But several very big and important questions remain. Just when and in what order did disease reduce the aboriginal populations? Epidemiological speculation still remains just that in the region. Did European disease cause the reduction of the Southeastern chiefdoms to the more familiar tribes of the eighteenth century, or was some other factor at work? The notable lack of models for social devolution makes this a crucial question for the region that must be accommodated by anthropological theory. And (although this question is not so mysterious in the Southeast as it is for Mexico and Peru) why did the Indians let the Europeans get away with abuse? This serious problem of the meeting of two very disparate cultures and the communication process between them has been dodged repeatedly as archaeologists reduced it to one of "acculturation" without asking what made acculturation begin and who it happened to.

These questions are hard to answer in the Southeast because many of the answers to them are to be found, if at all, in the period 1550–1680, between the major inland incursions of Europeans. The implied changes happened, in other words, "behind the scenes" of European expansion, and the only evidence for them is in archaeological remains that are so far largely unknown (survey coverage in the region is shockingly poor given the rate of site destruction) and that in any case cannot be reliably dated by any absolute method; sequence alone will not suffice because drastic population movements apparently occurred (cf. M. Smith 1984) and social organization took no single form across the region. It is for these reasons that the accounts of the earlier incursion are considered so important for a reconstruction of the "protohistory" of the region.

In general terms, this protohistoric period can be divided into three phases. The first saw an incursion by the Spanish expedition led by Hernando de Soto upon a relatively untouched inland population. This episode was followed by nearly one hundred years during which the inland Southeast is a black box for which even historical knowledge of inputs and outputs is limited. This "blank" period was in turn followed by full and continuing contact initiated by the journeys of La Salle and his Spanish and British rivals. Thus we know what things looked like at the end, and from three different and competing points of view, but historical knowledge of the conditions that obtained at the opening of the drama is basically dependent upon the evidence of a single expedition. It is true that there were several other expeditions—those of Juan Pardo and Tristan de Luna being most important—that caught glimpses of what was going on in the interior after Soto, but their contacts were limited in time and area and do not offer the kind of panorama the Soto accounts seem to make available, nor can their evidence always be securely linked with that of the earlier expedition (*pace* Hudson 1987).

Hence archaeologists have felt that it is vitally important to pay the closest attention to what information there is to be had from the first incursion. The promise is a very tempting one: if the living groups observed by Soto and later explorers can be identified with specific archaeological "cultures," then we will presumably know what they thought and how they arranged their lives as well as how they made pottery and traded in exotic metals. Then, of course, we will have no difficulty charting their trajectory into Western history.

The Direct Historical Approach

In the United States the attempt at a solution to difficult problems of late prehistoric social evolution and culture change through the use of historical documents has been called the Direct Historical Approach. Its goal is to connect named native tribes of the historic period with protohistoric and prehistoric archaeological remains, and this is generally held to be a simple matter of moving from the known to the unknown backward in time while moving at the same time from document to material artifact. Steward dates its beginnings with archaeological work in the Southwest and New York around 1915, but its real application came as a response or a corrective to the Midwestern Taxonomic System with its "set of timeless and spaceless categories" (Steward 1942:339); it was, ironically, an attempt to deal with such cultural intangibles as were ignored in that formalist approach. The Direct Historical Approach has been applied to two main problems: the location and identification of archaeological sites and the explanation of social organization. For finding and identifying archaeological sites information like travel time, distance estimates, and topographic features mentioned in early accounts are of interest, while for social organization the archaeologist turns rather to the behavior and lifeways of the aboriginal people as recorded by Europeans.

In the Southeast, the Direct Historical Approach has been the basis of a good deal of research into the cultural dynamics of the late prehistoric period. First in this field as in many others was the Lower Mississippi Survey, beginning with the work of Philip Phillips, James A. Ford, and James B. Griffin in 1951. These three scholars tried to approach the late prehistory of the segment of the Mississippi Valley of interest to them through the documentary evidence generated by both the Spanish expedition of Hernando de Soto (1539–1542) and the French expeditions that followed more than a hundred years later, intending to bracket the period with these two baselines. Continuing this tradition has been the work of Jeffrey P. Brain, who with various collaborators has been pursuing for nearly twenty years the historical and physical trajectory of the Tunica people who became eponymous of their ancestors in the eighteenth century (see especially Brain, Toth, and Rodriguez-Buckingham 1974; Williams and Brain 1983; Brain 1979, 1985). The hope of this long-range project has been to study culture change through the study of a people who may have been pioneers of the Mississippian culture complex in prehistory and who certainly were successful assimilators of certain aspects of European cultures after contact. In the process of pursuing it, Brain has paid some considerable attention to the theoretical underpinnings of what he terms "ethnohistoric archaeology" without really facing the shaky historical ground on which it is often built.

Charles Hudson and his students have been pursuing the eastern path of Hernando de Soto for many years and have recently turned to the task of taking on the remainder of the route of that expedition. This effort has had two goals. The first is the locational one: using the routes of Soto, Pardo, and other early explorers to put a name and cultural affiliation to known archaeological sites (see DePratter, Hudson, and Smith 1985; Hudson, Smith, and DePratter 1987). The second has been the use of that identification to anchor and thus make exploitable the cultural observations that can be teased out of the exploration accounts. So far this latter line of research has been most clearly exemplified in the team's account of the Coosa chiefdom (Hudson et al. 1985). These researchers have been especially interested in the work of the *Annales* historians without being aware of how seriously such a position should indict their favorite narrative sources.

The Problematic of the Contact Situation

Although the practitioners of the Direct Historical Approach in the Southeast have made use of European historical materials, and although Phillips, Ford, and Griffin warned of archaeological naïveté in the face of historical documents well over thirty years ago, archaeologists have never actually questioned more than the observational ability of these documents' authors. There has been no indication that their sincerity or indeed the historical status of their entire testimonies might be in doubt, and no effort has been made to examine these questions. Presumably because they have judged these Europeans to be like themselves as inheritors of the Western tradition, anthropologists have abandoned the cautions of their own discipline (and ignored the fact that the area and period have received no attention from modern historians) and accepted the transparency of these texts. Clearly this is a mistake, for historical evidence is never Direct.

Sixteenth-century Spaniards were not like us. Although no real anthropological study of the personnel of the conquest of the New World has been made, quite adequate data exist for doing so, and social historians have made a beginning in this direction with their "group studies" of conquest expeditions in Central and South America (cf. Lockhart 1972). Such studies have shown that the *mentalité* of the conquistador was peculiar to him and emerged from his unique historical formation.

Spaniards of the sixteenth century had barely emerged from feudalism and were still bound by the rigidities and limited horizons of a society based upon local manors farmed by peasants. Another important element in the immediate past history of the conquistador or his father or elder brother is that he had just completed the *Reconquista*, expelling the Moors from the southern part of Spain and taking over the lands they dominated by handing out their manors as *encomiendas* to the victorious reconquistadores. The pattern of the *Reconquista*, as more than one observer has remarked, was repeated in the New World—and this new conquest served to occupy warriors who found life a little tame at home.

Variations were introduced into the successful strategies of the *Reconquista* by the experience of the New World, and each new area of conquest entered by the Spaniards taught a new lesson. To take only the experiences of Soto, he made a beginning in Nicaragua with Pedrarias, and learned there to deal with heat and swamp and more dispersed populations than Cortés had found in Mexico. It is often unremarked that Soto was also one of the Men of Cajamarca, that elite led by Pizarro who shared both the honor and the spoils of the conquest of the Incas. This experience was significant not only because it enabled Soto to finance his Florida expedition; it taught him much about the organization of New World states and how to exploit that organization for the purposes of conquest (Lockhart 1972).

As the conquest of the Americas began with heroic and epic expeditions led by charismatic individuals, so it was recorded by and large in the genre of the individual narrative account so closely related in theme and structure to the chivalric romance that was popular during the age. One author of a Soto account (Garcilaso) was a literary man by profession (Henige 1986), while the editor of another (Oviedo) repented the frivolous romance he wrote in his youth (Merrim 1982). No rational case can be made for the independence of these narratives from the literary traditions of their age. Such texts are thus already two removes from "what happened."

If the thoughtworld of the sixteenth-century Spaniard was peculiar to his own place and time and quite different from that of a modern Western anthropologist, that of the protohistoric native of the Americas can by no stretch of the imagination have been much like anything we know. One need only rethink the contact situation itself as a cognitive problem to apprehend the difficulties it presents for obtaining a true account *of* either side *from* either side. The contact situation should be viewed as the meeting of cognitive styles supporting very different social formations, and nothing in it is more certain than mutual misunderstanding, as Todorov's analysis (1984) has suggested. Before tackling an analysis of the record of the ensuing interaction, I want to approach a more detailed formulation of this model of the contact situation. I am going to try to formulate in the same terms all of the various forms of discourse that meet in the "ethnohistoric archaeology" construct.

Anthropologists and archaeologists have found in Bourdieu's (1977) concept of the *habitus* a fruitful notion that has helped them recognize both nonlinguistic modes of culture transmission and nonlinguistic messages in the resulting material patterns (cf. Hodder 1986:72–73). But although Bourdieu has phrased and rephrased definitions of the *habitus*, he has not precisely come out and said what it is and where it resides; even his examples amount more to examples of the functioning of the *habitus* than to a description of the structure actually orchestrating behavior. If, however, one can suggest a close analogy between the many facets of *habitus* as defined by Bourdieu and recent mentalist schemes of knowledge acquisition and representation as proposed by cognitive scientists, it is possible to arrive at a model that retains all the generative capacity and improvisational virtuosity of Bourdieu's concept but that is far less impressionistically expressed. I am going to give a fairly detailed outline of this model because I am going to use it later in formulating the problem of historical narrative.

The model to which I am referring has roughly two categories of elements. First are the declarative data structures that contain the system's world knowledge—its semantics or memory—organized in more or less static structures called "frames," which may include situational frames or scripts (knowledge including sequences of normal actions about frequently encountered situations), state frames ("commonsense" knowledge about physics and psychology—"ethnoscience" in some senses), and object/person frames (permissible predications belonging to classes of objects and persons). Such frames are generalized structures containing "slots" that are filled in (instantiated) by the specific occurrences. They are built through repeated exposure to the kinds of entities they represent, and they may be altered, expanded, or newly generated in response to new experience.

The active, syntactic, and pragmatic side of the model is represented by the procedures that operate on the frames. At lowest level is a set of linguistic parsing procedures that refer both to input and to established knowledge in the shape of the currently instantiated frame(s) to comprehend what is happening and predict what will happen next. This pragmatics, to go beyond language understanding, must include procedures to decide what frame to instantiate and must also be able to "parse" nonlinguistic behavior. It also incorporates goal-orientation by including procedures for "planning" or predicting a course through contingencies without benefit of scripts, attempting to realize such goals as may apply.

An individual's practical knowledge of how to conduct himself in the world, then, amounts to a set of frame-based knowledge structures and the procedures for manipulating them. It is not claiming much more to characterize an individual's competence in his culture as the sum or the average of these representations of knowledge about it. If cultural competence can be formulated as a set of frame-based knowledge structures coupled with capacities for "planning" or orchestrating low-level frames containing commonsense knowledge to maximize performance in novel situations, we arrive at a model that can explain more clearly how the real behavioral flexibility of humans depends on what they know (Schank and Abelson 1977; Schank 1982; Minsky 1985).

If the introduction of this model seems extraneous, bear with me; like others here, I wonder why behavioral sciences other than psychology have not yet made more use of the findings of cognitive science, and I personally find it helpful to use its language as a lingua franca to mediate between anthropology and the "textual sciences" of literature and history. Structuralist and hermeneutic interpretations of texts and other semiotic structures often seem to me to drown in an indefensible self-referentiality, and I am afraid I am not satisfied with Barthesian *jouissance* as an adequate analysis of any discourse.

Using the equation of *habitus* with a set of scripts and a competence for planning, it is possible to describe the contact situation in a way that more directly addresses the internal social processes on both sides. Spaniard and Indian alike were faced at contact by novelty and the necessity for improvisation. The cognitive view of human interaction asserts that for each participant the first step in dealing with any situation is to attempt to find an appropriate script to instantiate, since the use of an already-learned structure reduces the effort required. The sort of structure that might come to mind on both sides can be suggested informally to give an idea of what I mean here. Clearly very different intentions may have been at work, and these intentions would lead to the selection of very different script structures.

For the Spaniard, "conquest" might have meant carrying out relatively newly developed scripts which—after Cajamarca—might include such variations as duplicitous seizure of a ruler to coerce the cooperation of his subjects. For the leader of a multilevel Southeastern chiefdom, "contact with powerful strangers" might mean extension of hospitality and the signs of kinship. But if human beings learn by modifying old frames and adding new ones, and if that means instantiating old ones until they start to go wrong and planning one's way out when they do, then there is room for improvised solutions to be introduced on both sides. It is of course quite probable that in unprecedented situations script selections may go disastrously wrong, as would be the case when the Spaniards adopted patterns of a conduct that had been successful in dealing with social formations that granted leaders such monopolistic control over symbolic capital that the man who controlled *them* thus easily dominated that capital and its implied obligations.

This same conduct could not be very effective when the chief's leadership rested less on a set of institutions than on a more constant day-to-day maintenance of obligation through the distribution and transmutation of real capital; imprisonment of such a leader stops the maintenance of his leadership and weakens it. Southeastern natives, too, seem to have been more or less bound by their own cultural conventions to choose initially an inappropriate "hospitality" script for coping with these marauding intruders (but not, one should stress, apparently a fully instantiated one), but this "mistake" is easier to understand in terms of a notion of obligatory choice subsumed under a dominant goal structure that classifies various "greeting" script choices as more or less honorable in a given situation.

But neither side was *required* to adhere to any first choice. In many cases the explorers appear to have been dealing with ranked societies: chiefdoms or the dependencies and devolved remnants of chiefdoms. Although at such levels an institutionalization of structures of dominance can be assumed to have taken place to a modest degree, manifested in terms of detailed obligatory scripts for some aspects of social life, chiefdoms were in some ways prepared to cope with novelty. By definition, some members of a ranked society must transcend the face-to-face *habitus* characterized by Calvin Martin as the "bio-logic" of hunters and gatherers (Martin 1987), and must undertake to specialize in managing not animals and the nonhuman world, but people. That is, elites become so and stay so because they have developed the knowledge to manipulate the *habitus* of other people and the flexibility to modify their techniques as their power grows and their trading networks expand. So even though their position and many of its appurtenances become institutionalized, their function as problem-solvers and appliers of the society's theories to reality actually makes them expert in the generative capacities of the *habitus*. The notion that native peoples of the Southeast met the intrusive Europeans trapped in the set habits of tradition like flies in amber simply does not take account either of the relative recency of parts of that tradition or of its potential ad hoc malleability in the shock of novel situations.

Other aspects of this particular contact situation are external to these considerations. Its brevity has been underemphasized. Soto and his men observed individual Southeastern groups for at most a few continuous months, but that was the rare exception, and in most cases those observations lasted no more than a few days. In addition, in spite of the arguments of Dobyns (1983) for the early spread into the Southeast of epidemic disease, there is no documentary evidence and certainly as yet no archaeological evidence to show that it definitely had or had not yet affected the groups of the interior. If it had, or if it had differentially, what the first interior expedition saw had already been altered radically: the likelihood that the bearers of the framesful of esoteric and other specialized knowledge had died means that the repertoire of knowledge possessed by the community would have been reduced to the common denominators of subsistence and kinship rules that would permit only partial reproduction of complex late prehistoric societies.

Thus in many respects the contact situation is by its nature one which cannot tell the archaeologist much about the cognitive implications of precontact archaeological remains, simply because the entire situation is novel and it warps behaviors on both sides accordingly. Unless we assume that native peoples naturally prostrated themselves before the obviously superior European, it is necessary that we admit that they might equally well have reacted creatively and interestedly, and that by doing so they altered "traditional" behavior. The story of Cortés's being "mistaken" for the god Quetzalcoatl and his exploitation of such a belief is taken by Todorov as a successful manipulation of the situation by Cortés (1984:116–119), but it certainly also represents a novel and creative manipulation by the Aztecs of their belief system to accommodate an unprecedented situation; Cortés could not have forced the belief on anyone. A very similar situation in which Captain Cook was taken also for a god who returned—but one who had to die ritually soon after—shows that such "mistakes" can be quite effective in coping with novelty (Sahlins 1981).

The Texts

In spite of the foregoing pessimistic analysis, there was certainly much of value to be observed in the contact situation, but the problem lies in identifying and extracting it. This information is preserved embedded in the texts produced by the European participants in the contact (Todorov 1984 offers an exceptional close reading of such texts). These texts lie at the heart of the enquiry here because as long as their status as evidence is in doubt, any linking of that evidence with archaeological referents is a futile exercise. As I have said, these texts are for the most part cast in the form of historical narratives; the specific narratives I will discuss here are those that pertain to the Soto expedition, since not only are they the earliest and most detailed and therefore the most interesting to archaeologists, but their status is also the most questionable.

Because it is of first importance to know the source of information, the initial problems are raised by unresolved questions of authorship. Of the extant four narratives of Soto, only one (Biedma) comes to us directly. Of the others, in order of presumed authenticity, the first (Ranjel) has been included with commentary in another man's history; the second (Elvas) leaves its authorship anonymous; while the third (Garcilaso) claims to represent mostly the direct testimony of a second anonymous participant. In no case except possibly the first can anyone be sure that the actual words of an expedition participant are thus made available.

It is almost as hard to find out why the narratives were written. The first of the four cited above was an official report and the second is supposed to have been, but the other two could have been written to satisfy any of a number of motives. This is a serious issue because narrative is an artistic form: it picks and chooses the things it will represent and the ways it will represent them, simply because there is not enough paper in the world to represent everything, even if an informant could remember it. Most archaeologists who have dealt with these sources have treated them as though they were simply compilations of discrete observations, without attention to the communicative purpose and overall structure of the text; much has been said about the necessity for reconstructing the whole of the expedition's route, but nothing at all about the necessity for grasping the import of the texts as a whole. But these texts are meaningful not piecemeal but whole—and to swallow one item from such a text is also to accept the assumptions that inform it, which could well invalidate the desired item if made explicit. Such problems can be clearly exposed in a closer examination of the use that has been made of the textual evidence.

Locational Evidence

These narratives have been minutely studied in order to settle the apparently simple question of where Soto went across the Southeast. Although American Babbitry has found almost no more fertile outlet than the Soto route question, several quite serious efforts have been made to study the possibilities. In this research several kinds of evidence have been pulled from the texts to be intercollated, weighed, and erected into a unified route structure. Perhaps the most carefully studied of this evidence has been the portrayal of time and distance. Lengthy debates have raged over the measurment of a Spanish league and the distance that could have been covered by the expedition in a day. Direction estimates and accuracy have been equally hotly debated, without to my knowledge any careful enquiry about the availability of adequate instrumentation. Finally, detailed note of the landforms observed and described by the Spaniards has been taken, and taken to signify more or less precise observation of the topography the explorers passed through. All of this discussion has led to characterizations of the authors themselves as "careless in his observation of direction" or guilty of giving "exaggerated distances"—phrases which suggest that the scholars themselves have prejudged the data.

From the beginning of serious study of the route for ethnographic purposes, it has seemed obvious to researchers that they would have to reconstruct the whole of the route before any part of it could be counted reliably identified. John R. Swanton and the De Soto Expedition Commission (Swanton 1939) met with local experts in the location of "Indian trails" and walked all over the Southeast in carrying out their task for the United States Congress, constructing at last a route that represented a consensus of many theories current in their day and that gave about equal weight to time, distance, direction, and topography. Their work was doomed from the outset to a certain extent, however, since the archaeological chronology of their time was so compressed that they were satisfied if their route crossed almost any kind of evidence of aboriginal occupation.

Charles Hudson and his colleagues have been particularly concerned to be sure that their findings coincide with archaeological remains that at least stand a chance of being of the right age, and they have made drastic revisions of the route by being more concerned with time, distance, and especially topography than with direction. Jeffrey Brain and his co-workers have similarly depended more on distances and topography and upon likely archaeological correspondences than they have on direction. The fact that the routes recommended by Hudson and Brain differ radically at several points, however, suggests what must be admitted about any such efforts: the evidence hardly supports replicable scientific research.

Cartographic theorists are acerbic in their strictures against the suitability of the narrative form for conveying spatial information (Robinson and Petchenik 1976). Although some of this aversion is attributable to a rather odd application of Piaget's discredited developmental topological-to-Euclidean space sequence, there are real cognitive problems with the reconstruction of maps from narrative sources. As numerous observers have pointed out, the fundamental sequentiality of narrative implies more than it can deliver in spatial terms; this is especially true of a narrative whose main focus is not spatial information. To avoid this problem, a document would have to approach the equivalent of "annalistic" form: that is, it would have to be a simple list of places and distances, from which a reasonable map could in fact be constructed depending upon the accuracy of the data (cf. Kendall 1971). But the narratives of Soto cannot be so characterized, and their capacity for representation of spatial information must be low, even if it be assumed that they were *intended* to represent spatial information.

It is obvious that this must be so if we merely consider the information actually available to the explorers. In simply moving through the landscape they encountered serious perceptual problems familiar to psychologists who study the human capacity for getting around in a strange place. Soto's expedition was perhaps most nettled by the rank and rampant vegetation they encountered in the uninhabited borderlands between groups, which often made it difficult to see the way ahead even for men on horseback. The topography of the Southeastern coastal plain is not unduly challenging (except for the numerous watercourses that had not at that time been subjected to the tender mercies of the U.S. Army Corps of Engineers), but there are several difficult obstacles further inland: the southernmost salient of the Appalachians, the Tombigbee-Alabama watershed, and the Mississippi River valley. The mountains would not have presented an undue problem to men who had tackled the Andes, but the rivers were another matter: the Guadalquivir is the best simile the authors can manage, and it was certainly no match for the Mississippi.

Both of these difficulties, joined to the problems of supervising reluctant bearers and a large herd of pigs and to concerns as to where food, booty, and women might next be found, were bound to affect the Spaniards' estimates of time and distance, both notoriously difficult for humans to encompass. Time could certainly be measured pretty accurately in days (though the narratives do not agree), but distance is the only important datum to be taken from such evidence, and there is no assurance that travel could have been at all constant in speed over different topographies or with different burdens of numbers or baggage. Hence, the distances in which archaeologists have been so interested require a much more critical analysis than they have so far seen.

But these are subjective issues. There are other issues that must also be raised, and they have to do with the mental and physical tools the Spaniards might have used to improve their grasp of spatiality. As adult Europeans the members of the expedition presumably possessed a commonsense model of hydrological behavior that included the facts that rivers flowed down from mountains and toward the sea. Probably many of them, and certainly their leaders, were familiar with the portolan charts of the Gulf of Mexico that had been made by Spanish pilots and that indicated the mouths of several rivers on the Atlantic and Gulf coasts. They would therefore expect that the sources of these same rivers would be found inland, probably in mountainous or hilly regions.

There is little indication in any of the narratives that the expedition possessed even a compass, but it seems astounding that it would not have had one, and Juan deAñasco is credited with having possessed a portable astrolabe according to Garcilaso and his own independent testimony (Weddle n.d.). But clearly readings of position were not the matter of course that they would be even a century later, as the importance of accurate observations to scientific mapmaking began to be appreciated.

Doubtless the Spaniards' perceptions were also shaped by what they hoped and expected to find in the way of portable wealth. Among the most important of these things were gold, for which they sought mountains, and pearls, for which they learned to seek rivers. And to these ends they certainly questioned Indian informants, but here again systems of spatial perception and representation are likely to have clashed, even when the Indian informants were not being purposefully misleading in their information.

In fact it would be very surprising if the members of Soto's expedition had had a clear notion of where they were, since contemporary mapmakers who not only spoke their language but had the opportunity to question expedition members themselves were confused. The so-called "De Soto" map made around 1544 by Alonzo de Santa Cruz, chief cartographer of the *Casa de Contratacion* in Seville (Boston 1941), is an excellent example of this misunderstanding. In order to square the number of rivers the explorers said they crossed with the number of mouths on the portolan charts, he had to wander them back and forth across multiplied tributaries. It is worth noting that Santa Cruz paid almost no attention to the distance and direction reports in the accounts; it is odd that we would give them so much more credence today.

More than a hundred and fifty years later, the confusion about Soto's route had not abated, and the Delisle family, cartographers to the king of France, spent much time considering the accounts and attempting to map them (Boston 1939). This was the first critical examination of this data of which evidence survives, and it is interesting to see what kind of route is constructed when a professional cartographer attempts to pay serious attention to the distance and direction estimates of the exploration narratives. The Delisles themselves saw that the results of such a practice were ludicrous, and they made notes to that effect. Hence on their published maps they mostly expunged the names that contemporary explorers were telling them were not relevant anyway, eventually adopting a route constructed as much by guess (dependent upon the eighteenth-century locations of the few Indian groups that had not changed their names) as by anything else—a route that is not so different from the modern one supposedly reconstructed by careful scholarship.

Finally, there is very good reason to discount the entire procedure of using multiple narratives to construct a composite route. First, only one of the narratives (Biedma) can even possibly be assumed to have been written with the *intention* of portraying where the expedition went. The rest of them offer this information no more seriously than as transitional phrases between portrayals of events and observations; we have no way of deciding now if the narrator mentions crossing a swamp between two named towns because there was one exactly there, or there was one in the vicinity, or there was difficulty getting from one town to another and a swamp sounded a likely obstacle, or the swamp represented some sort of moral turbidity in the decision making of the expedition leadership. Each account needs to be evaluated for the structure that it creates, and mutual agreement says nothing at all about the reliability of any of the narratives where they do not agree. The point is that, as we shall see in the subsequent discussion, these narratives are not obliged to present fact as we understand fact at all, and certainly not to present it uniformly.

"Ethnographic" Evidence

The major interest in these narratives is not in the locations, however—that information is only of interest so far as it can tie observations to specific archaeological remains. The goal of the whole exercise is to extract "ethnographic" information from the narratives. If there are serious problems with narrative as a vehicle for spatial information, the serious problems do not cease when we pass to the descriptive information, in spite of a nearly universal tendency to accept whatever descriptive data seem to suit the explanatory preferences of the researcher. Hayden White has examined the problem of historical narrative in great detail and has described the writing of it as the imposition on a sequence of events of a story or plot recognized as acceptable by the culture of the writer (White 1978:81–99). It is this culture-specific preinterpretation that opens the problematic of the narrative form itself for conveying historical ethnographic description.

What are these plots? If as White suggests they are patterns of event sequences that make sense, that have explanatory force, then they are quite easily equated with certain of the scripts that make up the writer's cultural repertoire. Since such scripts have a generative capacity, their slots may be instantiated in nearly infinite combinations and different stories generated (hence fiction, when the slots are instantiated with characters and things known to be imaginary). White does not mean to suggest that just any story will be used to mold the shape of a historical narrative, for this will not be the case. There are unspoken *topoi* at work in historical writing, which would not be taking place at all if it did not take its task as the presentation of the most important events. Likewise, the canons of tragic drama, for example, indicate to us that cultures have certain scripts that embody their most significant cultural themes; certain *habitus* that are ignored at peril of cultural disintegration (cf. Lévi-Strauss 1967:202–228). These "master scripts" (or "cultural root paradigms"—Turner 1980:154) will be the ones that serve the historian as interpretative templates. It is worth remarking also that this frequently tends to mean that historians write the same history over and over, clothed in different instantiations.

Perhaps a more serious problem for the archaeologist is the fact that narrative is of its nature selective in terms of the information it will present. It is instructive to look at some of the considerations that govern that selectivity. Because a story is being told, because a script is being instantiated, facts that do not conduce to the telling of the story are omitted. White remarks that "the social system . . . alone . . . provide[s] the diacritical markers for ranking the importance of events . . . " and thus their suitability for being chosen (White 1987:10)—but it is the social system of the *observer* that dictates these choices, not that of the people whose social system actually interests the archaeologist. The unfolding of every script is limited in the possible sequences it can support, and events may be shifted around or omitted if they do not fit the sequence. Finally, the authors of narratives choose their materials for relevance to the communicative situation of the telling itself. The prominent inclusion of an episode in which a detachment is sent to look for the gold that so obsessed the Spanish crown appears in all the narratives, but in each one it is attributed to a different point in the journey.

Above all, the particular situation of narrative plots as the master scripts of their cultures raises the ideological question that has impelled Western historians to write antihistory: that the very genre of connected linear narrative governed by a plot has a teleological force that binds it to Western ideologies, that makes it an expression of the master-scripts of Western culture in particular. Calvin Martin and those Indian historians who find narrative history alien in kind from what counts as history among nonliterate peoples have been vehement in their agreement with this assertion (Martin 1987), claiming that narrative is of its nature incapable of rendering the "thoughtworld" of their subjects.

But I would say that such a question is irrelevant here. Unlike the emerging state societies of Mesoamerica and South America, the Southeastern chiefdoms at their height did not require more than pictographic literacy and thus did not pass down a written record of what they thought their history was; and whenever it happened, the drastic wasting of disease must certainly have wiped out any esoteric traditions nurtured by elites, leaving behind as tradition only those mnemonic devices—scripts—known to the largest number of people, things like subsistence patterns and the gross rules of kinship. Hence it is useless to quibble over the fact that the narrative history we have does not represent the "thoughtworld" of native peoples: we know it doesn't. What we need to agree on is that it does represent the thoughtworld of the teller. If there is any way to correct for that, it may be possible at least to observe some of the things he or his informant saw. The way to apply such a corrective is to exploit what is known of narrative as a linguistic object to neutralize the culture-specificity of the form and a good deal of the content.

Both of these are very much ruled by the meaning to be conveyed, the story to be told. To decide what this story is, one must first know who is telling it and for whom it is being told. Concerns with authorship are of the first priority, as are bibliographic and codicological matters that further situate the event of the telling and identify the person—and thus possibly the concerns and predispositions—of the author. Unfortunately, so far few literary scholars have turned their interest to what they view as bibliographical donkeywork for the sake of only marginally literary works (even more unfortunately, the exception to this is the very literary Garcilaso), while historians have been very little concerned with the details that would reveal Spanish bias in portrayal of the Indians, since Indians are of marginal interest to them. But further information is available in the text. One school of poststructuralist literary criticism, taking its cue on the one side from the phenomenological *epoché* and on the other from linguistic pragmatics, has come to be called "reader-response" literary criticism: it envisions the narrative as a cooperative venture entered into by the mutual participation of writer and reader, and thus has attempted to deconstruct the interlocking strands of narrative that define the presence of an implied author, an implied audience, and perhaps also a narrator. This model of textual structure offers the tools for separating the *habitus* of teller and occasion from the tale, and its constructs fit very well with the cognitive model that has already been introduced in discussing the contact situation.

I have detailed elsewhere a mapping onto the cognitive process model of the version of reader-response theory advanced by Wolfgang Iser (Galloway 1983) and will only summarize it here. Iser's model of what happens as a reader apprehends a narrative is very detailed and includes the manipulation of the reader's apprehension process by the writer as well as the creative role of the reader's own activity: the reader brings to the narrative his world knowledge in terms of schemata or frames and a set of procedures for processing the text that are analogous to the procedures he uses in everyday life to call up frames matching real situations, instantiate their slots, and thus arrive at his options for what to do next, only in the case of reading he undertakes to plan what the characters will do next. The author, possessing the same competencies and aware of what the reader will be doing, orchestrates the reader's experience by manipulating the way he processes the text: a blatant example is the author's trickery in persuading the reader to instantiate an erroneous frame in a mystery story so that he can resolve the reader's growing confusion by leading him to the correct frame in the denouement (see Galloway 1979). There is a higher level of this processing model that is directed at least partially by the reader's model of story-reading itself, which includes a story grammar that would indicate the kinds of master-scripts that the reader could expect. The goal of this higher level is the reduction of the sequence of instantiated frames encountered in processing the narrative to a single structure, which Iser refers to as the ''primary gestalt'' but which will be in our terms one of the master-scripts or in White's the culturally approved story.

The point of all this is that the author so directs the reader's activity that he arrives at the same story or overall cultural meaning from the narrative that the author wants him to perceive, *and that this intention pervades the author's presentation of the events of the narrative*. But since we are not the author's or the reader's contemporaries, it is likely that the modern reader of an older text will not be receptive to this manipulative intention in the same way. Thus it must be the cultural context of the telling that offers additional clues for deciding what master-script is being invoked. It is imperative that the literary context be examined here for judging historical texts: in the period in question (and to the present, it might be added), historical discourse was judged by the same canons as other products of literary art, and it is just as legitimate to compare sixteenth-century historical narratives with fictional ones as it is to compare them with contemporaneous narrative histories (which were few in any case). Indeed, in a sense it is fiction that most clearly demonstrates in its choice of script/plot what contemporaries (the implied reader) viewed with interest and favor and hence what kind of *habitus* the culture aspired to reproduce—for the New World was as much a flight of the imagination for the sixteenth-century Iberian as was the court of the Grand Turk, and the historical claims of chivalric romance so seriously taken that some of them are only now being shown false (Henige 1986). What I am arguing is that the whole import of the narrative may have nothing at all to do with what actually happened: if we decide, for example, that Garcilaso de la Vega's *La Florida* has much in common with chivalric romances that portray the truimph of the hero over adversity (evil Moors, rapacious barons) through knightly conduct and piety, then we will begin to understand why conflict between Indian and Spaniard is portrayed as chivalric tournament.

Having identified the script that provides the plot of the narrative, the task that remains is to ''read out'' the cultural preinterpretation of the narrative: to return the sequence of events to a relatively neutral annalistic format of ''this happened and then this happened.'' For although in this format the sequential bias still remains, at least it can be made to bear no more than the implication of causality.

Here we come to the point where we have to bite the bullet and decide what shall be allowed to count as fact. Archaeologists have always done this with these texts as they selectively picked "descriptive" passages over the awkwardly inconvenient distances and directions as offering the unmediated reality the Spaniards saw; the difference here is that I am trying to make this process explicit and repeatable. The constructs of narrative theory make this possible. The task is simply to remove the interpretative apparatus constituted by all modifiers that express the narrator's and/or implied author's judgment of object, person, or action (Galloway 1973); to make conscious and thus to discard the frames that constitute the author's situational expectations and classificatory apparatus. In semantic terms, this means simply the removal of modifiers. To say, for example, that "the *cacique* approached boldly" is first to judge that the individual in question did actually hold and maintain any of a range of positions of dominance, which the Spaniard could not know. It is also to say that characteristics of the Indian's bearing and stride seem to have been read by the Spaniard as having an aspect of the masculine pride he understood, but again neither he nor we could know that this was an appropriate reading of the native's postural code. This sentence, then, can only validly yield "the man whom, by virtue of sumptuary distinction and his treatment by others, we assumed was the leader approached." Not very colorful or exciting, perhaps, but when such a process is carried out *in extenso* for one of these texts, an amazing thing happens: the story of Indian actions in response to invasion emerges from these tales of Spanish heroism like the transposition of figure and ground in a visual perception experiment. The resulting story of what the Indians did is still not comprehensible, nor should it be: we do not see all of it and it does not match our own or the Spaniards' master-scripts. But at last this version of events can be clearly seen to be incomprehensible in our terms, and we are no longer deluded by plausibility.

Limitations of the Direct Historical Approach

The Direct Historical Approach in archaeology, then, has serious limitations that are a direct consequence of the preinterpretation of the narrative sources used by the method. If the goal of such an effort is to wrest a nonmaterial interpretation from such archaeological cultures as can be tied to early contact documents, it must be recognized that an understanding of the document as an artifact of a process is indispensable and that the archaeology itself is going to have to help judge its truth.

Thus the archaeologist who has access to such materials will have to work harder than if he had none. He will have to find structure and implication in material remains that match what he finds in the "subtext" of the documents before he can use them with confidence. And above all, he will have to do some anthropology to the Europeans before he can understand the narrative artifacts they left. These Europeans, after all, were not participant observers. They wrote stories with themselves as the heroes and the Other as antagonist and background. They wrote stories for self-justification and glory; it was not necessary that they portray the places they went and the people they saw accurately— just that they do it convincingly. Unfortunately for archaeology, they succeeded.

Acknowledgment: I would like to thank the Hermon Dunlap Smith Center for the History of Cartography, Newberry Library, for a short-term fellowship that provided time and access to research materials for a good part of the work on this essay.

REFERENCES

Boston, B. 1939. "The route of de Soto: Delisle's interpretation," *Mid-America* **21,** 277–297.
———1941. "The 'de Soto map'," *Mid-America* **23,** 236–250.
Bourdieu, P. 1977. *Outline of a Theory of Practice*. R. Nice (tr.). Cambridge University Press, Cambridge.
Brain, J. P. 1979. *Tunica Treasure*. Peabody Museum of Archaeology and Ethnology Papers 71, Cambridge, MA.
———1985. "The archaeology of the Hernando de Soto expedition," in R. R. Badger and L. A. Clayton (eds.), *Alabama and the Borderlands: From Prehistory to Statehood*, pp. 96–107. University of Alabama Press, Tuscaloosa.
Brain, J. P., A. Toth, and A. Rodriguez-Buckingham 1974. "Ethnohistoric archaeology and the de Soto entrada into the Lower Mississippi Valley," *The Conference on Historic Site Archaeology Papers* (1972) **7,** 232–289.
Depratter, C. B., C. Hudson, and M. T. Smith 1985. "The Hernando de Soto Expedition: From Chiaha to Mabila," in R. R. Badger and L. A. Clayton (eds.), *Alabama and the Borderlands: From Prehistory to Statehood*, pp. 108–127. University of Alabama Press, Tuscaloosa.
Dobyns, H. 1983. *Their Number Become Thinned*. University of Tennessee Press, Knoxville.
Galloway, P. 1973. *Transaction Units: An Approach to the Structural Study of Narrative Through the Analysis of Percyvelle of Galles, Li Contes del Graal, and Parzival*. Ph.D. dissertation, University of North Carolina.
———1979. "Yngve's depth hypothesis and the structure of narrative: The example of detective fiction," in M. MacCafferty and K. Gray (eds.), *The Analysis of Meaning: Informatics 5*, pp. 104–110. ASLIB, London.
———1983. "Narrative theories as computational models: Reader-oriented theory and artificial intelligence," *Computers and the Humanities* **17,** 169–174.
———(ed.) 1989. *Southeastern Ceremonial Complex, Artifacts and Analysis: The Cottonlandia Conference*. University of Nebraska Press, Lincoln.
Henige, D. 1986. "The context, content, and credibility of *La Florida del Ynca*," *The Americas* **43,** 1–23.
Hodder, I. 1986. *Reading the Past*. Cambridge University Press, Cambridge.
Hudson, C. 1987. "The uses of evidence in reconstructing the route of the Hernando de Soto expedition," Alabama De Soto Commission Working Paper 1, Tuscaloosa.
Hudson, C., M. T. Smith, and C. B. DePratter 1987. "The Hernando de Soto expedition: From Mabila to the Mississippi River," unpublished manuscript of a paper given at the conference "Towns and Temples Along the Mississippi." Memphis, TN.
Hudson, C., M. Smith, D. Hally, R. Polhemus, and C. DePratter. 1985. "Coosa: A chiefdom in the sixteenth-century Southeastern United States," *American Antiquity* **50,** 723–737.
Kendall, D. G. 1971. "Construction of maps from 'odd bits of information'," *Nature* **231,** 158–159.
Lévi-Strauss, C. 1967. *Structural Anthropology*. C. Jacobson and B. Schoepf (trs.). Doubleday Anchor, New York.
Lockhart, J. 1972. *The Men of Cajamarca*. University of Texas Press, Austin.
Martin, C. 1987. "Introduction" and "Epilogue," in C. Martin (ed.), *The American Indian and the Problem of History*, pp. 3–26, 192–220. Oxford University Press, Oxford.
Merrim, S. 1982. "The castle of discourse: Fernandez de Oviedo's *Don Claribalte* (1519) *or* 'Los correos andan mas que los caballeros'," *Modern Language Notes* **97,** 329–346.

Minsky, M. 1985. *The Society of Mind*. Simon and Schuster, New York.

Peebles, C., and S. Kus 1977. "Some archaeological correlates of ranked societies," *American Antiquity* **42,** 421–448.

Phillips, P., J. A. Ford, and J. B. Griffin 1951. *Archaeological Survey in the Lower Mississippi Alluvial Valley, 1940–1947*. Peabody Museum of Archaeology and Ethnology Papers 25. Cambridge, MA.

Robinson, A. H., and B. B. Petchenik 1976. *The Nature of Maps: Essays Toward Understanding Maps and Mapping*. University of Chicago Press, Chicago.

Sahlins, M. 1981. *Historical Metaphors and Mythical Realities: Structure and Early History of the Sandwich Islands Kingdom*. University of Michigan Press, Ann Arbor.

Schank, R. C. 1982. *Dynamic Memory*. Cambridge University Press, Cambridge.

Schank, R. C., and R. Abelson 1977. *Scripts, Plans, Goals and Understanding: An Inquiry into Human Knowledge Structures*. Lawrence Erlbaum Associates, Hillsdale, NJ.

Smith, B. (ed.) 1978. *Mississippian Settlement Patterns*. Academic Press, New York.

Smith, M. T. 1984. *Depopulation and Culture Change in the Early Historic Period Interior Southeast*. Ph.D. dissertation, University of Florida, Gainesville.

Steward, J. H. 1942. "The direct historical approach to archaeology," *American Antiquity* **7,** 337–343.

Swanton, J. R. 1939. *Final Report of the U.S. De Soto Expedition Commission*. Government Printing Office, Washington, D.C.

Todorov, T. 1984. *The Conquest of America: The Question of the Other*. R. Howard (tr.). Harper and Row, New York.

Turner, V. 1980. "Social dramas and stories about them," *Critical Inquiry* **7,** 141–168.

Weddle, R. n.d. "Soto's problems of orientation: Maps, navigation, and instruments in the Florida expedition," in P. Galloway (ed.), *The Historiography of the Hernando de Soto Expedition*. In preparation.

White, H. 1978. *Tropics of Discourse*. Johns Hopkins University Press, Baltimore, MD.

———1987. *The Content of the Form: Narrative Discourse and Historical Representation*. Johns Hopkins University Press, Baltimore, MD.

Williams, S., and J. P. Brain 1983. *Excavations at the Lake George Site, Yazoo County, Mississippi, 1958–1960*. Peabody Musuem of Archaeology and Ethnology Papers 74. Cambridge, MA.

Wolf, E. R. 1982. *Europe and the People without History*. University of California Press, Berkeley.

Theoretical Archaeology and Rhetorical Archaeology

TOWARD A "HISTORY" OF ARCHITECTURE
IN THE ANCIENT NEAR EAST

This paper shows, with the aid of a case study, the impact of the new archaeological approaches (or the inclinations brought about by the new archaeology) on a "literary" archaeologist whose viewpoint has been shaped by the "classics" (the classical humanities). The fundament of this "rhetorical archaeology" consists in applying the methods of textual criticism to archaeological documents, through which one can hope to achieve a thorough "reading" of the past (cf. Hodder 1986).

Because the object of this study is prehistoric architecture of the ancient Near East from about 14,000 to 5500 BP, the application might seem paradoxical: indeed, the remains in question belong to cultures that existed before the discovery of writing and, therefore, left no written texts for analysis. But the application of textual analysis in this investigation is no less warranted than the appeal by archaeologists to other modes of analysis—to sciences, such as mathematics, physics, natural sciences, or social sciences (in the French sense of this last term).

The rhetorical approach to the analysis of archaeological remains involves a two-part process (here termed internal criticism and external criticism) and develops in three steps.

Step One: Internal Criticism of Archaeological Documents

In the case of architecture, internal criticism is applied on two levels. The first level is in the field, when the remains themselves are brought to light by excavation. Because this approach is quite similar for the whole discipline, I will not discuss it here. The second level is peculiar to architecture, and it requires the scrupulous application of an approach akin to that of textual criticism. In the Near East, architectural remains are, in fact, extremely perishable and generally do not survive once they have been exposed. They fade from view either because of their inherent fragility or because they are destroyed by the archaeologist, intent upon the discovery of other remains that lie below. Unlike other archaeological objects (potsherds, lithic industry, bone objects, etc.), it is not possible to remove most architectural features from the field, store them in museum cases, and reexamine them time and time again. They survive only through the texts that describe them and through the plans and sections that represent them. Literary description and graphic (or photographic) description are, on that account, equally important. Subsequent use of these documents depends on a textual criticism that leads to their decipherment, that focuses upon what lies behind the description or the drawing, and that will lead the archaeologist to a reality comparable to that found in the field.

As Molino says in this volume, "criticism operates first in a negative way: it aims at clearing the text of any additions or mistakes in order to regain its original features." Thus, this first step consists of criticizing two kinds of texts: (1) archaeological publications and (2) the traces in their original context, in the field. Both activities have a single, three-part goal, which is, again following Molino, first "identification," next "classification," and finally "chronology." These three activities correspond to what Molino calls the "neutral level" of archaeological research. This first step is also equivalent to what Alain Gallay, in his paper in this volume, calls the constitution of "scenarios" and then of "regularities."

Even the best of internal criticism is limited in its power. For example, properly applied, it might allow one to reassemble a human skeleton from mismatched bones, but one could not divine the color of the skin or the eyes of this person through such a process. The study of ancient architecture provides an analogous situation. The world discovered by the archaeologist is a desperately dead world.

Step Two: External Criticism; From the Text to the Context

At some point, the circularity of internal criticism must be broken and the text must be placed in a wider context. This process can be labeled external criticism. When viewed from the perspective of the French system of education, such an approach involves an excursion, a "crossing" through, if you will, into ethnology. Such a process may seem unexceptional to those trained in the Anglo-Saxon tradition, where courses in anthropology form a part of the curriculum for the study of both ancient and contemporary societies. In France, however, placing archaeological texts in ethnographic contexts is relatively recent.

In the case of architecture, external criticism comprises the careful study of contemporary, inhabited, living architecture. Thus, the label of "Living Archaeology" (Gould 1980) is quite appropriate. As with internal criticism, the study is conducted in two parts. First, the ethnological literature that describes this architecture is consulted. In the case of the Near East, this literature is rich with accounts from geographers, architects, and ancient travelers, whose testimony must be taken into account. As in the previous step, the methods of textual criticism are applied to assay and order the information (identification, classification, chronology, in Molino's terms) and to render it coherent.

It quickly becomes apparent that the ethnological literature is not fully appropriate and cannot solve all archaeological problems. To remedy these defects, some archaeologists have undertaken their own ethnographic research, and a new discipline, ethnoarchaeology, has arisen from such work. In such research, a particular importance should be granted, for instance, to the process of demolition: the creation of archaeological deposits. It also is important to follow the contemporary course of construction of a building, especially, for the case at hand, one that uses the same materials and techniques as those used in the ancient Near East. Such activity chains (Perlès, this volume), from the building of the house, through the period in which it is occupied, up to its abandonment and its ultimate demolition, allow one subsequently to "see the film backwards," and to relate floor plans to the three-dimensional house as it once stood upon the ground. The "game" of rebuilding could be played "in theory" on paper, but what could be better than a firsthand view of contemporary reality?

The comparison with "current reality" (as emphasized by Molino in this volume) has as its goal an increase in the number of potential answers and credible hypotheses. The aim is to constitute a kind of catalog of hypotheses which, for any given society, could be made more encompassing and more robust by testing and refining them through interviews with those who constructed and who actually inhabited the buildings. The advantage of ethnoarchaeology is that it does not rely solely on an observation of traces, but it also elicits their meaning from those who made and use them. Thus ethnoarchaeology produces a double reading: from the meaning to the traces, and from the traces to the meaning. Only this process will permit one to go from the archaeological object to its interpretation, because for the archaeologist the way of reading, on the contrary, is always one way (cf. "reverse problem" of Gallay, this volume).

Step Three: Back to Archaeology

It is after, and only after, this excursion into ethnography, this "crossing through," that the archaeologist, anxious to find a meaning for the traces he finds, can go back to the "text" that began the process. Indeed, in practice there is a constant movement between archaeological traces and ethnographic observations. Experience shows that the initial archaeological observations, objective though they may be, are modified by ethnoarchaeological observations, which suggest new sets of associations, and eventually new means of classification. As Molino points out (this volume), the goal is to establish a dialectical relationship among archaeological and ethnographic traces. This process again requires a two-part analysis. First, one must focus on the techniques of building, assuming that with identical materials and comparable technologies, architectural variations cannot be numerous. The bounds set by techniques are probably more important in a field such as architecture than elsewhere. To this end, one can note, for example, that in both the Neolithic and the present of the Near East, metrical constraints on the size of rooms are imposed by the properties of the wood that is available. Second, from these technological similarities, one could imagine the way the occupants of these buildings used the inhabitable space of individual buildings (houses) as well as the collective space of the community (village). That is to say, we could try, using Gallay's terminology, to give one or several "functional meanings" to the architecture. The example that follows employs such an approach.

Before presenting the example, a few words must be written about the form in which it is presented: here again rhetoric intrudes. The report of the archaeological activity here, as in the book from which it is drawn (Aurenche 1981a), takes on a "literary" form, or more precisely a "historical" form. But the word "history," as it is used here, is taken with both meanings of the single English word: "tale" and "history." If it cannot be true, would it be, at least, beautiful . . .

Through almost nine millennia (14,000 to 5500 BP) and across hundreds of thousands of hectares, the ancient Near East offers a vast corpus of architecture. Examples from all periods and places are sufficiently numerous to allow the formation of "series" for study.

The span of time chosen includes, at its beginning, cultures without permanent architecture, and ends with the first urban societies, for which another kind of document (texts) gives a complementary approach. Then "history" and "tale" have, here, as in a good story-board; it has a beginning, a middle, and an end.

The initial catalyst for this work was Kent Flannery's pioneering article (Flannery 1972). Our architectural inquiry is of the same kind. Although it builds directly on his work, and it uses much of the same data, it also takes into account discoveries that have taken place since Flannery wrote his article. The archaeological details and a full bibliography are given in two recent studies (Aurenche 1981a, 1982) and will not be repeated here.

Broadly speaking, three main steps can be distinguished in the development of permanent architecture in the Near East. Moreover, at the present time, it seems as though such buildings first appeared in this part of the world. These three stages can be defined as follows: (1) the birth of architecture and the original circular house, (2) the development of architecture and the universal rectangular house, (3) the florescence of architecture and the complex rectangular plan.

The Birth of Architecture and the Original Round House (14,000–9600 BP)

Two factors characterized this earliest architecture: its circular plan and its method of construction: together they produced semisubterranean pit houses. Three successive cultures developed this form of building in the Near East: the Kebaran (14,000 to 12,000 BP), the Natufian (12,000 to 10,300 BP), and earliest prepottery Neolithic (PPNA, 10,300 to 9600 BP), to use terms developed for the Levant. The similarities among these buildings are important: diameter (from 2 to 10 m), depth (from 0.5 to 2 m), material and building techniques (earth and wood, with walls sometimes faced with pebbles). That method of construction prevailed even in the peripheral regions (Mesopotamia and the Zagros), where it does not seem to have been the direct result of influences from the Levant.

Given the current state of knowledge, it seems that the first attempts to build permanent shelter from durable materials adopted similar solutions. Thus, to invest these similarities with "cultural" significance would produce a weak argument; instead, similar solutions seem to have been adopted over a broad area to a common set of problems. Without the masonry skills to construct a standing wall of stone (in French, *construire*, with the Latin etymological meaning of the word, *con-struere*, to pile), the alternative is to dig a hole that will provide its own walls. Moreover, as any field archaeologist knows, it is easier to dig a pit that is elliptical or close to round rather than one that is rectilinear and has perpendicular walls.

The evidence at hand confirms that these semisubterranean pit houses are the earliest form of durable construction in the region. At those sites where the evolution from earlier to later forms can be traced (Mureybet, Jericho) the later rectangular forms are super-imposed and stratigraphically above the circular forms. Thus the first major generalization in Flannery's paper is confirmed: circular houses precede rectilinear houses in the Near East. His second major proposition, that such construction is associated with nomadic or seminomadic tribes, is not fully confirmed. As currently understood, Near Eastern history indicates that the populations which adopted the original round house were sed-entary (the Natufian and the PPNA Neolithic). As for the earlier, mobile hunter-gatherer populations of the terminal Pleistocene, we know very little of the kinds of structures they built on their open-air sites. Consequently, Flannery's generalization must be quali-fied. We know the Kebarans, the terminal hunter-gatherer populations in the region, did build circular houses. This architectural form persisted through several millennia, and certainly was present among groups who became sedentary and established large villages, such as the populations of the PPNA who established settlements some two to three hectares in extent. It was at such settlements that the next step in the evolution of architecture took place.

The Development of Architecture and the Universal Rectangular House (9600–8000 BP)

After several millennia, during which only one kind of architecture "reigned," a rapid transformation in form occurred around 9600 BP. At that point semisubterranean, round pit houses were gradually replaced by rectangular houses with masoned walls built from "prepared" or "premanufactured" elements (stones or mud bricks). On reflection, the advantage of the rectangular over the circular plan is simple: the former allows an almost unlimited number of "modular" units to be added to a primary nucleus (Flannery 1972). The advantages of a rectangular building, however, depended on mastery of several building techniques, especially joining a pair of perpendicular walls at right angles. In this case there was a direct correlation between the development of building techniques and the invention of a new type of building.

   The earliest evidence for this rectangular plan occurs in the Euphrates Valley, at Mureybet, and seems to have spread from that general area throughout the Near East. The succession from round to rectangular houses is found, for example, at Jericho, Çayönü Tepesi, and Abdulhosein. Regional cultures can be distinguished (Aurenche 1981a and 1982; Aurenche and Calley 1988), but at that first stage, there is little "weight of tra-dition," little "cultural standardization" of these dwellings: some have one room, some have several rooms, but these latter structures generally have rooms with reduced floor area. Some observations (techniques of construction, organization of the space) allow the definition of cultural groups; among the better known of these are the first Neolithic communities of east Anatolia, which are known by the name "Taurus PPNB facies" (Aurenche and Calley 1988; Cauvin 1988), and the Levantine PPNB facies. For the first time, a type or architecture can be associated with contemporary populations spread over a quite large territory.

   In the main, this first Neolithic architecture is associated with farming communities that seem not to have had domesticated animals. Thus Flannery's second postulate is confirmed, at least in part. Yet this proposition must be explored in greater detail, because the domestication of plants and the domestication of animals seems not to have appeared in these communities in any set sequence. Consequently, at least at the present time, we cannot explain clearly relations between the appearance of rectangular house plans and birth of agriculture; we can only notice the link between these two "inventions."

The rhythm of development of rectangular architecture, which gradually but completely and definitively replaces the circular plan, was not uniform throughout the Near East. Indeed, there were some "pockets of resistance" where the population continued to build round houses at a time when their neighbors, who otherwise seemingly followed similar lifeways, had shifted to a rectangular plan. In such cases, we can examine more precisely the cultural significance of these architectural facts. Architecture can be viewed as a fossil with a slower rate of evolution; it can be seen to respond to cultural rhythms and social traditions, and perhaps as an indicator of psychological resistance to innovation (see also Perlès this volume; Stordeur this volume).

This observation takes on its real importance when we note that at *circa* 8000 BP some communities adopted—we do not dare say chose anew—a circular plan, while at the same time and in the same region the rectangular plan had been in existence for a long time. Two examples are meaningful: the Cypriote Neolithic and the Halaf culture in northern Mesopotamia.

Thus far, the Neolithic represents the first human occupation discovered on the island of Cyprus. We thus can consider the circular constructions of the Cypriote Neolithic as an "original" architecture and as a representative of the "first" permanent buildings in this region.

The case of Halafian culture is completely different. These populations can be recognized easily because they produced a pottery that is distinctive in both its aesthetic and its technical features. Halafian populations built rectangular buildings as well as a large number of circular buildings. This combination of forms contrasts markedly with the architectural complexes of neighboring groups who built only rectangular buildings. It is hard to explain such a phenomenon. However, I believe that it is important to be able to associate, unambiguously, specific types of architecture with particular human groups that also can be defined in terms of other archaeological criteria. The cultural significance of the architectural fact takes on its importance at this point and in these terms.

The next step in the discussion allows one to go further with this idea.

The Florescence of Architecture and the Complex Rectangular Plan (7600–5700 BP)

Mesopotamia, at a point near the middle of the eighth millennium BP, witnesses a new architectural transformation, the "invention" of the complex rectangular plan. It is a new kind of construction, not merely a minor modification of what went before. Whereas the previous buildings could be enlarged only through successive additions of a small number of modifiable spaces, these new buildings involve large-scale planning at the time of their conception. The houses include, at the time of the initial plan, fifteen to twenty rooms, and need a system of inner passageways, which also are included as a part of the planning process. In effect, a "spontaneous" architecture is replaced by one that is much more "rational" and "planned." These latter attributes can be seen as indications of a more formal and precise cultural tradition.

Three cultures, which existed at about the same time and in the same general region, solved the problems of architectural organization in different but homogeneous ways. The Samarra culture, which is not well defined and seems a bit ephemeral, employed the principle of "suite circulation" (*circulation en enfilade*) for movement between rooms (Aurenche 1982, 1981b, 1986). The Ubaid culture, which lasted several millennia, solved the problem of movement with a principle of "distribution circulation" from a large central room (Aurenche 1981b, 1986). The Susa culture (or pre-Susa, "Susiana" culture), which was equal in duration to that of the Ubaidian, solved their problem with the principle of "peripheral circulation" around a central nucleus (Aurenche 1985). In each case, other archaeological data let us distinguish these cultures one from another quite clearly. Once more, it is clear that there is a strong correlation between a particular architectural type and a homogeneous human group. Like pottery, which usually provides the principal criteria for cultural identification, architecture plays an important role in the identification of cultural facts. In the three examples employed here, "cultural meaning" is particularly important. It seems clear that from the beginning of the evolution of architecture in the Near East, "cultural meaning" increased with the growth of its complexity.

It is difficult to bring the significance of this architectural evolution into sharp focus. One can note the correspondence between socioeconomic and architectural change: two of the three cultures discussed above (Samarra and Ubaid) which incorporated new forms of dwellings were also among the first groups which practiced irrigated agriculture. It would be caricatural, and probably wrong, as ethnology shows, to associate "simple" architecture with "simple" society, and "complex" architecture with "complex" society. Nonetheless, the association is present in this case.

Finally, we should note that the first urban cultures (Uruk and Elam) were the direct successors of the Ubaid and Susa cultures, and heirs to not only the territories but the architectural traditions of their predecessors. The progression of architecture cannot be a simple coincidence. On the contrary, it seems that each of these steps, in the required order, constitutes not only a chronological but a logical evolution. History could not develop without this long but unavoidable prehistory.

Perhaps one can delve more deeply into the relationships between architecture and the human groups who raised and used the buildings. It is worthwhile to establish the cultural significance of architecture, not from the outside (in terms of relations with socioeconomic organization and adaptation) but from the inside (in terms of relations with the social organization of the group).

Architecture and Society: Some Elements for Reflection

There is nothing more difficult, in the absence of written records and oral traditions, than to estimate the internal organization of a human group. One approach that has been tried in the Near East is through an analysis of funerary customs (Forest 1983). It is also possible to approach problems of social organization through an observation of people in their "life spaces": a study of "living architecture." In this latter regard, two archaeological examples permit us to raise several hypotheses about "life spaces" in the ancient Near East. These examples rely upon what, for that part of the world, are extraordinary conditions—the complete excavation, or at least excavation of the principal parts—of a whole human settlement. The goal, then, is to examine the architectural remains from such excavations in terms of the information they might hold for differences in the organization of society itself.

The first traces of interest appear on Natufian sites (12,000–10,300 BP), where there are constructions of different sizes: there are both "large" and "small" round houses. When their topographic disposition is compared with contemporary ethnographic example, the variation in their size seems related to function (dwellings versus storage) rather than to the different social status of individuals and families. Later, during the PPNA (10,300–9600 BP), the famous Jericho tower and the wall that encircled the site contrasts with individual dwellings but suggests nonetheless a more collective and organized construction activity (Cauvin 1978:43). We can go quite a bit further with the Neolithic of the PPNB (9600–8000 BP). For example, the village of Çayönü, which is situated in the upper Tigris basin, has been excavated extensively and through several successive levels. There, in addition to "ordinary" buildings, there is a "particular" set of buildings which differ markedly in their morphology from the others. Three different buildings of this particular kind succeed one another in the history of the village. Their location in relation to the remainder of the settlement shows that they were always constructed beside a "square"—a sign of a "structuring" collective space. The function of these buildings is not obvious, but the presence of numerous skulls in one of them suggests a kind of "charnel house." Such buildings can be found today in some societies (Aurenche and Calley 1988). Whatever significance it carries, it is the first time in the history of architecture that we find a building for which the main function does not seem to be as a dwelling.

The second step occurs at approximately 6500–6000 BP, in the Ubaid culture of Mesopotamia. The "exceptional" building that can be seen there does not differ greatly from others either in construction or, probably, in general terms of use, but it does differ significantly in its size and in its architectural decoration. Such a building seems to suggest the notion of prestige in an "architectural hierarchy." It can be considered either as the house of a community leader (chief) or as a house for the community as a whole (collective). Whatever the case, it is clear that these two hypotheses are not contradictory.

In the examples employed here, there is a difference in kind (the charnel house at Çayönü) or a difference in degree (the "large house" from Ubaid) between a few structures and the vast majority of other structures. Architectural traces obviously do serve as signs relative to the organization of human groups; the full implications and translations of these signs are neither straightforward nor fully understood, but are easier to "read" than other kinds of archaeological documents. In the Near East, each crucial step of the socioeconomic evolution has been defined by architectural changes or innovations: sedentism, the birth of agriculture, the practice of irrigation, the beginning of urbanism. In each case, architecture was a "sign" of change, and this sign has been made perceptible, if not explained to some extent, by the archaeologist.

REFERENCES

Aurenche, O. 1981a. *La maison orientale. L'architecture du Proche-Orient ancien des origines au milieu du IVème millénaire*. Librarie orientaliste P. Geuthner, BAH 109, Paris.

———1981b. "L'architecture mésopotamienne du 7ème au 4ème millénaire," *Paléorient* **7/2,** 43–55.

———1982. "Les premières maisons et les premiers villages," *La Recherche* **135,** juillet-août 1982, 880–889.

———1985. "La tradition architecturale à l'est de la Mésopotamie (Iran-Turkmenistan) du 10ème au 4ème millénaires," in J.-C. Gardin (ed.), *l'Archéologie de la Bactriane ancienne*, pp. 235–245. Editions du C.N.R.S., Paris.

———1986. "Mesopotamian architecture from the 7th to the 4th millennia," *Sumer* **XLII N 1– 2,** 71–80.

Aurenche, O., and S. Calley 1988. "L'architecture de l'Anatolie du Sud-Est au Néolithique acéramique," *Anatolica* **XV, 1–2x.**

Cauvin, J. 1978. *Les premiers villages de Syrie-Palestine du IXème au VIIème millénaire avant J. C.* Maison de l'Orient, CMO 4, Lyon, Diffusion de Boccard, Paris.

———1988. "La néolithisation de l'Anatolie du Sud-Est," *Anatolica* **XV,** 69–80.

Flannery, K. V. 1972. "The origins of the village as a settlement type in Mesoamerica and the Near East: A comparative study," in P. J. Ucko, R. Tringham, and G. W. Dimbleby (eds.), *Man, Settlement and Urbanism*, pp. 23–53. Duckworth, London.

Forest, J.-D. 1983. *Les pratiques funéraries en Mésopotamie du 5ème millénaire au début du 3ème. Etude de cas*. ADPF, Paris.

Gould, R. A. 1980. *Living Archaeology*. Cambridge University Press, Cambridge.

Hodder, I. 1986. *Reading the Past*. Cambridge University Press, Cambridge.

Macaulay, D. 1979. *Motel of the Mysteries*. Houghton Mifflin, Boston.

Change and Cultural Inertia

FROM THE ANALYSIS OF DATA TO THE CREATION OF A MODEL

Preface

The goal of this paper is to show, stage by stage, the elaboration of a theoretical model founded on the direct analysis of archaeological data. The process followed could be defined as logicist in the sense that each stage gives rise to the next, in a progression going from the particular to the general, and with frequent steps backward, carried out with the purpose of examining and comparing partial conclusions. As for the model itself, it concerns the process of cultural change. It examines sites that were occupied over a long span of time and where there appears a continuity of technique and a "resistance to change" which we call "cultural inertia." Observed first in the domain of prehistoric bone, and told from a Middle Eastern perspective (of the Natufian, to be exact), this model is tested on other examples of technical activity (lithic industry), then on other periods. It remains meanwhile indispensable to verify it in other areas of human or natural science to make it eventually move from the value of a proposition to that of an explanatory precept.

Introduction

Archaeology today is turning inward upon itself. It indulges in self-criticism and self-analysis (self-psychoanalysis is not far away) by dissecting its own logical processes. It stops and turns to look for the "good approach." The definition of the "good approach" varies according to personal inclinations and to the systems of thought; it can be seen that this intellectual instability covers up cultural, geographic, even political realities.

There has appeared, in the recent work of Gallay (1986), an opinion which seems to me very positive. There exists not one good approach; on the contrary, several may co-exist, each in turn contributing to a scientific process. It is in exactly this spirit that the meeting in Bloomington, which produced this collection of papers, was concluded. Next to a so-called "cold" archaeology, above all European and in any case logicist, may be juxtaposed a so-called "hot" archaeology, symbolic, interpretive, even literary (Gardin).

Instead of hoping for a consensus of opinion (Hertzfeld) the archaeologists present welcomed the richness brought by diverse and complementary attitudes.

For my part, I situate myself (as Roux has suggested) in a position both "cold" and "hot," but at the same time avoiding a mixture of genres, or simply a mixture of stages of research, so that I do not attract to me the curse reserved for those who are "lukewarm."

The method which will be applied here is in effect anchored in a detailed analysis of material evidence. From the multiple elements which this analysis generates, a logicist approach develops point by point, permitting through an interplay of combinations, classifications, and diverse manipulations the transformation of an anarchic mass of information into a series of ordered images or scenarios. It is from this point that the "temperature changes." Indeed, it seems evident to me that the analysis and the constructions which follow it cannot constitute an end in themselves. On the contrary, they lead naturally to the stage of attempting explanations. Now these explanations do not inevitably (and still less mechanically) flow from the prolongation of logical reasoning. They can spring from intuition, but an intuition whose nature must be precisely stated. We call this "heavy intuition," to lay stress on its character, which is loaded with a past knowledge accumulated and more or less ordered which it represents as an instantaneous crystallization. Should this contraction in time have attributed to it an irrational character which it does not necessarily have? We leave this kind of question to philosophers, recalling only the Cartesian definition of intuition; our notion of "heavy intuition" refers expressly to it.[1]

The application of this method in the example that follows has its geographic setting in the Middle East and its chronological framework in the eleventh and tenth millennia B.C. It is deployed within the Natufian culture,[2] and more particularly in an area of technical creation: worked bone objects.

Although it is true that this type of artifact is difficult to study without using somewhat heavy strategies,[3] one can state that it is sometimes possible to extract from a thorough understanding of it information of a palaeoethnographic or historic order. It is necessary, however, to recognize that this information is often "micro-cultural," and that if it is invaluable at the level of a site, a group of related sites, or very coherent cultural systems, it generally loses much of its weight when the questions posed concern vast regions or widely spread cultures. This observation does not preclude one from offering interpretations that can be elaborated from a study of worked bone industry and that can not only be tested on other materials but even proposed as a more largely useful model.

Such a proposition will be presented here. We will follow the process of its formation from the basic data from which it sprung, and follow its elaboration to the new perspectives which it can open.

The construction comprised a seven-stage process, which we will deal with in order:

I- Analysis of worked bone objects from a site: Mallaha, occupied from the beginning to the end of the Natufian.[4]

II- Comparison with other Natufian sites, identification of regional and chronological differences through the Levant.

III- Interpretation of these regional differences: proposed explanation.

IV- Test of this proposition, always in the Natufian context, but extended to other categories of objects.

V- Test of this proposition in other space-time contexts.

VI- Comparing the proposition to other modes of explaining the observed phenomenon.

VII- Analysis of the importance to the model: limitation, validity, extension to other sectors, and analogies with explanatory laws known in other domains.

I- Analysis of Bone Artifacts from a Site

The basic data at the first level of the analysis come from the site of Mallaha (Israel),[5] which was occupied from the early Natufian (levels IV to II) to late and final Natufian (levels Ia, b, c),[6] and has produced a rich array of worked bone objects.

The tools have been analyzed in detail but could not, for reasons of conservation, be subjected to exhaustive physical study (experimentation, microwear analysis).

Several kinds of classification have been applied to the material: morphological and technical categories, mode of hafting, degree of elaboration of the tools, dimensions and indexes, techniques of fabrication, and heat treatment. From these classifications, information has been recovered directly—in the form of characteristics and the evolution of regrouped elements—or indirectly—as a combination of the characteristics and manifestation of types.

One notes at first that there are thirteen categories of tools, which are clearly differentiated (Table 1). Twelve of these categories are present in the early Natufian, but only seven are present in the late Natufian. There is, then, a decline in the variety of the tools. This decline, it is necessary to point out, concerns more particularly the most specialized tools.

On the other hand, one does not detect any evolution on a strictly technical level, that is to say in the method of fabrication of the objects. The Natufians knew a large range of fabrication techniques and practiced them freely, combining them apparently at random. A few objects, projectile points for example, for which the fabrication was subject to strict limitations (form and dimensions) were treated according to a rigid chain of operations.

One notes the same total absence of evolution in the use of a particular technique: in this case, heat treatment, which characterizes 32.7 percent of the tools. A highly controlled heat source is in effect imposed unequally on different categories of tools (almost 100 percent of projectile points, 32 percent of punches, and only 18 percent of cutting tools) but shows no chronological variation.

When one examines the domain of hafting and the fitting of handles on tools, one detects between the beginning and the end of the Natufian of Mallaha a slight reduction of indirect methods (fitting of handles) and an increase in more simple methods (integrated handles, that is to say being part of the bone tool itself).

Generally speaking, one notes a certain narrowing in the range of bone tools from the beginning to the end of the occupation of Mallaha; that is to say, from the beginning

BONE TOOL TYPE	EARLY NATUFIAN	LATE and FINAL NATUFIAN
Type I punch	●	★
Type III punch	●	★
Type IV punch	●	★
Standard smoothing tool	●	★
Flat knife	●	★
Composite tool	●	★
Type II punch	●	
Projectile point	●	
Retoucher	●	
Dagger	●	
Smoothing tool with diverging edges	●	
Chisel	●	
Spoon-spatula		★

Table 1. Bone tool types present in the Early, Late, and Final
Natufian at Mallaha.

to the end of the Natufian. This evolution is not particularly spectacular, and above all
is within the framework of technical practice. How is it on the other Natufian sites?

II- Evolution of Worked Bone on Natufian Sites

Bone artifacts from Natufian sites have rarely been studied in detail. The bases for
comparisons with Mallaha are thus sometimes difficult to establish. However, the publications enable, in the limited domain of bone objects, an evident Natufian cultural unity
to be brought to light, at the heart of which Mallaha naturally has its place.

It is possible to translate this "worked bone cultural unity" into a portrait-type with
"ten original traits" indicative of the Natufian and which one does not risk finding
regularly in all Neolithic cultures. These "traits" differ in nature: types of tools (barbed
points, composite tools, bipointed projectile points, retouchers, smoothing tools with
diverging edges, and fish hooks), technical processes (heat treatment), decorative pro-

	barbed point	composite tool	bipoint	bone ornament	decorated tool	art	heat treatment	retoucher	smoothing tool	fish hook
NATUFIAN (undifferentiated)										
El Wad B	○	○	○	○	○	○	○	○		
Hayonim Terrace	○			○	○	○	○	○		
Aîn Sakhri	○			○	○	○				
Zoueitina	○	○				○				
EARLY NATUFIAN										
Hayonim Cave I-II			●	●	●	●	●	●	●	●
Kebara B	●	●	●	●	●	●	●			●
El Wad B2			●		●	●	●			
Mallaha II-IV			●	●	●	●	●	●	●	●
Wadi Hammeh 27			●	●	●	●	●			
Jericho	●						●		●	
Erq El Ahmar A2	●			●	●					
Oumm Qaláa	●	●								
Jabrud	●									
LATE and FINAL NATUFIAN										
Hayonim Cave III	★	★	★		★					
Hayonim Cave IV	★	★	★							
El Wad B1	★		★				★			
Mallaha Ic, Ib		★		★		★	★			
Nahal Oren V	★		★		★	★				
Abu Hureyra			★	★		★				
Mureybet						★	★			
Hatoula			★				★			
Shukbah					★					
Saadeh 2						★				
Rosh Horesha			★							
Salibiyah				★						

Table 2. Distribution of typical characteristics of Natufian worked bone.

cesses (decorated tools), the existence of figurative art (which we have extended to include artistic expression in other materials), and finally, the existence of elements of particular ornament (pierced phalanges or oval pendants, brought together under a single heading).

These characteristics are found unequally distributed and in differing frequencies at eighteen of the Natufian sites presently known and published which have produced worked bone (Tables 2 and 3).

With what frequency do they appear on these sites? Do these frequencies vary with time?

It is to be noted that the most common characteristics, and above all the most stable, do not concern the categories of tools but more general factors: the custom of decorating the tools, the existence of figurative art, heat treatment, and the use of characteristic

Sites with worked bone; not differentiated chronologically		

○○○○○○○	El Wad B	
○○○○○	Hayonim Terrace	
○○○○	Ain Sakhri	
○○○	Zoueitina	

	EARLY NATUFIAN	LATE and FINAL NATUFIAN
Sites occupied during Early, Late, and Final Natufian		
Hayonim Cave	●●●●●●●●	★ ★ ★ ★
Mallaha	●●●●●●●●	★ ★ ★ ★
El Wad	●●●●●	★ ★ ★
Early Natufian Sites		
Kebara	●●●●●●●●	
Wadi Hammeh 27	●●●●●	
Erq El Ahmar	●●●●	
Jericho	●●●	
Oumm Qaláa	●●	
Jabrud	●	
Late˙ and Final˙˙ Natufian Sites		
Nahal Oren V˙˙		★ ★ ★ ★
Abu Hureyra˙		★ ★ ★
Mureybet˙˙		★ ★
Hatoula˙		★ ★
Shukbah˙		★
Saadeh 2˙˙		★
Rosh Horesha˙		★
Salibiyah˙˙		★

Table 3. Chronological distribution of Natufian sites with worked bone. Each symbol represents a typical Natufian characteristic.

ornaments. The types of tools or weapons appear more irregularly. If the barbed points, the groups of composite tools, and the bipointed projectile points are frequent, on the other hand the retouchers, the smoothing tools with diverging edges, and above all the curved fish hooks are much less frequent.

But what interests us most of all concerns a general decline of the pertinent cultural characteristics from early Natufian to final Natufian. If we find up to eight characteristics out of ten in the early Natufian on a site (or in a level corresponding to a site), for the late or final Natufian no site can summon up more than two characteristics. Some few sites are exceptions: for example, El Wad, Hayonim Cave, and Mallaha, which in their late levels show four traits of the Natufian.

MOUNT CARMEL and GALILEA												
El Wad	○	○	○	○	○	○	○					
Kebara	●	●	●	●	●	●	●	●				
Hayonim Cave	✪	✪	✪	✪	●	●	●	●				
Mallaha	✪	✪	✪	✪	●	●	●	●				
Hayonim Terrace	○	○	○	○	○							
Nahal Oren	★	★										

JUDEA and SAMARIA												
Wadi Hammeh 27	●	●	●	●	●							
Aîn Sakhri	○	○	○	○								
Erq El Ahmar	●	●	●	●								
Jericho	●	●	●									
Zoueitina	○	○	○									
Oumm Qal'aa	●	●										
Hatoula	★	★										
Shukbah	★											
Salibiyah	★											

NORTH LEVANT : SYRIA and LEBANON												
Abu Hureyra	★	★	★									
Mureybet	★	★										
Saadeh	★											
Jabrud	●											

NEGEV, SINAI and SOUTH JORDAN												
Rosh Horesha	★											

● Early Natufian   ○ Undifferentiated Natufian

★ Late and Final Natufian   ✪ Early, Late and Final Natufian

Table 4. Geographical distribution of Natufian sites with worked bone.
Each symbol corresponds to a typical Natufian characteristic.

To better understand this phenomenon of decline, we have regrouped the sites according to their situation (Table 4) by distinguishing three geographic zones (all phases of Natufian mixed):

1- Mount Carmel and the Galilee
2- Judea and Samaria
3- The northern Levant: Lebanon and Syria

These groups were created in order to examine the possibilities of effects other than those due simply to chronological factors.

This classification at once produces clear information: each zone is clearly differentiated from the others by the number of typical cultural characteristics which the sites bring together. In the first, one finds 2 to 8 characteristics, in the second, 1 to 4 characteristics, in the third, 1 to 2 characteristics.

Zone of Mount Carmel and the Galilee

This zone brings together the five sites which are the richest, the oldest, and the longest inhabited: El Wad, Kebara, Hayonim cave and terrace, and Mallaha, at which the occupation begins in the early Natufian and lasts until the late or final Natufian. Only one site is marginal to this group. This is Nahal Oren, which is attributed to the final Natufian.

Zone of Judea and Samaria

This very homogenous zone contains a majority of early Natufian sites and seems to have been abandoned in the late and final Natufian, as only two sites, the poorest, Shukbah and Hatoula, are representative of the late Natufian.

   The capacity of these sites, to give evidence of typical Natufian cultural characteristics, although often excavated to only a limited extent, is quite homogenous, all being less strong than in Galilee and on Mount Carmel. Several sites, however, like El Khiam, Fazael IV, or Tor Abu Sif, have not produced a single bone artifact, although they contain Natufian levels.

Northern Zone: Syria and Lebanon

The Natufian sites of Syria and Lebanon are much more dispersed, even after taking into account the fact that excavations in this region have been few (M. C. Cauvin 1987). These sites, which show at least one of the cultural characteristics which we have isolated, all belong, with the exception of Jabrud, to the late or final Natufian. They are, then, at once rare, poor, far from zones with high concentrations of typical Natufian characteristics, and late.

   There exists a fourth zone, also far from the major sites, which we cannot pass over in silence, even if its muteness in terms of bone tools tends to make us forget it. This is the Negev, Sinai, and the Southern Jordan zone. At present, we only know one Natufian site in that zone which produced bone tools, Rosh Horesha (Beidha, which has produced worked bone for later periods, allows us to dismiss natural causes of this absence).

III- Interpretation of Regional Differences: Proposed Explanation

The examination of the evolution of worked bone characteristic of the Natufian produces the following patterns. If the characteristics diminish from early to late Natufian, this diminution of variety is observed even more clearly when one considers it geographically: the farther from Mount Carmel, the more this is marked (even in Judea, where early Natufian sites are predominant).

   The geographic factor seems then to prevail over the chronological factor.

   How can this difference be interpreted?

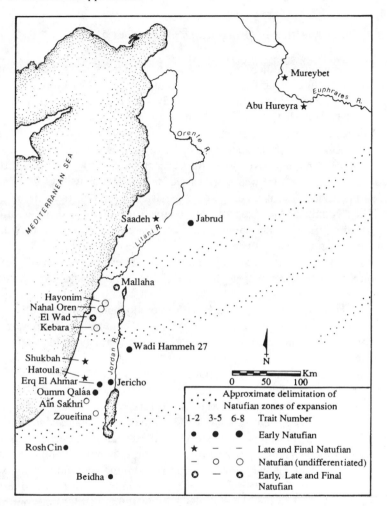

Map 1. Distribution of Natufian sites with worked bone.

Examination of Map 1 and Table 2 suggests the following explanation: in the zones with the longest history of occupation, and even more so in the sites occupied from the early to the end of the Natufian, the phenomenon of the decline of traits is reduced. It is as if in a zone playing the role of cultural center (Mount Carmel and Galilee) for the Natufian culture, the coherence of the most traditional "values" is maintained longer than elsewhere. Moreover, this conservatism seems more persistent in the sites of continuous occupation, as if "cultural inertia" slows down in places where generations succeed each other without rupture.

It may seem rash to put forth such a "model" on the basis of one sector of the artisanal activity of one culture and with a sample of only twenty sites. Convinced of the justness of such a criticism, I shall now test the model with reference to other areas of the activity of the Natufians.

IV- Test of the Proposition in Other Areas of Natufian Culture

The theme of the decline in the range of the cultural manifestations from the beginning to the end of the Natufian is far from being a recent discovery. Garrod (Garrod and Bates 1937) has already remarked upon this, particularly in reference to the worked bone from El Wad. Neuville, somewhat later, pointed out the richness of the worked bone of Natufian I "only to disappear almost totally in Natufian II" (Neuville 1951:117), that is to say, at the same time that the art disappeared. For Perrot (1966) the decline was general and more quantitative than qualitative. Valla, in a recent synthesis (1987), states that in the early Natufian the architecture was more varied, technically as well as in form, than in the late Natufian. He discerns a continuous, persistent evolution from the beginning to the end of the Natufian. My remarks only confirm an established observation which seems, apart from various shades of meaning, to be shared by all the prehistorians working or having worked in the Natufian.[7]

But does one note, as in the worked bone, a "difference of behavior" between the sites occupied from the beginning to the end of the Natufian and those settled in the later periods?

I have chosen to test this proposition in a microdomain of lithic tools, that of the retouching of lunates. This significant microdomain is without a doubt important, because it is upon this that Natufian cultural identifications and distinctions between early, late, and final often rest.

In the past it was thought that the oblique bifacial retouch, so-called "Heluan," only existed in the early Natufian, and the abrupt retouch characterized the late and final Natufian. Subsequently, many prehistorians have arrived at a more subtle position. In various articles (Bar-Yosef; Henry; Valla; M. C. Cauvin) percentage tables and diagrams show that the Heluan retouch does not always disappear in the late Natufian.[8] The question, which follows naturally from this statement, is simple: Were sites later in the chronology that exhibited Heluan retouch occupied from the beginning of the sequence?

Table 5 (to compare Table 4) permits an affirmative response to this question. The Heluan retouch was used on lunates after the early Natufian in 43.33 percent of cases at Mallaha,[9] 36.84 percent of cases at Hayonim Cave, 36.48 percent then 7.5 percent at Hayonim terrace, and finally 10.37 percent at El Wad. No other site of late or final Natufian shows such persistence except Zoueitina, which, as we have seen, may have problems in its chronological attribution and therefore should be used cautiously. Elsewhere, then, the Heluan retouch is reduced to less than 10 percent or, even more often, disappears completely (compare Maps 2 and 3).

In the example chosen it is less a matter of "decline" than of a "change" in technical practices. One can then state that in the sites occupied continuously there is a resistance to change, which parallels their resistance to the loss of cultural substance.

V- Test of the Proposition in Other Space-Time Contexts

The prestigious site of Jericho was occupied from the early Natufian to the Bronze Age (Kenyon 1960). The study of its worked bone for the earliest periods—Natufian, Proto-

	EARLY NATUFIAN			LATE AND FINAL NATUFIAN		
	0	50%	100%	0	50%	100%
MOUNT CARMEL and GALILEA						
Hayonim Cave						
Mallaha						
El Wad						
Kebara						
Nahal Oren						
JUDEA and SAMARIA						
Oumm Qaláa						
Erq El Ahmar						
Zoueitina˙						
Tor Abu Sif˙						
Taibe A4-A3						
Taibe A2						
Taibe A1						
Shukbah˙						
Salibiyah˙						
Fazael IV˙						
Hatoula˙						
BEKAA and EUPHRATES						
Jayroud J2						
Jayroud J1 ˙˙						
Abu Hureyra˙						
Dibsi Faraj˙						
Mureybet ˙˙						
NEGEV and SINAI						
Rosh Cin˙						
Rosh Horesha˙						

Table 5. Frequency of Heulan retouch on lunates, grouped by period and region. Percentages provided by Bar-Yosef and Valla (1979) and from M.-C. Cauvin (1987).

Neolithic, PPNA, and PPNB[10]—have led us to establish a continuity of technical practices. These appear most clearly in certain worked bone tools, of which the use crosses the frontiers of time and cultural features without apparent rupture.[11]

This continuity is particularly evident in the case of heavy bone tools, widely found, which were used for rubbing as well as for percussion. Descended from Natufian smoothing tools with diverging edges, they are found without interruption in the early Natufian as well as in Proto-Neolithic levels, in PPNA levels, where they become very numerous and diversified, and in PPNB levels. Their morphology, with a massive, globulous proximal part and a distal part with a cutting edge, is analogous to that of flint tools considered to be the most typical of the PPNA of Jericho (or Sultanian)—the tranchets ("tranchet-adzes" and "tranchet-chisels," Crowfoot-Payne 1984). But this analogy is not limited

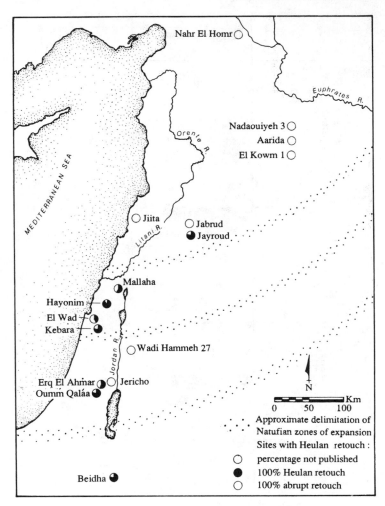

Map 2. Distribution of Early Natufian sites indicating Heulan retouch
in proportion to abrupt retouch.

to the morphology. In the two cases, in effect, a similar general form and an identical
feature, the terminal level (obtained, for the flint, by a "tranchet blow"), determine two
groups from the point of view of function. The first consists of tools of direct use which
are flint adzes and smoothing tools or hide-scrapers made of bone; the second brings
together tools of indirect use, bone chisels as well as flint chisels.

A last analogy, which interests us particularly, concerns the behavior of this ensemble
of flint and bone tools in the context of time. If they are particularly typical of the PPNA,
they persist also in the PPNB of Jericho. Moreover, in this period they are not limited
to this site only, and are even characteristic of all the PPNB of the south Levant (or
Tahounian), figuring in almost all the sites of this region. On the other hand, nothing is
known about them in northern Syria. We have there perhaps a new example of persistence

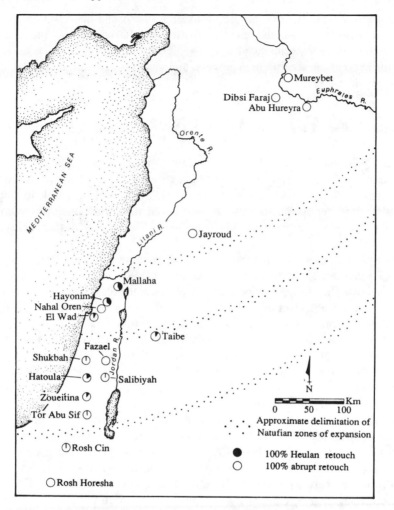

Map 3. Distribution of Late and Final Natufian sites indicating persistence of Heulan retouch in proportion to abrupt retouch on lunates.

of a local practice which crosses the limit of two successive cultural phases (the PPNA and the PPNB) without losing its substance. Thus this persistence reduces somewhat, and only on a local and circumscribed scale, the distinctness of a succession between two cultures. If very different factors contribute or create, within great cultural ensemble, that which is called "regional features" (J. Cauvin 1985), we would submit that it is possible that "cultural inertia" is one of these.

The example which has just been developed thus illustrates the persistence of a cultural trait in a limited context, across three cultures which succeed each other over four millennia: the Natufian, the PPNA, and the PPNB. It could be that the diagnosis of this persistence brings a significant element of comprehension to the understanding of PPNB.

One knows, in effect, that this culture, unlike the PPNA and the Natufian, is of Syrian origin (J. Cauvin 1978), and that it is largely diffused afterward across the south Levant. It appears thus to have encountered in this region local practices, which have persisted even at the heart of the acculturation process, and which in part account for the originality of the Palestinian PPNB.

VI- Confrontation of the Proposition with Other Modes of Explanation

The elements which I have just put forth seem to me to open the way to a necessary reconsideration of the model proposed. From a very focused perspective on the phenomenon of continually occupied sites, the question now is to back up a little to consider the problem in a broader spatial framework. We will achieve this breadth by coming back to the first example, the Natufian, which we have examined more thoroughly than the others.

In a spatial framework, the continually occupied sites where the phenomenon of "inertia" is detected are all found at the heart of the region of Galilee and Mount Carmel. This area shows the strongest concentration of Natufian sites. The farther from it, the number of sites, the number of typical attributes per site, and the rate of persistence of early Natufian retouching techniques diminish progressively (Figures 1, 2, and 3). The role of the region which encompasses the Galilee and Mount Carmel could well be defined by the term cultural center (as we have already suggested above). In this perspective, the particularly strong cultural inertia which characterizes the sites of this region could then be seen as a factor of the practices of a village which keeps to its patterns, as well as a factor of a group of close settlements which conserve strongly the basic patterns of their culture.[12] In this area then, our model could be enlarged.

On the other hand, this pattern is not the case for the region of Judea–Samaria–Hauran. Close to the Galilee–Mount Carmel region and occupied from the beginning of the Natufian, it is less rich in original (and fundamental) qualities. Besides, the loss of cultural substance between early and late Natufian is much more abrupt. Could this not be due to the fact that no continually occupied site has been found?

Finally, concerning the Negev, Sinai, and southern Jordan, the proposed model is of no use. What happened in this region could be explained through a spatiotemporal model of cultural diffusion from the center, the periphery having been occupied last, as well as in terms of differences in the way of life (many sites in this region are occupied only temporarily).

My proposition ought not then to make one lose from view the fact that no cultural phenomenon ever allows itself to be explained in a "simple" (in the sense of unique) manner, but on the contrary all progress in understanding it is accompanied without fail by "progress" in the complexity of explanations. Four models (at least) are already combined to give us a first glance at the organization of this vast Natufian cloth, which from the eleventh to the ninth millennium before our era was of such importance in Levant: the model (synchronic) of extension, with its typical succession of concentric zones becoming paler according to increasing distance from the center; the model (diachronic) of diffusion, which is valid only for the desert zones of the south; the model of progressive decline of a culture's values with time; and finally, the model of cultural inertia, which can, in sites long occupied, soften the effect represented by the preceding model.

I will conclude by pointing out that other explanations are still to be found. It is important to take account of the ecological conditions (completely untouched in this approach presented here) which concern the length and character of the settlements (base camp, etc.) or the economic data site by site. Our present perspective could, in the event of such research, be modified or, better, enriched.

VII- Analysis of the General Significance of the Proposed Model

For many years there has accumulated in my memory and in articles which are essentially descriptive and classificatory a body of data and of attributes which cannot but contribute to a familiarization with a difficult material. It is only from this kind of knowledge that an interpretative approach can be extracted.

This approach, as I have attempted to show here, rests irreducibly anchored in the handling of data which should not be held to superficial description or classification. In the example which I have chosen to present, the stages of the approach give rise to each other in a process which I will recapitulate here for the last time.

*The detailed analysis of a group of bone objects coming from a Natufian site has presented me with bodies of data of diverse nature.

*These data are ordered (or rather multiply classified) in several grids.

*These classifications are taken up again and transformed into one grid concerning the ensemble of Natufian sites.

*This last grid was reconstructed to order the classified attributes, according to chronological and geographic criteria.

*This reconstruction brought to light a chronological function: the decline of cultural attributes over time.

*A new construction centered on the geographic distribution of the sites brought forth a more powerful function: according to whether one variable, the continuity of occupation of a site, was positive or negative, this decline was weak or pronounced.

*This variable, then considered relevant, has been interpreted as follows: The fact that this variable slowed the process of decline means that the force of tradition opposed, at least momentarily, changes in the more conservative settlements. I gave to this interpretation the value of a model. It began then the process of testing of factors other than those which have allowed its creation.

*This testing has given positive results in a domain of Natufian lithic technology. It establishes that the theme of decline slowed down by cultural inertia could be developed. The phenomenon observed was, generally speaking, a resistance to change.

*Other verifications allow me to measure at the same time the possible import of the model in the framework of research on the dynamic of change, and the very preliminary state of my approach. They lead me to the impression that I have just broken into the deductive phase of my research and that there remains much to do in this sense. But also, in the inverse sense, they invite me to undertake a critical return to the data. I am conscious in effect of not having mastered all the variables present.

There is no question here of enlarging upon the import of the model which I have presented. Its presentation has as its essential end to rouse reflection or to suggest analogies. I will end this contribution by pointing out a certain analogy between my model and that which Gould (1980) and Eldredge (1982)[13] put forth on the subject of the macroevolution of species and the laws of selection: "The differences occur in very reduced populations situated generally at the periphery of the area of extension of the species, more rarely within the population concerned."

Could not one ask if this model rediscovers the "old law" which juxtaposes the conservatism of cultural centers to the flexibility and openness of the margins?

NOTES

1. Contrary to other, more "mystic" definitions (cf. Bergson), real intuition is not for Descartes the invasion into the domain of reason of elements foreign to it, but an abridgment of reasoning itself, when it contracts into an instantaneous vision of progressions ordinarily unfolding over time.

2. The Natufian, the last Epipalaeolithic culture of the Levant, is characterized by a lithic industry with geometric microliths (lunates), a rich and diversified worked bone industry, and a personal figurative art which is realistic or schematic. One is witnessing above all the beginnings of sedentarization with the installation of constructed villages, of which Mallaha (Isreal) is one of the best known.

3. In the Near Eastern Epipalaeolithic and Neolithic context one notes particularly that on the whole typological classifications are difficult to compose and use. On the contrary, the simultaneous regrouping of objects in several grills of classification established according to homogenous criteria gives precise information, confirming or invalidating the information coming from other domains of material culture (Stordeur 1976, 1985).

4. This analysis is the object of another work and is thus only presented in summary form here (Stordeur 1988a).

5. I wish to thank here J. Perrot, who entrusted me with the study of worked bone from this site. I also wish to thank A. Belpher-Cohen, N. Goring-Morris, O. Bar-Yosef, and I. Gilead, each of whom gave me useful advice concerning this paper.

6. Perrot (1966); Valla (1980, 1983, 1987). The early Natufian is dated, at Mallaha, to about 11,000 BP (LY 1661: 11,740 + or − 570 BP); the late Natufian lasted from 11,000 to 10,000 BP (it was dated at Rosh Horesha, Negev: SHU: 10,470 + or − 430 BP); the final Natufian follows immediately and lasted for only a short time.

7. This idea of decline is, moreover, almost a general law, which holds perhaps to a kind of inevitable entropy (as Gallay reminds us, 1986) which leads to the degeneration and death of cultures.

8. I have used principally the publications of Bar-Yosef and Valla (1979) for the south Levant and of M.-C. Cauvin (1987) for the north Levant.

9. Figure given by Bar-Yosef and Valla (1979). In the publication of Valla (1987) separate percentages are given for Mallaha Ic, late Natufian: 46.29 percent and Ib, final Natufian: 18.29 percent. Two values are also given for Hayonim terrace for two successive occupations of late

Natufian: 36.94 percent (loc 4) and 7.5 percent (sup). These figures are important, as they show the shrinking of the use of the Heluan retouch even within the late and final phases.

10. Proto-Neolithic, transition phase between the Natufian and the PPNA—Pre-Pottery Neolithic A (a seemingly arbitrary distinction as pointed out by Crowfoot-Payne 1984). PPNB—Pre-Pottery Neolithic B. All these terms are due to Kenyon (1960). The PPNA covers, in the southern Levant, the period from 10,000 to 9000 BP and the PPNB from 9000 to 8000 BP.

11. In spite of the absence of certain stages. Thus the absence of late Natufian has often been noted in stratigraphy of the site, an absence interpreted as a gap and a break in its occupation. It must be noted, however, that this very extensive level was only found in a very limited sounding. Future excavations may one day allow this void to be filled.

12. One could even ask if this conservation is not one of the conditions necessary to the functioning of a cultural epicenter.

13. Cited by Gallay (1986:106).

REFERENCES

Bar-Yosef O., and F. Valla 1979. "L'évolution du Natoufien, nouvelles suggestions," *Paléorient* **5**, 145–152.

Belpher-Cohen, A. 1988. *The Natufian Settlement and Hayonim Cave, a Hunter-Gatherer Band on the Threshold of Agriculture*. Thesis, Hebrew University, Jerusalem.

Cauvin, J. 1978. *Les premiers villages de Syrie-Palestine du IXe au VIIe millénaire av. JC*. Lyon, Maison de l'Orient (Coll. Maison de l'Orient, n 4).

———1985. "Civilisations protonéolithiques en Asie antérieure. Les cultures villageoises et les civilisations préurbaines d'Asie antérieure," in J. Lichardus et al., *La Protohistoire de l'Europe*, pp. 141–154 and 156–206. Presses Universitaires du France, Paris.

Cauvin, M.-C. 1987. "Chronologies relatives et chronologie absolue dans l'Epipaléolithique du Levant Nord," in O. Aurenche, J. Evin, and F. Hours (eds.), *Chronologies du Proche-Orient*, pp. 247–266. British Archaeological Reports International Series 379, Oxford.

Crowfoot-Payne, J. 1984. "The Flint industries of Jericho," in K. M. Kenyon and T. A. Holland (eds.), *Jericho V: The Pottery Phases of the Tell and Other Finds*, Vol. III, Appendix C, pp. 622–758. British School of Archaeology, London.

Eldredge, N. 1982. "La Macroévolution," *La Recherche* **13**, 616–626.

Gallay, A. 1986. *L'Archéologie demain*. Belfond, Paris.

Gardin J.-C. 1979. *Une archéologie théorique*. Hachette, Paris.

Garrod, D. A. E., and D. M. A. Bates 1937. *The Stone Age of Mount Carmel*. Clarendon, Oxford.

Gould, S. J. 1980. *Le pouce du Panda: les grandes énigmes de l'évolution*. Grasset, Paris.

Henry, D. O. 1973. *The Natufian of Palestine, Its Material Culture and Ecology*. Southern Methodist University Press, Dallas, TX.

Kenyon, K. 1960. *Archaeology in the Holy Land*. Ernest Been, London.

Neuville, R. 1951. *Le Paléolithique et le Mésolithique du désert de Judée*. (Archives I.P.H. n 24) Masson, Paris.

Perrot, J. 1966. "Le gisement Natoufien de Mallaha (Eynan) Israël," *L'Anthropologie* **70**, 5–6, 437–483.

Stordeur, D. 1976. "Classification multiple ou grilles mobiles de classification des objets en os," in H. Camps-Faber (ed.), *Méthodologie appliquée à l'industrie de l'os préhistorique*, pp. 235–238. Editions du C.N.R.S., Paris.

———1985. "Classification multiple des outillages osseux de Khirokitia, Chypre, VIe millénaire," in H. Camps-Faber (ed.), *L'industrie en os et bois de cervidés durant le Néolithique et les Ages des Métaux*, pp. 11–24, Aix-en-Provence (26–28 October 1983).

———1988a. *Outils et armes en os du village natoufien de Mallaha (Eynan) Israël*. Association Palèorient, Paris. (Memoires et Travaus du Centre de Recherche de Jérusalem No. 6.)

———1988b. "Des technologies nouvelles au service de la technologie? L'exemple des outils en os préhistoriques,'' in J. Tixier (ed.), *Technologies Préhistoriques*, pp. 127–150. Editions du C.N.R.S., Paris. (*Notes et monographies techniques de Centre de Recherche Archaéologiques No. 25.*)

Valla, F. 1980. "Les établissements Natoufiens dans le Nord d'Israël," in J. Cauvin and P. Sanlaville (eds.), *Préhistoire du Levant*, pp. 409–419. Colloque C.N.R.S., Lyon 1980.

———1983. *Les industries de silex de Mallaha (Eynan et du Natoufien du Levant*. Thèse de Doctorat d'Etat, Université Paris I, Paris.

———1987. "Chronologie absolue et chronologies relatives dans le Natoufien," in O. Aurenche, J. Evin, and F. Hours (eds.), "*Chronologies du Proche-Orient*," pp. 267–294. British Archaeological Reports International Series 379, Oxford.

In Search of Lithic Strategies

A COGNITIVE APPROACH TO
PREHISTORIC CHIPPED STONE ASSEMBLAGES

This paper is based on a straightforward observation: the role played by lithic industries in the so-called new approaches in archaeology has proved very limited. For the most part, lithic studies have remained basically descriptive in nature or they have limited their own role in archaeological inference because they have approached lithic variability from a purely typological perspective.

This observation is all the more paradoxical because:

— lithic industries, prior to the appearance of pottery, are by far the most abundant category of archaeological remains;

— these industries show great variability in spite of their limited number of functions;

— due to their physical nature, lithic implements retain exceptionally well traces of the successive production operations they undergo;

— from this perspective, these materials are good indicators of the intentions of their makers and users, and they can clearly reveal the technical traditions from which they come.

To the extent that lithic analyses have been limited to retouched pieces, and have been imprisoned in a narrow, typological framework, they underexploit the objects of their study. This is not to say that lithic studies have been frozen in the paradigms of the beginning of this century. On the contrary, they have developed in very important ways during the last few decades. Static, typological classifications have been replaced by dynamic analyses rooted in the careful study of complete operational sequences that begin with the acquisition of the raw materials and end with the discard of tools. In addition, use-wear analysis adds to this dynamic apprehension the dimension of functional purpose.

What these developments demonstrate is that typological variation is only the visible tip of the iceberg: much of the variability in lithic industries occurs at the following points along the production process: the modalities of raw material exploitation, the conceptual schemes underlying toolkit manufacture, the methods and techniques of production, and, finally, toolkit management. From this perspective, the problem of variability in lithic industries can be seen to rest on a much wider foundation, one no doubt closer to reality.

Because lithic variability is not exclusively typological, but simultaneously conceptual, technical, and economic, it is also likely that the underlying factors are themselves of a varied nature. Although most archaeologists would assent to this proposition, few actually apply it to their analyses of lithic industries. Instead, most diachronic and synchronic studies postulate single "explanatory" factors—e.g., functional needs, seasonality of occupation, cultural traditions, etc.—and account for all observational data in light of these "hypotheses." Such approaches are necessary at the methodological level to the extent that they demonstrate the *potential* relevance of a given factor.[1] On the other hand, these approaches lack the capacity to discriminate among various causal factors. Such arguments cannot establish either that the factor under consideration accounts for *all* of the observed variability or that it *alone* could produce it. Consequently, these approaches are too restricted for an efficient analysis of archaeological contexts in which lithic industries, their variations, and their transformations result, as do all human phenomena, from the interaction of multiple factors.

In contrast, recent studies which focus on *intentions* and take into account the ensemble of operative sequences seem better able to disentangle the diversity of purposes thus revealed, even when typological inventories are comparable. Consequently, lithic analysts should now be better able to grasp the mechanisms and causes of lithic variability (see, for example, Audouze et al. in press; Audouze and Cahen 1984; Cahen et al. 1980; Clark 1987; Clark and Lee 1982, 1984; Geneste 1985; Pelegrin 1986; van Noten et al. 1978).

The present study has a twofold objective. First, it examines how one may proceed from technological observations to interpretations phrased in terms of intentions—technological, economic, and others. In other words, it seeks to uncover the inferential bases of technological interpretations (rather than of technological analyses themselves). Second, it will provide an opportunity to present a more formalized method of approaching chipped stone industries so that one can discriminate among the *different* factors that are at work in the production of a given tool assemblage. To this end, when I use the term "intention," I do not mean more or less unconscious aims that are selected by holistic mechanisms, although such aims certainly do exist. Instead I refer to actual decisions taken by prehistoric individuals or groups of individuals when dealing with chipped stones. Consequently, it is a cognitive,[2] individualistic, decision-making approach to lithic industries.[3] At the same time, my claim is that such cognitive approaches are indeed amenable to scientific criteria, in the Popperian sense of falsifiable propositions, and even, as the conclusion will show, in the more demanding sense of the logicist approach.[4]

I. Background and Methods

This study, which is limited to aspects of lithic production and use,[5] is based on observations and fundamental propositions which, though classic, deserve to be presented here because they are its conceptual foundation.

1) For any given task, there are a number of potential tools and techniques that will accomplish the work satisfactorily.

2) Nonetheless, technical needs inevitably guide the production of tools, and the context of production (the social and economic contexts, for example) limit the range of effective solutions.

3) Likewise, the physical properties of the various raw materials may set additional constraints on the production of tools.

4) Finally, and perhaps most important, is that flaking hard rock is an activity that is learned, and practiced by individuals capable of critical judgment. Two basic consequences flow from this observation. Technical traditions, transmitted by training during childhood or adolescence, are limiting factors in the choice of technical and conceptual schemes by the prehistoric adult stone worker.[6] Nonetheless, given the conditions under which the tasks are carried out, critical judgment allows the stone worker to choose the most appropriate operational sequences (practical methods and techniques) known to him.[7]

Indeed, stone-working, like any other technical activity, presupposes the existence of a "conceptual schema." It requires an abstract plan of integrated actions, that can be implemented according to the design and the circumstances (for example, the nature of the desired tools, the nature of the original rock, etc.) as various operational sequences. As Audouze and her associates have shown:

> Since we are dealing here with the transition from a random shape—the raw material—to a volume partially dependent upon the natural shape of the raw material, the implication is that the conceptual scheme must be highly flexible. The operational chain changes from one piece of material to another with respect to the articulation of the different operations, although remaining grounded in the same principles and on the same evaluation of the qualities of the raw material. (Audouze et al. in press: 5)

This faculty of critical judgment, even if not consciously exercised as such, permits the assessment of various possible solutions in terms of savings of time or materials, risk of failure, technical or social advantages, etc. Without necessarily projecting our own contemporary rationality onto prehistoric decision-making, it nonetheless can be assumed that there was some form of rationality that animated individuals in the past. This rationality can be perceived in the options chosen and in their recurrence in similar contexts.

Thus, the manufacture of any stone tool is the result of a long series of technical, economic, social, and even symbolic options, the combination of which can be expressed in terms of "strategies." However, only the recurrent choices among these options—those arising from the socioeconomic context or, at the technical level, from the conceptual schema—can be analyzed in terms of strategies. The variants of operational sequences which can be explained in purely circumstantial terms are tactical choices. I am interested here in the first, strategic choices only.

These strategies are elaborated, implemented, and integrated into the behavior of a group, as long as they are judged satisfactory in light of a number of variables such as the quality and abundance of local raw materials, functional needs, and tool maintenance requirements. These variables take on definite values in each context, including the value "zero" (when, for example, raw materials can be obtained easily and, thus, "extraction cost" can be said to equal "zero"). By confronting the values taken by these variables in a given archaeological situation with the strategies revealed by the stone tool assemblages, it thus is possible to infer which variables have been judged to be the most constraining, and the principal factors in the implementation of these strategies: e.g., a reduction in the time spent in acquiring raw materials, the possibility of obtaining blanks of specific characteristics, the response to powerful technical constraints. A particular strategy will be implemented as long as it proves to be adequate; consequently there is no need to postulate that each time a series of tools is manufactured each variable is consciously reevaluated by the artisan. In fact, specific strategies may be transmitted across several generations and changed only when new circumstances and constraints make the adoption of a new strategy appropriate.

Throughout the operational sequence that leads to discarded lithic artifacts, the artisan is presented with numerous options. In practice, the operational sequence splits into three stages, which rest on different conceptual grounds and occur in temporal succession: raw material acquisition, tool production, and toolkit management. Thus every technical operation, even one of minimal complexity, is the result of not one but three complementary strategies, each of which reacts to and interacts strongly with the other two.[8]

These three stages, and the variables that potentially determine them, will be briefly examined and exemplified in the context of archaeological remains from two separate areas: the Late Upper Paleolithic Magdalenian sites of the Paris Basin (Audouze et al. in press); the lithic assemblages from Franchthi Cave in Greece[9] based on the author's own work.

II. Strategies of Raw Material Procurement

Raw materials suitable for the manufacture of stone tools are not evenly distributed over the face of the earth. Furthermore, neither are these materials all of the same flaking quality nor equally appropriate for specific tasks. Thus quality, abundance, and ease of procurement frequently can conflict one with another. As a consequence of this lack of harmony among means, there is frequently a need to make choices, and a need to elaborate strategies of raw material acquisition. The variables which are relevant in the development of these strategies are numerous but relatively easy to evaluate (Table 1, I.1—I.9). Therefore I shall discuss them only briefly below.

1) Abundance of locally available raw materials

A long line of investigation of procurement strategies shows that sources can be considered strictly "local" if they occur within a five-kilometer radius of a site (see, for example, Geneste 1985). This figure coincides with the "site catchment" as defined by Higgs and Vita-Finzi (1972) and it provides a framework within which the abundance of resources, including raw materials, can be evaluated (Bailey and Davidson 1983).

2) Flaking quality of locally available raw materials

Variation in flaking quality is important and can be evaluated both by observation and by experimentation. Nonetheless, the notion of quality is at best relative and can only be evaluated by taking into account the end product and the techniques employed to produce it.

3) Functional quality of locally available raw materials

Functional quality must be distinguished from flaking quality, because at times these two variables may in fact be in conflict with one another. Obsidian, for example, has

Table 1

Evaluation of variables in given archaeological situations:

Scientific grounds

I Strategies of raw material acquisition
    I.1 Abundance of locally available raw material: Observation
    I.2 Flaking quality of locally available raw materials: Observation
    I.3 Functional quality of locally available raw materials: Observation (microwear analysis in certain cases)
    I.4 Technical needs and functional constraints: Observation (microwear analysis in certain cases)
    I.5 Time available for the acquisition of raw materials: Inference
    I.6 Knowledge of distant sources of raw materials: Observation
    I.7 Socioeconomic context: Inference
    I.8 Cost of raw material acquisition: Observation
    I.9 Group traditions: Inference

II Tool production strategies
    II.1 Raw material available at the production site: quantity, quality, and acquisition cost: Observation
    II.2 Technical constraints: Observation
    II.3 Functional needs: Observation
    II.4 Necessities of tool maintenence: Observation
    II.5 Ease of transportation: Observation
    II.6 Tradition and cultural context: Inference

III Tool maintenance strategies
    III.1 The nature of resources exploited and temporal constraints: Observation plus inference
    III.2 Technical potential for transformation: Observation
    III.3 Functional constraints: Observation
    III.4 Cost of the tool: Observation
    III.5 Symbolic value of the tool: Observation plus inference

excellent flaking quality but does not hold up well to violent percussion during use; certain cherts on the other hand, although they may splinter during flaking, nevertheless make excellent drills or points (such as the micropoints in the Early Neolithic period at Franchthi discussed below).

4) Technical needs and functional constraints

It follows that the technical needs of a group at a particular site can orient strategies for the procurement of raw materials. When such needs are not met by local raw materials, a system of long-distance procurement may be established.

5) Time available for raw material acquisition

Even though the time taken to procure raw materials cannot be observed directly by the archaeologist, it may have been decisive in the orientation of strategies for their acquisition. Even if the local material is of poor quality, strong time constraints, linked to other, dominant activities such as hunting, may preclude the exploitation of distant sources of high quality material or nearby sources that are difficult to exploit.

6) Knowledge of more distant sources

Regular procurement of raw materials from sources more than thirty to fifty kilometers from a site usually involves only raw materials of a quality superior to those available either in the immediate site catchment or in the nearby region. Procurement of materials from distant sources requires either direct or indirect knowledge of their existence. This knowledge frequently can be demonstrated by the presence of imported raw materials or artifacts made from such materials.

7) Socioeconomic context

The exploitation of raw materials that lie beyond the catchment and more traditional territory of a group requires more than knowledge. It requires a socioeconomic context that either mediates exchanges among groups or allows one group to cross the territory of another. This context may also include various notions of rights in property and the rights to exploit sources of raw materials.

8) Costs of raw material acquisition

The several variables enumerated above determine the "acquisition cost" of raw materials. This cost can be expressed in terms of time or energy. High costs can be incurred in direct procurement, when the distances to be covered are great or when extraction is difficult, as well as in indirect procurement when the production of goods for exchange carry a high cost. The costs of various raw materials can be estimated and compared one to another, but these costs cannot be quantified directly and unambiguously.

9) Group traditions

The force of tradition may be manifested by a pronounced and recurring preference for a particular raw material which cannot be explained by either technical or economic considerations. One cannot exclude the possibility that in some cases the choice of raw material can have, in a broad sense, symbolic value.[10]

The respective values of these variables, and the importance assigned to them by a particular group, will affect the development of the strategy of raw material acquisition. Thus strong time constraints could lead to strategies that minimize the time spent acquiring raw materials. When taken in concert with the other parameters,[11] this choice could lead to two related strategies: either setting up camp right at the source, or practicing embedded procurement—that is, procurement integrated with other activities (Binford 1979). Conversely, if the technical constraints are given priority and the local resources are not satisfactory, the importance of the time constraint could be diminished and satisfaction of technical needs may become the primary factor in the implementation of the strategy. In much the same manner the strength of functional requirements can lead to the acceptance or rejection of high acquisition costs. In practice, especially in recent periods, one often observes complex strategies in which acquisition costs and the intensity of exploitation of each raw material are linked directly to its quality and to management of technical needs.

The long sequence at Franchthi offers a good example of changes in strategies in a context in which certain parameters—quality and abundance of raw materials—remain constant while others—technical needs and social context—change through time.

Strategies of Raw Material Procurement at Franchthi

The Franchthi cave was occupied from the beginning of the Upper Paleolithic through the Mesolithic, and from the Early through the Final Neolithic. The area outside the cave was occupied from the Early to Final Neolithic, either simultaneously or alternately with the interior (Jacobsen and Farrand 1987; Jacobsen forthcoming; Perlès 1987). Lithic raw material is abundant in the surrounding limestone and flysch hills, in river beds, and in conglomerate deposits, but it is generally of mediocre quality and always of small size.

i) Upper Paleolithic: from 23,000 to 9000 B.C. (lithic phases II to V)[12]

The cave was inhabited sporadically by large-game hunters and seems to have been used as a hunting camp. The abundance and variety of raw material found at the site, the simultaneous presence of pebbles, water-worn slabs, and sharp-ridged rocks, clearly indicate embedded procurement of lithic raw materials. Anything and everything was gathered, including blocks that proved to be useless at the first attempt to flake them. This nonselective acquisition resulted in serious technical problems when it came to the manufacture of tools, but rather than adapting the strategies of raw material acquisition to the technical needs (the production of bladelets), these hunters chose to adapt their techniques to the quality of the raw materials that were available nearby. The consequences of these choices will become apparent during the discussion of the production phase. The time saved in the acquisition of raw materials thus can be put forward as the determining factor of the whole strategy.

ii) Late Paleolithic and Mesolithic: from 9000 to 7000 B.C. (lithic phases VI and VII)

The cave still was inhabited by hunter-gatherers, but gathering (of plants, snails, shellfish, small fish, etc.) seems to have gained in importance. A tiny quantity of obsidian from the island of Milos was added to the local lithic assemblage. The presence of this obsidian indicates that seafaring capabilities existed among some group, though not necessarily one of the bands that inhabited Franchthi Cave (Perlès 1978). Although this imported obsidian was incomparably superior in terms of flaking properties and sharpness of edge to the local rocks, it played no particular functional role in the tool assemblage. Instead, local procurement of lithics, for the most part gathered from conglomerates and stream beds, provided the vast majority of the raw materials from which tools were made. The presence of the obsidian demonstrates a knowledge of high-quality, distant lithic resources on the part of the inhabitants, but the latter did not consider the technical gains offered by obsidian to be sufficiently high to justify markedly higher acquisition costs, whether through direct procurement or by exchange.

iii) Upper Mesolithic: 6500 B.C. (lithic phase VIII)

In the Upper Mesolithic the economic base was modified by the increasing importance of tuna fishing. Two subtle, concomitant transformations are apparent in the strategy of lithic raw material procurement.

— First, among locally collected materials, pebbles were replaced by small sharp-ridged blocks. The former probably were collected from stream beds and other derived contexts; the latter probably were acquired in a primary position—in bedrock.

— Second, obsidian was used more regularly and grew from one-tenth of one percent in the preceding period to approximately one percent in the Upper Mesolithic (a tenfold increase). Although it was used preferentially for certain categories of tools, especially microliths, there was still no exclusive use for any one type of tool.

To the extent that bedrock slabs can be said to be of better quality or to give a higher yield than blocks from secondary sources, then one can conclude from this and from the increase in obsidian that time constraints were less influential in the lithic procurement strategy. That is, a slight improvement in the quality of the raw material offset a higher acquisition cost.

The weakening of time constraints may be associated with the addition of tuna fishing to the subsistence system. Tuna fishing is an intermittent activity, and its products can be stored. Some of the time between fishing episodes could be used profitably to acquire raw material of better quality, and some of the fish could have been exchanged for obsidian.

iv) Early and Middle Neolithic: sixth to fifth millennium B.C. (lithic phases XI and XII)

The Final Mesolithic and "aceramic" or Initial Neolithic (lithic phases IX and X) will not be discussed here.

The Early and Middle Neolithic comprised major economic transformations and witnessed the establishment of an agro-pastoral economy. There were equally important changes in strategies of raw material procurement.

— Local materials continued to be exploited, but only in a minor way and for tools for which they were particularly appropriate: especially perforating tools and micropoints.

— Obsidian, which became the primary raw material, was acquired as preformed cores (Perlès in press). It then was reduced by indirect percussion and by pressure flaking to yield extremely sharp blades and light bladelets.

— Flint (both blond and honey flint) also was imported, but as large, already flaked blades. These blades were used first as sickles and then recycled into various other kinds of tools. The transport of the finished product is logical in this case when one considers the size and weight of the cores from which these blades were struck. Conversely, the importation of preformed obsidian cores is equally logical when the fragility of finished obsidian tools is taken into account.

Thus in the Early and Middle Neolithic the procurement strategies of the previous periods were reversed completely. A complex system based on the acquisition of distant and necessarily costly raw materials was put into place. This reversal can be explained in terms of perceptions of increased functional constraints, which became determining factors of the strategy even though they entailed higher acquisition costs. Indeed, foreign raw materials technically were not substitutes for local raw materials but, on the contrary, were used for new varieties of blade tools that would have been difficult to fabricate from local resources. Thus, rather than adapting technical goals to the constraints of local materials, the groups sought the necessary materials at great distances to fulfill these goals.

Still, the constraints imposed by this new agro-pastoral tool assemblage can be considered as a determining factor only in relation to another variable, that of technical traditions. Indeed it would have been possible to make sickles, for example, with microlithic inserts, which would have posed no procurement problem.

v) Late and Final Neolithic: fifth millennium B.C.

The last important change in strategies of raw material acquisition took place in the Late and Final Neolithic period: chipped stone tools were manufactured almost exclusively from obsidian. Data currently available from Franchthi Cave do not allow an analysis of concomitant changes in adaptation by the groups that occupied the site. If, however, information from other, contemporary sites in Greece is taken into account, then it is possible to suggest that there was a shift from sedentary agro-pastoralism to transhument pastoralism.

What factors can be proposed to justify the fact that a significant sector of the Final Neolithic economy was based on imported raw materials? One again could suggest technical factors: a modified mode of adaptation and settlement might create needs that could be served better by obsidian. Such, however, is not manifestly the case, at least from macroscopic observation of tool types and use-wear patterns. Moreover, the near exclusive use of obsidian for tools is not unique to Franchthi; on the contrary, it is found to a greater or lesser extent throughout southern Greece during the Final Neolithic. The dominant factors undoubtedly were more socioeconomic than functional, because they do not seem to be linked to specific changes in technical needs at any one site. It is equally clear that reliance on a single exogenous raw material meant that procurement was reliable in terms of frequency and quantity. Briefly stated, I suggest that the colonization of the Cycladic islands at that time made it possible to shift from indirect to direct procurement, thus explaining the greater availability of obsidian in southern Greece (Perlès in press).

III. Strategies of Tool Production

In their fine details, the modalities of tool production present almost infinite variations. Yet at their most inclusive level, such strategies can be analyzed in terms of a few very simple oppositions. At this latter level, one might find:

1) Evidence of hasty, rapid production or, conversely, deliberate, more careful production. The former minimizes production time, the latter gives evidence of greater technical investment and hence an increase in production time.

In cases of increased technical investment, production time can either be directed to the production of blanks that conform to set technical and morphometric standards (blades and flakes of predetermined form) or to the transformation through extensive retouch of blanks that do not conform initially to the requirements of the finished product. Because I consider these two options to be potentially opposite poles of a single strategy, I have grouped the successive phases of blank production, selection, and subsequent modification by retouch under the term "tool production strategies."

2) Increased productivity may or may not have been a goal of a particular strategy. Certain lithic reduction strategies, though the object of high technical investment, are limited in their production potential or yield. Such is the case, for example, for the classic Levallois method (Boëda 1986). Other conceptions of blank production (*débitage*) in contrast allow high production yields from a single core. These high yields are potentially possible with the production of lamellar blades from prismatic or cone-shaped cores, although experience shows that this goal rarely was pursued in the Upper Paleolithic.[13] On the other hand, pressure flaking is accompanied by a pronounced increase in productivity, a fact that could have been a decisive factor for its adoption (Pelegrin in press).

Variables which potentially can determine the implementation of these different strategies are presented in Table I. For the sake of brevity, I will discuss directly only cases where variables take on values capable of inducing either (A) an important investment in the production of blanks of predetermined form (lamellar blades in the case of interest here) or (B) an important investment in the transformation of blanks through retouch. The problem of increased productivity will be incorporated automatically into the first part of the discussion. It should be understood, however, that if these variables have a value of zero, then rapid production of blanks which either are not standardized or are not predetermined in shape should suffice.

A) Production of Blanks of Predetermined Form (Blade Production)

The basic question, then, is: What factors can induce groups to adopt a strategy of time-consuming blade production?

1) Raw material available at the production site: quantity, quality, and acquisition cost

This variable cannot be introduced independently, because it results from the strategies of raw material acquisition, themselves potentially determined by the nature of the desired tools. Yet as the Franchthi example showed, the latter is not always a determining factor in raw material acquisition. Consequently, the situation can be reversed; the quality and relative cost of raw materials may become essential elements in the elaboration of production strategies.

The quality of the raw material can either enhance or limit the choice of methods and techniques used. For instance, although the *débitage* of Pincevent corresponds to the same general conceptual schemes as those of other Magdalenian sites in the Paris Basin,

> The geometrization of shapes is less developed [in this case]. When the raw material is of lesser quality and of smaller dimensions, the tendency is not to invest too much time in cores which are not likely to produce long series of blades. (Audouze et al. in press:6)

In this case the relatively mediocre quality of the raw material led to nonintensive production. Conversely, high acquisition costs can lead to a choice of methods which permit optimum yields. Such high yields have been used to account for the pressure flaking of blades from flint (Pelegrin in press) and obsidian (Torrence 1986 and references therein) cores. Management strategies for finished tools of imported raw materials often confirm the importance of high acquisition costs: not only is such raw material used optimally, but the tools themselves are used intensively, reused, recycled, and transformed until little useful remains (Perlès and Vaughan 1983).

2) Technical constraints

The production of predetermined (often standardized) blades also can be stimulated by technical constraints that, strictly speaking, do not arise from the ultimate function of the tool but from its particular mode of utilization. Such constraints arise, for example, when hafts with cavities or grooves are cut for the insertion of interchangeable stone elements. The inserts must be standardized and morphometric norms observed during their manufacture. At the level of the production of blanks, greater technical investment and constraints therefore are imposed on the shaping of the core itself. Here is yet another factor that has been proposed to explain the introduction of the pressure flaking of blades (Cahen et al. 1980).

3) Functional needs

Several functions, principle among them cutting, require straight edges. Such edges can be regularly and repeatedly obtained either indirectly through retouch of irregular blanks or directly by the production of blanks of an appropriate predetermined form. In the latter case the different methods and constraints that go into the shaping of the core are well documented for the production of specific kinds of flakes, such as Levallois flakes (Boëda in press), as well as for blades (Collective 1984).

In the case of blades, the length and straightness of the edge are directly functional features. The unretouched edge of the tool constitutes the active part (either directly or as the continuation of a point), whereas retouch plays a role in the overall shaping of the tool (as, for example, a backed edge, a truncation, a retouched base). The most frequently sought products of this type are light blades or bladelets, but one also finds large, typically unretouched meat-carving blades.

4) Necessities of tool maintenance

Upper Paleolithic tool assemblages provide an instructive example of tool maintenance. Along with the previously mentioned light blades or carving blades, tool kits of this period are characterized by the high frequency of retouch on the distal end of blades: end-scrapers, burins, borers, beaks, etc. Retouch on these tools contrasts with that of earlier periods when lateral modifications were dominant: side-scrapers, denticulates, points, etc. In both these cases, however, the role of retouch is the opposite of that described above in terms of functional needs. It now modifies the *active* part of the tool rather than shaping the tool and leaving its active part untouched (as use-wear analysis shows).

Under such conditions, and especially if hafting is not used (the absence of which can be determined from microwear analyses, such as those done for the assemblage from Pincevent by Plisson [1987]), the length of the blade no longer has a directly functional role. The absence of strong functional constraints on length can be demonstrated through an examination of the range of measurements for blade tools, such as burins, taken from assemblages closely related to one another in time and space: from 30 to 120 mm at Verberie, from 30 to 130 mm at Pincevent (Habitation No. 1), and from 30 to 170 mm and Marsangy (N-19) to use the data from Audouze et al. (in press).

In these cases the higher cost of blade production cannot be justified in terms of functional constraints: there is no need for a long, straight cutting edge. Instead, the possibility of rapid and efficient tool maintenance seems to be a potentially determining factor. Indeed, the lamellar blank[14] here derives its value from the fact that it permits the rapid and frequent renovation of a tool while preserving unchanged its functional characteristics. It also permits the transformation of one tool into another—an end-scraper into a beak, a beak into a burin—without having to manufacture a suitable new blank (see van Noten et al. 1978; Gamble 1986:290). As Gamble has proposed, the longer life of the tool could compensate for the increased technical investment in its production (Gamble 1986:279). Yet this high cost of production is not borne in every case, as the discussion of Franchthi will show. Therefore, a concern for tool maintenance might be linked to the nature of the resources involved (Bleed 1986). For example, a link could be established with the exploitation of abundant natural resources that require relatively continuous and time-consuming exploitation: for example, the preparation of hides from a collective slaughter, or the harvesting of crops.

5) Ease of transportation

Among social groups whose adaptations demand frequent travel, ease of transportation of basic equipment yields considerable advantages.[15] To this end, a blade tool industry provides an excellent solution. First, blades are easy to pack in a limited space. Second, blade tools offer the longest cutting edge for a given volume (Leroi-Gourhan 1965). Third, as already stated, blades can be transformed easily into a wide variety of tools that might be required during the course of a trip.[16] In the Magdalenian sites mentioned above, one can demonstrate the introduction of good, already flaked blades made from exogenous raw materials; one can also show, where refitting is possible, that large blades produced at the site have been taken elsewhere (Cahen et al. 1980; Audouze and Cahen 1984)

6) Tradition and cultural context

Whatever the potential strength of the preceding variables, they cannot account entirely for tool production strategies. One must also consider technical traditions which, with the other factors held constant, can lead to stylistic variations among groups.

However, before ascribing the production of blades to cultural factors alone, it is necessary to examine the entire corpus of lithic production from the perspective of a "stone tool manufacturing economy" (économie de débitage, Inizan 1976; Collective 1980). A few studies which have taken this perspective have shown that strategies of production can be determined, not by the requirements of each class of tools, but by a single, predominant class of tools that dominates the system of productive strategies and modalities as a whole. The byproducts of their operational sequence then are used to manufacture other classes of tools. Those byproducts include flakes produced during the initial shaping of the core, preliminary blades, blades broken during the flaking process, etc. The dominant class of tools, whose production orients the remainder of the assemblage, can vary from site to site, even when such sites are closely related in space, time, and cultural contexts. For example, end-scrapers determine the production strategies at Pincevent (Habitation No. 1) and beaks determine the strategies at Verberie, yet both sites are closely related, Late Magdalenian localities in the Paris Basin (Audouze et al. in press). An analogous process has been demonstrated for Chatelperronian assemblages by J. Pelegrin (1986). He shows that the entire operational sequence was based on the production of Chatelperron points, and that all other tools (with the possible exception of bladelets) were made from the byproducts of this manufacturing sequence.

The identification of the principal factors that shape a production strategy, therefore, need not involve either every category or any arbitrarily chosen category of tool. Rather, in relevant cases, the category which alone is capable of determining the entire strategy must be isolated and identified. But, not all tools must or can be produced from blanks of predetermined shape that require little or no subsequent retouch to be functional. Even in carefully produced tool assemblages emphasis can be placed on retouch rather than on the production of "standardized" blanks.

B) Transformation of Blanks by Retouch

The direct production of preformed blanks is not the only solution to various technical constraints that require a piece of a particular size and shape. Either as an extension or as an alternative of such techniques, retouch makes it possible to achieve the proper correspondence between the shape of the blank and the form of the projected tool. It has been a longstanding observation that the frequency and importance of retouch varies greatly from one industry to another. Such is the case, for example, for the different *faciès* of the Mousterian (Dibble 1984). It is also remarkable that there is only a small investment in retouch in the majority of Neolithic industries except for bifacial projectile points.

Because we are still dealing with tool production strategies, the relevant factors and constraints are, by definition, the same ones that were presented earlier. For the present part of the analysis, however, differences in their values that lead to a reorientation of technical effort will be presented. In brief, these efforts, rather than being directed toward the production of standardized blanks, will be directed toward retouch.

1) Raw material

Technical constraints imposed by poor quality raw material are less of an obstacle in retouching, except for very particular types of retouch, than in the manufacture of blanks of a predetermined shape. Consequently, in some situations it can be easier to obtain the desired shape for a tool by retouch than by direct production of a blank of the appropriate shape. For example, at Franchthi certain "backed bladelets" are obtained by proximal truncation of flakes at their distal edge, a process that requires less investment in the production of the blank and more investment in its retouch.[17]

2) Technical constraints

The standardization of blanks is not always sufficient to satisfy the conditions and requirements created by certain modes of hafting. Tanged projectile points, shouldered points, and backed blades are classic examples where the application of retouch might prove indispensable.

3) Functional constraints

Some activities are better served by edges that have been retouched rather than by those that have not been retouched: tasks that require sturdy working edges or specific shapes provide ready examples. Yet technical investment and time spent on these transformations should not be overestimated. We know that the working part of an end-scraper or a burin can be fashioned in a few seconds, and cases are rare (if they exist at all) where functional constraints, in and of themselves, demand a high technical investment in retouch.

4) Tool maintenance

By definition, maintenance of noncomposite tools is carried out through retouch (whereas for composite tools it is possible to replace elements). Here again this factor alone does not justify a very important technical investment in retouch.

5) Ease of transportation

The earlier remarks under this subheading can be reproduced here without change.

6) Tradition and cultural context

In reality, important technical investment in retouch (invasive bifacial retouch on large pieces, pressure retouch, etc.) can rarely be justified completely in either economic or functional terms. The quality of the best Solutrean "laurel leaves," the best bifacial projectile points of the Neolithic, Chalcolithic "daggers," and the justly famous knives of Predynastic Egypt cannot be reduced to technical constraints or to purely functional needs. This fact is illustrated by the frequent association of these artifacts with pieces of more hasty workmanship. We have no reason to consider the poorer pieces as "nonfunctional": quite the opposite.

We are dealing here with instances of "technical overinvestment" which must be interpreted in the framework of social context in its broadest sense: the expression of a symbolic role, the expression of group status or identity by a consciously displayed style, the values of goods in codified exchanges, etc. A few case studies from very different cultural contexts offer archaeological support for these proposals (Hayden 1982; Midant-Reynes 1987).[18] Current investigations in the Greek Neolithic seem to indicate the existence of a comparable phenomenon in the production of certain arrowheads of the Late and Final Neolithic and the large, triangular foliate points that appear at the very end of the Neolithic.

Tool Production Strategies at Franchthi

As early as the twentieth or twenty-first millennium B.C., backed bladelets were by far the dominant tool group at Franchthi. Consequently, if a single tool group could determine the entire production strategy, it is this one. In practice, however, the actual situation is more complex. As their name indicates, backed bladelets are usually produced on lamellar blanks of predetermined form and dimensions: that is, on elongated blanks of a regular thickness, without curves and with at least one straight edge. These criteria presuppose homogenous raw materials of relatively good quality. Yet as we have already seen, the strategies for raw material procurement produced blocks of small sizes and of mediocre quality. Thus there is, *a priori*, a contradiction between technical needs and the strategies of raw material acquisition. Consequently the question becomes: How were these conflicts resolved?

In the earliest phases (phases II and III) there was indeed a specific reduction sequence for the production of bladelets, but it came at the expense of a high rate of discard among the blocks brought to the site: only the best were selected and the productivity per block was low. The low acquisition cost was "paid for" by the frequency of discard of raw material and by a low return from the technical investment during production. In the following two phases of the Upper Paleolithic (IV and V, eleventh and tenth millennia B.C.) there seems to have been only occasional bladelet production, and it was integrated within the general production of flakes. Nevertheless, tools remained, for the most part, lamellar in final form, although backed bladelets tended to be shorter and thicker than their earlier counterparts. Thus bladelet-shaped tools were no longer produced directly (by *débitage* alone) but by a sequence of retouch. For some "bladelets" very straight truncations on flakes play the role of a backed edge; others are actually backed flakes.

For the entire Upper Paleolithic period at Franchthi strategies of raw material procurement created real difficulties for the production of tools. Consequently, it was the strength of the functional constraints that determined the production strategy. When, for example, long obtuse backed bladelets were required, it was difficult to avoid true lamellar flaking (phases II, III, and part of VI). When, on the other hand, the dominant classes of backed bladelets were shorter, pointed bladelets with retouch on the distal end (a shape that can be obtained more easily from any bladelet or from a small flake), the difficulties of bladelet production were avoided and effort was transferred to their transformation by retouch (deep backing and sectioning by the microburin technique). In all cases, nonetheless, time-saving and effort-saving seem to have been predominant factors in the strategies.

During the Mesolithic, production strategies did not change markedly, but they do appear to be better adapted to the tools desired, because elongated pieces are found only rarely in the assemblage. Tools were manufactured rapidly from a collection of unstandardized flakes, and the main effort was devoted to retouch. In the absence of technical constraints and with no need for long-term maintenance, this strategy provided the simplest solution. Even during the Upper Mesolithic, when more homogenous materials were gathered, most of the production remained expedient in its productive organization.

The organization of production was reversed completely at the beginning of the Early Neolithic. The production of lamellar blanks of predetermined shape became the object of maximum investment. This emphasis, in turn, led to a reversal of strategies for raw material procurement. It resulted in the acceptance, for the first time, of a high acquisition cost for most items in the toolkit: the importation of obsidian from Milos for the lighter blades, and the acquisition of preflaked flint blades for the sickles.

During the Early and Middle Neolithic, obsidian was used to produce lamellar blades of predetermined shape, and only occasional marginal retouch was applied to them. Functional needs thus became the determining factor in the modalities of production and the major constraints in the reduction process. Moreover, the relatively high cost of obsidian goes together with the adoption of pressure flaking, a manufacturing process that conserved the raw material. In the meantime, the work with local raw materials remained as expedient as ever, but the notches, micropoints, borers, etc. made from this material were suited perfectly to the ends they served.

Late Neolithic tool assemblages from Franchthi are too fragmentary to apply the full range of analytical techniques advocated here. During the Final Neolithic a transformation of the production strategy is documented. Obsidian became the sole raw material, and tools previously made from flint were now made from obsidian. Obsidian was used even for tasks demanding relatively sturdy tools, although seemingly not for sickle blades, which were no longer present in the assemblage. The production of stronger blades was effected through soft percussion; light blades were made by pressure flaking and probably also by punch flaking. Yet flaking by soft percussion was less conservative of the raw material than the other techniques. This observation suggests that obsidian was less costly, a hypothesis supported by the fact that toolkit management in the Final Neolithic was less intensive than in the Middle Neolithic (see above) and by the greater abundance of obsidian in both relative and absolute terms.

In summary, throughout the sequence at Franchthi, one finds evidence of opposing strategies of tool production. There is an emphasis either on production of blanks or on retouch, each of which was influenced by the conflicting factors of minimizing production costs and finding answers to functional needs. In the Paleolithic, the minimization of production costs was paramount, even though it clashed with functional needs. In the Mesolithic no factor seemed to justify an important technical investment in manufacturing techniques, and the simplest solution that satisfied the available resources and the nature of the activities envisioned was used. Flakes were produced rapidly and modified by retouch according to need. In the first part of the Neolithic functional and technical constraints, coupled with the intensive use of imported raw materials, came to the fore. Long-distance procurement and technically more demanding manufacturing sequences led to higher costs, but these were taken in the context of a sedentary agro-pastoral economy which clearly was in a position to absorb the higher costs. Finally, at the end of the Neolithic, the production strategy was still conditioned by technical needs, but the intense exploitation of raw materials received a lower priority. The acquisition cost for obsidian appears to have diminished, and, at the same time, tool production strategies were modified. Only a few flint projectile points comprise a minor exception to this generalization. They are the product of a high investment in retouch rather than in the production of blanks: it is probable that they belong to a different conceptual domain.

IV. Strategies of Toolkit Management

The final stage in the operational sequence is toolkit maintenance. At this point, with the essential parts of the system already in place, the remaining options are necessarily limited by what has gone before.

Tools used directly after their fabrication (an operative sequence continuous through time) can first be opposed to tools manufactured in anticipation of future needs and then put to use after a more or less important period of time has elapsed (an operative sequence discontinuous through time). Paradoxically, this temporal discontinuity cannot be perceived by the archaeologist unless it is accompanied by a spatial discontinuity in which tools are discarded at a place away from the one where they were fabricated. Consequently, the archaeologist can only grasp the notion of "curation" (in the sense of Binford 1979) when it is manifest in its double, spatiotemporal sense.

A second contrast opposes tools used briefly and discarded rapidly thereafter with those kept in use as long as possible through replacement of elements, rejuvenation and resharpening, and an eventual recycling and transformation of the blades from which they were made. In many situations tools can be placed in one or the other category with the aid of microwear analysis (traceological analysis) and through refitting. Moreover, there often is a connection between the advance manufacture of a tool and its intensive use and reuse (which can be observed on articles made from imported materials), but the converse is not necessarily true: a readily made tool is not necessarily quickly discarded.

The variables which determine the elaboration of these strategies are relatively few (see Table 1, III.1 to III.5), and some of them in fact integrate the choices made in preceeding stages of the operative sequence.

1) The nature of the resources exploited and time constraints

Several recent studies based on ethnographic data have shown a relationship between a curated tool technology and the nature of the resources exploited, especially the mobility of the resources, the time constraints related to this exploitation, and the risks of failure (Oswalt 1976; Binford 1979; Bleed 1986; Torrence in press). I am tempted to propose that the constraints introduced by the nature of the resources exploited are so strong that there is virtually no room for choice on the part of those who use the tools. That is, there is no room for what could be called strategic choice on their part. One hardly can envision a hunter who waits to track down his prey before fabricating a weapon or a farmer who sets out to harvest his wheat without the necessary equipment. In contrast, it is easy to imagine that when the Early Neolithic inhabitants of Franchthi manufactured massive quantities of cardium shell beads their production of flint micropoints, which break easily, was keyed to the immediate requirements of their work.

On the other hand, time constraints can exert an effective influence on the strategy of toolkit *maintenance*. Indeed it is quicker to renovate a tool on a preexisting blank (burin, scraper, sickle element, etc.) than it is to manufacture a new one from scratch. During continuous activities, where there is a risk of spoilage or destruction (the preparation of hides, the harvest of grain), intensive use of existing tools holds certain advantages over a strategy of rapid discard followed by fabrication of new tools.

2) Technical possibilities of transformation

The possibility of maintenance through either resharpening or transformation depends, of course, on the nature of the blank. It would be futile, for example, to look for traces of consequential rejuvenation on a tool made from a microblade. As we have already seen, flake tools also are less suited than blade tools to repeated transformations. The rapid discard of bladelets and flake tools may therefore be due to inherent technical constraints rather than to choices made at the level of toolkit management.

3) Functional constraints

The choice between either prolonged use or rapid discard is not relevant in the case of tools that cannot undergo renovation without losing essential attributes such as very sharp edges. Each resharpening entails an increase in the working angle and hence the loss of acuteness. Thus a strategy of rapid discard may be due to functional constraints rather than to the absence of time constraints or to low production costs.

4) Tool cost

The "cost" of a tool is a synthetic value that comprises the acquisition costs of the raw material and the production or acquisition cost of the blank. An elevated cost can be the result of a high expenditure of energy as much as a high expenditure of time. These costs can be incurred either directly or indirectly, through the production of goods for exchange. A simple concern for a high return on capital expenditures leads to maximizing the life of a costly tool by successive resharpening and transformations. The effects of such actions are often directly observable in assemblages where local and imported materials occur together. As mentioned above, such is the case at Franchthi.

5) The symbolic value of the tool

By symbolic value, I mean, at least in the broad sense, the nontechnical functions of the tool, whether or not these attributes preclude actual use. In general, the symbolic value of a tool logically will have consequences opposed to those of its economic or technical costs. Such values would place a premium on keeping the tool in its original, optimal form; they would guard against radical transformations and manipulations that would disfigure the tool. The consequences of such conservation is attested to, for example, by certain polished stone axes that were exchanged over long distances yet bear no signs of ever having been used. I believe that similar forces are at work in the case of certain categories of flaked tools, especially those which show evidence of "technical overinvestment" in retouch.

The contrast between high cost and symbolic value can be clarified further. In general, high costs are not attached to the tool itself but to the blank, through its acquisition cost or the technical investment in its production. The blank therefore is the object of maximum exploitation. In some cases this maximization takes place through radical rejuvenation and transformation (for example, reflaking from a blade). In contrast, symbolic value involves the tool itself—if the term "tool" is appropriate in this case—whose production through very elaborate retouch requires considerable time and technical investment. Hence it is the tool itself that one seeks to maintain in its pristine, optimal form. In the Greek Neolithic, for example, I have found no evidence of either rejuvenation or transformation of the most carefully fashioned bifacial artifacts: i.e., flint or obsidian arrowheads retouched by pressure flaking and triangular foliate points. The situation is quite different in the case of arrowheads of less meticulous craftsmanship, some of which have been transformed into beaks, for example, or in the case of sickle blades which have been transformed from one tool type into another. It is to these questions of toolkit management strategies in the Neolithic levels of Franchthi that I now turn.

Strategies of Toolkit Maintenance at Franchthi during the Neolithic

From the very beginning of the ceramic-bearing levels of the Neolithic at Franchthi, most of the tools were manufactured from imported obsidian and flint. Nevertheless, nothing indicated a strategy of intensive tool use in the Early Neolithic. On the contrary, if one considers the group of sickle elements, which were well represented in both the Early and Middle Neolithic levels, one finds in the former period short tool life, little evidence of resharpening, and the virtual absence of retransformation of the blanks. Moreover, the strategy of rapid discard—which is a bit surprising because it includes both tools made from local material and tools made from imported obsidian and flint— was not unique to Franchthi but seems to characterize numerous assemblages from the Early Neolithic of Greece.

In the Middle Neolithic at Franchthi there was a complex tool management strategy with three modalities that corresponded to the three major categories of raw materials. Tools manufactured from local lithics continued to be used briefly and discarded without major resharpening or transformations. Tools manufactured from imported flint blades were very long-lived and went through intricate cycles of conservation. These large blades, which reached 4 cm in width, probably were imported as unretouched, "undifferentiated blanks" that were capable of being used for the fabrication of any type of tool. In practice these flints were used almost always first as sickle elements, and as such underwent several cycles of use and resharpening.[19] In fact, their edges became blunted through constant retouching. Yet even in this condition, the tool was kept in use until its working edges were dulled completely. A number of these dulled sickle blades were then used for working leather, a task for which the blunted edges were suited.[20] After this step, some of the blades were transformed into different tool types through retouch: beaks, end-scrapers, projectile points, etc. If at this point the blank was still long enough, the cycle ended with the blade being used either as raw material or as a splintered blade in a bipolar percussion process.

Obsidian tools occupied a position intermediate between the offhand treatment of tools made from local materials and the complex management cycles to which flint tools were subjected. Imported obsidian could not be subjected to complicated systems of use and multiple transformations because the tools made of this material were light, sharp blades. Nonetheless, obsidian tools were used intensively, and obsidian sickle blades were resharpened, although more delicately than those made from flint, and spent obsidian tools were reused in bipolar percussion.

Thus in the Middle Neolithic there was a direct correlation between the acquisition cost of blanks (either as raw material or as preforms) and tool maintenance, tool life, and the intensity of exploitation of the original blank. The more costly the tool in terms of acquisition and production, the longer it was kept active. The nature of the initial production, however, mediates the cost factor somewhat: small obsidian blades underwent less radical transformations than the stronger flint blades. Thus maximum exploitation was sought not just of the tool but of the reserve of raw material it represented. These strategies, then, appear to be regulated by two strongly correlated factors: the desire for maximum maintenance of costly tools and the desire for the maximum return from foreign raw materials.

If, however, tool management strategies in the Middle Neolithic can be explained in terms of the maximization of return on costs, it remains to account for the differences between the Early and Middle Neolithic periods, since the raw materials used were identical. The brief, "uneconomical" use of sickle blades in the Early Neolithic may have been due to functional constraints: they were abandoned when their usually unretouched cutting edge just was beginning to dull. In contrast, the sickle blades of the Middle Neolithic were removed from use only when their edges had become so blunt and dulled that it is hard to conceive how they could have been functional. I believe that the modalities of utilization (or even the nature of the work activities) were in fact different during these two periods and that these differences imposed radically different functional constraints and led to opposed tool maintenance strategies.

It is also true that the flint blades of the Early Neolithic were lighter than those of the Middle Neolithic and as a result would have been harder to rejuvenate and transform. Yet these factors alone cannot account for the differences in maintenance strategies between the two periods. It is nearly certain that the sickle blades of the early Neolithic could have been used more intensively, without losing their functionality, by merely turning the blade over and using the other edge. Yet this practice was not followed systematically. Moreover, obsidian blades show no signs of having been recycled into material for bipolar flaking, as they were in the Middle Neolithic. We thus are led to the conclusion that, in the eyes of the Early Neolithic users, the cost of their tools were not sufficiently high to justify extracting the last bit of value from them.

This comparative analysis leads to the introduction of two reasonably well defined problems and their attendant hypotheses that will be the subject of future investigations. First, there is the problem of the transformation in the use of "sickle blades" between the Early and Middle Neolithic. Second, there is the increase in the relative value of imported raw materials, perhaps caused by a change in economic modalities which rendered imports more expensive (perhaps due to an increase in demand set against a constant supply).[21] In other words, the analyses presented here establish new directions for research but they do not provide a solution to the current problems.

Conclusion

The approach presented here must be considered provisional, as part of a wider concern for methods of analysis of lithic assemblages. The goal has been to stimulate discussion and to guide future research. Consequently, the approach taken here—one based on decision-making—should be subjected to one final round of critical analysis. This discussion can be organized in three levels, each of which corresponds to a different stage in the analysis: the establishment of a set of variables; the evaluation of the value each takes on in a given archaeological context; and, finally, the relationships among the estimated values and their actual archaeological effects.

1) The establishment of relevant variables

The list of variables for each stage of the manufacturing sequence is based on my personal experience with lithic industries, on experimental data, and on the search for analytical measures used, either explicitly or implicitly, in several studies concerned with the interpretation of lithic assemblages. The variables proposed here do have operational validity in the sense that they are actually capable of guiding the process of production and the modalities of use of lithic tools. Nonetheless it is very probable that my list is incomplete and that additional variables will have to be added, not only for the assemblages discussed here but also for lithic strategies based on very different principles.[22]

2) The evaluation of variables in given archaeological contexts

Contrary to what intuition would lead one to expect, the values taken on by most of the variables discussed here are observable directly in the archaeological record, at least in qualitative terms: as zero, low, or high values. To be sure, these measures can be derived sometimes only by a combination of several approaches: prospection, experiment, use-wear analyses. Nonetheless, these approaches themselves produce observational measures, whatever the inherent risks of errors for each.

Yet it must be noted that certain variables cannot be apprehended directly but must be estimated through some process of inference. If inference were required for the majority of variables used here, then the whole process of analysis here would be called into question. Fortunately, as Table 1 shows, such is not the case. Furthermore, the grounds for inference can be explicitly established for most variables: temporal constraints (Table 1, I.5 and III.1), for example, are inferred for the dominant activities and a knowledge of the risks entailed by differential exploitation of some resources. The weight of traditions (Table 1, I.9 and II.6) can be inferred from observed regularities in a given cultural context and from their apparent contradictions with other factors. In my view, the most fragile inferences involve the existence of exchange networks or specialized production (Table 1, I.7), for which the evidentiary grounds have not yet been established satisfactorily by archaeologists. Nonetheless, on the whole, a satisfactory evaluation of each variable in a given archaeological context remains in the domain of direct observation or of first-degree inference.

3) The relationships between variables and their values on the one hand and their archaeological consequences on the other

The foundation of the approach taken here is the refusal to assume that there exists an *a priori*, mechanical relationship between a particular variable and its potential effects: i.e., a univocal relationship. A raw material will not be ignored necessarily because of its mediocre quality; a tool will not be used as long as possible merely because it is costly.

REPRESENTATIONS IN ARCHAEOLOGY

It is not a question of whether or not human behavior in the past followed contemporary standards of rationality,[23] but above all because practical decisions were the consequence of choices made from among competing ends that were conditioned by multiple and sometimes conflicting factors. For example, a raw material available at a greater distance but possessing a better quality may have proved advantageous for technical activities, but the time taken to acquire it may have conflicted directly with subsistence activities. Thus, factors that determined the lithic strategies actually implemented were the result of evaluations of the positive and negative aspects of each. It is this evaluation, this value judgment, that I have sought to elucidate here. At this stage I have had to leave the realm of direct observation and derive what can be called "determining factors." These factors can only be inferred from a confrontation of the values given to the several variables in a given archaeological context and the observed strategies of lithic production. Therefore, there arises the problem of the validity of inferential mechanisms in general. The principles followed here were to make the fewest number of inferences consistent with the actual variability that was observed in the archaeological data. Further evaluation of the structure of the analysis and its heuristic value must await its application to additional and different archaeological contexts.

NOTES

1. I shall rely on several such demonstrations.

2. In complete agreement with Th. N. Huffman's observation: "We do not dig up ideology, of course, but then we also do not dig up economy (in general terms how a people make their living) or technology (what a people make their living with). These two aspects of society are no less abstract than ideology" (Huffman 1986:84). It was only after this paper was written that I read about the "design theory" (Horsfall, in Hayden, ed. 1987), which appears to bear a narrow resemblance to the approach advocated here.

3. See chapters 2 and 3 by Bell and Sperber in this volume.

4. In the sense given this term by several authors in this volume and by Gardin (1980).

5. Before a lithic tool assemblage (that is, broadly speaking, equipment for the acquisition and transformation of resources) can be produced, it must be conceived. This conception can be expressed in terms of complexity, standardization, specialization, dependability, etc. Recent works have sought the factors that underlie the conceptualization of tool assemblages, in particular the equipment used for the acquisition of food resources (Bleed 1986; Oswalt 1976; Torrence 1983 and in press). Such studies logically precede the one presented here, which deals with the interpretation of operational sequences actively implemented in a given context.

6. The integration of these conceptual schemes occurs quite early in the life of a child, at an age when they value examples set by their elders (Pelegrin 1986:58).

7. Although the development of critical judgment is demonstrated easily for *Homo sapiens*, its gradual emergence in earlier species of the genus *Homo* is more difficult to chart. Similarly, it is hardly possible to prove that the principles of rationality which underlie the present analyses (*infra*) also apply to more ancient hominid forms. Consequently, this study is limited to *Homo sapiens*.

8. The definition of these three stages here, although drawing on earlier works, is slightly at variance with them (see Collective 1980; Binder 1983; Inizan 1976; Perlès 1987). Previously, strategies of raw material exploitation have been basically distinguished from strategies of blank production (*débitage*). When retouched tools have been analyzed in this light, the selection of blanks, the process of retouch, and the management of the tool kit have been seen as a single

productive process. For reasons discussed here, it seems more satisfactory to include the production of blanks and tool retouch under the heading of tool production strategies and to keep them separate from the strategies that guide the acquisition of raw materials on the one hand and those that determine toolkit management on the other.

9. The presentation of the Franchthi material will be oriented in terms of the problematic developed here. It is not meant to constitute a faithful summary of the sequence at that site. For a full discussion see Perlès (1984a, 1984b, 1987, in press).

10. It would be interesting to examine the particular place held by "yellow" or "honey" flint in the European Neolithic from this perspective.

11. Once evaluated, variables can in fact be considered parameters for a particular human group at a particular site at a particular time.

12. These phases express the lithic sequence at Franchthi used by the author in the report of the excavation (Perlès 1987).

13. Referring to Magdalenian sites in the Paris Basin, Audouze et al. state: "The study of *débitage* fails to reveal strong concerns for productivity. The goal is to obtain the product without respect to the time it takes" (Audouze et al. in press:8).

14. It is in this case that the term "blank" takes on its full meaning.

15. The introduction of this factor is due to fruitful discussions with J. Phillips.

16. We find here the "curated" tool assemblage of L. Binford (1979).

17. As a consequence, all flake tools cannot be identified as "expedient" in Binford's sense.

18. On the other hand, I do not agree with authors who take the frequency of simple lateral retouch as an indication of energy investment.

19. These cycles are visible to the naked eye, but they have been confirmed under microscopic examination by P. Vaughan.

20. This phase of reuse is visible only under the microscope (see Perlès and Vaughan 1983).

21. For reasons too extensive to explain here I consider the second of these alternatives to be the best. It seems that the same procurement networks were operative in both the Early and the Middle Neolithic (perhaps in the hands of groups whose frequency of travel and route of travel remained relatively constant) but that there was an increase in demand linked to a population increase in the Middle Neolithic. In contrast, the proposition that the costs of obsidian decreased in the Final Neolithic (see above) is confirmed by the existence of a process that produced fewer blades per unit of raw material and by a much less intensive use of the blades thus produced. In fact, utilization of obsidian in the Final Neolithic parallels that of the Early Neolithic. I believe that the explanation for a more unrestricted use of obsidian in the Final Neolithic is not identical to that applied to its use in the Early Neolithic. Consumption in the later period seems tied to technical progress that permitted greater and more regular procurement of obsidian.

22. This being said, one should note that the present list of variables is already quite long. Moreover, each variable can take on different values, even if the variables are evaluated only summarily (see above); therefore, the number of cases that are theoretically possible is extremely large. From my perspective, the large number of possibilities in each instance explains the failure of most attempts to approach the variability of lithic assemblages through preestablished models. If the real diversity of archaeological situations is granted, then either a great number of unwieldy models must be tested or greatly simplified models must be employed, which almost guarantees a loss of discriminatory capacity.

23. Although an underlying, common rationality seems to characterize all members of the species *Homo sapiens sapiens* past and present, it cannot be automatically extended to earlier hominid subspecies.

REFERENCES

Audouze, F., et al. in press. "Taille du silex et finalité du débitage dans le Magdalénian du Bassin Parisien," in M. Otte (ed.), *Les civilisations du Paléolithique final de la Loire à l'Oder*. British Archaeological Reports, Oxford.

Audouze, F., and D. Cahen 1984. "L'occupation Magdalénienne de Verberie et sa chronologie," in *Jungpaläolitische Siedlung Strukturen in Europa*, Koll. 8, pp. 143–159, 14 May 1983. Reisenburg/Günzburg, Tübingen.

Bailey, G. N., and I. Davidson 1983. "Site exploitation territories and topography: Two case studies from Paleolithic Spain," *Journal of Archaeological Science* **10,** 87–115.

Binder, D. 1983. *Approche des industries lithiques du Nèolithique ancien Provençal.* Doctoral thesis (troisième cycle), Université de Paris X, Paris.

Binford, L. R. 1979. "Organization and formation processes: Looking at curted technologies," *Journal of Anthropological Research* **35,** 255–273.

Bleed, P. 1986. "The optimal design of hunting weapons: Maintainability or reliability," *American Antiquity* **51(4),** 737–747.

Boëda, E. 1986. *Approche technologique du concept Levallois et évaluation de son champ d'application.* Doctoral thesis, Université de Paris X, Paris.

———in press. "Le concept laminaire: rupture et filiation avec le concept Levallois," pre-prints of the conference "*L'Homme de Neandertal,*" Liège 1986.

Cahen, D. 1984. "Aspects du débitage laminaire dans le Néolithique ancien de la Belgique," in *Préhistoire de la pierre taillée, 2: économie du débitage laminaire*, pp. 21–22. CREP, Paris.

Cahen, D. et al. 1980. "Méthodes d'analyse technique, spatiale et fonctionnelle d'ensembles lithiques," *Helinium* **XX,** 209–259.

Clark, J. E. 1987. "Politics, prismatic blades and Mesoamerican civilization," in J. K. Johnson and C. A. Morrow (eds.), *The Organization of Core Technology*, pp. 259–284. Westview Press, Boulder, CO.

Clark, J. E., and T. A. Lee 1982. "The changing role of obsidian exchange in Chiapas, Mexico: An experimental analysis of production." *New World Archaeological Foundation*, Brigham Young University, Provo, UT.

———1984. "Formative obsidian exchange and the emergence of public economies in Chiapas, Mexico," in K. Hirth (ed.), *Exchanges in Early Mesoamerica*, pp. 235–273. University of New Mexico Press, Albuquerque.

Dibble, H. L. 1984. "Interpreting typological variation of Middle Paleolithic scrapers: Function, style, or sequence of reduction?," *Journal of Field Archaeology* **11(4),** 431–436.

Gamble, C. 1986. *The Paleolithic Settlements of Europe.* Cambridge University Press, Cambridge.

Gardin, J.-C. 1980. *Archaeological Constructs.* Cambridge University Press, Cambridge.

Geneste, J. M. 1985. *Analyse lithique d'industries Moustériennes du Périgord: une approche technologique du comportement des groupes humains au Paléolithique moyen.* Doctoral thesis, Université de Bordeaux I, Bordeaux.

Hayden, B. 1982. "Interaction parameters and the demise of paleo-Indian craftsmanship," *Plains Anthropologist* **27,** 109–123.

———(ed.) 1987. *Lithic Studies Among the Contemporary Highland Mayas.* The University of Arizona Press, Tucson.

Higgs, E. S., and C. Vita-Finzi 1972. "Prehistoric economies: A territorial approach," in E. S. Higgs (ed.), *Papers in Economic Prehistory*, pp. 27–36. Cambridge University Press, Cambridge.

Huffman, T. N. 1986. "Cognitive studies of the Iron Age in Southern Africa," *World Archaeology* **18(1),** 84–95.

Inizan, M.-L. 1976. *Nouvelle étude d'industries lithiques du Capsien.* Doctoral thesis (troisième cycle), Université de Paris X, Paris.

Jacobsen, T. W. in press. *Excavations at the Franchthi Cave.* Indiana University Press, Bloomington.

Jacobsen, T. W., and W. R. Farrand 1987. *Franchthi Cave and Paralia: Maps, Plans, and Sections.* Indiana University Press, Bloomington.

Leroi-Gourhan, A. 1964. *Le geste et la parole, I. Technique et langage.* Albin Michel, Paris.

———1965. *Le geste et la parole, II. Mémoire et technique.* Albin Michel, Paris.

Midant-Reynes, B. 1987. "Contribution technologique à l'étude de la société prédynastique: le cas du couteau 'ripple-flake'," *Studien zur Altägyptischen Kultur* **14,** 185–224.

Oswalt, W. H. 1976. *An Anthropological Analysis of Food-getting Technology*. John Wiley and Sons, New York.

Pelegrin, J. 1986. *Technologie lithique: une méthode appliquée à l'étude de deux séries du Périgordien ancien. Roc de Combe couche 8. La Côte niveau III*. Doctoral thesis, Université de Paris X, Paris.

———in press. *Notes de recherche techniques sur le débitage par pression*.

Perlès, C. 1978. "Des navigateurs méditerranéens il y a 10.000 ans," *La Recherche* **96,** 82–82.

———1984a. "Etude préliminaire des industries paléolithiques de la grotte de Franchthi, Argolide, Grèce," in *Advances in Palaeolithic and Mesolithic Archaeology, Archaeologia interregionalis*, pp. 151–162. Warsaw-Cracow.

———1984b. "Aperçu sur les industries mésolithiques de Franchthi, Argolide, Grèce," in *Advances in Palaeolithic and Mesolithic Archaeology, Archaeologia interregionalis*, pp. 163–171. Warsaw-Cracow.

———1987. *Les industries lithiques taillées de la grotte de Franchthi (Grèce). Tome I: Présentation générale et industries paléolithiques*. Indiana University Press, Bloomington.

———in press. *Les industries lithiques taillées de la grotte de Franchthi (Grèce). Tome II: Industries du Mésolithique et du Néolithique initial*. Indiana University Press, Bloomington.

Perlès, C., and P. Vaughan 1983. "Pièces lustrées, travail des plantes et moissons à Franchthi, Grèce (Xème-IVème mill. B.C.)," in M.-C. Cauvin (ed.), *Traces d'utilisation sur les outils néolithiques du Proche-Orient*, pp. 209–224. Maison de l'Orient, Lyon.

Plisson, H. 1987. "L'emmanchement dans l'habitation n°1 de Pincevent," in D. Stordeur (ed.), *La main et l'outil*, pp. 75–88. Maison de l'Orient, Lyon.

Torrence, R. 1983. "Time budgeting and hunter-gatherer technology," in G. N. Bailey (ed), *Hunter-Gatherer Economy in Prehistory*, pp. 11–23. Cambridge University Press, Cambridge.

———1986. *Production and Exchange of Stone Tools*. Cambridge University Press, Cambridge.

———in press. "Hunter-gatherer technology and the management of risk." Paper presented at the World Archaeological Congress, Southampton, 1986.

Van Noten, F., et al. 1978. *Les chasseurs de Meer*. De Tempel, Bruges.

Collective 1980. *Préhistoire et technologie lithique*. Publications de l'URA 28, cahier no. 1. C.N.R.S., Paris.

Collective 1984. *Préhistoire de la pierre taillée, 2: économie du débitage laminaire*. CREP, Paris.

PART IV

Formal Analysis, Artificial Intelligence, and Cognitive Perspectives

Grammars of Archaeological Design

A GENERATIVE AND GEOMETRICAL APPROACH
TO THE FORM OF ARTIFACTS

> the only things that can stick into the Mind of
> Man are built upon impregnable Foundations of
> Geometry and Arithmetic: the rest is indigested
> Heaps and Labyrinths
>   (Peter Ackroyd, *Hawksmoor*)

1. Artifacts and Texts

The Bloomington meeting and other conferences and books are witness to an increasing interest in approaching archaeological artifacts after the manner of texts. The textual view of artifacts is touched upon by several contributors here, and much in the new literature takes a textual view, either directly or by a textual view of meaning, from *Writing Archaeology* (Sinclair 1989) to *The Recovery of Meaning* (Leone and Potter 1988).

Gardin et al. (1987) are applying formal methods that relate to textual analysis and criticism, echoing Gardin's (1987) other interests in the automation of logical processes in printed text. The work takes archaeology as an exemplar of the general character of studies within the humanities; and a criticism has been made (Voorrips 1987) of the focus of this work on artifacts from historical periods, that is, those about which we may have information that is textually derived.

From another school, Hodder's manifesto for a postmodern archaeology proposes a "con-textual" archaeology to which reading the meaning of artifacts—just as if they were texts—will be central, as its title, *Reading the Past*, affirms (Hodder 1986). Shanks and Tilley (1987), again from the "postprocessual" school, provide as their main example of the relations between material culture and society a study concerned not with artifacts at all, but with *written texts* (of a uniquely modern kind) and their accompanying graphic pictures. The postmodern approach poses many difficulties (Barrett 1987). The most misleading, in my opinion, is the easy assumption that texts and words and artifacts are

	1 music	2 spoken text	3 written text	4 pictures	5 artifacts	6 architecture	7 kinship
space a necessary variable?	no	no [usually 2D]	usually [often 3D]	yes [3D]	yes [3D]	yes	no
time a necessary variable?	yes	yes	no	no	no	no	yes
sequence essential?	yes	yes	yes	no	no	no	yes
fundamental physical variable	sound	sound [within narrow range]	shape	shape	shape	shape	sexual reproduction
basis of generation and study	sequential patterns of harmonics	meaning and its expression	meaning and its expression	geometric form; meaning	geometric form	space defined by geometric form	biological and social relationships

Figure 1. Some characteristics of seven human cultural systems.

much the same thing and are to be treated interchangeably, and with it the hope, contrary to much evidence (e.g., Goody 1972), that language and literacy changed nothing fundamental in human societies. And the meanings diagnosed from artifacts by postmodern methods are, in my view, simply restatements of inferred function.

Spoken words and written texts—even leaving aside the differences between oral and visual ways of using words—make one, but only one, of a large and diverse range of human cultural systems.

Figure 1 tabulates seven such systems, with some of their salient features. In the first column is music, which depends on the physical properties of sound, in particular its capacity for sequential patterns of harmonics. Notice that the fundamentals of the system depend, first, on the physical variables involved: sound has no equivalent of three-dimensional space, and sequence is fundamental: and, within that, on human capacities, in particular the range of frequencies ears hear and the human capacity to discriminate between close frequencies. Notice that meaning is not usually an element, even though the physical properties involved are those of sound, the same as used for spoken texts. (Music in particular times and places—such as the "program music" of the later European romantics—has been used to convey specific meanings after the manner of texts, and particular habits in music evoke in their own cultures some conventional associations; but this introduction of meaning into music is not essential to the *nature* of music.)

In the second column is spoken text, using the same physical variables but with meaning and its expression the basis of the system.

In the third column is written text, which conveys the sequence that is essential to language in a different manner, usually by the setting of conventional marks or letters in a series of two-dimensional spaces.

In the fourth column are pictures, which share with spoken text the same fundamental variable of shape but which are only partly concerned with the conveying of meaning: for the rest they deal with a greater variety of geometrical form.

In the fifth column are artifacts, again concerned with geometric form, but not necessarily with meaning—beyond, again, the conventional associations they may evoke.

In the sixth column is architecture, a special class of artifacts because people do not use or inhabit the solid structural elements of buildings, their walls and floors, in the way they directly deal with artifacts; rather, they use the space within and defined by those artifactual forms.

Finally, the seventh column notes kinship, as an example of the range of other and very different human systems which this paper and conference do not address.

To the extent that these are all expressions of some human fundamentals, so they all share fundamental structures. But they also have characteristics specific to each, and inescapably those that follow from the fundamental physical and biological properties they depend on. Kinship would have different possibilities if human reproduction were asexual or "trisexual," depending on the uniting of three individuals rather than two. Architectural design, because physical objects are three-dimensional, deals with the geometry of 3-D space rather than that of 2 or 4. Within these formal constraints are others of a practical nature: architecture deals not with all 3-D designs, but with that subset of 3-D designs which can be planned and built, given engineering realities and the size of the human beings who move in architectural spaces. Often, things in one system may be *expressed* in terms of another, as a piece of music is represented in its written score; but the music and its score, equivalent in some senses, are not actually the same thing. Nor is the essence of a play's performance to be found in its written text alone.

Insofar, then, as artifacts and texts are the same thing, the study of artifacts as if they were texts produces the same insights. Insofar as artifacts and texts are different, the study of artifacts as if they were texts ignores their artifactual character. Under the definition of archaeology as concerned specifically with the *artifactual* aspects of history and of anthropology, the artifactual is fundamental, especially in prehistory, where other direct evidence is lacking. It is the artifactual aspects which need to be concentrated on. At worst, the same insights will be made by an artifactual view, but by a longer route than the textual, and one which may involve the reinventing of some wheels. Further, we know that literacy, and the dominance of text which has followed in Western culture, has involved fundamental changes in many social and cognitive matters. The modern literate society and its texts make a special case, and other human cognitive systems are different worlds of their own, not remakings of text by inferior means. Further again, we have quantities—overwhelming quantities—of data about the *shapes* of artifacts; a systematics of artifact shape addresses the empirical evidence, while a systematics of artifact meaning will depend on, or be ruled out by, any uncertainty of articulation between the artifact and its meaning as we try to infer it.

The different nature of texts and of artifacts is so important that it is worth a re-statement in other terms and an analogy.

A restatement. All these systems can be seen as domains within formal logic. Each uses a particular subset of formal logic appropriate to its nature—those of syntax and semantics for written texts, those of 3-D geometry for architecture, those of harmonic patterns for music. Each subset of formal logic has some characteristics specific to that subset, and some characteristics general to formal logic. Any two domains share those elements which are general in formal logic, and those few or many which fall within the intersection of the two subsets.

An analogy. All computer systems deal, at a deep level, with arrays of "flip-flop" switches in one or other binary state (0–1, positive-negative, on-off). A computer system controlling a chemical-process plant is, at that deep level, identical to that used for word processing; indeed, the same machine and operational logic may be applied to both domains simultaneously. Yet the important characteristics of process plant and of word processing are not at the level of abstracted deep structure at which they are algorithmically identical, but at those higher levels at which they are quite distinct in nature. To understand either, they must be addressed at that high level. To understand texts and artifacts, they must be addressed at that high level at which they have major differences.

2. From Classifications of Attributes to the Means by Which They Were Generated

Classification, typological classification especially, has been a dominant tradition in archaeology from the beginning. Instructively, it seems to be a necessary first step in making sense of artifacts; on the rare occasions nowadays that wholly new varieties and classes of artifacts have to be dealt with, it is found that work has to start with classification in the nineteenth-century manner and then recapitulate the history of artifactual studies up to modern concerns. But there are more ways of working with shape than to classify.

The recent history of the study of British stone rings (Figure 2) is a valuable example of the possibilities and the limits of classificatory approaches. The rings (Burl 1976), of which Stonehenge is the most famous and the least typical, are settings of upright or recumbent stones, commonly ten or twenty, that are roughly circular in plan and commonly 30 m or 50 m in diameter (Figure 2A). They date to the third and second millennium BC. Locations, scanty artifactual associations, burials, and astronomical orientations relating to the moon suggest that they were ceremonial centers, partly to do with death and the lunar cycle, and perhaps functioning as territorial central places. Their "meaning" to their builders is not immediately apparent, and the faint inferences that can be made as to function are not of a nature that seems to be closely coupled to their spatial forms.

Thom, over many years of study (e.g., Thom, Thom and Burl 1980), found that the plans of most stone rings fitted, more or less, six shapes: circles; ellipses; flattened circles of two varieties; and egg-shapes of two varieties (Figure 2B). He noted that the complex shapes could all be derived from Pythagorean right-angled triangles, and he presented a set of formal geometric constructions by which the plan could be made. Thom concluded that the prehistoric builders of the circles knew those geometries and planned the rings that way, as part of a coherent and sophisticated "megalithic science," which implied a very full knowledge of mathematics, mensuration, and astronomy in prehistoric Britain.

Angell (1976) pointed out that circles are most easily laid out on the ground by scribing with a rope tied to a central post, and ellipses by a loop of rope running round two posts. He showed that scribing with ropes around arrays of a few posts generated a set of geometries almost identical to Thom's (Figure 2C). Their generation required a familiarity with ropes and posts, but no knowledge of formal or Pythagorean geometry.

Barnatt and Moir (1984) and Barnatt and Herring (1986) explored a third hypothesis, the laying-out of the rings by eye (Figure 2D). They noted that Thom's and Angell's schemes both generated sets of symmetrical designs; examining the plans, they found many to be asymmetrical. By simulating the planning of rings on the ground in a modern experiment, they showed that the fair judging of a circle by eye is not easy; the tendency was for their experimental subjects to generate circles with corners or "flat sides," many of them very closely approximating the formal Thom geometries. Apart from a few good circles, of such accuracy that they must have been laid out by, for example, scribing with peg and rope, the repertoire of megalithic geometry required only the laying-out of round shapes by eye.

Finally, new work at one celebrated site, Long Meg and Her Daughters (Soffe and Clare 1988), shows that the flattening from a circle of that ring follows from its having been built against the bank of an older earthwork whose perimeter was nearly straight. The geometry of this ring follows in part from the accident of an older topography.

Notice that it remains indisputable that the stones which make up the rings do fall near the perimeters of rather complex shapes; Thom's Pythagorean geometries are, to a defined degree of accuracy, perfectly fair *descriptions* of the shapes of the rings. (Indeed, if one insists on higher accuracies than has been customary, then the rings are described better by much more *recherché* geometries.)

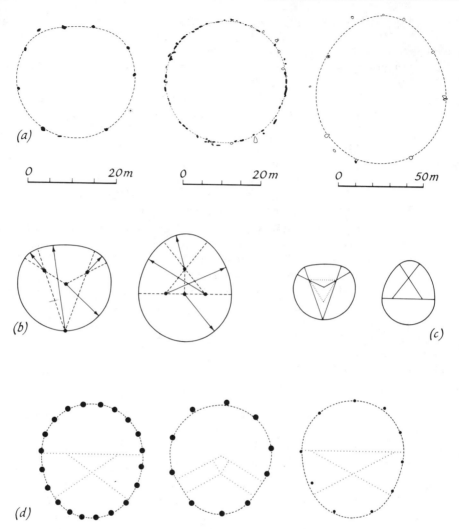

Figure 2. Order in the plans of prehistoric British stone rings. (a) Plans of three rings: Seascale (flattened circle), Rollright (circle), Twelve Apostles (egg-shape). (b) Two Thom geometries for rings: flattened circle, egg-shape. (c) Cowan configurations for rings made by scribing with rope and posts: flattened circle, egg-shape. (d) Egg shapes arrived at in the laying-out of rings by eye. After Thom et al. 1980; Heggie 1981; Cowan 1970; Barnatt and Herring 1986.

The point, then, is not in the *characteristics* of the rings as such, but the inferences that can be made from those characteristics as to how the artifacts were *generated*. Barnatt and colleagues were able to concentrate on symmetry because it was this characteristic which set their proposal apart from the Thom and Angell hypotheses.

Any artifact, however small and simple, possesses an indefinitely large number of characteristics. Almost all of them are trivial when considered in relation to how the artifact is generated. A few are important. The purpose of description and classification is to isolate significant variability, and significant variability is that which concerns those characteristics which are informative about the generation, the use, and the degeneration of the artifact.

Equifinality applies to generative systems, of course: any artifact, however small and simple, can be generated by an indefinitely large number of procedures. Almost all of the distinctions between the procedures are trivial, considered in relation to how the artifact is generated. A few are important. The value of understanding how the artifact is generated, and of focusing the research interest on this, is in linking the active process of its making—the ancient process that is the proper purpose of study—closely to the characteristics we choose to describe.

The danger, perfectly inescapable in the study of archaeology, is that a *pattern can always be found in any set whatever of characteristics that artifacts present*. The set of replica stone-ring designs generated by Barnatt and Herring's experiment did follow Thom's Pythagorean geometry. A random distribution of spot points, artifact find-spots for example, across a geographical area can easily appear to be clustered or scattered (Hodder and Orton 1976:4–9; and see discussion in Chippindale 1986)—with good reason, since it may well be either a clustered or a scattered distribution whose original order has been lost through taphonomic loss and sampling biases. Part of a random, haphazard or unstructured distribution, suitably selected, will always present some illusory structure. And more than one kind of pattern can be identified, as a domestic example illustrates. My children are of an age to enjoy arithmetic and we have sometimes passed the time on car journeys by making equations from license plates, which in Britain usually have three-digit numbers. The idea is to make an equation out of the number on a passing car, which is sometimes easy:

111   $1 = 1 = 1$
437   $4 + 3 = 7$

and can become trickier:

238   2 to the power of 3 is 8
667   6.6 to the nearest whole number $= 7$

The numbers can be made sense of, one by one, and could be classified by their arithmetical characteristics into classes created by addition, by subtraction, and so on. Such a study and classification, although it fairly describes characteristics of the numbers presented, has made illusory order out of a pattern which was actually generated by a simpler process; the licensing office simply issues numbers one by one up to 999, and then starts again at the beginning.

The point, then, is not the characteristics of the numbers as such, but the correct and incorrect inferences that can be made from those characteristics as to *how they were generated*. But once clear ideas have been put forward as to likely means of generation, the *significant* variability in the pattern can be identified. The same goes for artifacts and their regularities: the point is not in the characteristics as such, but in the inferences that can be made about how the artifacts were generated—information about their active life.

3. Requirements of a Generative Approach to the Characteristics of Artifacts

The first section set out the view, which should be quite unremarkable, that the fundamental character of artifacts, as they are presented archaeologically, is their shape; the appropriate means to study them is therefore geometrical, broadly defined. The second section asserted, by example, that the interest is not in those shapes and their regularities *per se*, but in how they have been generated, for it is in the ways that artifacts are generated, used, and degenerated that archaeologists can find the information they want about past societies, as well as past artifacts. The success of grammars, rule-based means to order complex systems, is such that no full argument should be needed here to justify a wish to use grammatical methods.

The need, in short, is to deal with the shape of artifacts by

> *geometrical*
>
> *generative*
>
> *grammars.*

Meaning, in the sense of what ancient societies thought their artifacts stood for, does not immediately come into it. Even if we had a rather good idea of what stone circles symbolized, even if we wanted to call Stonehenge by its proper ancient name rather than by an early medieval invented name, this would not be of much help *unless we could closely connect those 'meanings' to the variability in shape for which we have so much, if so recalcitrant, empirical evidence.*

Function can also be helpful but not always: the functional requirements for human burial are the provision of a space into which a human body, in whole or in part, as one piece or many, raw or burnt, may be placed—requirements which can be, and have been, fulfilled by an immense range of built and unbuilt forms.

4. Architectural Grammars

More important and more numerous people than archaeologists are concerned with the generation of artifacts—the potters, dressmakers, builders, and assembly workers who make things, and the engineers and designers who are concerned with the theory of making things.

Design can be seen as the inverse of artifactual archaeology (Figure 3). The designer and maker of things, in a given social context, generates artifacts whose form is to do with practical matters of function and the properties of materials, with social and economic values, and with expectations (a kettle, as for boiling water, needs to *look* like a kettle to the people who are to use it), all these within a certain state of technical knowledge; that is,

> *from society to the artifact.*

Design: moves from formal, informal, and implicit brief to make an artifact

from "brief"	through design possibilities	to made artifact
specifying, for example function material context 'style' expectations and habits (within a craft tradition) technical knowledge symbolism and "meaning" efficiency (?) minimal cost	"range of designs suitable for the job"	design that is made

Archaeology: moves from found artifact toward formal, informal, and implicit brief

from made artifact	through design possibilities	to "brief, as reconstructed"
found object	contemporary range of design variability	indicating, for example function material context "style" date geographical origin expectations and habits (within an archaeological tradition) technical knowledge efficiency (?) minimal cost (?) social context (?) symbolism and "meaning"

Figure 3. Design of artifacts and archaeological study of artifacts as inverse processes. Design moves from society to the made artifact. Archaeology moves from the found artifact to society. After Chippindale 1986.

The artifacts, once created, degenerate by degrees and may survive for archaeological study. The archaeologist has the inverse task, of studying the artifact and inferring

from the artifact to society.

The orthodox view of design, as conventional in Western society, starts with function and social value, reasonably enough. If one wishes to build a house, the essential of the brief is function, a house not a railway station, and with that function a set of social expectations as to what houses are and are not like. But archaeologists do not know the functions and social contexts of the artifact they study; so most designers' insight in these matters depends on the things an archaeologist does not know, rather than on an interest in the form alone that the archaeologist is presented with.

The wide context to this paper, and this conference, is the closeness of the coupling between objects and the societies that make them. At one end of the range of opinion are those like Hodder (1986) who seem to think that past societies can be read rather easily from their objects: the coupling is consistent and clear. In the middle, where I also am, are those like Sabloff, Binford (Sabloff, Binford and McAnany 1987), Gardin (Gardin et al. 1987) and Renfrew (1985) who think major deductions can be made about past societies, given enough care and study as to just what is linked and exactly how: the coupling is variable and takes much care to clarify. At the other end are those, still dominant by number in many fields of European archaeology, for example, who doubt if social inference in any detail is useful to attempt: the coupling is too variable to make clear.

Architects face the same issues. Past and present opinion in that profession has a broad spread, as does archaeology's, and the closeness of some of the equivalent schools of thought is startling. In archaeology, for example, the idea has been put up (e.g., Shanks and Tilley 1987) that the past is something we invent more to suit ourselves than reconstruct from any real information, and the archaeologist's professional authority in these matters is minimal. In architecture, Christopher Alexander is following the parallel path: he thinks that communities should themselves build together the buildings they want, and the architect's role is to help the community articulate its own wishes, rather than to provide an authority of professional competence.

The difference is that architects actually build their models of relations between artifact and society into physical structures, and societies live with the results. Experience this century has been mixed, and on balance hostile to the view of a close and easy coupling. The modern movement tried to develop a rational, functionalist architecture rationally to function in a rational society. Society was not always sure, and did not consistently react as it was supposed to. (But notice that the same classes of built forms, such as tower blocks for public housing, have been variously successful or calamitous in different Western countries, and regions of countries, according, it appears, to rather small differences in social lives and in design.) The postmodern movement of the 1970s and 1980s has moved against this; its touchstones are eclecticism and capriciousness: there is no single form rationally to fulfill a particular function or social need, but there is a great variety of forms, old or new or both, from which to draw, and none with an absolute claim to efficiency. Nor ought the postmodern architect, if he or she is consistent, expect society to regard or use a postmodern building in the way the architect planned. Postmodernism is a realistic recognition of the looseness of the coupling between form and function.

It was noticed above that the usefulness of architectural experience is limited by its common point of departure, a brief of function and social context that archaeologists have no equivalent of. But there is one school of architectural design whose work precisely fits the archaeological question, the group of "formal morphologists" associated with the journal *Planning and Design*, with the UCLA architecture department and Open University research center, and with the persons of Gips, Hillier, March, Mitchell, Steadman, and Stiny (March and Steadman 1971 is an early survey, Steadman 1983 a more recent one, Stiny 1986 a key collection of papers; *Planning and Design* is also publishing work in this manner by archaeologists, e.g. Chippindale 1986, and the papers in Boast and Steadman 1987). The morphologists take as premises two particular opinions. The first is that an intuitive knowledge of the coupling of form and function is not to be trusted; from this follows an interest in form, and the particular character of form, as proper primary concerns. The second is a concern for the value of explicit formal methods; from this follows a concern, for example, with "algorithmic aesthetics" and with the making explicit of the mysteries of architectural creativity which is the necessary preliminary to automated creative design. Notice that *both* interests match archaeological requirements as I see them—the interest in the particularities of form, and the value of explicit formal methods.

There are several elements to formal morphology and several techniques. The most directly attractive for the study of ancient architecture is the study of access with built forms by Hillier's methods (Figure 4) (Hillier and Hanson 1985). Characteristically, it starts with a geometric aspect of spatial layout, the access from one defined space to another, and from that morphological aspect works toward functional and social matters; so it provides archaeologists with one sophisticated means to explore architectural design and the social relations it embodies *without having to guess at function and meaning* as a preliminary.

Here I wish to mention two other elements, the specific of *enumerating rectilinear dissections*, and the general formalism of *Stiny shape-grammars*.

First, though, three vital consequences of the morphological point of view.

A first is a respect for the *particular* character of individual geometries (Figure 5). Circular plans have a bundle of related properties: they have the highest ratio of area to perimeter of any geometric form; they do not pack solidly together; they cannot be subdivided into smaller circles, as multiples of the same class; and so on. Rectangles have other properties: they have a lower, and variable, ratio of area to perimeter; they do "pack"; they can be divided into smaller rectangles. Triangles have different properties again. All these properties have implications for design. Where area to periphery ratios are important, and inability to pack is not, circular forms have the edge: hence scattered round huts inside round defended enclosures. Where subdivision into shape of the same nature is required, and packing matters, rectangular forms have the edge: hence rectangular enclosed fields, city gridirons, and multiply subdivided buildings. Where demands conflict, a subform may combine advantageous elements of two geometries: hence

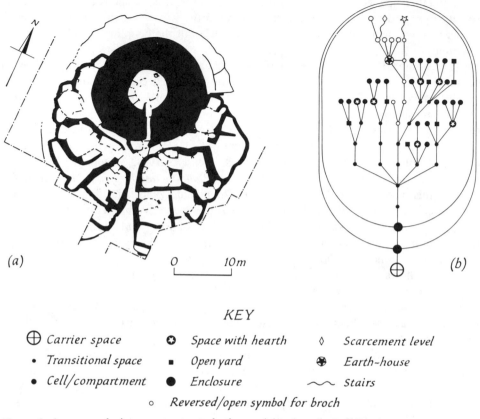

(a)   *(b)*

0   10m

KEY

⊕ *Carrier space*   ✪ *Space with hearth*   ◊ *Scarcement level*

• *Transitional space*   ▪ *Open yard*   ✬ *Earth-house*

● *Cell/compartment*   ● *Enclosure*   ⌇ *Stairs*

○ *Reversed/open symbol for broch*

Figure 4. Access analysis, a means to study the spatial order of a building in terms of the access between existing spaces. (a) Plan of the Iron Age broch at Howe, Scotland. (b) Access map showing how the various spaces within the broch are related on the basis of its essential geometry. After Carter et al. 1984; Foster 1989.

square towers, castles, and defended places, for the square is that rectangular form which most closely nears the area to perimeter ratio of a circle. And there are engineering strengths and weaknesses that go along with particular geometries.

Second, these characteristics are *bundled* together. Suppose—and this is the kind of vague social assertion the morphologists hate—that it is in the nature of circular space to be democratic and of rectangular spaces to be autocratic (think of the audience halls of kings and princes; of debating chambers of elected assemblies; and of the shift in church plans from central-place to rectangular and back again, as the Church's power grew and shrank again). Suppose that a circular form is chosen for good geometric or engineering reasons, such as the stability of an underground kiva against the pressure of earth against its walls. Then a built form appears with substantial social consequences that are both inescapable and unintended when the form was preferred—social consequences that follow from the artifact form rather than any dynamic internal to the society.

A third concern, neatly phrased by W. R. Lethaby (1922) as "systematic research into the possibilities," is the exploring of all varieties of a class, usually as a specific

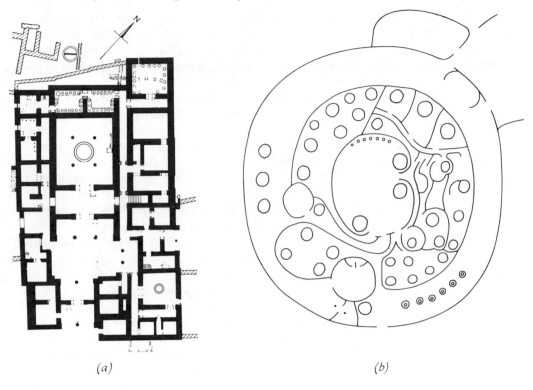

(a) (b)

Figure 5. The nature of rectilinear and of circular geometries has consequence for how space can be divided, and therefore for how structures that follow these geometries behave. Rectilinear structures may themselves be divided into smaller rectilinear spaces. Circular spaces, if divided, make shapes which are generally not circular. (a) Portions of the palace at Pylos, Crete, thirteenth century B.C. (b) Chiefly krall of the Mabo people, recent. After Blegen and Rawson 1966; Walton 1956.

consequence of interest in the particular characteristics of a geometry. Knowing the full number or range of designs that exist in any one class is most useful for archaeology, since it makes possible the fair study of similarities and differences between groups; one can only say "how similar is similar," "how different is different" in light of the number of possibilities that may exist. A simple example concerns the pyramids found in ancient Egypt and in ancient Mesoamerica, whose similar form from time to time prompts claims for transatlantic contact or colonization. But consider: firstly, ancient Egyptian and ancient Mesomerican cities and large buildings were built to rectilinear plans; secondly, since ancient Egyptian and ancient Mesomerican building technology lacked any means to secure very high vertical faces, any very tall and heavy structure had to be of a form that would stand by its own mass, that is, sloped to a stable grade. Given the impetus to build massive stone structures, a pyramid is the *only* building form which is possible, and the similarity of form carries no inference whatever of contact. There are some options: the base plan, within a rectilinear principle, can be square and rectangular; the slope can be smooth or stepped; a sacred place, if required, can be buried within the mass of the structure or set instead on the pyramid apex. In all three aspects Egyptian and Mesoamerican practices were different, so one can conclude, *having systematically researched* (a little) *into the possibilities*, that the striking and obvious similarity means nothing, and that the Egyptian and Mesomerican pyramids are in fact practically as different as they could be. If more precision is needed, the means exists to give a numerical value to that degree of difference.

Among the British sites, the word "pyramid" evokes Silbury Hill (Whittle in press), the largest prehistoric mound of Europe, a monument of broadly the same date as the Egyptian pyramids. In profile, Silbury Hill resembles the pyramids—again for the same engineering reason: it is a pile mound, made up of chalk rubble with some internal walling to maintain its stability, and it is therefore obliged to follow the natural angle of repose in the same way as do the pyramids of Egypt and America. No internal chamber has been found inside the Hill, and it has a flat top, so it seems the American rather than the Egyptian choice was made as to where a sacred space of the pyramid was located. Where Silbury Hill differs from both Egyptian and American pyramids is that it is round rather than rectangular in plan. This is congruent with the geometrical habits of its builders, whose other earthworks are of varied shape, round and rectangular, who had no urban or quasi-urban centers, who did not follow rectangular grids for large-scale buildings, and who chose a round plan for the smaller burial mounds which are the closest local analogue in geometry to Silbury Hill. In the Hill, then, one sees similarities to, and differences from, the pyramids of Egypt and of America, and these similarities and differences again make every sense in terms of geometrical and engineering possibilities that exist and the choices that different societies make from among those possibilities.

Rectilinear dissections (Steadman 1973) (Figure 6)

Take a rectangle. Divide it, by a line parallel to one side, into two rectangles (order 2, Figure 6A). The line may be placed in many places, producing two rectangles of different sizes, so there are many *metrical* possibilities. But *topologically* these are all the same, two rectangles, 1 and 2, which are mutually adjacent.

Divide the rectangle again, to make three rectangles (order 3, Figure 6B). Again there are metric variants; there are now two topologically distinct dissections: in one, 1, 2, and 3 are mutually adjacent; in one, 1 is adjacent to 2, and 2 to 3, but 1 is not adjacent to 3.

With the dissection of order 4, there are six possibilities (Figure 6C), for order 5 there are 23 possibilities, for order 6, 119 possibilities (Steadman 1983:31)—and for any given order a fixed and calculable number.

So what? For the archaeologist, here is a means to some exact knowledge about the possibilities that exist for the layout of buildings of a few rooms. Knowing how many dissections of order 6 exist, one can exactly quantify the probabilities and possibilities involved if one finds, say, eight six-room structures all of the same dissection, or none of the same dissection. With the help of contemporary ethnoarchitectural study as to what dissections are advantageous in small-building layouts, such knowledge can provide a route to the rational reconstruction of what designs were preferred—and therefore as to the reasons for that preference. The metric attributes of the dissections can be explored, and so can the consequences of particular building technologies; for example, in roof-

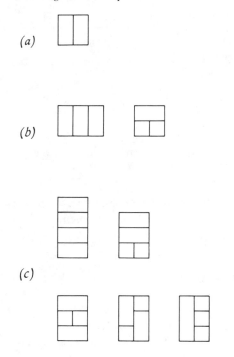

Figure 6. Rectilinear dissections: geometrical properties of the spaces generated by subdividing a rectangular shape, in terms of their adjacency. (a) Order 2: only one rectilinear dissection exists, of two adjacent spaces. (b) Order 3: two relations exist; in one the three spaces are mutually adjacent, in the other they are not. (c) Order 4: six relations exist. After Bloch 1979.

access or pueblo kinds of single-story buildings, the usual requirement of access between rooms may be suspended, since rooms in the center of buildings are still directly accessible from the exterior via the roof.

The methodology is, in the morphologists' manner: from the study of the form and its geometrical characteristics, to systematic exploration of possibilities (in this case by enumeration), to study of what has been chosen from among the possibilities, to social inference.

Stiny shape-grammars (Stiny 1986) (Figures 7 and 8)

Stiny and his collaborators have developed a mathematical formalism for the generation of shapes, the Stiny shape-grammar. A shape-grammar consists of a set of shapes and a set of rules by which a shape may be transformed into another shape. The rudimentary grammar of Figure 7, for example, creates a family of shapes, squares inside squares, by the repeated application of a transforming rule.

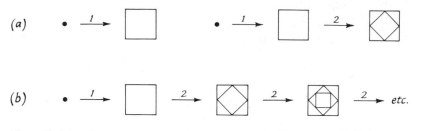

Figure 7. Stiny shape-grammars to generate squares inside squares. (a) Rule 1 creates a square, and rule 2 places a square inside the square. (b) Rule 1 followed by repeated applications of rule 2 creates a shape of nested squares.

The full Stiny formalism will not always be appropriate, or worth the considerable labor of its derivation, but it provides an ideal formal statement, for which a less formal, and less precise, approximation will sometimes suffice.

5. Four Generative Geometric Grammars

All this is empty theory until it is shown actually to work. I cannot do more, in a paper of this nature and length, than to point to a little of what is being done; and this may be more useful as summaries, however abrupt and inadequate, than referring to work published elsewhere. So here are four examples of generative geometrical grammars dealing with historical architecture and artifacts. Only the first and third follow the Stiny formalism and are shape-grammars in the proper sense. We use the vaguer term "design-grammar" to cover both Stiny shape-grammars and other grammars, either less rigorous or of a different formalism, of a geometric and generative character.

The Palladian Grammar (Stiny and Mitchell 1978) (Figure 8)

Figure 8 summarizes the Palladian grammar of Stiny and Mitchell (1978). A series of transforming rules generate a rather complex shape from a spot point. That final shape is the plan of one of Palladin's neoclassical villas, among the supreme designs of the classical revival. The Palladian grammar sets out, by rigorous geometry, the derivation and character of Palladian villa design, by the evidence of the villas Andrea de Palladio built and by the principles of his own treatise on architecture (Palladio [1738]). This grammar exactly defines the Palladian style, insofar as that resides in the floor plan (complementary grammars can be written for elevations, decorative treatments, etc.); it indicates the common elements in the corpus of villas of that style, and the variability; it supplies criteria to judge if other buildings follow the style; it provides the compositional machinery to design new buildings that would be instances of the style. All these aspects of the grammar are *descriptive*, though at a very high level of rigor and exactness. And from this secure knowledge of what Palladian villas amount to can be built a variety of comparative and analytical studies. Intuitive judgments that two villas are "similar" or "different" may be made precise, and inferences may follow from the information that description offers as to the design process, units of length, geometric proportions, and

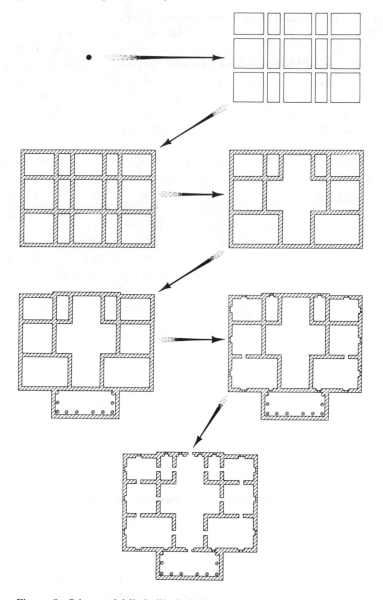

Figure 8. Stiny and Mitchell's Palladian grammar. The ground plan of a neoclassical building generated by a series of geometric transformations, here abridged in a summary form. After Stiny and Mitchell 1978.

so on. Equally, these intuitive judgments provide a sure basis for developing inference as to the function and "meaning" of the villas, which are unlikely to be obvious to a prehistorian if he were to come across them anew as an unrecognized building type. (Notice that we are misled by the appearance of the villas, as they "obviously" appear to us today: they were neither academic exercises of architectural indulgence nor pretty country retreats for the urban aristocracy, but a novel fusion of the architectural requirements of the educated gentleman and the working farmer, analogous to the smaller provincial villas of late Roman landed gentry [Ackerman 1966:40–45].) This analytical or systematic description is the key to exploring inferences: in particular, it forces the question, whenever social inference is concerned, "where in the geometry, in what aspects of the physical building, is this social element concerned?" And if social aspects are *not* expressed, with some decent clarity, in some aspect or other of the physical building, then it follows that the social aspect—however fascinating—cannot usefully be illuminated by study of the architectural, the artifactual evidence.

A previous section of this paper set out the requirements of artifact grammars. The Stiny formalism provides the vital elements: the mathematical rigor, a focus on physical form, a generative approach. And the papers in Stiny's collection (Stiny 1986) and elsewhere now present a number of shape-grammars applied to a wide range of historical architecture and artifacts: the Stiny shape-grammar is well tested and experienced as a technique.

Brown's London grammar (Brown 1986) (Figure 9)

An instructive example of a grammar approach, though not using the Stiny formalism, is Brown's study of the characteristic urban form of medieval London. Within near-rectangular blocks defined by main thoroughfares, the layout is a chaos of little plots and buildings with a maze of alleys and courts within the block (Figure 9A). Brown analyzed the characteristics of this layout and developed a set of algorithms by which to simulate the generation of the pattern (Figure 9B); his grammar therefore provides both a systematic description of the characteristics of the London plan, and an account of how it may be generated. Beyond this, his elegant model shows valuable points. First, it identifies the key variables in determining the particular form which results: land boundaries, the division of street boundaries into plots, the need for natural lighting, the technology of building. It also identifies the geometric problem fundamental to such layouts: the need to provide easy access from the street to the center of the block despite the preference for building on the frontage. Fine-tuning of the model identifies those choices which are critical in deriving the form, or the variant within the range of forms, that results.

An accident of history is particularly revealing as to social inference. This area of London, built up in medieval times, was leveled by the Great Fire of 1666 and was subsequently rebuilt from the ground. Individual structures, as surviving pre- and post-Fire plans show, do not correspond, yet the overall *character* of the urban form is unchanged (this can be neatly shown by introducing a stochastic element into the model, and showing what range of variability it naturally may fall within). But consider. The great transformation in European society is, it is often said, that between the medieval and the early modern world. The structures of pre-Fire London were largely medieval,

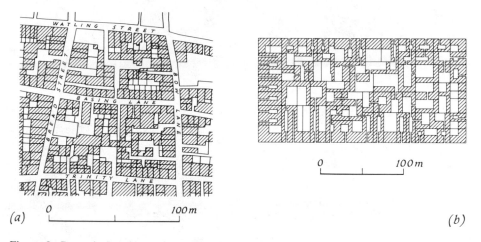

Figure 9. Brown's London grammar. (a) Detail of London street plan. (b) Portion of generated plan. After Brown and Johnson 1985.

so that social transformation ought to show itself in a changed spatial order after the Fire: it *must*, as a woman once said to me in a seminar discussion on these matters, be in that plan somewhere. But why? The fundamentals that control the urban form did not change: the characteristics of 2-D geometry are unchanging; the land boundaries, and the social attitudes that respected them, did not move; the need for natural daylighting and access remained; and so on—all these factors that directly relate to the urban form were the same after the Fire. That is why the fundamental forms did not change. The social transformation probably *is* in there somewhere, but it will not be found until it can be linked to some *significant* factor influencing the urban geometry. This is why similar forms are to be found in other urban contexts, such as Arab cities and modern shanty towns, where similar geometrical and technical constraints apply. The revolution in the urban form of London had to wait until artificial lighting, changed building technology, new transport systems, and other real variables made their impact—not because those are social transformations, but because they are changes which upset the major controlling variables of the system under study. For an urban form of utterly different character, one must look, for example, to the cities of ancient Mesoamerica. In those societies, with attitudes to land ownership and access that really were fundamentally different, different rules applied and different urban forms arose.

The megalithic grammar (Boast and Chippindale forthcoming) (Figure 10)

The megalithic chambered tombs of northwestern Europe provide classic problems of affinity. As varying typologies, evolutionary trees, and guesses at chronology have shown over many decades, the monuments indicate how intractable are the basic questions: How similar is similar? How different is different? How and why do artifactual similarity and difference matter? Nowhere is this truer than in the Orkney Islands, whose well-preserved Neolithic chambered tombs have shaken off several attempts to order them.

We tried a shape-grammar approach, as a means of systematic description and as a

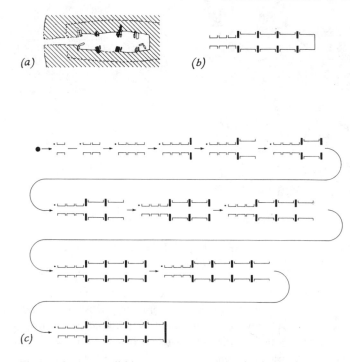

Figure 10. A megalithic grammar generates the form of a
later prehistoric chamber-tomb from northwestern Europe.
(a) Plan of the east chamber at Calf of Eday Long, Eday,
Orkney, Scotland, a "stalled chamber" of Neolithic date.
(b) The plan redrawn with units of construction made of a
regular size. (c) Grammatical derivation of the plan. At each
stage of the derivation a new element is attached following
a rule of the grammar. Plan after Davidson and Henshall
1989.

preliminary to an algorithmic study of affinity. Figure 10a shows the plan of an Orkney
megalithic chamber, built largely of flat stone slabs and with a characteristic rectilinear
layout of adjoining "modules." In Figure 10b the same plan is drawn to a standardized
grid. In Figure 10c the plan is generated by a series of grammatical steps. At each step
either a new module is added or an additional feature, such as a pair of slabs, is added
to an existing module. In this way, the whole plan can be generated by applying a small
number of rules, each enlarging or modifying the plan by geometrical transformation.
All essential features of the chamber plan, as indicated in Figure 10a and regularized in
Figure 10b, are accounted for in the grammatical derivation of Figure 10c. In a further
step in the analysis, each rule that makes a geometrical transformation can be referenced
by a number, and the set of ordered transformations that describe the chamber plan can
therefore be stated as a number-string. If the essential character of a chamber plan is
indeed encapsulated in the grammatical description, as we believe it is, then the corpus
of Orkney chambers can be presented and compared as a set of number-strings. In that

fact is explanation of the diversity of schemes that can be devised to classify and make sense of the megalithic architecture of Orkney; there are at least as many reasonable ways to do this as there are rational ways to compare number-strings, a reality which we find disconcerting. Our response has been to develop and to depend on those algorithms for comparing the strings that seem to us to be directed by those elements we believe most pertinent.

The picture problem and the inverse picture problem (Hagen 1986) (Figure 11)

Early in this paper (Figure 1), pictures were noted as having characteristics intermediate between those of written texts and those of artifacts. They are directly to do with meaning in a way that artifacts are not, yet they work with geometry and with geometrical possibilities in a way that artifacts do. For pictures from familiar places, which we really do know and understand, the approach from meaning is clearly right: medieval religious painting, for example, can be seen in terms of Christian iconography and symbolism. For pictures from unfamiliar places and contexts, and certainly for all prehistoric art, the approach from meaning depends at best on analogy and inference, and may often amount to simple guessing.

The "picture problem," as Hagen neatly calls it, is the basis for a geometric and formal approach to prehistoric pictures. Why can we recognize what a picture is a picture of? Because it is the same shape as the thing it depicts. But not often *exactly* the same shape, and certainly not the same shape when, as is usual, the picture is a 2-D and simpler version of a complex 3-D shape. The "picture problem," for the ancient or modern artist, is how to express in the picture the *essentials* of the shape, of the geometry of what is depicted. There are many coherent geometric transformations, or projections, which generate from an original 3-D shape a variety of 2-D pictures: each preserves some elements, though not all, of the geometry of the original, and each is perfectly recognizable as a picture of what it is a picture of to anyone familiar with the basis of transformation. But because there is some loss of information in the transforming, and especially in reduction from three dimensions to two (Figure 11B), there is ambiguity in the shapes that result. But the fact that pictures can be recognized ("read") even when they come from cultures we do not know, or when they contain depictions of things we have never seen, underlines the dependence of the picture problem on underlying geometrical regularities: contrast this with the utter opacity of texts in languages one does not understand. A *coherent* solution to the picture problem may be defined as one which applies a simple geometrical to the initial shape, such as presenting its silhouette as seen by an observer; conversely, an *incoherent* solution presents a shape of a different character, say, transforming a sphere into a wiggly line. The coherent solutions turn out to be manageably small in number, the incoherent ones to be indefinitely numerous.

The "picture problem" and its various solutions, among them profile drawing, Western artificial perspective, isometric projections and many more, amounts to

an initial shape x (subject)
under a coherent transforming geometry y (projection system)
generates a final shape z (picture)

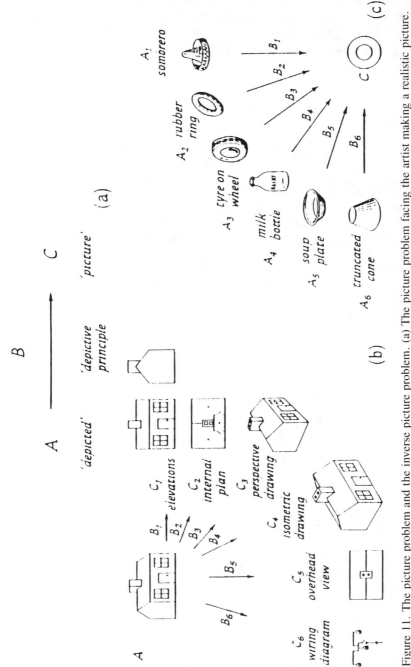

Figure 11. The picture problem and the inverse picture problem. (a) The picture problem facing the artist making a realistic picture. A three-dimensional shape A is projected as a two-dimensional picture C by means of some depictive principle B. (b) Several solutions for the picture problem, when the three-dimensional shape to be depicted is a little house, A. Under a variety of projective principles, B1 to B6, that same shape generates a variety of pictures, C1 to C6—all of them equally reasonable representations of A. The archaeologist will encounter a range of different pictures, C1 to C6, that all derive from the same A. (c) The archaeologist may also be faced with the same picture, C, deriving from a variety of different shapes, A1 to A6. After Chippindale 1988.

$$y$$
$$x \rightarrow z$$

The archaeologist, wishing to study ancient pictures, faces the inverse picture problem:

$$y$$
$$z \rightarrow x$$

that is, reconstructing both

an initial shape x (subject)
and a transforming geometry y (projection system)
from the evidence of a final shape z (picture).

If the transformations are incoherent, and especially if they are very variable also, it will be hard to determine x and y. If the transformations are coherent, reconstructing aspects of x and y will be possible by comparative methods, which Schafer (1986) does most beautifully for the formal and very coherent rules of ancient Egyptian art.

These are very early days for this geometrical approach to prehistoric pictures, with only one example worked out very far (Chippindale 1987) within this statement of the formal problems and further work in progress (Chippindale forthcoming). That paper explored whether petroglyphs, which had the appearance of maps, actually were maps. By exploring the geometrical character of the petroglyphs, it was possible to show that they were not coherent transformations of real ancient places, that is, maps in the usual sense; the possibility must remain either that they are incoherent transformations of real places (maps which don't map what they map) or that they are coherent transformations of unreal ancient places (maps which map things that do not exist). However, a great deal of work on ancient art has been done in this spirit, and much mainstream work in art history and analysis (and in art itself!) amounts to studies of various geometric aspects of the picture problem.

6. In Conclusion

I do not propose that design-grammars of this character are obviously appropriate for anthropological studies of material culture or for those with a good basis in ethnohistorical information. Where function, social values, "meaning" are known to us, they are more obvious points of departure than morphology. But archaeology is its own subject, with its own, largely artifactual world to study. In all but the best-documented contexts, and that means almost always in prehistory, it may be better to depend on morphology than on what amounts often to guesses about function, social values, or "meaning."

Underlying the morphological approach are two sets of uniformitarian principles. First are the absolute verities of geometry: there are, always have been, and always will be, by the nature of 2-D space, only two topologically distinct ways to divide a rectangle into three rectangles. Second are the less absolute, but reasonably secure, verities of the physical properties of materials: the shapes that flint will flake to, the engineering properties of post-and-beam building techniques; and of human requirements of artifacts: containers need to contain things, roofs need to keep the weather out.

The insider's approach, by prior knowledge of social context and function, can be called "informed"; the second, which assumes little knowledge, can be called "formal." The informed approach offers, or seems to offer, satisfying explanations in terms of what human beings do to artifacts, and demands much prior understanding; the formal offers less, preferring to stop at systematic descriptions, but depends on minimal prior understanding. Those two aspects go together: the informed offers much and requires much; the formal offers less and requires less. Almost all the literature on the semiotics of artifacts and architecture comes from the informed school: I have for that reason not referred to it in this discussion of formal methods. In prehistory we are inescapably ill-informed, and therefore must turn to the formal. It may be limited, bleak even, but at least it is safe as far as it goes. For this reason, I have not looked at those methods, said to be of general archaeological application, which are informed in character and therefore applicable only to those few contexts, mostly in recent historical archaeology, where there is already a good knowledge.

Stiny's collected papers (1986), the key body of historical studies of a formal and morphological character, are entitled, *Computing with Form and Meaning in Architecture*. If form is the natural domain of formal approaches, what is meaning doing there of all places?—since meaning is the key word that defines the other, the informed school. Here is the deeper point, which is to do with what we mean by "meaning." Two Cambridge colleagues, Renfrew and Hodder, have published extensively on these matters and from opposed viewpoints, the one processual, the other postprocessual. What they have in common is an interest in prehistoric minds; they see as fundamental how prehistoric people saw and understood the world. So what an artifact means is, in large or whole part, what it meant to the people who made and understood it. That is a part of the story but it is not the whole story. For more than two centuries now the human sciences have been studying those regularities in the world that its actors are *not* aware of, whether the hidden hand of economics that guides the markets, or the unconscious forces of psychology that steer the market-maker. To go back to what people *thought* they were doing, as if that alone makes a truth, is to set aside the understanding gained in a couple of centuries of the human sciences. The meaning of artifacts lies more deeply in their fundamental character, their shapes, and in how those shapes and artifacts are treated. It is the case of taking note of what people did and do, rather than guessing at what they might have thought they were doing.

Archaeology is, by the nature of what it studies, concerned with the anonymous and the long-term. Those two things go together. As the *Annales* historians have often shown, what matters is not what kings and princes think or mean or think they mean, but how those human actors behave in relation to the great realities of history: topography, climate, landscape, subsistence, means of production, demography. The great regularities of prehistory take place over so many human generations that one can be sure that larger regularities are involved than anything people were aware of, or consciously chose to do at the time. No *Homo erectus* ever said, "We've had the Acheulean for quite long enough now; it's really time we went on to the Middle Palaeolithic." The real questions, the real issues of "meaning" in artifacts, are in the means by which consistency in design was maintained, and not maintained, over *la longue durée*: there is much more to these things than what people thought they were doing; there is much more to their study than guessing at what people thought they were doing.

REFERENCES

Ackerman, J. 1966. *Palladio*. Penguin, Harmondsworth.

Angell, I. O. 1976. "Stone circles," *Mathematical Gazette* **60**, 189–193.

Barnatt, J., and P. Herring 1986. "Stone circles and megalithic geometry," *Journal of Archaeological Science*.

Barnatt J., and G. Moir 1984. "Stone circles and megalithic mathematics," *Proceedings of the Prehistoric Society* **50**, 197–216.

Barrett, J. 1987. "Contextual archaeology," *Antiquity* **61**, 468–473.

Blegen, C. W., and M. Rawson 1966. *The Palace of Nestor at Pylos in Western Messenia*. Vol. 1, part 2. Princeton University Press, Princeton, NJ.

Blegen, C. W., M. Rawson, S. P. Carter, D. Haigh, N. R. J. Neil, and B. Smith 1984. "Interim Report on the structures at Howe, Stromness, Orkney," *Glasgow Archaeological Journal* **11**, 61–73.

Bloch, C. J. 1979. *A Formal Catalogue of Small Rectangular Plans: Generation, Enumeration, and Classification*. Unpublished Ph.D. thesis, University of Cambridge.

Boast, R., and C. R. Chippindale in press. "A shape-grammar approach to architecture and artifacts; with a worked example from megalithic Orkney," *Journal of Anthropological Archaeology*.

Boast, R., and J. P. Steadman (eds.) 1987. Special issue of *Planning and Design* on analysis of building plans in history and prehistory, *Planning and Design* **14 (4)**, 359–390.

Brown, F. E., and J. H. Johnson 1985. "An interactive computermodel of urban development: The rules governing the morphology of medieval London," *Planning and Design* **12**, 377–400.

Burl A. 1976. *The Stone Circles of the British Isles*. Yale University Press, New Haven.

Carter, S. P., D. Haigh, N. R. J. Neil, and B. Smith 1984. "Interim report on the structures at Howe, Stromness, Orkney," *Glasgow Archaeological Journal* **11**, 61–73.

Chippindale, C. R. 1986. "Archaeology, design-theory and the reconstruction of prehistoric design-systems," *Planning and Design* **14**, 445–485.

———1987. "Formal geometries and the identifying of prehistoric maps." Paper presented at the Annual Meeting of the Society for American Archaeology, Toronto.

———1988. *The Later Prehistoric Rock-Engravings of Val Fontanalba, Mont Bégo, Tende, Alpes-Maritimes, France*. Unpublished Ph.D. dissertation, University of Cambridge.

———forthcoming. *Looking at Prehistoric Pictures: The Bronze Age Rock Engraving of Mont Bégo, Alpine France*. Cambridge University Press, Cambridge.

Chippindale, C. R., and D. Read (eds.) forthcoming. *Grammars of Archaeological Design*.

Cowan, T. M. 1970. "Megalithic rings: Their design and construction," *Science* **168**, 321–325.

Davidson, J. L., and A. S. Henshall 1989. *The Chambered Cairns of Orkney: An Inventory of the Structures and Their Contents*. Edinburgh University Press, Edinburgh.

Foster, S. M. 1989. "Analysis of spatial patterns in buildings (access analysis) as an insight into social structure: Examples from the Scottish Atlantic Iron Age," *Antiquity* **63**, 40–50.

Gardin, J.-C. 1987. *Expert Systems and Scholarly Publications*. British Library, London.

Gardin, J.-C., O. Guillaume, P. O. Herman, A Hesnard, M -S Lagrange, M. Renaud, and E. Zadora-Rio 1987. *Systèmes experts et sciences humaines: le cas de l'archéologie*. Eyrolles, Paris.

Goody, J. 1972. *The Domestication of the Savage Mind*. Cambridge University Press, Cambridge.

Hagen, M. 1986. *Varieties of Realism*. Cambridge University Press, Cambridge.

Heggie, D. C. 1981. *Megalithic Science: Ancient Mathematics and Astronomy in North-West Europe*. Thames and Hudson, London.

Hillier, W., and J. Hanson 1985. *The Social Logic of Space*. Cambridge University Press, Cambridge.

Hodder, I. 1986. *Reading the Past*. Cambridge University Press, Cambridge.

Hodder, I., and C. Orton 1976. *Spatial Analysis in Archaeology*. Cambridge University Press, Cambridge.

Leone, M. P., and P. B. Potter (eds.) 1988. *The Recovery of Meaning: Historical Archaeology in the Eastern United States*. Smithsonian Institution Press, Washington, D.C.

Lethaby, W. R. 1922. *Form in Civilization*. John Muray, London.

March, L. J., and J. P. Steadman 1971. *The Geometry of Environment*. RIBA, London.

Palladio, A. de 1738. *The Four Books of Architecture*. I. Ware (tr.). Isaac Ware, London.

Renfrew, A. C. 1985. *The Archaeology of Cult*. British School at Athens, London.

Sabloff, J. R., L. R. Binford, and P. R. McAnany 1987. "Understanding the archaeological record," *Antiquity* **61**, 203–209.

Schafer, H. 1986. *Principles of Egyptian Art*. Griffith Institute, Oxford.

Shanks, M., and C. Tilley 1987. *Re-constructing Archaeology: Theory and Practice*. Cambridge University Press, Cambridge.

Sinclair, A. 1989. *Writing Archaeology*. Thematic issue of *Archaeological Review from Cambridge* **8, 2**.

Soffe, G., and T. Clare 1988. "New evidence of ritual monuments at Long Meg and Her Daughters, Cumbria," *Antiquity* **62**, 552–557.

Steadman, J. P. 1973. *Architectural Morphology*. Pion, London.

Stiny, G. (ed.) 1986. *Computing with Form and Meaning in Architecture*. UCLA Graduate School of Architecture, Los Angeles.

Stiny, G., and W. J. Mitchell 1978. "The Palladian grammar," *Environment and Planning* **85**, 5–18.

Thom, A., A. S. Thom, and A. Burl 1980. *Megalithic Rings*. British Archaeological Reports British Series 81, Oxford.

Voorrips, A. 1987. "Review of Gardin et al. 1987," *Antiquity* **61** 481–482.

Walton, J. 1956. *African Villages*. Van Shaik, Pretoria.

Whittle, A. W. R. in press. "Silbury Hill, Wiltshire: Excavations in 1968–70 by R. J. C. Atkinson," *Proceedings of the Prehistoric Society*.

Logicist Analysis, Exterior Knowledge, and Ethnoarchaeological Research

> En philosophie, il faut distinguer entre les proposi-
> tions qui expriment la pente de notre pensée et
> celles qui *résolvent* le problème.
> Wittgenstein (1985:52)

This paper will illustrate, through a case study, the method of "logicist reconstruction" and will illuminate (a) the benefits offered by this type of analysis for assessing the epistemological value of our archaeological interpretations and (b) the importance of reference to the regularities upon which we found our hypotheses.

Let it be recalled that the basic principle of logicist analysis (see also Gardin et al. 1981) is that archaeological (or any other) knowledge should be "well formed" and empirically verifiable. The principle of "well formed" necessitates the development of explicit derivations which enable the transition from the initial propositions (the facts mobilized in the construction) to the terminal proposition (the final interpretation). The implied rewriting of archaeological reasoning, and the consequent demonstration of log-ico-semantic operations, will reveal the bases on which inferences are made and will allow us to evaluate the validity of our interpretations in comparison with the principle of verifiability. In this sense, logicist analysis comes under practical epistemology, which is its major point.

The example chosen is based on an ethnoarchaeological study which approaches the concept of craft specialization on the basis of material facts. The procedure adopted for approaching this problem is as follows:
— observation in the ethnographic field of a relationship between ceramic material and the concept of craft specialization;
— comprehension of the mechanism responsible for the relationship and definition of the context in which this relationship is a univocal one;
— definition of the traits intrinsic to ceramics which are significant to the relationship; transfer of the relationship on to comparable archaeological material.

Reference to an exterior knowledge for the interpretation of archaeological data does not present epistemological problems, in the sense that it is a necessary fact, as Gallay has underlined (1986). According to him, all archaeological interpretations make use of "regularities": these are relations or correlations between properties (intrinsic and/or extrinsic properties of the material facts) and attributes (significances of all types). These regularities are formulated following ethnoarchaeological, experimental, or historical studies. When transferred on to archaeological data, they serve as a basis for building up interpretative constructions. It is the regularities that will become the subject of laws, although the historical scenarios will remain local and undetermined.

Considering the importance of exterior knowledge in the process of interpretation, ethnoarchaeology provides a choice approach for dealing with problems of archaeological interpretation. Its task, strictly speaking, is to formulate regularities or, again, to propose an exterior knowledge which complies with the specificity of archaeological matters.

Logicist analysis, reference to an exterior knowledge, and ethnoarchaeological research are thus the three components of our study, logicist analysis bringing out the importance and the merits of ethnoarchaeological reasoning.

1. Example of Logicist Analysis: The Phenomenon of Craft Specialization

The ethnoarchaeological investigations reviewed in this paper were conducted in India with the collaboration of Daniela Corbetta, researcher in developmental psychology at Geneva University.

In this paper, only the main stages of reasoning are presented. The details of the investigation are available in Roux (1989).

The definition adopted for craft specialization is the following: the taking over, by a part of the population, of a craft activity whose products are consumed by the community. This definition does not make a judgment about the economic status (full-time, part-time) or the social context of the craftsmen. It only describes the distribution of knowledge within a community.

The theoretical hypothesis is as follows: if it is demonstrated that, prior to the appearance of the wheel, coiled ceramics were made domestically, it should be possible to describe the phenomenon of craft specialization among potters of prehistoric times through a diachronic study of wheel-thrown ceramics. This hypothesis overlaps the following one: while the coiling technique can be executed by all domestic groups of a community, the wheel-throwing technique can be performed only by specialists.

In order to evaluate the validity of these hypotheses, observational and experimental data have been collected. The data were selected in terms of their relevance to the following hypotheses: it is possible to base the "wheel-throwing technique/craft specialization" relationship on a comparison between the learning processes witnessed in the wheel-throwing technique and the coiling technique, respectively. The comparison will have to do with the degrees of difficulty and of motor complexity inherent to each of these techniques. The observational data are the information gathered about the apprenticeship process in the wheel-throwing technique and in the coiling technique in the state of Haryana (northwest India). The experimental data include: (a) perceptual motor tests on children of potters and of nonpotters; these tests have been devised in terms of the various bimanual activities or motor aptitudes executed in throwing pottery; (b) the reproduction of pots by children who learn the wheel-throwing technique; the children had to make not only the pots characteristic of their highest stage of learning, but also those of earlier stages. Video films have been made of this production. These recordings have made it possible to conduct a detailed study of the gestures involved in the execution of the different phases of manufacturing a pot (centering, hollowing, throwing, shaping); (c) also filmed was the reproduction of jars, pots, hearths, and silos made by coiling.

The Initial Propositions or "Facts"

The initial propositions are the facts mobilized by the interpretative construction. We have here two categories of facts: ethnographic facts (observational and experimental facts) and archaeological facts. These latter have been invented. Indeed, it has not been possible to examine the archaeological material in accordance with the desired criteria. For purposes of ethnoarchaeological reasoning, we have therefore devised an imaginary archaeological situation which is expressed in propositions PO8 and PO9.

The following are, in a simplified manner, the main propositions (PO) which express these facts:

PO1: According to the indigenous setting, apprenticeship in the wheel-throwing technique involves three main stages. The markers for these are the types of pots. These types are of simple shapes (flower-pot type), the entire skill of the potter consisting in throwing a higher and higher vertical surface. The apprenticeship starts about the age of eight and the last stage is only achieved in adulthood.

PO2: The three major apprenticeship stages are expressed through the transition from bimanual activities which take place on both sides of the axis of rotation of the turning wheel (stage 1) to the bimanual activities which take place to the right of the axis of rotation of the turning wheel (stage 2), and through the control of stronger and stronger pressures on larger and larger lumps of clay (stage 3).

PO3: The number of manufacturing operations and the time taken for manufacture increase according to the size of the pot. On the other hand, operations and times decrease as the children advance through the apprenticeship stages.

PO4: The perceptual motor tests show:
— an improvement, during the apprenticeship stages, of the motor abilities relating to the bimanual activities involved in the different phases of manufacture of the pots. These are stability of the forearms and control over pressures;
— among potters, the development of bimanual activities specific to their craft, which is seen in their performance during tests, as compared to the performance of nonpotters;
— a right-hand specialization among potters, marked by lateralization. This is expressed through a greater firmness of the right hand required for throwing clay surfaces.

PO5: The experimental ceramic production shows intrinsic traits which vary according to the different apprenticeship stages. These are: the height, the opening, the height/thickness ratio, the index of regularity of throwing (established on the basis of the sum of the squares of the differences between the right and left thickness of the surfaces), the index of standardization (value of the root-mean-squares that are seen in the absolute dimensions from one stage to the other for each type of pot).

PO6: Apprenticeship in the coiling technique is of short duration. There is essentially one stage to be reached and the difficulty lies not in acquiring the gestures, but in the capacity to juxtapose the coils in the desired alignment, that is to say, in terms of the lower part and of the shape of the vase planned to be made.

PO7: The gestures employed for making a coiled pot are similar to the gestures which are executed naturally since childhood and for household activities (any gestures for gripping). These gestures, when compared to those related to the wheel-throwing technique, are all the more natural, because it is the hand which moves and the pot which is stationary, and not the other way around, as is the case for the wheel-throwing technique. In this sense, the gestures used for making a coiled pot are much easier as they do not require an absolute firmness of the arms and they are organized around a single parameter, which is the pressure of the fingers.

PO8: The archaeological assemblages under examination have wheel-thrown pots whose traits are comparable to the traits significant to the different stages of apprenticeship (progressive increase in the height of the pots turned, regularity of throwing, etc.). The stages of technical development of wheel-thrown pottery are thus comparable to the stages followed today in the apprenticeship of wheel-thrown pottery.

PO9: Before the appearance of the potter's wheel, ceramics were made by nonspecialists.

The Intermediary Propositions

The intermediary propositions make it possible to connect the initial data with the conclusion. The initial data from which these propositions are derived are in brackets.

(PO1, PO2, PO3, PO4) P1: Apprenticeship in the wheel-throwing technique is long and difficult. The throwing activity requires (a) bimanual activity executed to the right of the axis of rotation of the wheel, which is complicated; (b) some prerequisites (strength of the potter) and control over a series of motor and physical parameters which are interdependent: speed of rotation of the turning wheel, centering, steadfastness of pressures, immobility of forearms, bimanual coordination, size of the lump. All the activities connected with the throwing must take these factors into account. They are difficult to learn and take time to acquire. Only the skillful are capable of executing them.

(PO6, PO8, PO9, P2) P3: Description of craft specialization process according to the descriptive traits of wheel-thrown ceramics found on archaeological sites.

(P3, Pi, Pj) P4: Proposition on the craft specialization phenomenon in the techno-economic context observed (indicated by Pi, Pj).

This last proposition represents the terminal proposition.

The bases for the intermediary propositions can be set forth as follows:
— for P1: the wheel-throwing technique implies a long and difficult apprenticeship. This is a relationship of a universal character, considering the experimental data which corroborate in causal terms the implicit hypothesis about the transcultural value of the empirically observed correlation. This relationship is verifiable through experimentation. It is univocal and necessary in the sense that physiological constraints prevent a short and easy learning of the wheel-throwing technique. Its context of univocity and appli-

cation is the universe of *Homo sapiens sapiens*: it exists on account of physiological constraints which are postulated as being identical through the ages.

— for P2: the wheel-throwing technique implies craft specialization. This is also a univocal relationship, recalling P1. It is not reciprocal, at least in the sense that craft specialization can be a fact of other techniques such as the coiling technique. Moreover, the relationship is not necessary, at least in the sense that the appearance of the wheel-throwing technique does not necessarily imply that it is a consequence of specialization. A favorable sociocultural environment is required for the adoption of an inventive technique and its consequences (Leroi-Gourhan 1945, 1973). The context of application of the relationship is the context in which P1 is univocal: it includes every community of *Homo sapiens sapiens*. To refute this relationship or to restrict the context of its application, it would suffice that we find some examples of ceramic assemblages which are entirely wheel-thrown and produced on the domestic scale.

To support the argument which is at the basis of this relationship, there should be either other examples of apprenticeship in which the "duration and difficulty" variables are decisive to a craft specialization, or there should be apprehension of craft specialization by another measurement whose application to the archaeological data would give the same results.

— for P3: the similarity of context (*Homo sapiens sapiens* community) and of material (wheel-thrown ceramics PO5 and PO8)), and the univocal nature of the "wheel-throwing technique/craft specialization" relationship validate the transfer of the ethnographic attributes to the archaeological data.

For P3 to be valid, PO9 must be attested. Studies have yet to be made to this end, which would enable the presenting of a univocal relationship between the coiling technique (in particular) and the "domestic or specialized" attributes.

P4 is an inferential proposition whose validity is dependent on P3 and the other propositions taken into account (Pi, Pj).

The initial propositions are also susceptible to clarification as regards their bases (relevance of the observational data, validity of the experiment, etc.). Without going into details, a short account of the bases for the seven ethnographic propositions will be given (PO8 and PO9 have been put aside, since they relate to an imaginary archaeological situation):

PO1, PO6: The apprenticeship stages of the wheel-throwing and the coiling techniques are described on the basis of oral data. Indian potters themselves consider different apprenticeship stages to be indicated by the type of vessel.

PO2, PO3, PO7: The apprenticeship stages of the wheel-throwing technique are described in terms of empirically observable data (the gestures, the number of operations, and the throwing time involved in the making of the vessels characteristic of each stage of apprenticeship). The correlations brought out between these empirical data and the apprenticeship stages are the result of observations made on the ceramic production of thirty subjects at different levels of skill. As for the gestures characteristic to the coiling technique, these were observed for only six subjects. However, the products of manufacture were diverse, lending a general character to the observations

PO4: The perceptual motor tests were devised to evaluate the activities specific to the wheel-throwing technique. These tests were conducted under homogeneous conditions.

The different subjects submitted themselves to these tests at the same place and on the same wheel. From a methodological point of view, they are therefore admissible. One criticism against the validity of the results could relate to the size of the sample (we were able to interview only thirty potter subjects and thirty nonpotter subjects).

PO5: The wheel-thrown ceramic assemblage on which we observed a correlation between intrinsic traits and the different stages of apprenticeship represents a body of experimental data gathered under controlled conditions. It has the advantage:

a) of representing each stage of apprenticeship. We asked several subjects from each stage to reproduce three specimens of the different types of pots learned in the course of the various stages;
b) of having been obtained under homogeneous conditions. We asked each potter subject to come and make the vessels at the house of our potter informant, who himself prepared the lumps of clay.

Once again, criticism of the correlations that were observed could be related to the size of the sample.

2. Comments and Conclusions

2.1 The three components of the study: logicist analysis, reference knowledge, and ethnoarchaeology

Logicist Analysis

Figure 1 recapitulates in the form of a diagram the preceding analysis and illustrates the method of logicist reconstruction of our reasoning. Only the elements necessary for the interpretative construction are taken into account. The basis of each logico-semantic operation is clearly expressed. Lastly, the interpretative propositions are verifiable and decidable. P3 and P4 are verifiable on account of the verifiability of P2 and P1; they are decidable on the basis of the analogy between PO5 and PO8 and of the univocal character of the "wheel-throwing technique/craft specialization" relationship which makes valid the transfer of P2 on to PO8 and validates the P3 inference, keeping PO9 in mind.

The epistemological value of the interpretative propositions is assessable in terms of the logico-semantic problems characteristic of these propositions. The logicist diagram of the interpretative reasoning enables the easy and rapid detection of the strong and weak points of the construction, the widening at will of the base, and the modifying of the inferences according to new data, whether by the author himself or by other researchers.

Reference Knowledge

Reference knowledge is of prime importance in the process of archaeological interpretation. This process is made up of three stages:

1. Observation of an analogy between ethnographic and archaeological material facts,

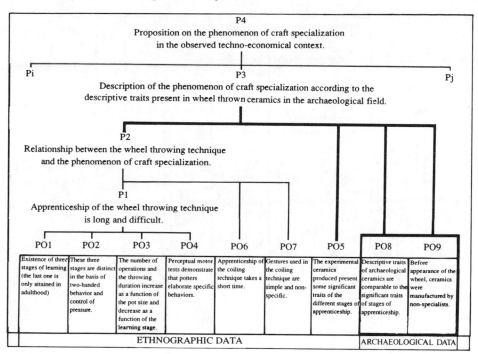

P4 Proposition on the phenomenon of craft specialization in the observed techno-economical context.								
Pi	**P3** Description of the phenomenon of craft specialization according to the descriptive traits present in wheel thrown ceramics in the archaeological field.							Pj
P2 Relationship between the wheel throwing technique and the phenomenon of craft specialization.								
P1 Apprenticeship of the wheel throwing technique is long and difficult.								
PO1	PO2	PO3	PO4	PO6	PO7	PO5	PO8	PO9
Existence of three stages of learning (the last one is only attained in adulthood)	These three stages are distinct in the basis of two-handed behavior and control of pressure.	The number of operations and the throwing duration increase as a function of the pot size and decrease as a function of the learning stage.	Perceptual motor tests demonstrate that potters elaborate specific behaviors.	Apprenticeship of the coiling technique takes a short time.	Gestures used in the coiling technique are simple and non-specific.	The experimental ceramics produced present some significant traits of the different stages of apprenticeship.	Descriptive traits of archaeological ceramics are comparable to the significant traits of stages of apprenticeship.	Before appearance of the wheel, ceramics manufactured by non-specialists.
ETHNOGRAPHIC DATA							ARCHAEOLOGICAL DATA	

Figure 1. Logicist diagram of the interpretive construction on craft specialization.

and between the contexts of these facts. The term ethnographic has to be understood in its wider sense: historical, geographic, sociological, ethnographic, etc. In this study, the facts compared are PO5 and PO8. The context is represented by the *Homo sapiens sapiens* community.

2. Transfer of the attributes of the ethnographic facts on to the archaeological facts. The term attribute encompasses here not only the attributes of time, of place, and of function, but also complex anthropological propositions. In our study, the transfer is that of P2 on to PO8, taking account of the univocal character that P2 presents (determined by P1) and of PO9.

3. From this analogical base, an inference operation which leads to the conclusion. In this case P3 is the analogical base and P4 the inference.

We have converted this procedure of interpretation into the form of a diagram in Figure 2. It expresses the extent to which archaeological interpretation depends in its essence on a reasoning by analogy. The roles played by deduction and induction relate to the ethnographic and archaeological facts and to the analogical base obtained through the transfer of attributes. This reasoning can be formalized in the following manner:

$$\text{if } p \text{ in context } C \rightarrow q \text{ or } q \text{ and only } q$$
$$\text{and if } (p, C) \text{ is analogous to } (p', C')$$
$$\text{then } p' \text{ in context } C' \rightarrow q$$

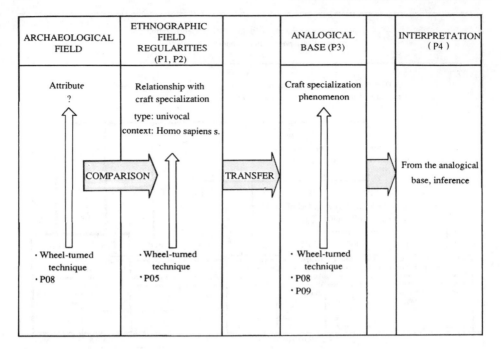

Figure 2. Structure of the interpretation procedure.

The verifiability and the decidability of interpretative propositions therefore depend essentially on regularities. The interpretations are verifiable in comparison with the regularity invoked (for example, P2). They are decidable in terms of archaeological facts (for example, PO5 and PO9) and of the context of univocity of the regularity which defines the conditions for the transfer of the attribute on to the archaeological data. When regularities are posed in univocal terms (univocal relationship between properties and attributes), problems of interpretation which arise out of the multivocal nature of the material facts are overcome. If the relationship invoked is not univocal in the context of observation, this implies that other relationships can be applied to the material facts. The transfer of a non-univocal relationship will not make the interpretation false, but will place it in the category of the plausible.

To pose the univocity of a relationship between properties and attributes, one is required to go beyond empirical observations and to understand the mechanisms which explain the existence of the relationship. Thus the ''wheel-throwing technique/craft specialization'' relationship has been posed as a univocal one, taking onto account the learning problems of individuals and the solution required by these problems on the scale of the community.

Ethnoarchaeology

Ethnoarchaeology is an ideal discipline to formulate regularities and to understand the mechanisms which explain them, because of the nature of its field of observation: properties, attributes, and context are well known to it. The conditions are therefore perfect for observing and understanding the extent to which relationships between properties and attributes are valid in a given context.

In other words, ethnoarchaeological investigations enable us to demarcate, by a context, the transcultural character of regularities that allow their transfer on to archaeological data. This is the context in which regularities are observed. Thus every regularity displays a strictly "local," non-"universal" character which is to be defined by understanding the mechanisms of the regularity. The context is always subject to respecification during the course of research, following a comparison with new situations. In the case of our study, the context of validity of the regularity "long and difficult apprenticeship/craft specialization" should be restricted if we are to apply it to any craft. Following a comparison between hunter-gatherers and agriculturalists, the variable "number of crafts achieved in the community" can be retained as pertinent to restrict the context of our regularity to communities in which the whole of technical knowledge cannot be possessed by each individual but is necessarily distributed among them. Regularities are enclosed in original and complex socioeconomic systems. Such originality and complexity will be described by archaeologists on the basis of the archaeological data and the present regularities.

2.2 Objections to the Logicist Approach

In the course of preparing this text, a few objections have been voiced, and these are examined at this point. They address essentially the use of the logicist approach for archaeological interpretations.

One objection relates to the severity of the logicist requirement which implies a knowledge based on empirical data. The belief is that the human phenomenon is so complex that it can never be described as a whole through the use of such methods. It is a fact that our study is very limited in terms of sociocultural information. It only demonstrates the validity of the "wheel-throwing technique/craft specialization" relationship, a relationship whose semantics are weak in comparison with the meaningful relationships in terms of sociocultural explanations: e.g., "emergence of an elite/craft specialization," "urbanization/craft specialization," "maximization of profits/craft specialization," etc.

The point is that the proposed relationship can be assessed from the epistemological point of view. Consequently it permits a description of the craft specialization phenomenon, whose validity can be verified. Subsequently, to study the conditions in which the wheel-throwing technique developed, the types of communities which adopted this technique, and the form of specialization established, one should call upon other constructions, other reference knowledge, and propose complementary constructions. An example of complementary construction can be found in the study of PO9 and of the craft specialization problem prior to the appearance of the potter's wheel. Elements other than apprenticeship should be suggested for distinguishing the techniques which are practiced on the domestic scale from those which are practiced by specialists. This construction would come as a fortunate complement to the one presented here, which itself has to be considered as a preliminary study of the phenomena of craft specialization one can observe in different socioeconomic systems. Here the belief is that the knowledge of human phenomena can be based on the analyses of relationships between variables which are empirically verifiable and that will be inserted in a general interpretative construction.

A second objection concerns the reductionist aspect of the knowledge of human phenomena formed in this manner. As a matter of fact, in this study, it has not been suggested that the craft specialization phenomenon is of a strictly preceptual motor nature or again that its explanation is to be found in only this point of view. No attempt has been made to isolate and identify the different causes responsible for the emergence of the craft specialization phenomena, or even to suggest why its development was slow (in the archaeological example invented). No explanatory hypothesis of the phylogenesis/ontogenesis type has been proposed. An awareness of the importance of the sociocultural context in the appearance of such phenomena has been maintained and the proposed study aims only at comprehending the functional links between the wheel-throwing technique and the craft specialization phenomenon.

A third objection, of a more general order, that has been raised concerns the principles of logicist analysis and the fact that it may restrict creative abilities out of which arise theoretical explanations. The power of imagination need not be bridled by strict epistemology. The point is that our ambitions for interpretation are bridled when one accepts the principle of verifiability.

2.3 Other Approaches

Other ways have been suggested for interpretations of the history of society. These fall into two general categories. The first brings together approaches which seek to validate interpretations through material facts. Such approaches lay stress on the structuring or classification of data and the significance of the structures or typologies brought to light. The second category unites approaches which do not consider validation by material facts as the only criteria for an appropriate interpretation. The first category of approaches will now be examined with reference to studies of craft specialization. Three works representative of this form of archaeological reasoning are Rice 1981, Torrence 1986, and Tosi 1984. These three studies relate to the procedures to be followed in order to arrive at an inference about the presence of craft specialization on the basis of material facts gathered from the archaeological record.

For Rice, craft specialization is related to the emergence of an elite and to their subsequent control over ceramic resources (reserves of clay and production of vessels). This control would be exercised first on the ceramics produced by one particular group of potters. This is the beginning of specialization. When this first group is given the responsibility for manufacturing the entire corpus of ceramics, the control will become total and specialization will become complete. To study the craft specialization phenomenon in this way, Rice retains two descriptive features which characterize the control of the resources by an elite: (1) the degree of standardization and (2) the degree of diversification in the properties of ceramics (paste, technology, decoration, shape).

Torrence considers craft specialization in terms of the maximization of profits. Craft specialization is treated as one of the significant elements in different types of exchange.

To evaluate the degree of maximization of profits, Torrence examines lithic assemblages from the point of view of (1) efficiency (incidence of errors, technique of preparation of the core, degree of standardization of the finished tools and of *débitage*), (2) the density of production, and (3) the rate of consumption. The density of production is calculated from the number of hours required to obtain the waste byproducts observed, taking into account the duration of occupation during which these waste byproducts were deposited. The rate of consumption is calculated from the number of tools on the site. Assemblages involving an efficient technology (gain in time, concentration of effort, and ready availability of raw material) and a large corresponding labor force (according to the rates of production and consumption) are interpreted as resulting from the work of craftsmen who are more specialized than those whose lithic output shows the opposite characteristics.

For Tosi, craft specialization is a phenomenon connected to the progressive control by the elite over craftsmanship. In this sense, craft specialization is responsible for the emergence of class societies. To study craft specialization within an archaeological context, Tosi proposes to distinguish several forms of organization of craft production which are indicative of the degree of its control by an elite. The archaeological evidence taken into account on a site includes the surface area covered by indicators relating to the craft, the density of those indicators and the degree of spatial coherence of products indicating a technological process. Depending on the formal configurations observed, craft production can be interpreted in terms of the degree of control exercised over it by the elite and, in this sense, in terms of the degree of specialization.

Only the broad outlines of these studies have been presented. They will suffice to bring out the problems of verifiability that arise out of this type of interpretation.

Rice and Tosi seek to infer from material data the degree of control exercised by an elite over craft production, and they postulate that this expresses the degree of craft specialization. Table 1 presents the material data from which Rice infers control over production.

One objection to this approach is related to the postulate used to define craft specialization: the degree of specialization is defined by the degree of control over production. Ethnographic data do not justify the validity of the definition, since there are examples of groups of specialized craftsmen independent of any central control, thus invalidating the univocal nature of the "craft specialization/control over the production by an elite" relationship. The proposed postulate seems to correspond in fact to a hypothesis or a correlation whose explanation could enable us to define its context of application on to archaeological data.

The material facts used to infer the degree of control over the production by an elite will now be examined.

The descriptive traits used by Rice are standardization and diversification. For example, the standardization of paste and of shapes of utilitarian pottery is considered to be significant to craft specialization, since standardization would appear only following the restriction of ceramic production to a single group of potters. This reorganization of tasks would be due to the elite gaining control over ceramic production. This reasoning implies that the relationship between standardization and the restriction of ceramic production to one group of potters is universal. It also implies that there is a relationship

MATERIAL FACTS	FIRST INFERENCE LEVEL	SECOND INFERENCE LEVEL
- variation in technique - variation in decoration and shape in accordance with idiosyncratic factors - no standardization of paste, shape, or decoration - no elite pottery	There is no control over production.	No specialization
- more skill in technique - less variation in decoration and shape - more standardization of paste - wider distribution of standardized products	Potters situated near the clay sources are more highly productive; this becomes associated with a lineage.	Nascent specialization
- diversification of ceramic assemblage - irregular distribution of pottery classes - elite pottery recognizable by some characteristic decorations; standardized paste - imitation of elite pottery	Emergence of an elite leads to control of the clay sources and a part of the ceramic production.	Craft specialization in the making
- specialized tools; utility pottery; shapes which facilitate storage and transport; mass-production of finished products - standardized work area - large distribution of standardized products - elite pottery with elaborate decoration	The potters produce a surplus, whose distribution is controlled by the elite.	Process of craft specialization has reached completion.

Table 1. Material facts noted by Rice (1981) as important when making an inference about craft specialization on archaeological sites.

between this "restriction" and the control of the production by an elite. The phenomenon of standardization can be connected to other factors as well: for example, an improvement in the technique, or again an increase in production (something which has been observed with the wheel-throwing technique). To verify these hypotheses, the context in which standardization shows a univocal relationship with a particular distribution of the tasks should be specified, as should the context in which the reorganization of the tasks presents such a relationship with a control of ceramic production by an elite.

Tosi's approach to documenting craft specialization in the archaeological record has problems of a magnitude similar to those of Rice. The significance of the material facts is treated as universal, whereas it could be only local. The result is that counterexamples can invalidate the inferences. Thus the concentration of workshops on the principal sites of a region does not necessarily mean that craft production was in the hands of a central authority. It could result from the presence of a group of craftsmen who are independent of a central government.

Torrence's study also raises problems of validity resulting from an interpretation based on inferences whose context of validity is not sufficiently restricted. To evaluate the validity of the "maximization of profits/craft specialization" relationship, it would be necessary to study the basis of this relationship within an ethnographic context.

An evaluation of the validity of these approaches to the documentation of the presence of craft specialization on archaeological sites can be reduced in all cases to two questions: What are the bases for the inferences; and how do we verify the interpretations empirically? In other words, although the interpretations retained are rich and stimulating from an anthropological and intellectual point of view, they leave open the question of their own validity. One can hope that in the future it will be possible to verify them. To this end, it seems that regularities are needed, and that these must be defined either in ethnographic or in experimental contexts.

Other approaches in archaeological interpretation exist which make no reference to the verification procedures. For example, symbolic approaches (Hodder 1982) consider the comprehension of human phenomena as a more important matter than the validation of the interpretations. Such approaches relate to the symbolic structure of societies. They cannot be validated, as there is no means of posing univocal relationships between material facts and their symbolic value. Moreover, they are not verifiable, as no regularities exist on the basis of which it is possible to infer symbolic structures particular to each society.

3. Conclusion

Approaches within which verification procedures are ignored make it difficult to choose from among interpretations. In the same way, it appears difficult to choose among interpretations whose context of validity is not locally restricted and defined by reference to ethnographic or experimental studies. Such a definition implies an explanation of the mechanisms that produce the regularities. Such explanations will allow the demarcation of the local context in which regularities present a transcultural value that permits their application to archaeological data. It is not illusory to think that numerous regularities can be brought to light: physical, biological, and ecological variables can present numerous functional links in various combinations when considered within different technoeconomic systems that are analyzed in terms of different constraints and different possible strategies. As an example, the duration of apprenticeship is a significant part of craft specialization in complex technoeconomic systems when analyzed in terms of the necessary distribution of knowledge within a community. These regularities are all the more interesting since they open the way to the construction of a reference knowledge which should allow us (a) on the basis of archaeological data to study the conditions under which technoeconomic systems evolved, as well as the solutions adopted by different sociocultural systems, and (b) to assess the epistemological value of our writings when judged against the principles of logicist analysis.

REFERENCES

Gallay, A. 1986. *L'archéologie demain*. Belfond, Paris.
Gardin, J.-C. 1979. *Une archéologie théorique*. Hachette, Paris.
Gardin, J.-C., M.-S. Lagrange, J. M. Martin, J. Molino, and J. Natali 1981. *La logique du plausible*. La Maison des Sciences de l'Homme, Paris.
Hodder, I. (ed.) 1982. *Symbols in Action*. Cambridge University Press, Cambridge.
Leroi-Gourhan, A. 1945 and 1973. *Milieu et techniques*. Albin Michel, Paris.

Rice, P. M. 1981. "Evolution of specialized pottery production: A trial model," *Current Anthropology* **22**, 219–240.
Roux, V., in collaboration with D. Corbetta 1989. *The Potter's Wheel: Craft Specialization and Technical Competence*. Oxford and IBH, New Delhi.
Torrence, R. 1986. *Production and Exchange of Stone Tools*. Cambridge University Press, Cambridge.
Tosi, M. 1984. "The notion of craft specialization and its representation in the archaeological record of early states in the Turanian basin," in M. Spriggs (ed.), *Marxist Perspectives in Archaeology*, pp. 22–52. Cambridge University Press, Cambridge.
Wittgenstein, L. 1985. *Etudes préparatoires à la 2ème partie des recherches philosophiques*. G. H. von Wright and N. Nyman (eds.). Trans-Europ-Repress, Paris.

The Sense of Measure in Archaeology

AN APPROACH TO THE ANALYSIS OF PROTO-URBAN SOCIETIES
WITH THE AID OF AN EXPERT SYSTEM

1. Introduction

The present contribution takes a modest but deliberate cognitive perspective insofar as it attempts to reconstruct, through simulation, certain elements of (contemporary) archaeological reasoning on the one hand, and certain manifestations of the mental functioning of humans from times past on the other. Of these two aspects, the contemporary and the ancient, the former is more methodological and the latter more thematic, but they are not, essentially, categorically different, at least on the time scale used here, which does not extend beyond the limits of the last eight thousand years (i.e., well within the span of fully modern humans, *Homo sapiens sapiens*).

These two aspects of mentation, the contemporary and the ancient, will be termed, in the body of this paper, doxography and physiography, respectively.[1] These terms indicate a measured ambition, one which is to describe (not explain) opinions (not theories) and things. That is to say, by fixing these limits, we will leave aside the adjectives ending in "—ic" and "—ical" (e.g., theoretic, methodological, numerical, etc.), which are readily appended to various aspects of contemporary archaeology, and we will apply ourselves to understanding how it is done, *hic et nunc*, without hesitating to employ *ad hoc* means.

In other words, we will maintain a strictly archaeological outlook, but one that is situated on a level of representation that is both lower than those of encompassing sociocultural reconstructions, and higher than those of stratigraphies and taxonomies. Indeed, the latter pair, although they can be discussed, multiplied, and refined *ad infinitum*, may be considered as being almost universally taken for granted, whereas the former are rarely taken for granted, and can generally be repeated and multiplied *ad nauseam*. These large sociocultural reconstructions, which abound in symbolism, but not much more, are generally unsuited to archeological applications in the field: they therefore must be manipulated within the structure of sociocultural theories, as models that continue to function no matter what, since they are perfectly untestable. Work by

D. Miller in India provides two instructive examples (1985a, 1985b), but these are only two of many.

The present analysis is situated at the level of mental representations—at a cognitive level—which, following Howard Gardner, is "wholly separate from the biological or neurological, on the one hand, and the sociological or cultural, on the other" (Gardner 1985:6). Given the goals of this analysis, the choice of this level, and this is an important point, is absolutely necessary for operational reasons (see Gardner 1985:383–392). This cognitive level of images, schemes, rules, and transformations, excludes the wider concerns of mood and belief, at least for the present (see Fodor 1983; Pylyshyn 1984), but inclusion of these aspects of mentation are not inconceivable in the future (Gardner 1985:390–392). Furthermore, there are good reasons for keeping our goals modest at the moment: as Douglas Hofstadter notes: "It is both baffling and disturbing to me to see so many people working on imitating cognitive functions at the highest level of sophistication when their programs cannot carry out cognitive functions at much lower levels of sophistication" ("Waking up from the Boolean Dream, or, Subcognition as Computation" in Hofstadter 1985:638).

Hence, beyond the skepticism of the contemporary "affaire Dreyfus"[2] (McCorduck 1979), but short of the "dream" of Simon and Newell (Hofstadter 1985:638), we will pose for our subject a level of operational representation on which the notions will be calculable, appraisable, measurable, and on which the sequence of inferences will be verifiable. We find here the exigencies formulated by Gardin (1979) about the verification of the inferences, which are akin, to a certain extent, to the demands made by Binford for instruments of measurement (1982:129) and for the "middle range theories" (1981; 1983), as well as the prediction made by Gallay (1986:280) about an archaeology "in which we will be able to broach only those matters whose replies are liable to be verified in facts."

To these limits, placed above by "the present state of the art" and below by our choice, is added the one which is imposed by the necessity of working on a representation of knowledge. This constraint is nothing but our supposedly scientific representation of remains of the past. Consequently, we never analyze anything other than our thought: "my thought is that the thought of men of earlier times was . . . " There would be nothing in this, other than banality, were it not that we have to admit also the conventional character of this representation and hence that the "fact" and the "object" itself are conventional.

Wittgenstein has written that "establishing the method of measurement precedes the accuracy or the inaccuracy of the data of length" (1983:91) and that "calculation determines what the empirical facts are" (1983:306).

In spite of its shocking appearance, Wittgenstein's attitude is the only one which will enable us to advance within a cognitive perspective. Indeed, far from adopting the constructivist theory of Piaget, and still less the tenets of behaviorism, we feel that an innatism, an appeal to innate, inborn mental structures, in the manner of Chomsky and Fodor (see Piatelli-Palmarini 1979; Fodor 1983, and more recent publications), is likely to supply a theoretical support, suitable to a cognitive enterprise, even in archaeology. Why should this be the case? And why is it necessary to make reference to it at all?

In other words, at what level should such a measurable representation be situated for archaeology? Let us return for a moment to the cognitive sciences. Gardner (1983), in his *Frames of Mind*, sets out the theory of multiple intelligence in which there is a convergence of "linguistic intelligence," "musical intelligence," "logico-mathematical intelligence," "spatial intelligence," and "bodily-kinesthetic intelligence": he develops the question of the socialization of intelligence and of its development through education. Now, technical intelligence is missing in this panorama—perhaps because technical intelligence is only a synthesis of the linguistic, logico-mathematical, spatial, and bodily-kinesthetic intelligences. Yet, whether it be singular and basic or composite, this technical intelligence is at the heart of the matter, as Leroi-Gourhan had noted in *Le geste et la parole* (Gesture and Speech) (1964; 1965), a prophetic work which unfortunately created much less of a stir than did the interpretations of prehistoric art by its author. On the scale of the individual, as much as on that of society, technical intelligence, *technics*, is a gigantic part of the human adventure which, in addition, leaves remarkable traces in relics of bygone times (Leroi-Gourhan 1964:187–198; 1965:35ff). Even more, the symbolic acts themselves, once they have been divested of their meaning and their capacity for abstraction, can be reduced, at this extreme, to structured technical sequences. These are the "mechanical operational sequences" of Leroi-Gourhan (1965:29) as they relate to learning and memory (1965:29, 66) and to language (1965:260). More recently, P. Scheurer has repeated the ideas of Leroi-Gourhan: "The object functions as a memory of all the interactions which affected it from the time of its formation . . . " (1979:310), and " . . . henceforth, neither economics, nor sociology can do without the triplet, time-energy-information, which has become essential for the analysis of the physical world" (*ibid.*).

Time, energy, and information may appear to be very abstract notions to those who are attempting, as we are trying to do, to restore them in their proper proportion to certain archaeological approaches. Yet each is fundamental to our quest.

Time is a basic notion, in archaeology as in history, which is more or less difficult to measure and on which we will not dwell at length. To say too little would result in banalities; to say enough would fill more space than is available. Recall when Augustine posed the question to himself: "What then is time?" He answered: "If no one asks me, I know. If I wish to explain it to someone who asks, I know it not" (*Confessions*, Book II, section 14).

Energy is much more difficult to apprehend, except under certain very precise conditions and within very strict limits, which we will fix more precisely further on. Let us indicate now, however, that archaeology is not required to distinguish energy from matter—a position that contrasts strongly with the practice of most authors, who, although having the best of intentions, then find a stumbling block in the systems of measurement and calculations whose unknown elements are too numerous for a satisfactory solution to be found for their equations (White 1959; Adams 1975, 1978, 1981; van der Leeuw 1981:283ff).

Information appears better suited to an archaeological approach, but, here again, its measurement is not devoid of serious problems, in spite of a few, limited successes, such as those of Johnson (1982). Here, however, information will not be measured in terms of levels within institutions—that is, in terms of general levels of sociocultural organization—but instead in the much narrower, technical sense of information. We apprehend this technical information by measuring "technological operational sequences," sequences of technical acts which result in two aspects of the archaeological object, its form and its spatial position. These two aspects are the only ones which enable one to distinguish an archaeological object from a natural object, because both are the result of "technological operational sequences." The first aspect, the form or phase, is the result of sequences of acts having culminated in the object or in the remnant; the second aspect, the spatial position, is the state of completion of a sequence of events which configures in space the corpus of the archaeological object up to the point it is recovered by the researcher. By way of an inadequate approximation, we could say that the first aspect is the one of "production," and the second is that of "consumption," which concludes with final abandonment. However, in our opinion, the use of expressions such as the production-consumption combination, or terms like cost-profit, optimization, maximization, etc., which are semi-abstractions drawn mainly from the socioeconomic field, is not relevant to archaeological research. Indeed, in the final analysis, their archaeological usage rests only on the more or less synthetic and intuitive perception and evaluation of technological operational sequences. We will not broach here the more or less skillful grafting of socioeconomic or cultural models onto archaeological remains: rhetoric apart, such tactics usually are reduced to an appeal to simplistic patterns.

One example of the problem noted above is provided by the use in archaeology of models of the center/periphery type, like the Modern World-Economy of Wallerstein, which reduces to a small, concentric, Ptolemaic system with an Omphalos and a Tartar, but whose heuristic potential is small. We will take the liberty of contrasting it with Gallay's analysis of the hearths of the Tuareg of the Sahara (Gallay 1988), structures of a deceptive simplicity, in order to measure the divergence between the truly archaeological approach and that of the socioeconomic veneer. Yet the information, formulated in technological operational sequences, in no way excludes the study of vast techno-structures, even those of a symbolic nature. Such an approach does not limit us to the gestures of isolated individuals. Its goal is construction of a sort of generative technology, although we are still far from reaching such points in our analysis. This approach may appear quite limited on account of its relatively low representational level, and on account of a reduction of the object into technical terms (taxonomy and stratigraphy being taken for granted), in which the human actor has been all but cast out. To such criticism we can reply first that we do not seek to dehumanize but rather to deanthropomorphize our practice of archaeology. Second, to seek the limits of the scientifically verifiable field is, for us, an epistemological priority which engenders other heuristic and practical limits, which will be presented in the following paragraphs.

The application of various theories and the selection of certain approaches themselves set limits. Thus, for example, some broad-scale propositions, like those of the coevolution of the mind and culture, or of genes and culture (Lumsden and Wilson 1984), or again those of the codevelopment of speech and tools, are no longer applicable, without new, fine-scale methods from the moment of the appearance of *Homo sapiens sapiens*. When they are draped over Neolithic societies, or even more inappropriately over those from protohistoric periods, such macro-propositions become evanescent. The power of these approaches fades even further as the glimmer appears of what we must truly call the scientific enticement of the significance of symbols and of myths, which tends to reduce the study of techniques to a descriptive archaeometry (alloys, origins, etc.) and reserves the comprehensive (and the fine) parts of research to the most elevated aspects of what is considered human. We take exception to the validity of such research designs, because we consider that technique, when taken as the application of information to matter over the course of time, expresses in the most direct manner the highest manifestations of the human mind in its effort toward creative exactitude and calculation (in the wide sense).

Therefore, the point of view adopted here is one that locates archaeology within the perspective of the cognitive sciences. It establishes a level of representation at which epistemological as well as heuristic measurements are indispensable, simply because it becomes necessary to express the evaluations which are implicit in the whole of archaeology, where there is neither theory, concept, notion, nor fact that is not the result of measurement, even including the minutest of descriptive traits taken from the most lowly of ancient debris.

The discussion that follows is based on principles laid down in the foregoing discussion. It includes an examination, through simulation with the aid of an expert system, of doxography as regards epistemology (§5) and physiography as regards heuristics (§4). These examinations will be followed by the exposition of some rules for the correct use of the expert system (§6) and, last, by a discussion of certain limits of the inferential constructions which can be contemplated in the field under consideration (§7).

It is necessary to begin, however, with a rapid examination of current practices of mensuration in archaeology—methods which have been refined for decades in the discipline (§2) but which are being overtaken by powerful theoretical tools from mathematics and physics (§3). Here again the difficulty of joining the *physis* to the *doxa* will appear and, to express oneself in scholastic terms, already was apparent in the *disputatio* which pitted Panurge against Thaumaste (Rabelais, *Pantagruel*, chaps. XVIII–XX).

2. Measures Which Give No Meaning

We will not speak here about archaeometry, but only and briefly in a summary way about the processing of data.

Reading through contributions in a few specialized publications—such as *Advances in Computer Archaeology, Computer Applications in Archaeology, Science and Archaeology, Informatique et Sciences Humaines, Panorama des traitements de données en archéologies* (published by H. Ducasse for 1981, 1983, 1985), *Informatique et mathématiques appliquées en archéologie* (seminar notes by F. Djindjian, 1986), etc.—enables us to make a few interesting observations. The applications reported therein can be divided into five groups: (a) fieldwork; (b) the databases that result from field and laboratory work (SGBD);[3] (c) graphics produced as a result of these operations; (d) algorithms; and (e) applications.

These algorithms and these applications all have their merits, their faults, and their ardent followers; they have become indispensable, but they do not automatically produce meaning. F. Djindjian, who practices and teaches mathematics and computer science to archaeologists, and who writes in a lucid manner, has said: "On the other hand, the difficulty in execution is to be found on the level of the archaeological formalization of the problem to be dealt with: quality of the corpus, choice of the variables, search for the more or less complex structures of seriation, and above all, definition of procedures for validation of the results" (conclusion of the seminar: Djindjian 1986). On the whole, the difficulty does not lie in the formal tried and tested methods themselves, but in their application by archaeologists. The choice of the variables, the search for structures of seriation, and the procedures of validation are all problems of evaluation and of measurement, on which the interpretation depends, but which are exterior to the methods of calculation utilized. As Thom has pointed out: "In Physiology, Ethnology, in Psychology and Social Sciences, mathematics hardly appears in a form other than statistical recipes whose very legitimacy is suspect" (Thom 1980:113). Thus, in present-day archaeology, calculation, in spite of its sophistication, gives no meaning. What, then, of meaning produced by the grand theories and systems?

3. The Measures Which Give Too Much Meaning

Big physico-mathematical systems (models) have appeared recently in archaeology (see Renfrew, Rowlands, and Seagraves 1982; van der Leeuw 1981b). These models can be grouped under the broad headings of (a) general system theory, (b) catastrophe theory, and (c) what has come to be called Chaos theory—the theory of order that is created through fluctuation.

a) The application of general system theory and other broadly "systemic" approaches by archaeologists has been discussed by Gardin (1979:170ff) and Gallay (1986:78ff) and will not be dwelt upon here. The varieties of system theory employed merely dress old problems in new garb, but they do not provide solutions. Moreover, the deterministic differential equations, each with numerous unknowns, that are a part of system theory cannot be evaluated for almost all archaeological data. Lastly, the mathematician Thom does not even consider these models as worthy of the name "theory": " . . . there is nothing but banality in the notion of system . . . " (Thom 1980:295). In short, the metaphorical use of a pseudo-theory in archaeology cannot be considered a major contribution.

b) Thom's "Catastrophe theory," which is a spatial morphogenetic theory that has its origin in algebraic topology, has been imported recently into the social sciences, including archaeology (Zeeman 1977; Renfrew and Cooke 1979; Zeeman 1982). It has served to "explain" the decline of the proto-state formations (Renfrew 1979:481ff). Reservations about the use of this theory have been expressed (Francfort et al. 1989:334–335); it has been shown that its use is purely metaphorical and, given the way in which it has been applied, it could as well have been replaced by a model of the cycles of the internal combustion engine. Indeed, the choice of one catastrophe (constriction) rather than another is never justified—no more so than that of other types of variables ("allegiance," etc.)—and neither verification nor even measure is ever possible. As Thom writes (1980:123), a qualitative theory is judged subjectively, according to the degree of intellectual satisfaction that it brings. Thus, Thom takes us back to the starting point. Let us remove catastrophic paraphrases and archaeological pseudo-explanations, because in doing so we will show them for what they truly are: pure products of our sociocultural subjectivity. Their stimulating side is not even apparent in the replacement of the semantic intuition by unverified geometrical intuition (Thom 1980:123).

c) The theory of "self-organizing, non-equilibrium, thermodynamic systems" (what has come to be called the Science of Chaos) advanced by I. Prigogine (Prigogine and Stengers 1979) has also slipped into archaeology (van der Leeuw 1981b; Allen 1982). There is no need to go into the details of the "theory" here: such would only recount the catastrophe of the theory and its applications in archaeology. One must note in passing, however, that in archaeology it has been employed to explain the State (van der Leeuw 1981b), through the intermediary of a vortex representing the flow of information and of organization in the "system," which itself is a rather vague entity (see Thom 1980:285–286 on complexity). A flood of seventy pages of qualitative, therefore metaphorical banalities follows in the wake of this vortex: organization, specialization, center and periphery, etc. following closely on one another. However, becoming more practical toward the end of his essay, van der Leeuw (1981b:304–305) suggests some measures of complexity that are interesting but heteroclite and, for the most part, incapable of being used or executed in his optics of the vortex. We will wait to read the publication of the details of the actual results of van der Leeuw's work with theories of self-organization in archaeology before we discuss further, not the vortex, but the work of an archaeologist.

At this point we will leave these "grand" approaches, whose only support lies in the metaphorical use of physico-mathematical theories, and which lack the means of evaluation that support them in the exact sciences—calculations or measures. With measures being near-absent, these theories give too much meaning to the data, as against the abundant measures presented in §1, which gave none whatsoever. These models (theories) have the same epistemological status as the large sociocultural explanatory systems, which admit all functions but which are not verifiable and are seemingly interchangeable with one another through the passage of the years. They are like the automatic pilot of a plane, leaving to the "calculation" the care of interpretation and guidance.

Measure and sense, in the practices that we have just reviewed, are scarcely related in a scientific manner. There is nothing unfortunate in this statement: that is, if we know how to reach an understanding in regard to things (and words) and recognize local successes. We will not draw up an inventory of these, just as we have not attempted to make a complete exposition of all the methods and theories making use of measure. The fact we would note would always be the same: there exists a gap separating, on the one hand, the use of precise formal scientific methods that are rigorous, and testable in archaeology, and, on the other hand, the inferences and interpretations for which they serve as a support, a guarantee, or a pretext. The problem is therefore archaeological; It concerns archaeological reasoning. Perhaps, with a practical objective in view, it would be good to give up, at least provisionally, and unless there is a verified favorable case,

seeking explanations and causes in the sociocultural field, at least as long as we do not
know how to describe phenomena precisely at a level of intermediary representation such
as that which we have posed above.

4. Measure in Search of Meaning: Physiography

The preliminary experiment that we present here arose from a sense of unease created
by an epistemological anomaly (Francfort 1984; Francfort et al. 1989). From 1976 to
1979, we excavated the small protohistoric site of Shortughaï (in northeast Afghanistan),
whose existence extended from ca. 2200 to ca. 1800 B.C. The sequence of eleven levels,
grouped in four periods, could be synthesized neatly into two successive phases, A and
B, in terms of taxonomic and stratigraphic analyses. Curiously, for this region, phase A
belonged to the mature, unmixed Indus civilization, and phase B, although it showed
evidence of continuity, represented a local Bactrian culture of the Bronze Age.

The unease arose from the following situation. Phase A, which could be attributed
to the wider Indus civilization, evidently belonged to what is called urban civilization
(or proto-urban, or proto-state society, all of which matters little, here), but on so small
a site (less than 2 ha.) that none of the distinctive urban traits appeared clearly. We could
have restricted ourselves to extending the urban concept of the Indus cities to the village
of Shortughaï (on the basis of the artifacts found there) if phase B had not been present
to add an additional difficulty. This phase B, as a representative of the generalized Central
Asian village, could not be further associated with any established body of knowledge
on cultures of this period and area, whether urban or nonurban. This problem was made
all the more difficult by the fact that no consensus could be arrived at over the existence
of a form of urban development in Central Asia outside Turkmenistan.

Without going into the details (see Francfort op. cit.), we can compare the present
difficulty with that presented by C. Kramer (1981) for the description of settlements of
greater or lesser complexity at a scale confined to villages. We thus were led to the
creation of a scale of measurement that allows the comparison of phases A and B at
Shortughaï, without having to invoke the unverifiable sociocultural equivalence of urbanism = class-society = State, and without having recourse to any of the ten archaeological criteria proposed by Childe (1950), even as revised by Tosi (1977), which do not
enable the detection of urban civilization except in the presence of cities.

a) Physiography

It soon became apparent that the criteria traditionally used to define urbanism have neither
clear archaeological correlates nor straightforward means of evaluation. For example,
how large would some manifestation have to be (ziggurats excluded) to be considered
"public," "collective," and "large"?

We therefore have had to concentrate on the study of what is commonly called "craft
specialization," a subcategory of Childe's more inclusive criteria of "broad, non agricultural classes." Because this is a small site, however, it is not possible to distinguish
an "elite quarter" from that of the "craftsmen," as is so often possible at larger sites.
As a consequence, we have restricted our ambitions to a relative evaluation of two orders

of archaeological determinants: one contextual and stratigraphic, that is, topographic, and the other technological. Our determinants enable measurements whose interpretation, although approachable in sociocultural terms, will allow us to revise the vague notion of "craft-specializaton" (see below).

— The topography of the site for phases A and B was searched, level by level, for markers of the following three functions: domestic, craft, and prestige. Markers of the domestic function included the remains of daily life; craft functions were identified by the tools and the remnants of manufacture that were located in appropriate contexts; various markers of prestige were taken in the usual sense of the term, and included ritual deposits, obvious items of great value ("riches"), and various other components commonly associated with wealth and prestige. We rejected the usual kinds of interpretations that depended on the identification of materials located in "elite" or "craftsmen's" quarters; in this way we could retain the level of greater or smaller differentiation provided by the simple topographic and stratigraphic units.

— In the case of technology, questions of sophistication and intensification of production were structured in a manner that did not depend on the fragile paralogical scaffolding that eventually works its way up to "full-time specialized artisans." Stress was laid on the measurement of the total data: the technological operational sequences, the types of artifacts produced, and the mass of material recovered from various deposits.

The various artifact types employed were those defined in the usual taxonomies; the total number of types present was used as a measure of the variety of production. The mass (of a type of object) was defined as the total weight of objects (or remnants) of a single type found in a unit of excavation expressed as weight per cubic meter. Variation, which is a derivative of the functions of production, reflects the growth, the stability, or the decrease of intensity of the production of a type of object. To obtain it, we weighed all the finds by categories and reduced the measured mass to a density per cubic meter in order to compare phases A and B.

The technological operational sequence (TOS) for a particular type of object is the length of the sequence of technical gestures required for its production. Thus, for example, beads have a TOS of 6 and ceramics usually have a TOS of 4. The TOS measurements of materials from Shortughaï are still quite primitive, but they are also deliberately conventional and coherent. With the aid of archaeometric studies of technology, ethnoarchaeological investigations of traditional production, a study of the nature of apprenticeships, and through experimental archaeology, this approach will be improved in the future (see Roux, chapter 16 this volume). At any rate, the magnitude of the whole of TOS measures (the technostructures) is in agreement with the degree of sophistication (complexity, diversity) of the production.

We thus have constructed tools of relative measurement by which we can compare the two phases, A and B. In doing so, at least for this discussion, I have put aside the technical questions of their application: the details of measurement and sampling methods.

b) Simulation with an Expert System

The expert system (see Francfort 1987; Francfort, Lagrange, and Renaud 1989 for details) uses the SNARK inference engine (Laurière 1985); it is made up of two subsystems called HPF 1 (topography) and HPF 2 (technology), each possessing its own fact base (FB) and rule base (RB). The FB and RB are constructed from information extracted from a written work (Francfort 1984). The schematization based on this information was obtained through a logicist analysis on a part of this text carried out by M.-S. Lagrange. The expert system was implemented in collaboration with M. Renaud (LISH, CNRS).

The topographic study enables the enumeration of the locations at which one of the three functions (domestic, craft, prestige) is predominant, and their adding up per phase, expressing the global relative variation in the specialization of the areas toward more or less "domestic" functions (that is, toward nonspecialization). The results about Shortughaï show a relative decrease of the specialization in the areas from phase A to phase B.

The fact base is not much more than a catalogue of the antiquities and the contexts in which they were found. It also contains values that set minimum thresholds that must be surpassed in order to attribute a functional qualification (domestic, craft, prestige), as well as the means to choose the scale of observation, from that of the small local topostratigraphic unit (location) up to the totality of the A or B phases.

The rule base comprises six groups of rules designed to link together inferences from the fact base to the terminal propositions, or from the **P0** to the **Pn** according to the terminology of Gardin (1979). The first group of rules enables the assignment of a numerical coefficient to three function counters (Domestic, Craft, Prestige) according to the nature of each find at each location. Certain conditional rules reinforce the incrementation of the counters: those above a certain threshold of value, for example.

This manner of proceeding is conventional, but no more so than any other dissection of reality, like that of a taxonomy; it enables the expression of intuitive evaluations, in a manner that can be discussed and is verifiable. A second group of rules brings out the dominant function of each of the locations: domestic, craft or prestige. The third group of rules sums the counter per level, then per phase, and makes a calculation of their percentages. The fourth group of rules brings out the totals and the percentages of the number of locations at which one of the three functions dominates, per level and per phase.

The fifth group of rules compares the A and B phases through time and highlights any variations in functions, from A toward B, or from B toward A, that are above a certain minimum threshold value. Anything below that value is considered unchanging. Thus each one of the three functions (domestic, craft, prestige) can, from one phase to another, grow, decrease, or remain stable; the result is a table of the variations that consists of eighteen lines of three columns each. This table is interpreted in terms of the sixth group of rules, which establishes, according to the variation of the functions, whether the specialization of the areas is increasing or decreasing.

The final rule contains the instruction to write the results. In the case of Shortughaï, the results show that as one moves from phase A to B, the craft function is stable, the indicators of prestige decrease strongly, and the markers of domesticity increase. Taken together, these three measures show that specialization diminishes through time there. This result was intuitively perceptible, but compared to the "manual" study (Francfort 1984), the simulation brings out the global stability of the craft activity, which I formerly believed had diminished in intensity. On the basis of this conclusion, which was obtained in a verifiable manner, there remain propositions to be derived that would serve to interpret the decrease of specialization in the several areas in sociocultural terms. We will return to this problem later, but we can note here that "specialization of the areas" is, for us, a metaterm obtained from the sum of the transformations presented above; it is not conceived as a socioeconomic or cultural term, even if we discern intuitively a plausible relationship between the two fields.

— The technological study enables us to approach an evaluation of the intensity of production and of the elaboration of its products. In this case, as before, we begin with the topo-stratigraphy and from the known taxonomy of the finds. In addition, we have measures for the weight of the objects by type as well as for the remnants of each type; we have as well the TOS for each type of object. Without going into detail, we should note that the weight of the objects ranges from a few grams (gold) to several tons (ceramics and pebbles). To avoid the samples that are too small (in units of space and time), we again compared the A and B phases in such a way as to obtain trends over several centuries.

The fact base contains the length of the TOS for each type of artifact, the density of finds per type per cubic meter, and the density of finds per type per phase.

The rule base is made up of three groups of rules. First, for each phase, the cumulative total of the number of types ("diversification of the products"), the mass "quantities produced" (per cubic meter), and the mass of the TOS are collected. An index, M. I. (mass × TOS), is calculated, which yields an abstract measure of the quantity of technological information applied to the materials that was necessary for their production. Lastly, the quantity of the TOS, comprising from one to six segments, is enumerated (this application does not allow sequences of more than six segments).

The application of other rules produce, for each of the two phases, A and B, additional indices: (1) "the average elaboration of the products," from the calculation of the TOS/type ratio; (2) an index that comprises a "weighted average of technicity" (M. I./mass ratio); (3) the percentages of the TOS of each length. Lastly, to differentiate the A and B phases, thresholds are established for the following five factors: "diversification of products," "quantity produced," "elaboration of the products," "weighted average of production," and "weighted average of technicity." The values obtained indicate either an increase ($+1$), a decrease (-1), or stability (0) in these factors from phase A to B. The value of the results is totalled together to bring out "the intensification of production" ("quantity produced" + "weighted average of production") and the "sophistication of the production" ("diversification of the products" + "elaboration" + "weighted average of technicity").

At Shortughaï, as one moves from phase A toward B, there is a decrease in "the intensification of the production" and a slight decrease in the "sophistication of the production," while "the elaboration of the products" and the "weighted average of technicity" remain stable. These results do not take into account the deposit of large quantities of rough pebbles on the site in phase A: taking them into account increases the "weighted average of technicity" and stabilizes the "sophistication of production."

These conclusions, when compared to those we had obtained intuitively, "by hand," show that we had overestimated the decrease in "sophistication." Lastly, this technological study is consistent with the topographical and contextual evidence, which shows a stability in areas of craft production during the two phases (but which does not necessarily indicate that craft production itself remained stable, as the morphology of the objects themselves did change).

Let us repeat, here again, that we are using terms such as "intensification," "sophistication," etc. as constructed metaterms, that are far removed from their use in natural language. To the predictable criticism about the representativity of the sample, we contrast the techniques of collection (extensive excavation), of verification (by additional excavation), and of enlargement of scale (the phase), which we will not speak about in detail here. To the reproach about the arbitrariness of the divisions in the definition of the TOS, we answer that their rejection implies, ipso facto, the rejection of all taxonomic segmentations of the real, which themselves comprise conventional evaluations based on agreement. To the objection about the arbitrariness of measurements and to the application of the rules in relation to the terminal propositions, we reply that such criticism hardly holds ground in the face of the much greater but commonly practiced arbitrariness of the process which consists in being content with vague, implicit, or worthless evaluations, and in establishing thereupon a relationship with sociocultural propositions drawn from natural language, without further ceremony, as if they were taken for granted.

As Tosi described it lucidly at the end of a study on craft specialization based upon the division of the finds at Shahr-i Sokhta, in the Iranian Seistan: he concludes that his hypothesis can as yet hardly go beyond the level of a statement of political faith (Tosi 1984:49).

The verification of inferences beyond a certain level eludes the archaeological approach, which is why we have chosen the intermediate level, one at which the archaeological correlates are related to notions apparently in conformity with protohistoric urbanism, a phenomenon whose exploration is far from complete. At each stage, at each level of inference, more or less conventional choices, as well as measures of evaluation, force themselves upon the investigation. The price to pay for mastery over inferences is the impoverishment of the significance of notions, through a narrowing of the field which keeps pace with the local and relative aspect of the approaches. The experiment which has been presented here has a field of application limited to the archaeological sites of preliterate, protohistoric (or Neolithic?) cultures; it does not exclude, however, any other traditional approach. These limits in application in no way take away from the universality of the structures such as the TOS (and application of information on matter, which will come in the course of time).

The exploration of physiography ends here, in the relatively low profile of the terminal propositions, which themselves are not necessarily the final ones that we can expect. To attempt to know them, we have constructed a doxography, on the basis of which the bridging will be attempted (§5).

5. Sense in Pursuit of Measure: Doxography

The study of theories that account for the emergence or the existence of proto-state societies should, on no account, be taken as a criticism of the substance of the studies in which they are embedded. We are attempting to analyze, by logicist schematization and simulation, and with the aid of an expert system, good theories which are well-known and widely disseminated. To prevent our undertaking from being misunderstood, we have chosen studies that have systematized various of the theories (e.g., Wright 1978 for those of Wittfogel, Carneiro, Adams, and for his own work) or those which can be easily systematized (e.g., that of Claessen in Claessen and Skalnik 1985 and in Claessen, van de Velde and Smith 1985; Childe 1950; Tosi 1977, 1984; Johnson 1973; Wright and Johnson 1975).

The simulation presented here is one which captures our schematization of the reasoning of the several authors. It is quite possible, if not probable, that they could reproach us for having excessively simplified their thought or selected out-of-date versions of their theories. It matters little, since we are seeking here to specify, to fix, and to evaluate our reasoning processes and not theirs. We concede willingly to all the right to keep to their ideas.

Whatever the case, a preliminary observation demands recognition: there is a common nucleus of notions related to the concept of the ''proto-state.'' This fact is both reassuring and disturbing; reassuring because of the professional ''consensus'' which emerges; disturbing because of the quantitative poverty of the concepts deployed in these powerful constructions which contrasts with their semantic richness (or nebulousness). In the present state of our task, which is still preliminary, we have worked with a dictionary of only 140 notions (many of which are almost synonyms), which is capable of being enriched. The fact base that activates the rules in the expert system consists of extracts from this dictionary. (We will see below how to widen the procedure).

These rules in the rule base are fourteen in number (after the names of the authors): WITT; DIAK; WRI-1; WRI-2; CARN; WRI-3; TOS; ADAM; TOSCHILD; CHLD; JON; WRIJON; CLAES-1; CLAES-2.

Neither the details of the schematization nor those of the rules (see Gardin et al. 1986 for examples; see Francfort, Lagrange, and Renaud 1989 for the complete version) are given here. Instead, an attempt is made to give an idea of the sort of results obtained using these rules and to evaluate them.

These fourteen sets of rules can be activated individually, all together (general RB), or in groups.

— Utopia (or test-country) is the minimal facts base which activates the triggering of all the rules (general RB).[4] Utopia is made up of 16 facts; together they trigger the rules 71 times and produce 46 additional facts; thus the final fact base (FB) contains 62 facts.

Utopia is described as follows:

CONSTRUCTION	PLANNED	existence of planned constructions
IRRIGATION	LARGE	presence of large-scale irrigation
SPE-RAIS	GROWS	growth of specialization in stock breeding

SOPH-PRODUC	GROWS	growth in the sophistication of production
AGRIC	STABLE	stability of agricultural production
GOODS	STOCKED	stocking of goods
GOODS	EXCHANGE	regional exchange of goods
TRADE	LONG-DIST	long-distance trade
POPULATION	GROWS	population growth
SOCIETY	CITIZEN	existence of citizenship
LAND	INSUF	shortage of land
WAR	ACTIVITY	existence of warlike activities
SOCIETY	SLAVE	presence of slaves
SYMBOL	ARTIST-PRO	artistic and symbolic production
RELIGION	COM-IDEOLO	existence of a common religious ideology

This Utopia, despite the possibility of some disagreement, encompasses the common core of the notions about the emergence of the state. It should be noted that we have not distinguished the dynamic theories of the origins of the state from the static theories that lead to the recognition of the existence of the state (Childe or Claessen type). Indeed, both the one and the other call on the same notions, "appearing" or "growing" in the first case while they "exist" or "are present" in the second. The details of the final FB of Utopia, obtained through the general RB, become apparent if we attribute an arbitrary and uniform likelihood coefficient (LC) of 0.5 to each one of the facts about Utopia; by this means, the facts get reinforced, or not, acquiring LC which go from 0.5 to 1 (a likelihood of 100 percent). Here the LC enable us to pick out the facts which are reinforced the most during the activation of the general RB.

The following obtained an LC of 1:

SOCIETY	RUL-CLAS	ruling class
SOCIETY	CLAS	class society
POLIT-STATE	ORGANIZED	organized political state
ADMINSTR	PRESENT	administration
SOCIETY	ELITE	presence of an elite in society

The other LC are of 0.98; 0.97; 0.5; 0.75; 0.87 for the 52 remaining facts.

Hence, the recurrent, reinforced facts that have been inferred relate to social inequalities, to administration and power, as well as to irrigation, which itself turns out to be the "strongest" archaeological fact.

These inferred facts do not deviate from the propositions habitually met with in the pertinent archaeological literature. The propositions about proto-state societies are therefore easily generated by the general RB as it is activated by the test-country (Utopia) FB.

— To continue the test of the general FB, we expanded our activities through the creation of two additional FB, one produced by the schematization of a study on the Iron Age in Europe (van de Velde 1985), called EUROPE-IRON-AGE, the other emanating from an analysis of a work on the Neolithic of Wessex (Renfrew 1973b), called NEO-OF-WESSEX. In both of these cases no likelihood coefficients were used initially.

The EUROPE-IRON-AGE FB is made up of 11 facts, which trigger the rules 32 times and thereby produce 18 new facts and a final FB of 29 facts. The facts concerning the administration and society are recurrently activated. In this process the WITT, CLAES, CHLD, and JON sets of rules are not activated at all. We are led, however, to the "fact" of the appearance of irrigation(!).

The NEO-OF-WESSEX FB is made up of 14 facts that trigger the rules 45 times and produce 26 new facts. The final FB comprises 40 facts. As with the Iron Age FB, the WITT, CLAES, CHLD, and JON sets of rules are not activated. Nonetheless, the final FB describes a magnificent proto-state society (with irrigation!). It may be noted in passing that we have not retained in the initial FB a fact such as "no true government" which would have automatically excluded NEO-OF-WESSEX from our analysis. The reason for this modification will be discussed below.

— The experiment was extended by grouping the RB in a manner which enabled the global clarification of the functioning of the various chains of inferences. Thus, WITT was grouped with DIAK; WRI 1,2,3, JON, and WRIJON were grouped; TOS, CHLD, and TOSCHILD; CARN remained alone, as did ADAM; CLAES was excluded altogether. This time, we assigned an LC of 0.5 to each fact of the initial FB of NEO-OF-WESSEX.

During this phase of the experiment, the WITT-DIAK RB remained inactive, as did the set of rules labeled ADAM. CARN, for its part, triggered 9 rules relating to social classes, administration, and defence, which with LC reinforcement (max 0.75), led to the generation of 8 new facts. The group of RB WRI-JON triggered 13 rules, of which ADMINISTR PRESENT has a LC of 0.94 and URB POP has a LC of 0.87, and produced 10 new facts. The group of RB TOS-CHILD created 12 new facts through 20 activations of the rules and the strong reinforcement of LC. Thus, ORGANIZED POLIT-STATE received a value of 1.0, CLAS SOCIETY 0.98, ELITE SOCIETY 0.94, and UNEQUAL SOCIETY 0.87.

Having obtained these results with NEO-OF-WESSEX, we considered that the problem of evaluation and of handling of the criteria raised by this Neolithic case should be generalized.

We extracted two RB concerning very organized and complex animal societies, those of termites and of ants (Sire 1960; Chauvin 1985). Without straining the vocabulary employed by the authors, the following results are obtained:

With the termites, the initial FB TERMITARY, which comprised 19 facts, generated 14 additional facts (among them irrigation!). These results came from use of the general RB, but without ADAM (15 rules read), CARN (11 rules read), WITT-DIAK (15 rules read), and WRI-JON (23 rules read) being activated. The result was obtained through

29 activations of the rules; the final FB accounted for 35 facts. The group of RB TOS-CHILD produced 6 new facts as the result of 17 activations: ORGANIZED POLIT-STATE, URBAN POPULATION, PLANNED LAND, CONCENTRATED POWER, CLAS SOCIETY, CENTR AUTHORITY, ORGANIZED POLIT-STATE.

The anthill FB ANTHILL of 22 facts produced 30 activations of the rules in the general RB thus giving rise to 14 new facts, one among these being irrigation (!), and a five-time confirmation of the fact CLAS SOCIETY. However, WITT-DIAK, CARN, and ADAM were not activated at all. The RB group WRI-JON was read 23 times and its rules were activated 5 times and 2 new facts were engendered: URBAN POPULATION and ADMINISTR PRESENT. The RB group TOS-CHILD, which was read 27 times and produced 17 activations of its rules, yielded 6 new facts: ORGANIZED POLIT-STATE, URBAN POPULATION, PLANNED LAND, CONCENTRATED POWER, CLAS SO-CIETY, CENTR AUTHORITY, ORGANIZED POLIT-STATE.

These collective experiments illustrate the problem that, for a given FB, the rules of derivation (or of inferences) work for the Neolithic, for termite colonies, and for anthills. For example, irrigation, the most aberrant fact derived for the insects, came from the following sequence in the general RB:

- Rule x →   CLASS SOCIETY
- Rule TOS 8   CLASS SOCIETY → ORGANIZED POLIT-STATE
- Rule DIAK 5   ORGANIZED POLIT-STATE → IRRIGATION PRESENT

Similarly, the recurrent reinforcement of "class" society arises out of the privileged status of this social fact, to which practically all the RB lead, not to mention the synonymous, equivalent, or encompassing terms such as "ruling classes," "elite," "inegalitarian society," "hierarchized" etc.

— The experiment was continued by taking as the FB the single and only strictly archaeological fact, LARGE IRRIGATION. This single fact triggered the rules 28 times in the general RB, which generated 23 facts. CHLD, JON, CLAES, and WRIJON were not activated. On this single fact, the RB group of WITT-DIAK and the ADAM RB were activated, whereas they remained inert during the Neolithic, termitary, and anthill experiments. The rules were activated 6 times in ADAM, which concerned social classes, regional economic symbiosis, the redistribution of goods, and the purchase of lands, and produced 9 additional facts. WITT-DIAK derived 14 facts through 12 activations of the rules concerning all the fields of proto-state societies.

This simulation experiment shows first of all that neither the schematization of the reasoning nor the writing of our FB and RB is absurd, since the results of the process are very widely compatible with the conclusions of the authors being considered. The details of this procedure will be published elsewhere (see Francfort, Lagrange, and Renaud 1989).

The problem that we wish to raise here is epistemological and not heuristic, as was announced at the start of this doxography. The computer scientists who collaborated with us in this work were struck by the small size of the initial FB as compared to the respectable size of the final FB, even when applied to fields situated at the limits of inference (Neolithic, insects). A simple means of avoiding such a conceptual drift would be to introduce some *ad hoc* rules stipulating "no true government" for the Neolithic or the rejection of nonhuman societies from the relevant field, or to restrict "irrigation."

These restrictions, however, would amount to ignoring the importance of the real question, which is that of the historical continuum on the one hand and the continuity of concepts on the other hand. The historical continuum results in our furtive passage from the Neolithic to what are called the State societies by way of some transitional forms to which the label "proto" has been attached to "State." This descriptive process, however, is not an adequate explanation of the origin of the state. To take a known example, the variety of ideas associated with the interpretation of the Neolithic site of Çatal Hüyük as "too developed" shows the difficulty inherent in sociocultural interpretations when the facts deviate from certain well-recognized norms or prototypes. Such problems are magnified for the state societies and for the lists of traits that are associated with them in peripheral fringes like Central Asia, the Neolithic, or animal societies.

We could choose to solve this problem by rejecting schematization and simulation (by expert systems or by other means) because they are too restrictive, if not too simplistic, and by keeping and amplifying the sociocultural interpretations of the literary and historical types. This, however, is not our attitude.

We also could choose to open up the field of sociocultural interpretations to the point of including literature and to devote ourselves to connecting this level, insofar as that is possible, to the archaeological base: from doxography to physiography. The predictable consequence would be a reduction in the number of interpretations that could be related firmly to the facts.

If we choose this latter path, it becomes evident that we will be faced immediately with questions of evaluations, of degrees, of measures, and of meaning. This measure, for which natural language and the current applications of formal methods are ill-adapted, demands a clear conceptual effort.

Such bridges are being built in the field which interests us, that of the protohistoric Indus and Central Asia. This work has convinced us that there is no alternative to measurement; moreover, at present, these can only be numerical measures (probabilistic if we like), as we are going to see.

The role of expert systems in such a task can be an aid to reasoning, at least under certain conditions. Indeed, a privileged field for this type of approach is being revealed, which measures the capacity to calculate, to organize, and to put to work the information and the energy of protohistoric individuals and communities. To this end, expert systems are of great help, in spite of certain limitations which necessitate that they be used with circumspection.

6. The Limits of Expert Systems and of Their Proper Use

We should remember that the primary archaeological problem, which begins with a known database (typology and topo-stratigraphy), is to verify the chains of inference by way of successive transformations.

At this point we have chosen to ignore the use of expert systems as an aid to typological and chronological classification, although we must note that such applications do exist. We also bypass a discussion of the use of expert systems as systemic models, as a means to analyze discourse, and as a means to reproduce reasoning processes, each of which can be accomplished with their aid. For our purposes here, the main importance in the use of expert systems lies elsewhere.

It is important to take as a starting point the article by Huggett and Baker (1985), which is quite lucidly critical of expert systems, as well as the one by Gardin et al. (1986), which presents demonstrations of their applications in archaeology.

For Huggett and Baker, the elucidation of knowledge and the rigorous system of reasoning imposed by expert systems are seen as salutary. However, as they point out, limits do exist. According to them, the representation of knowledge poses problems, because few experts are capable of explaining their knowledge in any systematic way. Moreover, simulation has little in common with human reasoning processes, thus the human expert has to conform to the model of reasoning and to the knowledge of the system, rather than the other way round.

In our opinion, the shortcomings highlighted by Huggett and Baker are not necessarily a major disadvantage, since all science proceeds in such a manner, and, as with any other craft, requires an apprenticeship. Given the fact that an empirical practice, like that of mental calculation, proceeds through several methods to obtain a result, where, then, is *the* human reasoning? Moreover, the question is not to copy but to simulate with differences that are as large as those which distinguish, respectively, a plane and Vaucanson's duck (an eighteenth-century automaton) from real birds. The first simulates, whereas the second copies. I do not think that the exact replication of alchemic reasoning would lead one to physics or to chemistry, nor that the analysis and the simulation of the texts of Apollonius of Pergè would be of great help for deriving the equations of conics. The main importance of simulations in archaeology is to bring to light the gaps and the interpretative jumps that are a part of its current practice. Their use as an aid to reasoning will follow later. Indeed, the limitations of expert systems in our discipline are still very large: e.g., confinement to narrow fields; problems of conflict resolution by the algorithm; question of the introduction of common sense ("the least well distributed thing in the world").

The crucial question is that of the management of uncertainty and of "approximations." In this respect, expert systems are guilty of excessive simplification, of forcing knowledge, of distorting it, and of failing to exploit fully the knowledge of the expert. Similar accusations are to be found scattered through the history of sciences since Galileo, each perfectly justified from the academic point of view, but none worthy of additional discussion here.

Huggett and Baker have identified a number of shortcomings in the application of expert systems: "The problems of elicitation [of knowledge] are recognized in the 'scientific' domain areas and are likely to be seen even greater in the humanities . . . with their traditional distrust of the dehumanizing effects of anything seen as 'scientific'. The resolution of these problems is an important research topic" (Huggett and Baker 1985:5).

The problems of evaluation of hypotheses are raised by these authors as well; they criticize procedures for weighing facts and rules and conclude that " . . . numerical values are unreliable measures of confidence, and however reliable the statistical techniques that manipulate them may be . . . [a]rchaeologists already abstract and simplify in order to construct discrete models, but these models can be freely discussed, modified, accepted and rejected, while arguably those models within a machine will be less accessible for these processes . . . [and will be] hidden from the user . . . ''(Huggett and Baker 1985:6).

The whole course of our work leads us to conclusions quite opposite to those reached by Huggett and Baker. For us, natural language permits dissimulation, enables shifts in meaning, makes dodging issues possible, and embraces implicit meaning, synonymy, and polysemy. In short, it provides a means suitable for endless discussion. An expert system, on the other hand, which has been constructed to simulate and to aid reasoning, puts at the disposal of the user all stages in the sequence of inferences. Moreover, such systems can aid in the evaluation of their diagnoses and permit the elimination of conceptual gaps and jumps in the stages of thought they simulate (see Lagrange and Renaud 1983, 1986). If the quantified evaluations of the facts and of the rules are not ideal (but the likelihood coefficients are not the only procedures!), they are at least perfectly explicit, discussable, modifiable, and acceptable or rejectable. Besides, the "danger of fossilization of the conceptual canvas" is at least as great with natural language, but in a much more insidious manner. The discourses on the origin of social inequality at ca. 6000 B.C. or on the center-periphery dialectics are good examples of conceptual fossilizations, draped in diverse and mottled phraseology. Lastly, the argument that logical reduction is epistemologically inadequate does not hold: between the "Boolean dream" and the literary ineffable of the irreducible domains, there is much that remains to be done.

Logical reduction is a necessity which affects every discipline claiming to be a science. To this end, expert systems enable us to avoid some of the snares of natural language discussed above, thanks precisely to their flexibility, provided we consider them as adapted to a limited objective and as an aid to the art of good guidance of our thought. Moreover, we must recognize that expert systems are not yet good archaeologists. In archaeology, which does not appear to us to be a part of the field that is forever decreed as being outside the pale of science, expert systems have been applied mainly to the diagnosis of typological reasoning and to the analysis of discourse. This second point is going to hold our attention now by bringing us back to our problem, that of the sense of measure.

— Why measure?

A number of contemporary scholars provide a variety of answers to this question and to the relationships among rules and measures. For example, '' . . . the rules that experts call upon in their decision making process are only approximate . . . the data involved in these uncertain rules are themselves imprecise . . . '' (Gallaire 1987:273). J.-C. Gardin (1986a:88) suggests, in connection with the evaluation of numerous analogies, a rule of the $N > T$ type, where N = the number of parallels and T is a relative or absolute standard threshold. However, he rejects this "primitive process . . . exposing itself to criticisms about its arbitrariness or its circularity" and prefers to declare these "numerous analogies" as a basic "fact." The problem is real and is discussed by a number of authors. O. Guillaume (1986:102) notes that "in all the rules (without exception) are to be found measures of the sort: 'very numerous,' 'very diverse,' 'little tested,' 'the large majority,' 'numerous,' 'rare,' etc." These deserve, to say the least, to be specified more exactly. P. Herman (1986:123) seeks to avoid too synthetic a fact base by establishing

rules of resemblance through counters with relation to a prototype; thereby he attempts
to evaluate the "weight of the elements of the context" and develops the evaluation of
the resemblances through coefficients of likelihood (Herman 1986:133). M.-S. Lagrange
and M. Renaud (1986:216) weigh the diagnosis through the application of coefficients
of likelihood, and E. Zadora-Rio (1986:185–187) wonders about the problem of the
"relative value of rules."

It is obvious that the problem of the evaluation of uncertainty is at the center of the
analysis of archaeological reasoning, and that simulation by means of an expert system
is a good means to identify the sources of such uncertainty. If, however, it is granted
that one's facts are chosen based on one's understanding, then how are the objections
of primitivism, arbitrariness, and circularity of numerical evaluations to be met?

Leaving out of consideration the sophistication of certain calculations or instruments,
many measures are "primitive": the degrees of difference between ice and steam account
nevertheless for a multitude of experiments. Is that not the main thing? These degrees
are arbitrary, whether Fahrenheit, Celsius, or Kelvin, but they are conventional. This
does not bring any impediment. As for circularity, every definition of measurement being
by definition tautological, it hardly disturbs us.

Finally, given the fact that the utility of, even the necessity for, measurement is
unanimously recognized, everything depends on the manner in which measurement is
expressed. Should it be quantified a little, a lot . . . not at all? The necessity for measurement has many consequences for the manner of designing and constructing the facts
and rules of expert systems.

We have gotten into the daily habit of receiving information that has been translated
into numbers showing indexes and ratings (to the extent of measuring the "popularity"
of political personalities) to which we give a meaning (and they even more so). Everything
is therefore a matter of convention, between the measurement and its meaning. The
important point is to underline that in our field each "fact" possesses a value. This value
can be expressed in the form of numbers or in a primitive, verbal form ("a little, a
lot . . . "). We will give some details about the different aspects of the value assigned
to facts below. Moreover, and this is less apparent intuitively, each fact possess a proximity, which enables the existence, and therefore the writing, of the rules of inferences
and of the transfer of attributes in archaeology. Indeed "what we call 'logical inference'
is a transformation of expression" (Wittgenstein 1983:37).

The six reservations about expert systems expressed by J.-C. Gardin (1986b:237–
238) be divided into two groups. The first group concerns the fragmentary and *ad hoc*
nature of representations, the arbitrary nature of the fact base that could be produced by
rules, and the awkwardness of rules themselves. The second group concerns the construction of definitions from vague terms, the use of analogies that are not constructed
from underlying calculations based upon measured quantities and likelihood coefficients,
and a sense of the undertaking that is " . . . judged to be closer to improvisation than
to a real science of reasoning." These reservations represent the real limits of expert
systems, and there is no choice possible but to admit them and to use conventional but
verifiable measurements, since we cannot do without them. What could be more puerile
than the meter or the kilogram? They are conventions. These acknowledged conventions
(expert systems or not) give us free play to know which yardstick to employ to measure

our archaeological interpretations. We see already that many large sociocultural interpretations, which come under the *doxa* (Veyne 1971), should be left to their ambitious excessiveness. For that which remains and which is capable of being considered as science, the most important theoretical problem that comes from a consideration of artificial intelligence is, to my mind, that of the representation of knowledge in a perspective wider than that of the present expert systems. From this perspective, one can ask: How can one choose from among these facts and the facts produced by these rules? To what extent are the latter only a slippage of the former? And, hence, where are their limits?

7. The Limits of Constructions

One could conclude that the preceding views are, on balance, negative and, above all, that the proposed simulations are poverty-stricken and even simplistic. That is why it appears important to return to these questions and to widen consideration of them without, at the same time, binding ourselves to expert systems. Indeed, we admit absolutely that expert systems are not capable of reproducing the richness of all interpretative constructions in archaeology, but we categorically reject the reduction of the interpretative process exclusively to the rhetoric of contemporary social sciences. While waiting for wider, better formed, and verifiable scientific constructions to come and take account of the sociocultural and symbolic interpretative levels, we have to measure our ambitions for rigor and restrict them to levels of thought that are both less elevated and less untrustworthy.

As an end to this study, we propose a program of exploration and experiment. The exploration program aims at cleaning the quasi or pseudo concepts at the level of intermediary representations; it involves the analysis of technoeconomic structures through diverse historical approaches (texts) and ethnological observations (tradition; apprenticeship; experimentation) to sift from them an archaeological practice. The technoeconomic structures could be integrated, from the object up to the archaeological culture (material totality) and the supracultural, symbolic levels through rules of verified inferences.

The experiments will relate to simulation, opening the road to future aid to reasoning, thanks to the expert system, with the limits and the exigencies that go with it, combining facts understood as possessing a proximity and a value, with rules of derivation mastered as rules of rewriting.

It is at this price that we can hope to attain the sense of measure/measurement/in archaeology, by which we evaluate how man molds matter in the course of time (or matter molds itself through the intermediary of the human agent). Between the descriptions to which larger or smaller numbers have been given and the interpretations that have been more or less well shaped, there can emerge the measure of meaning in archaeology.

The predictable outcome of such assemblies of work is the birth of a new scientific language, as there is no field, not even that of the humanities, which cannot take advantage of the services of artificial intelligence, through which we will make a litter of what are nothing short of stupendously amazing speeches.

NOTES

1. Physiography is a term used by some pre-Socratic philosophers to refer to the functioning of the material world; *doxa*, initially attributable to philosophers of the Hellenistic period, refers to catalogs of philosophical opinions.

2. Which relates to books by Hubert L. Dreyfus that attack the notion and the foundations of artificial intelligence, especially his *What Computers Can't Do: The Limits of Artificial Intelligence*, Harper and Row, New York, 1972; see also Hubert L. Dreyfus and Stuart E. Dreyfus, *Mind Over Machine*, Free Press, New York 1986.

3. *Système de Gestion de Base de Données*, which in English would correspond to DBMS, Database Management System.

4. Note that this and the implementations that follow were programmed in French (tr.).

REFERENCES

Adams, R. N. 1975. *Energy and Structure. A Theory of Social Power*. University of Texas Press, Austin.
———1978. "Man energy and anthropology: I can feel the heat but where's the light?," *American Anthropologist* **80,** 297–309
———1981. "Natural selection, energetics and 'Cultural Materialism'," *Current Anthropology* **22** 603–624.
Allen, P. M. 1982. "The genesis of structure in social systems: The paradigm of self-organization," in C. Renfrew, M. Rowlands, and B. A. Seagraves (eds.), *Theory and Explanation in Archaeology*, pp. 347–388. Academic Press, New York.
Binford, L. R. 1981. *Bones: Ancient Men and Modern Myths*. Academic Press, New York.
———1982. "Objectivity-Explanation-Archaeology 1981," in C. Renfrew, M. Rowlands, and B. A. Seagraves, (eds.) *Theory and Explanation in Archaeology*, pp. 125–137. Academic Press, New York.
———1983. *Working at Archaeology*. Academic Press, New York.
Chauvin, R. 1985. *La biologie de l'esprit*. Editions du Rocher, Monaco.
Childe, V. G. 1950. "The urban revolution," *Town Planning Review* **21,** 3–17.
Claessen, H. J., and P. Skalnik (eds.) 1978. *The Early State*. Mouton, Paris.
Claessen, H. J., P. van de Velde, and M. E. Smith 1985. *Development and Decline. The Evolution of Sociopolitical Organization*. Bergin and Garvey, South Hadley, MA.
Cohen, S., and E. Service (eds.) 1978. *Origins of the State*. Institute for the Study of Human Issues, Philadelphia.
Djindjian, F. 1986. Unpublished seminar notes.
Ducasse, H. 1981, 1983, 1985. "Panorama des traitements de données en archéologie." *Archéologie et ordinateurs*. C.N.R.S., Paris.
Fodor, J. 1983. *Modularity of Mind*. MIT/Bradford Press, Cambridge, MA.
Francfort, H.-P. 1984. *Recherches sur l'Asie centrale protohistorique. L'Age du Bronze en Bactriane orientale et le déclin des civilisations urbaines du 3ème millénaire*. Thèse de doctorat d'Etat, Université de Lille III, Lille.
———1987. "Un système expert pour l'analyse archéologique de sociétés proto-urbaines. Première étape: le cas de Shortughaï," *Informatique et Sciences Humaines* **74,** 73–91.
Francfort, H.-P., M.-S. Lagrange, and M. Renaud 1989. *PALAMEDE. Application des systèmes experts à l'archéologie de civilisations urbaines protohistoriques*. Document de travail no. 9, C.N.R.S., LISH/UPR 315, Paris.
Francfort, H.-P., with contributions by C. Boisset, L. Buchet, J. Desse, J. Echallier, A. Kermorvant, and G. Willcox 1989. *Fouilles de Shortughaï: recherches sur l'Asie centrale protohistorique*. Diffusion de Boccard, Paris.

Gallaire, H. 1987. "La représentation des connaissances," in *La Recherche en intelligence artificielle*. Seuil, Paris,

Gallay, A. 1986. *L'archéologie demain*. Belfond, Paris.

———1988 "Vivre autour d'un feu: analyse ethnoarchéologique de campements Touaregs du Hoggar," *Bulletin de Centre genevois d'Anthropologie* **1**, 35.

Gardin, J.-C. 1979. *Une archéologie théorique*. Hachette, Paris.

———1986a. "Les relations entre la Grèce et l'Asie centrale à l'époque hellénistique d'après les données céramologiques," in J.-C. Gardin et al., *Systèmes experts et sciences humaines*, pp. 59–90. Eyrolles, Paris.

———1986b. "Epilogue," in J.-C. Gardin et al., Systèmes experts et sciences humaines, pp. 233–258, Eyrolles, Paris.

Gardin, J.-C., O. Guillaume, P. Q. Herman, A. Hesnard, M.-S. Lagrange, M. Renaud, and E. Zadora-Rio 1986. *Systèmes experts et sciences humaines*. Eyrolles, Paris.

Gardner, H. 1983. *Frames of Mind: The Theory of Multiple Intelligence*. Heinemann, London.

———1985. *The Mind's New Science. A History of the Cognitive Revolution*. Basic Books, New York.

Guillaume, O. 1986. "L'artisanat métallurgique en Bactriane à l'age du fer," in J.-C. Gardin et al., *Systèmes experts et sciences humaines*, pp. 93–109. Eyrolles, Paris.

Herman, P. Q. 1986. "Que les ancêtres des figurines chypriotes lèvent les bras," in J.-C. Gardin et al., *Systèmes experts et sciences humaines*, pp. 113–136. Eyrolles, Paris.

Hofstadter, D. R. 1979. *Gödel, Escher, Bach: An Eternal Golden Braid*. Harvester Press, Brighton, East Sussex.

———1985. *Metamagical Themas. Questing for the Essence of Mind and Pattern*. Basic Books, New York.

Huggett, J., and K. Baker 1985. "The computerized archaeologist: The development of expert system," *Science and Archaeology* **27,** 3–7.

Johnson, G. A. 1973. *Local Exchange and Early State Development in Southwestern Iran*. University of Michigan Museum of Anthropology, Anthropological Papers No. 51, Ann Arbor, MI.

———1982. "Organizational structure and scalar stress," in C. Renfrew, M. Rowlands, and B. A. Seagraves (eds.), *Theory and Explanation in Archaeology*, pp. 389–421. Academic Press, New York.

Kramer, C. 1981. "Variability, complexity and spatial organization in Southwest Asian settlements," in S. E. van der Leeuw (ed.), *Archaeological Approaches to the Study of Complexity*, pp. 100–116. IPP, Universiteit van Amsterdam.

Lagrange, M.-S., and M. Renaud 1983. "Deux expériences de simulation des raisonnements en archéologie au moyen d'un système expert: le système SNARK," *Informatique et Sciences Humaines* **59–60,** 161–188.

———1986. "Superikon, essai de cumul de six expertises eniconographie," in J.-C. Gardin et al., *Systèmes experts et sciences humaines*, pp. 191–220. Eyrolles, Paris.

Laurière, J. L. 1985. *Intelligence artificielle. Résolution de problèmes par l'Homme et la machine*. Eyrolles, Paris.

van der Leeuw, S. E., 1981a. "Information flows, flow structures and the explanation of change in human institution," in S. E. van der Leeuw (ed.), *Archaeological Approaches to the Study of Complexity*, pp. 230–328. IPP, Universiteit van Amsterdam.

———(ed.) 1981b. *Archaeological Approaches to the Study of Complexity*. IPP, Universiteit van Amsterdam.

Leroi-Gourhan, A. 1964, 1965. *Le geste et la parole*: Vol 1 *Technique et langage*; Vol 2 *La mémoire et les rythmes*. Albin Michel, Paris.

Lumsden, C., and E. O. Wilson 1984. *Le feu de Prométhée. Réflexions sur l'origine de l'esprit*. Mazarino, Paris.

McCorduck, P. 1979. *Machines Who Think*. W. H. Freeman, San Francisco.

Miller, D. 1985a. *Artefacts as Categories. A Study of Ceramic Variability in Central India*. Cambridge University Press, Cambridge.

———1985b. "Ideology and the Harappan civilization," *Journal of Anthropological Archaeology* **4,** 34–71.

Piatelli-Palmarini, M. (ed.) 1979. *Théories du langage. Théories de l'apprentissage. Le débat entre Jean Piaget et Noam Chomsky*. Seuil, Paris.

Prigogine, I., and I. Stengers 1979. *La Nouvelle Alliance. Métamorphose de la Science*. Gallimard, Paris.

Pylyshyn, Z. 1984. *Computation and Cognition: Toward a Foundation for Cognitive Science*. MIT Press, Cambridge, MA.

Renfrew, C. (ed.) 1973a. *The Explanation of Culture Change*. Duckworth, London.

———1973b. "Social organization in Neolithic Wessex," in C. Renfrew (ed.), *The Explanation of Culture Change*, pp. 539–558. Duckworth, London.

———1979. "Systems collapse as social transformation: Catastrophe and anastrophe in early state societies," in C. Renfrew and K. L. Cooke (eds.), *Transformations: Mathematical Approaches to Culture Change*, pp. 481–505. Academic Press, New York.

———1982a. "Explanation revisited," in C. Renfrew et al., *Theory and Explanation in Archaeology*, pp. 5–23. Academic Press, New York.

———1982b. "Comment: The emergence of structure," in C. Renfrew et al., *Theory and Explanation in Archaeology*, pp. 459–464. Academic Press, New York.

Renfrew, C., and K. L. Cooke (eds.) 1979. *Transformations. Mathematical Approaches to Culture Change*. Academic Press, New York.

Renfrew, C., M. Rowlands, and B. A. Seagraves (eds.) 1982. *Theory and Explanation in Archaeology*. Academic Press, New York.

Scheurer, P. 1979. *Révolutions de la science et permanence du réel*. Presses Universitaires du France, Paris.

Sire, M. 1960. *La vie sociale des animaux*. Seuil, Paris.

Thom, R. 1980. *Modèles mathématiques de la morphogenèse*. Christian Bourgois, Paris.

Tosi, M. 1977. "The archaeological evidence for protostate structures in Eastern Iran and Central Asia at the end of the 3rd millennium B.C.," in J. Deshayes (ed.), *L'Asie Centrale et le plateau iranien des origines à la conquête islamique*, pp. 45–66. Editions du C.N.R.S., Paris.

———1984. "The notion of craft specialization and its representation in the archaeological record of early states in the Turanian Basin," in M. Spriggs (ed.), *Marxist Perspectives in Archaeology*, pp. 22–52. Cambridge University Press, Cambridge.

van de Velde, P. 1985. "Early state formation in Iron Age Central Europe," in H. J. Claessen, P. van de Velde, and M. E. Smith, *Development and Decline: The Evolution of Sociopolitical Organization*, pp. 176–177. Bergin and Garvey, South Hadley, MA.

Veyne, P. 1971. *Comment on écrit l'histoire*. Seuil, Paris

White, L. A. 1959. *The Evolution of Culture*. McGraw Hill, New York.

Wilson, E. O. 1971. *The Insect Societies*. Harvard University, Belknap Press, Cambridge, MA.

Wittgenstein, L. 1983. *Remarques sur les fondements des mathématiques*. G. E. M. Anscombe, R. Rhees, and G. H. von Wright (eds.). Gallimard, Paris.

Wright, H. 1978. "Toward an explanation for the origin of the state," in S. Cohen and E. Service (eds.), *Origins of the State*, pp. 49–69. Institute for the Study of Human Issues, Philadelphia.

Wright, H. T., and G. A. Johnson 1975. "Population, exchange and early state formation in Southwestern Iran," *American Anthropologist* **LXXVII,** 267–329.

Zadora-Rio, E. 1986. "L'identification d'une construction médiévale," in J.-C. Gardin et al., *Systèmes experts et sciences humaines*, pp. 169–188. Eyrolles, Paris.

Zeeman, E. C. 1977. *Catastrophe Theory: Selected Papers 1972–1977*. Addison-Wesley, London.

———1982. "Decision Making and Evolution," in C. Renfrew, M. Rowlands, and B. A. Seagraves (eds.), *Theory and Explanation in Archaeology*, pp. 315–346. Academic Press, New York.

A Computational Investigation of Three Models of Specialization, Exchange, and Social Complexity

Introduction

In Doran 1982 I suggested that multiple actor systems theory, a branch of Distributed Artificial Intelligence, could form the basis of a model of sociocultural dynamics including the growth of social complexity. Since 1982 Distributed Artificial Intelligence itself (henceforth DAI) has developed substantially (Huhns 1987). On the archaeological side there has been interest in what Renfrew (1986) has called "Peer Polity Interaction," and "cognitive" archaeology has also become more prominent, involving attention to the mental states, beliefs, and ideology of those comprising sociocultural systems. Further, Brumfiel and Earle (1987) have identified three basic models currently employed by those studying growth of social complexity.

These have been important and highly relevant developments. Since they seem to offer some support to my 1982 proposal, it is timely to look again at that proposal to see whether it may now be pursued in greater detail and to greater effect. This is the more likely since computer programs now exist which permit simple experiments of the type conceived in my 1982 paper. Accordingly, after a brief preliminary discussion I shall review relevant DAI concepts and then look in some detail at the three models discussed by Brumfiel and Earle (1987). I shall ask how these models might be interpreted in relation to my 1982 proposal and to a development of that proposal, the EOS (Emergence of the State) scenario (Doran 1988).

Underlying my investigation is the assumption that better and more rigorous sociocultural theory is needed to support archaeological practice. The reasons for seeking formal theories and models, by which I mean theories or models expressed within some formal language of logic, mathematics, or computer science, are quite simply that their specification can be made testably coherent and that their consequences are derivable in a rigorous, repeatable way. It has frequently been pointed out that archaelogical theories and models are typically informally specified, structurally simple, and too imprecise for their implications to be derived in any other than a subjective and unreliable way.

My approach is explicitly a processual one. But even postprocessualists (e.g., Hodder

1985) may be sympathetic to the emphasis on the role played by the beliefs of social participants.

Interpretation Within a Formal Conceptual Repertoire

There have been many attempts to bring quantification and formalization into archaeological research and not all of them have been fruitful (Doran 1986b). Hence some preliminary explanation and attempted justification of my line of attack here will not be out of place.

Any model will embody certain structural assumptions about the target system being modeled. These assumptions specify the elements or components discerned within the target system and the relationships discerned between them. Clearly, a good choice of structural assumptions is crucial to the success of the modeling exercise. In a formal modeling study, structural assumptions must themselves be expressed within a symbolic language or formalism (if they are to be subject to logical or mathematical inference, or to computation) and this symbolic language or formalism will in turn embody a **formal conceptual repertoire** (henceforth FCR), for example that of catastrophe theory, or discrete-event simulation or mathematical programming. The FCR which provides the matrix for the particular structural assumptions to be adopted must be appropriate to these assumptions. This **choice** of underlying FCR is arguably the most important part of a formal modeling study but, alas, is commonly made merely on the basis of immediate practical convenience.

Important criteria for the choice of an FCR in a particular context include adequacy, the requirement that all the structural assumptions are expressible within it, and tractability, the requirement that there exists a reliable mechanism for deriving conclusions from the assumptions made. My suggestion that the DAI conceptual repertoire is appropriate to the study of the social phenomena behind the archaeological record is based primarily on its adequacy: not only does it immediately address the behavior of structured communities, it can express assumptions about the specific beliefs and social models held by their participants. Tractability rests on the ability of DAI models to be programmed and run on a computer.

A difficulty is that DAI itself is a research area rather than a well established and tried body of concepts and techniques. This means that conventional modeling studies are not feasible. However, there is evidence that an emerging conceptual repertoire can usefully be deployed in "exploratory engineering mode." This is the lesson to be drawn, for example, from artificial intelligence (in relation to cognitive psychology) and aircraft engineering (in relation to bird flight). In these disciplines the immediate aim has been to build working systems to display specific behaviors rather than to build realistic models. Although not always successful, the attempts almost invariably illuminate the original domain of study. By exploring the implications of an FCR oriented to a particular application area, an understanding is gained of those conceivable process combinations which are feasible and of their behavior.

When an FCR is chosen to support theories and models existing ideas must be interpreted within it. In a sociocultural context, for example, concepts such as "exchange" or "political elite" must be interpreted within the repertoire. Inadequate interpretations undermine the value of the study. But unless a study has a clear practical outcome whose value can be measured, assessment of interpretations is bound to be largely subjective.

Formal models can be created using direct formal interpretations of the concepts of the anthropological or archaeological formulation—which implies that the model can have no explanatory power for these concepts (though it may, of course, say things about their implications)—or the model can be set at a more fundamental level which enables study of the origins of the entities and relationships, especially causal relationships, of interest. Consider, for example, a model of warfare between two polities. At the simplest it might be no more than a random variable indicating the possible outcome. But it might also unpack the internal structure and decision processes of the polities in question and predict the outcome of the struggle accordingly. Unlike the former model, this latter would be able to offer some explanation of the outcome it predicts.

In what follows I shall consider essential low-level processes, seeking to derive the behavior of the social whole from the behavior of its participants, their interconnections and context.

Distributed Artificial Intelligence

DAI is a rapidly growing research area. It is a branch of Artificial Intelligence studies, in turn a branch of Computer Science. In the words of Les Gasser:

> "DAI is a continuum of study, both scientific research (reflective or examining) and engineering research (design-oriented), focused on how to understand and organise groups of intelligent problem-solvers. Groups of people, groups of automated intelligent processes, and human-computer interactive systems are all a part of DAI research. The best research in each of these areas tends to reinforce research in the others." (quoted in Sridharan 1987:76)

DAI has a number of different branches. That at issue here concerns the design and properties of multiple actor systems (henceforth MAS), in which a number of autonomous but communicating programmed problem-solvers, **actors,** concurrently collect information, reason with it, and act in a shared context. Most MAS work is not (yet) aimed at modeling human social systems but rather is oriented to building a system capable of performing some specific task. Typical tasks are distributed sensing (for example, for vehicle tracking) and control of multiple autonomous vehicles. In the former the core problem is the coordination of spatially distributed actors who collectively must acquire raw data and integrate and interpret it. Coordination implies negotiated task delegation typically leading to a hierarchical organization of actors, together with individual planning of data processing operations and collective plan reconciliation by way of exchange and modification of individual plans (see, for example, Durfee and Lesser 1987).

More generally, to specify such a multiple actor system the the DAI specialist (and ultimately the computer programmer) must specify:

— the actors themselves, their "physical" and "cognitive" abilities, and their beliefs/knowledge. Programmed actors are typically able (in very limited ways) to accept and set themselves goals, to generate, reason about, and execute plans of action in pursuit of those goals, and to maintain and update individual world models. Commonly actors will be partly adaptable, if only by having the ability to acquire and retain for future use new (to them) facts about the system in which they are embedded.

— communication channels between actors, and possible communications that may be sent between actors: for example, requests for information or for action.

— the shared environment of the actors and the way it behaves in response to the actions the actors perform upon it. This environment may be simulated as part of the multiple actor system (perhaps as one or more ''environment'' actors) or it may be a real applications environment.

There is no agreed classification of MAS (but see Sridharan 1987; Doran in press). However, natural dimensions of classification are by the capabilities of the individual programmed actors (for example, planning abilities, adaptability), by the properties of the community of actors (for example, their number and their dynamics), by communication properties (for example, fixed against varying communication links, density of linkage), and finally by the purpose of the MAS (for example, modeling, applications, theoretical investigation).

The non-DAI specialist must keep in mind that the various possible attributes of the actors in an MAS cannot yet be programmed to anything like human range and performance. They can, however, be programmed in limited forms sufficient for interesting and informative systems behavior to emerge, for example stable patterns of communication and action, and for useful work to be performed in applications contexts.

Also, the use of the word *actor* does not imply that where an MAS is used to model a human system each actor in the MAS will correspond to an individual human being. An actor might well correspond to a settlement or a social class, say. A specific example is the computer simulation study reported by Allen (1982) where the actors correspond to towns. By contrast Mithen (1988) has programmed a computer simulation of a hunting group where the actors correspond to specific hunters. Neither of these studies draws upon AI concepts, and the ''cognitive'' structure of the actors is correspondingly, and I would suggest inappropriately, limited. Renfrew (1986) considers, in effect, multiple actor system models in which the actors correspond to polities. He does focus on cognitive aspects, but without attempting to deploy the DAI conceptual repertoire.

MAS Testbeds at Essex University

Because of the substantial programming effort typically required to set up an MAS on a computer, **testbeds** (analogous to expert system shells) have been developed which facilitate the specification of particular MAS either for immediate applications use or for research experimentation. To illustrate these, I shall now briefly describe the TEAMWORK2/MCS and EXCHANGE testbeds developed at Essex University.

The TEAMWORK2/MCS testbed, written in Prolog (Doran 1985; Doran in preparation), associates with each actor its own database of ''beliefs'' about actions, the world, and other actors, together with a unified hierarchical planning and plan execution system

(IPEM—Ambros-Ingerson 1987; Ambros-Ingerson and Steel 1988), and provides facilities whereby the actions executed by one actor can access the database of any other actor. It thus enables an MAS to be set up which features relatively sophisticated planning and plan execution by the actors (including simultaneous handling of several plans), and structured message passing between actors, but in which the structure of the simulated world in which the actors exist is left entirely to the discretion of the user. The testbed provides a range of online commands which make it easy to use in experimental mode.

By contrast, the EXCHANGE testbed (also written in Prolog—Doran and Corcoran 1985) is considerably simpler and more directly relevant to this paper. It is oriented toward research into multiple actor exchange systems in which the actors are "spatially" distributed, which means merely that each actor has only a small number of neighbors for the purposes of communication and exchange. The actors have (abstract) resources, (abstract) technological production knowledge, (abstract) consumption goals, and they are able to exchange resources and products with their neighbors. The actors can independently and concurrently generate and execute plans, but the planner program involved is much simpler and more restricted than that embodied in the TEAMWORK2/MCS system just sketched. An "exchange handler" is provided to resolve situations where many exchange proposals are made, but only a subset can possibly be achieved. Finally, actors have and can acquire knowledge (more strictly beliefs—they can be in error) about their neighbors.

To illustrate what can be done, here follows a description of a small scenario which is typical of many run in the EXCHANGE testbed. The scenario is directed at the abstract concepts of a "central place" and of "deferred exchange."

Scenario: a "solar" exchange network implemented using the EXCHANGE testbed

There are 5 actors A,B,C,D,E in the system. Notionally E is a 'central place' and A,B,C, and D are 'peripheral.' A,B,C,D can exchange directly with E, but not with one another. A,B,C, and D have p1,q1 through to p4,q4 respectively as basic resources, but have no production (technological) knowledge except that they know respectively how to produce p5 from p1, p6 from p2, p7 from p3, and p8 from p4. E has no resources but knows how to produce p11 from p1 through p4 via intermediate products p9 and p10. A,B,C,D all wish to consume quantities of p11 in addition to whichever q it is they have as a basic resource, while E wishes to consume q1 through q4 as well as p11.

*A,B,C,D know that E can produce p11. E knows the resources that A,B,C, and D have. Using the knowledge they have, the actors independently and simultaneously try to achieve their consumption goals by forming and executing appropriate plans. A,B,C,D each aim at an exchange with E for p11. Meanwhile, E, in order to achieve its goal of consuming q1,q2,q3,q4, and p11, plans that it must exchange with A obtaining p1 against a **promise** of p11, obtain quantities of p2,p3,p4 similarly from B,C, and D, then produce an appropriate amount of p11, then pay off its 'p11' debts and then use more p11 to exchange for what it really wants, q1,q2,q3,q4, and for its own consumption. And in due course this is what happens. Note that although the peripheral actors have the knowledge and resources to produce p5 through p8, there is no point in their doing so and accordingly these products are not created.*

Simple though the processes just described may seem, the computational design issues are not trivial. Giving a programmable but nontrivial interpretation to such words as *knowledge, goals, plans,* and *decisions* opens a plethora of alternatives, some easily handled but of limited interest, others much more interesting but correspondingly more difficult to make work. Implementing the idea of a promise is particularly tricky. And typically it is not until the example is actually run that subtle and often very important interactions are recognized.

Like all such experiments, that described provokes many further questions. I shall not discuss here such issues as rates of exchange, and the extension of the scenario to "down the line" exchange or to redistribution. For some consideration of such topics and more details of the EXCHANGE testbed see Doran and Corcoran 1985.

Five Key Concepts

There are a number of important general concepts that naturally emerge from DAI work and yet also have manifest significance in social theory. I shall briefly discuss five which have particular relevance for what follows: **potential technology, social model, cognitive economy, interactor contract, and organization.**

Computer experiments of the type illustrated by the foregoing testbed example highlight the idea of **potential technology,** that is, the "technology" that is there for the actors to discover. Thus, in the example it is a fact that p11 may be produced from p1,p2,p3,p4 via intermediate stages, though only one of the five actors knows this. The importance of the potential technology in an MAS is that for any particular mechanism of technological discovery there will be an interaction between this mechanism and the structure of the potential technology itself. This interaction will, one may reasonably hypothesize, play an important role in the social dynamics. For example, a plateau in the potential technology—where discoveries are hard to come by—will perhaps manifest itself as a plateau in the development of social complexity. We seem to know almost nothing about this interaction even from studies of prehistoric human technology.

Potential technology is an aspect of the shared environment in the MAS. It may well be that an interaction between "spatial" environment and potential technology (e.g., raw materials are widely dispersed) forces wide spatial cooperation.

That part of a programmed actor's internal world model (variously 'world view,' 'belief system,' 'cognized model,' or 'mental map' in human terms) which is concerned with other actors in the MAS I shall refer to as its **social model.** The design of social models is a key issue in DAI since, in an obvious way, it is the basis of an actor's reasoning as it relates to communication with and manipulation of other actors. Further, an actor's social model may embody a view of the actor community (as regards, say, groupings and subgroupings) which may be both a simplification and a distortion of the "reality," with major implications both for the individual actor's behavior and for the behavior of the community. I shall refer to an actor with a developed social model as **aware.**

The origin of the simplification and possible distortion in actors' social models lies not just in an actor's possibly limited access to information (depending upon the circumstances of the particular MAS), but also in straightforward computational limitations.

Each actor can only do so much processing in a given time and has only so much memory space. In consequence there is a need for **cognitive economy** (Lenat, Hayes-Roth and Klahr 1979): heuristic strategies which reduce processing and memory storage requirements without too great a cost in accuracy and effectiveness. Important examples are the use of focusing techniques, aggregation and storage of knowledge in terms of object prototypes, and the reuse of suitably generalized successful plans of action. In any substantial system (including the human system) strategies of cognitive economy are obligatory. Yet the impact of the distortions and inflexibility that these strategies clearly imply is poorly understood. However, both Johnson (1982) and Cohen (1985) provide insightful anthropological discussions of aspects of cognitive economy.

Also important in DAI work is the notion of a **contract.** In the influential CNET system of Davis and Smith (1983) a contract is an automatically negotiated agreement between two programmed actors whereby one performs a task for another. In Doran 1982 I suggested a rather different concept: "a recurring piece of behavior, standardized by schemata in the actors participating in it" (p383). Contracts in this latter sense derive partly from cognitive economy, since the schemata mentioned are executable representations of past successful behavior and thus the product of one of the basic strategies of cognitive economy.

A collection of contracts (in either sense) within a community of actors yields a type of **organization.** However, there are differing DAI conceptions of what organizations essentially are. A typical interpretation is that an organization is a stable pattern of relationships between actors such that the actions of the actors achieve some discernible collective goal—though this leaves open the question of just what constitutes a collective goal. It is important that an organization persists even with change of actors. Thus the relationships are really between **roles,** where a role is a restricted piece of behavior which is a fixed part of the collective goal-oriented behavior of the whole organization.

It is natural to distinguish between information collecting organizations and action performing organizations, accepting that most organizations are intermediate between these two extremes. It is also useful to distinguish between unaware and aware organizations. In the former, the actors are purely reactive without social models, that is, without the ability to build or use permanent internal representations of their fellow actors and the organization of which they are a part. An ant community is an unaware organization in this sense. If at least some of the actors do possess nontrivial social models, are aware, then we have the more interesting case in which actors have a manipulable view of their own organization and expectations about the behavior of their fellow actors. It is plausible that aware organizations possess greater stability in the presence of varying conditions.

As will appear, each of these concepts has a bearing upon the growth of social complexity.

EOS: A DAI-Based Scenario for the Emergence of Complexity

From a DAI viewpoint, organizational emergence occurs where the actors programmed in an MAS have not been initialized within organizations, but are so contrived that they "spontaneously" combine in one or more organizations in ways that are, in effect, unpredictable. Assuming an MAS embodying an initially unstructured community of similarly architectured actors distributed in a shared environment, how might aware organizations emerge?

The EOS scenario (Doran 1988; and see Doran 1982) identifies the following four key steps of a possible emergence path for an MAS programmed in something like the EXCHANGE testbed. There is no suggestion that this is the only possible path. The emphasis is on key abstract processes, the basic assumption being that **organization emerges as a ''side effect'' of individual actors attempting to achieve local consumption goals in the presence of a ''spatially'' distributed ''technological'' environment.**

1. Developing awareness of (neighboring) actors—actors acquire knowledge of their local context, most importantly of neigboring actors and their abilities. This is the process of social model building and may be seen as an extension of nonsocial model building. Technically it seems to require situation-event rule induction from past state representations, with the rules induced then deployed as spontaneous operators in plan formation. Although complex models of others are not necessarily implied, the process of rule induction is potentially combinatorially explosive.

2. Goal oriented manipulation of others by exchange—to achieve their individual goals, actors find it effective to persuade, possibly to plan to persuade, other actors to act on their behalf. Exchange of information, action, or products is thus a particular means to persuasion. A core technical issue is to specify exactly the learning process by which an actor acquires a representation of the process of exchange, regarded as a spontaneous operator, and its preconditions and effects.

3. Dominance and cumulative dominance—the structure of the potential technology in combination with the ''spatial'' distribution of basic resources then enables effective cooperative organizations. These emerge by way of suitably located actors with relatively rich resources or technological knowledge being able to ''buy'' the specialization of their neighbors and in this sense dominate them (as illustrated in a minor way in the solar exchange scenario discussed earlier). This is particularly so if an emerging lead actor can ''buy'' additional technological knowledge by exchange. Local dominance of an actor over neighboring actors can become recursively cumulative **if local lead actors can communicate directly,** and exchange on behalf of their followers, yielding one or more hierarchical organizations exploiting the technology on a large scale. The degree of awareness shown by an organization will depend upon the effectiveness of the actors' social model-building processes. The more awareness lead actors have, the more they will, in principle, be able to **plan** reorganization of the actors they dominate.

4. Stability—in addition to any constraints imposed by the spatial structure of the environment and by the potential technology, a newly emerged organization will be stabilized by the processes of cognitive economy internal to its actors.

This scenario, sketchy though it is, is in touch with and arises from current AI and DAI research. Thus it is primarily a DAI product, not an attempt to model human social processes. From the viewpoint of social science, its most unexpected feature is perhaps the attention it focuses on learning processes within the actors, especially in the first two steps of the path. Another possibly surprising feature is that no technological innovation is presumed. Rather, the growth of hierarchical complexity is seen as more effective exploitation of the existing (i.e., currently known to the actors) technology (compare the accumulation of beneficial contracts considered in Doran 1986a).

The EOS scenario has not been programmed in its entirety and therefore everything said about its behavior is subject to revision. However, simple versions of it certainly could be programmed and no doubt will be. I assume that a fully working version could in principle be informative about human social processes in just the way that a more conventional mathematical model might be. My limited aim in the remainder of this paper is to match the DAI conceptual repertoire, and this EOS scenario in particular, against models of growth in social complexity currently used by anthropologists and archaeologists to see what, if anything, can be learned.

The Brumfiel and Earle Models

Brumfiel and Earle (1987) have identified in the (extensive) literature three recurring outline models which seek to explain, or at least describe, the growth of social complexity via specialization and exchange. Brief formulations of the models which identify what seem to be the essentials are as follows (all quotations are taken from Brumfiel and Earle 1987):

The first model takes the root cause of social complexity as **commercial development** "dictated by economic efficiency and the pursuit of individual advantage." The key observation is that commercial development generates increased specialization and exchange, which in turn provokes the central authority needed to order it.

In the second or **adaptionist model,** "powerful centralised leadership" arises specifically in those environmental or demographic contexts where economic management is either necessary for survival or especially beneficial. Management is directed to the good of all. Management may be of redistribution, or markets, or production, or long-distance trade. It is important that in this model specialization and exchange are as much a consequence of central management as a cause of it.

Finally, the **political model** is similar to the adaptionist, with the important difference that central control is directed to the well-being of the elite leadership with disregard for the well-being of the remainder of the population. "It is proposed that political elites **conciously** and strategically employ specialisation and exchange to create and maintain social inequality, ... " (my emphasis). "Mobilisation, the transfer of goods from producers to political elites, is seen as lying at the heart of political development." Mobilization enables rulers to create new institutions of political control, to become patrons of craft specialities, and to sponsor long-distance trade. Alternative versions of this model stress monopoly of foreign trade; monopoly of certain food crops, tools, or weaponry; control and manipulation of wealth; control over prestige goods or wealth combined with a regional marketing system.

In their discussion of these models Brumfiel and Earle make a number of important observations and distinctions. Thus they distinguish between subsistence goods and wealth, including within the latter "primitive valuables used in display, ritual, and exchange and special rare and highly desired subsistence goods" (p. 4), and follow Douglas in suggesting that "the political importance of wealth derives from its essential role in validating social status'' (p. 4). They discuss specialization and exchange for both subsistence goods and wealth, and conclude that specialization in the production of subsistence goods is of little political significance, whereas the procurement and distribution of wealth rival the mobilization and distribution of subsistence goods in political impact. They also distinguish between independent and attached specialists, the latter serving patrons amongst the political elite. They see production by attached specialists as developing first and foremost in response to "*needs for control* in the political economy'' (p. 5—italics in original).

A DAI Assessment of the Brumfiel and Earle Models

There is an obvious major difference in the nature of the EOS scenario and the Brumfiel and Earle models. The latter are essentially simple, imprecise descriptions of complex economic and social phenomena. The EOS scenario is a considerably more precise description of a complex computational process. My claim is that at a sufficient level of abstraction the difference between them is much less important than may at first appear.

Since the Brumfiel and Earle models are built upon considerations of exchange, specialization, and wealth, some preliminary discussion of these topics from the DAI standpoint is appropriate before the growth of social complexity itself is addressed.

DAI and Exchange

From the DAI perspective, simple exchange raises technical problems but is conceptually clear. It may be seen as a particular form of requesting as a means to goal achievement by the requesting actor. This actor must know what the effects of an exchange are likely to be and how to initiate one. It must have sufficient knowledge of the goals and resources of the target actor to realize that an exchange with it is feasible. The target actor has the rather simpler task of deciding whether or not to agree to the exchange offered. A DAI view of exchange is illustrated by the EXCHANGE testbed scenario given earlier, and, as already discussed, exchange is central to the EOS scenario, in which it appears both as a necessity for "technological" cooperation and as a mechanism of dominance.

The natural interpretation of an exchange system is a number of actors motivated and able to take part in exchanges one with another—as envisaged, of course, in the design of the EXCHANGE testbed. The central issue in such a system is the relationship between the elements of the system—for example, actor planning abilities and the potential technology—and the patterns of exchange which emerge—for example, redistribution and chains of exchanges which implement long-distance trading (Doran and Corcoran 1985; and compare Plog 1977).

More complex types of exchange, for example, deferred exchange and generalized exchange, pose more complex computational design problems—as in the deferred exchange in the EXCHANGE example scenario. It is technically difficult fully to capture the difference between an actor having a thing and having a promise of a thing. A different dimension of difficulty concerns **what** is exchanged. The foregoing remarks largely address the exchange of material commodities. What about the exchange of information?

This is, at first glance, rather easily addressed within a DAI system: each actor has information, and an exchange between part of that information and commodities or other information supplied by another actor is easily programmed. There are, of course, problems of valuation. More important, there are problems associated with the handling within the actors of objects of exchange which are at the same time pieces of knowledge later to be used as such. Many of the technical issues are unresolved.

DAI and Specialization

If specialization is taken to mean that an actor performs only a narrow range of actions, then in the DAI perspective several different causes or mechanisms of specialization are discernible. At its simplest, specialization may be inbuilt (the actor can only perform a few actions) or determined by a restrictive environment. Alternatively, the actor may have the "physical" ability to act widely but have only limited knowledge, for example, it may have representations of only a small number of actions. More interestingly, the actor may be a specialist, because that is cognitively economical in a highly complex situation. Finally, the actor may have accepted a limiting role in a cooperative organization. This last possibility implies that the specialization is a matter of goal-driven choice, and is technically much more complex. Specialization in what? Just production? Or planning, for example? This would imply specialization in meta-knowledge, that is, in knowledge of how to reason. If the knowledge is inbuilt and fixed, then this is not problematic. But manipulation of meta-knowledge is never simple.

Specialization would certainly be part of step three of the EOS development path, and appears to involve attached specialists according to the Brumfiel and Earle distinction. However, an element of "possession" in the attachment relationship suggests that it should in some way be explicitly represented and marked as desirable in the social model of the dominant actor.

DAI and Wealth

The EOS scenario makes no reference to wealth and therefore suggests the existence of a path to social complexity without it. This seems consistent with the view that the importance of wealth is its role in validating (rather than creating) social status. Perhaps wealth serves primarily to stabilize an already existing organization and does so by the invocation of aspects of human cognition other than those reflected in EOS, for example, contextual rather than logical association.

The Commercial Development Model

After these preliminaries, I now turn to a consideration of the models themselves. There is little process detail in the commercial development model. Recall that it proposes just two successive stages. First comes "spontaneous" economic growth, including increase in specialization and exchange. This growth involves the pursuit of individual advantage and possibly also involves technological innovation. Only later comes central authority, primarily in order to control the complexity that has already appeared.

The first of these stages seems compatible with the EOS scenario even though the latter makes no assumption of technological innovation. Specifically, step two of the EOS scenario may loosely be related to "spontaneous economic growth." However, the proposed emergence of central authority to perform an overall regulatory function is certainly not compatible with EOS. The commercial development model seems (it is not specific) to imply lead actors motivated and able to exercise regulatory power. As regards motivation, while it is certainly possible to set up programmed actors with goals oriented to the well-being of the entire actor system, it is less easy to devise processes by which such goals could emerge in actors with much more local initial goals. The ability to exercise regulatory power implies lead actors with complex social models, kept updated and supported by a correspondingly sophisticated planning ability and the ability to act upon the entire system or some substantial part of it. This is far from trivial, and goes far beyond anything envisaged in the EOS scenario. EOS, it will be recalled, envisages a hierarchy structured by exchange relationships with only limited awareness even by actors at its summit.

The Adaptionist Model

The adaptionist model is similar to the commercial development model just discussed in that it also proposes "altruistic" lead actors with the ability and power to take management decisions with wide-ranging impact. But again nothing specific is said about processes by which such a power structure might come into existence and how the information flow it requires might be sustained.

An important aspect of the adaptionist model is the suggestion that the environmental or demographic context must be suitable. This in not a problem from the DAI point of view. In the EOS scenario dispersion of basic resources and the structure of the technology would certainly be determining factors on the emergence path.

The Political Model

The DAI interpretation of the political model identifies the same unexamined information collection, information processing, and effective action requirements for the lead actor or actor group as in the other two models. However, the abandonment of the "altruistic" element in the motivation assigned to the leadership is more in line with the EOS scenario.

The notion of a "political elite" is itself somewhat problematic. Is a political elite to be interpreted in MAS terms merely as a subset of the actors with particular characteristics (and should one envisage sharp boundaries to the elite?), or is it "really" a representation in the social models of all the actors in the system? Either or both is possible. The Brumfiel and Earle discussion seems to concentrate of the former possibility, but the latter, which is very different, seems of equal potential significance.

Discussion

The major problem with all three of the models discussed by Brumfiel and Earle is that while they embody central authority, they say nothing about the process mechanisms by which that authority must function: how the lead actors collectively represent the current economic situation (if that is what is at issue), how they acquire the knowledge to keep that representation moderately accurate, and how their decisions can be put into effect. These are not minor issues. They constitute much of the social complexity the emergence of which the models are intended to explicate. It may perhaps be argued that these are psychological matters and not the business of social science. But if there is one thing that DAI research has already made clear—and these topics are at the heart of DAI— it is that the information processing of the individual and of the system are deeply interconnected and that the one cannot be understood without the other.

Another aspect of the interconnection between the processing of the individual and of the system is the prominence in the EOS scenario of the learning processes within the actor. These are not mentioned in the Brumfiel and Earle models, although it is obvious that individuals must learn new ideas and behavior as part of the growth of social complexity. Indeed, the ability of individuals to learn such things, and internally to represent the knowledge acquired through learning, is a necessary condition for the growth of complexity. The archaeological models implicitly assume these cognitive abilities.

On the other hand, the EOS scenario, and the DAI conceptual repertoire behind it, have nothing yet to say about a multitude of anthropological topics including those as fundamental as wealth, goods, markets, and security. How far these concepts can be interpreted in the DAI conceptual repertoire remains largely unconsidered. Equally, we do not know how central they are to some or all possible emergence paths.

It is worth remarking that, incomplete though the three Brumfiel and Earle models are, nothing in them seems impossible in DAI terms. This does not mean that anything goes. Rather, it suggests that there are many pathways to complexity and we must search for less obvious constraints, probably centered on the interface between the individual and the system, to distinguish between what is possible and what is not.

If there are multiple paths to social complexity, as just suggested, why do some societies seem to stick at a particular level of complexity? There are several possibilities compatible with the DAI viewpoint. One is variation in the processing abilities of the actors. If the actors in a given system cannot support the learning process presumed in the EOS scenario, say, then certainly that growth path is ruled out. Another possibility is a bottleneck or plateau in the potential technology as mentioned earlier. And cognitive economy may be significant. As part of my 1982 proposal I suggested that one effect of the individual actor's need for cognitive economy would be that an MAS would often "lock into" a suboptimal pattern of contracts. A further, more subtle, possible consequence of cognitive economy is the emergence of substantially distorting social models. By a distorting model I mean one that does not correctly or even approximately reflect the actor's context as it really is in the MAS. A coherent set of such models might be stable and yet so distort actor decision making that the basic causal link embodied in the EOS scenario between individual goal seeking and the emergence of cooperative organization is disrupted.

The Interpretation of the Archaeological Record

Something must be said about the implications of such investigations as this for the interpretation of the archaeological excavation record. Put simply, such investigations are intended as a contribution to the identification of a limited number of possible paths for the emergence and growth of social complexity. Should it then prove possible to identify archaeological indicators characteristic of each path, it will be possible to determine which was followed, when, and why.

Of course, the identification of key archaeological indicators is not at all easy (for an excellent and particularly relevant discussion see Peebles and Kus 1977). Specialization, exchange, and wealth are all partially identifiable in the excavation record. Unfortunately, such key factors as goals, social models, and effective central control are not (yet). This differential access is reflected in the current archaeological models.

The hard problem of linking theory to the excavation record is not going to go away. But to interpret excavation evidence as if there could be no relevant social theory is no solution. We shall only find the crucial insights by looking for them.

Conclusions

This has been an initial attempt to put DAI and archaeological models of the growth of organization complexity alongside one another. In spite of the largely speculative nature of the exercise I believe that certain important conclusions may be drawn.

First, the two domains of study can indeed inform each other. There are fundamental concepts that appear in both. In particular, the formal conceptual repertoire of DAI can serve as a matrix for models of human social dynamics, and computer-based experiments can establish their properties. That the associated technical problems are themselves far from easy and at the research frontier is only to be expected—one should not expect the proverbial free lunch!

Secondly, the archaeological models described by Brumfiel and Earle are consistently deficient in their failure to address the information processing details (any of the details!) of how a power structure might emerge and be sustained. This is partly because they fail to address the role played by the cognitive abilities and inabilities of individual actors. I believe that unless we are very lucky, no deep understanding will be gained until this deficiency is put right. DAI can help.

Acknowledgments: I am grateful to Jose Ambros-Ingerson, Graham Clarke, and Chris Trayner for numerous helpful discussions concerning the modeling of exchange systems, and to Horacio Carvajal-Sanchez-Yarza for helpful discussions concerning the structure of social models. The TEAMWORK project was funded by the UK Science and Engineering Research Council under grant number GR/C/44938.

REFERENCES

Allen, P. M. 1982. "The genesis of structure in social systems: The paradigm of self-organisation," in C. Renfrew, M. Rowlands, and B. A. Segraves (eds.), *Theory and Explanation in Archaeology*, pp. 347–374. Academic Press, New York.
Ambros-Ingerson, J. A. 1987. *IPEM: Integrated Planning Execution and Monitoring*. M.Phil. dissertation, Department of Computer Science, University of Essex, Colchester.
Ambros-Ingerson, J. A., and S. Steel 1988. "Integrating planning, execution and monitoring." Paper presented at the AAAI-88 Conference. In press.

Brumfiel, E. M., and T. K. Earle 1987. "Specialisation, exchange and complex societies: An introduction," in E. M. Brumfiel and T. K. Earle (eds.), *Specialisation, Exchange and Complex Societies*, pp. 1–9. Cambridge University Press, Cambridge.

Cohen, M. N. 1985. "Prehistoric hunter-gatherers: The meaning of social complexity," in T. D. Price and J. A. Brown (eds.), *Prehistoric Hunter-Gatherers: The Emergence of Cultural Complexity*, pp. 99–119. Academic Press, New York.

Davis, R., and R. G. Smith 1983. "Negotiation as a metaphor for distributed problem solving," *Artificial Intelligence* **20,** 63–109.

Doran, J. E. 1982. "A computational model of sociocultural systems and their dynamics," in C. Renfrew, M. Rowlands, and B. A. Segraves (eds.), *Theory and Explanation in Archaeology*, pp. 375–388. Academic Press, New York.

———1985. "The computational approach to knowledge, communication and structure in multi-actor systems," in N. Gilbert and C. C. Heath (eds.), *Artificial Intelligence and Sociology*, pp. 160–171. Gower, London.

———1986a. "A contract-structure model of sociocultural change," in S. Laflin (ed.), *Computer Applications in Archaeology 1986*, pp.171–178. University of Birmingham Computer Centre, Birmingham.

———1986b. "Formal methods and archaeological theory: A perspective," *World Archaeology* **18,** 21–37.

———1988. "The structure and emergence of hierarchical organisations." Alvey Workshop on Multiple Agent Systems, Philips Research Laboratories, Redhill, April 14th and 15th, 1988.

———in press. "Distributed artificial intelligence and the modelling of sociocultural systems," in L. Murray and J. Richardson (eds.), *Human Implications of Intelligent Systems*. Oxford University Press, Oxford.

———in preparation. *The TEAMWORK/MCS Testbed User Guide*. Department of Computer Science, University of Essex.

Doran, J. E., and G. Corcoran 1985. "A computational model of production exchange and trade," in A. Voorrips and S. Loving (eds.), *To Pattern the Past*. Special volume of the Journal of the European Study Group on Physical, Chemical and Mathematical Techniques Applied to Archaeology *(PACT)* **11,** 349–359.

Durfee, E. H., and V. Lesser 1987. "Using partial global plans to coordinate distributed problem solvers," *International Joint Conference on Artificial Intelligence 1987*, pp. 875–883.

Hodder, I. 1985. "Postprocessual archaeology," *Advances in Archaeological Method and Theory* **8,** 1–25.

Huhns, M. N. (ed.) 1987. *Distributed Artificial Intelligence*. Morgan Kaufmann, Los Altos, CA.

Johnson, G. A. 1982. "Organisational structure and scalar stress," in C. Renfrew, M. Rowlands, and B. A. Segraves (eds.), *Theory and Explanation in Archaeology*, pp. 389–421. Academic Press, New York.

Lenat, D. B., F. Hayes-Roth, and P. Klahr 1979. "Cognitive economy," *Proceedings of the Sixth International Joint Conference on Artificial Intelligence*, pp. 531–536. Tokyo.

Mithen, S. J. 1988. "Simulation as a methodological tool: Inferring hunting goals from faunal assemblages," in C. L. N. Ruggles and S. P. Q. Rhatz (eds.), *Computer and Quantitative Methods in Archaeology 1987*, pp. 119–137. British Archaeological Reports International Series 393, Oxford.

Peebles, C. S., and S. M. Kus 1977. "Some archaeological correlates of ranked societies," *American Antiquity* **42,** 421–448.

Plog, F. 1977. "Modelling economic exchange," in T. K. Earle and J. Ericson (eds.), *Exchange Systems in Prehistory*, pp. 127–140. Academic Press, New York.

Renfrew, C. 1986. "Introduction: Peer polity interaction and socio-political change," in C. Renfrew and J. F. Cherry (eds.), *Peer Polity Interaction and Socio-Political Change*, pp. 1–18. Cambridge University Press, Cambridge.

Sridharan, N. S. 1987. "1986 Workshop on Distributed AI," *AI Magazine*, Fall 1987, 75–85.

Symbolic Data and Numerical Processing

A CASE STUDY IN ART HISTORY BY MEANS OF
AUTOMATED LEARNING TECHNIQUES

Introduction

This research has been conducted in collaboration with Monique Renaud, computer research consultant at the Laboratoire d'Informatique pour les Sciences de l'Homme, CNRS, Paris. All calculations have taken place at the Centre Inter Régional de Calcul Electronique (CIRCE), in Orsay, near Paris. The APL Automated Learning Program, called TRINITA, was written by Jean Sallantin, from the Centre de Recherche en Informatique de Montpellier (CRIM), CNRS, Montpellier, and developed by his colleagues, Frédérique Van Bokstaele and Henri Soldano.

The automated learning experiment described here is based upon a classification of previously published and perfectly well-known Cistercian church plans. No new important archaeological or historical questions are raised. In regard to the automated classification procedures, our intention is not to bring forth a new one, since archaeologists nowadays are quite familiar with a number of successful tools for classification. Our reasons for starting this research, and, partly, for describing its results at this conference, are the following:

(1) Having used expert systems since 1982, as a means to analyze and reproduce different kinds of archaeological reasoning (Lagrange and Renaud 1985), we wanted to test other AI techniques that might be beneficial to the study of cognitive mechanisms in a domain that was familiar to us. Automated learning, as such, is most certainly at the core of AI research, and can be one of the most daring or utopian ways to approach modeling of human brain activity. Concerning the impact of automated learning on expert systems, first their development is slowed seriously by the difficulty of transferring knowledge from man to machine; thus the idea of machine self-learning. Second, expert systems must, in the near future, be able to maintain current control over the coherence of the knowledge which is imparted to them—when new rules are being added to a rule base—and this control capacity is closely associated with the learning function (Lagrange and Renaud 1987). Third, from a more theoretical point of view, we all hope that we may build AI tools (or models) which not only might imitate us, as expert systems do,

but also be capable of induction (generalization) or discovery. This is the inspiration that guides those who work in the area of machine self-learning: "Learnists," if you will.

(2) As an incentive, we were familiar with what looked like a suitable set of data: they are part of a corpus of 355 Cistercian church plans (Dimier 1949), empirically classified by the author (Appendix 1). A close critical study of this first classification, with the help of automatic classification techniques, had already been published (Lagrange 1973). Starting from there, we were able to build up a model of an empirical classification, with all possible "natural" defects: uncertainties in regard to a suitable description for church plans, lack of extrinsic (historical and geographical) information, weakness of hypotheses, and so on. The automated learning experiment, thus, consisted first in submitting examples of empirically classified objects (plans) to a computer program, in order that it might build up its own knowledge of classification, and then in checking the consistency of this knowledge by asking the program to classify new objects.

(3) TRINITA, the method for machine learning very kindly proposed to us by Jean Sallantin (see §I below), seemed to suit our project. In particular, the use of examples and counterexamples seemed close enough to our own approach to classification.

(4) The fact that the output of the learning phase in TRINITA consists in explicit production rules was a great help; it provides a means to analyze the interface between descriptive traits, mostly symbolic, and the learning procedure proper, which makes use of statistics.

I. The Functioning of TRINITA

I.1. A summary of statistico-syntactic learning techniques is presented by Sallantin and Quinqueton (1984), and by Soldano and Moisy (1985); see also a recent application to ecological data by Varone (1987).

Automated learning procedures comprise two phases: the learning phase proper, when knowledge is built by the program from input data (for instance, generalization based on a number of particular cases), and the operational phase, when the program applies its knowledge to new objects. In the present case, input data are lists of examples (or objects) described by sequences of binary attributes linked by the logical connector $\wedge$ (AND). Through these lists an extensive knowledge is expressed that the program must use comprehensively for treating objects which are not part of the initial lists.

(1) Statistico-syntactic techniques may be briefly described as follows: suppose a set of objects and their description (d_i, d_j, . . . d_n). Let A be a property of these objects (for instance belonging to a given group of church plans; see §II below). The question which is being asked is: Does an object x, known through its description $d(x)$, verify property A?

Learning consists of finding what the examples of A have in common in their description, or, in other words, in diagnosing a degree of consistency in the description of the objects which possess property A. The first step is to try to build up approximations to the description of objects. These are called "points of view." A point of view associated to a descriptive attribute d_i of an object is defined as a prediction of the value of d_i from the values taken by the other attributes of this object. A correct prediction of d_i is considered as an argument in favor of the hypothesis "the object has property A" (or "the object is assimilable to A").

(2) Two approaches may then be considered: "assimilation" and "discrimination." In the first case, one tries to build up "points of view" that are arguments in favor of property A (or hypothesis A), from a list of examples of A. In the second case, one selects points of view which are arguments in favor of A and not in favor of property B, from a list of examples of A and a list of counterexamples which are assimilable to B. This second approach precisely is the one we have followed with TRINITA. The preference given to discrimination rests on the following idea: an argument in favor of A is not sufficient to infer A, because some examples of A may not verify the premises of the argument; conversely, there may exist some examples of B which actually verify the premises of an argument in favor of A and still are assimilable to B (and not to A). TRINITA accepts these two types of contradiction.

(3) Discrimination consists of building up of "points of view" (i.e., "rules"). Starting from lists A and B, the problem is to build a set of arguments (called "rules") which may be often true of objects in A and seldom true of objects in B. These rules are singlets (one attribute), doublets (two attributes), triplets (three attributes), etc., selected as a function of the number of examples (objects) in A in which they occur, and of the number of examples in B in which they do not (or seldom) occur. The syntax of rules includes $\wedge$ (AND; *ET*) and $\sim$ (NOT; *NON*). In order that attributes or combinations of attributes be selected as rules, their "counts" (number of occurrences and nonoccurrences in objects) must be greater than some minimum score in A and less than some maximum score in B. A measure of the divergence of value distributions in A and B is also taken into account. The following is an example of a rule in our application (see also Appendix 2):

(VABACO) $\wedge$ ($\sim$SICLFA) STAT: 67 7; DIV: 197.7

Which means: "If the attribute VABACO (nave with aisles) is present, and the attribute SICLFA (separate chancel, with rounded lateral chapels) is not present, then the rule is true for 67 percent in list A (examples), and for 7 percent in list B (counterexamples)."

As in our application, let us suppose that list A is composed of church plans belonging to three groups out of four, and that list B includes plans belonging to the fourth group. This rule "refutes" the fourth group, from a "point of view" (combination of attributes) which "originates" from the first three groups.

The higher value of STAT indicates the count of the rule in the list of examples (A); the lower value indicates its count in the list of counterexamples (B).

The high value of DIV (divergence of value distribution) indicates a marked contrast between list A and list B, from the "point of view" stated in the rule. Note that STAT and DIV are necessary to evaluate the strength of such "refutation" rules, for instance when they are being selected (manually), but that these indicators are no longer meaningful when rules apply to new objects (i.e., which are not part of the learning set. See §I.2.B below).

For clarity's sake, we must also remark that the above example of rule is the equivalent of the two following expressions, closer to classical production rules:

"IF VABACO is true
IF SICLFA is false
THEN the refutation of list B (i.e., the fourth group of church plans) is true"; or:
"IF VABACO takes value 1
IF SICLFA takes value 0
THEN the rule (i.e., the refutation of list B) takes value 1"

I.2. Description of TRINITA

The program called TRINITA is a set of learning modules, written in APL by Jean Sallantin and his team, which we have applied to a classification of Cistercian church plans. A somewhat similar program, CALM, was written more recently in FORTRAN by J.-L. Moisy, a member of the same research team (Varone 1987). TRINITA's main modules are DISTILLE, the learning module proper, FRANCAIS, which prints rules in clear text, and DECIDE, the expert system (built up from DISTILLE) which applies itself to new objects.

I.2.A. The Learning Module DISTILLE

For each couple S1/S2 of sets of objects which are being confronted, DISTILLE produces two sets of rules:

$TRAIT1: rules issued with S1 as examples (A) and S2 as counterexamples (B), i.e., rules that "refute" S2 from the points of view of S1
$TRAIT2: rules issued with Sl as counterexamples (B), and S2 as examples (A), i.e., rules which refute S1 from the points of view of S2

$TRAIT1 and $TRAIT2 include three sets of rules:

STRAIT: singlets (for instance "Transept")
DTRAIT: doublets (for instance "Transept and lateral chapels with rounded shapes")
bTRAIT: triplets (for instance "Transept and lateral chapels with rounded shapes and three chapels")

In practice, each time DISTILLE is run on a descriptive matrix, 6 files of rules are produced: $TRAIT1 and $TRAIT2 for singlets, doublets, and triplets.

Example of application of DISTILLE:
The instruction "A DISTILLE B", where A and B are matrices filled with 0, 1, or 2 (not applicable), which describe already classified objects, means that A is defined as a set of examples and B as a set of counterexamples.
In order to obtain, for instance, TRAIT1 triplet rules expressing the points of view of Group 1 of Cistercian church plans on another group, the following instruction is typed:

FRANCAIS 3 TRAIT1

An example of rule printed by FRANCAIS 3 is the following:

(~LARGTOTl) $\wedge$ (~LONGSE3) $\wedge$ (~TR) STAT: 100 0; DIV: 182.3

which means: "If the total width is less than 30m and if the total length is less than 78m and if there is no transept, then the rule is true for 100 percent of the cases in Group 1 and for 0 percent of the cases in the other group."

Which, in turn, implies that any new object (church plan) for which the three attributes LARGTOTl, LONGSE3, and TR have a zero value would belong to Group 1, from the point of view of this rule.

Since we used this example, we must observe that rules with such clear-cut statistics would be of interest if they disclosed unheard-of descriptive associations. In our case study, such was not the case. Moreover, the absence of transept, which only occurs in Group 1, would tend to strongly minimize other, less evident criteria.

I.2.B. The Expert System DECIDE

DECIDE functions like an inference engine (without variables): it matches the rules issued by DISTILLE to a descriptive matrix filled with 0, 1, and 2 (for attributes which are not relevant), where objects appear in lines and attributes in columns. This matrix functions as a fact base. Results (i.e., the "diagnosis" of DECIDE) are printed in the shape of a new matrix, also filled with 0, 1, and 2: 0 if a rule does not apply, 1 if a rule applies, 2 if a rule is not applicable (for cases of inapplicability, see below §I.2.D).

In our case study, the rules produced by DISTILLE are classification rules: the "properties" A and B to be verified are whether a plan belongs to a particular group or not. DECIDE thus is a classifying tool. In practice, the following instruction:

(RR, refutation rules) DECIDE (S, set of objects)

produces a matrix of results which is composed of as many lines as there are objects in (S), and as many columns as there are rules in (RR). Results are interpreted in the following manner:

— occurrences of 0, 1, and 2 are totaled on each line. The three totals represent the "score" of an object;

— if the rules are highly discriminant, it clearly shows on the matrix: many 1 and few 0 on a line mean that the corresponding object is adequately classified (formally, at least). The abundance of 1 indicates that the corresponding object is refuted by several groups, and the small number of zeros shows that there exists at least a group to which the object may belong since not all refutation rules apply (see below, §II.4).

I.2.C. The "refutation" approach

As can be seen, lists A (examples) and B (counterexamples) which are submitted to DISTILLE in the first place are freely defined by the user. Given our input data, which are composed of four groups of church plans, we could either successively oppose one group (as A) to the three other groups cumulated as B (strategy 1), or oppose all groups two by two (strategy 2). It so happened that strategy 2 produced rules which were easier to understand and evaluate than did strategy 1 (first tried). Thus, only strategy 2, where each group is refuted by all others, will be described here.

The number of sets of rules issued, according to this strategy, is the number of arrangements of four objects two by two, that is, in principle:

$$A^{p=2}_{m=4} = \frac{m!}{(m-p)!}$$

which amounts to twelve sets of singlets, twelve sets of doublets, etc.

For clarity's sake, we shall call "rules of group X" the rules produced by DISTILLE when objects belonging to group X are chosen as examples, and objects of another group are used as counterexamples (module $TRAIT1).

Thus, "rules of group X" do not refute objects belonging to group X, but refute objects belonging to another group. We shall call "refutation rules for group X" the rules produced when objects belonging to group X are chosen as counterexamples and objects belonging to another group are chosen as examples (module $TRAIT2). These rules refute objects belonging to group X.

The strategy defined above, and the fact that we are dealing with the process of classification, imply the following interpretation of final results: we must consider as formally "well classified" an object which is homogeneously refuted by rules of all groups except one. In the case of a seriation, i.e., when groups are supposed to be ordered according to some kind of gradual affinity, it seems not unreasonable to assume that a group can be considered as formally "ordered" if the number of refutations issued by other groups is gradual.

I.2.D. Inapplicability (coded as 2)

Although the problem is not new, sad to say, cases of inapplicability are not treated properly by TRINITA. When DISTILLE builds up rules, descriptive attributes associated with the value 2 in the learning matrix are altogether neglected, as if the program confused those coded 2 with those coded 1 when looking for those coded 0, and confused them with code 0 when looking for code 1.

Example: A rule of group 1 is:

(SICFLA) ∧ (~RPRSANG) STAT: 54.0;

which means: "If the chancel is separate, with lateral chapels with rounded shapes, and if the ratio length of chancel/total length is less than 0.26, etc. . . . "

First it is necessary to explain how the attributes mentioned have been coded (see also §II.2 below).

SICLFA: the value of this variable is 1 when the chancel is separate, with rounded chapels on each side; its value is 0 when the chapels on each side are square. The value is 2 (not applicable) (a) when the chancel is not separate (i.e., when the walls of the chancel are just prolongations of those of the nave vessel; this also implies that there are no lateral chapels); (b) when the chancel is separate from the nave vessel, but without any side chapels.

RPRSANG: the value is 1 when the ratio length of chancel/total length is equal to or greater than 0.26 and 0 if this ratio is less than 0.26. The value is 2 (inapplicable) when the chancel is not separate (i.e., cannot be measured as a separate structure).

The above rule has been built by DISTILLE on the basis of the following descriptive matrix (with fifteen church plans appearing in columns):

SICLFA 1 1 2 2 1 1 2 1 2 1 1 2 2 1 0
RPRSANG 0 0 2 0 0 0 1 0 2 0 0 0 1 0 1

It is clear, from the value of STAT (54.0) for this rule, that only the eight 1/0 combinations have been taken into account by DISTILLE out of the fifteen values for each of the two attributes. As a consequence, whenever a group happens to include a number of objects with many 2 values, the number of highly discriminating rules of this group is considerably lower than it should be.

II. Description of the Application

II.1. A description of the empirical classification and a definition of the problem to be solved.

Leaving aside Dimier's original classification (1949), which was not suitable as it stood (see Lagrange 1973), we tried to construct our own typology of the published church plans, one which made use of all the published information that was available. This information concerns two aspects of the study of Cistercian church plans:

a. The description of plans, i.e., the most suitable level of analysis, the selection of "important" descriptive criteria, the choice of "typical" examples. Our work consisted of a systematization of the available concepts and vocabulary, and then completing an entirely new description for the church plans.

b. The meaning, or rather, the possible meaning of the original scheme of classification was examined closely. Dimier (1949) hints at the possibility that the types of church plans he defined might illustrate a chronological evolution, from the earlier churches, the "simplest" (at the beginning of the twelfth century), to the latest (sixteenth century), already of considerable size and far away from the original austerity willed by Saint Bernard. From the published plans, all of which had dates assigned—either the year they were built or a building period that spanned two dates—we already knew that we could not devise a proper chronological seriation. Nonetheless, we defined four groups of plans which actually reflected a growing complexity from Group 1 to Group 4. Chronological information was included in our descriptions as a guide and a cross-check. On the other hand, the filiation of each church, which always was indicated along with the geographical area in which it was located, was included because one could not exclude, *a priori*, the possibility that something like an order of diffusion of types from one region to another might be revealed by the program. Accordingly, geographical information also was included in our description.

The main morphological criteria which have been selected to define our 4 groups are the following (see examples in Appendix 1):

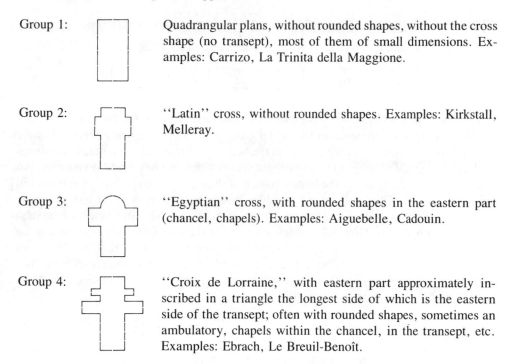

Group 1: Quadrangular plans, without rounded shapes, without the cross shape (no transept), most of them of small dimensions. Examples: Carrizo, La Trinita della Maggione.

Group 2: "Latin" cross, without rounded shapes. Examples: Kirkstall, Melleray.

Group 3: "Egyptian" cross, with rounded shapes in the eastern part (chancel, chapels). Examples: Aiguebelle, Cadouin.

Group 4: "Croix de Lorraine," with eastern part approximately inscribed in a triangle the longest side of which is the eastern side of the transept; often with rounded shapes, sometimes an ambulatory, chapels within the chancel, in the transept, etc. Examples: Ebrach, Le Breuil-Benoît.

At this stage, the question which we wanted answered through the use of TRINITA was the following: Was it possible to teach a program the knowledge invested in this classification, despite all its defects?

The answer to this question required two steps:

— first TRINITA must learn our criteria of classification from a description of plans, including the information about their assignment to one or another of the four groups.

— then we had to check TRINITA's knowledge, by making it classify new plans. We knew, of course, that statistically based learning programs such as TRINITA only show one side of automated learning. More precisely, we knew that this kind of program could not strictly reproduce our own classifying behavior. This behavior, in fact, did not have much to do with statistics, in spite of our considerable efforts to be systematic in regard to the description and in the choice of the learning sample. However, since in TRINITA the results of learning take the shape of linguistic rules, as in an expert system, we expected to get back, at worst, a surface model of the underlying reasoning. This model then could be compared without difficulty to our own.

II.2. The descriptive matrices

A model of the scheme which we actually used for the description of each of the (120) plans is included as Appendix 3. Three or four different versions were tested initially,

Table 1

(LONGTOT)	< 60m		>/ = 60m	
	< 48m	>/ = 48m	< 78m	>/ = 78m
LONGTOT1	0	0	1	1
LONGTOT2	0	1	0	1

but without much success. All were unsuitable for one or another variant of two primary reasons. First, a limited number of variables was allowed (47 were first selected, 33 were finally kept). Then we were not clear as to the best way of translating numerical attributes (dates, numbers of chapels, etc.) and geographical names into binary (0/1) variables. An example of this difficulty is the binary coding of dimensions and ratios (16 variables in the first version). Obviously, these variables first had to be transcribed into intervals; intervals, in turn, could be turned into a dichotomous, binary code. To define the intervals, we used a program (MONIQUE) which allowed for the best discrimination among the 60 plans of the learning sample based upon their dimensions and ratios. Starting from there, three coding schemes were tried, the third of which was finally chosen. The numerical variable LONGTOT (total length of church) provides an example of this problem. It was coded, successively, as follows:

First coding:

LONGTOT   is divided into LONGTOT1 and LONGTOT2

LONGTOT1   has value 0 when total length is < 60m and value 1 when total length is >/ = 60m.

If LONGTOT1   = 0, LONGTOT2 has value 0 when total length is < 48m, and value 1 when total length is >/ = 48m.

If LONGTOT1   = 1, LONGTOT2 has value 0 when total length is < 78m and value 1 when total length >/ = 78m (see Table 1).

This first coding scheme had serious drawbacks. Singlet rules mentioning LONGTOT2, for instance, may have a double meaning: whenever the value stated in the rule for this attribute is 0, one does not know whether it means a total length with a value equal to or less than 48m, or between 60m and 78m.

Second coding:
Plans were distributed into four classes: LONGPE (short), LONGMP (middle short), LONGMG (middle long), and LONGG (long), according to the same intervals as in the first coding scheme (see Table 2).

This coding scheme also has drawbacks. Suppose that in a given group the value of LONGPE is 1 for 45 percent of plans and the value of LONGMPE is 1 for 48 percent. The statistical weight of each variable, taken separately, is too weak to be taken into account by DISTILLE (i.e., no rules will mention either of them), and the fact that 93

Table 2

	L < 48m	48 < L < 60m	60m < L < 78m	L >/ = 78m
LONGPE	1	0	0	0
LONGMP	0	1	0	0
LONGMG	0	0	1	0
LONGG	0	0	0	1

Table 3

	L < 48m	48 < L < 60m	60m < L < 78m	L >/ = 78m
LONGSE1	0	1	1	1
LONGSE2	0	0	1	1
LONGSE3	0	0	0	1

percent of plans in this group have a total length which is less than 60m will be totally lost.

Third coding (see Appendix 3):

The original variable LONGTOT (total length) has been split into three variables, LONGSE1, LONGSE2, LONGSE3, which are "nested." Values vary according to the same intervals as previously defined (see Table 3).

Additional changes in the original descriptive sheet were necessary. As can be seen in Appendix 3, chronological indications are reduced to only one binary variable (values: 1 if the twelfth century, 0 if later), and geographical information is coded in terms of broad areas: France, Southern Europe (EURSUD), Northern Europe (EURNORD), Central Europe (EURCEN). More details are given on measurements and the morphology of plans (28 variables).

Since the question of the treatment of inapplicable variables has been mentioned above (see §I.2.D; see also §III.B below), we must point out the considerable number of variables in Appendix 3 which are "dependent," i.e., which become inapplicable when the variable which they imply (or on the presence of which they depend) has a 0 value. There are 16 of those in Appendix 3: variables 12 to 22, which describe the "separate chancel" (SI, "sanctuaire individualisé") and are not applicable when the value of SI is 0; and variables 24 to 29, which depend on variable 23 (TR, presence of transept).

Obviously, if the present corpus had been more homogeneous—for instance, if all Cistercian churches selected had transepts—the number of variables with the potential of becoming inapplicable would have been much lower. We assumed, however, that the lack of applicability or relevance of some variables is diagnostic of the rather fuzzy situations in which archaeologists or historians of art find themselves when they try to rationalize their own classifying mechanisms.

The 120 plans, each assigned to one of the four groups defined above (see §II.1), were analyzed according to the descriptive sheet in Appendix 3. The **learning matrix** (called BABA) thus was composed of 60 plans (15 plans in each group) and comprised 33 variables per plan. The **test matrix** (called BIBI) described the remaining 60 plans in similar terms.

II.3. Evaluation of rules (output of DISTILLE)

II.3.1 Selection scheme

Triplet rules have been left out entirely, for two reasons: first, they are redundant if compared to doublets (the latter also are much easier to analyze), and second, the sorting programs (see below) did not work on triplets.

As for the rest of the rules produced by DISTILLE (440 rules, mainly doublets, singlet rules being few; see Table 4), it was first necessary to sort them (online) so that all rules refuting the same group were printed together. Starting from there, we selected (by hand) what looked like the most satisfactory rules. To make it easier, two routines were available: LES MEMES and SYNONYMIE. The first routine lists together "truly synonymous" rules (TS), i.e., two or more identical rules that originate from different groups. The second lists together "falsely synonymous rules" (FS), i.e., rules which have been built on exactly the same distribution of 0s and 1s in the learning matrix. The user may set whatever level of "false synonymy" is desired; for instance, we chose 90 percent: this setting implies that rules listed as FS originate from the same distribution of values in no less than 50 plans out of 60.

After much hesitation, we decided upon the following selection procedure:

a. TS rules: if there were 2 or 3 examples, one rule was kept no matter the value of STAT.

b. Isolated rules and FS rules: they were kept if the higher value of STAT was superior to the lower value of at least 60, and if the lower value was not more than 7.

c. When we found a singlet rule, together with doublets all stating the same variable as the singlet, only the singlet was kept, whatever the value of STAT. This situation comes about when the common variable has a sufficiently strong statistical weight to draw with it other variables which are co-occurrent but much less statistically significant. In this case, the doublets are assumed to be redundant when compared to the singlet. Example: (from refutation rules for Group 4):

R1: (~SILAl)   STAT: 74 0; DIV: 110.0
R2: (~SILA1) $\wedge$ (~LONGSE3)   STAT: 74 0; DIV: 110.0
R3: (~SILAl) $\wedge$ (~LARGTOTl) STAT: 74 0; DIV: 110.0

Which means:
R1: "If there is a separate chancel with a width less than 11m,"
R2: "If (as R1) and if total length is less than 60m,"
R3: "If (as R1) and if total width is less than 30m,"
"Then the rule (resp. 1, 2, 3) is true for 74 percent in other groups of plans, and for 0 percent in Group 4."

Table 4. Results of the rule selection scheme.

Origin of rules → Refuted Groups	Groups				Total number of rules produced	Total number of rules retained
	1	2	3	4		
1		50	50	50	150	59
2	50		22	50	122	37
3	11	23		18	52	26
4	50	35	31		116	41
Totals →	111	108	103	118	440	163

In this particular case at least, redundancy is rather obvious if one looks at church plans in Group 4: the enormous width of chancels is striking, definitely more so than the total length or width of most plans.

d. Rules mentioning geographical areas ("geographical rules"): due to uncertainties about the relevance of geographical information, we had decided initially to run DECIDE first with geographical rules and then without them (see §III.C below). However, some geographical rules have been left out entirely, because they made no sense. Example: (from refutation rules for Group 1):

$$(\text{SICL}) \land (\sim\text{EURSUD}) \text{ STAT: } 0 \ 87; \text{ DIV: } 136.7$$

Which means: "If there is a separate chancel with side chapels and if the area is not Southern Europe, then the rule is true for 0 percent in Group 1 and for 87 percent in Group 2."

In brief, such rules are difficult to evaluate for two reasons:

— Since we had no clues as to the influence of geographical areas upon the morphology of Cistercian church plans, we have tried to define regions as systematically as possible, but definitely without inspiration. Less systematic or finer geographical divisions might have revealed diffusion centers or historical turning points.

— The level of description of morphological attributes, such as it is, very well may be inadequate for the study of morphological variability across the several regions.

e. Rules mentioning the chronological period are few and, for most of them, the value STAT is low. Half a dozen have been kept.

II.3.2 Comments on selected rules

Table 4 shows the actual number of rules selected, including geographical rules, for each group.

Note that the 63 percent of the rules were excluded, which is a significant proportion of the total. This decrease is due to the redundancy in the set of rules produced by DISTILLE: it often is the case that three groups refute the fourth through identical rules.

Significant contrasts are evident in Table 4: although the numbers of rules of all groups are more or less the same (a hundred), numbers of actual refutations are not even. The group with the most refutations is Group 1; the group with the fewest refutations is Group 3. These contrasts indeed are in keeping with the learning sample and our scheme of classification (see Appendix 1): Group 1 stands much apart (smallish plans, simplified outline); Group 3 seems "average" in every aspect (dimensions, morphological complexity).

II.4. The running of DECIDE

DECIDE, thus fed with 163 rules, was run successively, first on the learning matrix BABA (minus group information), and then on the new matrix (BIBI). The testing of DECIDE on the original sample was necessary to verify whether the expert system still made sense after so many rules had been taken out, and also to make sure that the number of cases of inapplicability had not altogether wrecked the whole learning mechanism. The new matrix (BIBI) had the plans in groups, as they were in BABA, but no indication of this was included in the information given to DECIDE. In order that results would be easier to read, the group indications were given by the position of plans on the lines in both matrices: the first 15 plans belong to Group 1, the following 15 plans belong to Group 2, and so on.

The matrices that resulted were too cumbersome and difficult to read, so we have obtained (by program) two tables which summarize the results: Listing M1 and Listing M2.

Listing M1: this is a matrix of 120 lines (60 lines for BABA and 60 lines for BIBI) and four columns filled with numbers. The first column indicates the number of applications of rules of Group 1, the second column the number of applications of rules of Group 2, etc. This matrix allowed us to judge the overall quality of the automated classification, with respect to formal propriety and conformity to our classifying scheme. We have distinguished three degrees of classification (see Table 5):

(1) "Best classified" (BC): A BC object has a minimal score (0 at best) in one column, the one which indicates the number of applications of rules of its own group. This means that this object is not (or is seldom) rejected by these rules, and that it is rejected in terms of the rules of other groups.

(2) "Indecisive" (I): An I object simultaneously has (a) a low score (or a 0 score) in the column which indicates the number of applications of rules of its own group, and (b) an identical score in another column.

(3) "Misclassified" (MC): An MC object has a relatively high score in the column which indicates the number of applications of rules of its own group, and a low score in one or two other columns.

Listing M2 (see Table 6): this matrix gives more detailed information than that given in Listing M1. In particular, cases where rules do not apply because they are inapplicable with respect to an object (answer 2), are separate from those where they do not apply because there is no match (answer 0). Table 6 is an extract from Listing M2 (which actually includes 240 lines, since DECIDE successively applies rules of Groups 1,2,3,4 to BABA and BIBI). This extract shows the results of the application of rules of Group 1 to Group 1 itself, which accounts for the small number of answers 1 (at least in BABA;

Table 5. Examples of "best classified" (BC) plans, "indecisive" (I) plans, and "misclassified" (MC) plans, in matrices BABA and BIBI, after Listing AI1 (application with geographical rules included).

Name of church	Original group	TRINITA's results	Origin of rules and number of applications			
			Group 1	Group 2	Group 3	Group 4
(BABA)						
La Trappe	1	BC	0	12	12	4
Camp		I	0	0	8	28
Valvisciolo		I	4	3	10	29
Buch	2	BC	41	0	16	27
Droiteva		I	0	0	7	27
Jervaulx		MC	57	12	19	3
Aiguebelle	3	BC	10	14	0	25
Beaulieu Abbey		I	48	30	0	0
Bonneva		MC	28	0	13	32
Doberan II	4	BC	34	27	10	0
Cherlieu		I	47	33	0	0
Varnhem		I	21	27	0	0
(BIBI)						
Junquera	1	I	0	11	1	24
Magdenau		I	1	0	5	23
Salem		MC	3	0	0	0
Abbaye Blanche	2	BC	16	0	11	27
Fontenay		BC	42	0	14	28
Strata Florida		BC	38	3	13	21
Bronnbach	3	BC	26	14	0	20
Heisterbach		I	31	28	1	1
Falleri		MC	0	12	2	32
Fontaine Jean	4	BC	19	15	14	0
Baumgartenberg		I	21	28	0	0
Heiligenkreuz		MC	3	3	9	13

Table 6. Classification by DECIDE of Group 1 plans (extract from Listing M2, application of rules of Group 1 with and without geographical rules).

	Results of the running of DECIDE on BABA								Results of the running of DECIDE on BIBI							
	(with geogr. rules)				(without geogr. rules)				(with geogr. rules)				(without geogr. rules)			
N of plans	Number of			Total	Number of			Total	Number of			Total	Number of			Total
	0	1	2		0	1	2		0	1	2		0	1	2	
1	59	0	0	59	48	0	0	48	48	0	11	59	41	0	7	48
2	59	0	0	59	48	0	0	48	47	1	11	59	42	0	6	48
3	43	0	16	59	38	0	10	48	53	6	0	59	42	6	0	48
4	42	0	17	59	36	0	12	48	59	0	0	59	48	0	0	48
5	59	0	0	59	48	0	0	48	45	1	13	59	39	1	8	48
6	59	0	0	59	48	0	0	48	51	8	0	59	43	5	0	48
7	52	0	7	59	43	0	5	48	33	1	25	59	29	1	18	48
8	59	0	0	59	48	0	0	48	47	1	11	59	42	0	6	48
9	34	0	25	59	30	0	18	48	51	8	0	59	40	8	0	48
10	59	0	0	59	48	0	0	48	47	1	11	59	38	1	9	48
11	59	4	0	59	48	0	0	48	20	3	36	59	17	2	29	48
12	44	0	15	59	38	0	10	48	29	1	29	59	26	1	21	48
13	44	0	15	59	37	0	11	48	56	3	0	59	48	0	0	48
14	59	0	0	59	48	0	0	48	45	1	13	59	40	0	8	48
15	55	4	0	59	44	4	0	48	55	4	0	59	47	1	0	48
.	.				.				.				.			
.	.				.				.				.			

see left part of Table 6). As before, there were two separate runs of DECIDE, one with geographical rules included, the other without.

III. Evaluation of Results

Four main points will be examined here: A, the overall quality of the classification obtained in BABA and BIBI; B, the influence of cases of nonapplicability on the quality of results; C, the question of relevance (or irrelevance) of geographical rules; D, the degree of conformity of automated classification when compared to our own approach.

III.A. The quality of the classification obtained

As can be seen in Table 7, results are most satisfactory for Groups 2, 3, 4, in both BABA and BIBI. "Perfection" is reached when we look at Group 2 in BIBI.

— Results are not bad for Group 1 in BABA when geographical rules are included in the run. However, they clearly deteriorate in the same matrix when the geographical rules are left out. With or without geographical rules, the results are definitly bad for Group 1 in BIBI. At this stage, the adequacy of Group 1 as part of a learning sample seems dubious.

III.B. Influence of variables scored as inapplicable

We have said before (see §II.2) that the observed number of code 2s (variables not relevant or inapplicable) for Group 1 was high, in both BABA and BIBI, on average double the number in other groups. This distribution is reproduced almost exactly in the DECIDE matrix, except that the rates are altogether much higher (see Table 8).

As a consequence of this observation, we must assume that a link exists between the poor results obtained for Group 1 and the high number of cases of inapplicable variables in the description of this group. The observed increase of rate for code 2s in the DECIDE matrix can be explained as follows: nearly all rules are doublets, i.e., consisting in two variables linked by connector $\wedge$ (AND), so that if one of the variables happens to be inapplicable, then the rule too becomes inapplicable, i.e., receives an answer coded 2.

We also assume, however, that if a group is homogeneous, and is described as such, objects in this group may be adequately classified by TRINITA, even if there exists a certain number of 2s in the description of most objects in this group. In this case, as we have already seen, refutation rules are built up irrespective of 2s. Their number is lower, but they still get a 0 answer for objects in this group and, as the case may be, a 1 answer from other groups.

Moreover, if this homogeneous group is not too distant from other groups, the rules of these groups should normally apply to it and the number of 2 answers should be low.

III.C. The question of the relevance of geographical rules

Leaving out geographical rules seems to have no effect whatsoever on the classification of Groups 2,3,4, either in BABA or in BIBI. In each matrix the same plans are, respectively, BC, I, and MC after both runs (with and without geographical rules). How-

Table 7. Total number of "best classified" (BC) plans, of "indecisive" (I) plans, and of "misclassified" (MC) plans in matrices BABA and BIBI.

		GROUP 1			GROUP 2			GROUP 3			GROUP 4		
		BC	I	MC	BC	I	MC	BC	I	MC	BC	I	MC
BABA	with geogr. rules	7	8	0	12	1	2	10	4	1	10	5	0
	without geogr. rules	1	13	1	12	1	2	8	6	1	10	5	0
BIBI	with geogr. rules	1	8	6	15	0	0	13	2	0	9	5	1
	without geogr. rules	1	11	3	15	0	0	12	3	0	9	5	1

Table 8. Distribution of irrelevance (coded 2) in the two descriptive matrices and in the DECIDE matrices.

	Number of variables coded 2 in the description of plans		Number of answers coded 2 in the DECIDE matrices	
	BABA	BIBI	BABA	BIBI
Group 1	146	135	253	517
Group 2	78	78	131	130
Group 3	51	74	14	124
Group 4	26	45	58	141

ever, leaving out geographical rules tends to lead to the deterioration of the classification of Group 1, especially in BIBI. Here again, we must assume that, in view of the scarcity of 1s and the high number of 2s in the description of Group 1 in BABA, DISTILLE "made do" with geographical variables instead, in order to produce some sort of discrimination from other groups. Geographical information, which probably was fortuitous in the learning matrix, could not convey rules that really discriminated.

III.D. Degree of conformity of automated classifying as compared to our own approach

In cognitive psychology, the study of automated learning is currently considered as one of the most fruitful approaches to the study of mental processes. Our questions here are less ambitious, and we are going to ask only whether TRINITA has indeed constructed generalizations from the information given it, such as it was.

In the present case we can answer that it has done so, and that it definitely is a good learning program (and a good tool for classification, if need be). It still remains to be seen whether we are better off after this experiment with respect to the study of archaeological reasoning, but we will leave that question for discussion in the conclusions to this chapter. To support our present judgment of TRINITA, we shall propose four arguments:

III.D.1 Plans which we assigned, without hesitation, to one or the other of the four groups are precisely those which are "best classified" (BC) by TRINITA. One can consult, for example, Appendix 1 for the plans listed in Table 9.

III.D.2. If we look at the list of plans which were called "indecisive" (I), 17 plans in BABA and 15 in BIBI, this list includes all plans which were particularly difficult for us to classify, most of them having affinities with both Group 3 and Group 4.
Examples (see also Appendix 1): Beaulieu Abbey, which we classified as Group 3, has affinities with Group 4 because of its enormous chancel; Veruela, which we assigned to Group 4 because of its general shape (similar to that of a "croix de Lorraine"), could also belong to Group 3, its dimensions being close to the average in this group.

III.D.3. Anomalies, that is divergences, from our own classificatory behavior in the results, are few. They are as follows:

Table 9

Group 1	Group 2	Group 3	Group 4
(BABA)			
La Badiazza	Kirkstall	Aiguebelle	Le Breuil-Benoît
Carrizo	Melleray	Cadouin	Ebrach
La Trinita della Maggione	Monte de Ramo	Ruremonde	Royaumont
(BIBI)			
La Maigrauge	Fontenay	Flaran	Altenberg II
	Mores	Mazan	Bonport
	Noirlac	Meira	Dore

a. TRINITA sometimes is far from decisive in the assignment of an object to one of three groups, and the lack of a decision concerns plans which belong without any doubt to Group 1 (no transept).

Examples: Rein and Beauvoir (in BABA), are "indecisive" between Groups 1,2,3. This anomaly may be explained by a high rate of inapplicable variables in the descriptive matrix (16 values out of 33 for both plans), and in the DECIDE matrix (53 for Beauvoir and 70 for Rein).

b. A few anomalous cases, where there was a lack of decision between Group 1 and another group, also were due to cases of inapplicability.

Examples: Gigean (in BIBI), indecisive between Groups 1 and 3 (12 values of 2 in the descriptive matrix, 23 in the DECIDE matrix).

c. Misclassifications (MC plans, or anomalous indecisions): from the total of 120 objects, TRINITA made 9 mistakes (2 in BABA and 7 in BIBI). The reasons for these mistakes, beyond perturbations caused by inapplicability, seem to be the following:

— Except for plans belonging to Group 4, which are of considerable dimensions, we unconsciously gave more importance to the general shape of plans than to their size when devising our typology. TRINITA, which is much more systematic, assigns to Groups 2,3, or 4 several churches which we had associated with Group 1 because of their shape: for instance Rueda, misclassified in Group 2, or Salem, which could be equally assigned to Groups 2,3,4.

— As do other statistical tools, TRINITA picks out significant combinations of attributes (rules) which we had overlooked. Though these sometimes shift plans from what we thought was their rightful group to another, we must say TRINITA is often right. See, for instance, Jervaulx, from Group 2 ("croix latine"), which TRINITA puts in Group 4, due both to the considerable size of its chancel and to its ambulatory.

TRINITA also puts right one or two of our own mistakes: Bouchet, for instance, which we erroneously assigned to Group 2, is put back where it belongs (Group 3).

III.D.4. The ordering of groups

Our four groups had been defined to represent a morphological evolution, from the "simplest" churches in Group 1 to the most sophisticated in Group 4, according to what

Table 10. "Affinities" between groups in TRINITA's classification of plans.

Groups of origin		Number of "affinities" between groups of origin and other groups, from indecisive and misclassified plans			
		Group 1	Group 2	Group 3	Group 4
(BABA)	Group 1	—	5	5	0
	Group 2	1	—	0	2
	Group 3	2	1	—	2
	Group 4	0	0	5	0
(BIBI)	Group 1	—	9	6	0
	Group 2	0	—	0	0
	Group 3	3	0	—	0
	Group 4	0	1	5	—

seemed to be Dimier's (1949) main hypothesis. However, no indications in regard to the degrees of complexity were given in our description of plans. In order to check if specific attractions or affinities between groups appeared in TRINITA's results, we listed all "indecisive" (I) or "misclassified" (MC) plans in each group, together with indications about the groups which "attracted" them (see Table 10). Note that an I or MC plan may be simultaneously attracted by two or three groups.

Nothing really conclusive resulted regarding an order between groups; except that Group 1 is never attracted by Group 4, and that Group 4 is preferentially attracted by Group 3.

IV. Conclusions

IV.1. Statistico-learning techniques were first used to discover regularities or structures in domains such as the study of chemical molecules, the analysis of biological sequences, seismic prediction, etc. However, learning based on examples and counterexamples is often cited in the literature (Michalski, Carbonnell and Mitchell 1983). According to the authors of TRINITA, this approach is a guarantee against the indifferent quality of information, i.e., the lack of inspiration at the descriptive stage, inadequate questions, fuzzy hypotheses, mistakes, etc. In this sense, TRINITA fitted our case study beautifully, its only frustrating aspect being the treatment of inapplicable scores. Indeed, this problem is not new nor is it specific to archaeological data. Though we know it cannot be solved in the near future (a new kind of logic must be devised for the purpose) we would suggest that a module be incorporated which would be capable of adjusting the statistical weight of rules as a function of the rate at which variables that lacked applicability occurred.

IV.2. From a practical point of view, if we compare TRINITA to the various programs for classification that we had applied in the past to the same Cistercian corpus, its most important advantage is the explicit nature of the "expertise" in classification obtained through automated learning (i.e., linguistic rules). This characteristic is most useful, as some attribute combinations with a considerable statistical weight may make no sense at all for the archaeologist (see above, §II.3.1). In those cases, either the user removes the corresponding rules, in order to be in complete control of reasoning, but then he is in danger of wrecking the whole procedure, or he slackens his hold and lets calculations take charge. We have tried to follow both methods: our selection scheme for rules was "blind" when we systematically left out rules with low STAT values, but also critical, when, for instance, we left out geographical rules because they were meaningless. We were lucky enough not to wreck the procedure, but it must be clear also that we probably would have wrecked it entirely if we had tried to poke too much.

IV.3. From the point of view of AI proper, it must be recalled first that the hypothesis of statistical control of the working of the brain, which would correspond to various kinds of inductive learning processes, remains to be established: TRINITA was not chosen because it makes use of statistics (currently believed to be conducive of good results), but precisely because it was not strictly based on them (it allows the use of a syntax), and because of its flexibility (as illustrated by the fact that a number of rules can be suppressed by the user). In regard to the modeling of learning processes, we agree with critics who have already objected that, in such a domain as history of art, the knowledge which should be summoned to achieve a somewhat likely model is possibly unmeasurable. However, as we said before, we were never very ambitious when it came to the depth of modeling in this precise case study. What seemed important to us, as in the case of expert systems, is to avail ourselves, as quickly as possible, of current AI techniques in order to get a better grip on our reasoning habits, and perhaps to pull down barriers standing between our "soft" sciences and the so called "hard" sciences of others.

IV.4. From a methodological point of view, let us recall that the most difficult part of this experiment was the construction of the learning matrix, even if, at this stage, we were already clear as to the overall definition of groups. Though we tried to make good use of Dimier's erudition, the selection of attributes for the special purpose of automated learning could only be achieved by trial and error, i.e., by running both DISTILLE and DECIDE over and over. The same can be said of the coding of attributes (see §II.2). This effort has taught us more about the various approaches to knowledge representation in artificial intelligence. This confirms our favorite assumption that AI specialists should first insist on a systematic study of various schemes of knowledge representation, in specialized areas, with the help of scientists themselves (should these have a taste for lengthy, humble, and tedious tasks). They would then be able to go on with more accurate, if less ambitious, simulation projects.

IV.5. As regards epistemology and history of art (or archaeology), TRINITA reminds us that, in those domains where conclusions seldom can be validated by empirical facts, one way to appraise the outputs of our elaborate reasoning behavior is to try to simulate (repeat) them in the fashion of computers. Though we now know that a computer will obediently learn and simulate any rubbish, going through the tasks of simulation is indeed conducive to a healthy critical approach to our own mental workings.

APPENDIX 1

Examples of Cistercian church plans, after A. Dimier (1949)

The Plans are arranged by group of origin according to the empirical classification which has been defined in the text (§II.1) and by alphabetical order within groups.

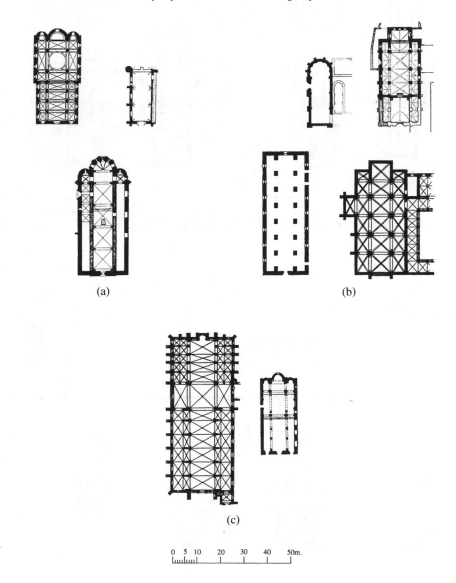

(a)   (b)

(c)

0 5 10   20   30   40   50m.

GROUP 1, **Figure 1a** *La Badizza* (upper left), *Beauvoir* (upper right), *Carrizo* (lower center);
Figure 1b *Gigean* (upper left), *La Maigrauge* (upper right), *Rein* (lower left), *Rueda* (lower right);
Figure 1c *Salem* (upper left), *La Trinita della Maggione* (upper right).

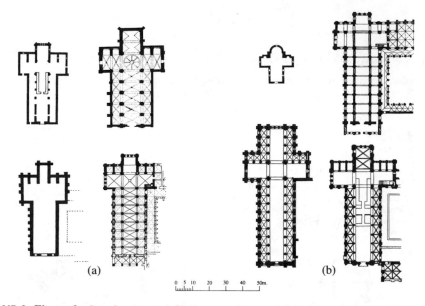

GROUP 2, **Figure 2a** *Bouchet* (upper left) *Fontenay* (upper right), *Jervaulx* (lower left), *Kirkstall* (lower right); **Figure 2b** *Melleray* (upper left), *Monte de Ramo* (upper right), *Mores* (lower left), *Noirlac* (lower right).

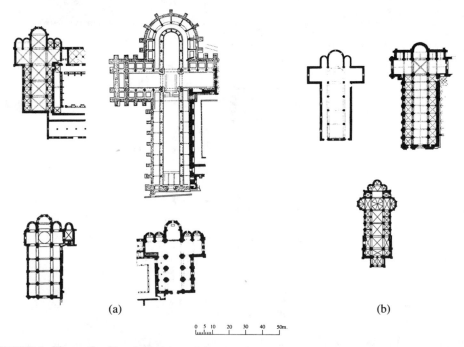

GROUP 3, **Figure 3a** *Aiguebelle* (upper left), *Beauliey Abbey* (upper right), *Cadouin* (lower left), *Flaran* (lower right); **Figure 3b** *Mazan* (upper left), *Meira* (upper right), *Ruremonde* (lower center).

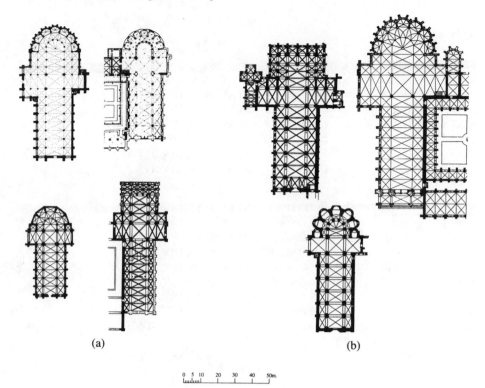

(a)   (b)

0 5 10   20   30   40   50m.

GROUP 4, **Figure 4a** *Altenberg* II (upper left), *Bonport* (upper right), *Le Breuil-Benoît* (lower left), *Dore* (lower right); **Figure 4b** *Ebrach* (upper left), *Royaumont* (upper right), *Veruela* (lower center).

APPENDIX 2

FRANCAIS2 DTRAIT1
REG.1 : (~TRCL   ) ∧ (SICOR   ) STAT :74 9; DIV.:218.4
REG.2 : (~TRCOC   ) ∧ (SICOR   ) STAT :60 7; DIV.:158.6
REG.3 : (RPRSANG   ) ∧ (LONGSE2) STAT :60 7; DIV.:158.6
REG.4 : (SICOR   ) ∧ (LONGSE3) STAT :60 9; DIV.:138.7
REG.5 : (SICOR   ) ∧ (RPRSANG) STAT :67 9; DIV.:175.3
REG.6 : (VAPOR   ) ∧ (RPRSANG) STAT :60 7; DIV.:158.6
REG.7 : (VAL1   ) ∧ (SICOR   ) STAT :67 9; DIV.:175.3

FRANCAIS2 DTRAIT2
REG.1 : (~SICOR   ) ∧ (~DATE   ) STAT :0 52; DIV.:722.6
REG.2 : (~SICOR   ) ∧ (~LONGSE2) STAT :0 52; DIV.:722.6
REG.3 : (~SISAIL1   ) ∧ (~LONGSE3) STAT :0 54; DIV.:754.7
REG.4 : (~SILA1   ) ∧ (~LONGSE3) STAT :0 56; DIV.:787.2
REG.5 : (~SICOR   ) ∧ (~LONGSE3) STAT :0 74; DIV.:1100
REG.6 : (~VAPOR   ) ∧ (~LONGSE3) STAT :7 54; DIV.:129.1
REG.6 : (~VAPOR   ) ∧ (~LONGSE3) STAT :7 54; DIV.:129.1
REG.7 : (~SICOR   ) ∧ (~RPRSANG) STAT :0 72; DIV.:1063
REG.7 : (~SICOR   ) ∧ (~RPRSANG) STAT :0 72; DIV.:1063
REG.8 : (~SISAIL1   ) STAT :0 54; DIV.:754.7
REG.9 : (~SICOR   ) ∧ (~SISAIL1   ) STAT :0 52; DIV.:722.6
REG.10 : (~SILA1   ) STAT :0 56; DIV.:787.2
REG.11 : (~SICOR   ) ∧ (~SILA1   ) STAT :0 54; DIV.:754.7
REG.12 : (~SICOR   ) STAT :0 80; DIV.:1216
REG.13 : (~SICOR   ) ∧ (LONGSE1) STAT :0 54; DIV.:754.7

Examples of doublet rules associated with Group 4.

DTRAIT1 : rules which originate from Group 4 and refute other groups.
DTRAIT2 : rules which refute Group 4.

APPENDIX 3

N D'IDENTIFICATION DU PLAN:
 1 DATE   1 si 12ème siècle
                     0 si date plus tardive
 2 FRANCE   oui 1   0 non
 3 EURSUD   oui 1   0 non
 4 EURNORD   oui 1   0 non
 5 EURCEN   oui 1   0 non
 6 LONGSE1   0 si longueur totale < 48m
                     1 si longueur totale ≥ 48m
 7 LONGSE2   0 si longueur totale < 60m
                     1 si longueur totale ≥ 60m
 8 LONGSE3   0 si longueur totale < 78m
                     1 si longueur totale ≥ 78m
 9 RPRSANG   0 si rapp. long.sanctuaire/long.tot. < 0,26
                     1 si rapp. long.sanctuaire/long.tot. ≥ 0,26
10 LARGTOT   0 si largeur totale < 30m
                     1 si largeur totale ≥ 30m
11 SI   oui 1   0 non (sanct. individualisé)
12 SISAIL1   0 si saillie sanctuaire < 8m
                     1 si saillie sanctuaire ≥ 8m
13 SILA1   0 si largeur sanctuaire < 11m
                     1 si largeur sanctuaire ≥ 11m
14 SIFA   oui 1   0 non (sanct. forme arrondie)
15 SICOR   oui 1   0 non (chapelles orientales)
16 SICORN1   0 si nombre de chapelles orientales < 7
                     0 si nombre de chapelles orientales ≥ 7
17 SICORFA   oui 1   0 non (ch. orient. forme arrondie)
18 SICORDE   oui 1   0 non (ch. orient. + déambul.)
19 SICL   oui 1   0 non (chapelles latérales)
20 SICLN   0 si nombre de chapelles latérales ≤ 2
                     1 si nombre de chapelles latérales > 2
21 SICLFA   oui 1   0 non (ch. lat. forme arrondie)
22 SICLOT   oui 1   0 non (ch. lat. occupant toute la largeur du transept ou de la partie
                     occidentale)
23 TR   oui 1   0 non (transept)
24 TRLA1   0 si largeur transept < 34m
                     1 si largeur transept ≥ 34m
25 TRLO1   0 si longueur transept < 14m
                     1 si longueur transept ≥ 14m
26 TRCL   oui 1   0 non (transept avec chap. latérales)
27 TRCLFA   oui 1   0 non (av. chap. lat. forme arrondie)
28 TRCOC   oui 1   0 non (av. chap. lat. occidentales)
29 TRCOCFA   oui 1   0 non (ch. occident. forme arrondie)
30 VAL1   0 si largeur vaisseau < 22m
                     1 si largeur vaisseau ≥ 22m
31 VALO1   0 si longueur vaisseau < 39m
                     1 si longueur vaisseau ≥ 39m
32 VABACO   oui 1   0 non (bas-côtés)
33 VAPOR   oui 1   0 non (porche, narthex)

REFERENCES

Dimier, A. 1949. *Recueil de plans d'églises cisterciennes*. Librairie d'Art Ancien et Moderne, Vincent, Fréal et Cie, Paris.

Lagrange, M.-S. 1973. *Analyse sémiologique et histoire de l'art*. Klincksieck, Paris.

Lagrange, M.-S., and M. Renaud 1985. "Intelligent knowledge-based systems in archaeology: A computerized simulation of reasoning by means of an expert system," *Computers and the Humanities* **19,** 37–52.

———1987. "SUPERIKON: Essai de cumul de six experts en iconographie," in J.-C. Gardin, O. Guillaume, P. Q. Herman, A. Hesnard, M.-S. Lagrange, M. Renaud, and E. Zadora-Rio, *Systèmes experts et sciences humaines*, pp. 191–232. Eyrolles, Paris.

Michalski, R. S., J. Carbonnell, and T. M. Mitchell 1983. *Machine Learning*. Tioga Publishing Company, Palo Alto, CA.

Sallantin, J., and J. Quinqueton 1984. *Généralisation par points de vue et apprentissage de concepts*. Rapport de recherche INRIA, 1265, Rocquencourt.

Soldano, H., and J. L. Moisy 1985. "Statistico-syntactic learning techniques," *Biochimie* **67,** 493–498.

Varone, S. 1987. *Un système d'apprentissage appliqué à des données écologiques et forestières*. Mémoire de D.E.A. en Informatique. Option Intelligence Artificielle, Université des Sciences et Techniques du Languedoc—CRIM, Montpellier.

Rooting Out Latent Behaviorism in Prehistory

> From the point of view of evolutionary episte-
> mology, the principal lesson of both special and
> general relativity theories is this: Human beings
> are organisms capable of manipulating internal rep-
> resentations of the world by means of concrete op-
> erations and can transcend the bounds of their
> biologically given perception. They can liberate
> themselves and construct a view of reality that
> conflicts with intuition, yet gives a truer, more en-
> compassing view.
>
> (Delbruck 1986:277)

Today, significant segments of the archaeological community lurch from intellectual fad to scholarly fancy, with hardly a pause for reflection and evaluation. In less than a generation the "Old" archaeology has given way to the "New." Culture-history has become an epithet for outmoded methods and has been replaced by processual archaeology. Processual archaeology in turn is yielding to postprocessual, structural, decon-structural, and other up-to-the-minute schemes. Amid the stratified ruins of earlier archaeologies lie the corpses of history and humankind.

I believe it worthwhile to ask why archaeologists—at least most archaeologists in North America—have abandoned the notion of history and historical methods as worth-while pursuits.[1] I believe it also necessary to ask why mental events—human intention, cognition, and representation—play little or no role in much of contemporary archaeo-logical reasoning. In answering these two broad questions, I hope to show that they are linked in rather special ways by the twin concepts of positivism and behaviorism: two loosely connected (Smith 1986), messianic[2] movements in twentieth-century science; two eroded pillars of what Popper has called "promissory materialism" (Popper and Eccles 1977:96–98). Furthermore, I hope to show that neither positivism nor behaviorism is necessary to the practice of archaeology as a science, and that strong adherence to either or both in fact precludes rational thought and discourse about archaeological remains.

The position adopted in this paper is that history, representations, mind, and mental events have been eliminated from archaeological research, not because they lack theo-retical interest or have no analytical utility, but because they did not fit into a very restrictive definition of just what comprised a properly "scientific" archaeology. Their exclusion was in large measure part of the quest to distance archaeology from history and embed it firmly in the scientific as opposed to the symbolic part of anthropology. To this end, archaeologists focused on what they perceived as crucial distinctions between the humanistic understanding of historians and the kinds of scientific explanation sought by anthropologists, especially those who looked toward the natural sciences for exemplars. In mapping a course for their field, they rejected both the methods of history and the humanistic path as unproductive and unrewarding.

Many North American archaeologists seized on what they believed were important differences between historical narrative and scientific argument on the one hand and between ideographic and nomothetic reasoning on the other. In part, the rhetorical force of these distinctions was founded on mistaken notions of the ontological status of written sources versus archaeological remains. They argued that the documents used by historians provided an essentially "subjective" view of the world, and that archaeological remains were a far more "objective" source of data about the past. The methods and goals of archaeology and history as disciplines were juxtaposed in ways that made them incompatible and that cast history in the role of the loser.

It was assumed that historians generally sought their explanations in the realm of individual, subjective mental episodes and discrete events, and that these explanations were grounded in an empathic understanding of "the other," the historical actor set in the framework of single events and individual lifetimes. In short, it became a tenet of archaeology that historians produced idealized, psychological narratives based on individual thoughts and actions that were only short-term descriptions of limited aspects of the past. The goals of archaeology, it was argued, were more encompassing than those of history; the methods of archaeology, it was concluded, were significantly different from those of history. To make the boundaries between the disciplines impenetrable, a narrow view of "scientific" methods became the touchstone against which the products of archaeology could be measured.

Positivism, especially the version championed by Carl Hempel, became the model for archaeological reasoning in North America (and in parts of Western Europe). To the extent that archaeologists adopted his version of logical empiricism, with its emphasis on directly observable phenomena, history and human cognition were pushed even farther from archaeological theory. Consistent with this methodological stance, many archaeologists adopted a version of operationalism coupled with the assumptions of behaviorism to guide their research. In rough form, their reasoning went from the material record itself, to the activities that produced and modified these materials, to a direct coupling with prehistoric behavior (as cause), to contemporary analytic and replicative behavior (as confirmation), and, finally, to the operations necessary to reproduce the items and patterns in the prehistoric record (as epistemological warrant). These events, with a depth no greater than the overt manifestations of human behavior, then became the material implications within a wider, theoretical argument. The goals of this exercise were the production of a uniquely archaeological science and verifiable "laws of human behavior." In their quest for the empirical and the objective, archaeologists mistakenly took the substantial character of the archaeological record as a warrant for a crude version of materialism.[3]

The adoption of behaviorism, which has been overtly shorn of all reference to objective knowledge and human intention, is largely responsible for the poverty of much of contemporary archaeological theory. Therein, reconstructed behaviors form the theoretical entities of archaeological reasoning. The process of this construction is termed "middle range theory" (Binford 1983b). The result of this stance is a science of the "artifact," without reference to intention, representation, and other aspects of thought. In this scheme, humans are reduced to the status of cultural epiphenomena and knowledge becomes a response mechanism to environmentally induced stimuli Neither the one nor the other is an acceptable conclusion for the discipline (anthropology) that Kant (1885) gave the task of posing the most important question of all: What is human?

In this paper I suggest that archaeology can employ both reductive and holistic research strategies simultaneously. It can focus on the biological constraints on human life, and it can construct explanations for the place of humans within their ecosystem. It can focus on broadly social and cultural concerns and the symbolic dimensions of human existence, and it can seek understanding in terms of knowledge and its representations. Yet in addition to these biological and cultural levels of analysis, a cognitive level must be added to the methods of research in prehistory. It is this level of analysis that unites the other two: it is cognition that mediates between the representational (artificial) and the natural aspects of human life.

This paper comes in four parts. The first surveys the philosophical muddles that characterize much of contemporary archaeological thought. It attempts to account for the antipathy toward history and psyche that characterizes the work of so many archaeologists in North America. The second presents a unified "metaphysical research program" for archaeology that admits both mind and matter, determinism, indeterminism, contingency, and cognition. This part is based in large measure on the work of Karl Popper. The third outlines the concerns and some accomplishments of the emergent "cognitive sciences" and the role they might play in theory and methods for the study of prehistory. The fourth looks at the evidence that can be marshaled for the coevolution of the human brain, mind, and knowledge. It also looks at the general problems of mind in prehistory and at the mental products of contemporary archaeologists who contemplate the evidence of the past. This sketch draws on the work of archaeologists, cognitive scientists, and philosophers in approximately equal measure.

Positivism and Contemporary Archaeology

It has been fashionable of late to criticize the so-called New Archaeology for its adoption of logical empiricism, and then offer one or another brand of irrational relativism as a substitute. Critics who attempt to make this case are far off the mark in their condemnation (see Peebles 1990). Archaeological methods have not been crippled by an insistence on well formed explanatory arguments and the regulatory notion of "truth." Instead, they have been hamstrung by an insistence on employing an inappropriate version of empiricism: the one that relies *solely* on rules of confirmation and empirical evidence to establish *completely* the sense and acceptability of a proposition. A disavowal of positivism does not automatically entail rejection of the role of a well-constructed argument in scientific reasoning.[4] There is unity of scientific method, but it rests neither completely on the calculus of verification nor solely on the tautological nature of correct "theories." Instead, as Popper (1965, 1983) repeatedly has pointed out, science rests on bold conjectures and on the methods established for their refutation. Neither the "New Archaeology" nor the epistemological value of "Scientific Methods" can be eliminated by appeals to relativism.

There is much in the current corpus of archaeological knowledge to which individuals who have identified themselves as "New Archaeologists" can point with pride. Despite their disavowal of metaphysics (as part and parcel of their adoption of the positivist program), they have maintained an essentially metaphysical position that there was a "real" past that could be approached, in all its dimensions, through the application of theory and reason to evidence. This position, which ignored earlier pronouncements on the so-called logical limits to the archaeological record, instilled a methodological optimism in the discipline. Conversely, their insistence on explicit theory, rigorously defined measures, and clear descriptions provided a check on their optimism and provided a necessary corrective to the then current practice. Finally, their initial sense of proper explanatory form as an argument that conjoined theory and evidence in an abductive manner (see Fritz and Plog 1970) must be counted as a real contribution to the discipline.

This admirable program went wrong when efforts were made to rationalize and give philosophical justification to the initial methodological prescriptions. The tenets of logical positivism[5] were adopted in order to invest archaeological arguments with the mantle of science. Therein, only tautological (analytically true) theories, so-called bridge principles (to connect theory with data), and directly observable phenomena were to be admitted in the conduct of science. Mental events were excluded because they could not be observed directly; metaphysical statements and systems were excluded because they were neither true by definition nor uniformly subject to empirical test. To the extent that history and historical explanations were seen primarily as mental phenomena, they too were excluded from science. As a consequence, insofar as the prescriptions of logical empiricism were followed, bad scholarship generally resulted;[6] insofar as these prescriptions were ignored, and the methodological optimism and critical spirit that formed the core of contemporary archaeology were followed, productive and innovative research was accomplished.

Alison Wylie, in her dissertation *Positivism and the New Archaeology*, has reached much the same conclusion, but she has done so in a far more elegant and complete manner.

> . . . positivism is a stringent form of empiricism so that, in espousing it, New Archaeologists have unwittingly reinstated, as the epistemological underpinning of their own program, precisely the presuppositions that they resist in traditional forms of research. (Wylie 1982:374)

She too believes that archaeological research is successful to the extent that it ignores positivist prescriptions and gets about the business of science.

> . . . archaeologists can achieve an understanding of the cultural past and they can contribute, through this, to anthropological theory . . . only insofar as they are able to reconstruct and

elucidate the causal properties of cultural systems in what amounts to a radical departure
from the official positivism of the New Archaeology. (Wylie 1982:372)

In fact, Wylie has concluded (ibid:340) that the abductive method of "question and
answer" proposed by Collingwood (1961) for history is the proper approach for archaeology as well. In Collingwood's scheme, written material and material remains are taken
as "testimony," to be turned into proper evidence through cross-examination by the
scholar, much as an attorney examines a witness in a trial. History is then constructed
from this evidence, and historical constructs are modified in light of this evidence. The
foundations of the scheme involve sequential generalizations and modification based on
a cycle of problems, questions, and the answers to these questions. In this scheme both
concepts (theories) and evidence are mutually important.

The appreciative assessment of Collingwood's historical method by Wylie is instructive, especially in light of Lewis Binford's equally strong antipathy toward him (Binford
1983a:60). In a concerted effort to discredit historical methods, and to forestall any
movement by archaeology toward what he derisively calls "paleopsychology," Binford
constructs an argument that inverts the clear meaning and intent of several historians,
archaeologists, and philosophers, including those of Collingwood, who was an accomplished scholar in all three disciplines.

Binford lumps all of Collingwood's historical method under the rubric of "empathic
understanding," in which subjective psychic propensities are seen as the crucial explanatory variables in historical understanding (Binford 1983a:60).[7] He continues by
faulting Childe for the same mentalistic shortcomings, and he clearly implies that Childe
agrees with Collingwood on this matter (ibid:61). For the record, Collingwood specifically
disavows the subjectivism of Windelband and the empathic, psychic explanations of
Dilthey (Collingwood 1978:165–168, 171–176). Moreover, Childe specifically disavows
the particular brand of idealism served up by Collingwood, especially the latter's focus
on reenactment (Childe 1949:24–25). These misreadings, as Toulmin implies (see note
7 above), are misguided at best and malicious at worst. They are, in fact, designed to
advance a particular cause in the absence of either reason or evidence.

The irony of this situation is that Binford's use and misuse of Collingwood does not
stop here. Collingwood argues—correctly, I believe—that the ontological status of history is as "the past encapsulated in the present" (Collingwood 1978:100). In effect, the
past is here today in documents, films, books, artifacts, and archaeological sites. Moreover, our only access to this past is what has been preserved on the "thin edge of the
present."[8] If I have read Binford correctly, he would only allow *archaeological* materials
to have such a present, objective existence. Without so much as a passing reference to
Collingwood, Binford writes:

> *The archaeological record is here with us in the present.* . . . . They are not direct observations
> that remain from the past (as in the case of the historian who uses information from a 15th
> century diary which conveys information made by an author in the 15th century). (Binford
> 1983b:19, emphasis in the original)

This is a blatant and completely illegitimate attempt to separate archaeology from history. Binford endows written documents with a status radically different from that of archaeological remains. A charitable reading of his intent is: conscious (but perhaps misguided) thought is represented in the former, and unconscious "behavior" (the meaning of which the archaeologist makes manifest) is present in the latter. A further implication is that the historian must take the content of the written document at face value (a conclusion with which no historian would agree), but that the archaeologist can impose scientific meaning on material remains (presumably producing an objective rather than subjective reading). The conclusion, which certainly is unwarranted, is that the archaeological past differs in kind rather than degree from the historical past.

The penultimate irony is provided by Binford's attempt to incorporate Kuhn's notion of "paradigm" as the centerpiece of archaeological reasoning. In doing so, he and his coauthor Jeremy Sabloff assert: "What is interesting in these developments is the very paradigmatic distinctions which Kuhn so insightfully introduced were ignored by many who have accepted or elaborated his arguments (see, for example, Feyerabend 1975; Toulmin 1972)" (Binford 1983a:397).

To set the record straight, the reference to "Toulmin 1972" is to his book *Human Understanding*. Therein, not only does Toulmin discuss Kuhn and *The Structure of Scientific Revolutions* for some fifty pages, but he specifically and categorically rejects the relativistic notion of paradigms. Toulmin himself provides the ultimate irony when he argues that Kuhn can be styled the empiricist successor to the relativistic idealism of Collingwood and his "absolute presuppositions," a position which, I must add, Toulmin rejects (Toulmin 1972:98–130).

These and the other philosophical muddles, which run amok in contemporary archaeology, have far-reaching consequences for research. On the one hand, reliance on the positivist criteria of meaningfulness through verification based upon sense-data has closed off whole avenues of investigation. On the other hand, the failure to see the implications of various metaphysical choices has produced conceptual (theoretical) structures that are little more than anecdotal frameworks for what might have been. These problems, which are manifest in the discipline, led Michael Schiffer (1981) to call for archaeologists and philosophers to reach some kind of *rapprochement*. For the archaeologist "The first task . . . is to identify questions and issues that are potentially amenable to philosophic analysis" (Schiffer 1981:901). For their part, "As additional philosophers of science begin testing their formulations using archaeology as a source of data, it is likely that significant contributions will be made to both archaeology and philosophy" (Schiffer 1981:906). The naïveté may be overlooked, but again the consequences are profound. Philosophers are interested in questions of history and humankind (which, recall, are excluded from several schools of contemporary archaeology, almost by definition), but they are neither interested in nor equipped to referee arguments among archaeologists about the status of ethnoarchaeological materials.[9]

It seems as though archaeologists have come to treat philosophy like a giant intellectual toolbox full of useful things. They choose the methodological equivalents of socket wrenches, but they do so irrespective of whether or not they are all from the same "standard": Metric, Whitworth, or SAE sizes, they are treated as all the same. In doing so, they ignore the implications of their choices. The reliance on behavior, "behaviorism," and the primacy of the effects of behavior (artifacts) is the case in point.

The clearest argument for the role of "behaviorism" in a "behavioral archaeology" is set out in a textbook by Michael Schiffer[10] and William Rathje (Rathje and Schiffer 1982):

> Living societies are an interrelated mix of behaviors and artifacts; dead societies are just artifacts. For archaeologists, therefore, whole societies consist of two halves, one usually invisible—behavior, one usually visible—artifacts. Taken by themselves, artifacts are like a jumble of letters without meaning, so that archaeologists studying a dead society are like someone learning to read a new language. It is only when linked to common behaviors of manufacture, use, and discard, that patterns in artifacts begin to make sense. (Rathje and Schiffer 1982:44)

There is no room in this model for either representations or intentions but only for observable behavior and its products.

Mental states and dispositions have no place in this science; instead, in the parlance of B. F. Skinner, reinforced "operants" are the engines of behavioral stasis and change. Moreover, as Lawrence Smith has argued in his recent book *Behaviorism and Logical Positivism* (1986), behaviorism and logical positivism have common cause, although they do not necessarily have common intellectual roots. Specifically, both privilege sense-data, both abjure metaphysics, and both hold an essentially Darwinian view of nature and culture.

In brief, both behaviorism and positivism are empiricist and relativist, instrumentalist and operationalist. In fact, Lewis Binford explicitly adopts many of these ills when he argues that "middle range research" [or middle range theory] should seek " . . . accurate means of identification and good instruments for measuring specified properties of past cultural systems" (1983a:49). Yet most theoretical archaeologists who would give primacy to behavior as the focal point of analysis, including Binford, would deny vehemently instrumentalism and would not embrace operationalism fully. Adherence to either the one or the other would deny them most of historical and social theory upon which they implicitly base their work and would even restrict their access to ecological theory, itself built upon realist assumptions. To take this part of the argument to a conclusion, if one posits that there is a "real" past[11] against which the truth of the historian's product can be measured, then neither relativism nor instrumentalism provides the tools necessary to write prehistory.

Short of a return to a narrowly descriptive, unreflective discipline, is there a consistent philosophical position that can provide archaeology—as a historical science—with a metaphysic for judgment of its methods and products? I believe the answer is yes, and, as I will attempt to demonstrate in the next section, it can be found in the philosophy of Karl Popper and some of his students. Their "evolutionary epistemology," with its emphasis on the theoretical foundations of all knowledge, their insistence on empirical "truth" as the measure of all theories, and their conclusion that all theories are fallible and transitory, escape the contradictions inherent in logical empiricism as well as the intellectual anarchy that pervades relativism. In somewhat more pragmatic terms: Can prehistory find a method that will include human behavior and its biological foundations, as well as culture and its framework of knowledge, in the context of individual human actors, their cognition and intentions, and the unintended consequences of their actions? Again I believe the answer is yes. It is distributed widely in the work of contemporary cognitive scientists as well as in the work of Popper, his students, and his colleague John Eccles.

Karl Popper and the Philosophy of Science

In outline form, and in its rich specifics, the philosophy of Karl Popper is clear and straightforward.[12] He is a realist—he says "historical realist"—and his philosophy of science places great emphasis on the fallibility of knowledge. He gives rational criticism and the identification and elimination of error the primary role in scientific research. He ties the advance of knowledge to the refutation of theories rather than to their confirmation: a false consequent falsifies its antecedent; a true consequent does not establish, necessarily, the truth of its antecedent.

For him, good science consists of problems and their solutions. This process is, at its base, abductive—in the sense of Peirce (1940:150–156)—and it comprises (1) the recognition of a problem, (2) the proposal of a tentative theory to solve the problem, (3) a match of expectations generated from the theory with the "real world," (4) elimination of error in the fit between the expectations and the world, (5) and so on, *ad infinitum*. Progress comes when old theories fall and new theories fail to fall, at least for the moment. The regulative notion in this process is truth: Tarski's "truth"; the correspondence or lack thereof of a statement with the facts. For Popper, falsification—the lack of correspondence—is more important than verification. His fallibilist stance sets him apart from the positivists and their emphasis on verification and places him in the tradition of Peirce (1940:42–59).

The best theories for Popper are those that have "risky" predictions. They should contain implications that say "this" or "that" should never happen. Good scientific practice then comprises the construction of such theories, the crafting of rigorous deductive arguments that connect these premises to their conclusions, and the unrelenting search for the consequences that will falsify the theory. The very best among the current crop of theories are those that have withstood this process and which also have high information content, low probability, and a number of disparate predictions at risk.[13]

Perhaps the greatest difference between Popper and the "positivists" is in the high value which Popper assigns metaphysics:

> In science, problem situations are the result, as a rule, of three factors. One is the discovery of an inconsistency within the ruling theory. A second is the discovery of an inconsistency between theory and experiment—the experimental falsification of the theory. The third, and perhaps the most important one, is the relation between the theory and what may be called the '*metaphysical research programme*.'
>
>   In using this term I want to draw attention to the fact that in almost every phase of the development of science we are under the sway of metaphysical—that is, untestable—ideas;

ideas which not only determine what problems of explanation we shall choose to attack, but also what kinds of answers we shall consider as fitting or satisfactory or acceptable, and as improvements of or advances on earlier answers. (Popper 1982b:161)

The emphasis here is on rational criticism of unverifiable propositions. It is not a re-statement of Kuhn's "paradigms," and Holton's (1973) "themata"; although it is far closer to the latter than to the former. Popper's metaphysical research programmes, although they may not be subject to disconfirmation through empirical evidence, none-theless carry the same fallibility as theories. They are at risk from criticism, they are subject to correction, and, unlike paradigms, they cannot be immunized and insulated through appeals to relativism. In summary, Popper sees a vast universe—in fact, an infinite universe—of ignorance from which we carve little illuminated patches of knowl-edge through bold conjectures and diligent attempts at their refutations.[14]

A second important aspect of Popper's metaphysics is his ontology of "Three Worlds." His trinitarian categorical framework comprises (1) the material, (2) the con-scious—for humans consciously subjective—and (3) the corpus of objective knowledge.

By 'World 1' I mean what is usually called the world of physics: of rocks and trees and physical fields of forces. I also mean to include here the worlds of chemistry and biology. By 'World 2' I mean the psychological world. It is studied by students of the human mind. . . . It is the world of feeling of fear and hope, of dispositions to act, and of all kinds of subjective experiences, including subconscious and unconscious experiences. (Popper 1982b:114)

By "World 3" I mean the world of the products of the human mind [e.g., objective knowledge] (ibid).

World 3 begins only with the evolution of a specifically human language. I will take the world of *linguistically formulated human knowledge* as being most characteristic of World 3. It is the world of problems, theories, and arguments. . . . (op. cit.:116)

Transitions from the lower to the higher among these Three Worlds must be counted as "emergent phenomena," and the explanation of these transitions defies reduction to principles that govern the the level below. Moreover, there are levels of complexity within World 1—e.g., the emergence of life—and World 2—e.g., the emergence of human, self-awareness as distinct from animal consciousness—that also defy reduction to principles of nonliving matter and simple animal awareness. For the purposes of this paper, however, it is the interaction among the Three Worlds—matter, self-awareness, and knowledge—that is of interest.

Popper and Eccles (1977) and Eccles (1979, 1980) have presented an extended, interactionist argument for the existence of mind as distinct from brain.[15] Their argument, for the most part due to Popper, is that mind is the product of the interaction of a con-scious, sentient World 2 "self" with its brain. It is this conscious self that links World 3 objective knowledge with the living and nonliving materials of World 1. That is, World 1 phenomena and objects are open to and affected by World 3 phenomena only through the mediation of World 2 minds.

$$World_1 \leftrightarrow World_2 \leftrightarrow World_3$$

In this framework, mind cannot be reduced to brain, and knowledge cannot be reduced solely to brain function; likewise, extending the argument, life cannot be reduced to either chemistry or physics, and even the structure of something as "simple" as crystals cannot be completely reduced to the laws of physics and chemistry.[16]

All three of Popper's worlds are set in an indeterministic universe. In this universe the future—especially the human and cultural future—cannot be predicted through the application of ever more powerful laws and theories. He argues that we cannot predict the shape of new theories, thus we cannot predict the inventions and discoveries that will flow from them over the next fifty years. Moreover, even if we could make such "hard," scientific predictions, we could not predict the unintended consequences such discoveries would have on humankind and society. Consequently, from Popper's perspective, history (and prehistory) can be scientific and retrodictive, but they cannot be predictive in the ways envisioned by logical empiricists.[17]

The interplay of self, mind, and language are at the heart of Popper's arguments about the production of knowledge. First, there is the recognition that the conscious, human, subjective self is ontologically prior to and necessary for the development of mind.[18] Second, the development of language (in the broadest, representational, semiotic sense) is logically prior to the production of objective knowledge (intersubjective knowledge). Third, as humans act in a world mediated by objective knowledge, and as expectations are either met or not met and communicated to others, the corpus of objective knowledge grows. Fourth, this process of growth is essentially "Darwinian":[19] the production of novelty is essentially random, and these variants are subject to selection both in the symbolically mediated World 3 and by the things and situations of World 1. Fifth, in this process, the only difference between scientific knowledge and ordinary, everyday knowledge is that the former usually is couched in terms of a deductive argument—which can be judged in terms of logical validity and match with the "real" world (e.g., truth)—and the latter, like the products of engineering and those of Lévi-Strauss's *bricoleur*, is judged pragmatically.

The notion that all knowledge and most action is hypothetical in one way or another can be found throughout the human sciences. As Richard Gregory observes: "We now see predictions as a vital element of intelligent behavior, and indeed of Mind. We have suggested that intelligence may be defined as the 'generation of successful novelty'; and of course predictions that turn out right are successful and were novel" (Gregory 1981:563). Jerome Bruner, although in profound disagreement with Popper's realism, registers both support and alarm at the central position Popper gives to hypotheses in the production of knowledge:

It is this staggering gift for creating hypotheses that makes Popper's view of science more right than wrong—that and the ease with which by the very selectivity of our senses, our minds, and our language, we accept our hypotheses as right. We have extraordinary faith in one-shot instantiation. Milton's Satan in "Paradise Lost" may have been the forerunner of Karl Popper's falsificationism. (Bruner 1986:51)

Popper's ontology and epistemology is complete, consistent, subject to criticism, and open to correction. It can give a metaphysical foundation for prehistory as a historical science, and it not only allows but demands that the makers of the prehistoric record—both then and now—be endowed with minds and with intentions that transcend their overt behaviors.

As W. W. Bartley III, a student and interpreter of Popper and his philosophy, has summarized:

> The chief ideas of Popper's philosophy all relate to the basic theme that something can come from nothing. Scientific theories introduce new forms into the universe and cannot be reduced to observations: there is no such thing as scientific induction. The future is not contained in the present or the past. There is indeterminism in physics; and there is indeterminism in history, *ipso facto*, and also because new scientific ideas affect history and thus the course of the physical universe. There is genuine emergence in biology. Value cannot be reduced to fact. Mind cannot be reduced to matter. Descriptive and argumentative levels of language cannot be reduced to expressive and signal levels. Consciousness is the spearhead of evolution, and the products of consciousness are not determined. (Bartley 1978:676)

In effect, there can be human sciences, including history and prehistory, but they cannot call upon timeless "laws" of human behavior for self-justification and validation. Although their methods must be those of science in general, and although they can be intensely theoretical, they must take into account that the "initial conditions" change with each generation, and that the "unintended consequences" of even the most mundane acts sometimes can outnumber the intended outcomes. In effect, both the biological and the intellectual foundations of humankind are changing constantly, and future states, although founded on current states, cannot be extrapolated directly from such current states.

The Cognitive Sciences

Although ambitious and expansive—and perhaps the academic "growth industry" of the 1980s and 1990s—cognitive science is neither a passing fad nor an eclectic thing of shreds and patches that has no academic department to call home. As Neil Stillings and his colleagues argue in their text *Cognitive Science, An Introduction*, from their vantage point, the proper focus for scholars in this interdisciplinary movement is on the mind as "a complex system that receives, stores, retrieves, transforms, and transmits information" (Stillings et al. 1987:1). They argue that understanding of mind is based on the study of formal information processes, that these processes are representational, and that for purposes of study they can be separated from physical and biological processes (ibid:1–15). Howard Gardner, in his book *The Mind's New Science*, takes a somewhat less formalist perspective and defines cognitive science as "the empirically based effort to answer long-standing epistemological questions—particularly those concerned with the nature of knowledge, its components, its sources, its development, and its deployment" (Gardner 1985:6). Central to all branches and sects within the wider cognitive sciences is the belief that cognition, representation, and intention comprise phenomena "wholly separate from the biological or neuronal on the one hand, and the sociological or cultural on the other'' (Gardner 1985:6). As such, they deserve and demand study in their own right.

Daniel Dennett, a philosopher and important contributor to the cognitive sciences, has argued that human beings are intentional systems (1987:13–35). As intentional systems, their (our) actions cannot be understood from a "physical stance," where the laws of nature are sufficient to predict outputs from any given input. Likewise, their actions cannot be predicted from a "design stance," where knowledge of the design, but ignorance of the actual internal works, is sufficient to predict the behavior. Instead, one must impart rational beliefs to the agent and, from those beliefs, purposes, and place in the world, predict the agent's behavior from those considerations. That is, one must adopt an "intentional stance" in order to understand human actions and activities. John Searle (1983), who disagrees with Dennett on many things, has come to essentially the same conclusion. In the "Preface" to his book *Intentionality*, and in his later Reith Lectures, he says:

> Ordinary human behavior has proven to be particularly recalcitrant to explanations by the methods of the natural sciences. Why? Why is it that the methods of the natural sciences have not given results comparable to physics and chemistry when applied to the study of individual and collective human behavior? There are many attempts to answer this question in contemporary philosophy, none of them in my view completely satisfactory. I believe that the direction of the correct answer lies in seeing the role of Intentionality in the structure of action; not just in the description. (Searle 1983:x)

In summary, problems of intentionality are problems of mind; problems of mind are what animate the several disciplines that have formed the loose confederation known as the cognitive sciences.

Thus far computer science has provided the greatest range of methods and metaphors for cognitive science. Under the rubric of Artificial Intelligence (AI), computers and computation have been used as either analogues or homologues for human thought processes.[20] Computers have provided the means for experimentation—a way in which possibilities, potentials, and limits of cognition might be explored—where such intervention would be unthinkable with a human subject. Above all, use of computers to model human mind(s) and logic(s) has shown that a good representation is far superior to "brute force" in the solution of most problems, even when the computing power available is many orders of magnitude greater than that of the human brain.

There are six propositions that comprise a foundation for a cognitive approach to human thought and action. These six elements are by no means the only contributions that can be appropriated from the cognitive sciences, but they are directly applicable and important to prehistoric studies. Individually and together, several of them marked or hastened the end of behaviorism in psychology; they should serve much the same rôle in the elimination of behaviorism from the study of prehistory. They are presented here in order of increasing complexity and decreasing experimental support.

The first proposition, which many see as crucial to the demise of behaviorism, is contained in Karl Lashely's 1948 paper "The Problem of Serial Order in Behavior"

(1951). Therein he demonstrates that most human sequences of behavior above the level of the simple reflex arc must be planned and organized in advance of their execution. That is, thought and ratiocination are necessary for and prior to action.

Second, and in the same vein, is the observation and experimental confirmation that voluntary movement is activated by the conscious mind *in advance* of the actual movement of a particular limb. If such simple movements require some form of thought, more complex actions cannot be reduced solely to external stimuli, no matter how complex they might be (Eccles in Popper and Eccles 1977:§19; Eccles 1979, 1980).

The third proposition, due to George Miller and his famous paper "The Magical Number Seven, Plus or Minus Two: Some Limits on Our Capacity for Processing Information" (1956), presents the concepts of short- and long-term memory and the relationships among these two very different mechanisms for storing, retrieving, and processing information. This paper asserts, and experimental evidence subsequently has confirmed, that an average human being can hold approximately five separate and independent notions in short-term memory at one time for mental processing. This proposition has very important implications for the organization and content (the categorical frameworks) of human knowledge in light of some very real limitations of the human brain and its ability to retrieve and process information.

The fourth proposition, which comes from the work of Herbert Simon and Alan Newell, comprises what they call the "Physical Symbol System Hypothesis" where " . . . a physical symbol system has the necessary and sufficient means for generating intelligent action" (Newell and Simon 1987:293). In effect, they argue for a materialist basis for symbols and symbolic action. They propose that human symbolic behavior is a direct result of such a physical symbol system. Moreover, they posit that humans solve problems " . . . by generating potential solutions and then testing them, that is, by searching. Solutions are usually sought by creating symbolic expressions and modifying them sequentially until they satisfy the conditions for a solution" (Newell and Simon 1987:311). The source of these symbolic expressions lies at what Newell has defined as the "knowledge level" (1982).

> The focus here is on the knowledge level. Knowledge is the medium. Each primitive system consists of a body of knowledge, including some knowledge of the system's goals. If knowledge is input at some time, then it becomes a permanent part of the body of knowledge of the system. The law of behavior is that each system acts (within its physical constraints) to use its knowledge to attain its physical goals (a simple form of rationality). Primitive knowledge-level systems and their interconnections are realized by symbol-level systems. (Newell 1988:521)

Representations, at least for Newell, are generated from knowledge and the means to access that knowledge (Newell 1982:114).

In the work of Newell and Simon cognition, language, and the analogy with computation come together. For them humans are systems with representations and with memory which can match internal and stored information with their environment as the means to reach various goals. They (we) are the most complex examples, at least thus far, of Ashby's principle of "requisite variety"—of the necessary match of internal symbolic variety of a system with the variety that is present in its "effective" environment. Humans also can be characterized in terms of Wilden's semantic reformulation of Ashby:

> Ashby's principle of 'requisite variety' can therefore be restated as a principle of representation, using the more general term 'requisite diversity': The capacity of any system, R, to represent the diversity of another system, S, cannot exceed the flexibility of R as a coding system. This is the principle of requisite diversity of representation. (1987:192)

In Wilden's terms, 'R' must come to grips with and represent the basic diversity within any one level of an environment. These representations must differentiate among levels in a hierarchy in that environment (if such levels exist), and they must be capable of representing one level in terms of another by crossing boundaries and effecting a reduction of one to the other: e.g., a simple calendar that might sum up (predict) the ebb and flow of nature throughout a seasonal cycle; a classification of kin that orders individuals in terms of those who are potential mates and those who are not. To the extent that the semantic (representational) code is adequate, so then is the agent that produces and incorporates that code.

The fifth proposition asserts that brain and mind are not comprised of a single, undifferentiated human cognitive faculty or capacity. Instead, there seems to be a plurality of "faculties" that characterize human mental competence. Marvin Minsky has dubbed these *The Society of Mind* (1986); Michael Gazzaniga has called these *The Social Brain*:

> The data suggest that our mental lives amount to a reconstruction of the independent activities of the many brain systems we all possess. A confederation of mental systems resides within us. Metaphorically, we humans are more of a sociological entity than a single unified psychological entity. We have a social brain. (Gazzaniga 1985:x)

He is not alone in proposing a variety of faculties for the human brain and mind. Zenon Pylyshyn (1984) argues for a three-part (-level) approach to cognition: first, the level of the functional architecture of the brain, which he sees as specialized and relatively unchanging; second, the syntactic or functional level; third, the semantic or "knowledge" level.[21]

Sixth, and finally, is the "representational materialism" proposed by Arthur C. Danto (1989), which can be used to give added perspective to many of the points sketched above. For him, the basic cognitive episode comprises three components—(1) subject, (2) representation, and (3) the world; these three components, in turn, yield three relationships—(1) self, (2) causality, and (3) truth (1989:xii–xiii) (see Figure 1). As representing beings " . . . we are connected to the world in terms of causality and truth—*inside* the world, one might say, under causality and outside the world under truth-relationship" (ibid).

Although Danto might disagree, there are elements of Popper's Three Worlds scheme here. The most notable convergence is the notion that awareness of self is a product of an interaction between the subject and its representations. Where Danto parts from Popper is over the notion of a dualist-interactionist view of mind as the result of an interaction

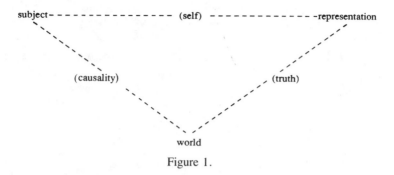

Figure 1.

between the self and its brain. Instead, Danto prefers to see the cognitive, representational act as one ultimately "written" in the neuronal tissue—in his terms, a "representational materialism" (Danto 1989:Chapter 35).

In his discussion of humans as representational beings, Danto examines cause and effect relationships between representational and nonrepresentational states as they enter into cognition. For example, representational states can be both cause and effect; such would be the case when an individual believes **x** because that same individual believes **y**. An example of a nonrepresentational cause and a representational effect would be when events in the world produce certain representations in an individual (the empiricist view of mind). There are, however, representational causes and nonrepresentational effects, when, for example, the arm is raised in a salute to a passing flag. Finally there are nonrepresentational causes and effects, such as eating, respiration, and most other life processes, the dynamics of the solar system, the movement of billiard balls, etc. The point to be made here is that Danto sees all these causal pairs and triplets as evolving together: as part of subjects, representations, and the world. He argues that the ability to form "true representations" is every bit as important for survival of an organism as is a particular kind of "metabolism" or "protective coloration" (op. cit.:269). Put the other way around, beings which hold some significant number of "false" representations are those that do not survive.

Humans are separated from the remainder of the living world to the extent that their representational states cause other representational states and form belief systems. "What cannot be sought in the genetic material is the contribution that history and culture make to our identities" (op. cit.:273). "There are limits assigned by historical locations in human affairs that have no counterparts in the natural world" (op. cit.:274). In summary, for Danto:

Folk psychology explains our conduct with reference to inference, knowledge, and action. All of these involve us as held together within ourselves by logical relations, and held together with the world by means of semantical relations. The materialist is right, in that unless representations were embodied, perhaps even neurally embodied, making the neurophilosopher right, representations would and could make nothing happen. Causality holds between material states. But the idealist is right as well: If no representations were embodied, we would be mere physical systems. It is the metaphysical relationship between matter and representations, and then the causal relationships through which representations are effective, that a repre-

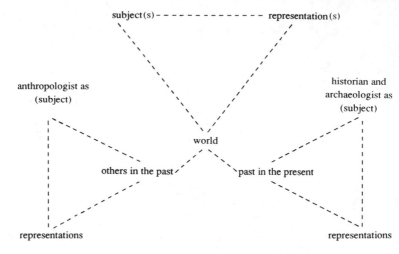

Figure 2

sentational materialism of the sort that I have been advancing here must work out. But once
there are representations, a factor or set of factors enters to complicate the materialist position.
Truth becomes, as it were, a causal force (so, of course, does falsity). The way we represent
the world becomes a factor in the way the world is. (op. cit.:269)

Again there is an echo of Popper's Three Worlds and the role of the subject in the
application of objective knowledge to the material world.

From the perspective of the cognitive sciences, the development of human capacities
for culture can be viewed as the evolution of a collection of faculties and not as an all-
or-nothing phenomenon which had to cross a cerebral Rubicon to be counted as human.

If Danto's outline can be expanded to incorporate two aspects of anthropological
inquiry, the ensuing schema might look like Figure 2.

Anthropologists, archaeologists as anthropologists, and archaeologists as historians
operate with specialized subsets of representations that they take to the world of the
living and the world of the dead—the latter taken as the past in the present. In each of
these cases, to the extent that knowledge of the world and of others in the world is
created, the stock of representations is increased and the world itself is remade, if even
only a bit. In geological time, however, each of these three major components has
expanded and evolved many times over, and each has served as a selective "environment"
for the others. An examination of these relationships between mind and brain and the
world in the evolutionary context of our lives and their lives, in geological time and time
present, forms the final section of this paper.

Cognition in the Pleistocene; Cognition in the Present

It is reasonably clear that the development of brain-mind and that of culture-knowledge
have been linked (or at least mutually constrained) over the last few million years. The

rough details and sequence of this mutual development can be sketched, but the fine points and precise chronology are not apparent, at least not at present. Given Popper's ontology of Three Worlds and the central position of World 2, the human psyche and sentience, as mediation between the materiality of World 1 and the objective knowledge of World 3, it stands to reason that the evolutionary forces on the human brain would come from both the natural and cultural environments. As Clifford Geertz has observed:

> Tools, hunting, family organization, and later, art, religion, and "science" molded man somatically; and they are, therefore, necessary not merely to his survival but to his existential realization.
> The application of this revised view of human evolution leads to the hypothesis that cultural resources are ingredient, not accessory, to human thought. (Geertz 1973:83)

This insight by Geertz, one of the founders of "symbolic anthropology," is echoed by Simon, one of the founders of Artificial Intelligence:

> Symbol systems are the almost quintessential artifacts, for adaptivity to an environment is their whole *raison d'etre*. They are goal-seeking, information processing systems, usually enlisted in the service of the larger system in which they are incorporated. (Simon 1981:27)

Thus rather than the behaviorist's simple operant, reinforcement, and fixation model, one is faced with multiple "environments" and multiple cognitive faculties that begin with the brain and end in representations which have referents and interpretants in even wider environments. Moreover, following Fodor, Gardner, Minsky, and Pylyshyn, the somatic realization of the selective forces should be distributed among different areas and faculties of the brain. Each and all then would be cast in the wider environments of the "real" world.

John Gowlett (1984) has examined the problem of the evolution of mind from an uncompromising archaeological perspective. Therefrom he has searched for evidence of human abilities not only to make more and more complex tools but to master and "navigate" in space and time. He concludes his analysis of the Human Career with:

> The human mind reflects the human way of life: complexity reflects complexity. Complex routines and practices observable in the Lower Pleistocene are best accounted for by the progress of natural selection itself, rather than by single shot mechanisms, such as the hunting hypothesis or the foodsharing hypothesis. In a demanding environment, there is every incentive to develop more foresight, better planning abilities. The archaeological record enables us to demonstrate that the foundations for these had been laid at least two million years ago.

The earliest hints at the development of human faculties is found in the "handedness" of early hominids. Nicholas Toth (1985) has shown from an analysis of early Paleolithic, Oldowan, and Acheulean assemblages that the vast majority of the flint knappers were right-handed. Given the association of handedness with the lateralization of the human brain, this perhaps is evidence for the nascent specialization of the hemispheres.

Andre Leroi-Gourhan has linked the faculties necessary to craft tools with those of speech and, ultimately, with those necessary for writing (Leroi-Gourhan 1965). The concept of an ''operational chain,'' a finite series of steps necessary for the production of a tool, occupies a position of great importance in his analytical scheme. Such programs, with their various subroutines, decision points, and contingencies, as they develop in length and complexity, place a premium on representation, communication, and memory. Leroi-Gourhan believes that the development of fine motor skills in humans is connected to cortical expansion and neural reorganization; in turn, increase in complexity of tasks and tools provides the problem situation in which language develops.

The concept of ''operational chains'' can be found in several of the papers that comprise this volume, although they are applied to products of rather recent vintage (e.g., Perlès, Chapter 14). In evolutionary time, these chains range from the relatively simple operations that yield Oldowan tools to those very complex programs that generated the tools and ornaments characteristic of Upper Paleolithic, Aurignacian assemblages (see White 1989). Larry Kimball and Lawrence Keely (1988) have looked at the increasing complexity not only of tools and their manufacture throughout the Paleolithic but of the spatial and temporal separation of their production and use. They find that not only do operational chains increase in length and complexity, but that their applications can be radically discontinuous in space and time. Items may be ''roughed out'' in one place, finished at another, modified at yet a third, remodified at a fourth, and discarded at a fifth. In Lewis Binford's terms, tools in a particular assemblage are ''curated'' not only in general but at different points in their manufacture and life-cycle.

Gazzaniga (1985) too sees nascent human skills in early hominids in their ability to control and reshape small parts of their environment. He, however, posits that the crucial development in the hominization process was the development of the ability to make inferences (the evolution of the hardware for an ''inference engine,'' if you will). He correlates this ability, plus linguistic competence, to the development of Wernicke's area of the brain. Following Coppens, he argues that it was not until *Homo sapiens sapiens* that this area of the brain became fully developed, although the vascularization of this portion of the cerebral hemispheres began earlier in human evolution.

> In summary, the view is that the archaeological record is suggesting specific brain areas evolved to carry out specific functions that in turn produced new capacities for our species. These capabilities, such as inference and aesthetics, are manifestly present in *Homo sapiens sapiens*. Their origins can be traced all the way back to *Homo erectus*, perhaps further. The ensuing cognitive skills came slowly, and in prehistory early man was capable of making more associative responses than inferential leaps. Once inference was possible, however, modern man was born into and doomed to a most difficult way to live. The inferential capacity led to the formation of beliefs, not only about his own behavior but also about past and present behavior of others within his group. Such mental activities in turn begin the process of decoupling man from the influence of environmental forces. (Gazzaniga 1985:164)

For Gazzaniga, the notion of ''self'' develops from the ability to make inferences. This conclusion inverts the Cartesian universe and the causal order proposed by Popper and Eccles.

Gazzaniga sees the increase in tool types and sophistication in their manufacture as the essential markers for a flowering of skills and abilities in the Middle Paleolithic. He also posits that some inferential capacities are present among the Neanderthals, and these faculties are evident in seasonality of settlement, which bespeaks of mental maps of the landscape, and in aesthetic (stylistic) dimensions to tools. Recall, however, that Popper asserts causal priority to the "self." Mind, for him, is the interaction of the "self" with "its brain." Thus, for Popper, the conscious "self" of World 2 should logically precede World 3 phenomena.

Nicholas Humphrey, a psychologist and gifted naturalist, asserts the priority of the self, but he does so from the vantage point of an evolutionary biologist:

> In evolutionary terms it [human consciousness] must have been a major breakthrough. Imagine the biological benefits to the first of our ancestors to develop the ability to make realistic guesses about the inner life of his rivals: to be able to picture what another was thinking about, and planning to do next, to be able to read the minds of others by reading his own. The way was open to a new deal in human social relationships: sympathy, compassion, trust, treachery, and double-crossing—the very things which make us human. (Humphrey 1986:76)

Richard Alexander, who takes a position close to that of Humphrey, casts the social basis of human consciousness in sociobiological terms:

> The central evolved function of the human psyche, then, is to yield an ability to anticipate or predict the future—explicitly the social future—and to manipulate it in the (evolutionary, reproductive) interest of self's genetic success. (Alexander 1989:459)

For both Humphrey and Alexander, the ability to predict the states of other's minds and the development of an introspective self arose together—each in service to the other.

For Popper (Popper and Eccles 1977:153), the knowledge of self implies not only the existence of other selves but also an apprehension of death. [Perhaps the Neanderthals of Shanidar engaged in the first Cartesian meditation.] Eccles, who does believe in the supernatural (in contrast to Popper's agnosticism), summarized the crucial points of their view of biological and cultural evolution:

> As a transcendence in the evolutionary process [in which] there appeared an animal differing fundamentally from other animals because he had attained propositional speech, abstract thought and consciousness, which are all signs that a being of transcendent novelty had appeared in the world—creatures existing not only in World 1 but realizing their existence in the world of self-awareness (World 2) and so having in the religious concept, souls. And simultaneously these human beings began utilizing their World 2 experiences to create very effectively another world, the third world of the objective spirit. (Eccles 1979:121)

World 3 knowledge, as Popper has taken great pains to demonstrate, has an existence independent of the individual selves who created it and who employ it. World 3 knowledge is objective in the strictest sense of the word. Moreover, as the quantity of World 3 knowledge has grown, various ploys, devices, and structures have been developed to handle the "knowledge explosion" in the context of limitations in human cognitive capacities. Various preliterate peoples distribute knowledge differentially among the sexes, among appropriate age grades, and among individuals deemed "experts." Mnemonic devices, and, eventually, hard copy, give independent existence to knowledge, thus mediating transmission from one long-term memory to another and assuring a greater quantity of intergenerational messages. In computer parlance, both distributed processing and denser, less volatile storage devices, some of which had built-in error correcting codes, were used to store and transmit knowledge among members of one generation and from one generation to the next. Today, the amount of declarative and procedural knowledge, even in narrowly defined fields, is generally too great to be mastered by a single individual: hence databases, abstracting services, and information centers.

Perhaps the great art of the Upper Paleolithic was the first hard copy. As Leroi-Gourhan and his associates have shown, at least in outline, it is an art that has continuity through time and a structure (syntax) that is reasonably coherent. Alexander Marshack, echoing in part the themes of Leroi-Gourhan's *Le Geste et la Parole* (1965), has concluded that both the portable and wall art of the Upper Paleolithic are the ultimate development of visual and motor skills that began to evolve some 2 million years before, with the first tool makers. That is, handedness, lateralization, and cross-modal associations came together in visual representations that had symbolic, referential dimensions:

> Here it is important to note that these images, the observations and concepts of which they were a part, and the relations among them were essentially nonlinguistic. They were recognitions derived from the vision-oriented categorizing and abstracting capacity of the right and left hemispheres, though it is likely that such other aspects of categorization as the naming of the species and the differential details of anatomy, sex, and behavior would have been encoded in language. Language, when used in such contexts, would have been referential, marking categories and processes that were recognized and differentiated nonlinguistically and visually. Language would have served, in such use, as a contribution to what was in essence, a *visual* form of symboling with its own syntax, modes of use and association, and vocabulary or iconography. The capacity for language and the capacity for visual symboling and problem solving are separate, highly evolved referential modalities, utilizing different areas of the brain, though the evaluation of production in either mode involves equally complex bilateral function. (Marshack 1985:32–33)

The foundations of this art are representations based in time: seasonal time, maturational time for both animals and humans, and generational time, in which animal and human groups reproduce. The roots of this "time-factoring" competence are in the "mosaic" evolution of different parts of the human brain, each of which contributed to "the human capacity" (Marshack 1985:31–50). Marshack, however, separates the development of material symbols from the development of language, and he assigns the former temporal priority in the development of the symbolic-representational capacities of humans.

Finally, Kant, Toulmin, and Fodor, Bruner, Childe, and Leroi-Gourhan, Popper, Gazzaniga, and Marshack come together, in the frameworks that are common to all human reason: the great Kantian *a priori* intuitions of space, time, and cause, and other general categories, such as self and other, male and female, life and death. In their widest interpretation, these are the categories that can be extracted from the content of Upper Paleolithic art (Leroi-Gourhan 1982; Pfeiffer 1982; Marshack 1985). They are the frameworks that can form the foundations of a cognitive and a symbolic archaeology. As Colin

Renfrew stressed in his Inaugural Lecture,[22] these reasonably constant frameworks, plus evidence of conscious planning, are the places one should begin the analysis. They are the many times of human experience and imagination.[23] They are Bachelard's *Poetics of Space* (1964) and Barel's "socialization of space" (1973). They are Marshack's image of the cliffs of the Dordogne as the framework for marking the position of the waxing and waning of the moon, and then transferring these measures onto bone, thereby producing a calendar.

It is the evolution of the human capacity for producing knowledge, and knowledge itself—not just human behavior, which springs from that knowledge—that form the archaeological record. As Danto has argued: "To be human is to belong to a stage of history and to be defined in terms of the prevailing representations of that period. And the human sciences must, among other things, arrive at historical explanations of historically indexed representations" (Danto 1989:273). Furthermore, as Childe has written: " . . . as a pre*historian* I must treat my objects always and exclusively as concrete expressions and embodiments of human thoughts and ideas—in a world of knowledge" (Childe 1956:1). These materials represent the intentions of those who produced them in the past, and they represent the intentions of those who seek to interpret them in the present—the archaeologists. They thus become elements in a two-part archaeological equation. They are part of the answer to the contemporary question about the knowledge it took for those in a past bereft of written records to live out their lives; they also are an element in the knowledge contemporary archaeologists deploy in the service of that past in the present (Peebles 1991:108).

Acknowledgments: The prose and reasoning in this paper have been improved by the careful reading and critical comments of Jim Bell, Jeffrey Cohen, Jean-Claude Gardin, L. Halles, Michael Herzfeld, Stephen Miller, and Catherine Perlès. I thank them for their suggestions, even the ones that I did not adopt. They have helped to make this a better paper, but I alone am responsible for the shortcomings that remain.

NOTES

1. Two notable examples seem to signal a reversal of this trend. I refer to the dual Distinguished Lectures of the Society for American Archaeology in 1987 given by T. Cuyler Young, Jr. (1988) and James Deetz (1988) on the topic of "History and Archaeological Theory."

2. If you do not believe that behaviorism is a messianic movement, read B. F. Skinner's *Walden Two* (1948) and his three-volume autobiography, *Particulars of My Life, The Shaping of a Behaviorist*, and *A Matter of Consequences* (1984a, 1984b, 1984c).

3. V. Gordon Childe escaped the problem of subjectivism, and at the same time retained "knowledge" as a crucial factor in his reasoning, by stressing the social, public, and objective nature of what he called "real thought":

In effect, the separation of subject from object is transcended. Real thoughts of the past have been issued in action. Real thinking has already been objectified. To study a past society there is no need to turn its real thoughts into objects, for that has already been done. The relics and monuments studied by archaeology are patently objects, and need no translation into an alien conceptual framework. (Childe 1949:25)

4. See, for example, *The Uses of Argument* by Stephen Toulmin (1958).
5. At least as these tenets have been presented by Carl Hempel in a series of publications that began with "Studies in the Logic of Explanation" (Hempel and Oppenheim 1948) and ended with *Aspects of Scientific Explanation* (Hempel 1965). Little attention was paid to the work of others of the Vienna Circle such as Carnap and Richenbach. The choice of Hempel and his philosophy of science was consistent with similar movements in the other social sciences, including history. At that time Karl Popper was not read widely by archaeologists, although his *Logic of Scientific Discovery* (1959) was available in English. Of greater moment was the fact that although Albert Spaulding, who with W. W. Taylor can be counted among the major figures of contemporary archaeology, recommended, assigned, and taught from an essentially antipositivist text, Abraham Kaplan's *The Conduct of Inquiry* (1964), few archaeologists seem to have read it, let alone incorporated its message in their work.
6. Hilary Putnam has observed, with devastating effect:

. . . the logical positivist criterion of significance was *self-refuting*: for the criterion itself is neither (a) analytic (unless, perhaps, it is analytically *false!*) nor (b) empirically testable. Strangely enough this criticism had very little impact on the logical positivists and did little to impede the growth of their movement. I want to suggest that the neglect of this particular philosophical gambit was a great mistake; that the gambit is not only correct, but it contains a deep lesson, and not just a lesson about logical positivism. (Putnam 1981:100)

7. Stephen Toulmin (1972:491, fn 3) observes:

In the *Idea of History*, part V, Section 3, 'Historical Evidence', Collingwood makes it clear that the procedures by which a historian reaches his conclusions involves hypotheses and the appraisal of evidence, in just the same way as those used by the other rational investigator; in Section 4, 'History as Re-enactment of Past Experience', by contrast he speaks explicitly about the *outcome* of the historian's work, not about his *methods*. One really has to be somewhat wilful, in order to overlook the clear distinction between these two separate arguments.

8. I borrowed this line from something I read recently, and I cannot find the reference. So, I beg the indulgence of the original author.
9. Ronald N. Giere takes this position to its ultimate, logical conclusion:

. . . there are no special philosophical methods for plumbing the depths of any science. There are only the methods of the sciences themselves. Moreover, the people best equipped to engage in such pursuits are not those trained as philosophers, but those totally immersed in the subject matter—namely, scientists. (Giere 1988:xvi)

10. Schiffer's first book was entitled *Behavioral Archaeology* (Schiffer 1976). The core of this book was a study of cultural and natural transformations that could be held to account for the pattern in the archaeological record.
11. As does Ricoeur in his *The Reality of the Historical Past* (1984).
12. To say that Karl Popper and his philosophy have been misunderstood and misapplied is an understatement. He has been classified variously as a positivist and an empiricist, a relativist and a negativist. Not a single one of these terms fits either the man or his philosophy.
13. See especially Popper (1983), *Realism and the Aim of Science*, from the Postscript to the *Logic of Scientific Discovery*.
14. The phrasing is taken from the title of a collection of his articles: *Conjectures and Refutations: The Growth of Scientific Knowledge* (Popper 1965).

15. If you wish, so as to avoid various problems, read "mind" as "they posit the existence of individual minds as distinct from their respective individual brains."

16. Heinz Pagels, in his recent book *The Dreams of Reason*, is very uncomfortable with both Popper's brand of dualism and the concept of "emergence." Without doing Pagels an injustice, I believe that he arrives at roughly the same position as Popper on the relative autonomy of mind. In his argument for "epistemic dualism" in opposition to what he calls Popper's "substance dualism," he says:

> Two key notions that help support epistemic dualism and are exemplified by physical systems are: first, the notion that there is a "causal decoupling" between material levels that makes radical physical reductionism and the identity theory [mind = brain] practically unrealizable; and second, the notion of the "barrier of complexity" that allows the mind its practical freedom in spite of the fact that its material support, the brain, is completely governed by biological laws. (Pagels 1988:222)

17. Note that the first part of Popper's metaphysics eliminated the positivism of Mach—in which explanation is equivalent to description, and cause is equal to function—and the second part eliminated the positivists who insist that explanation and prediction are equivalent except for their position in a temporal sequence.

18. Philip N. Johnson-Laird, in his book *The Computer and the Mind*, sees the conscious self in terms of a high-level "operating system" that has limited access to itself: " . . . the conscious mind is the result of a special mode of processing that creates the subjective experience of awareness. Once an operating system had evolved, it could take on such a function, and this mode of processing, I believe, is our capacity for *self-awareness*" (Johnson-Laird 1988:360).

19. Popper, a number of his students, and Donald Campbell argue strongly for the Darwinian rather than Lamarckian model of the evolution of objective knowledge. The most recent statement of their position can be found in a collection of their papers edited by W. W. Bartley III and Gerard Radnitzky, *Evolutionary Epistemology, Theory of Rationality, and the Sociology of Knowledge* (Radnitzky and Bartley 1987).

Some scholars argue that although biological phenomena are cast in a Darwinian universe, cultural phenomena are essentially Lamarckian in their mode of production and transmission. Such a view is clearly wrong. Habitual use generates boredom, not new theories. Necessity may be the mother of invention, but she rarely produces viable children on demand, and when she does, they take on lives of their own that differ markedly from the reasons that begat them.

As Pagels points out, even in the most goal-directed of all enterprises,

> Science rarely progresses because it has a direct goal in mind. It is, like the evolutionary system, blind as to where it is headed. There is a kind of randomness in its progress, a randomness severely constrained by previous experience [in the same ways mutations operate on the gametes of an existing genotype]. But, when an idea works, the individual and the profession lock into it—the random searching stops, and research becomes more goal-oriented. The ideas that work are selected, in the end, not so much by human beings but by the Demiurge—the order of nature itself. And therein lies the unique peculiarity of science: its truth is not regulated exclusively by us. (Pagels 1988:266)

20. Margaret Boden, in her book *Computer Models of Mind* (1988), has proposed a triad of theories common to what she calls computational psychology (the human aspect of the wider realm of AI and machine intelligence).

> First, computational psychologists adopt a functionalist approach to the mind, in which mental states are abstractly defined in terms of their causal role (with respect to other mental states and observable behavior). Second, computational psychologists conceive of the mind as a representational system, and see psychology as the study of the various computational processes whereby mental representations are constructed. And third, they think about neuroscience (if they think about it at all) in a broadly computational way, asking what sorts of

logical operations or functional relations might be embodied in neural networks. (Boden 1988:5–6)

Although these three propositions form a common core for work in AI, other strongly held theories and methods tend to divide the field into several competing schools.

Three cross-cutting classifications can be applied to those cognitive scientists who use the computer as model of human thought and thought processes: "wet" versus "dry," "strong" versus "weak," and the "neat" versus the "scruffy." The last pair can be characterized quickly. There are those who see formal logic and "neat" computer algorithms as the center of AI research. Those labeled "scruffies" claim that " . . . AI is more likely to be successful if it eschews the rigor of formal logic and investigates instead the more varied structures and processes found in human thought" (Thagard 1988:3).

The "wet" versus "dry" camps take a bit longer to describe. There are those who employ the computer as a model of actual brain processes. To that end, they attempt to instantiate neuronal processes in hardware and software. They are called "connectionists," and most are practitioners of what is called "wet AI." They " . . . rejected the notion that rule-governed sign manipulation can simulate complex intelligent action as not being a very useful idea [which places them in the "scruffy" camp as well]. Instead they see intelligence as a property of the design of a network" (Pagels 1988:118). They explicitly relate the strengths of connections among computer processors with the inhibitory and excitatory synapses among neurons.

Then there are those who see the computer only as a device to emulate human thought. They see the computer as a device that manipulates information in terms of programs. They are called "computationalists," and most among this group are proponents of a "neat" and a "dry AI." This latter lineage begins, perhaps, with Alan Turing, who saw thought as a purely logical process.

> The Turing model did not seek to explain one kind of phenomena, that of mind, in terms of another. It did not seek to 'reduce' psychology to anything. The thesis was that 'mind' or psychology could properly be described in terms of Turing machines because they both lay on the *same* level of description of the world, that of discrete logical systems. It was not a reduction, but an attempt at transference, when he imagined embodying such systems in an artificial 'brain.' (Hodges 1983:291)

In the forty years since Turing wrote, human thought, knowledge structures, and perception have been shown to be far more complex than he thought. [See, for example, Roger Schank and Robert P. Abelson, *Scripts, Plans, Goals, and Understanding: An Inquiry into Human Knowledge Structures* (1977) and Marvin Minsky, *The Society of Mind* (1988).] Yet by attacking problems of mind through the computer—through attempts to impart to machines the declarative and procedural knowledge that is available to all humans—computer scientists have gained fundamental insights about the operation of brain and mind.

Proponents of both "wet" and "dry" AI can be sorted into those who profess a "strong" version of AI and those who are content with a "weak" version. Those in the first group assert that at some point in the future, computers will replicate every important aspect of the human mind. In fact, some AI researchers adhere to a radically strong position; they believe that computers can be constructed that will outdistance all facets of human competence and performance. The second group comprise those who see the computer as a device that is useful for studying the human mind and reason, but who do not advance the proposition that computers will ever replicate human thought processes. They are proponents of what is called "weak AI."

It seems, at least for the moment, that the arguments *against* the proponents of strong and superstrong AI are compelling. The critics hinge their arguments on the fact that computers—either in serial or in parallel—work at the level of syntax, not at the level of semantics and meaning. As a consequence, they argue that computers will never be able to "understand" in the same ways that humans "understand." Searle, who has presented this position most strongly, says: "In a word, the mind has more than syntax, it has semantics. The reason that no computer program can ever be a mind is simply that a computer program is only syntactical, and minds are more than syntactical. Minds are semantical, in the sense that they have more than a formal structure, they have content'' (Searle 1984:31). One might add, it is unlikely that computers as they are now constituted will master the pragmatics of human communication. Along the same lines, but in a far more polemical manner, the brothers Dreyfus, who are outspoken opponents of all AI, assert that computers can never replicate either the semantics or the extralogical intuitions that human "experts" develop after long training and practice in a particular field of endeavor (Dreyfus and Dreyfus 1986:101–121).

The position adopted here, which is far less extreme than that of the Dreyfuses, is that of "scruffy, dry, and weak AI": the computer is seen as a useful analog for human reasoning, whether it be in the form of Lévi-Strauss's *bricolage* or the logic of the sciences. In fact, attempts to program computers to emulate human patterns of thought have underscored just how complex these processes are in their biological instantiations. Thus, to borrow Ross Ashby's felicitous phrase, we can use computers as an "intelligence amplifier," but not, I suspect, as a complete replacement.

21. One of the points made by Pylyshyn is presented in even stronger terms by Jerry Fodor. He proposes that much of the functional architecture of the brain, such as that devoted to vision and hearing, is narrowly specialized and coordinated only at higher levels of brain function. Fodor, in fact, presents a model for the *Modularity of Mind* (1983). His model for the mind, in addition to a store of representations, also has specialized and relatively independent cognitive modules for spatial apprehension and language acquisition. In computer terms, he sees these modules as having their own specialized input, output, and processing hardware as well as an immediate cache of memory, each with its own store of highly specific representations. Finally, Howard Gardner, who like Gazzaniga has worked with brain-damaged patients, presents a theory of multiple intelligences (faculties). In his book *Frames of Mind* (1983), Gardner postulates that humans have separate faculties for language, music, logico-mathematical operations, the apprehension of space, kinesthetics and the body, and the knowledge of the self.

22. *Toward an Archaeology of Mind*, given on the occasion of his elevation to the Disney Professorship at the University of Cambridge, 30 November 1982.

23. See, for example, *Winston Churchill's Afternoon Nap: A Wide Awake Inquiry into the Human Nature of Time* by Jeremy Campbell (1986).

REFERENCES

Alexander, R. 1989. "Evolution of the human psyche," in P. Mellars and C. Stringer (eds.), *The Human Revolution*, pp. 455–513. Princeton University Press, Princeton, NJ.

Bachelard, G. 1964. *The Poetics of Space*. Beacon Press, Boston.

Barel, Y. 1973. *La reproduction sociale*. Editions Anthropos, Paris.

Bartley, W. W., III 1978. "Critical study: The philosophy of Karl Popper: Part II: Consciousness and physics," *Philosophia* **7**, 675–716.

Binford, L. R. 1983a. *Working At Archaeology*. Academic Press, New York.

———1983b. *In Pursuit of the Past*. Thames and Hudson, New York.

Boden, M. A. 1988. *Computer Models of the Mind*. Cambridge University Press, Cambridge.

Bruner, J. 1986. *Actual Minds, Possible Worlds*. Harvard University Press, Cambridge, MA.

Campbell, J. 1986. *Winston Churchill's Afternoon Nap*. Simon and Schuster, New York.

Childe, V. G. 1949. "The sociology of knowledge," *Modern Quarterly* **IV**, 302–309.

———1956. *Society and Knowledge*. Harper & Brothers, New York.

Collingwood, R. G. 1978 [orig. 1939]. *An Autobiography*. Oxford University Press, Oxford.

——— 1961 [orig. 1946]. *The Idea of History*. Oxford University Press, Oxford.

Conkey, M. 1989. "Structural analysis of Paleolithic art," in C. C. Lamberg-Karlovsky (ed.), *Archaeological Thought in America*, pp. 135–154. Cambridge University Press, Cambridge.

Danto, A. C. 1989. *Connections to the World*. Harper & Row, New York.

Deetz, J. 1988. "History and archaeological theory: Walter Taylor revisited," *American Antiquity* **53**, 12–22.

Delbruck, M. 1986. *Mind from Matter?* Blackwell Scientific Publications, Palo Alto, CA.

Dennett, D. C. 1987. *The Intentional Stance*. MIT Press, Cambridge, MA.

Dreyfus, H., and S. E. Dreyfus 1986. *Mind Over Machine*. Free Press, New York.

Eccles, J. 1979. *The Human Mystery*. Springer International, New York.

———1980. *The Human Psyche*. Springer International, New York.

Feyerabend, P. 1975. *Against Method*. Verso, London.

Fischler, M. A., and O. Firschein 1987. *Intelligence: The Eye, the Brain, and the Computer*. Addison Wesley, New York.

Fodor, J. A. 1984. *The Modularity of Mind*. MIT Press, Cambridge, MA.

Fraser, J. T. 1987. *Time the Familiar Stranger*. Tempus Books, Redmond, WA.

Fritz, J. M., and F. Plog 1970. "The nature of anthropological explanation," *American Antiquity* **35**, 405–412.

Gardner, H. 1983. *Frames of Mind: The Theory of Multiple Intelligences*. Basic Books, New York.

———1985. *The Mind's New Science*. Basic Books, New York.

Gargett, R. H. 1989. "Grave shortcomings: The evidence for Neanderthal burial," *Current Anthropology* **30**, 157–190.

Gazzaniga, M. 1985. *The Social Brain: Discovering the Networks of the Mind*. Basic Books, New York.

Geertz, C. 1973. *The Interpretation of Cultures*. Basic Books, New York.

Giere, R. N. 1988. *Explaining Science, a Cognitive Approach*. University of Chicago Press, Chicago.

Gowlett, J. A. F. 1984. "Mental abilities of early man: A look at some hard evidence," in R. Foley (ed.), *Hominid Evolution and Community Ecology*, pp. 167–192. Academic Press, London.

Gregory, R. L. 1981. *Mind in Science*. Cambridge University Press, Cambridge.

Heath, A. F. (ed.) 1981. *Scientific Explanation*. [The Herbert Spencer Lectures]. Clarendon Press, Oxford.

Hempel, C. G. 1965. *Aspects of Scientific Explanation*. Free Press, New York.

Hempel, C. G., and P. Oppenheim 1948. "Studies in the logic of explanation," *Philosophy of Science* **15**, 135–175.

Hodges, A. 1983. *Alan Turing: The Enigma*. Simon and Schuster, New York.

Holton, G. 1973. *Thematic Origins of Scientific Thought*. Harvard University Press, Cambridge, MA.

Humphrey, N. 1986. *The Inner Eye*. Faber and Faber, London.

Johnson-Laird, P. N. 1988. *The Computer and the Mind*. Harvard University Press, Cambridge. MA.

Kant, I. 1885. *Kant's Introduction to Logic and his Essay on the Mistaken Sublity of the Four Figures*. T. K. Abbot (tr.). Longmans Green and Company, London.

Kaplan, A. 1964. *Conduct of Inquiry: Methodology for Behavioral Science*. Chandler Publishing Co., San Francisco.

Kimball, L., and L. H. Keely 1988. "Detection of planning in Paleolithic assemblages." Manuscript in possession of the author.

Lashley, K. 1951. "The problem of serial order in behavior," in L. A. Jeffress (ed.), *Cerebral Mechanisms in Behavior: The Hixon Symposium*, pp. 112–135. John Wiley, New York.

Leroi-Gourhan, A. 1964–1965. *Le geste et la parole* (2 vol.). Albin Michel, Paris

———1982. *The Dawn of European Art*. Cambridge University Press, Cambridge.

Lorenz, K. 1973. *Behind the Mirror*. Harcourt Brace Jovanovich, New York.

Marshack, A. 1985. *The Hierarchical Evolution of the Human Capacity: The Paleolithic Evidence*. Fifty-Fourth James Arthur Lecture on the Evolution of the Human Brain. American Museum of Natural History, New York.

McClelland, J. L., and D. Rummelhart 1986. *Parallel Distributed Processing*. Volume 2: *Psychological and Biological Models*. MIT Press, Cambridge, MA.

Miller, G. A. 1956. "The magical number seven, plus or minus two: Some limits on our capacity for processing information," *Psychological Review* **63**, 81–97.

Minsky, M. 1986. *The Society of Mind*. Simon and Schuster, New York.

Newell, A. 1982. "The knowledge level," *Artificial Intelligence* **18**, 87–127.

————1988. "The intentional stance and the knowledge level," *Behavioral and Brain Science* **11**, 520–522.

Newell, A., and H. Simon 1987. "Computer science as empirical enquiry: Symbols and search," [1975 Turing Award Lecture], in *ACM Turing Award Lectures: The First Twenty Years*, pp. 287–316. ACM Press [Addison-Wesley Publishing Company], New York.

Pagels, H. 1988. *The Dreams of Reason*. Simon and Schuster, New York.

Peebles, C. 1990. "From history to hermeneutics: The place of theory in the later prehistory of the Southeast." *Southeastern Archaeology* **9**, 23–34.

————1991. "*Annalistes*, hermeneutics and positivists: Squaring circles or dissolving problems," in J. Bintliff (ed.), *The Annales and Archaeology*, pp. 108–124. Leicester University Press, Leicester.

Pfeiffer, J. 1982. *The Creative Explosion: An Inquiry into the Origins of Art and Religion*. Harper and Row, New York.

Peirce, C. S. 1940. *The Philosophy of Peirce: Selected Writings*. Selected and edited by Justus Buchler. Routledge and Kegan Paul, London.

Popper, K. R. 1959. *The Logic of Scientific Discovery*. Harper and Row, New York.

————1965. *Conjectures and Refutations*. Harper and Row, New York.

————1982a. *The Open Universe: An Argument for Indeterminism*. Rowman and Littlefield, Totowa, NJ.

————1982b. *Quantum Theory and the Schism in Physics*. Rowman and Littlefield, Totowa, NJ.

————1983. *Realism and the Aim of Science*. Rowman and Littlefield, Totowa, NJ.

Popper K. R., and J. C. Eccles 1977. *The Self and Its Brain*. Springer International, New York.

Putnam, H. 1981. *Reason, Truth, and History*. Cambridge University Press, Cambridge.

Pylyshyn, Z. W. 1984. *Computation and Cognition*. MIT Press, Cambridge.

Radnitzky, G., and W. W. Bartley III (eds.) 1987. *Evolutionary Epistemology, Theory of Rationality and the Sociology of Knowledge*. Open Court, La Salle, IL.

Rathje, W. L., and M. B. Schiffer 1982. *Archaeology*. Harcourt Brace Jovanovich, New York.

Renfrew, C. 1982. *Towards an Archaeology of Mind*. Cambridge University Press, Cambridge.

Ricoeur, P. 1984. *The Reality of the Historical Past*. [The Aquinas Lecture, 1984]. Marquette University Press, Milwaukee.

Rumelhart, D. E., and J. McClelland 1986. *Parallel Distributed Processing*. Volume 1: *Foundations*. MIT Press, Cambridge, MA.

Schank, R. C. 1984. *The Cognitive Computer*. Addison Wesley, New York.

Schank, R. C., and R. P. Abelson 1977. *Scripts, Plans, Goals, and Understanding*. Lawrence Erlbaum Associates, Hillsdale, NJ.

Schiffer, M. B. 1976. *Behavioral Archaeology*. Academic Press, New York.

————1981. "Some issues in the philosophy of archaeology," *American Antiquity* **46**, 899–908.

Searle, J. 1983. *Intentionality: An Essay in the Philosophy of Mind*. Cambridge University Press, Cambridge.

————1984. *Minds, Brains, and Science*. Harvard University Press, Cambridge, MA.

Simon, H. A. 1981. *The Sciences of the Artificial*, 2nd ed. MIT Press, Cambridge, MA.

Skinner, B. F. 1948. *Walden Two*. Macmillan, New York.

————1984a. *Particulars of My Life*. New York University Press, New York.

————1984b. *The Shaping of a Behaviorist*. New York University Press, New York.

————1984c. *A Matter of Consequences*. New York University Press, New York.

Smith, L. D. 1986. *Behaviorism and Logical Positivism: A Reassessment of the Alliance*. Stanford University Press, Palo Alto, CA.

Stillings, N., M. H. Feinstein, J. L. Garfield, E. L. Rissland, D. A. Rosenbaum, S. E. Weisler, and L. Baker-Ward 1987. *Cognitive Science: An Introduction*. MIT Press, Cambridge, MA.

Thagard, P. 1988. *Computational Philosophy of Science*. MIT Press, Cambridge, MA.

Toth, N. 1985. "Archaeological evidence for preferential right-handedness in the Lower and Middle
    Pleistocene and its possible implications," *Journal of Human Evolution* **14,** 607–614.
Toulmin, S. 1958. *The Uses of Argument*. Cambridge University Press, Cambridge.
———1972. *Human Understanding*. Princeton University Press, Princeton, NJ.
White, R. 1989. "Visual thinking in the Ice Age," *Scientific American* **261,** 92–99.
Wilden, A. 1987. *The Rules Are No Game: The Strategy of Communication*. Routledge & Kegan
    Paul, London.
Wylie, A. 1982. *Positivism and the New Archaeology*. Ph.D. dissertation, Department of Philoso-
    phy, State University of New York, Binghamton.
Young, T. C. 1988. "Since Herodotus, has history been a valid concept?," *American Antiquity*
    53, 7–12.

Jean-Claude Gardin and Christopher S. Peebles

Epilogue

We leave it to the reader to decide which of the papers represent the main contributions to the domain of deliberation we chose: an exploration of new interpretive approaches in archaeology. Some readers, however, might wish to know our views on this subject as well as on the substance of the summary discussions that took place during the final session of the seminar.

1. One observation, certainly positive and perhaps unexpected, was that the participants had no difficulty whatsoever in avoiding internecine conflicts that all too often plague adherents of different "schools" of archaeology when they find themselves thrown together in the same meeting room. Instead, a common purpose emerged quickly and easily: it was neither to defend the merits of one or another of the "new-new" archaeologies nor to proclaim yet one more "revolution" in archaeological thought, but simply to try, together, to understand the mechanisms, assumptions, and limits of various interpretations, regardless of the paradigms and guiding principles from which they sprang. Approaches usually regarded as "traditional" were admitted on the same terms as were "postmodern" enterprises. In this regard, however, we should point out that space-time-form systematics and culture-history have played important roles in archaeology for more than a century, and they will continue to have a productive place in the constitution of our knowledge of prehistoric societies for the indefinite future. Similarly, "hyperscientific" approaches, including various brands of positivism and logical empiricism, which have fallen into disrepute of late, were juxtaposed with exemplars of freer and more personal ways of grappling with human affairs. We believe that the changing membership of the several "sides" in these comparisons benefited from the process, and we hope that the substance of this observation will become apparent in the discussion that follows.

2. Some divisions nevertheless appeared during our discussions. In particular there seemed to be two distinct methods—or perhaps merely styles—of approaching problems of interpretation, one Anglo-Saxon and the other Gallic, without either nationalistic or chauvinistic overtones. We alluded to one aspect of this duality in the Introduction, when we wrote of the differences between the American and the French versions of our common proposals as independently formulated on each side of the Atlantic. At the risk of being charged with gross oversimplification, we can summarize the main features of the opposition as follows. (i) On the "anglophone" side, great hermeneutic ambitions were expressed; these, at times, held out a hope that one could understand some aspects of

the development of "mind" and cognition as forces in human history. These ambitions were tempered with an acute perception of the variety of "biases" that influence our interpretative constructions and can deprive them of the claims to "truth" and "reality" accorded scientific theories. (ii) On the "francophone" side there was an almost excessive concern for moderation, which renounced any desire to push inferences beyond the thresholds imposed by the limits of archaeological observations, but also much less fear of ideological deviation in interpretation. Such positions are in fact a curious reversal of commonly held stereotypes: a reversal where the taste for philosophical and sociopolitical speculations was more on the "anglophone" side—nourished with references to Merleau-Ponty, Foucault, Bourdieu, etc.—whereas our "francophone" archaeologists displayed a pragmatic perspective that in the past would have been called Anglo-Saxon—one through which the shade of John Stuart Mill might have strolled comfortably. This perspective was offered without any theoretical backing save the anonymous idea of scientific reasoning in general, judged, rightly or wrongly, to be one and indivisible, in human as well as in natural orders.

3. In rough outline, this dual division could be supported on the basis of a quick reading of the papers submitted in advance of the seminar; several fell clearly on one or the other side of the interpretative line, while others tended to occupy a middle ground and thereby resisted allocation except by default. Yet it was the principal goal of the seminar to go beyond these first impressions, to reach a common vision of interpretative approaches in archaeology, new or not so new, and to do so without making distinctions based on labels—symbolic, structural, semiotic, or *any other*. The key word (and central concept) that unified our discussions is the one that we have chosen for the title of this book: "representations." As our discussions progressed over that week, it became clear that one multifaceted but dominant theme was emerging, namely the nature of representations of the world, which necessarily shape our archaeological constructs as they do those of any science. The notion of representation, however, was applied in different ways by various participants.

(A) Amongst those allied to symbolic or contextual archaeology, there was a belief that the interpretation of vestiges of the past ought to be pushed as far as the reconstitution of the symbolic universes particular to past populations. Their methods could be seen as analogous to those of a social anthropologist who studies the mental representation of a group in order to "explain" the actions and material products of present-day individuals within a given cultural context.

(B) Others, however, pointed out the obvious difficulties of such an approach: (i) at some levels it becomes impossible to confirm or refute hypotheses; (ii) even at lower levels of reasoning, inference is biased by the presuppositions of the observer, and as a result it can become an exercise in wishful thinking.

This second point can be approached from two directions: (ii.a) from an ethnological perspective, where such presuppositions are seen as a reflection of the conceptual categories on which the observer necessarily depends, even unconsciously, through language, and as the product of education or professional training—in short, through culture in its widest sense; (ii.b) from an ideological point of view, where the emphasis is put on systems of thought, paradigms, and schools that vie for the interpreters' favor within the same culture—especially Western culture.

(C) Yet there is more. Some of the participants have a keen interest in the knowledge shared by members of a scientific community that transcends the particulars of their cultural and scholastic backgrounds. The hypothesis here is that even in the human sciences the notion of "science" includes the potential to constitute this common knowledge, under one name or another, in such a way that it would allow archaeologists from vastly different backgrounds to agree, for example, on the interpretation of Stonehenge. In essence this perspective seeks to overcome the notion that each group, gender, race, religion, and class should have its own archaeology. Justified or not, this perspective has its followers, who are thus *also* interested in representations: the case in point comprises those durable ideas that transcend particular ages and, in the end, constitute the notions essential to a science and form the hard core of its didactic works.

Representations have become a key topic in philosophy, history, and the cognitive sciences. In his most recent book, the philosopher Arthur C. Danto (1989) has argued strongly for a "representational materialism," in which the ability to construct representations plays a key role in human relations with the world. He presents a schema that comprises the triad of subject, representation, and the world. Therein the link between the subject and its representations is the "self," that between the subject and the world is "causality," and that between representations and the world is "truth" (Danto 1989:iii). In his scheme of things, *bricolage* and linear, logical thought are both parts of human rationality. The human capacity for representations—their dynamic instantiation in the brain—and representations themselves are the products of evolution and subject to selection. "We have the concept of knowledge because we need there to be not simply representations but true ones, and not only true ones but those that are true because of the way the world causes us to have those representations in the first instance" (Danto 1989:268).

Perhaps speaking to the points raised in this section, Danto concludes: "All sciences aim at true representations. But a science which deals with scientific representation as its subject aspires to true representations or representational truth, where truth and such a relationship enter into the structure of what this sort of representational science undertakes to represent" (Danto 1989:272). In brief, a philosophy of science must include itself and its representations in that which it tries to represent. We are a part of what we study, and what we study is a part of us, in ways that are very different from those of physics or biology and more akin to cosmology, where, as Danto points out, it regards itself as part of its problem. Thus to preface what follows, from this perspective "The inside and the outside are one" (Danto 1989:256).

4. Between all these systems of thought, the links are not only the common reference to mental representations of differing origins and functions, but also the far from absurd idea that we can aim at a logically necessary but unattainable point of convergence of different classes of representations. Nothing prevents one, in effect, from considering that there exists in way **A** as in way **B** a threshold beyond which one may in time be able to locate points of correspondence between the symbolic universes they represent: that of the "Other" (way **A**), that of the observer (way **B**), so that the established or divided-up knowledge aimed at in way **C** is constituted. Those most attached to the "scientific" model, but convinced nevertheless of the value of research of types **A** or **B**, find in this question-begging a means of satisfying their twofold impulses. The others,

for whom the scientific model is repulsive—either in and of itself or, for the more moderate, when it is applied to humankind—are also satisfied, since they are free to declare that the threshold is so low that it is better to place oneself *above* it, even if it means—this time for the more radical—that the ways of interpretation are then open to any current of human imagination or sensibility, for better or for worse.

How do we tell better from worse in these areas? Is it even necessary to tell them apart? The most persistent of all the questions raised during our discussions were: If logico-empirical objectivity cannot be applied above our threshold, should we not at least define the criteria of the intersubjectivity that will take over? And if, in turn, these criteria seem inadmissible for other reasons, would it not be more honest just to ban any discussion of validation in archaeology, because, as several excellent authors have stressed, it is simply beyond our means? During the last session the discussions on this topic took the form of a "mini-tragedy" (the label is that of J.-C. Gardin), in the sense that we all seemed to be torn between two irreconcilable intellectual passions. On one side, a "warm" vision of humanity reigned, where some *persons*, used to categories which they recognize as specifically theirs—yet also equipped with a sensibility and a spiritual intelligence that modesty forbids them to acknowledge in themselves—met *individuals*, and by means of the dialogue with the Other, understood them through categories no less *particular* that were suggested through empathy. On the other side, the "cold" vision reigned, where more or less interchangeable researchers were collectively trying to establish interpretations relative to the same objects, through common categories, established by means of constructions submitted to empirical and logical constraints, and ultimately perceived in the same terms by both observer and observed. In addition there were moral and political resonances: here the redress of wrongs between Celts and Romans, Choctaw and Spaniards, Pilgrim Fathers and modern Yankees, etc.; there, on the contrary, a detached interest in the ways of life of others, apprehended without mention of the guilt of the West.

Nearly all participants showed equal respect for both sides of the debate in ways that transcended their particular inclinations for either clime. Clearly, the personal sympathies that had begun and matured on both sides during our stay in Bloomington played a role in this pleasant syncretic impulse; the fact remained, however, that we were finally facing a duality and not a synthesis, even if this opposition of "warm" and "cold" was only one way among many others of designating an ancient and today trite diptych (Dionysian/ Apollonian, *anima/animus*, Eros/Thanatos, etc.). Closer to our time and our subject, C. P. Snow's Rede Lecture for 1959, *The Two Cultures*, comes to mind: Arts and Literature on one side; Science on the other (Snow 1969). J. Bruner (1986:11) formalized this division as two distinct modes of thought or "natural kinds." He regards paridigmatic, scientific thought, cast in terms of well-formed *argument*, as fundamentally different from a good story, formed from a believable, lifelike *narrative*. He sees these two modes as complementary but "irreducible to one another" (*ibid.*). For Bruner, both science and literature can be judged by criteria of well-formedness, but the former requires empirical and formal evaluation, whereas the latter is evaluated in terms of lifelikeness. The matter, however, is more complicated that this simple outline suggests: Bruner's narrative mode of thought is, as he stresses, poorly defined at this point (but see Bruner 1990); it is clear, however, that it is not solely restricted to artistic and literary contributions to knowledge. It is just as well that Bruner does not do so, because many of the authors here who express an aversion to logico-scientific paradigms do not at the same time insist that their work falls under either great literature or the fine arts. The problem of the existence of a "third genre," represented by our explanations of the past, arises when there are challenges to the mutual exclusivity of the arts and sciences and to paradigmatic and narrative dichotomies. C. P. Snow (1969) admits of the possibility of a third culture when, in *The Two Cultures: A Second Look*, he provisionally grants this status to those disciplines that "are concerned with how human beings are living or have lived—and concerned, not in terms of legend, but of fact" (Snow 1969:70). Yet his admission of such a possibility of a "third culture" carries with it major problems, as Wolf Lepenies has shown in his recent book, rendered in English as *Between Literature and Science: the Rise of Sociology* (Lepenies 1988). Aspects of this discussion also can be found above, in the chapter by Gardin (Chapter 5, §4.1 et seq.), where it is presented in very much the same terms. Yet it goes one step further and suggests that there are as yet no critical rules for the evaluation of this "third genre" that would permit us to judge its products. Hence, at least for the foreseeable future, we should concentrate on one of the two genres available and not live on a faithful hope of a third. It is significant that in the course of the final discussion, no voice was raised to present either a defense or an illustration of this hybrid, third genre.

5. Should we see in this silence an acknowledgment of failure? We think not. The reduction of the apparent diversity among our "new approaches" to two or three interpretative genres that are truly distinct from an epistemological point of view would, if it were more widely understood, already represent significant progress. Yet, is not this progress, to use the French expression, *accoucher d'une souris*, merely a mountain giving birth to a mouse? What then remains of the unifying objective painted in glowing colors in the announcement of the seminar?

Let us begin with the second question. To us, the appropriate answer seems to be the following: the reduction we contemplate achieves unification to the extent that it can be applied equally to any approach, to any school or philosophy of interpretation, by asking the same questions about the nature and origin of the representations which make each unique. In other words, our vision of the field is unitary, even if, in the final analysis, it leads to the recognition of two or three categories of discourse among which synthesis is neither possible nor desirable—so long as we can agree on the appropriate function of each. Some of the participants, those more convinced than others of the reality of a unitarian rather than a trinitarian approach, thought they could affirm their position by showing that it was fully subsumed by semiotics, one of the titles under which our seminar had been organized. Indeed, it is easy to demonstrate that the field of research thus named encompasses within its diversity the study of symbolic systems in general, and more particularly those that underlie human works and actions. This very broad definition has the merit of being applicable to all the variants of semiotics brought up during our discussions: as a science of symbolic forms (J. Molino), as part of a symbolic anthropology (M. Herzfeld), as an analysis of symbolic constructions (J.-C. Gardin), which in this last sense includes the constructions of semiotics itself when it offers us original views on the hidden structures and senses of all things.

The risk of such a general perspective, however, is that it might remain nothing more than that: a perspective with neither methodological content nor cognitive originality, except those inherited from semiotics, or the disciplines which provide the latter with its objects of study—literature, anthropology, archaeology, etc. On the whole, the participants proved to be too sensible to risk their future projects on an investment in a "unified semiotic perspective"; in fact, the great majority urged that the limits of such an approach be emphasized clearly and boldly. In this regard, one of the participants had an incisive formulation of the situation: "in the last analysis, the semiotics of archaeology's material objects or discursive products is nothing other than archaeology."

6. There remained nonetheless a feeling that it might be possible to agree on a more precise definition of the role that representations play in the constitution of archaeological data and in the exercise of interpretative functions. If it were necessary to find an established disciplinary sponsor for this particular perspective, would it not be judicious to search for it in the cognitive sciences or even better within the broader cognitive movement that is currently undergoing an exponential growth in practitioners and publications? Indeed, there were numerous allusions to the latter during our discussions, and it is clearly significant that this general perspective surfaces in the papers of several authors in this volume, each of whom tackled interpretation from independent and differing viewpoints: for example, ontological (D. Sperber), semiological (J. Molino), logicist (J.-C. Gardin), metric (H.-P. Francfort), computer science (J. Doran), mind-brain (C. S. Peebles), etc. By referring to the broad cognitive movement rather than to the sciences that have been invested with the qualifier "cognitive," we can avoid once again the risk of confusion, where one could have the illusion of a direct contribution from any of the disciplines concerned to the interpretative apparatus of ours. In fact, there was no move to make archaeology a part of the cognitive sciences, even on the part of the authors just listed. The constructions used to illustrate their discussions really are archaeological or anthropological, nothing more, so that specialists in cognitive sciences—in any branch, psychology, neurology, linguistics, etc.—would probably be surprised that we found in them some "family resemblance" with their own works. Yet the danger we mentioned before arises once more: are we not "giving birth to a mouse" when we suggest as a conclusion to the week of intensive discussions that archaeology should show more concern in the origin and the nature of the representations that nurture it, in the name of a "self-reflection" or a "reflexivity," which the cognitivist movement certainly made popular, yet did not create? Opinions on this question (over)heard behind the scene of the seminar and elsewhere encompass all possible answers, from the most derisive skepticism to the conviction that a new revolution in archaeology is on its way: the latest, after so many others, following the "cognitive revolution" itself, as some wits think it necessary to call it.

Most participants, however, seemed to adopt a middle of the road position; one where it is accepted that there is more in this program than a "concern for rigor" or other such platitudes, while admitting the existence of antecedents which, today as well as yesterday, make any appeal to revolution ridiculous. As for us, we will consider that we have reached our goal if the publication of this book contributes to an increase in the number of our colleagues who practice a more reflective archaeology: an archaeology that is as far from the conformity of some—Ancients and Moderns together—as it is from the radicalism of others. In short, we hope for a discipline less preoccupied with cultivating the diversity of its "approaches" than with discovering what they have in common in the substance and the form of their representations.

REFERENCES

Bruner, J. 1986. *Actual Minds, Possible Worlds*. Harvard University Press, Cambridge, MA.
————1990. *Acts of Meaning*. Harvard University Press, Cambridge, MA.
Danto, A. C. 1989. *Connections to the World*. Harper & Row, New York.
Lepenies, W. 1988. *Between Literature and Science: The Rise of Sociology*. Cambridge University Press, Cambridge.
Snow, C. P. 1969. *The Two Cultures and A Second Look*. Cambridge University Press, Cambridge.

Contributors

OLIVIER AURENCHE, Professor of Archaeology, Maison de l'Orient, 1 rue Raulin, F 69007 Lyon, France.

JAMES A. BELL, Professor and Chair, Department of Philosophy, University of South Florida, Tampa, Florida 33620 USA.

CHRISTOPHER CHIPPINDALE, Assistant Curator, Museum of Archaeology and Anthropology, University of Cambridge, and Editor, *Antiquity*, 85 Hills Road, Cambridge CB2 1PG, England.

WHITNEY DAVIS, Associate Professor of Art History, Department of Art History, Northwestern University, Evanston, Illinois 60208, USA.

JAMES DORAN, Professor of Computer Science, Department of Computer Science, University of Essex, Colchester CO4 3SQ England.

MICHAEL FOTIADIS, Rackham Postdoctoral Fellow, Classical Studies, University of Michigan, 2016 Angel Hall, Ann Arbor, Michigan 48109, USA.

HENRI-PAUL FRANCFORT, Director of Research, C.N.R.S., E.R. 315, 23 rue du Maroc, 75940 Paris, Cedex 19, France.

ALAIN GALLAY, Professor of Anthropology, Department of Anthropology, University of Geneva, 12 rue Gustave Revilliod, 1227 Carouge-Geneve, Switzerland.

PATRICIA GALLOWAY, Special Projects Officer, Mississippi Department of Archives and History, P.O. Box 571 Jackson, Mississippi 39205 USA.

JEAN-CLAUDE GARDIN, Director of Research, C.N.R.S., 23 Rue du Maroc, 75940 Paris, Cedex 19, France.

MICHAEL HERZFELD, Professor of Anthropology, Department of Anthropology, Harvard University, Cambridge, Massachusetts 02138, USA.

ELIZABETH KRYDER-REID, Instructor of Anthropology, Department of Anthropology, University of Maryland, College Park, Maryland 20742, USA.

SUSAN KUS, Associate Professor of Anthropology, Department of Anthropology and Sociology, Rhodes College, 2000 N. Parkway, Memphis, Tennessee 38112, USA.

MARIE-SALOMÉ LAGRANGE, Director of Research, C.N.R.S., 23 rue du Maroc, 75019 Paris, Cedex 19, France.

MARK P. LEONE, Professor of Anthropology, Department of Anthropology, University of Maryland, College Park, Maryland 20742, USA.

JEAN MOLINO, Professor of Semiotics, Faculté des Lettres, Université de Lausanne, BFSH 2 CH-1015, Switzerland.

CHRISTOPHER S. PEEBLES, Director, Glenn A. Black Laboratory of Anthropology, Indiana University, 9th and Fess Streets, Bloomington, Indiana 47405, USA.

CATHERINE PERLÈS, Professor of Anthropology, University of Paris X, Nanterre, and Director of the Laboratory of Prehistory and Technology, U.R.A. 28 du C.R.A., 1, Place Aristide Briand, 92190 Meudon, France.

VALENTINE ROUX, Research Scholar, Laboratory of Prehistory and Technology, U.R.A. 28 du C.R.A., 1, Place Aristide Briand, 92190 Meudon, France.

DAN SPERBER, Director of Research, C.N.R.S., 2 Square de Port-Royal, 75013 Paris, France.

DANIELLE STORDEUR, Research Scholar, Institut de Prehistoire Orientale, Jalès F 07460 Berrias, France.

JEAN-CLAUDE GARDIN is Director of Research, Centre National de la Recherche Scientifique and Director of Studies, Ecole des Hautes Etudes en Sciences Sociales, Paris. His books include *Archaeological Constructs, Le calcul et la raison*, and with his colleagues of the CNRS, *La logique du plausible* and *Artificial Intelligence and Expert Systems: Case Studies in the Knowledge Domain of Archaeology*.

CHRISTOPHER S. PEEBLES is Director, Glenn A. Black Laboratory of Archaeology and Associate Dean/Executive Director, University Computing, Indiana University.